KARL MARX
FREDERICK ENGELS

COLLECTED WORKS
VOLUME
36

KARL MARX
FREDERICK ENGELS

COLLECTED
WORKS

INTERNATIONAL PUBLISHERS

NEW YORK

KARL MARX
FREDERICK ENGELS

Volume
36

KARL MARX: *CAPITAL*, VOL. II

INTERNATIONAL PUBLISHERS

NEW YORK

This volume has been prepared jointly by Lawrence & Wishart Ltd., London, International Publishers Co. Inc., New York, and Progress Publishing Group Corporation, Moscow, in collaboration with the Russian Independent Institute of Social and National Problems (former Institute of Marxism-Leninism), Moscow.

Editorial commissions:

GREAT BRITAIN: Eric Hobsbawm, John Hoffman, Nicholas Jacobs, Monty Johnstone, Jeff Skelley, Ernst Wangermann, Ben Fowkes.
USA: James E. Jackson, Victor Perlo, Betty Smith, Dirk J. Struik.
RUSSIA: for Progress Publishing Group Corporation— Yu. V. Semyonov, Ye. N. Vladimirova; for the Russian Independent Institute of Social and National Problems—L.I. Golman, M.P. Mchedlov, V.N. Pospelova, G.L. Smirnov.

Copyright © Progress Publishing Group Corporation, Moscow, 1997
© Lawrence & Wishart, London, 1997
© International Publishers, New York, 1997

Library of Congress Cataloging in Publication Data

Marx, Karl, 1818-1883.
　　Karl Marx, Frederick Engels: collected works.

　　1. Socialism — Collected works. 2. Economics — Collected works. I. Engels, Friedrich, 1820-1895. Works. English. 1975. II. Title.
HX 39. 5. A 16 1975　　　335.4　　　73-84671
ISBN 0-7178-0536-0　　　(v. 36)

Printed in the USA

Contents

KARL MARX

CAPITAL

A Critique of Political Economy

Volume II

BOOK II

THE PROCESS OF CIRCULATION OF CAPITAL

PART I

THE METAMORPHOSES OF CAPITAL AND THEIR CIRCUITS

PART II

THE TURNOVER OF CAPITAL

PART III

THE REPRODUCTION AND CIRCULATION
OF THE AGGREGATE SOCIAL CAPITAL

NOTES AND INDEXES

ILLUSTRATIONS

Note: Pages 1-5 and 26-31 have been consolidated
to meet U.S. production requirements.

Preface

Volume 36 of the *Collected Works* of Marx and Engels contains the second volume of Marx's *Capital* published by Engels on the basis of the author's rough manuscripts. It also includes Engels' prefaces to the first and second German editions, as well as a short compilation of passages taken by Engels from the author's Manuscripts II-VIII. Volume II deals with the circulation of individual and social capital, its metamorphoses and its realisation in the form of value and material objects.

Marx divides the total social production into two major departments: the production of the means of production and that of the articles of consumption. He establishes the necessary proportions between them and between their component parts (constant and variable capital and surplus value) and clarifies the general conditions of simple and expanded reproduction, that is, reproduction on the same scale and on an extended scale.

Volume II of *Capital* is a link between an analysis of the process of the production of capital made in Volume I and that of its concrete types and forms in bourgeois society (profit, ground rent, interest) in Volume III. The subject of Volume III, according to Marx himself, is the process of capitalist production as a whole.

* * *

The present English edition of Volume II follows the second German edition published in 1893 under Engels' editorship. It is based on the English edition published by Progress Publishers, which made extensive use of the English translation of the second volume of *Capital* by Ernest Untermann printed by Charles H. Kerr & Co., Chicago, 1907.

When comparing the first and second German editions with Marx's manuscripts and with the final version edited by Engels, the editors discovered a number of misprints and printers' errors in the 1893 edition, checked factual data and calculations and corrected inaccuracies. Obvious slips of the pen in Marx's text have been corrected without comment.

Marx's and Engels' footnotes are indicated by numbers in superscript with a bracket, while the editors' footnotes are indicated by index letters, and editorial notes by numbers in superscript. The insertions made by Engels in Marx's text when preparing it for the press and in quotations are given in double oblique lines.

Foreign words and expressions are given as used by Marx, with the translation supplied in footnotes where necessary. English phrases, expressions and individual words occurring in the original are set in small capitals. Longer passages and quotations in English are enclosed within asterisks.

All quotations from English and American authors have been checked with the original sources.

In all cases the form of quotation used by Marx is respected. The language in which Marx quotes is indicated in footnotes unless it is German.

In this volume the editors have preserved the terminology used in the Engels-authorised English translation of Volume I of *Capital*, which is published in Volume 35 of the present edition.

The volume was compiled, the preface, notes and indexes written by Tatyana Vasilyeva (Russian Independent Institute of Social and National Problems) and edited by Lydia Belyakova, Mzia Pitskhelauri (Progress Publishing Group Corporation) and Alexander Malysh, scientific editor (Russian Independent Institute of Social and National Problems).

The volume was prepared for the press by Mzia Pitskhelauri (Progress Publishing Group Corporation).

KARL MARX

CAPITAL

A CRITIQUE OF POLITICAL ECONOMY [1]

VOLUME II

BOOK TWO

THE PROCESS OF CIRCULATION OF CAPITAL

Edited by Frederick Engels

First published in Hamburg in 1885   Printed according to the book: K. Marx, *Das Kapital. Kritik der politischen Oekonomie*, Zweiter Band, Zweite Auflage, Hamburg, 1893

Das Kapital. *S. Moore.*

Kritik der politischen Oekonomie.

Von

Karl Marx.

Zweiter Band.

Buch II: Der Cirkulationsprocess des Kapitals.

Herausgegeben von Friedrich Engels.

Das Recht der Uebersetzung ist vorbehalten.

Hamburg
Verlag von Otto Meissner.
1885.

Title page of the First German Edition
of Volume II of *Capital*

Frederick Engels

PREFACE TO THE FIRST GERMAN EDITION

It was no easy task to prepare the second book of *Capital* for publication, and do it in a way that on the one hand would make it a connected and as far as possible complete work, and on the other would represent exclusively the work of its author, not of its editor. The great number of available, mostly fragmentary, texts worked on added to the difficulties of this task. At best one single text (Manuscript IV) had been revised throughout and made ready for the press, but the greater part of even this manuscript had become obsolete through subsequent revision. The bulk of the material was not finally polished, in point of language, although in substance it was for the greater part fully worked out. The language was that in which Marx used to make his excerpts: careless style full of colloquialisms, often containing coarsely humorous expressions and phrases, interspersed with English and French technical terms or with whole sentences and even pages of English. Thoughts were jotted down in the form in which they developed in the brain of the author. Some parts of the argument would be treated in detail, others of equal importance only indicated. Factual material for illustration would be collected, but barely arranged, much less worked out. At conclusions of chapters, in the author's anxiety to get to the next, there would often be only a few disjointed sentences to mark the further development here left incomplete. And finally there was the well-known handwriting which the author himself was sometimes unable to decipher.

I have contented myself with reproducing these manuscripts as literally as possible, changing the style only in places where Marx would have changed it himself and interpolating explanatory sentences or connecting statements only where this was absolutely necessary, and where, besides, the meaning was clear beyond any doubt. Sentences whose interpretation was susceptible of the slightest doubt were preferably copied word for word. The passages which I have remodelled or interpolated cover barely ten pages in print and concern only matters of form.

The mere enumeration of the manuscript material left by Marx for Book II proves the unparalleled conscientiousness and strict self-criticism with which he endeavoured to elaborate his great economic discoveries to the point of utmost completion before he published them. This self-criticism rarely permitted him to adapt his presentation of the subject, in content as well as in form, to his ever widening horizon, the result of incessant study. This material consists of the following:

First, a manuscript entitled *A Contribution to the Critique of Political Economy*, containing 1,472 quarto pages in 23 notebooks, written from August 1861 to June 1863.[a] It is the continuation of a work of the same title, the first part of which appeared in Berlin, in 1859.[b] It treats, on pages 1-220 (notebooks I-V) and again on pages 1,159-1,472 (notebooks XIX-XXIII), of the subjects examined in Book I of *Capital*, from the transformation of money into capital to the end, and is the first extant draft thereof. Pages 973-1,158 (notebooks XVI-XVIII) deal with capital and profit, rate of profit, merchant's capital and money capital, that is to say with subjects which later were developed in the manuscript for Book III. The themes treated in Book II, and very many of those which are treated later, in Book III, are not yet arranged separately. They are treated in passing, namely, in the section which makes up the main body of the manuscript, viz., pages 220-972 (notebooks VI-XV), entitled *Theories of Surplus Value*. This section contains a detailed critical history of the pith and marrow of political economy, the theory of surplus value, and develops parallel with it, in polemics against predecessors, most of the points later investigated separately and in their logical connection in the manuscript for Books II and III. After eliminating the numerous passages covered by Books II and III, I intend to publish the critical part of this manuscript as *Capital*, Book IV.[2] This manuscript, valuable though it is, could be used only very little in the present edition of Book II.

---

[a] See present edition, vols 30-34. - [b] Ibid., Vol. 29, pp. 257-417.

The manuscript chronologically following next is that of Book III. It was written, at least the greater part of it, in 1864 and 1865. Only after this manuscript had been completed in its essential parts did Marx undertake the elaboration of Book I, the first volume published in 1867. I am now getting this manuscript of Book III in shape for the press.

The following period — after the publication of Book I — is represented by a collection of four folio manuscripts for Book II, numbered I-IV by Marx himself. Manuscript I (150 pages), presumably written in 1865 or 1867, is the first separate, but more or less fragmentary, elaboration of Book II as now arranged. Here too nothing could be used. Manuscript III is partly a compilation of quotations and references to Marx's notebooks containing excerpts, most of them relating to Part I of Book II, partly elaborations of particular points, especially a critique of Adam Smith's propositions on fixed and circulating capital and the source of profit; furthermore an exposition of the relation of the rate of surplus value to the rate of profit, which belongs in Book III. Little that was new could be garnered from the references, while the elaborations for volumes II and III were superseded by subsequent revisions and had also to be discarded for the greater part.

Manuscript IV is an elaboration, ready for the press, of Part I and the first chapters of Part II of Book II, and has been used where suitable. Although it was found that this manuscript had been written earlier than Manuscript II, yet, being far more finished in form, it could be used with advantage for the corresponding part of this book. All that was needed was a few addenda from Manuscript II.— The latter is the only somewhat complete elaboration of Book II and dates from the year 1870. The notes for the final editing, which I shall mention immediately, say explicitly: "The second elaboration must be used as the basis."

There was another intermission after 1870, due mainly to Marx's ill health. As usual, Marx employed this time for studies; agronomics, rural relations in America and, especially, Russia, the money market and banking, and finally natural sciences such as geology and physiology, and above all independent mathematical works, form the content of the numerous excerpt notebooks of this period.[3] By the beginning of 1877 he had recovered sufficiently to resume his main work. Dating back to the end of March 1877 there are references and notes from the above-named four manuscripts intended as the basis of a new elaboration of Book II, the beginning of which is represented by Manuscript V (56 folio pages). It comprises the first four chapters and is still little worked out. Essential points are treated in footnotes. The material is rather collected than sifted, but it is the last complete presentation of this, the most important section of Part I.

A first attempt to prepare from it a manuscript ready for the press was made in Manuscript VI (*after* October 1877 and before July 1878), embracing only 17 quarto pages, the greater part of the first chapter. A second and last attempt was made in Manuscript VII, "July 2, 1878", only 7 folio pages.

About this time Marx seems to have realised that he would never be able to finish the elaboration of the second and third books in a manner satisfactory to himself unless a complete revolution in his health took place. Indeed, manuscripts V-VIII show far too frequent traces of an intense struggle against depressing ill health. The most difficult bit of Part I had been worked over in Manuscript V. The remainder of Part I and all of Part II, with the exception of Chapter XVII, presented no great theoretical difficulties. But Part III, dealing with the reproduction and circulation of social capital, seemed to him to be very much in need of revision; for Manuscript II had first treated reproduction without taking into consideration money circulation, which mediates it, and then gone over the same matter again, but with money circulation taken into account. This was to be eliminated and the whole part to be reconstructed in such a way as to conform to the author's enlarged horizon. Thus Manuscript VIII came into existence, a notebook containing only 70 quarto pages. But the vast amount of matter Marx was able to compress into this space is clearly demonstrated when we compare that manuscript with Part III, in print, after leaving out the pieces inserted by me from Manuscript II.

This manuscript is likewise merely a preliminary treatment of the subject, its main object having been to ascertain and develop the points of view newly acquired in comparison with Manuscript II, with those points ignored about which there was nothing new to say. An essential portion of Chapter XVII, Part II, which anyhow is more or less relevant to Part III, was included and expanded. The logical sequence is frequently interrupted, the treatment of the subject gappy in places and very fragmentary, especially the conclusion. But what Marx intended to say is said there, somehow or other.

This is the material for Book II, out of which I was supposed "to make something", as Marx remarked to his daughter Eleanor shortly before his death. I have construed this task in its narrowest meaning. So far as this was at all possible, I have confined my work to the mere selection of a text from the available versions. I always based my work on the last available edited manuscript, comparing this with the preceding ones. I only encountered real difficulties, i. e., of more than a merely technical nature, in the first and third parts, but these were indeed considerable. I have endeavoured to solve them exclusively in the spirit of the author.

I have mostly translated quotations in the text [into German] whenever they are cited in confirmation of facts or when, as in passages from Adam Smith, the original is available to everyone who wants to go thoroughly into the matter. This was impossible only in Chapter X, because it is precisely the English text that is criticised. The quotations from Book I are paged according to its second edition, the last one to appear in Marx's lifetime.[a]

For Book III, only the following materials are available, apart from the first elaboration in manuscript form of *A Contribution to the Critique*..., from the above-mentioned parts of Manuscript III, and from a few occasional short notes scattered through various excerpt notebooks: the folio manuscript of 1864-65, referred to previously, which is about as fully worked out as Manuscript II of Book II; furthermore, a notebook dated 1875: The Relation of the Rate of Surplus Value to the Rate of Profit, which treats the subject mathematically (in equations). The preparation of this book for publication is proceeding rapidly. So far as I am able to judge up to now, it will present mainly technical difficulties, with the exception, it is true, of a few very important sections.

I consider this an opportune place to refute a certain charge which has been raised against Marx, first only in whispers, sporadically, but more recently, after his death, proclaimed an established fact by German armchair and State socialists[4] and by their followers — the charge that Marx plagiarised the work of Rodbertus. I have already

---

[a] In the Engels-authorised English edition of Volume I of *Capital* (Volume 35 of the present *Collected Works*) the division into parts and chapters is different from that in the German edition. Therefore references to the English edition are given in the footnotes here.

stated elsewhere [1] what was most urgent in this regard, but not until now have I been able to adduce conclusive proof. As far as I know this charge was made for the first time in R. Meyer's *Emancipationskampf des vierten Standes*, p. 43:

"It can be *proved* that Marx has gathered the greater part of his critique from these publications" (the works of Rodbertus dating back to the last half of the thirties).

I may well assume, until further evidence is produced, that the whole "proof" of this assertion consists in Rodbertus having assured Herr Meyer that this was so. In 1879 Rodbertus himself appears on the scene [5] and writes the following to J. Zeller (*Zeitschrift für die gesammte Staatswissenschaft*, Tübingen, 1879, p. 219), with reference to his work *Zur Erkenntniss unsrer staatswirtschaftlichen Zustände*, 1842:

"You will find that this" // the line of thought developed in it // "has been very nicely used ... by Marx, without, however, giving me credit for it."

The posthumous publisher of Rodbertus' works, Th. Kozak, repeats his insinuation without further ceremony (*Das Kapital* von Rodbertus. Berlin, 1884, Introduction, p. XV).

Finally in the *Briefe und sozialpolitische Aufsätze von Dr. Rodbertus-Jagetzow*, published by R. Meyer in 1881, Rodbertus says point-blank:

"Today I find I have been *robbed* by Schäffle and Marx without having my name mentioned" (letter No. 60, p. 134).

And in another place, Rodbertus' claim assumes a more definite form:

"In my third social letter I have shown *virtually in the same way* as Marx, only more briefly and clearly, whence the *surplus value* of the capitalist *originates*" (letter No. 48, p. 111).

Marx had never heard anything about any of these charges of plagiarism. In his copy of the *Emancipationskampf* only that part had been cut open which related to the International. The remaining pages were not opened until I cut them myself after his death. He never saw

---

[1] In the preface to *Das Elend der Philosophie. Antwort auf Proudhons Philosophie des Elends von Karl Marx*. Deutsch von E. Bernstein und K. Kautsky. Stuttgart, 1885.[a]

[a] See present edition, Vol. 26, pp. 278-91.

the Tübingen *Zeitschrift*. The *Briefe, etc.*, to R. Meyer likewise remained unknown to him, and I did not learn of the passage referring to the "robbery" until Dr. Meyer himself was good enough to call my attention to it in 1884. However, Marx was familiar with letter No. 48. Dr. Meyer had been so kind as to present the original to the youngest daughter of Marx. When some of the mysterious whispering about the secret source of his criticism having to be sought in Rodbertus reached the ear of Marx, he showed me that letter with the remark that here he had at last authentic information as to what Rodbertus himself claimed; if that was all Rodbertus asserted he, Marx, had no objection, and he could well afford to let Rodbertus enjoy the pleasure of considering his own presentation the briefer and clearer one. In fact, Marx considered the matter settled by this letter of Rodbertus.

He could think so all the more since I know for certain that he was not in the least acquainted with the literary activity of Rodbertus until about 1859, when his own critique of political economy had been completed, not only in its fundamental outlines, but also in its more important details. Marx began his economic studies in Paris, in 1843, starting with the great Englishmen and Frenchmen. Of German economists he knew only Rau and List, and he did not want any more of them. Neither Marx nor I heard a word of Rodbertus' existence until we had to criticise, in the *Neue Rheinische Zeitung*,[a] 1848, the speeches he made as Berlin Deputy and his actions as Minister. We were both so ignorant that we had to ask the Rhenish deputies who this Rodbertus was that had become a Minister so suddenly. But they too could not tell us anything about the economic writings of Rodbertus. That on the other hand Marx knew very well already at that time, without the help of Rodbertus, not only whence but also *how* "the surplus value of the capitalist" originated is proved by his *Poverty of Philosophy*, 1847,[b] and by his lectures on wage labour and capital, delivered in Brussels the same year and published in Nos. 264-69 of the *Neue Rheinische Zeitung*, in 1849.[c] It was only around 1859, through Lassalle, that Marx learned of the existence of an economist named Rodbertus and thereupon Marx looked up the "third social letter" in the British Museum.

---

[a] See present edition, Vol. 7, pp. 174, 188, 195, 273, 419, 425, 427; Vol. 8, p. 4. - [b] Ibid., Vol. 6, pp. 105-212. - [c] Ibid., Vol. 9, pp. 197-228.

These were the actual circumstances. And now let us see what there is to the content, of which Marx is charged with "robbing" Rodbertus.

"In my third social letter", says Rodbertus, "I have shown in the same way as Marx, only more briefly and clearly, whence the surplus value of the capitalist originates."

This, then, is the crux of the matter: The theory of surplus value. And indeed, it would be difficult to say what else there is in Marx that Rodbertus might claim as his property. Thus Rodbertus declares here that he is the real originator of the theory of surplus value and that Marx robbed him of it.

And what has the third social letter to say about the origin of surplus value? Simply this: That "rent", his term which lumps together ground rent and profit, does not arise from an "addition of value" to the value of a commodity, but

"from a deduction of value from wages; in other words, because wages represent only a part of the value of a product",

and if labour is sufficiently productive

"wages need not be equal to the natural exchange value of the product of labour in order to leave enough of this value for the replacing of capital" (!) "and for rent".[a]

We are not informed however what sort of a "natural exchange value" of a product it is that leaves nothing for the "replacing of capital", consequently, for the replacement of raw material and the wear and tear of tools.

It is our good fortune to be able to state what impression this stupendous discovery of Rodbertus produced on Marx. In the manuscript *A Contribution to the Critique...*, Notebook X, pp. 445 et seqq. we find a "Digression. Herr Rodbertus. A New Ground-Rent Theory". This is the only point of view from which Marx considers the third social letter there. The Rodbertian theory of surplus value in general is dismissed with the ironical remark: "Mr. Rodbertus first investigates

---

[a] [J. K.] Rodbertus, *Sociale Briefe an von Kirchmann. Dritter Brief: Widerlegung der Ricardo'schen Lehre von der Grundrente und Begründung einer neuen Rententheorie*, Berlin, 1851, S. 87.

the situation in a country where there is no separation between land ownership and ownership of capital, and then comes to the *important*[a] conclusion that rent (by which he means the entire surplus value) is simply equal to the unpaid labour or the quantity of products which it represents."[b]

Capitalistic man has been producing surplus value for several hundred years and has gradually arrived at the point of pondering over its origin. The view first propounded derived directly from commercial practice: surplus value arises out of an addition to the value of the product. This view was current among the mercantilists.[6] But James Steuart already realised that in that case what the one gains the other necessarily loses. Nevertheless, this view persisted for a long time afterwards, especially among the socialists. But it was thrust out of classical science by Adam Smith.

He says in the *Wealth of Nations*, Vol. I, Ch. VI [7]:

"As soon as STOCK[c] has accumulated in the hands of particular persons, some of them will naturally employ it in setting to work industrious people, whom they will supply with materials and subsistence, in order to make a *profit* by the sale of their work, or by *what their labour adds to the value of the materials*.... The *value* which the workmen *add to the materials*, therefore, resolves itself in this case into *two parts*, of which the one pays *their wages*, the other the *profits of their employer* upon the whole stock of materials and wages which he advanced."

And a little further on he says:

"As soon as the land of any country has all become private property, the landlords, like all other men, love to reap where they never sowed, and demand a rent even for its natural produce...." The labourer "...must *give up* to the landlord *a portion* of what his *labour* either collects or produces. This portion, or, what comes to the same thing, the price of this portion, constitutes the *rent of land*."

Marx comments on this passage in the above-named manuscript *A Contribution to the Critique...*, etc., p. 253: "Thus Adam Smith conceives *surplus value*—that is, surplus labour, the excess of labour performed and objectified in the commodity *over and above* the paid labour, the labour which has received its equivalent in the wages—as the *general category*, of which profit proper and rent of land are merely branches."[d]

Adam Smith says furthermore (Vol. I, Ch. VIII) [8]:

[a] Marx has "right". - [b] See present edition, Vol. 31, p. 251. - [c] Engels uses the German word *Kapital* and gives "stock" in parentheses. - [d] See present edition, Vol. 30, p. 388.

"As soon as land becomes private property, the landlord demands a share of almost all the produce which the labourer can either raise, or collect from it. His rent makes the *first deduction* from the *produce of the labour which is employed upon land.* It seldom happens that the person who tills the ground has the wherewithal to maintain himself till he reaps the harvest. His maintenance is generally advanced to him from the STOCK of a master, the farmer who employs him, and who would have no interest to employ him, unless he was to *share in the produce of his labour,* or unless his stock was to be replaced to him with a profit. This profit makes a *second deduction* from [the produce of] the labour which is employed upon land. The produce of almost all other labour is liable to the like deduction of profit. In all arts and manufactures the greater part of the workmen stand in need of a master to advance them the materials of their work, and their wages and maintenance till it be completed. He *shares* in the *produce of their labour,* or in the value which it adds to the materials upon which it is bestowed; and in this share consists his profit."

Marx's comment (manuscript, p. 256): "Here therefore Adam Smith in plain terms describes rent and profit on capital as mere *deductions* from the workman's product or the value of his product, which is equal to the quantity of labour added by him to the raw material. This deduction however, as Adam Smith has himself previously explained, can only consist of that part of the labour which the workman adds to the materials over and above the quantity of labour which only pays his wages, or which only provides an equivalent for his wages; that is, the surplus labour, the unpaid part of his labour." [a]

Thus even Adam Smith knew "whence the surplus value of the capitalist originated", and furthermore that of the landlord. Marx openly acknowledged this as early as 1861, while Rodbertus and the swarming mass of his admirers, who grew like mushrooms under the warm summer showers of state socialism, seem to have forgotten all about that.

"Nevertheless," Marx continues, "Smith does not distinguish surplus value as such as a category on its own, distinct from the specific forms it assumes in profit and rent. This is the source of much error and inadequacy in his inquiry, and of even more in the work of Ricardo." [b]

This statement fits Rodbertus to a T. His "rent" is simply the sum of ground rent and profit. He builds up an entirely erroneous theory of ground rent, and he accepts profit without any examination of it, just as he finds it among his predecessors.

___
[a] See present edition, Vol. 30, p. 391. - [b] Ibid., pp. 388-89.

Marx's surplus value, on the contrary, represents the *general form* of the sum of values appropriated without any equivalent by the owners of the means of production, and this form splits into the distinct, *converted* forms of profit and ground rent in accordance with very specific laws, which Marx was the first to discover. These laws will be expounded in Book III. We shall see there that many intermediate links are required to arrive from an understanding of surplus value in general at an understanding of its transformation into profit and ground rent; in other words at an understanding of the laws of the distribution of surplus value within the capitalist class.

Ricardo goes considerably further than Adam Smith. He bases his conception of surplus value on a new theory of value contained in embryo in Adam Smith, but generally forgotten when it comes to applying it. This theory of value became the starting-point of all subsequent economic science. From the determination of the value of commodities by the quantity of labour realised in them he derives the distribution, between the labourers and capitalists, of the quantity of value added by labour to the raw materials, the division of this value into wages and profit (i. e., here surplus value). He shows that the value of the commodities remains the same no matter how proportion of these two parts changes, a law which, in his opinion, has but few exceptions. He even establishes a few fundamental laws, although couched in too general terms, on the mutual relations of wages and surplus value (taken in the form of profit) (Marx, *Das Kapital*, Buch I, Kap. XV, A),[a] and shows that ground rent is an excess — accruing under certain circumstances — over and above profit.

In none of these points did Rodbertus go beyond Ricardo. He either remained wholly unaware of the internal contradictions of the Ricardian theory, which caused the downfall of that school, or they only misled him into raising utopian demands (his *Zur Erkenntniss, etc.*, p. 130) instead of inducing him to look for economic solutions.

But the Ricardian theory of value and surplus value did not have to wait for Rodbertus' *Zur Erkenntniss, etc.* in order to be utilised for socialist purposes. On page 609 of the first volume of *Das Kapital* (2nd ed.),[b] we find the following quotation, "THE POSSESSORS OF SURPLUS PRODUCE OR CAPITAL," taken from a pamphlet entitled *The Source and Remedy of the National Difficulties. A Letter to Lord John Russell*, London, 1821.[9] In this pamphlet of 40 pages, the importance of which should

---

[a] English edition: Vol. I, Ch. XVII, 1 (see present edition, Vol. 35). - [b] Ibid., Vol. I, Ch. XXIV, 1.

have been noted if only on account of the one expression SURPLUS PROD-
UCE OR CAPITAL, and which Marx tore from oblivion, we read the following statements:

"...Whatever may be due to the capitalist" //from the standpoint of the capitalist//
"he can only receive the SURPLUS LABOUR ᵃ of the labourer; for the labourer
must live" (p. 23).

But *how* the labourer lives and hence how much the surplus labour
appropriated by the capitalist can amount to are very relative things.

"If capital does not decrease in value as it increases in amount, the capitalists will
exact from the labourers the produce of every hour's labour beyond what it is possible
for the labourer to subsist on ... the capitalist may ... eventually say to the labourer,
'You shan't eat bread [...] because it is possible to subsist on beet root and potatoes.'
And to this point have we come" (pp. 23-24). "Why, if the labourer can be brought to
feed on potatoes instead of bread, it is indisputably true that more can be exacted from
his labour; i. e., if when he fed on bread, he was obliged *to retain* for the maintenance of
himself and family *the labour of Monday and Tuesday*, he will, on potatoes, require only
the *half of Monday*; and the remaining half of Monday and the whole of Tuesday are
available either for the service of the state or *the capitalist*" (p. 26). "IT IS ADMITTED ᵇ
that the interest paid to the capitalists, whether in the nature of rents, interests on
money, or profits of trade, is paid out of the labour of others" (p. 23).

Here we have, exactly, Rodbertus' "rent", except that "interest" is
used instead of "rent".

Marx makes the following comment (manuscript *A Contribution to
the Critique...*, p. 852): "This scarcely known pamphlet — which appeared at a time when the 'incredible cobbler' MacCulloch ¹⁰ began
to make a stir — contains an important advance on Ricardo. It
bluntly describes surplus value, or 'profit' as Ricardo calls it (often
also SURPLUS PRODUCE ᶜ), or INTEREST, as the author of the pamphlet
terms it, as SURPLUS LABOUR,ᶜ the labour which the worker performs
gratis, which he performs over and above the quantity of labour by
which the value of his labour power is replaced, i. e. by which he produces an equivalent for his wages. Important as it was to reduce
value to *labour*, it was equally important to reduce SURPLUS VALUE,ᶜ
which manifests itself in *SURPLUS PRODUCE,*ᶜ to *SURPLUS LABOUR.*ᶜ This was in
fact *already stated by Adam Smith and constitutes one of the main elements in*

ᵃ Engels gives the English term in parentheses after the German equivalent. - ᵇ Engels gives the English words in parentheses after their German equivalent.
- ᶜ Both the German and the English terms are given in the text.

Ricardo's argumentation. But nowhere did they clearly express it and record it in an *absolute form*."[a] We read further on, on page 859 of the manuscript: "For the rest, the author remains a captive of the economic categories as he finds them. Just as in the case of Ricardo the confusion of surplus value with profit leads to undesirable contradictions, so in his case the fact that he christens surplus value the interest of capital. To be sure, he is in advance of Ricardo in that he first of all reduces all surplus value to surplus labour, and when he calls surplus value *interest of capital*, he at the same time emphasises that by INTEREST OF CAPITAL he understands the general form of surplus labour in contrast to its particular forms—rent, interest of money and profits of trade. [...] But on the other hand, he applies the name of one of these particular forms—INTEREST—to the general form. And this suffices to make him relapse into economic gibberish //SLANG in the manuscript//."[b]

This last passage fits our Rodbertus like a glove. He, too, remains a captive of the economic categories as he finds them. He, too, applies to surplus value the name of one of its converted sub-forms, rent, and makes it quite indefinite at that. The result of these two mistakes is that he relapses into economic gibberish, that he does follow up his advance over Ricardo critically, and that instead he is misled into using his unfinished theory, even before it got rid of its egg-shell, as the basis for a utopia with which, as always, he comes too late. The pamphlet appeared in 1821 and anticipated completely Rodbertus' "rent" of 1842.

Our pamphlet is but the farthest outpost of an entire literature which in the twenties turned the Ricardian theory of value and surplus value against capitalist production in the interest of the proletariat, fought the bourgeoisie with its own weapons. The entire communism of Owen,[11] so far as it engages in polemics on economic questions, is based on Ricardo. Apart from him, there are numerous other writers, some of whom Marx quoted as early as 1847 against Proudhon (*Misère de la Philosophie*, p. 49[c]), such as Edmonds, Thompson, Hodgskin, etc., etc., "and four pages more of etceteras". I select the following at random from among this multitude of writings: *An Inquiry into the Principles of the Distribution of Wealth, Most Conducive to Human Happiness*, BY William Thompson; A NEW EDITION, London,

---

[a] See present edition, Vol. 32, p. 374. - [b] Cf. present edition, Vol. 32, pp. 388-89. - [c] See present edition, Vol. 6, p. 138.

1850.[12] This work, written in 1822, first appeared in 1824. Here likewise the wealth appropriated by the non-producing classes is described everywhere as a deduction from the product of the labourer
and rather strong words are used.

"The constant effort of what has been called society, has been to deceive and in-
duce, to terrify and compel, the productive labourer to work for the smallest possible
portion of the produce of his own labour" (p. 28). "Why not give him the whole absolute produce of his labour?" (p. 32). "This amount of compensation, exacted by capitalists from the productive labourers, under the name of rent or profits, is claimed for the
use of land or other articles... Since all the physical materials on which, or by means of
which, the propertiless productive labourer, with no other possession than his capability of producing, can make use of this capability, are in the hands of others with interests opposed to his, and their consent is a necessary preliminary to any exertion on his
part, is he not, and must he not always remain, at the mercy of these capitalists for
whatever *portion of the fruits of his own labour* they may think proper to leave at his disposal in compensation for his toils?" (p. 125). "... in proportion to the amount of *products withheld*, whether these defalcations are called profits, or taxes, or theft" (p. 126),
etc.

I must admit that I do not write these lines without a certain mor-
tification. I will not make so much of the fact that the anti-capitalist
literature of England of the twenties and thirties is so totally unknown
in Germany, in spite of Marx's direct references to it even in his
Poverty of Philosophy, and his repeated quotations from it, as for instance
the pamphlet of 1821, Ravenstone,[13] Hodgskin, etc., in the first volume of *Capital*. But it is proof of the grave deterioration of official
political economy that not only the *literatus vulgaris*,[a] who clings
desperately to the coat-tails of Rodbertus and "really has not learned
anything",[b] but also the officially and ceremoniously installed professor,[c] who "boasts of his erudition", has forgotten his classical political
economy to such an extent that he seriously charges Marx with having purloined things from Rodbertus which may be found even in
Adam Smith and Ricardo.

But what, then, is new in Marx's utterances on surplus value? How is
it that Marx's theory of surplus value struck home like a thunderbolt
out of a clear sky, and this in all civilised countries, while the theories
of all his socialist predecessors, Rodbertus included, vanished without
having produced any effect?

The history of chemistry offers an illustration which explains this.

---

[a] Rudolf Meyer - [b] A remark Talleyrand is supposed to have made about the
Bourbons. - [c] Adolph Wagner (for Marx's critique of his book *Lehrbuch der politischen Oekonomie* see present edition, Vol. 24, pp. 531-59).

We know that late in the past century the phlogistic theory still prevailed. According to it, combustion consisted essentially in this: that a certain hypothetical substance, an absolute combustible named phlogiston, separated from the burning body. This theory sufficed to explain most of the chemical phenomena then known, although it had to be considerably strained in some cases. But in 1774 Priestley described a certain kind of air

"which he found to be so pure, or so free from phlogiston, that common air seemed adulterated in comparison with it".

He called it "dephlogisticated air". Shortly after him Scheele in Sweden described the same kind of air and demonstrated its existence in the atmosphere. He also found that this kind of air disappeared when some body was burned in it or in ordinary air and therefore he called it "fire-air".

"From these facts he drew the conclusion that the combination arising from the union of phlogiston with one of the components of the atmosphere" //that is to say, from combustion// "was nothing but fire or heat which escaped through the glass."[2]

Priestley and Scheele had described oxygen without knowing what they had laid their hands on. They "remained captives of the" phlogistic "categories as they found them". The element which was destined to upset the whole phlogistic theory and to revolutionise chemistry remained barren in their hands. But Priestley had immediately communicated his discovery to Lavoisier in Paris, and Lavoisier now analysed the entire phlogistic chemistry in the light of this new fact and discovered, first, that this new kind of air was a new chemical element, and that combustion was not a case of the mysterious phlogiston *departing* from the burning body, but of this new element *combining* with that body. Thus he placed all chemistry, which in its phlogistic form had stood on its head, squarely on its feet. And although he did not describe oxygen simultaneously and independently of the others, as he claimed later on, he nevertheless is the real *discoverer* of oxygen vis-à-vis the two, who had only *described* it without knowing *what* they had described.

Marx stands in the same relation to his predecessors in the theory of surplus value as Lavoisier stood to Priestley and Scheele. The *exist-*

[2] Roscoe-Schorlemmer, *Ausführliches Lehrbuch der Chemie*. Brunswick, 1877, I, pp. 13, 18.[14]

ence of that part of the value of products which we now call surplus value had been ascertained long before Marx. It had also been stated more or less clearly what it consisted of, namely of the product of the labour for which its appropriator had not given any equivalent. But they did not get any further. Some — the classical bourgeois economists — investigated at most the proportion in which the product of labour was divided between the labourer and the owner of the means of production. Others — the socialists — found that this division was unjust and looked for utopian means of abolishing this injustice. They all remained captives of the economic categories as they had found them.

Now Marx appeared on the scene. And he took a view directly opposite to that of all his predecessors. Where they had seen a *solution*, he only saw a *problem*. He saw that this was a case neither of dephlogisticated air nor of fire-air, but of oxygen — that here it was not simply a matter of stating an economic fact or of pointing out the conflict between this fact and eternal justice and true morality, but of explaining a fact which was destined to revolutionise all political economy, and which offered to him who knew how to use it the key to an understanding of all capitalist production. In the light of this fact he examined all the economic categories which he found in existence, just as Lavoisier, proceeding from oxygen, had examined the existing categories of phlogistic chemistry. In order to understand what surplus value was, Marx had to find out what value was. He had to criticise above all the Ricardian theory of value. Hence he analysed labour's value-producing property and was the first to ascertain *what kind* of labour it was that created value, and why and how it did so. He found that value was nothing but congealed labour of *this* kind, and this is a point which Rodbertus never grasped to his dying day. Marx then investigated the relation between commodity and money and demonstrated how and why, owing to the property of value immanent in the commodity, the commodity and commodity exchange must engender the opposition of commodity and money. His theory of money, based on this realisation, is the first exhaustive one and has been tacitly accepted everywhere. He analysed the transformation of money into capital and demonstrated that this transformation is based on the purchase and sale of labour power. By substituting labour power, the value-creating property, for labour he solved with one stroke one of the difficulties which brought about the downfall of the Ricardian school, viz., the impossibility of harmonising the mutual exchange of capital and labour with the Ricardian law that value is determined by labour. By stating the division of capital into constant and variable he was enabled to trace the process of the formation of surplus value in its minutest details as it really takes place, and thus to explain it — something none of his predecessors had accomplished.

Thus he stated the existence of a division within capital itself with which neither Rodbertus nor the bourgeois economists knew in the least what to do, but which furnishes the key for the solution of the most complicated economic problems, as is strikingly proved again by Book II and will be proved still more by Book III. He analysed surplus value itself further and found its two forms, absolute and relative surplus value. And he showed that they had played a different, but in either case a decisive role, in the historical development of capitalist production. On the basis of surplus value he developed the first rational theory of wages we have, and for the first time gave an outline of the history of capitalist accumulation and an exposition of its historical tendency.

And Rodbertus? After he has read all this, he — like the tendentious economist he always is — declares that this is "an assault on society",[a] that he himself has said much more briefly and clearly what surplus value evolves from, and finally that all this does indeed apply to "the present form of capital", that is to say to capital as it exists historically, but not to the "concept of capital", namely the utopian idea which Mr. Rodbertus has of capital. Just like old Priestley, who swore by phlogiston to the end of his days and refused to have anything to do with oxygen. The only thing is that Priestley had actually been the first to describe oxygen, while Rodbertus had merely rediscovered a commonplace in his surplus value, or rather his "rent", and that Marx, unlike Lavoisier, disdained to claim that he was the first to discover the *fact* of the existence of surplus value.

The other economic feats performed by Rodbertus are on about the same plane. His elaboration of surplus value into a utopia has already been unintentionally criticised by Marx in his *Poverty of Philosophy*. What else may be said about it I have said in my preface to the German edition of that work.[b] Rodbertus' explanation of commercial crises as outgrowths of the underconsumption of the working class

---

[a] [J. K.] Rodbertus, *Briefe und sozialpolitische Aufsätze.* Herausgegeben von Dr. R. Meyer. Berlin, Bd. I, [1881,] S. 111. - [b] See present edition, Vol. 26, pp. 278-91.

may already be found in Sismondi's *Nouveaux Principes de l'Économie Politique*, Book IV, Ch. IV.[3] However, Sismondi always had the world market in mind, while Rodbertus' horizon does not extend beyond the Prussian border. His speculations as to whether wages are derived from capital or income belong to the domain of scholasticism and are definitely settled in Part III of this second book of *Capital*. His theory of rent has remained his exclusive property and may rest in peace until the manuscript of Marx criticising it is published.[a] Finally his suggestions for the emancipation of the old Prussian landed property from the oppression of capital are also entirely utopian; for they evade the only practical question raised in this connection, viz.: How can the old Prussian landed junker have a yearly income of, say, 20,000 marks and a yearly expenditure of, say, 30,000 marks, without running into debt?

The Ricardian school suffered shipwreck about the year 1830 on the rock of surplus value. And what this school could not solve remained still more insoluble for its successor, vulgar economy. The two points which caused its failure were these:

First. Labour is the measure of value. However, living labour in its exchange with capital has a lower value than the objectified labour for which it is exchanged. Wages, the value of a definite quantity of living labour, are always less than the value of the product which this same quantity of living labour produces or in which it is embodied. The question is indeed insoluble, if put in this form. It has been correctly formulated by Marx and thereby answered. It is not labour which has a value. As an activity which creates values it can no more have any special value than gravity can have any special weight, heat any special temperature, electricity any special strength of current. It is not labour which is bought and sold as a commodity, but labour *power*. Once labour power becomes a commodity, its value is determined by the labour embodied in it as a social product. This value is equal to the labour socially necessary for its production and reproduction. Hence the purchase and sale of labour power on the basis of its value thus defined does not at all contradict the economic law of value.

---

[3] "Thus the concentration of wealth in the hands of a small number of proprietors narrows the home market more and more, and industry is more and more compelled to look for foreign markets to dispose of its goods, where even greater revolutions threaten it" (namely, the crisis of 1817, which is described immediately afterwards). *Nouveaux Principes*, I, ed. 1819, p. 336.

---

[a] See ibid., Vol. 37.

Second. According to the Ricardian law of value, two capitals employing equal quantities of equally paid living labour, all other conditions being equal, produce products of equal value, and likewise surplus value, or profit, of equal quantity, in equal periods of time. But if they employ unequal quantities of living labour, they cannot produce equal amounts of surplus value, or, as the Ricardians say, equal amounts of profit. Now in reality the opposite takes place. In actual fact, equal capitals, regardless of how much or how little living labour they employ, produce equal average profits in equal times. Here there is therefore a contradiction of the law of value which had been noticed by Ricardo himself, but which his school also was unable to resolve. Rodbertus likewise could not but note this contradiction. But instead of resolving it, he made it one of the starting-points of his utopia (*Zur Erkenntniss*, p. 131). Marx had resolved this contradiction already in the manuscript of *A Contribution to the Critique....*[a] According to the plan of *Capital*, this solution will be provided in Book III.[b] Months will pass before that will be published. Hence those economists who claim to have discovered in Rodbertus the secret source and a superior predecessor of Marx have now an opportunity to demonstrate what Rodbertus' political economy can accomplish. If they can show how an equal average rate of profit can and must come about, not only without a violation of the law of value, but rather on the very basis of it, we are willing to discuss the matter further with them. In the meantime they had better make haste. The brilliant investigations of the present Book II and their entirely new results in fields hitherto almost untrod are merely introductory to the contents of Book III, which develops the final conclusions of Marx's analysis of the process of social reproduction on a capitalist basis. When this Book III appears, little mention will be made of the economist called Rodbertus.

The second and third books of *Capital* were to be dedicated, as Marx repeatedly told me, to his wife.

Frederick Engels

London, on Marx's birthday, May 5, 1885

---

[a] See present edition, vols 31-32. - [b] See ibid., Vol. 37 (*Capital*, Vol. III, parts I and II).

Frederick Engels

[PREFACE TO THE SECOND GERMAN EDITION]

The present second edition is, in the main, a faithful reprint of the first. Typographical errors have been corrected, a few stylistic blemishes eliminated, and several short paragraphs containing only repetitions struck out.

The third book, which presented quite unforeseen difficulties, is now almost finished in manuscript. If my health holds out it will be ready for the press this autumn.

F. Engels

London, July 15, 1893

———

For the sake of convenience there follows here a short compilation of passages, each with an indication of the particular manuscript (II-VIII) taken from.

Part I

Pp.31-32 [1] [a] from Ms. II; pp. 32-42 [2-12], Ms. VII; pp. 42-46 [12-16], Ms. VI; pp. 46-122 [16-89], Ms. V; pp. 122-25 [89-92], note found among excerpts from books; pp. 125-26 [92] to the end of this part, Ms. IV; there have, however, been inserted pp. 133-34 [100-

---

[a] The page numbers in square brackets refer to the 1893 German edition.

01], a passage from Ms. VIII; pp. 138 and 144 [105 and 111], notes from Ms. II.

Part II

The beginning, pp. 156-65 [123-33], is the end of Ms. IV. From here on to the end of this part, pp. 165-348 [324], all from Ms. II.

Part III

Chapter 18: (pp. 349-57) [324-32] from Ms. II.
Chapter 19: I and II (pp. 357-88) [332-64] from Ms. VIII; III (pp. 388-90) [364-66] from Ms. II.
Chapter 20: I (pp. 390-94) [366-69] from Ms. II, only the concluding paragraph from Ms. VIII.
II (pp. 394-97) [370-72] in the main from Ms. II.
III, IV, V (pp. 397-420) [373-97] from Ms. VIII.
VI, VII, VIII, IX (pp. 420-36) [397-412] from Ms. II.
X, XI, XII (pp. 436-80) [413-56] from Ms. VIII.
XIII (pp. 480-88) [457-65] from Ms. II.
Chapter 21: (pp. 488-523) [465-500] entirely from Ms. VIII.

Das Kapital.

Kritik der politischen Oekonomie.

Von

Karl Marx.

Zweiter Band.

Buch II: Der Cirkulationsprocess des Kapitals.

Zweite Auflage.

Herausgegeben von Friedrich Engels.

Das Recht der Uebersetzung ist vorbehalten.

Hamburg
Verlag von Otto Meissner.
1893.

Title page of the Second German Edition
of Volume II of *Capital*

BOOK II
THE PROCESS OF CIRCULATION OF CAPITAL

Part I

THE METAMORPHOSES OF CAPITAL
AND THEIR CIRCUITS

Chapter I

THE CIRCUIT OF MONEY CAPITAL

The circular movement [1] of capital takes place in three stages, which, according to the presentation in Volume I, form the following series:

First stage: The capitalist appears as a buyer on the commodity and the labour market; his money is transformed into commodities, or it goes through the circulation act M—C.

Second stage: Productive consumption of the purchased commodities by the capitalist. He acts as a capitalist producer of commodities; his capital passes through the process of production. The result is a commodity of more value than that of the elements entering into its production.

Third stage: The capitalist returns to the market as a seller; his commodities are turned into money, or they pass through the circulation act C—M.

Hence the formula for the circuit of money capital is: M—C ... P ... C′—M′, the dots indicating that the process of circulation is interrupted, and C′ and M′ designating C and M increased by surplus value.

The first and third stages were discussed in Book I only in so far as this was necessary for an understanding of the second stage, the process of production of capital. For this reason, the various forms which capital takes on in its different stages, and which it now assumes and now strips off in the repetition of its circuit, were not considered. These forms are now the direct object of our study.

In order to conceive these forms in their pure state, one must first of all discard all factors which have nothing to do with the changing or building of forms as such. It is therefore taken for granted here not only that the commodities are sold at their values but also that this

[1] From Manuscript II.

takes place under the same conditions throughout. Likewise disregarded therefore are any changes of value which might occur during the movement in circuits.

I. FIRST STAGE. M—C[2]

M—C represents the conversion of a sum of money into a sum of commodities; the purchaser transforms his money into commodities, the sellers transform their commodities into money. What renders this act of the general circulation of commodities simultaneously a functionally definite section in independent circuit of some individual capital is primarily not the form of the act but its material content, the specific use character of the commodities which change place with the money. These commodities are on the one hand means of production, on the other labour power, material and personal factors in the production of commodities whose specific nature must of course correspond to the special kind of articles to be manufactured. If we call labour power L, and the means of production MP, then the sum of commodities to be bought, C, is equal to L + MP, or more briefly $C <^L_{MP}$. M—C, considered as to its substance, is therefore represented by $M—C <^L_{MP}$, that is to say M—C breaks up into M—L and M—MP. The sum of money M is separated into two parts, one of which buys labour power, the other means of production. These two series of purchases belong to entirely different markets, the one to the commodity market proper, the other to the labour market.

Aside from this qualitative division of the sum of commodities into which M is transformed, the formula $M—C <^L_{MP}$ also represents a most characteristic quantitative relation.

We know that the value, or price, of labour power is paid to its owner, who offers it for sale as a commodity, in the form of wages, that is to say as the price of a sum of labour containing surplus labour. For instance, if the daily value of labour power = the product of five hours' labour valued at 3 marks, this sum figures in the contract between the buyer and seller as the price, or wages, for, say, ten hours of labour. If such a contract is made for instance with 50 labourers, they are supposed to work altogether 500 hours per day for the purchaser, and one half of this time, or 250 hours = 25 days of labour of 10 hours each, represents nothing but surplus labour. The quantity and the volume of the means of production to be pur-

---

[2] Beginning of Manuscript VII, started July 2, 1878.

chased must be sufficient for the utilisation of this mass of labour. $M—C <^{L}_{MP}$, then, does not merely express the qualitative relation indicating that a certain sum of money, say £ 422, is transformed into a corresponding sum of means of production and labour power, but also a quantitative relation between L, the part of the money spent for labour power, and MP, the part spent for means of production. This relation is determined at the outset by the quantity of excess labour, of surplus labour to be expended by a certain number of labourers.

If for instance in a spinning-mill the weekly wage of its 50 labourers amounts to £ 50, £ 372 must be spent for means of production, if this is the value of the means of production which a weekly labour of 3,000 hours, 1,500 of which are surplus labour, transforms into yarn.

It is quite immaterial here how much additional value in the form of means of production is required in the various lines of industry by the utilisation of additional labour. The point merely is that under all circumstances the part of the money spent for means of production— the means of production bought in M—MP—must be sufficient, i. e., must at the outset be calculated accordingly, must be procured in corresponding proportion. To put it another way, the quantity of means of production must suffice to absorb the amount of labour, to be transformed by it into products. If the means of production at hand were insufficient, the excess labour at the disposal of the purchaser could not be utilised; his right to dispose of it would be futile. If there were more means of production than available labour, they would not be saturated with labour, would not be transformed into products.

As soon as $M—C <^{L}_{MP}$ is completed, the purchaser has at his disposal more than simply the means of production and labour power required for the production of some useful article. He disposes of a greater capacity to set labour power in motion, or a greater quantity of labour than is necessary for the replacement of the value of this labour power, and he has at the same time the means of production requisite for the realisation or objectification of this quantity of labour. In other words, he has at his disposal the factors making for the production of articles of a greater value than that of the elements of production—the factors of production of a mass of commodities containing surplus value. Thus the value advanced by him in money form has now assumed a natural form in which it can be realised as a value generating surplus value (in the shape of commodities). In brief, value exists here in the condition or form of *productive capital*, which has the faculty of creating value and surplus value. Let us call capital in this form P.

Now the value of P is = to that of L + MP, it is = to M transformed into L and MP. M is the same capital value as P, only it has a different mode of existence, it is capital value in the state or form of money—*money capital*.

$M—C <^L_{MP}$, or its general form M—C, a sum of purchases of commodities, an act of the general circulation of commodities, is therefore at the same time—as a stage in the independent circuit of capital—a transformation of capital value from its money form into its productive form or, more briefly, it is the transformation of *money capital* into *productive capital*. In the diagram of the circuit which we are here discussing, money appears as the first depository of capital value, and money capital therefore represents the form in which capital is advanced.

Capital in the form of money capital is in a state in which it can perform the functions of money, in the present case the functions of a universal means of purchase and universal means of payment. (The last-named inasmuch as labour power though first bought is not paid for until it has been put into operation. To the extent that the means of production are not found ready on the market but have to be ordered first, money in M—MP likewise serves as a means of payment.) This capacity is not due to the fact that money capital is capital but that it is money.

On the other hand capital value in the form of money cannot perform any other functions but those of money. What turns the money functions into functions of capital is the definite role they play in the movement of capital, and therefore also the interrelation of the stage in which these functions are performed with the other stages of the circuit of capital. Take, for instance, the case with which we are here dealing. Money is here converted into commodities the combination of which represents the natural form of productive capital, and this form already contains latently, potentially, the result of the process of capitalist production.

A part of the money performing the function of money capital in $M—C <^L_{MP}$ assumes, by consummating this act of circulation, a function in which it loses its capital character but preserves its money character. The circulation of money capital M is divided into M—MP and M—L, into the purchase of means of production and the purchase of labour power. Let us consider the last-named process by itself. M—L is the purchase of labour power by the capitalist. It is also the sale of labour power—we may here say of labour, since the form of wages is assumed—by the labourer who owns it. What is M—C (= M—L) for the buyer, is here, as in every other purchase, L—M (= C—M) for the seller (the labourer). It is the sale of his labour power. This is the first stage of circulation, or the first metamorphosis, of the commodity (Buch I, Kap. III, 2a).[a] It is for the seller of labour a transformation of his commodity into the money form. The labourer spends the money so obtained gradually for a number of commodities required for the satisfaction of his needs, for articles of consumption. The complete circulation of his commodity therefore appears as L—M—C, that is to say first as L—M (= C—M) and secondly as M—C; hence in the general form of the simple circulation of commodities, C—M—C. Money is in this case merely a passing means of circulation, a mere medium in the exchange of one commodity for another.

M—L is the characteristic moment in the transformation of money capital into productive capital, because it is the essential condition for the real transformation of value advanced in the form of money into capital, into a value producing surplus value. M—MP is necessary only for the purpose of realising the quantity of labour bought in the process M—L, which was discussed from this point of view in Book I, Part II, under the head of "The Transformation of Money into Capital." We shall have to consider the matter at this point also from another angle, relating especially to money capital as the form in which capital manifests itself.

Generally M—L is regarded as characteristic of the capitalist mode of production. However not at all for the reason given above, that the purchase of labour power represents a contract of purchase which stipulates for the delivery of a quantity of labour in excess of that needed to replace the price of the labour power, the wages; hence delivery of surplus labour, the fundamental condition for the capitalisation of the value advanced, or for the production of surplus value, which is the same thing. On the contrary, it is so regarded because of its form, since *money* in the form of wages buys labour, and this is the characteristic feature of the money economy.

Nor is it the irrationality of the form which is taken as character-

---

[a] English edition: Vol. I, Ch. III, 2a (present edition, Vol. 35).

istic. On the contrary, one overlooks the irrational. The irrationality consists in the fact that labour itself as a value-creating element cannot have any value, nor can therefore any definite amount of labour have any value expressed in its price, in its equivalence to a definite quantity of money. But we know that wages are but a disguised form, a form in which for instance the price of one day's labour power presents itself as the price of the labour set in motion by this labour power in one day. The value produced by this labour power in, say, six hours of labour is thus expressed as the value of twelve hours' functioning or operation of the labour power.

M—L is regarded as the characteristic feature, the hallmark of the so-called money economy, because labour there appears as the commodity of its owner, and money therefore as the buyer—hence on account of the money relation (i. e., the sale and purchase of human activity). Money however appears very early as a buyer of so-called services, without the transformation of M into money capital, and without any change in the general character of the economic system.

It makes no difference to money into what sort of commodities it is transformed. It is the universal equivalent form of all commodities which show, if only by their prices, that ideally they represent a certain sum of money, anticipate their transformation into money, and that they only acquire the form in which they may be converted into use values for their owners by changing places with money. Once labour power has come into the market as the commodity of its owner and its sale takes the form of payment for labour, assumes the shape of wages, its purchase and sale is no more startling than the purchase and sale of any other commodity. The characteristic thing is not that the commodity labour power is purchasable but that labour power appears as a commodity.

By means of $M—C <^{L}_{MP}$, the transformation of money capital into productive capital, the capitalist effects the combination of the objective and personal factors of production so far as they consist of commodities. If money is transformed into productive capital for the first time or if it performs for the first time the function of money capital for its owner, he must begin by buying means of production, such as buildings, machinery, etc., before he buys any labour power. For as soon as labour power passes into his control, he must have means of production to which he can apply it as labour power.

This is the capitalist's presentation of the case.

The labourer's case is as follows: The productive application of his labour power is not possible until the moment when it is sold and brought into connection with means of production. Before its sale, labour power exists therefore separately from the means of production, from the material conditions of its application. In this state of separation it cannot be used either directly for the production of use values for its owner or for the production of commodities, by the sale of which he could live. But from the moment that as a result of its sale it is brought into connection with means of production, it forms part of the productive capital of its purchaser, the same as the means of production.

True, in the act M — L the owner of money and the owner of labour power enter only into the relation of buyer and seller, confront one another only as money owner and commodity owner. In this respect they enter merely into a money relation. Yet at the same time the buyer appears also from the outset in the capacity of an owner of means of production, which are the material conditions for the productive expenditure of labour power by its owner. In other words, these means of production are in opposition to the owner of the labour power, being property of another. On the other hand the seller of labour faces its buyer as labour power of another which must be made to do his bidding, must be integrated into his capital, in order that it may really become productive capital. The class relation between capitalist and wage labourer therefore exists, is presupposed from the moment that the two face each other in the act M — L (L — M on the part of the labourer). It is a purchase and sale, a money relation, but a purchase and sale in which the buyer is assumed to be a capitalist and the seller a wage labourer. And this relation arises out of the fact that the conditions required for the realisation of labour power, viz., means of subsistence and means of production, are separated from the owner of labour power, being the property of another.

We are not concerned here with the origin of this separation. It exists as soon as M — L goes on. The thing which interests us here is this: If M — L appears here as a function of money capital or money as the form of existence of capital, it is not for the sole reason that money here assumes the role of a means of paying for a useful human activity or service; hence by no means in consequence of the function of money as a means of payment. Money can be expended in this form only because labour power finds itself in a state of separation from its means of production (including the means of subsistence as means of production of the labour power itself), and because this separation can be overcome only by the sale of the labour power to the owner of the means of production; because therefore the functioning of labour power, which is not at all limited to the quantity of labour required for the reproduction of its own price, is likewise the concern of its buyer. The capital relation only emerges during the process of production because it is inherent in the act of circulation, in the different fundamental economic conditions in which buyer and seller confront each other, in their class relation. It is not money which by its nature creates this relation; it is rather the existence of this relation which permits of the transformation of a mere money function into a capital function.

In the conception of money capital (for the time being we deal with the latter only within the confines of the special function in which it faces us here) two errors run parallel to each other or cross each other. In the first place, the functions performed by capital value in its capacity of money capital, which it can perform precisely owing to its money form, are erroneously derived from its character as capital, whereas they are due only to the money form of capital value, to its form of appearance as money. In the second place, on the contrary, the specific content of the money function, which makes it simultaneously a capital function, is traced to the nature of money (money being here confused with capital), while the money function premises social conditions, such as are here indicated by the act $M — L$, which do not at all exist in the mere circulation of commodities and the corresponding circulation of money.

The purchase and sale of slaves is formally also a purchase and sale of commodities. But money cannot perform this function without the existence of slavery. If slavery exists, money can be invested in the purchase of slaves. On the other hand the mere possession of money by a buyer cannot make slavery possible.

In order that the sale of one's own labour power (in the form of the sale of one's own labour or in the form of wages) may constitute not an isolated phenomenon but a socially decisive premise for the production of commodities, in order that money capital may therefore perform, on a social scale, the above-discussed function $M — C <_{MP}^{L}$, historical processes are assumed by which the original connection of the means of production with labour power was dissolved — processes in consequence of which the mass of the people, the labourers, have, as non-owners, come face to face with the non-labourers as the owners of these means of production. It makes no difference in this case whether the connection before its dissolution was such in form that the labourer, being himself a means of production, belonged to the other means of production or whether he was their owner.

What underlies $M - C <^{L}_{MP}$ is distribution; not distribution in the ordinary meaning of a distribution of articles of consumption, but the distribution of the elements of production itself, the material factors of which are concentrated on one side, and labour power, isolated from them, on the other.

The means of production, the material part of productive capital, must therefore face the labourer as such, as capital, before the act $M - L$ can become a universal, social one.

We have seen on previous occasions[a] that in its development capitalist production, once it is established, not only reproduces this separation but extends its scope further and further until it becomes the generally prevailing social condition. However, there is still another side to this question. In order that capital may be able to arise and take control of production, a definite stage in the development of trade is assumed. This applies therefore also to the circulation of commodities, and hence to the production of commodities; for no articles can enter circulation as commodities unless they are produced for sale, hence as commodities. But the production of commodities does not become the normal, dominant type of production until capitalist production serves as its basis.

The Russian landowners, who as a result of the so-called emancipation of the peasants[15] are now compelled to carry on agriculture with the help of wage labourers instead of the forced labour of serfs, complain about two things: First, about the lack of money capital. They say for instance that comparatively large sums must be paid to wage labourers before the crops are sold, and just then there is a dearth of ready cash, the prime condition. Capital in the form of money must always be available, particularly for the payment of wages, before production can be carried on capitalistically. But the landowners may take hope. Everything comes to those who wait, and in due time the industrial capitalist will have at his disposal not only his own money but also *l'argent des autres*.[b]

---

[a] English edition: *Capital*, Vol. I, parts VII and VIII, especially Ch. XXXII. - [b] the money of others

The second complaint is more characteristic. It is to the effect that even if one has money, not enough labour power is to be bought at any time. The reason is that the Russian farm labourer, owing to the common ownership of land in the village community, has not yet been fully separated from his means of production and hence is not yet a "free wage labourer" in the full sense of the word. But the existence of the latter on a social scale is a *sine qua non* for M — C, the conversion of money into commodities, to be able to represent the transformation of money capital into productive capital.

It is therefore quite clear that the formula for the circuit of money capital, M — C ... P ... C′ — M′, is the matter-of-course form of the circuit of capital only on the basis of already developed capitalist production, because it presupposes the existence of a class of wage labourers on a social scale. We have seen that capitalist production does not only create commodities and surplus value, but also reproduces to an ever increasing extent the class of wage labourers, into whom it transforms the vast majority of direct producers. Since the first condition for its realisation is the permanent existence of a class of wage labourers, M — C ... P ... C′ — M′ presupposes a capital in the form of productive capital, and hence the form of the circuit of productive capital.

II. SECOND STAGE. FUNCTION
OF PRODUCTIVE CAPITAL

The circuit of capital, which we have here considered, begins with the act of circulation M — C, the transformation of money into commodities — purchase. Circulation must therefore be complemented by the antithetical metamorphosis C — M, the transformation of commodities into money — sale. But the direct result of M — C $<^{\text{L}}_{\text{MP}}$ is the interruption of the circulation of the capital value advanced in the form of money. By the transformation of money capital into productive capital the capital value has acquired a bodily form in which it cannot continue to circulate but must enter into consumption, viz., into productive consumption. The use of labour power, labour, can be materialised only in the labour process. The capitalist cannot resell the labourer as a commodity because he is not his chattel slave and the capitalist has not bought anything except the right to use his labour power for a certain time. On the other hand the capitalist cannot use this labour power in any other way than by utilising means of production to create commodities with its help. The result of the first stage is therefore entrance into the second, the productive stage of capital.

The movement is represented by $M - C <_{MP}^{L}$ ... P, in which the dots indicate that the circulation of capital is interrupted, while its circular movement continues, since it passes from the sphere of the circulation of commodities into that of production. The first stage, the transformation of money capital into productive capital, is therefore merely the harbinger and introductory phase of the second stage, the functioning of productive capital.

$M - C <_{MP}^{L}$ presupposes that the individual performing this act not only has at his disposal values in any use form, but also that he has them in the form of money, that he is the owner of money. But the act consists precisely in giving away money, and the individual can remain the owner of money only in so far as the latter flows back implicitly to him through that very act. But money can return to him only through the sale of commodities. Hence the above act presupposes his existence as a producer of commodities.

$M - L$. The wage labourer lives only by the sale of his labour power. Its preservation — his self-preservation — requires daily consumption. Hence payment for it must be continually repeated at rather short intervals in order that he may be able to repeat acts $L - M - C$ or $C - M - C$, repeat the purchases needed for his self-preservation. For this reason the capitalist must always meet the wage labourer in the capacity of a money capitalist, and his capital as money capital. On the other hand if the wage labourers, the mass of direct producers, are to perform the act $L - M - C$, they must constantly be faced with the necessary means of subsistence in purchasable form, i. e., in the form of commodities. Consequently this state of affairs necessitates a high degree of development of the circulation of products in the form of commodities, hence also of the volume of commodities produced. When production by means of wage labour becomes universal, commodity production is bound to be the general form of production. The production of commodities, once it is assumed to be general, carries in its wake an ever increasing division of social labour, that is to say an ever growing differentiation of the products which are produced in the form of commodities by a definite capitalist, ever greater division of complementary processes of production into independent processes. $M - MP$ therefore develops to the same extent as $M - L$ does, that is to say the production of means of production is divorced to that extent from the production of commodities whose means of production they are. And the latter themselves stand opposed to every producer of commodities as commodities which he does not produce but buys for his particular process of production. They come from branches of production which, operated independently, are entirely divorced from his own, enter into his own branch as commodities, and must therefore be bought. The material conditions of commodity production face him more and more as products of other commodity producers, as commodities. And to the same extent the capitalist must assume the role of money capitalist, in other words there is an increase in the scale on which his capital must assume the functions of money capital.

On the other hand, the same conditions which give rise to the basic condition of capitalist production, the existence of a class of wage workers, facilitate the transition of all commodity production to capitalist commodity production. As capitalist production develops, it has a disintegrating, resolvent effect on all older forms of production, which, designed mostly to meet the direct needs of the producer, transform only the excess produced into commodities. Capitalist production makes the sale of products the main interest, at first apparently without affecting the mode of production itself. Such was for instance the first effect of capitalist world commerce on such nations as the Chinese, Indians, Arabs, etc. But, secondly, wherever it takes root capitalist production destroys all forms of commodity production which are based either on the self-employment of the producers, or merely on the sale of the excess product as commodities. It first makes the production of commodities general and then, by degrees, transforms all commodity production into capitalist production. [3]

Whatever the social form of production, labourers and means of production always remain factors of it. But in a state of separation from each other either of these factors can be such only potentially. For production to go on at all they must unite. The specific manner in which this union is accomplished distinguishes the different economic epochs of the structure of society from one another. In the present case, the separation of the free worker from his means of production is the starting-point given, and we have seen how and under what conditions these two elements are united in the hands of the capitalist, namely, as the productive mode of existence of his capital. The actual

[3] End of Manuscript VII. Beginning of Manuscript VI.

process which the personal and material creators of commodities enter upon when thus brought together, the process of production, becomes therefore itself a function of capital, the capitalist process of production, the nature of which has been fully analysed in the first book of this work. Every enterprise engaged in commodity production becomes at the same time an enterprise exploiting labour power. But only the capitalist production of commodities has become an epoch-making mode of exploitation, which, in the course of its historical development, revolutionises, through the organisation of the labour process and the enormous improvement of technique, the entire economic structure of society in a manner eclipsing all former epochs.

The means of production and labour power, in so far as they are forms of existence of advanced capital value, are distinguished by the different roles assumed by them during the process of production in the creation of value, hence also of surplus value, into constant and variable capital. Being different components of productive capital they are furthermore distinguished by the fact that the means of production in the possession of the capitalist remain his capital even outside of the process of production, while labour power becomes the form of existence of an individual capital only within this process. Whereas labour power is a commodity only in the hands of its seller, the wage labourer, it becomes capital only in the hands of its buyer, the capitalist who acquires the temporary use of it. The means of production do not become the material forms of productive capital, or productive capital, until labour power, the personal form of existence of productive capital, is capable of being embodied in them. Human labour power is by nature no more capital than are the means of production. They acquire this specific social character only under definite, historically developed conditions, just as only under such conditions the character of money is stamped upon precious metals, or that of money capital upon money.

Productive capital, in performing its functions, consumes its own component parts for the purpose of transforming them into a mass of products of a higher value. Since labour power acts merely as one of its organs, the excess of the product's value engendered by its surplus labour over and above the value of productive capital's constituent elements is also the fruit of capital. The surplus labour of labour power is the gratuitous labour performed for capital and thus forms surplus value for the capitalist, a value which costs him no equivalent return. The product is therefore not only a commodity, but a commodity pregnant with surplus value. Its value is equal to $P + s$, that is to say equal to the value of the productive capital P consumed in the production of the commodity plus the surplus value s created by it. Let us assume that this commodity consists of 10,000 lbs of yarn, and that means of production worth £372 and labour power worth £50 were consumed in the fabrication of this quantity of yarn. During the process of spinning, the spinners transmitted to the yarn the value of the means of production consumed by their labour, amounting to £372, and at the same time they created, in proportion with the labour expended by them, new value to the amount of, say, £128. The 10,000 lbs of yarn therefore represent a value of £500.

III. THIRD STAGE. C′—M′

Commodities become *commodity capital* as a functional form of existence—stemming directly from the process of production itself—of the already expanded capital value. If the production of commodities were carried on capitalistically throughout society, all commodities would be elements of commodity capital from the outset, whether they were crude iron, Brussels lace, sulphuric acid or cigars. The problem of what kinds of commodities out of the vast host available are destined by their nature to rank as capital and what other kinds to serve as ordinary commodities, is one of the self-created lovely ills of scholastic political economy.

Capital in the form of commodities has to perform the function of commodities. The articles of which capital is composed are produced from the outset for the market and must be sold, transformed into money, hence go through the process C — M.

Suppose the commodity of the capitalist to consist of 10,000 lbs of cotton yarn. If £372 represent the value of the means of production consumed in the spinning process, and new value to the amount of £128 has been created, the yarn has a value of £500, which is expressed in its price of the same amount. Suppose further that this price is realised by the sale C — M. What is it that makes of this simple act of all commodity circulation at the same time a capital function? No change that takes place inside of it, neither in the use character of the commodity — for it passes into the hands of the buyer as an object of use — nor in its value, for this value has not experienced any change of magnitude, but only of form. It first existed in the form of yarn, while now it exists in the form of money. Thus a substantial distinction is evident between the first stage $M-C$ and the last stage $C-M$. There the advanced money functions as money capital, because it is transformed by means of the circulation into commodities of a specific use value. Here the commodities can serve as capital only to the extent that they bring this character with them in ready shape from the process of production before their circulation begins. During the spinning process, the spinners create yarn value to the amount of £ 128. Of this sum, say £ 50 represent to the capitalist merely an equivalent for his outlay for labour power, while £ 78 — when the degree of exploitation of labour power is 156% — form surplus value. The value of the 10,000 lbs of yarn therefore embodies first the value of the consumed productive capital P, the constant part of which = £ 372, the variable = £ 50, their sum = £ 422 = 8,440 lbs of yarn. Now the value of the productive capital $P = C$, the value of its constituent elements, which in the stage $M-C$ confronted the capitalist as commodities in the hands of their sellers.

In the second place, however, the value of the yarn contains a surplus value of £ 78 = 1,560 lbs of yarn. C as an expression of the value of the 10,000 lbs of yarn is therefore = to $C + \Delta C$, or C plus an increment of C (= £ 78), which we shall call c, since it exists in the same commodity form as now the original value C. The value of the 10,000 lbs of yarn, equal to £ 500, is therefore represented by $C + c = C'$. What turns C, the expression of the value of the 10,000 lbs of yarn, into C' is not the absolute magnitude of its value (£ 500), for that is determined, as in the case of any other C standing for the expression of the value of some other sum of commodities, by the quantity of labour objectified in it. It is its relative value magnitude, its value magnitude as compared with that of capital P consumed in its production. This value is contained in it plus the surplus value supplied by the productive capital. Its value is greater, exceeds that of the capital value by this surplus value c. The 10,000 lbs of yarn are the bearers of the capital value expanded, enriched by this surplus value, and they are so by virtue of being the product of the capitalist process of production. C' expresses a value relation, the relation of the value of the commodities produced to that of the capital spent on their production, in other words, expresses the fact that its value is composed of capital value and surplus value. The 10,000 lbs of yarn represent commodity capital, C', only because they are a converted form of the productive capital P, hence in a connection which exists originally only in the circuit of this individual capital, or only for the capitalist who produced the yarn with the help of his capital. It is, so to say, only an internal, not an external relation that turns the 10,000 lbs of yarn in their capacity of vehicles of value into a commodity capital. They exhibit their capitalist birthmark not in the absolute magnitude of their value but in its relative magnitude, in the magnitude of their value as compared with that possessed by the productive capital embodied in them before it was transformed into commodities. If, then, these 10,000 lbs of yarn are sold at their value of £ 500, this act of circulation, considered by itself, = C — M, a mere transformation of an unchanging value from the form of a commodity into that of money. But as a special stage in the circuit of an individual capital, the same act is a realisation of the capital value embodied in the commodity to the amount of £ 422 + the surplus value, likewise embodied in it, of £ 78. That is to say it represents C′—M′, the transformation of the commodity capital from its commodity form into the money form.[4]

The function of C′ is now that of all commodities, viz.: to transform itself into money, to be sold, to go through the circulation stage C— M. So long as the capital, now expanded, remains in the form of commodity capital, lies immovable in the market, the process of production is at rest. The capital acts neither as a creator of products nor as a creator of value. A given capital value will serve, in widely different degrees, as a creator of products and value, and the scale of reproduction will be extended or reduced commensurate with the particular speed with which that capital throws off its commodity form and assumes that of money, or with the rapidity of the sale. It was shown in Book I that the degree of efficiency of any given capital is conditional on the potentialities of the productive process, which to a certain extent are independent of the magnitude of its own value.[a] Here it appears that the process of circulation sets in motion new forces independent of the capital's magnitude of value and determining its degree of efficiency, its expansion and contraction.

The mass of commodities C′, being the depository of the expanded capital, must furthermore pass in its entirety through the metamorphosis C′ — M′. The quantity sold is here a main determinant. The individual commodity figures only as an integral part of the total mass.

---

[4] End of Manuscript VI. Beginning of Manuscript V.

---

[a] English edition: *Capital*, Vol. I, Ch. XXIV, 4 (present edition, Vol. 35).

The £500 worth of value exists in the 10,000 lbs of yarn. If the capitalist succeeds in selling only 7,440 lbs at their value of £372, he has replaced only the value of his constant capital, the value of the expended means of production. If he sells 8,440 lbs he recovers only the value of the total capital advanced. He must sell more in order to realise surplus value, and he must sell the entire 10,000 lbs in order to realise the entire surplus value of £78 (= 1,560 lbs of yarn). In £500 in money he therefore receives merely an equivalent for the commodity sold. His transaction within the circulation is simply C — M. If he had paid his labourers £64 in wages instead of £50 his surplus value would be only £64 instead of 78, and the degree of exploitation would have been only 100% instead of 156. But the value of his yarn would not change; only the relation between its component parts would be different. The circulation act C — M would still represent the sale of 10,000 lbs of yarn for £500,, their value.

$C' = C + c$ (= £422 + £78). C equals the value of P or the productive capital, and this equals the value of M, the money advanced in M — C, the purchase of the elements of production, amounting to £422 in our example. If the mass of commodities is sold at its value, then C = £422 and c = £78, the value of the surplus product of 1,560 lbs of yarn. If we call c, expressed in money, m, then $C' — M' = (C + c) — (M + m)$, and the circuit M — C ... P ... C' — M', in its expanded form, is therefore represented by $M — C <^L_{MP} ... P ... (C + c) — (M + m)$.

In the first stage the capitalist takes articles of consumption out of the commodity market proper and the labour market. In the third stage he throws commodities back, but only into one market, the commodity market proper. However the fact that he extracts from the market, by means of his commodities, a greater value than he threw onto it originally is due only to the circumstance that he throws more commodity value back onto it than he first drew out of it. He threw in value M and drew out the equivalent C; he throws C + c back, and draws out the equivalent M + m.

In our example M was equal to the value of 8,440 lbs of yarn. But he throws 10,000 lbs of yarn onto the market, and therefore he returns a greater value than he took. On the other hand he threw this increased value onto the market only because through the exploitation of labour power in the process of production he had created surplus value (as an aliquot part of the product expressed in surplus product). It is only by virtue of being the product of this process that the mass of commodities becomes commodity capital, the bearer of the expanded capital value. By performing C′ — M′ the advanced capital value as well as the surplus value are realised. The realisation of both takes place simultaneously in a series of sales or in a lump sale of the entire mass of commodities which is expressed by C′ — M′. But the same circulation act C′ — M′ is different for capital value and for surplus value, as it expresses for each of them a different stage of their circulation, a different section of the series of metamorphoses through which they must pass in the sphere of circulation. The surplus value c came into the world only during the process of production. It appeared for the first time in the commodity market, and moreover in the form of commodities. This is its first form of circulation, hence the act c — m is its first circulation act, or its first metamorphosis, which remains to be supplemented by the antithetical act of circulation, or the reverse metamorphosis, m — c.[5]

It is different with the circulation which the capital value C performs in the same circulation act C′ — M′, and which constitutes for it the circulation act C — M, in which C is = to P, equal to the M originally advanced. Capital value has opened its first circulation act in the form of M, money capital, and returns through the act C — M to the same form. It has therefore passed through the two antithetical stages of the circulation, 1) M — C, 2) C — M, and finds itself once more in the form in which it can begin its circular movement anew. What for surplus value constitutes the first transformation of the commodity form into that of money, constitutes for capital value its return, or retransformation, into its original money form.

By means of M — C $<^L_{MP}$ money capital is transformed into an equivalent sum of commodities, L and MP. These commodities no longer perform the function of commodities, of articles for sale. Their value exists now in the hands of the capitalist who bought them as the value of his productive capital P. And in the function of P, productive consumption, they are transformed into a kind of commodity differing materially from the means of production, into yarn, in which their value is not only preserved but increased, from £422 to £500. By means of this real metamorphosis, the commodities taken from the market in the first stage, M — C, are replaced by commodities of different substance and value, which now must perform the function of

---

[5] This is true no matter how we separate capital value and surplus value. 10,000 lbs of yarn contain 1,560 lbs = £78 worth of surplus value; likewise one lb., or one shilling's worth of yarn, contains 2.496 ounces = 1.872 pence worth of surplus value.

commodities, must be transformed into money and sold. The process of production therefore appears to be only an interruption of the process of circulation of capital value, of which up to that point only the first phase, M—C, has been passed through. It passes through the second and concluding phase, C—M, after C has been altered in substance and value. But so far as capital value, considered by itself, is concerned, it has merely suffered an alteration of its use form in the process of production. It existed in the form of £422 worth of L and MP, while now it exists in the form of £422 worth, or 8,440 lbs of yarn. If we therefore consider merely the two circulation phases of capital value, apart from its surplus value, we find that it passes through 1) M—C and 2) C—M, in which the second C has a different use form but the same value as the first C. Hence it passes through M—C—M, a form of circulation which, because the commodity here changes place twice and in the opposite direction—transformation from money into commodities and from commodities into money—necessitates the return of the value advanced in the form of money to its money form—its reconversion into money.

The same circulation act C'—M' that constitutes the second and concluding metamorphosis, a return to the money form, for the capital value advanced in money, represents for the surplus value—borne along by the commodity capital and simultaneously realised by its change into the money form—its first metamorphosis, its transformation from the commodity to the money form, C—M, its first circulation phase.

We have, then, two kinds of observations to make here. First, the ultimate reconversion of capital value into its original money form is a function of commodity capital. Secondly, this function includes the first transformation of surplus value from its original commodity form to its money form. The money form, then, plays a double role here. On the one hand it is the form to which a value originally advanced in money returns, hence a return to that form of value which opened the process. On the other hand it is the first converted form of a value which originally enters the circulation in commodity form. If the commodities composing the commodity capital are sold at their values, as we assume, then C + c is transformed into M + m, its equivalent. The realised commodity capital now exists in the hands of the capitalist in this form: M + m (£422 + £78 = £500). Capital value and surplus value are now present in the form of money, the form of the universal equivalent.

At the conclusion of the process capital value has therefore resumed the form in which it entered it, and as money capital can now open and go through a new process. Just because the initial and final forms of this process are those of money capital (M), we call this form of the circuit process the circuit of money capital. It is not the form but merely the magnitude of the advanced value that is changed at the close.

M + m is nothing but a sum of money of a definite magnitude, in this case £ 500. But as a result of the circuit of capital, as realised commodity capital, this sum of money contains the capital value and the surplus value. And these values are now no longer inseparably united as they were in the yarn; they now lie side by side. Their realisation has given both of them an independent money form; $^{211}/_{250}$ of this money represent the capital value of £422 and $^{39}/_{250}$ constitute the surplus value of £ 78. This separation, effected by the realisation of the commodity capital, has not only the formal content to which we shall refer presently. It becomes important in the process of the reproduction of capital, depending on whether m is entirely or partially or not at all lumped together with M, hence depending on whether or not it continues to function as a component part of the advanced capital value. Both m and M may pass through quite different processes of circulation.

In M′ capital has returned to its original form M, to its money form, a form however in which it is materialised as capital.

There is in the first place a difference of quantity. It was M, £ 422. It is now M′, £ 500, and this difference is expressed by M ... M′, the quantitatively different extremes of the circuit, whose movement is indicated only by the three dots. M′ > M, and M′ — M = s, the surplus value.—But as a result of this circular movement M ... M′ it is only M′ which exists now; it is the product in which its process of formation has become extinct. M′ now exists by itself, independently of the movement which brought it into existence. That movement is gone; M′ is there in its place.

But M′, being M + m, £ 500, composed of £ 422 advanced capital plus an increment of the same amounting to £ 78, represents at the same time a qualitative relation, although this qualitative relation itself exists only as a relation between the parts of one and the same sum, hence as a quantitative relation. M, the advanced capital, which is now once more present in its original form (£ 422), exists as realised capital. It has not only preserved itself but also realised itself as capital by being distinguished as such from m (£ 78), to which it stands in the same relation as to an increase *of its own*, to a fruit *of its own*, to an increment to which it has given birth itself. It has been realised as capital because it has been realised as a value which has created value. M′ exists as a capital relation. M no longer appears as mere money, but is expressly posited as money capital, expressed as a self-expanded value, which therefore possesses the property of self-expansion, of hatching a higher value than it itself has. M became capital by virtue of its relation to the other part of M′, which it has brought about, which has been effected by it as the cause, which is the consequence of it as the ground. Thus M′ appears as a sum of values differentiated within itself, functionally (conceptually) distinguished within itself, expressing the capital relation.

But this is expressed only as a result, without the intervention of the process of which it is the result.

Parts of value as such are not qualitatively different from one another, except in so far as they appear as values of different articles, of concrete things, hence in various use forms and therefore as values of different commodities — a difference which does not originate from them themselves as mere parts of value. In money all differences between commodities are extinguished, because it is the equivalent form common to all of them. A sum of money in the amount of £ 500 consists solely of uniform elements of £ 1 each. Since the intermediate links of its origin are obliterated in the simple existence of this sum of money and every trace has been lost of the specific difference between the different component parts of capital in the process of production, there exists now only the distinction between the conceptual form of a PRINCIPAL[a] equal to £ 422, the capital advanced, and an excess value of £ 78. Let M′ be equal to, say, £ 110, of which 100 may be equal to M, the principal, and 10 equal to s, the surplus value. There is an absolute homogeneity, hence an absence of conceptual distinctions, between the two constituent parts of the sum of £ 110. Any £ 10 of this sum always constitute $1/_{11}$ of the total sum of £ 110, whether they are $1/_{10}$ of the advanced principal of £ 100 or the excess of £ 10 above it. Principal and excess sum, capital and surplus sum, may therefore be expressed as fractional parts of the total sum. In our illustration, $10/_{11}$ form the principal, or the capital, and $1/_{11}$ the surplus sum. In its money expression realised capital appears therefore at the end of its process as an irrational expression of the capital relation.

---

[a] This English term in the original is given in parentheses after its German equivalent.

True, this applies also to C' (= C + c). But there is this difference: that C', of which C and c are only proportional value parts of the same homogeneous mass of commodities, indicates its origin in P, whose immediate product it is, while in M', a form derived directly from circulation, the direct relation to P is obliterated.

The irrational distinction between the principal and the incremental sum, which is contained in M', so far as that expresses the result of the movement M ... M', disappears as soon as it once more functions actively as money capital and is therefore not fixed as a money expression of expanded industrial capital. The circuit of money capital can never begin with M' (although M' now performs the function of M). It can begin only with M, that is to say it can never begin as an expression of the capital relation, but only as a form of advance of capital value. As soon as the £ 500 are once more advanced as capital, in order again to produce s, they constitute a point of departure, not one of return. Instead of a capital of £ 422, a capital of £ 500 is now advanced. It is more money than before, more capital value, but the relation between its two constituent parts has disappeared. In fact a sum of £ 500 instead of the £ 422 might originally have served as capital.

It is not an active function of money capital to appear as M'; to appear as M' is rather a function of C'. Even in the simple circulation of commodities, 1) C_1 — M, 2) M — C_2, money M does not figure actively until the second act, M — C_2. Its appearance in the form of M is only the result of the first act, by virtue of which it only then appears as a converted form of C_1. True, the capital relation contained in M', the relation of one of its parts as the capital value to the other as its value increment, acquires functional importance in so far as, with the constantly repeated circuit M ... M', M' splits into two circulations, one of them a circulation of capital, the other of surplus value. Consequently these two parts perform not only quantitatively but also qualitatively different functions, M others than m. But considered by itself, the form M ... M' does not include what the capitalist consumes, but explicitly only the self-expansion and accumulation, so far as the latter expresses itself above all as a periodical augmentation of ever renewed advances of money capital.

Although M', = to M + m, is the irrational form of capital, it is at the same time only money capital in its realised form, in the form of money which has generated money. But this is different from the function of money capital in the first stage, M—C $<^L_{MP}$. In this first stage, M circulates as money. It assumes the functions of money capital because only in its money state can it perform a money function, can it transform itself into the elements of P, into L and MP, which stand opposed to it as commodities. In this circulation act it functions only as money. But as this act is the first stage of capital value in process, it is simultaneously a function of money capital, by virtue of the specific use form of the commodities L and MP which are bought. M′, on the other hand, composed of M, the capital value, and m, the surplus value begotten of M, stands for self-expanded capital value—the purpose and the outcome, the function of the total circuit of capital. The fact that it expresses this outcome in the form of money, as realised money capital, does not derive from its being the money form of capital, *money* capital, but on the contrary from its being money *capital*, capital in the form of money, from capital having opened the process in this form, from its having been advanced in the money form. Its reconversion into the money form is, as we have seen, a function of commodity capital C′, not of money capital. As for the difference between M′ and M, it (m) is simply the money form of c, the increment of C. M′ is = to M + m only because C′ was = to C + c. In C′ therefore this difference and the relation of the capital value to the surplus value generated by it is present and expressed before both of them are transformed into M′, into a sum of money in which both parts of the value come face to face with each other independently and may, therefore, be employed in separate and distinct functions.

M′ is only the result of the realisation of C′. Both M′ and C′ are merely different forms of self-expanded capital value, one of them the commodity form, the other the money form. Both of them have this in common: that they are self-expanded capital value. Both of them are realised capital, because capital value as such exists here together with the surplus value, the fruit obtained through it and differing from it although this relation is expressed only in the irrational form of the relation between two parts of a sum of money or of a commodity value. But as expressions of capital in relation and contradistinction to the surplus value produced by it, hence as expressions of self-expanded value, M′ and C′ are the same and express the same thing, only in different forms. They do not differ as money capital and commodity capital but as money and commodities. In so far as they represent self-expanded value, capital acting as capital, they only express the result of the functioning of productive capital, the only function in which capital value generates value. What they have in common is that both of them, money capital as well as commodity capital, are modes of existence of capital. The one is capital in money form, the other in commodity form. The specific functions that distinguish them cannot therefore be anything else but differences between the functions of money and of commodities. Commodity capital, as the direct product of the capitalist process of production, is reminiscent of its origin and is therefore more rational and less incomprehensible in form than money capital, in which every trace of this process has vanished, as in general all special use forms of commodities disappear in money. It is therefore only when M' itself functions as commodity capital, when it is the direct product of a productive process instead of being the converted form of this product, that it loses its bizarre form, that is to say, in the production of the money material itself. In the production of gold for instance the formula would be $M - C <^{L}_{MP}$ ... P ... M' $(M + m)$, where M' would figure as a commodity product, because P furnishes more gold than was advanced for the elements of production of the gold in the first M, the money capital. In this case the irrational nature of the expression M ... M' $(M + m)$ disappears. Here a part of a sum of money appears as the mother of another part of the same sum of money.

IV. THE CIRCUIT AS A WHOLE

We have seen that the process of circulation is interrupted at the end of its first phase, $M - C <^{L}_{MP}$, by P, in which the commodities L and MP bought in the market are consumed as the material and value components of productive capital. The product of this consumption is a new commodity, C', altered in respect of substance and value. The interrupted process of circulation, $M - C$, must be completed by $C - M$. But the bearer of this second and concluding phase of circulation is C', a commodity different in substance and value from the original C. The circulation series therefore appears as 1) $M - C_1$; 2) $C'_2 - M'$, where in the second phase of the first commodity, C_1, another commodity of greater value and different use form, C'_2, is substituted during the interruption caused by the functioning of P, the production of C' from the elements of C, the forms of existence of productive capital P. However, the first form of appearance in which capital faced us (Buch I, Kap. IV, 1),[a] $M - C - M'$ (extended: 1) $M -$

---

[a] English edition: Vol. I, Ch. IV (present edition, Vol. 35).

Facsimile of a page of the manuscript
of *Capital*, Volume II, by Karl Marx

C_1; 2) $C_1 - M'$) shows the same commodity twice. Both times it is the same commodity into which money is transformed in the first phase and reconverted into more money in the second phase. In spite of this essential difference, both circulations share this much: that in their first phase money is transformed into commodities, and in the second commodities into money, that the money spent in the first phase returns in the second. On the one hand both have in common this reflux of the money to its starting-point, on the other hand also the excess of the returning money over the money advanced. To that extent the formula $M - C \ldots C' - M'$ is contained in the general formula $M - C - M'$.

It follows furthermore that each time equally great quantities of simultaneously existing values face and replace each other in the two metamorphoses $M - C$ and $C' - M'$ belonging in circulation. The change of value pertains exclusively to the metamorphosis P, the process of production, which thus appears as a real metamorphosis of capital, as compared with the merely formal metamorphoses of circulation.

Let us now consider the total movement, $M - C \ldots P \ldots C' - M'$, or, $M - C <^L_{MP} \ldots P \ldots C' (C + c) - M' (M + m)$, its more expanded form. Capital here appears as a value which goes through a series of interconnected, interdependent transformations, a series of metamorphoses which form just as many phases, or stages, of the process as a whole. Two of these phases belong in the sphere of circulation, one of them in that of production. In each one of these phases capital value has a different form for which there is a correspondingly different, special function. Within this movement the advanced value does not only preserve itself but grows, increases in magnitude. Finally, in the concluding stage, it returns to the same form which it had at the beginning of the process as a whole. This process as a whole constitutes therefore the process of moving in circuits.

The two forms assumed by capital value at the various stages of its circulation are those of *money capital* and *commodity capital*. The form pertaining to the stage of production is that of *productive capital*. The capital which assumes these forms in the course of its total circuit and then discards them and in each of them performs the function corresponding to the particular form, is *industrial capital*, industrial here in the sense that it comprises every branch of industry run on a capitalist basis.

Money capital, commodity capital, and productive capital do not therefore designate independent kinds of capital whose functions form the content of likewise independent branches of business separated from one another. They denote here only special functional forms of industrial capital, which assumes all three of them one after the other.

Capital describes its circuit normally only so long as its various phases pass uninterruptedly into one another. If capital stops short in its first phase M — C, money capital assumes the rigid form of a hoard; if it stops in the phase of production, the means of production lie without functioning on the one side, while labour power remains unemployed on the other; and if capital is stopped short in its last phase C′ — M′, piles of unsold commodities accumulate and clog the flow of circulation.

However, it is in the nature of things that the circuit itself necessitates the fixation of capital for certain lengths of time in its various phases. In each of its phases industrial capital is tied up with a definite form: money capital, productive capital, commodity capital. It does not acquire the form in which it may enter a new transformation phase until it has performed the function corresponding to each particular form. To make this plain, we have assumed in our illustration that the capital value of the quantity of commodities created at the stage of production is equal to the total sum of the value originally advanced in the form of money; or, in other words, that the entire capital value advanced in the form of money passes on in bulk from one stage to the next. But we have seen (**Buch I, Kap. VI**) [a] that a part of the constant capital, the labour instruments proper (e. g., machinery), continually serve anew, with more or less numerous repetitions of the same processes of production, hence transfer their values piecemeal to the products. It will be seen later to what extent this circumstance modifies the circular movement of capital. For the present the following suffices: In our illustration the value of the productive capital amounting to £ 422 contained only the average wear and tear of factory buildings, machinery, etc., that is to say only that part of value which they transferred to the yarn in the transformation of 10,600 lbs of cotton into 10,000 lbs of yarn, which represented the product of one week's spinning of 60 hours. In the means of production, into which the advanced constant capital of £ 372 was transformed, the instruments of labour, buildings, machinery, etc., figured as

---

[a] English edition: Vol. I, Ch. VIII (present edition, Vol. 35).

NY 30 a

NY 30 b

Facsimile of a page of the manuscript of *Capital*,
Volume II, edited and copied by Frederick Engels

if they had only been rented in the market at a weekly rate. But this does not change the gist of the matter in any way. We have but to multiply the quantity of yarn produced in one week, i. e., 10,000 lbs of yarn, by the number of weeks contained in a certain number of years, in order to transfer to the yarn the entire value of the instruments of labour bought and consumed during this period. It is then plain that the advanced money capital must first be transformed into these instruments, hence must have gone through the first phase M — C before it can function as productive capital P. And it is likewise plain in our illustration that the capital value of £ 422, embodied in the yarn during the process of production, cannot become a part of the value of the 10,000 lbs of yarn and enter the circulation phase C′ — M′ until it is ready. It cannot be sold until it has been spun.

In the general formula the product of P is regarded as a material thing different from the elements of the productive capital, as an object existing apart from the process of production and having a use form different from that of the elements of production. This is always the case when the result of the productive process assumes the form of a thing, even when a part of the product re-enters the resumed production as one of its elements. Grain for instance serves as seed for its own production, but the product consists only of grain and hence has a shape different from those of related elements such as labour power, implements, fertiliser. But there are certain independent branches of industry in which the product of the productive process is not a new material product, is not a commodity. Among these only the communications industry, whether engaged in transportation proper, of goods and passengers, or in the mere transmission of communications, letters, telegrams, etc., is economically important.

A. Chuprov [6] says on this score:

"The manufacturer may first produce articles and then look for consumers".

//his product, thrust out of the process of production when finished, passes into circulation as a commodity separated from it//.

"Production and consumption thus appear as two acts separated in space and time. In the transportation industry, which does not create any new products but merely transfers men and things, these two acts coincide; its services" //change of place// "are consumed the moment they are produced. For this reason the area within which railways can sell their services extends at best 50 versts" (53 kilometres) "on either side of their tracks." [16]

The result, whether men or goods are transported, is a change in

___

[6] A. Čuprov: *Železnodorožnoje chozjajstvo*, Moskva, 1875, pp. 69, 70.

their whereabouts. Yarn, for instance, may now be in India instead of in England, where it was produced.

However, what the transportation industry sells is change of location. The useful effect is inseparably connected with the process of transportation, i. e., the productive process of the transport industry. Men and goods travel together with the means of transportation, and this travelling, this locomotion, constitutes the process of production effected by these means. The useful effect can be consumed only during this process of production. It does not exist as a utility different from this process, a use thing which does not function as an article of commerce, does not circulate as a commodity, until after it has been produced. But the exchange value of this useful effect is determined, like that of any other commodity, by the value of the elements of production (labour power and means of production) consumed in it plus the surplus value created by the surplus labour of the labourers employed in transportation. This useful effect also entertains the very same relations to consumption that other commodities do. If it is consumed individually its value disappears during its consumption; if it is consumed productively so as to constitute by itself a stage in the production of the commodities being transported, its value is transferred as an additional value to the commodity itself. The formula for the transport industry would therefore be $M - C <^L_{MP} \ldots P - M'$, since it is the process of production itself that is paid for and consumed, not a product separate and distinct from it. Hence this formula has almost the same form as that of the production of precious metals, the only difference being that in this case M' represents the converted form of the useful effect created during the process of production, and not the bodily form of the gold or silver produced in this process and extruded from it.

Industrial capital is the only mode of existence of capital in which not only the appropriation of surplus value, or surplus product, but simultaneously its creation is a function of capital. Therefore with it the capitalist character of production is a necessity. Its existence implies the class antagonism between capitalists and wage labourers. To the extent that it seizes control of social production, the technique and social organisation of the labour process are revolutionised and with them the economico-historical type of society. The other kinds of capital, which appeared before industrial capital amid conditions of social production that have receded into the past or are now succumbing, are not only subordinated to it and the mechanism of their functions altered in conformity with it, but move solely with it as their basis, hence live and die, stand and fall with this basis. Money capital and commodity capital, so far as they function as vehicles of particular branches of business, side by side with industrial capital, are nothing but modes of existence of the different functional forms now assumed, now discarded by industrial capital in the sphere of circulation — modes which, due to social division of labour, have attained independent existence and been developed one-sidedly.

The circuit M ... M′ on the one hand intermingles with the general circulation of commodities, proceeds from it and flows back into it, is a part of it. On the other hand it forms an independent movement of the capital value for the individual capitalist, a movement of its own which takes place partly within the general circulation of commodities, partly outside of it, but which always preserves its independent character. First, because its two phases that take place in the sphere of circulation, M — C and C′ — M′, being phases of the movement of capital, have functionally definite characters. In M — C, C is materially determined as labour power and means of production; in C′ — M′, the capital value is realised plus the surplus value. Secondly, because P, the process of production, embraces productive consumption. Thirdly, because the return of the money to its starting-point makes of the movement M ... M′ a circuit complete in itself.

Every individual capital is therefore, on the one hand, in its two circulation halves M — C and C′ — M′, an agent of the general circulation of commodities, in which it either functions or lies concatenated as money or as a commodity, thus forming a link in the general chain of metamorphoses taking place in the world of commodities. On the other hand it describes within the general circulation its own independent circuit in which the sphere of production forms a transitional stage and in which this capital returns to its starting-point in the same form in which it left that point. Within its own circuit, which includes its real metamorphosis in the process of production, it changes at the same time the magnitude of its value. It returns not simply as money value, but as augmented, increased money value.

Let us finally consider M — C ... P ... C′ — M′ as a special form of the circular course of capital, alongside the other forms which we shall analyse later. We shall find that it is distinguished by the following features:

1. It appears as the *circuit of money capital*, because industrial capital in its money form, as money capital, forms the starting-point and

the point of return of its total process. The formula itself expresses the fact that the money is not expended here as money but is merely advanced, hence is merely the money form of capital, money capital. It expresses furthermore that exchange value, not use value, is the determining aim of this movement. Just because the money form of value is the independent, tangible form in which value appears, the form of circulation M ... M′, the initial and terminal points of which are real money, expresses most graphically the compelling motive of capitalist production — money-making. The process of production appears merely as an unavoidable intermediate link, as a necessary evil for the sake of money-making. //All nations with a capitalist mode of production are therefore seized periodically by a feverish attempt to make money without the intervention of the process of production.//

2. The stage of production, the function of P, represents in this circuit an interruption between the two phases of circulation M — C ... C′ — M′, which in its turn represents only the intermediate link in the simple circulation M — C — M′. The process of production appears in the form of a circuit-describing process, formally and explicitly as that which it is in the capitalist mode of production, as a mere means of expanding the advanced value, hence enrichment as such as the purpose of production.

3. Since the series of phases is opened by M — C, the second link of the circulation is C′ — M′. In other words, the starting-point is M, the money capital that is to be self-expanded; the terminal point is M′, the self-expanded money capital M + m, in which M figures as realised capital along with its offspring m. This distinguishes the circuit of M from that of the two other circuits P and C′, and does so in two ways. On the one hand by the money form of the two extremes. And money is the independent, tangible form of existence of value, the value of the product in its independent value form, in which every trace of the use value of the commodities has been extinguished. On the other hand the form P ... P does not necessarily become P ... P′ (P + p), and in the form C′ ... C′ no difference whatever in value is visible between the two extremes.— It is, therefore, characteristic of the formula M — M′ that for one thing capital value is its starting-point and expanded capital value its point of return, so that the advance of capital value appears as the means and expanded capital value as the end of the entire operation; and that for another thing this relation is expressed in money form, in the independent value form, hence

money capital as money begetting money. The generation of surplus value by value is not only expressed as the Alpha and Omega of the process, but explicitly in the form of glittering money.

4. Since M′, the money capital realised as a result of C′ — M′, the complementary and concluding phase of M — C, has absolutely the same form as that in which it began its first circuit, it can, as soon as it emerges from the latter, begin the same circuit over again as an increased (accumulated) money capital: M′ = M + m. And at least it is not expressed in the form M ... M′ that, in the repetition of the circuit, the circulation of m separates from that of M. Considered in its one-time form, formally, the circuit of money capital expresses therefore simply the process of self-expansion and of accumulation. Consumption is expressed in it only as productive consumption, by M — C $<^{L}_{MP}$, and it is only this consumption that is included in this circuit of individual capital. M — L is L — M or C — M on the part of the labourer. It is therefore the first phase of circulation which brings about his individual consumption, thus: L — M — C (means of subsistence). The second phase, M — C, no longer falls within the circuit of individual capital, but is initiated and premised by it, since the labourer must above all live, hence maintain himself by individual consumption, in order to be always in the market as material that the capitalist can exploit. But this consumption itself is here only assumed as a condition for the productive consumption of labour power by capital, hence only to the extent that the worker maintains and reproduces himself as labour power by means of his individual consumption. However the MP, the commodities proper which enter into the circuit of capital, are nutriment for the productive consumption only. The act L — M promotes the individual consumption of the labourer, the transformation of the means of subsistence into his flesh and blood. True, the capitalist must also be there, must also live and consume to be able to perform the function of a capitalist. To this end, he has, indeed, to consume only as much as the labourer, and that is all this form of the circulation process presupposes. But even this is not formally expressed, since the formula concludes with M′, i. e., a result which can at once resume its function of money capital, now augmented.

C′ — M′ directly contains the sale of C′; but C′ — M′, a sale on the one part, is M — C, a purchase, on the other part, and in the last analysis a commodity is bought only for its use value, in order to enter (leaving intermediate sales out of consideration) the process of consumption, whether this is individual or productive, according to the nature of the article bought. But this consumption does not enter the circuit of individual capital, the product of which is C′. This product is eliminated from the circuit precisely because it is a commodity for sale. C′ is expressly designed for consumption by others than the producer. Thus we find that certain exponents of the mercantile system[6] (which is based on the formula $M — C ... P ... C′ — M′$) deliver lengthy sermons to the effect that the individual capitalist should consume only as much as the labourer, that the nation of capitalists should leave the consumption of their own commodities, and the consumption process in general, to the other, less intelligent nations but that they themselves should make productive consumption their life's task. These sermons frequently remind one in form and content of analogous ascetic expostulations of the fathers of the church.

———

Capital's movement in circuits is therefore the unity of circulation and production; it includes both. Since the two phases $M — C$ and $C′ — M′$ are acts of circulation, the circulation of capital is a part of the general circulation of commodities. But as functionally they are definite sections, stages in capital's circuit, which pertains not only to the sphere of circulation but also to that of production, capital goes through its own circuit in the general circulation of commodities. The general circulation of commodities serves capital in the first stage as a means of assuming that shape in which it can perform the function of productive capital; in the second stage it serves to strip off the commodity function in which capital cannot renew its circuit; at the same time it opens up to capital the possibility of separating its own circuit from the circulation of the surplus value that accrued to it.

The circuit of money capital is therefore the most one-sided, and thus the most striking and typical form in which the circuit of industrial capital appears, the capital whose aim and compelling motive — the self-expansion of value, the making of money, and accumulation — is thus conspicuously revealed (buying to sell dearer). Owing to the fact that the first phase is $M — C$ it is also revealed that the constituents of productive capital originate in the commodity market, and in general that the capitalist process of production depends on circulation, on commerce. The circuit of money capital is not merely the production of commodities; it is itself possible only through circulation and presupposes it. This is plain, if only from the fact that the form M belonging in circulation appears as the first and pure form of advanced capital value, which is not the case in the other two circuit forms.

The circuit of money capital always remains the general expression of industrial capital, in so far as it always includes the self-expansion of the advanced value. In P ... P, the money expression of capital appears only as the price of the elements of production, hence only as a value expressed in money of account and is fixed in this form in bookkeeping.

M ... M′ becomes a special form of the industrial capital circuit in so far as newly active capital is first advanced in the form of money and then withdrawn in the same form, either in passing from one branch of business to another or in retiring industrial capital from a business. This includes the functioning as capital of the surplus value first advanced in the form of money, and becomes most evident when surplus value functions in some other business than the one in which it originated. M ... M′ may be the first circuit of a certain capital; it may be the last; it may be regarded as the form of the total social capital; it is the form of capital that is newly invested, either as capital newly accumulated in the form of money, or as some old capital which is entirely transformed into money for the purpose of transfer from one branch of industry to another.

Being a form always contained in all circuits, money capital performs this circuit [M ... M′] precisely for that part of capital which produces surplus value, viz., variable capital. The normal form of advancing wages is payment in money; this process must be renewed in comparatively short intervals, because the labourer lives from hand to mouth. The capitalist must therefore always confront the labourer as money capitalist, and his capital as money capital. There can be no direct or indirect balancing of accounts in this case such as we find in the purchase of means of production and in the sale of produced commodities (so that the greater part of the money capital actually figures only in the form of commodities, money only in the form of money of account and finally in cash only in the balancing of accounts). On the other hand, a part of the surplus value arising out of variable capital is spent by the capitalist for his individual consumption, which pertains to the retail trade and, however circuitous the route may be, this part is always spent in cash, in the money form of surplus value. It does not matter how large or small this part of surplus value is. Variable capital always appears anew as money capital invested in wages (M — L) and m as surplus value spent to defray the cost of the individual consumption of the capitalist. Hence M, advanced variable capital value, and m, its increment, are necessarily held in the form of money to be spent in this form.

The formula $M — C ... P ... C' — M'$, with its result $M' = M + m$, is deceptive in form, is illusory in character, owing to the existence of the advanced and self-expanded value in its equivalent form, money. The emphasis is not on the self-expansion of value but on the *money form* of this process, on the fact that more value in money form is finally drawn out of the circulation than was originally advanced to it; hence on the multiplication of the mass of gold and silver belonging to the capitalist. The so-called monetary system [17] is merely an expression of the irrational form $M — C — M'$, a movement which takes place exclusively in circulation and therefore can explain the two acts: 1) $M — C$, 2) $C — M'$ in no other way than as a sale of C above its value in the second act and therefore as C drawing more money out of the circulation than was put into it by its purchase. On the other hand $M — C ... P ... C' — M'$, fixed as the exclusive form, constitutes the basis of the more highly developed mercantile system, in which not only the circulation of commodities but also their production appears as a necessary element.

The illusory character of $M — C ... P ... C' — M'$ and the correspondingly illusory interpretation exists whenever this form is fixed as occurring once, not as fluent and ever renewed; hence whenever this form is considered not as one of the forms of the circuit but as its exclusive form. But it itself points toward other forms.

In the first place this entire circuit is premised on the capitalist character of the process of production, and therefore presupposes this process together with the specific social conditions brought about by it as the basis. $M — C = M — C <^{L}_{MP}$; but $M — L$ assumes the existence of the wage labourer, and hence the means of production as part of productive capital. It assumes therefore that the process of labour and self-expansion, the process of production, is a function of capital.

In the second place, if $M ... M'$ is repeated, the return to the money form appears just as evanescent as the money form in the first stage. $M — C$ disappears to make room for P. The constantly recurrent advance in the form of money and its constant return in the form of money appear merely as fleeting moments in the circuit.

In the third place

$$M - C \ldots P \ldots C' - M'. \quad M - C \ldots P \ldots C' - M'. \quad M - C \ldots P \ldots \text{etc.}$$

Beginning with the first repetition of the circuit, the circuit P ... C′ — M′. M — C ... P appears before the second circuit of M is completed, and all subsequent circuits may thus be considered under the form of P ... C′ — M — C ... P, so that M — C, being the first phase of the first circuit, is merely the passing preparation for the constantly repeated circuit of the productive capital. And this indeed is so in the case of industrial capital invested for the first time in the form of money capital.

On the other hand before the second circuit of P is completed, the first circuit, that of commodity capital, C′ — M′. M — C ... P ... C′ (abridged C′... C′) has already been made. Thus the first form already contains the other two, and the money form thus disappears, so far as it is not merely an expression of value but an expression of value in the equivalent form, in money.

Finally, if we consider some newly invested individual capital describing for the first time the circuit M — C ... P ... C′ — M′, then M — C is the preparatory phase, the forerunner of the first process of production gone through by this individual capital. This phase M — C is consequently not presupposed but rather called for or necessitated by the process of production. But this applies only to this individual capital. The general form of the circuit of industrial capital is the circuit of money capital, in so far as the capitalist mode of production is taken for granted, hence in social conditions determined by capitalist production. Therefore the capitalist process of production is assumed as a *prius*,[a] if not in the first circuit of the money capital of a newly invested industrial capital, then outside of it. The continuous existence of this process of production presupposes the constantly renewed circuit P ... P. Even in the first stage, $M - C <^{L}_{MP}$, this premise plays a part, for this assumes on the one hand the existence of the class of wage labourers; and then, on the other, that which is M — C, the first stage, for the buyer of means of production, is C′ — M′ for their seller; hence C′ presupposes commodity capital, and thus the commodities themselves as a result of capitalist production, and thereby the function of productive capital.

---

[a] a precondition

Chapter II

THE CIRCUIT OF PRODUCTIVE CAPITAL

The circuit of productive capital has the general formula P ... C′ — M′ — C ... P. It signifies the periodical renewal of the functioning of productive capital, hence its reproduction, or its process of production as a process of reproduction aiming at the self-expansion of value; not only production but a periodical reproduction of surplus value; the function of industrial capital in its productive form, and this function performed not once but periodically repeated, so that the renewal is determined by the starting-point. A portion of C′ may (in certain cases, in various branches of investment of industrial capital) re-enter directly as means of production into the same labour process out of which it came in the shape of a commodity. This merely saves the transformation of the value of this portion into real money or token money or else the commodity finds an independent expression only as money of account. This part of value does not enter into the circulation. Thus values enter into the process of production which do not enter into the process of circulation. The same is true of that part of C′ which is consumed by the capitalist *in natura* as part of the surplus product. But this is insignificant for capitalist production. It deserves consideration, if at all, only in agriculture.

Two things are at once strikingly apparent in this form.

For one thing, while in the first form, M ... M′, the process of production, the function of P, interrupts the circulation of money capital and acts only as a mediator between its two phases M — C and C′ — M′, here the entire circulation process of industrial capital, its entire movement within the phase of circulation, constitutes only an interruption and consequently only the connecting link between the productive capital, which as the first extreme opens the circuit, and that which closes it as the other extreme in the same form, hence in the form in which it starts again. Circulation proper appears but as an instrument promoting the periodically renewed reproduction, rendered continuous by the renewal.

For another thing, the entire circulation presents itself in a form which is the opposite of that which it has in the circuit of money capital. There it was: M — C — M (M — C. C — M), apart from the determination of value; here it is, again apart from the value determination: $C — M — C$ ($C — M$. $M — C$), i. e., the form of the simple circulation of commodities.

I. SIMPLE REPRODUCTION

Let us first consider the process $C' — M' — C$, which takes place in the sphere of circulation between the two extremes P ... P.

The starting-point of this circulation is commodity capital: $C' = C + c = P + c$. The function of commodity capital $C' — M'$ (the realisation of the capital value contained in it = P, which now exists as the constituent part C of C', as well as of the surplus value contained in it, which exists as a constituent part of the same quantity of commodities and has the value c) was examined in the first form of the circuit. But there this function formed the second phase of the interrupted circulation and the concluding phase of the entire circuit. Here it forms the second phase of the circuit but the first phase of the circulation. The first circuit ends with M', and since M' as well as the original M can again open the second circuit as money capital, it was not necessary at first to see whether M and m (surplus value) contained in M' continue in their course together or whether each of them pursues its own course. This would only have become necessary if we had followed up further the first circuit in its renewed course. But this point must be decided in the circuit of the productive capital, because the determination of its very first circuit depends on it and because $C' — M'$ appears in it as the first phase of the circulation, which has to be complemented by $M — C$. It depends on this decision whether the formula represents simple reproduction or reproduction on an extended scale. The character of the circuit changes according to the decision made.

Let us, then, consider first the simple reproduction of productive capital, assuming that, as in the first chapter, conditions remain constant and that commodities are bought and sold at their values. On this assumption the entire surplus value enters into the individual consumption of the capitalist. As soon as the transformation of the commodity capital C' into money has taken place, that part of the money which represents the capital value continues to circulate in the circuit of industrial capital; the other part, which is surplus value changed into money, enters into the general circulation of commodities, constitutes a circulation of money emanating from the capitalist but taking place outside of the circulation of his individual capital.

In our illustration we had a commodity capital C′ of 10,000 lbs of yarn, valued at £ 500; £ 422 of this represent the value of the productive capital and continue, as the money form of 8,440 lbs of yarn, the capital circulation begun by C′, while the surplus value of £ 78, the money form of 1,560 lbs of yarn, the excess of the commodity product, leaves this circulation and describes a separate course within the general circulation of commodities.

$$C' \begin{pmatrix} C \\ + \\ c \end{pmatrix} \begin{matrix} - \\ - \\ - \end{matrix} M' \begin{pmatrix} M \\ + \\ m \end{pmatrix} \begin{matrix} -C <^{L}_{MP} \\ \\ -c \end{matrix}$$

m — c represents a series of purchases by means of money which the capitalist spends either for commodities proper or for personal services to his cherished self or family. These purchases are made piecemeal at various times. The money therefore exists temporarily in the form of a supply, or hoard, destined for current consumption, since money whose circulation has been interrupted assumes the form of a hoard. Its function as a medium of circulation, which includes its transient form of a hoard, does not enter the circulation of capital in its money form M. This money is not advanced but spent.

We have assumed that the total advanced capital always passes wholly from one of its phases to the other; and so here too we assume that the commodities produced by P represent the total value of the productive capital P = £ 422 + £ 78 of surplus value created in the process of production. In our illustration, which deals with a discrete commodity, the surplus value exists in the form of 1,560 lbs of yarn; if computed on the basis of one pound of yarn, it would exist in the form of 2.496 ounces of yarn. But if the commodity were for instance a machine valued at £ 500 and having the same value composition, one part of the value of this machine, = £ 78, would be surplus value, but these £ 78 would exist only in the machine as a whole. This machine cannot be divided into capital value and surplus value without breaking it to pieces and thus destroying its value together with its use value. For this reason the two value components can be represented only ideally as components of the commodity, not as independent elements of the commodity C′, like any pound of yarn, which represents a separable independent element of the 10,000 lbs of commodity. In the first case the aggregate commodity, the commodity capital, the machine, must be sold in its entirety before m can enter upon its separate circulation. On the other hand when the capitalist has sold 8,440 lbs, the sale of the remaining 1,560 lbs would represent a wholly separate circulation of the surplus value in the form of c (1,560 lbs of yarn) — m ($£$ 78) — c (articles of consumption). But the elements of value of each individual portion of the 10,000 lbs of yarn, the product, can be represented by parts of the product as well as by the total product. Just as the latter, 10,000 lbs of yarn, can be divided into the value of the constant capital (c), 7,440 lbs of yarn worth $£$ 372, variable capital value (v) of 1,000 lbs of yarn worth $£$ 50, and surplus value (s) of 1,560 lbs of yarn worth $£$ 78, so every pound of yarn may be divided into c = to 11.904 ounces worth 8.928 d., v = to 1.600 ounces of yarn worth 1.200 d., and s = to 2.496 ounces of yarn worth 1.872 d. The capitalist might also sell various portions of the 10,000 lbs of yarn successively and successively consume the successive portions of the surplus value elements contained in them, thus realising, also successively, the sum of c + v. But in the final analysis this operation likewise premises the sale of the entire lot of 10,000 lbs, that therefore the value of c and v will be replaced by the sale of 8,440 lbs (Buch I, Kap. VII, 2[a]).

However that may be, by means of C′ — M′ both the capital value and surplus value contained in C′ acquire a separable existence, the existence of different sums of money. In both cases M and m are really a converted form of the value which originally in C′ had only a peculiar, an ideal expression as the price of the commodity.

c — m — c represents the simple circulation of commodities, the first phase of which, c — m, is included in the circulation of commodity capital, C′ — M′, i. e., included in the circuit of capital; its complementary phase m — c falls, on the contrary, outside of this circuit, being a separate act in the general circulation of commodities. The circulation of C and c, of capital value and surplus value, splits after the transformation of C′ into M′. Hence it follows:

First, while the commodity capital is realised by C′ — M′ = C′ — (M + m), the movement of capital value and surplus value, which in C′ — M′ is still united and carried on by the same quantity of commodities, becomes separable, both of them henceforth possessing independent forms as separate sums of money.

[a] English edition: Vol. I, Ch. IX, 2 (present edition, Vol. 35).

Secondly, if this separation takes place, m being spent as the revenue of the capitalist, while M as a functional form of capital value continues its course determined by the circuit, the first act, C′ — M′, in connection with the subsequent acts, M — C and m — c, may be represented as the two different circulations C — M — C and c — m — c; and both of these series, so far as their general form is concerned, belong in the usual circulation of commodities.

By the way, in the case of continuous, indivisible commodities, it is a matter of practice to isolate the value constituents ideally. For instance in the London building business, which is carried on mainly on credit, the building contractor receives advances in accordance with the stage of construction reached. None of these stages is a house, but only a really existing constituent part of an inchoate future house; hence, in spite of its reality, it is but an ideal fraction of the entire house, but real enough to serve as security for an additional advance (see on this point Chapter XII below[a]).

Thirdly, if the movement of capital value and surplus value, which still proceeds unitedly in C and M, is separated only in part (a portion of the surplus value not being spent as revenue) or not at all, a change takes place in the capital value itself within its circuit, before it is completed. In our illustration the value of the productive capital was equal to £422. If that capital continues M — C, as, say, £480 or £500, then it strides through the latter stages of its circuit with an increase of £58 or £78 over its initial value. This may also go hand in hand with a change in the composition of its value.

C′ — M′, the second stage of the circulation and the final stage of circuit I (M ... M′), is the second stage in our circuit and the first in the circulation of commodities. So far as the circulation is concerned, it must be complemented by M′ — C′. But not only has C′ — M′ the process of self-expansion already behind it (in this case the function of P, the first stage), but its result, the commodity C′, has already been realised. The process of the self-expansion of capital and the realisation of the commodities representing the expanded capital value are therefore completed in C′ — M′.

And so we have premised simple reproduction, i. e., that m — c separates entirely from M — C. Since both circulations, c — m — c as well as C — M — C, belong in the circulation of commodities, so far as their general form is concerned (and for this reason do not show

---

[a] See this volume, pp. 235-36.

any value differences in their extremes), it is easy to conceive the process of capitalist production, after the manner of vulgar economy, as a mere production of commodities, of use values designed for consumption of some sort, which the capitalist produces for no other purpose than that of getting in their place commodities with different use values, or of exchanging them for such, as vulgar economy erroneously states.

C′ acts from the very outset as commodity capital, and the purpose of the entire process, enrichment (the production of surplus value), does not by any means exclude increasing consumption on the part of the capitalist as his surplus value (and hence his capital) increases; on the contrary, it emphatically includes it.

Indeed, in the circulation of the revenue of the capitalist, the produced commodity c (or the fraction of the produced commodity C′ ideally corresponding to it) serves only to transform it, first into money, and from money into a number of other commodities serving private consumption. But we must not, at this point, overlook the trifling circumstance that c is commodity value which did not cost the capitalist anything, an incarnation of surplus labour, for which reason it originally stepped on the stage as a component part of commodity capital C′. This c is, by the very nature of its existence, bound to the circuit of capital value in process, and if this circuit begins to stagnate or is otherwise disturbed, not only is the consumption of c restricted or entirely arrested, but also the disposal of that series of commodities which serve to replace c. The same is true when C′ — M′ ends in failure, or only a part of C′ can be sold.

We have seen that c — m — c, representing the circulation of the revenue of the capitalist, enters into the circulation of capital only so long as c is a part of the value of C′, of capital in its functional form of commodity capital; but, as soon as it acquires independence through m — c, hence throughout the form c — m — c, the circulation of that revenue does not enter into the movement of the capital advanced by the capitalist, although it stems from it. This circulation is connected with the movement of advanced capital inasmuch as the existence of capital presupposes the existence of the capitalist, and his existence is conditioned on his consuming surplus value.

Within the general circulation C′, for example yarn, functions only as a commodity; but as an element in the circulation of capital it performs the function of *commodity capital*, a form which capital value alternately assumes and discards. After the sale of the yarn to a merchant, it is extruded out of the circular movement of the capital whose product it is, but nevertheless, as a commodity, it moves always in the sphere of the general circulation. The circulation of one and the same mass of commodities continues, in spite of the fact that it has ceased to be a phase in the independent circuit of the spinner's capital. Hence the real definitive metamorphosis of the mass of commodities thrown into circulation by the capitalist, C — M, their final exit into consumption may be completely separated in time and space from that metamorphosis in which this mass of commodities functions as his commodity capital. The same metamorphosis which has been accomplished in the circulation of capital still remains to be accomplished in the sphere of the general circulation.

This state of things is not changed a bit if this yarn enters the circuit of some other industrial capital. The general circulation comprises as much the intertwining of the circuits of the various independent fractions of social capital, i. e., the totality of the individual capitals, as the circulation of those values which are not thrown on the market as capital but enter into individual consumption.

The relation between a circuit of capital forming part of a general circulation and a circuit forming links in an independent circuit is shown further on when we examine the circulation of $M' = M + m$. M as money capital continues capital's circuit; m, being spent as revenue $(m — c)$, enters into the general circulation, but comes flying out of the circuit of capital. Only that part enters the latter circuit which performs the function of additional money capital. In c — m — c money serves only as coin; the object of this circulation is the individual consumption of the capitalist. It is typical of the idiocy of vulgar economy that it gives out this circulation, which does not enter into the circuit of capital — the circulation of that part of the value produced which is consumed as revenue — as the characteristic circuit of capital.

In the second phase, M — C, the capital value M = P (the value of the productive capital that at this point opens the circuit of industrial capital) is again present, delivered of its surplus value, therefore having the same magnitude of value as it had in the first stage of the circuit of money capital M — C. In spite of the difference in place the function of the money capital into which the commodity capital has now been transformed is the same: its transformation into MP and L, into means of production and labour power.

In the functioning of commodity capital C' — M', the capital value, simultaneously with c — m, has consequently gone through the phase C — M and enters now into the complementary phase M — C $<^{\text{L}}_{\text{MP}}$. Its complete circulation is therefore C — M — C $<^{\text{L}}_{\text{MP}}$.

First: Money capital M appeared in Form I (circuit M ... M′) as the original form in which capital value is advanced; it appears here from the outset as a part of that sum of money into which commodity capital transformed itself in the first circulation phase C′ — M′, therefore from the outset as the transformation of P, the productive capital, through the medium of the sale of commodities, into the money form. Money capital exists here from the outset as that form of capital value which is neither its original nor its final one, since the phase M — C, which concludes the phase C — M, can only be performed by again discarding the money form. Therefore that part of M — C which is at the same time M — L appears now no longer as a mere advance of money by the purchase of labour power, but as an advance by means of which the same 1,000 lbs of yarn, valued at £50, which form a part of the commodity value created by labour power, are advanced to labour power in the form of money. The money advanced here to the labourer is only a converted equivalent form of a part of the commodity value produced by himself. And for that reason if no other the act M — C, so far as it means M — L, is by no means simply a replacement of a commodity in the form of money by a commodity in the use form, but it includes other elements which are independent of the general commodity circulation as such.

M′ appears as a converted form of C′, which is itself a product of a previous function of P, the process of production. The entire sum of money M′ is therefore a money expression of past labour. In our illustration, 10,000 lbs of yarn = £500 are the product of the spinning process. Of this quantity, 7,440 lbs of yarn are = to the advanced constant capital c = £372; 1,000 lbs of yarn are = to the advanced variable capital v = £50; and 1,560 lbs of yarn = the surplus value s = £78. If of M′ only the original capital of £422 is again advanced, other conditions remaining the same, then the labourer is advanced the following week, in M — L, only a part of the 10,000 lbs of yarn produced in the given week (the money value of 1,000 lbs of yarn). As a result of C — M, money is always the expression of past labour. If the complementary act M — C takes place at once in the commodity market, i. e., M is given in return for commodities existing in the market, this is again a transformation of past labour, from one form (money) into another form (commodities). But M — C differs in the matter of time from C — M. They may exceptionally take place at the same time, for instance when the capitalist who performs M — C and the capitalist to whom this act means C — M ship their commodities to each other at the same time and M is used only to square the balance. The difference in time between the performance of C — M and M — C may be more or less considerable. Although M, as the result of C — M, represents past labour, it may, in the act M — C, represent the converted form of commodities which are not as yet in the market, but will be thrown upon it in the future, since M — C need not take place until C has been produced anew. M may likewise stand for commodities which are produced simultaneously with the C whose money expression it is. For instance in the exchange M — C (purchase of means of production) coal may be bought before it has been mined. In so far as m figures as an accumulation of money, is not spent as revenue, it may stand for cotton which will not be produced until the following year. The same holds good on spending the revenue of the capitalist, m — c. It also applies to wages, to L = to £50. This money is not only the money form of the past labour of the labourers but at the same time a draft on simultaneous or future labour which is just being realised or should be realised in the future. The labourer may buy with his wages a coat which will not be made until the following week. This applies especially to the vast number of necessary means of subsistence which must be consumed almost as soon as they have been produced to prevent spoilage. Thus the labourer receives, in the money which is paid to him as his wages, the converted form of his own future labour or that of other labourers. By giving the labourer a part of his past labour, the capitalist gives him a draft on his own future labour. It is the labourer's own simultaneous or future labour that constitutes the not yet existing supply out of which he will be paid for his past labour. In this case the idea of hoarding disappears altogether. [a]

Secondly: In the circulation $C — M — C <^{L}_{MP}$ the same money changes place twice; the capitalist first receives it as a seller and passes it on as a buyer; the transformation of commodities into the money form serves only for the purpose of retransforming it from the money form into the commodity form; the money form of capital, its existence as money capital, is therefore only a transient phase in this movement; or, so far as the movement is fluent, money capital appears

---

[a] Here Marx made the following note in the manuscript (in square brackets): "All this, however, belongs to the last part of the second book."

only as a medium of circulation when it serves as a means of purchase; it acts as a paying medium proper when capitalists buy from one another and therefore only have to square accounts.

Thirdly: The function of money capital, whether it is a mere circulating medium or a paying medium, effects only the replacement of C by L and MP, i. e., the replacement of the yarn, the commodity which represents the result of the productive capital (after deducting the surplus value to be used as revenue), by its elements of production, in other words, the retransformation of capital value from its form as a commodity into the elements that build this commodity. In the last analysis, the function of money capital promotes only the retransformation of commodity capital into productive capital.

In order that the circuit may be completed normally, C′ must be sold at its value and in its entirety. Furthermore, C — M — C includes not merely replacement of one commodity by another, but replacement with value relations remaining the same. We assume that this takes place here. As a matter of fact, however, the values of the means of production vary. It is precisely capitalist production to which continuous change of value relations is peculiar, if only because of the ever changing productivity of labour that characterises this mode of production. This change in the value of the elements of production will be discussed later on, [a] and we merely mention it here. The transformation of the elements of production into commodity products, of P into C′, takes place in the sphere of production, while the retransformation from C′ into P occurs in the sphere of circulation. It is brought about by a simple metamorphosis of commodities, but its content is a phase in the process of reproduction, regarded as a whole. C — M — C, being a form of the circulation of capital, involves a functionally determined exchange of matter. The transformation C — M — C requires further that C should be equal to the elements of production of the commodity quantum C′, and that these elements should retain their original value relations to one another. It is therefore assumed that the commodities are not only bought at their respective values, but also do not undergo any change of value during the circular movement. Otherwise this process cannot run normally.

In M ... M′, M represents the original form of the capital value, which is discarded only to be resumed. In P ... C′ — M′ — C ... P, M represents a form which is only assumed in the process and which is discarded before this process is over. The money form appears here

---

[a] See Section V of Chapter XV of this volume.

only as a transient independent form of capital value. Capital in the form of C′ is just as anxious to assume the money form as it is to discard it in M′, after barely assuming that garb in order again to transform itself into productive capital. So long as it remains in the garb of money, it does not function as capital and its value does not therefore expand. The capital lies fallow. M serves here as a circulating medium, but as a circulating medium of capital. [a] The semblance of independence which the money form of capital value possesses in the first form of its circuit (the form of money capital) disappears in this second form, which thus is a criticism of Form I and reduces it to merely a special form. If the second metamorphosis, M — C, meets with any obstacles (for instance if there are no means of production in the market) the circuit, the flow of the process of reproduction, is interrupted quite as much as when capital is held fast in the form of commodity capital. But there is this difference: It can remain longer in the money form than in the transitory form of commodities. It does not cease to be money, if it does not perform the functions of money capital; but it does cease to be a commodity, or a use value in general, if it is delayed too long in the exercise of its function of commodity capital. Furthermore, in its money form it is capable of assuming another form in place of its original one of productive capital, while it cannot budge at all if held in the form of C′.

C′ — M′ — C includes acts of circulation only for C′ in accordance with its form, acts which are phases of its reproduction; but the real reproduction of C, into which C′ transforms itself, is necessary for the performance of C′ — M′ — C. This however is conditioned on processes of reproduction which lie outside of the process of reproduction of the individual capital represented by C′.

In Form I the act $M — C <^L_{MP}$ prepares only the first transformation of money capital into productive capital; in Form II it prepares the retransformation from commodity capital into productive capital; that is to say, so far as the investment of industrial capital remains the same, retransformation of the commodity capital into the same elements of production as those from which it originated. Consequently here as well as in Form I, that act appears as a preparatory phase of the process of production, but as a return to it, as a renewal of it, hence as a precursor of the process of reproduction, hence also of a repetition of the process of self-expansion of value.

---

[a] Here Marx made the following note in the manuscript: "Against Tooke."

It must be noted once more that $M-L$ is not a simple exchange of commodities but the purchase of a commodity, L, which is to serve for the production of surplus value, just as $M-MP$ is only a procedure which is materially indispensable for the attainment of this end.

With the completion of $M-C <^{L}_{MP}$ M is reconverted into productive capital, into P, and the circuit begins anew.

The expanded form of $P \ldots C'-M'-C \ldots P$ is therefore:

$$P \ldots C' \begin{pmatrix} C \\ + \\ c \end{pmatrix} - \begin{pmatrix} M \\ + \\ m \end{pmatrix} \begin{matrix} -C <^{L}_{MP} \ldots P \\ \\ -c \end{matrix}$$

The transformation of money capital into productive capital is the purchase of commodities for the production of commodities. Consumption falls within the circuit of capital itself only in so far as it is productive consumption; its premise is that surplus value is produced by means of the commodities so consumed. And this is something very different from production and even commodity production, which has for its end the existence of the producer. A replacement — commodity by commodity — thus contingent on the production of surplus value is quite a different matter from a bare exchange of products brought about merely by means of money. But the economists take this matter as proof that no overproduction is possible.

Apart from the productive consumption of M, which is transformed into L and MP, the circuit contains the first member $M-L$, which signifies, from the standpoint of the labourer, $L-M = C-M$. In the labourer's circulation, $L-M-C$, which includes his consumption, only the first member falls within the circuit of the capital as a result of $M-L$. The second act, namely $M-C$, does not fall within the circulation of individual capital, although it springs from it. But the continuous existence of the working class is necessary for the capitalist class, and so is therefore the consumption of the labourer made possible by $M-C$.

The only condition which the act $C'-M'$ stipulates for capital value to continue its circuit and for surplus value to be consumed by the capitalist is that C' shall have been converted into money, shall have been sold. Of course, C' is bought only because the article is a use value, hence serviceable for consumption of any kind, productive or individual. But if C' continues to circulate for instance in the hands of the merchant who bought the yarn, this at first does not in the least affect the continuation of the circuit of the individual capital which produced the yarn and sold it to the merchant. The entire process continues and with it the individual consumption of the capitalist and the labourer made necessary by it. This point is important in a discussion of crises.

For as soon as C′ has been sold, been converted into money, it can be reconverted into the real factors of the labour process, and thus of the reproductive process. Whether C′ is bought by the ultimate consumer or by a merchant for resale does not affect the case. The quantity of commodities created in masses by capitalist production depends on the scale of this production and on the need for constantly expanding this production, and not on a predestined circle of supply and demand, on requirements that have to be satisfied. Mass production can have no other direct buyer, apart from other industrial capitalists, than the wholesaler. Within certain limits, the process of reproduction may take place on the same or on an extended scale even when the commodities expelled from it did not really enter individual or productive consumption. The consumption of commodities is not included in the circuit of the capital from which they originated. For instance, as soon as the yarn is sold the circuit of the capital value represented by the yarn may begin anew, regardless of what may next become of the sold yarn. So long as the product is sold, everything is taking its regular course from the standpoint of the capitalist producer. The circuit of the capital value he is identified with is not interrupted. And if this process is expanded — which includes increased productive consumption of the means of production — this reproduction of capital may be accompanied by increased individual consumption (hence demand) on the part of the labourers, since this process is initiated and effected by productive consumption. Thus the production of surplus value, and with it the individual consumption of the capitalist, may increase, the entire process of reproduction may be in a flourishing condition, and yet a large part of the commodities may have entered into consumption only apparently, while in reality they may still remain unsold in the hands of dealers, may in fact still be lying in the market. Now one stream of commodities follows another, and finally it is discovered that the previous streams had been absorbed only apparently by consumption. The commodity capitals compete with one another for a place in the market. Latecomers, to sell at all, sell at lower prices. The former streams have not yet been disposed of when payment for them falls due. Their owners must declare their insolvency or sell at any price to meet their obligations. This sale has nothing whatever to do with the actual state of the demand. It only concerns the *demand for payment*, the pressing necessity of transforming commodities into money. Then a crisis breaks out. It becomes visible not in the direct decrease of consumer demand, the demand for individual consumption, but in the decrease of exchanges of capital for capital, of the reproductive process of capital.

If the commodities MP and L, into which M is transformed to perform its function of money capital, of capital value destined to be re-transformed into productive capital — if those commodities are to be bought or paid for on different terms, so that M — C represents a series of successive purchases and payments, then a part of M performs the act M — C, while another part persists in the form of money and does not serve to perform simultaneous or successive acts of M — C until such time as the conditions of this process itself may determine. This part is only temporarily withheld from circulation, in order to go into action, perform its function, in due time. This storing of it is then in its turn a function determined by its circulation and intended for circulation. Its existence as a fund for purchase and payment, the suspension of its movement, the interrupted state of its circulation, will then constitute a state in which money exercises one of its functions as money capital. As money capital; for in this case the money temporarily remaining at rest is itself a part of money capital M (of $M' - m = M$), of that portion of the value of commodity capital which is = to P, to that value of productive capital from which the circuit starts. On the other hand all money withdrawn from circulation has the form of a hoard. Money in the form of a hoard therefore becomes here a function of money capital, just as in M — C the function of money as a means of purchase or payment becomes a function of money capital. This is so because capital value exists here in the form of money, because the money state here is a state in which industrial capital finds itself at one of its stages and which is prescribed by the interconnections within the circuit. At the same time it is here proved true once more that money capital within the circuit of industrial capital performs no other functions than those of money and that these money functions assume the significance of capital functions only by virtue of their interconnections with the other stages of this circuit.

The representation of M' as a relation of m to M, as a capital relation, is not directly a function of money capital, but of commodity capital C′, which in its turn, as a relation of c and C, expresses but the result of the process of production, of the self-expansion of capital value which took place in it.

If the continuation of the process of circulation meets with obstacles, so that M must suspend its function M — C on account of external circumstances, such as the conditions of the market, etc., and if it therefore remains for a shorter or longer time in its money form, then we have once more money in the form of a hoard, which happens also in simple commodity circulation whenever the transition from C — M to M — C is interrupted by external circumstances. It is an involuntary formation of a hoard. In the case at hand money has the form of fallow, latent money capital. But we will not discuss this point any further for the present.

In either case however persistence of money capital in its money state appears as the result of interrupted movement, no matter whether this is expedient or inexpedient, voluntary or involuntary, in accordance with its functions or contrary to them.

II. ACCUMULATION AND REPRODUCTION ON AN EXTENDED SCALE

Since the proportions which the expansion of the productive process may assume are not arbitrary but prescribed by technology, the realised surplus value, though intended for capitalisation, frequently can only by dint of several successive circuits attain such a size (and until then must therefore be accumulated) as will suffice for its effective functioning as additional capital or for entrance into the circuit of functioning capital value. Surplus value thus congeals into a hoard and in this form constitutes latent money capital — latent because it cannot act as capital so long as it persists in the money form. [6a] The formation of a hoard thus appears here as a factor included in the process of capitalist accumulation, accompanying it but nevertheless essentially differing from it; for the process of reproduction itself is not expanded by the formation of latent money capital. On the contrary, latent money capital is formed here because the capitalist producer cannot directly expand the scale of his production. If he sells his sur-

---

[6a] The term "latent" is borrowed from the idea of latent heat in physics, which has now been almost replaced by the theory of the transformation of energy. Marx therefore uses in the third part (a later version) another term, borrowed from the idea of potential energy, viz: "potential", or analogous to the virtual velocities of D'Alembert, "virtual capital".— F. E.

plus product to a producer of gold or silver, who puts new gold or silver into circulation or, what amounts to the same thing, to a merchant who imports additional gold or silver from foreign countries for a part of the national surplus product, then his latent money capital forms an increment of the national gold or silver hoard. In all other cases, the £78 for instance, which were a circulating medium in the hands of the purchaser, assume only the form of a hoard in the hands of the capitalist. Hence all that has taken place is a different distribution of the national gold or silver hoard.

If in the transactions of our capitalist the money serves as a means of payment (the commodities having to be paid for by the buyer on longer or shorter terms), then the surplus product intended for capitalisation is not transformed into money but into creditor's claims, into titles of ownership of an equivalent which the buyer may already have in his possession or which he may expect to possess. It does not enter into the reproductive process of the circuit any more than does money invested in interest-bearing securities, etc., although it may enter into the circuits of other individual industrial capitals.

The entire character of capitalist production is determined by the self-expansion of the advanced capital value, that is to say, in the first instance by the production of as much surplus value as possible; in the second place however (see Buch I, Kap. XXII)[a] by the production of capital, hence by the transformation of surplus value into capital. Accumulation, or production on an extended scale, which appears as a means for constantly more expanded production of surplus value — hence for the enrichment of the capitalist, as his personal aim — and is comprised in the general tendency of capitalist production, becomes later, however, as was shown in the first book, by virtue of its development, a necessity for every individual capitalist. The constant augmentation of his capital becomes a condition of its preservation. But we need not revert more fully to what was previously expounded.

We considered first simple reproduction, assuming that the entire surplus value is spent as revenue. In reality under normal conditions a part of the surplus value must always be spent as revenue, and another part must be capitalised. And it is quite immaterial whether a certain surplus value produced in any particular period is entirely consumed or entirely capitalised. On the average — and the general formula can represent only the average movement — both cases oc-

---

[a] English edition: Vol. I, Ch. XXIV (present edition, Vol. 35).

cur. But in order not to complicate the formula, it is better to assume that the entire surplus value is accumulated. The formula $P \ldots C' - M' - C' <^{\mathrm{L}}_{\mathrm{MP}} \ldots P'$ stands for productive capital, which is reproduced on an enlarged scale and with greater value, and which as augmented productive capital begins its second circuit, or, what amounts to the same, renews its first circuit. As soon as this second circuit is begun, we once more have P as the starting-point; only this P is a larger productive capital than the first P was. Hence, if in the formula M ... M′ the second circuit begins with M′, M′ functions as M, as an advanced money capital of a definite magnitude. It is a larger money capital than the one with which the first circular movement was opened, but all reference to its augmentation by the capitalisation of surplus value ceases as soon as it assumes the function of advanced money capital. This origin is expunged in its form of money capital, which begins its circuit. This also applies to P′ as soon as it functions as the starting-point of a new circuit.

If we compare P ... P′ with M ... M′, or with the first circuit, we find that they have not the same significance at all. M ... M′, taken by itself as an isolated circuit, expresses only that M, the money capital (or industrial capital in its circuit as money capital), is money generating money, value generating value, in other words, produces surplus value. But in the P circuit the process of producing surplus value is already completed upon the termination of the first stage, the process of production, and after going through the second stage (the first stage of the circulation), C′ — M′, the capital value + surplus value already exist as realised money capital, as M′, which appeared as the last extreme in the first circuit. That surplus value has been produced is depicted in the first-considered formula P ... P (see expanded formula, p. 47)[a] by c — m — c, which, in its second stage, falls outside of the circulation of capital and represents the circulation of surplus value as revenue. In this form, where the entire movement is represented by P ... P, where consequently there is no difference in value between the two extremes, the self-expansion of the advanced value, the production of surplus value, is therefore represented in the same way as in M ... M′, except that the act C′ — M′, which appears as the last stage in M ... M′ and as the second stage of the circuit, serves as the first stage of the circulation in P ... P.

In P ... P′, P′ does not indicate that surplus value has been produced but that the produced surplus value has been capitalised, hence that capital has been accumulated and that therefore P′, in contrast to P, consists of the original capital value plus the value of the capital accumulated because of the capital value's movement.

M′, as the simple close of M ... M′, and also C′, as it appears within all these circuits, do not if taken by themselves express the movement but its result: the self-expansion of capital value realised in the form of commodities or money, and hence capital value as M + m, or C + c, as a relation of capital value to its surplus value, as its offspring. They express this result as various circulation forms of the self-expanded capital value. But neither in the form of C′ nor of M′ is the self-expansion which has taken place itself a function of money capital or of commodity capital. As special, differentiated forms, modes of existence corresponding to special functions of industrial capital, money capital can perform only money functions and commodity capital only commodity functions, the difference between them being merely that between money and commodity. Similarly industrial capital in its form of productive capital can consist only of the same elements as those of any other labour process which creates products: on the one hand objective conditions of labour (means of production), on the other productively (purposively) functioning labour power. Just as industrial capital can exist in the sphere of production only in a composition which corresponds to the production process in general, hence also to the non-capitalist production process, so it can exist in the sphere of circulation only in the two forms corresponding to it, viz., that of a commodity and of money. But just as the totality of the elements of production announces itself at the outset as productive capital by the fact that the labour power is labour power that belongs to others and that the capitalist purchased it from its proprietor, just as he purchased his means of production from other commodity owners; just as therefore the process of production itself appears as a productive function of industrial capital, so money and commodities appear as forms of circulation of the same industrial capital, hence their functions appear as the functions of its circulation, which either introduce the functions of productive capital or emanate from them. Here the money function and the commodity function are at the same time functions of money capital and commodity capital, but solely because they are interconnected as forms of functions which industrial capital has to perform at the different stages of its circuit. It is therefore wrong to attempt to derive the specific properties and functions which characterise money as money and commodities as commodities from their quality as capital, and it is equally wrong to derive on the contrary the properties of productive capital from its mode of existence in means of production.

As soon as M′ or C′ have become fixed as M + m or C + c, i. e., as the relation between the capital value and surplus value, its offspring, this relation is expressed in both of them, in the first case in the money form, in the second case in the commodity form, which does not change matters in the least. Consequently this relation does not have its origin in any properties or functions inherent in money as such or commodities as such. In both cases the characteristic property of capital, that of being a value generating value, is expressed only as a result. C′ is always the product of the function of P, and M′ is always merely the form of C′ changed in the circuit of industrial capital. As soon therefore as the realised money capital resumes its special function of money capital, it ceases to express the capital relation contained in M′ = M + m. After M ... M′ has been passed through and M′ begins the circuit anew, it does not figure as M′ but as M even if the entire surplus value contained in M′ is capitalised. The second circuit begins in our case with a money capital of £ 500, instead of £ 422, as in the first circuit. The money capital, which opens the circuit, is £ 78 larger than before. This difference exists on comparing the one circuit with the other, but no such comparison is made within each particular circuit. The £ 500 advanced as money capital, £ 78 of which formerly existed as surplus value, do not play any other role than would some other £ 500 with which another capitalist inaugurates his first circuit. The same happens in the circuit of the productive capital. The increased P′ acts as P on recommencing, just as P did in the simple reproduction P ... P.

In the stage $M′—C′ <_{MP}^{L}$, the augmented magnitude is indicated only by C′, but not by L′ or MP′. Since C is the sum of L and MP, C′ indicates sufficiently that the sum of L and MP contained in it is greater than the original P. In the second place, the terms L′ and MP′ would be incorrect, because we know that the growth of capital involves a change in the constitution of its value and that as this change progresses the value of MP increases, that of L always decreasing relatively and often absolutely.

III. ACCUMULATION OF MONEY

Whether or not m, the surplus value turned into money, is immediately added to the capital value in process and is thus enabled to enter the circuit together with capital M now having the magnitude M′, depends on circumstances which are independent of the mere existence of m. If m is to serve as money capital in a second independent business, to be run side by side with the first, it is evident that it cannot be used for this purpose unless it is of the minimum size required for it. And if it is intended to be used for the expansion of the original business, the relations between the material factors of P and their value relations likewise demand a minimum magnitude for m. All the means of production employed in this business have not only a qualitative but also a definite quantitative relation to one another, are proportionate in quantity. These material relations as well as the pertinent value relations of the factors entering into the productive capital determine the minimum magnitude m must possess to be capable of transformation into additional means of production and labour power, or only into the former, as an accretion to the productive capital. Thus the owner of a spinning-mill cannot increase the number of his spindles without at the same time purchasing a corresponding number of carders and roving frames, apart from the increased expenditure for cotton and wages which such an expansion of his business demands. To carry this out the surplus value must therefore have reached a considerable figure (generally calculated to be £1 per newly installed spindle). If m does not reach this minimum size the circuit of the capital must be repeated until the sum of m successively produced by it can function together with M, hence $M'—C' <^L_{MP}$. Even mere changes of detail, for instance in the spinning machinery, introduced to make it more productive, require greater expenditures for spinning material, more roving machinery, etc. In the meantime m is accumulated, and its accumulation is not its own function but the result of repeated P ... P. Its own function consists in persisting in the money state until it receives sufficient increment from the repeated surplus-value-creating circuits, i. e., from outside, to possess the minimum magnitude necessary for its active function, the magnitude in which alone it can really enter as money capital—in the case at hand as the accumulated part of the functioning money capital M—into the function of M. But in the interim it is accumulated and exists only in the shape of a hoard in process of formation, of growth. Hence the accumulation of money, hoarding, appears here as a process by which real accumulation, the extension of the scale on which industrial capital operates, is temporarily accompanied. Temporarily, for so long as the hoard remains in the condition of a hoard, it does not function as capital, does not take part in the process of creating surplus value, remains a sum of money which grows only because money, come by without its doing anything, is thrown into the same coffer.

The form of a hoard is simply the form of money not in circulation, of money whose circulation has been interrupted and which is therefore fixed in its money form. As for the process of hoarding, it is common to all commodity production and figures as an end in itself only in the undeveloped, pre-capitalist forms of this production. In the present case, however, the hoard appears as a form of money capital and the formation of a hoard as a process which temporarily accompanies the accumulation of capital because and so far as the money here figures as *latent money capital*; because the formation of a hoard, the state of being a hoard, in which the surplus value existing in money form finds itself, is a functionally determined preparatory stage gone through outside of the circuit described by the capital and required for the transformation of the surplus value into really functioning capital. By its definition it is therefore latent money capital. Hence the size it must acquire before it can take part in the process is determined in each case by the value constitution of the productive capital. But so long as it remains in the condition of a hoard it does not yet perform the functions of money capital but is still idle money capital; not money capital whose function has been interrupted, as was the case before, but money capital not yet capable of performing it.

We are here discussing the accumulation of money in its original real form of an actual hoard of money. It may also exist in the form of mere outstanding money, of claims on debtors by capitalists who have sold C′. As for other forms in which this latent money capital may exist in the meantime even in the shape of money-breeding money, such as interest-bearing bank deposits, bills of exchange or securities of any description, these do not belong here. Surplus value realised in the form of money in such cases performs special capital functions outside the circuit described by the industrial capital which originated it—functions which in the first place have nothing to do with that circuit as such but which in the second place presuppose capital functions which differ from the functions of industrial capital and which have not yet been developed here.

IV. RESERVE FUND

In the form we have just discussed, the hoard, in which the surplus value exists, is a fund for the accumulation of money, the money form temporarily assumed by capital accumulation and to that extent a condition of this accumulation. However this accumulation fund can also perform special services of a subordinate nature, that is to say can enter into capital's movement in circuits without this process assuming the form of P ... P′, hence without an expansion of capitalist reproduction.

If the process C′ — M′ is prolonged beyond its normal duration, if therefore the commodity capital is abnormally delayed in its transformation into the money form or if, for instance, after the completion of this transformation, the price of the means of production into which the money capital must be transformed has risen above the level prevailing at the beginning of the circuit, the hoard functioning as accumulation fund can be used in the place of money capital or of part of it. Thus the money-accumulation fund serves as a reserve fund for counterbalancing disturbances in the circuit.

As such a reserve fund it differs from the fund of purchasing or paying media discussed in the circuit P ... P. These media are a part of functioning money capital (hence forms of existence of a part of capital value in general going through the process) whose parts enter upon their functions only at different times, successively. In the continuous process of production, reserve money capital is always formed, since one day money is received and no payments have to be made until later, and another day large quantities of goods are sold while other large quantities are not due to be bought until a subsequent date. In these intervals a part of the circulating capital exists continuously in the form of money. A reserve fund on the other hand is not a constituent part of capital already performing its functions, or, to be more exact, of money capital. It is rather a part of capital in a preliminary stage of its accumulation, of surplus value not yet transformed into active capital. As for the rest, it needs no explaining that a capitalist in financial straits does not concern himself about what the particular functions of the money he has on hand are. He simply employs whatever money he has for the purpose of keeping his capital circulating. For instance in our illustration M = £422, M′ = £500. If a part of the capital of £422 exists as a fund of means of payment and purchase, as a money reserve, it is intended, other conditions remaining the same, that it should enter wholly into the circuit, and besides should suffice for this purpose. The reserve fund however is a part of the £78 of surplus value. It can enter the circular course of the capital worth £422 only to the extent that this circuit takes place under conditions not remaining the same; for it is a part of the accumulation fund, and figures here without any extension of the scale of reproduction.

Money-accumulation fund implies the existence of latent money capital, hence the transformation of money into money capital.

The following is the general formula for the circuit of productive capital. It combines simple reproduction and reproduction on a progressively increasing scale:

$$\overset{1}{P\ldots C'\overset{\frown}{-}M'.} \qquad \overset{2}{M\overset{\frown}{-}C<\overset{L}{_{MP}}\ldots P\,(P')}$$

If P = P, then M in 2) = M′ − m; if P = P′, then M in 2) is greater than M′ − m; that is to say m has been completely or partially transformed into money capital.

The circuit of productive capital is the form in which classical political economy examines the circular process of industrial capital.

Chapter III

THE CIRCUIT OF COMMODITY CAPITAL

The general formula for the circuit of commodity capital is:

$$C' — M' — C \ldots P \ldots C'.$$

C′ appears not only as the product but also as the premise of the two previous circuits, since that which M — C means for the one capital, C′ — M′ means for the other, inasmuch as at least a part of the means of production is itself the commodity product of other individual capitals describing their circuits. In our case for instance coal, machinery, etc., represent the commodity capital of the mine-owner, of the capitalist machine-manufacturer, etc. Furthermore we have shown in Chapter I, IV, that not only the circuit P ... P but also the circuit C ... C′ is assumed even in the first repetition of M ... M′, before this second circuit of money capital is completed.

If reproduction takes place on an extended scale, then the final C′ is greater than the initial C′ and should therefore be designated here as C″.

The difference between the third form and the first two is as follows: First, in this case the total circulation with its two antithetical phases opens the circuit, while in Form I the circulation is interrupted by the process of production and in Form II the total circulation with its two mutually complementary phases appears merely as a means of effecting the process of reproduction and therefore constitutes the movement mediating between P ... P. In the case of M ... M′, the form of circulation is M — C ... C′ — M′ = M — C — M. In the case of P ... P it has the inverted form C′ — M′. M — C = C — M — C. In the case of C′ — C′ it likewise has this last form.

Secondly, when circuits I and II are repeated, even if the final points M′ and P′ form the starting-points of the renewed circuit, the form in which M′ and P′ were produced disappears. M′ = M + m and P′ = P + p begin the new process as M and P. But in Form III the starting-point C must be designated as C′, even if the circuit is renewed on the same scale, for the following reason. In Form I, as soon as M′ as such opens a new circuit it functions as money capital M, as an advance in money form of the capital value that is to produce surplus value. The size of the advanced money capital, augmented by the accumulation achieved during the first circuit, has increased. But whether the size of the advanced money capital is £422 or £500 does not alter the fact that it appears as simple capital value. M′ no longer exists as self-expanded capital or a capital pregnant with surplus value, as a capital relation. Indeed, it is to expand itself only during its process. The same is true of P ... P′; P′ must steadily continue to function as P, as capital value which is to produce surplus value, and must renew its circuit.

The commodity-capital circuit, on the contrary, does not open with just capital value but with capital value augmented in the commodity form. Hence it includes from the start the circuit of not only capital value existing in the form of commodities, but also of surplus value. Consequently if simple reproduction takes place in this form, the C′ at the terminal point is equal in size to the C′ at the starting-point. If a part of the surplus value enters into the capital circuit, C″, an enlarged C′, appears at the close instead of C′, but the now succeeding circuit is once more opened by C′. This is merely a larger C′ than that of the preceding circuit, with a larger accumulated capital value. Hence it begins its new circuit with a relatively larger, newly created surplus value. In any event C′ always inaugurates the circuit as a commodity capital which is = to capital value + surplus value.

C′ as C does not appear in the circuit of an individual industrial capital as a form of this capital but as a form of some other industrial capital, so far as the means of production are the product of the latter. The act M — C (i. e., M — MP) of the first capital is C′ — M′ for this second capital.

In the circulation act M — C $<_{MP}^{L}$ L and MP bear identical relations, as they are commodities in the hands of their sellers — in the one case the labourers who sell their labour power, in the other the owner of the means of production, who sells these. For the purchaser, whose money here functions as money capital, L and MP function merely as commodities until he has bought them, hence so long as they confront his capital, existing in the form of money, as commodities of others. MP and L differ here only in this respect, that MP may be C′, hence capital, in the hands of its seller, if MP is the commodity form of his capital, while L is always nothing else but a commodity for the labourer and becomes capital only in the hands of its purchaser as a constituent part of P.

For this reason C′ can never open any circuit as a mere C, as a mere commodity form of capital value. As commodity capital it is always twofold. From the point of view of use value it is the product, in the present case yarn, of the functioning of P whose elements L and MP, coming as commodities from the sphere of circulation, have functioned only as factors in the creation of this product. Secondly, from the point of view of value, it is the capital value P plus the surplus value s produced by the functioning of P.

It is only in the circuit described by C′ itself that C equal to P and equal to the capital value can and must separate from that part of C′ in which surplus value exists, from the surplus product in which the surplus value is lodged. It does not matter whether the two things can be actually separated, as in the case of yarn, or whether they cannot, as in the case of a machine. They always become separable as soon as C′ is transformed into M′.

If the entire commodity product can be separated into independent homogeneous partial products, as in the case of our 10,000 lbs of yarn, and if therefore the act C′ — M′ can be represented by a number of successive sales, then the capital value in the form of commodities can function as C, can be separated from C′, before the surplus value, hence before C′ in its entirety, has been realised.

Of the 10,000 lbs of yarn worth £500, the value of 8,440

lbs $= £422 =$ the capital value, independently of the surplus value. If the capitalist sells first 8,440 lbs of yarn at £422, then these 8,440 lbs of yarn represent C, the capital value in commodity form. The surplus product, of 1,560 lbs of yarn, contained besides in C′ and equal to a surplus value of £78, does not circulate until later. The capitalist could accomplish $C—M—C<^L_{MP}$ before the circulation of the surplus product c — m — c has taken place.

Or if he sells first 7,440 lbs of yarn worth £372, and then 1,000 lbs of yarn worth £50, he might replace the means of production (the constant capital c) with the first part of C, and the variable capital v, the labour power, with the second part of C, and then proceed as before.

But if such successive sales take place and the conditions of the circuit permit it, the capitalist, instead of separating C′ into c + v + s, may make such a separation also in the case of aliquot parts of C′.

For example the 7,440 lbs of yarn $= £372$, which as parts of C′ (10,000 lbs of yarn worth £500) represent the constant part of the capital, may themselves be separated into 5,535.360 lbs of yarn worth £276.768, which replace only the constant part, the value of the means of production used up in producing 7,440 lbs of yarn; 744 lbs of yarn worth £37.200, which replace only the variable capital; and 1,160.640 lbs of yarn worth £58.032, which, being surplus product, are the depositories of surplus value. Consequently on selling the 7,440 lbs of yarn, he can replace the capital value contained in them out of the sale of 6,279.360 lbs of yarn at the price of £313.968, and he can spend as his revenue the value of the surplus product amounting to 1,160.640 lbs, or £58.032.

In the same way, he may divide up another 1,000 lbs of yarn $= £50 =$ the variable capital value, and sell them accordingly: 744 lbs of yarn worth £37.200, constant capital value contained in 1,000 lbs of yarn; 100 lbs of yarn worth £5.000, variable capital value ditto; hence 844 lbs of yarn worth £42.200, replacement of the capital value contained in the 1,000 lbs of yarn; finally, 156 lbs of yarn worth £7.800, representing the surplus product contained in it, which may be consumed as such.

Finally, he may divide up the remaining 1,560 lbs of yarn worth £78, in such a way, provided he succeeds in selling them, that the sale of 1,160.640 lbs of yarn, worth £58.032, replaces the value of the means of production contained in those 1,560 lbs of yarn, and that 156 lbs of yarn, worth £7.800, replaces the variable capital value; altogether 1,316.640 lbs of yarn = £65.832, replacement of the total capital value; finally the surplus product of 243.360 lbs = £12.168, remains to be spent as revenue.

All the elements — c, v, and s — contained in the yarn are divisible into the same component parts, and so is every individual pound of yarn, worth 1 s., or 12 d.

$$
\begin{aligned}
c &= 0.744 \text{ lbs} &\text{of yarn} &= 8.928 \text{ d.} \\
v &= 0.100 \text{ lbs} &\text{of yarn} &= 1.200 \text{ d.} \\
s &= 0.156 \text{ lbs} &\text{of yarn} &= 1.872 \text{ d.}
\end{aligned}
$$

$$c + v + s = 1 \quad \text{lb.} \quad \text{of yarn} = 12 \text{ d.}$$

If we add the results of the above three partial sales we obtain the same result on selling the entire 10,000 lbs at one sweep.

We have of constant capital

at the first sale:	5,535.360 lbs	of yarn = £276.768
at the second sale:	744.000 lbs	of yarn = £ 37.200
at the third sale:	1,160.640 lbs	of yarn = £ 58.032
Total	7,440 lbs	of yarn = £372

Of variable capital:

at the first sale:	744.000 lbs	of yarn = £37.200
at the second sale:	100.000 lbs	of yarn = £ 5.000
at the third sale:	156.000 lbs	of yarn = £ 7.800
Total	1,000 lbs	of yarn = £50

Of surplus value:

at the first sale:	1,160.640 lbs	of yarn = £58.032
at the second sale:	156.000 lbs	of yarn = £ 7.800
at the third sale:	243.360 lbs	of yarn = £12.168
Total	1,560 lbs	of yarn = £78

Grand Total:

Constant capital . . .	7,440 lbs	of yarn = £372
Variable capital	1,000 lbs.	of yarn = £ 50 . .
Surplus value	1,560 lbs.	of yarn = £ 78 . .
Total	10,000 lbs	of yarn = £500

$C' — M'$ in itself stands merely for the sale of 10,000 lbs of yarn. These 10,000 lbs of yarn, like all other yarn, are a commodity. The purchaser is interested in the price of 1 s. per lb., or of £500 for 10,000 lbs. If during the negotiations he goes into the value composition of the yarn, he does so simply with the insidious intention of proving that it could be sold at less than 1 s. per pound and would still be a good bargain for the seller. But the quantity purchased by him depends on his requirements. If he is for example the owner of a weaving-mill, it depends on the composition of his own capital functioning in this enterprise, not on the composition of the spinner's of whom he buys. The proportions in which C' has to replace on the one hand the capital used up in its production (or the various component parts of this capital), and on the other to serve as surplus product either for the spending of surplus value or for the accumulation of capital, exist only in the circuit of the capital which has as its commodity form the 10,000 lbs of yarn. These proportions have nothing to do with the sale as such. In the present case it is assumed besides that C' is sold at its value, so that it is only a question of its transformation from the commodity form into the money form. It is of course of decisive importance with regard to C', as the functional form in the circuit of this individual capital out of which the productive capital is to be replaced, to what extent, if at all, there is a discrepancy between price and value in the sale. But this does not concern us here in the examination of mere distinctions of form.

In Form I, M ... M′, the process of production intervenes midway between the two complementary and mutually opposite phases of the circulation of capital. It is past before the concluding phase $C' — M'$ begins. Money is advanced as capital, is first transformed into elements of production and from these into the commodity product, and this commodity product in its turn is changed back into money. It is a full and complete business cycle that results in money, something everyone can use for everything. A new start is therefore only a possibility. M ... P ... M′ may be either the last circuit that concludes the functioning of some individual capital being withdrawn from business, or the first circuit of some new capital entering upon its function. The general movement is here M ... M′, from money to more money.

In Form II, P ... C′—M′—C ... P (P′), the entire circulation process follows after the first P and precedes the second P; but it takes place in the opposite order from that of Form I. The first P is the productive capital, and its function is the productive process, the prerequisite of the succeeding circulation process. The concluding P on the other hand is not the productive process; it is only the renewed existence of the industrial capital in its form of productive capital. And it is such as a result of the transformation, during the last phase of circulation, of the capital value into L + MP, into the subjective and objective factors which by combining constitute the form of existence of the productive capital. The capital, whether P or P′, is at the end once more present in a form in which it must function anew as productive capital, must again perform the productive process. The general form of the movement P ... P is the form of reproduction and, unlike M ... M′, does not indicate the self-expansion of value as the object of the process. This form makes it therefore so much easier for classical political economy to ignore the definite capitalistic form of the process of production and to depict production as such as the purpose of this process; namely that as much as possible must be produced and as cheaply as possible, and that the product must be exchanged for the greatest variety of other products, partly for the renewal of production (M — C), partly for consumption (m — c). It is then possible to overlook the peculiarities of money and money capital, for M and m appear here merely as transient media of circulation. The entire process seems simple and natural, i. e., possesses the naturalness of a shallow rationalism. In the same way profit is occasionally forgotten in commodity capital and the latter figures merely as a commodity when the production circuit as a whole is under discussion. But as soon as the constituents of value are debated, commodity capital figures as commodity capital. Accumulation, of course, is seen in the same light as production.

In Form III, C′ — M′ — C ... P ... C′, the two phases of the circulation process open the circuit, and do so in the same order which obtains in Form II, P ... P; next follows P, with its function, the productive process, the same as in Form I; the circuit closes with the result of the process of production, C′. Just as in Form II the circuit closes with P, the merely renewed existence of productive capital, so here it closes with C′, the renewed existence of commodity capital. Just as in Form II capital, in its concluding form P, must start the process over again as a process of production, so here upon the reappearance of industrial capital in the form of commodity capital the circuit must re-open with the circulation phase C′ — M′. Both forms of the circuit are incomplete because they do not close with M′, the capital value retransformed into *money* and self-expanded. Both must therefore be continued and consequently include the reproduction. The total circuit in Form III is C′ ... C′.

The third form is distinguished from the first two by the fact that it is only in this circuit that the self-expanded capital value — and not the original one, the capital value that must still produce surplus value — appears as the starting-point of its expansion. C′ as a capital relation is here the starting-point and as such relation has a determining influence on the entire circuit because it includes the circuit of the capital value as well as that of the surplus value already in its first phase, and because the surplus value must at least in the average, if not in every single circuit, be expended partly as revenue, go through the circulation c — m — c, and must partly perform the function of an element of capital accumulation.

In the form C′ ... C′ the consumption of the entire commodity product is assumed as the condition of the normal course of the circuit of capital itself. The individual consumption of the labourer and the individual consumption of the unaccumulated part of the surplus product comprise the entire individual consumption. Hence consumption in its totality — individual as well as productive — enters into circuit C′ as a condition of it. Productive consumption (which essentially includes the individual consumption of the labourer, since labour power is a continuous product, within certain limits, of the labourer's individual consumption) is carried on by every individual capital. Individual consumption, except in so far as it is required for the existence of the individual capitalist, is here assumed to be only a social act, but by no means an act of the individual capitalist.

In Forms I and II the aggregate movement appears as a movement of advanced capital value. In Form III the self-expanded capital, in the shape of the total commodity product, forms the starting-point and has the form of moving capital, commodity capital. Not until its transformation into money has been accomplished does this movement branch out into movements of capital and of revenue. The distribution of the total social product, as well as the special distribution of the product for each individual commodity capital, into an individual consumption fund on the one hand and into a reproduction fund on the other, is included in this form in the circuit of · capital.

In M ... M′ possible enlargement of the circuit is included, depending on the volume of m entering into the renewed circuit.

In P ... P the new circuit may be started by P with the same or perhaps even a smaller value and yet may represent a reproduction on an extended scale, for instance when certain elements of commodities become cheaper on account of increased productivity of labour. Vice versa, a productive capital which has increased in value may, in a contrary case, represent reproduction on a materially contracted scale as for instance when elements of production have become dearer. The same is true of C′ ... C′.

In C′ ... C′ capital in the form of commodities is the premise of production. It re-appears as a premise within this circuit in the second C. If this C has not yet been produced or reproduced the circuit is obstructed. This C must be reproduced, for the greater part as C′ of some other industrial capital. In this circuit C′ exists as the point of departure, of transition, and of the conclusion of the movement; hence it is always there. It is a permanent condition of the process of reproduction.

C′ ... C′ is distinguished from Forms I and II by still another feature. All three circuits have this in common, that capital begins its circular course in the same form in which it concludes it, and thus finds itself in the initial form in which it opens the circuit anew. The initial form M, P or C′ is always the one in which capital value (in III augmented by its surplus value) is advanced, in other words its original form in regard to the circuit. The concluding form M′, P or C′ is always a changed form of a functional form which preceded in the circuit and is not the original form.

Thus M′ in I is a converted form of C′, the final P in II is a converted form of M (and this transformation is accomplished in I and II by a simple act of commodity circulation, by a formal change of position of commodity and money); in III, C′ is a converted form of the productive capital P. But here, in III, the transformation, in the first place, does not merely concern the functional form of capital but also the magnitude of its value; in the second place, however, the transformation is not the result of a merely formal change of position pertaining to the circulation process, but of a real transformation experienced by the use form and value of the commodity constituents of the productive capital in the process of production.

The form of the initial extreme M, P or C′ is the premise of the corresponding circuit I, II or III. The form returning in the final extreme is premised and consequently brought about by the series of metamorphoses of the circuit itself. C′, as the terminal point in the circuit of an individual industrial capital, presupposes only the non-circulation form P of the same industrial capital of which it is the product. M′, as the terminal point of I, as the converted form of C′ (C′ — M′), presupposes that M is in the hands of the buyer, exists outside of the circuit M ... M′, and is drawn into it and made its own terminal form by the sale of C′. Thus the terminal P in II presupposes that L and MP (C) exist outside and are incorporated in it as its terminal form by means of M — C. But apart from the last extreme, the circuit of individual money capital does not presuppose the existence of money capital in general, nor does the circuit of individual productive capital presuppose the existence of productive capital. In I, M may be the first money capital; in II, P may be the first productive capital appearing on the historical scene. But in III,

$$C' \begin{cases} C- \\ -M' \\ c- \end{cases} \begin{cases} M-C <^{L}_{MP} \ ... \ P \ ... \ C' \\ \\ m-c \end{cases}$$

C is presupposed twice outside of the circuit. The first time in the circuit C′ — M′ — C $<^{L}_{MP}$. This C, so far as it consists of MP, is commodity in the hands of the seller; it is itself commodity capital, so far as it is the product of a capitalist process of production; and even if it is not, it appears as commodity capital in the hands of the merchant. The second time, in the second c of c — m — c, which must likewise be at hand as a commodity so that it can be bought. At any rate, whether they are commodity capital or not, L and MP are just as much commodities as is C′ and bear to each other the relation of commodities. The same is true of the second c in c — m — c. Inasmuch therefore as C′ = C (L + MP), it has commodities as elements for its own production and must be replaced by the same commodities in the circulation. In the same way the second c in c — m — c must be replaced by similar commodities in the circulation.

On the basis that the capitalist mode of production is the prevailing mode, all commodities in the hands of the seller must, besides, be commodity capital. And they continue to be so in the hands of the merchant or become such if they were not such before. Or they have to be commodities — such as imported articles — which replace original commodity capital and hence bestow upon it merely another form of existence.

As forms of existence of P the commodity elements L and MP, of which the productive capital P consists, do not possess the same form as in the various commodity markets where they are fetched. They are now united, and so combined they can perform the functions of productive capital.

That C appears as the premise of C only in this Form III, within the circuit itself, is due to capital in commodity form being its starting-point. The circuit is opened by the transformation of C′ (in so far as it functions as capital value, regardless of whether it has been increased by the addition of surplus value or not) into those commodities which are its elements of production. But this transformation comprises the entire process of circulation, C — M — C (= L + MP), and is its result. C here stands at both extremes, but the second extreme, which receives its form C by means of M — C from outside, the commodity market, is not the last extreme of the circuit but only of its first two stages comprising the process of circulation. Its result is P, which then performs its function, the process of production. It is only as the result of this process, hence not as that of the circulation process, that C′ appears as the terminal point of the circuit and in the same form as the starting-point, C′. On the other hand in M ... M′ and P ... P, the final extremes M′ and P are the direct results of the process of circulation. Here therefore it is presupposed only at the end that one time M′ and the other time P exist in the hands of others. In so far as the circuit is made between the extremes, neither M in the one case nor P in the other — the existence of M as the money of another person and of P as the production process of another capital — appears as the premise of these circuits. C′ ... C′ on the contrary presupposes the existence of C (= L + MP) as commodities of others in the hands of others — commodities drawn into the circuit by the introductory process of circulation and transformed into productive capital, as a result of whose functioning C′ once more becomes the concluding form of the circuit.

But just because the circuit C′ ... C′ presupposes within its sphere the existence of other industrial capital in the form of C (= L + MP) — and MP comprises diverse other capitals, in our case for instance machinery, coal, oil, etc.— it clamours to be considered not only as the *general* form of the circuit, i. e., not only as a social form in which every single industrial capital (except when first invested) can be studied, hence not merely as a form of movement common to all individual industrial capitals, but simultaneously also as a form of movement of the sum of the individual capitals, consequently of the aggregate capital of the capitalist class, a movement in which that of each individual industrial capital appears as only a partial movement which intermingles with the other movements and is necessitated by them. For instance if we regard the aggregate of commodities annually produced in a certain country and analyse the movement by which a part of it replaces the productive capital in all individual businesses, while another part enters into the individual consumption of the various classes, then we consider $C' \ldots C'$ as a form of movement of social capital as well as of the surplus value, or surplus product, generated by it. The fact that the social capital is equal to the sum of the individual capitals (including the joint-stock capital or the state capital, so far as governments employ productive wage labour in mines, railways, etc., perform the function of industrial capitalists), and that the aggregate movement of social capital is equal to the algebraic sum of the movements of the individual capitals, does not in any way preclude the possibility that this movement, as the movement of a single individual capital, may present other phenomena than the same movement does when considered from the point of view of a part of the aggregate movement of social capital, hence in its interconnection with the movements of its other parts, and that the movement simultaneously solves problems the solution of which must be assumed when studying the circuit of a separate, individual capital instead of being the result of such study.

$C' \ldots C'$ is the sole circuit in which the capital value originally advanced constitutes only a part of the extreme that opens the movement and in which the movement from its inception thus reveals itself as the total movement of the industrial capital — as the movement of that part of the product which replaces the productive capital as well as of that part which forms surplus product and which on the average is spent in part as revenue and employed in part as an element of accumulation. Included in this circuit is the expenditure of surplus value as revenue and to that extent individual consumption is likewise included. The latter however is also included for the reason that the starting-point C, commodity, exists in the form of a useful article, of whatever kind, but every article produced by capitalist methods is commodity capital, no matter whether its use form destines it for productive or for individual consumption, or for both. $M \ldots M'$ indicates only the value side, the self-expansion of the advanced capital value, as the purpose of the entire process; $P \ldots P$ (P') indicates the process of production of capital as a process of reproduction with a productive capital of the same or of increasing magnitude (accumulation). Revealing itself already in its initial extreme as a form of capitalist commodity production, C′ ... C′ comprises productive and individual consumption from the start; productive consumption and the self-expansion of value therein included appear only as a branch of its movement. Finally, since C′ may exist in a use form which cannot enter any more into any process of production, it is indicated at the outset that the various value constituents of C′, expressed by parts of the product, must occupy a different position, according to whether C′ ... C′ is regarded as the form of the movement of the total social capital or as the independent movement of an individual industrial capital. All these peculiarities of the circuit lead us beyond its own confines as an isolated circuit of some merely individual capital.

In the formula C′ ... C′, the movement of the commodity capital, that is to say, of the total product created capitalistically, appears not only as the premise of the independent circuit of the individual capital but also as required by it. If therefore this formula and its peculiarities are grasped, it is no longer sufficient to confine oneself to indicating that the metamorphoses C′ — M′ and M — C are on the one hand functionally defined sections in the metamorphosis of capital, on the other are links in the general circulation of commodities. It becomes necessary to elucidate the intertwining of the metamorphoses of one individual capital with those of other individual capitals and with that part of the total product which is intended for individual consumption. On analysing the circuit of an individual industrial capital, we therefore base our studies mainly on the first two forms.

The circuit C′ ... C′ appears as the form of a single individual capital, for instance in agriculture, where calculations are made from crop to crop. In Formula II, the sowing is the starting-point, in Formula III the harvest, or, to speak with the Physiocrats, Formula II starts out with the *avances*, and Formula III with the *reprises*. The movement of capital value appears in III from the outset only as a part of the movement of the general mass of products, while in I and II the movement of C′ constitutes only a phase of the movement of some isolated capital.

In Formula III commodities in the market are the continuous premise of the process of production and reproduction. Hence, if attention is fixed exclusively on this formula all elements of the process of production seem to originate in commodity circulation and to consist only of commodities. This one-sided conception overlooks those elements of the process of production which are independent of the commodity elements.

Since in $C' \dots C'$ the starting-point is the total product (total value), it turns out here that (if foreign trade is disregarded) reproduction on an extended scale, productivity remaining otherwise constant, can take place only when the part of the surplus product to be capitalised already contains the material elements of the additional productive capital; that therefore, so far as the production of one year serves as the premise of the following year's production or so far as this can take place simultaneously with the process of simple reproduction within one year, surplus product is at once produced in a form which enables it to perform the functions of additional capital. Increased productivity can increase only the substance of capital but not its value; but therewith it creates additional material for the self-expansion of that value.

$C' \dots C'$ is the groundwork for Quesnay's *Tableau économique*, and it shows great and true discretion on his part that in contrast to $M \dots M'$ (the isolatedly and rigidly retained form of the mercantile system) he selected this form and not $P \dots P$.

Chapter IV

THE THREE FORMULAS OF THE CIRCUIT

The three formulas may be set down in the following manner, using Tc for total circulation process:

$$\text{I)} \quad M — C \dots P \dots C' — M'$$
$$\text{II)} \quad P \dots Tc \dots P$$
$$\text{III)} \quad Tc \dots P \ (C').$$

If we combine all three forms, all premises of the process appear as its result, as a premise produced by it itself. Every element appears as a point of departure, of transit, and of return. The total process presents itself as the unity of the processes of production and circulation. The process of production becomes the mediator of the process of circulation and vice versa.

All three circuits have the following in common: The self-expansion of value as the determining purpose, as the compelling motive. In

I this is expressed in its form. Formula II begins with P, the very process of self-expansion of value. In III the circuit begins with the self-expanded value and closes with new self-expanded value, even if the movement is repeated on the same scale.

As C — M means M — C for the buyer, and M — C means C — M for the seller, the circulation of capital presents only the ordinary metamorphosis of commodities, and the laws evolved with regard to it (Buch I, Kap. III, 2)[a] on the mass of money in circulation are valid here. However, if we do not cling to this formal aspect but rather consider the actual connection between the metamorphoses of the various individual capitals, in fact, if we study the connection between the circuits of individual capitals as partial movements of the process of reproduction of the total social capital, then the mere change of form of money and commodities cannot explain the connection.

In a constantly revolving circle every point is simultaneously a point of departure and a point of return. If we interrupt the rotation, not every point of departure is a point of return. Thus we have seen that not only does every individual circuit presuppose the others (*implicite*), but also that the repetition of the circuit in one form comprises the performance of the circuit in the other forms. The entire difference thus appears to be a merely formal one, or as a merely subjective distinction existing solely for the observer.

Since every one of these circuits is considered a special form of the movement in which various individual industrial capitals are engaged, this difference always exists only as an individual one. But in reality every individual industrial capital is present simultaneously in all three circuits. These three circuits, the forms of reproduction assumed by the three forms of capital, are made continuously side by side. For instance, one part of the capital value, which now performs the function of commodity capital, is transformed into money capital, but at the same time another part leaves the process of production and enters the circulation as a new commodity capital. The circuit form C′ ... C′ is thus continuously described; and so are the other two forms. The reproduction of capital in each one of its forms and stages is just as continuous as the metamorphosis of these forms and the successive passage through the three stages. The entire circuit is thus really a unity of its three forms.

---

[a] English edition: Vol. I, Ch. III, 2 (present edition, Vol. 35).

We assumed in our analysis that capital value in its entire magnitude acts either as money capital, productive capital or commodity capital. For instance, we had those £422 first entirely as money capital, then we transformed them wholly into productive capital, and finally into commodity capital, into yarn of the value of £500 (containing £78 worth of surplus value). Here the various stages are just so many interruptions. So long as, e. g., those £422 retain their money form, that is to say, until the purchases M — C (L + MP) are made, the entire capital exists and functions only as money capital. As soon as it is transformed into productive capital, it performs neither the functions of money capital nor of commodity capital. Its entire process of circulation is interrupted, just as on the other hand its entire process of production is interrupted, as soon as it functions in one of its two circulation stages, either as M or as C′. Consequently, the circuit P ... P would represent not only a periodical renewal of the productive capital but also the interruption of its function, the process of production, up to the time when the process of circulation is completed. Instead of proceeding continuously, production would take place in jerks and would be renewed only in periods of accidental duration, according to whether the two stages of the process of circulation were performed quickly or slowly. This would apply for instance to a Chinese artisan who works only for private customers and whose process of production ceases until he receives a new order.

This is indeed true of every single part of capital that is in motion, and all parts of capital go through this motion in succession. Suppose that the 10,000 lbs of yarn are the weekly product of some spinner. These 10,000 lbs of yarn leave the sphere of production entirely and enter the sphere of circulation; the capital value contained in it must all be converted into money capital, and so long as this value continues in the form of money capital it cannot enter anew into the process of production. It must first go into circulation and be reconverted into the elements of productive capital, L + MP. The circuit-describing process of capital means constant interruption, the leaving of one stage and the entering into the next, the discarding of one form and the assuming of another. Each one of these stages not only presupposes the next but also excludes it.

But continuity is the characteristic mark of capitalist production, necessitated by its technical basis, although not always absolutely attainable. Let us see then what happens in reality. While, e.g., the 10,000 lbs of yarn appear in the market as commodity capital and are

transformed into money (regardless of whether it is a paying or purchasing medium or only money of account), new cotton, coal, etc.,
take the place of the yarn in the process of production, have therefore
already been reconverted from the money form and commodity form
into that of productive capital, and begin to function as such. At the
same time that these 10,000 lbs of yarn are being converted into
money, the preceding 10,000 lbs of yarn are going through the second
stage of their circulation and are being reconverted from money into
the elements of productive capital. All parts of capital successively describe circuits, are simultaneously at its different stages. The industrial capital, continuously progressing along its orbit, thus exists simultaneously at all its stages and in the diverse functional forms corresponding to these stages. That part of capital which is converted
for the first time from commodity capital into money begins the circuit C′ ... C′, while industrial capital as a moving whole has already passed through that circuit. One hand advances money, the other receives it. The inauguration of the circuit M ... M′ at one place
coincides with the return of the money at another place. The same is
true of productive capital.

The actual circuit of industrial capital in its continuity is therefore
not only the unity of the processes of circulation and production but
also the unity of all its three circuits. But it can be such a unity only if
all the different parts of capital can go through the successive stages of
the circuit, can pass from one phase, from one functional form to
another, so that the industrial capital, being the whole of all these
parts, exists simultaneously in its various phases and functions and
thus describes all three circuits at the same time. The succession [*das
Nacheinander*] of these parts is here governed by their co-existence [*das
Nebeneinander*], that is to say, by the division of capital. In a ramified
factory system the product is constantly in the various stages of its
process of formation and constantly passes from one phase of production to another. As the individual industrial capital has a definite size
which depends on the means of the capitalist and which has a definite
minimum magnitude for every branch of industry, it follows that its
division must proceed according to definite proportions. The magnitude of the available capital determines the dimensions of the process
of production, and this again determines the dimensions of the commodity capital and money capital in so far as they perform their functions parallel with the process of production. However co-existence,
by which continuity of production is determined, is only due to the

movement of those parts of capital in which they successively pass through their different stages. Co-existence is itself merely the result of succession. If for instance C'—M' stagnates as far as one part is concerned, if the commodity cannot be sold, then the circuit of this part is interrupted and no replacement by its means of production takes place; the succeeding parts, which emerge from the process of production in the shape of C', find the change of their functions blocked by their predecessors. If this lasts for some time, production is restricted and the entire process brought to a halt. Every stagnation in succession carries disorder into co-existence, every stagnation in one stage causes more or less stagnation in the entire circuit of not only the stagnant part of the capital but also of the total individual capital.

The next form in which the process presents itself is that of a succession of phases, so that the transition of capital into a new phase is made necessary by its departure from another. Every separate circuit has therefore one of the functional forms of capital for its point of departure and point of return. On the other hand the aggregate process is in fact the unity of the three circuits, which are the different forms in which the continuity of the process expresses itself. The aggregate circuit presents itself to every functional form of capital as its specific circuit and every one of these circuits is a condition of the continuity of the total process. The cycle of each functional form is dependent upon the others. It is a necessary prerequisite for the aggregate process of production, especially for the social capital, that it is at the same time a process of reproduction and hence a circuit of each one of its elements. Various fractional parts of capital pass successively through the various stages and functional forms. Thanks to this every functional form passes simultaneously with the others through its own circuit, although always a different part of capital finds its expression in it. One part of capital, continually changing, continually reproduced, exists as a commodity capital which is converted into money; another as money capital which is converted into productive capital; and a third as productive capital which is transformed into commodity capital. The continuous existence of all three forms is brought about by the circuit the aggregate capital describes in passing through precisely these three phases.

Capital as a whole, then, exists simultaneously, spatially side by side, in its different phases. But every part passes constantly and successively from one phase, from one functional form, into the next and thus functions in all of them in turn. Its forms are hence fluid and their simultaneousness is brought about by their succession. Every form follows another and precedes it, so that the return of one capital part to a certain form is necessitated by the return of the other part to some other form. Every part describes continuously its own cycle, but it is always another part of capital which exists in this form, and these special cycles form only simultaneous and successive elements of the aggregate process.

The continuity — instead of the above-described interruption — of the aggregate process is achieved only in the unity of the three circuits. The aggregate social capital always has this continuity and its process always exhibits the unity of the three circuits.

The continuity of the reproduction is at times more or less interrupted so far as individual capitals are concerned. In the first place the masses of value are frequently distributed at various periods in unequal portions over the various stages and functional forms. In the second place these portions may be differently distributed according to the character of the commodity to be produced, hence according to the particular sphere of production in which the capital is invested. In the third place the continuity may be more or less broken in those branches of production which are dependent on the seasons, either on account of natural conditions (agriculture, herring catch, etc.) or on account of conventional circumstances, as for instance in so-called seasonal work. The process goes on most regularly and uniformly in the factories and mines. But this difference in the various branches of production does not cause any difference in the general forms of the circular process.

Capital as self-expanding value embraces not only class relations, a society of a definite character resting on the existence of labour in the form of wage labour. It is a movement, a circuit-describing process going through various stages, which itself comprises three different forms of the circuit-describing process. Therefore it can be understood only as motion, not as a thing at rest. Those who regard the gaining by value of independent existence as a mere abstraction forget that the movement of industrial capital is this abstraction *in actu*. Value here passes through various forms, various movements in which it maintains itself and at the same time expands, augments. As we are here concerned primarily with the mere form of this movement, we shall not take into consideration the revolutions which capital value may undergo during its circuit. But it is clear that in spite of all the revolutions of value, capitalist production exists and can endure only so long as capital value is made to create surplus value, that is, so long as it describes its circuit as a value that has gained independence, so long therefore as the revolutions in value are overcome and equilibrated in some way. The movements of capital appear as the action of some individual industrial capitalist who performs the functions of a buyer of commodities and labour, a seller of commodities, and an owner of productive capital, who therefore promotes the circuit by his activity. If social capital experiences a revolution in value, it may happen that the capital of the individual capitalist succumbs to it and fails, because it cannot adapt itself to the conditions of this movement of values. The more acute and frequent such revolutions in value become, the more does the automatic movement of the now independent value operate with the elemental force of a natural process, against the foresight and calculation of the individual capitalist, the more does the course of normal production become subservient to abnormal speculation, and the greater is the danger that threatens the existence of the individual capitals. These periodical revolutions in value therefore corroborate what they are supposed to refute, namely, that value as capital acquires independent existence, which it maintains and accentuates through its movement.

This succession of the metamorphoses of capital in process includes continuous comparison of the change in the magnitude of value of the capital brought about in the circuit with the original value. If value's acquisition of independence of the value-creating power, labour power, is inaugurated by the act M—L (purchase of labour power) and is effected during the process of production as exploitation of labour power, this acquisition of independence on the part of value does not re-appear in that circuit, in which money, commodities, and elements of production are merely alternating forms of capital value in process, and the former magnitude of value is compared with capital's present changed magnitude of value.

    * "Value," * argues Bailey [18] against the acquisition of independence by value, an independence which is characteristic of the capitalist mode of production and which he treats as an illusion of certain economists,* "value is a relation between contemporary commodities, because such only admit of being exchanged for each other." *[a]

This he says against the comparison of commodity values of differ-

---

[a] S. Bailey, *A Critical Dissertation on the Nature, Measures, and Causes of Value; Chiefly in Reference to the Writings of Mr. Ricardo and His Followers. By the Author of Essays on the Formation and Publication of Opinions*, London, 1825, p. 72 (cf. present edition, Vol. 30, p. 101).

ent epochs, a comparison which amounts only to comparing the expenditure of labour required in various periods for the production of the same sort of commodities, once the value of money has been fixed for every period. This comes from his general misunderstanding, for he thinks that exchange value = value, that the form of value is value itself; consequently commodity values can no longer be compared, if they do not function actively as exchange values and thus cannot actually be exchanged for one another. He has not the least inkling of the fact that value functions as capital value or capital only in so far as it remains identical with itself and is compared with itself in the different phases of its circuit, which are not at all "CONTEMPORARY" but succeed one another.

In order to study the formula of the circuit in its purity it is not sufficient to postulate that commodities are sold at their value; it must also be assumed that this takes place with other things being equal. Take for instance the form P ... P, disregarding all technical revolutions within the process of production by which the productive capital of a certain capitalist might be depreciated; disregarding furthermore all reactions which a change in the elements of value of the productive capital might have on the value of the existing commodity capital, which might appreciate or depreciate if a stock of it is on hand. Suppose the 10,000 lbs of yarn, C′, have been sold at their value of £500; 8,440 lbs = £422 replace the capital value contained in C′. But if the value of cotton, coal, etc., has increased (we do not consider mere fluctuations in price), these £422 may not suffice for the full replacement of the elements of productive capital; additional money capital is required, money capital is tied up. The opposite takes place when those prices fall. Money capital is set free. The process takes a wholly normal course only when the value relations remain constant; its course is practically normal so long as the disturbances during the repetitions of the circuit balance one another. But the greater these disturbances the greater the money capital which the industrial capitalist must possess to tide over the period of readjustment; and as the scale of each individual process of production and with it the minimum size of the capital to be advanced increases in the process of capitalist production, we have here another circumstance to be added to those others which transform the function of the industrial capitalist more and more into a monopoly of big money capitalists, who may operate singly or in association.

We remark incidentally that if a change in the value of the elements of production occurs, a difference appears between the form M ... M′ on one side and P ... P and C′ ... C′ on the other.

In M ... M′, the formula of newly invested capital, which first appears as money capital, a fall in the value of the means of production, such as raw material, auxiliary material, etc., will permit of a smaller expenditure of money capital than before this fall for the purpose of starting a business of a definite size, because the scale of the process of production (productive power development remaining the same) depends on the mass and volume of the means of production which a given quantity of labour power can cope with; but it does not depend on the value of these means of production nor on that of the labour power (the latter value affects only the magnitude of self-expansion). Take the reverse case. If there is a rise in the value of the elements of production of the commodities which constitute the elements of the productive capital, then more money capital is needed for the establishment of a business of definite proportions. In both cases it is only the amount of the money capital required for new investment that is affected. In the former case money capital becomes surplus, in the latter it is tied up, provided the accession of new individual industrial capital proceeds in the usual way in a given branch of production.

The circuits P ... P and C′ ... C′ present themselves as M ... M′ only to the extent that the movement of P and C′ is at the same time accumulation, hence to the extent that additional m, money, is converted into money capital. Apart from this they are affected differently from M ... M′ by a change in value of the elements of productive capital; here, too, we do not take into consideration the reaction of such changes in value on those constituent parts of capital which are engaged in the process of production. It is not the original expenditure which is directly affected here, but an industrial capital engaged in its process of reproduction and not in its first circuit; i.e., $C′ ... C <^{\text{L}}_{\text{MP}}$, the reconversion of commodity capital into its elements of production, so far as they are composed of commodities. When values (or prices) fall three cases are possible: The process of reproduction is continued on the same scale; in that event a part of the money capital existing hitherto is set free and money capital is accumulated, although no real accumulation (production on an extended scale) or transformation of m (surplus value) into an accumulation fund initiating and accompanying such accumulation has previously taken place. Or the process of reproduction is carried on on a more extensive scale than ordinarily would have been the case, provided the technical proportions admit it. Or, finally, a larger stock of raw materials, etc., is laid in.

The opposite occurs if the value of the elements of replacement of a commodity capital increases. In that case reproduction no longer takes place on its normal scale (e. g., the working day gets shorter); or additional money capital must be employed in order to maintain the old volume of work (money capital is tied up); or the money fund for accumulation, when one exists, is employed entirely or partially for the operation of the process of reproduction on its old scale instead of for the enlargement of this process. This is also tying up money capital, except that here the additional money capital does not come from the outside, from the money market, but from the means of the industrial capitalist himself.

However, there may be modifying circumstances in $P \ldots P$ and $C' \ldots C'$. If our spinning-mill proprietor for example has a large stock of cotton (a large proportion of his productive capital in the form of a stock of cotton), a part of his productive capital is depreciated by a fall in the prices of cotton; but if on the contrary these prices rise, this part of his productive capital appreciates. On the other hand, if he has tied up huge quantities in the form of commodity capital, for instance of cotton yarn, a part of his commodity capital, hence of his circuit-describing capital in general, is depreciated by a fall of cotton, or appreciated by a rise in its prices. Finally take the process C'—M—$C <_{MP}^{L}$. If C'—M, the realisation of the commodity capital, has taken place before a change in the value of the elements of C, then capital is affected only in the way indicated in the first case, namely in the second act of circulation, M—$C <_{MP}^{L}$; but if such a change has occurred before C'—M has been effected, then, other conditions remaining equal, a fall in the price of cotton causes a corresponding fall in the price of yarn, and a rise in the price of cotton means conversely a rise in the price of yarn. The effect on the various individual capitals invested in the same branch of production may differ widely, according to the circumstances in which they find themselves.

Money capital may also be set free or tied up on account of differences in the duration of the process of circulation, hence also in the speed of circulation. But this belongs in the discussion on turnover. At this point we are only interested in the real difference that becomes evident, with regard to changes of values of the elements of productive capital, between $M \ldots M'$ and the other two circuit forms.

In the circulation section M—$C <_{MP}^{L}$, in the epoch of the already developed and hence prevailing capitalist mode of production, a large portion of the commodities composing MP, the means of production, is itself functioning as the commodity capital of someone else. From the standpoint of the seller, therefore, C′—M′, the transformation of commodity capital into money capital, takes place. But this is not an absolute rule. On the contrary. Within its process of circulation, in which industrial capital functions either as money or as commodities, the circuit of industrial capital, whether as money capital or as commodity capital, crosses the commodity circulation of the most diverse modes of social production, so far as they produce commodities. No matter whether commodities are the output of production based on slavery, of peasants (Chinese, Indian ryots), of communes (Dutch East Indies), of state enterprise (such as existed in former epochs of Russian history on the basis of serfdom) or of half-savage hunting tribes, etc.— as commodities and money they come face to face with the money and commodities in which the industrial capital presents itself and enter as much into its circuit as into that of the surplus value borne in the commodity capital, provided the surplus value is spent as revenue; hence they enter into both branches of circulation of commodity capital. The character of the process of production from which they originate is immaterial. They function as commodities in the market, and as commodities they enter into the circuit of industrial capital as well as into the circulation of the surplus value incorporated in it. It is therefore the universal character of the origin of the commodities, the existence of the market as world market, which distinguishes the process of circulation of industrial capital. What is true of the commodities of others is also true of the money of others. Just as commodity capital faces money only as commodities, so this money functions vis-à-vis commodity capital only as money. Money here performs the functions of world money.

However two points must be noted here.

First: As soon as act M—MP is completed, the commodities (MP) cease to be such and become one of the modes of existence of industrial capital in its functional form of P, productive capital. Thereby however their origin is obliterated. They exist henceforth only as forms of existence of industrial capital, are embodied in it. However it still remains true that to replace them they must be reproduced, and to this extent the capitalist mode of production is conditional on modes of production lying outside of its own stage of development. But it is the tendency of the capitalist mode of production to transform all production as much as possible into commodity production. The mainspring by which this is accomplished is precisely the involvement of all production into the capitalist circulation process. And developed commodity production itself is capitalist commodity production. The intervention of industrial capital promotes this transformation everywhere, but with it also the transformation of all direct producers into wage labourers.

Secondly: The commodities entering into the process of circulation of industrial capital (including the requisite means of subsistence into which variable capital, after being paid to the labourers, is transformed for the purpose of reproducing their labour power), regardless of their origin and of the social form of the productive process by which they were brought into existence, come face to face with industrial capital itself already in the form of commodity capital, in the form of commodity dealer's or merchant's capital. And merchant's capital, by its very nature, comprises commodities of all modes of production.

The capitalist mode of production presupposes not only large-scale production but also, and necessarily so, sales on a large scale, hence sale to the merchant, not to the individual consumer. If this consumer is himself a productive consumer, hence an industrial capitalist, i. e., if the industrial capital of one branch of production supplies some other branch of industry with means of production, direct sale by one industrial capitalist to many others takes place (in the form of orders, etc.). To this extent every industrial capitalist is a direct seller and his own merchant, which by the way he also is when he sells to a merchant.

Trading in commodities as the function of merchant's capital is a premise of capitalist production and develops more and more in the course of development of such production. Therefore we occasionally take its existence for granted to illustrate particular aspects of the process of capitalist circulation; but in the general analysis of this process we assume direct sale, without the intervention of a merchant, because this intervention obscures various facets of the movement.

Cf. Sismondi [19] who presents the matter somewhat naively:

"Commerce employs considerable capital, which at first sight does not seem to be a part of that capital whose movement we have described in detail. The value of the cloth accumulated in the stores of the cloth-merchant seems at first to be entirely foreign to that part of the annual production which the rich gives to the poor as wages in order to make him work. However this capital has simply replaced the other of which we have spoken. For the purpose of clearly understanding the progress of wealth, we have begun with its creation and followed it to its consumption. Then the capital employed in cloth manufacturing, for instance, always seemed the same to us; and when it was exchanged for the revenue of the consumer, it was divided into only two parts, one of them serving as revenue of the manufacturer in the form of the profit, the other serving as revenue of the labourers in the form of wages for the time they were manufacturing new cloth.

"But it was soon found that it would be to the advantage of all if the different parts of this capital were to replace one another and that, if 100,000 écus were sufficient for the entire circulation between the manufacturer and the consumer, they should be divided equally between the manufacturer, the wholesale merchant, and the retail merchant. The first then did with only one-third of this capital the same work as he had done with the entire capital, because as soon as his work of manufacturing was completed he found that a merchant would rather buy from him than a consumer would. On the other hand the capital of the wholesaler was much sooner replaced by that of the retailer... The difference between the sums advanced for wages and the purchase price paid by the ultimate consumer was considered the profit of those capitals. It was divided between the manufacturer, the merchant, and the retailer, from the moment that they had divided their functions among themselves, and the work performed was the same, although it had required three persons and three parts of capital instead of one" (*Nouveaux Principes*, I, pp. 139, 140).

"All of them" (the merchants) "contributed indirectly to the production; for having consumption for its object, production cannot be regarded as completed until the thing produced is placed within the reach of the consumer" (ibid., p. 137).[a]

In the discussion of the general forms of the circuit and in the entire second book in general, we take money to mean metallic money, with the exception of symbolic money, mere tokens of value, which are designed for specific use in certain states, and of credit money, which is not yet developed. In the first place, this is the historical order; credit money plays only a very minor role, or none at all, during the first epoch of capitalist production. In the second place, the necessity of this order is demonstrated theoretically by the fact that everything of a critical nature which Tooke and others hitherto expounded in regard to the circulation of credit money compelled them to hark back again and again to the question of what would be the aspect of the matter if nothing but metal money were in circulation. But it must not be forgotten that metal money may serve as a purchasing medium and also as a paying medium. For the sake of simplicity, we consider it in this second book generally only in its first functional form.

The process of circulation of industrial capital, which is only a part of its individual circuit, is determined by the general laws previously set forth (Buch I, Kap. III),[b] in so far as it is only a series of acts

---

[a] Marx quotes in French. - [b] English edition: Vol. I, Ch. III (present edition, Vol. 35).

within the general circulation of commodities. The greater the velocity of the currency of money, the more rapidly therefore every individual capital passes through the series of its commodity or money metamorphoses, the more numerous are the industrial capitals (or individual capitals in the form of commodity capitals) started circulating successively by a given mass of money, for example £500. The more the money functions as a paying medium, the more therefore — for instance in the replacement of some commodity capital by its means of production — nothing but balances have to be squared, and the shorter the periods of time when payments fall due, as for instance in paying wages, the less money a given mass of capital value therefore requires for its circulation. On the other hand, assuming that the velocity of the circulation and all other conditions remain the same, the amount of money required to circulate as money capital is determined by the sum of the prices of the commodities (price multiplied by the volume of commodities), or, if the quantity and value of the commodities are fixed, by the value of the money itself.

But the laws of the general circulation of commodities are valid only when capital's circulation process consists of a series of simple acts of circulation; they do not apply when the latter constitute functionally determined sections of the circuit of individual industrial capitals.

In order to make this plain, it is best to study the process of circulation in its uninterrupted interconnection, such as it appears in the following two forms:

$$\text{II) } P \ldots C' \left\{ \begin{array}{l} C- \\ -M' \\ c- \end{array} \right. \left\{ \begin{array}{l} M-C <^{L}_{MP} \ldots P \ (P') \\ \\ m-c \end{array} \right.$$

$$\text{III) } C' \left\{ \begin{array}{l} C- \\ -M' \\ c- \end{array} \right. \left\{ \begin{array}{l} M-C <^{L}_{MP} \ldots P \ldots C' \\ \\ m-c \end{array} \right.$$

As a series of acts of circulation in general, the process of circulation (whether in the form of C—M—C or of M—C—M) represents merely the two antithetical series of commodity metamorphoses, every single one of which in its turn implies an opposite metamorphosis on the part of the alien commodity or alien money confronting the commodity.

C—M on the part of the owner of a commodity means M—C on the part of its buyer; the first metamorphosis of the commodity in C—M is the second metamorphosis of the commodity appearing in the form of M; the opposite applies to M—C. Hence, what has been shown concerning the intertwining of the metamorphosis of a certain commodity in one stage with that of another in another stage applies to the circulation of capital so far as the capitalist functions as a buyer and seller of commodities, and his capital on that account functions in the form of money opposed to the commodities of another, or in the form of commodities opposed to the money of another. But this intertwining is not to be identified with the intertwining of the metamorphoses of capitals.

In the first place M—C (MP), as we have seen, may represent an intermingling of the metamorphoses of different individual capitals. For instance the commodity capital of the spinning-mill owner, yarn, is partly replaced by coal. One part of his capital exists in the form of money and is converted into the form of commodities, while the capital of the capitalist producer of coal is in the form of commodities and is therefore converted into the form of money; the same act of circulation represents in this case opposite metamorphoses of two industrial capitals (in different branches of production), hence an intertwining of the series of metamorphoses of these capitals. But as we have seen the MP into which M is transformed need not be commodity capital in the categorical sense, i. e., need not be a functional form of industrial capital, need not be produced by a capitalist. It is always M—C on one side and C—M on the other, but not always an intermingling of metamorphoses of capitals. Furthermore M—L, the purchase of labour power, is never an intermingling of metamorphoses of capitals, for labour power, though the commodity of the labourer, does not become capital until it is sold to the capitalist. On the other hand in the process C′—M′, it is not necessary that M′ should represent converted commodity capital; it may be the realisation in money of the commodity labour power (wages), or of the product of some independent labourer, slave, serf, or community.

In the second place however it is not at all required for the discharge of the functionally determined role played by every metamorphosis occurring within the process of circulation of some individual capital that this metamorphosis should represent the corresponding opposite metamorphosis in the circuit of the other capital, provided we assume that the entire production of the world market is carried on capitalistically. For instance in the circuit P ...· P, the M′ which converts C′ into money may be to the buyer only the realisation in money of his surplus value (if the commodity is an article of consumption); or, in M'—$C' <^{L}_{MP}$ (where therefore already accumulated capital enters) M' may, as far as the vendor of MP is concerned, enter into the circulation of his capital only to replace his advanced capital or it may not re-enter at all by being diverted into revenue expenditure.

Therefore the manner in which the various component parts of the aggregate social capital, of which the individual capitals are but constituents functioning independently, mutually replace one another in the process of circulation—in regard to capital as well as surplus value—is not ascertained from the simple intertwinings of the metamorphoses in the circulation of commodities—intertwinings which the acts of capital circulation have in common with all other circulation of commodities. That requires a different method of investigation. Hitherto one has been satisfied with uttering phrases which upon closer analysis are found to contain nothing but indefinite ideas borrowed from the intertwining of metamorphoses common to all commodity circulation.

———

One of the most obvious peculiarities of the movement in circuits of industrial capital, and therefore also of capitalist production, is the fact that on the one hand the component elements of productive capital are derived from the commodity market and must be continually renewed out of it, bought as commodities; and that on the other hand the product of the labour process emerges from it as a commodity and must be continually sold anew as a commodity. Compare for instance a modern farmer of the Scotch lowlands with an old-fashioned small peasant on the Continent. The former sells his entire product and has therefore to replace all its elements, even his seed, in the market; the latter consumes the greater part of his product directly, buys and sells as little as possible, fashions tools, makes clothing, etc., so far as possible himself.

Natural economy, money economy, and credit economy have therefore been placed in opposition to one another as being the three characteristic economic forms of movement in social production.

In the first place these three forms do not represent equivalent phases of development. The so-called credit economy is merely a form of the money economy, since both terms express functions or modes of exchange among the producers themselves. In developed capitalist production, the money economy appears only as the basis of the credit economy. The money economy and credit economy thus correspond only to different stages in the development of capitalist production, but they are by no means independent forms of exchange vis-à-vis natural economy. With the same justification one might contrapose as equivalents the very different forms of natural economy to those two economies.

In the second place, since it is not the economy, i. e., the process of production itself that is emphasised as the distinguishing mark of the two categories, money economy and credit economy, but rather the mode of exchange — corresponding to that economy — between the various agents of production, or producers, the same should apply to the first category. Hence exchange economy instead of natural economy. A completely isolated natural economy, such as the Inca state of Peru,[20] would not come under any of these categories.

In the third place the money economy is common to all commodity production and the product appears as a commodity in the most varied organisms of social production. Consequently what characterises capitalist production would then be only the extent to which the product is created as an article of commerce, as a commodity, and hence the extent also to which its own constituent elements must enter again as articles of commerce, as commodities, into the economy from which it emerges.

As a matter of fact capitalist production is commodity production as the general form of production. But it is so and becomes so more and more in the course of its development only because labour itself appears here as a commodity, because the labourer sells his labour, that is, the function of his labour power, and our assumption is that he sells it at its value, determined by its cost of reproduction. To the extent that labour becomes wage labour, the producer becomes an industrial capitalist. For this reason capitalist production (and hence also commodity production) does not reach its full scope until the direct agricultural producer also becomes a wage labourer. In the relation of capitalist and wage labourer, the money relation, the relation between the buyer and the seller, becomes a relation inherent in production. But this relation has its foundation in the social character of production, not in the mode of exchange. The latter conversely emanates from the former. It is, however, quite in keeping with the bourgeois horizon, everyone being engrossed in the transaction of shady business, not to see in the character of the mode of production the basis of the mode of exchange corresponding to it, but vice versa.[7]

———

The capitalist throws less value in the form of money into the circulation than he draws out of it, because he throws into it more value in the form of commodities than he withdrew from it in the form of commodities. Since he functions simply as a personification of capital, as an industrial capitalist, his supply of commodity value is always greater than his demand for it. If his supply and demand in this respect covered each other it would mean that his capital had not produced any surplus value; that it had not functioned as productive capital; that the productive capital had been converted into commodity capital not big with surplus value; that it had not drawn any surplus value in commodity form out of labour power during the process of production, had not functioned at all as capital. The capitalist must indeed "sell dearer than he has bought", but he succeeds in doing so only because the capitalist process of production enables him to transform the cheaper commodity he bought — cheaper because it contains less value — into a commodity of greater value, hence a dearer one. He sells dearer, not because he sells above the value of his commodity, but because his commodity contains value in excess of that contained in the ingredients of its production.

The rate at which the capitalist makes the value of his capital expand is the greater, the greater the difference between his supply and his demand, i. e., the greater the excess of the commodity value he supplies over the commodity value he demands. His aim is not to equalise his supply and demand, but to make the inequality between them, the excess of his supply over his demand, as great as possible.

What is true of the individual capitalist applies to the capitalist class.

In so far as the capitalist merely personifies industrial capital, his own demand is confined to means of production and labour power. In point of value, his demand for MP is smaller than his advanced capital; he buys means of production of a smaller value than that of his capital, and therefore of a still smaller value than that of the commodity capital which he supplies.

[7] End of Manuscript V. What follows, to the end of the chapter, is a note contained in a notebook of 1877 or 1878 amid extracts from various books.

As regards his demand for labour power, it is determined in point of value by the relation of his variable capital to his total capital, hence $= v : C$. In capitalist production this demand therefore grows relatively smaller than his demand for means of production. His purchases of MP steadily rise above his purchases of L.

Since the labourer all too often converts his wages almost wholly into means of subsistence, and for the overwhelmingly larger part into absolute necessities, the demand of the capitalist for labour power is indirectly also a demand for the articles of consumption essential to the working class. But this demand is equal to v and not one iota greater (if the labourer saves a part of his wages — we necessarily discard here all credit relations — he converts part of his wages into a hoard and *pro tanto*[a] does not act as a bidder, a purchaser). The upper limit of a capitalist's demand is $= to$ $C = c + v$, but his supply is $c + v + s$. Consequently if the composition of his commodity capital is $80_c + 20_v + 20_s$, his demand is $= to$ $80_c + 20_v$, hence, considered from the angle of the value it contains, $1/5$ smaller than his supply. The greater the percentage of the mass of surplus value m produced by him (his rate of profit) the smaller becomes his demand in relation to his supply. Although with the further development of production the demand of the capitalist for labour power, and thus indirectly for necessary means of subsistence, steadily decreases compared with his demand for means of production, it must not be forgotten on the other hand that his demand for MP is always smaller than his capital. His demand for means of production must therefore always be smaller in value than the commodity product of the capitalist who, working with a capital of equal value and under equal conditions, furnishes him with those means of production. That many capitalists and not only one do the furnishing does not alter the case. Take it that his capital is £1,000, and its constant part $= £800$; then his demand on all these capitalists is $= to$ £800. Together they supply means of production worth £1,200 for each £1,000 (regardless of what share in each £1,000 may fall to each one of them and of the fraction of his total capital which the share of each may represent), assuming that the rate of profit is the same. Consequently his demand covers only $2/3$ of their supply, while his own total demand amounts to only $4/5$ of his own supply, measured in value.

It still remains for us, incidentally, to investigate the problem of

---

[a] to that extent

turnover. Let the total capital of the capitalist be £5,000, of which £4,000 is fixed and £1,000 circulating capital; let these £1,000 be composed of $800_c + 200_v$, as assumed above. His circulating capital must be turned over five times a year for his total capital to turn over once. His commodity product is then = £6,000, i. e., £1,000 more than his advanced capital, which results in the same ratio of surplus value as above:

5,000 C : $1,000_s = 100_{(c+v)} : 20_s$. This turnover therefore does not change anything in the ratio of his total demand to his total supply. The former remains $^1/_5$ smaller than the latter.

Suppose his fixed capital has to be renewed in 10 years. So the capitalist pays every year $^1/_{10} = $ £400 into a sinking fund and thus has only a value of £3,600 of fixed capital left + £400 in money. If the repairs are necessary and do not exceed the average, they represent nothing but capital he has invested later. We may look at the matter the same as if he had allowed for the cost of repairs beforehand, when calculating the value of his investment capital, so far as this enters into the annual commodity product, so that it is included in that $^1/_{10}$ sinking fund payment. (If his need of repairs is below average he has done a good piece of business, and the reverse if it is above average. But this evens out for the entire class of capitalists engaged in the same branch of industry.) At any rate, although his annual demand still remains £5,000, equal to the original capital value he advanced (assuming his total capital is turned over once a year), this demand increases with regard to the circulating part of the capital, while it steadily decreases with regard to its fixed part.

We now come to reproduction. Let us assume that the capitalist consumes the entire surplus value m and reconverts only capital C of the original magnitude into productive capital. Then the demand of the capitalist is equal in value to his supply; but this does not refer to the movement of his capital. As a capitalist he exercises a demand for only $^4/_5$ of his supply (in terms of value). He consumes $^1/_5$ as a noncapitalist, not in his function as capitalist but for his private requirements or pleasures.

His calculation, expressed in percentages, is then as follows:

Demand as capitalist	= 100, supply	= 120
Demand as man about town =	20, supply	= —
Total demand	= 120, supply	= 120

This assumption is tantamount to assuming that capitalist production does not exist, and therefore that the industrial capitalist himself does not exist. For capitalism is abolished root and branch by the bare assumption that it is personal consumption and not enrichment that works as the compelling motive.

But such an assumption is impossible also technically. The capitalist must not only form a reserve capital to cushion price fluctuations and enable him to wait for favourable buying and selling conditions. He must accumulate capital in order to extend his production and build technical progress into his productive organism.

In order to accumulate capital he must first withdraw in money form from circulation a part of the surplus value which he obtained from that circulation, and must hoard it until it has increased sufficiently for the extension of his old business or the opening of a side-line. So long as the formation of the hoard continues, it does not increase the demand of the capitalist. The money is immobilised. It does not withdraw from the commodity market any equivalent in commodities for the money equivalent withdrawn from it for commodities supplied.

Credit is not considered here. And credit includes for example deposits by the capitalist of accumulating money in a bank on current account paying interest.

Chapter V

THE TIME OF CIRCULATION [8]

We have seen that the movement of capital through the sphere of production and the two phases of the sphere of circulation takes place in a series of periods of time. The duration of its sojourn in the sphere of production is its time of production, that of its stay in the sphere of circulation its time of circulation or rotation. The total time during which it describes its circuit is therefore equal to the sum of its time of production and its time of circulation.

The time of production naturally comprises the period of the labour process, but is not comprised in it. It will be remembered first of all that a part of the constant capital exists in the form of instruments of labour, such as machinery, buildings, etc., which serve the same

[8] Beginning of Manuscript IV.

constantly repeated labour processes until they are worn out. Periodical interruptions of the labour process, by night for instance, interrupt the functioning of these instruments of labour, but not their stay at the place of production. They belong to this place when they are in function as well as when they are not. On the other hand the capitalist must have a definite supply of raw material and auxiliary material in readiness, in order that the process of production may take place for a longer or shorter time on a previously determined scale, without being dependent on the accidents of daily supply from the market. This supply of raw material, etc., is productively consumed only by degrees. There is, therefore, a difference between its time of production[9] and its time of functioning. The time of production of the means of production in general comprises, therefore, 1) the time during which they function as means of production, hence serve in the production process; 2) the stops during which the process of production, and thus the functioning of the means of production embodied in it, are interrupted; 3) the time during which they are held in readiness as prerequisites of that process, hence already represent productive capital but have not yet entered into the process of production.

The difference so far considered has in each case been the difference between the time which the productive capital stays in the sphere of production and that it stays in the process of production. But the process of production may itself be responsible for interruptions of the labour process, and hence of the labour time — intervals during which the subject of labour is exposed to the action of physical processes without the further intervention of human labour. The process of production, and thus the functioning of the means of production, continue in this case, although the labour process, and thus the functioning of the means of production as instruments of labour, have been interrupted. This applies, for instance, to the grain, after it has been sown, the wine fermenting in the cellar, the labour material of many factories, such as tanneries, where the material is exposed to the action of chemical processes. The time of production is here longer than the labour time. The difference between the two consists in an excess of the production time over the labour time. This excess always arises from the *latent* existence of productive capital in the sphere of

---

[9] Time of production is here used in the active sense: The time of production of the means of production does not mean in this case the time required for their production, but the time during which they take part in the production process of a commodity product.— *F. E.*

production without functioning in the process of production itself or from its functioning in the production process without taking part in the labour process.

That part of the latent productive capital which is held in readiness only as a requisite for the production process, such as cotton, coal, etc., in a spinning-mill, acts as a creator of neither products nor value. It is fallow capital, although its fallowness is essential for the uninterrupted flow of the process of production. The buildings, apparatus, etc., necessary for the storage of the productive supply (latent capital) are conditions of the production process and therefore constitute component parts of the advanced productive capital. They perform their function as conservators of the productive components in the preliminary stage. Inasmuch as labour processes are necessary in this stage, they add to the cost of the raw material, etc., but are productive labour and produce surplus value, because a part of this labour, like of all other wage labour, is not paid for. The normal interruptions of the entire process of production, i. e., the intermissions during which the productive capital does not function, create neither value nor surplus value. Hence the desire to keep the work going at night, too (Buch I, Kap. VIII, 4).[a]

The intervals in the labour time which the subject of labour must endure in the process of production itself create neither value nor surplus value. But they advance the product, form a part of its life, a process through which it must pass. The value of the apparatus, etc., is transferred to the product in proportion to the entire time during which they perform their function; the product is brought to this stage by labour itself, and the employment of these apparatus is as much a condition of production as is the reduction to dust of a part of the cotton which does not enter into the product but nevertheless transfers its value to that product. The other part of the latent capital, such as buildings, machinery, etc., i. e., the instruments of labour whose functioning is interrupted only by the regular pauses of the production process — irregular interruptions caused by the restriction of production, crises, etc., are total losses — adds value without entering into the creation of the product. The total value which this part of capital adds to the product is determined by its average durability; it loses value, because it loses its use value, both during the time that it performs its functions as well as during that in which it does not.

---

[a] English edition: Vol. I, Ch. X, 4 (present edition, Vol. 35).

Finally the value of the constant part of capital, which continues in the production process although the labour process is interrupted, re-appears in the result of the production process. Labour itself has here placed the means of production in conditions under which they pass of themselves through certain natural processes, the result of which is a definite useful effect or a change in the form of their use value. La-bour always transfers the value of the means of production to the pro-duct, in so far as it really consumes them in a suitable manner, as means of production. And it does not change the matter whether la-bour has to bear continually on its subject by means of the instru-ments of labour in order to produce this effect or whether it merely needs to give the first impulse by providing the means of production with the conditions under which they undergo the intended altera-tion of themselves, in consequence of natural processes, without the further assistance of labour.

Whatever may be the reason for the excess of the production time over the labour time — whether the circumstance that means of pro-duction constitute only latent productive capital and hence are still in a stage preliminary to the actual production process or that their own functioning is interrupted within the process of production by its pauses or finally that the process of production itself necessitates interruptions of the labour process — in none of these cases do the means of production function as absorbers of labour. And if they do not absorb labour, they do not absorb surplus labour, either. Hence there is no expansion of the value of productive capital so long as it stays in that part of its production time which exceeds the labour time, no matter how inseparable from these pauses the carrying on of the process of self-expansion may be. It is plain that the more the pro-duction time and labour time cover each other the greater is the pro-ductivity and self-expansion of a given productive capital in a given space of time. Hence the tendency of capitalist production to reduce the excess of the production time over the labour time as much as possible. But while the time of production of a certain capital may dif-fer from its labour time, it always comprises the latter, and this excess is itself a condition of the process of production. The time of production, then, is always that time in which a capital produces use values and expands, hence functions as productive capital, although it includes time in which it is either latent or produces without expanding its value.

Within the sphere of circulation, capital abides as commodity capi-tal and money capital. Its two processes of circulation consist in its transformation from the commodity form into that of money and from the money form into that of commodities. The circumstance that the transformation of commodities into money is here at the same time a realisation of the surplus value embodied in the commodities, and that the transformation of money into commodities is at the same time a conversion or reconversion of capital value into the form of its elements of production does not in the least alter the fact that these processes, as processes of circulation, are processes of the simple metamorphosis of commodities.

Time of circulation and time of production mutually exclude each other. During its time of circulation capital does not perform the functions of productive capital and therefore produces neither commodities nor surplus value. If we study the circuit in its simplest form, as when the entire capital value passes in one bulk from one phase into another, it becomes palpably evident that the process of production and therefore also the self-expansion of the capital value are interrupted so long as its time of circulation lasts, and that the renewal of the process of production will proceed at a faster or a slower pace depending on the length of the circulation time. But if on the contrary the various parts of capital pass through the circuit one after another, so that the circuit of the entire capital value is accomplished successively in the circuits of its various component parts, then it is evident that the longer its aliquot parts stay in the sphere of circulation the smaller must be the part functioning in the sphere of production. The expansion and contraction of the time of circulation operate therefore as negative limits to the contraction or expansion of the time of production or of the extent to which a capital of a given size functions as productive capital. The more the metamorphoses of circulation of a certain capital are only ideal, i. e., the more the time of circulation is equal to zero, or approaches zero, the more does capital function, the more does its productivity and the self-expansion of its value increase. For instance, if a capitalist executes an order by the terms of which he receives payment on delivery of the product, and if this payment is made in his own means of production, the time of circulation approaches zero.

A capital's time of circulation therefore limits, generally speaking, its time of production and hence its process of generating surplus value. And it limits this process in proportion to its own duration. This duration may considerably increase or decrease and hence may restrict capital's time of production in a widely varying degree. But political economy sees only what is *apparent*, namely the effect of the time of circulation on capital's process of the creation of surplus value in general. It takes this negative effect for a positive one, because its consequences are positive. It clings the more tightly to this appearance since it seems to furnish proof that capital possesses a mystic source of self-expansion independent of its process of production and hence of the exploitation of labour, a spring which flows to it from the sphere of circulation. We shall see later that even scientific political economy has been deceived by this appearance of things. Various phenomena, it will turn out, give colour to this semblance: 1) The capitalist method of calculating profit, in which the negative cause figures as a positive one, since with capitals in different spheres of investment, where only the times of circulation are different, a longer time of circulation tends to bring about an increase of prices, in short, serves as one of the causes of equalising profits. 2) The time of circulation is but a phase of the time of turnover; the latter however includes the time of production or reproduction. What is really due to the latter seems to be due to the time of circulation. 3) The conversion of commodities into variable capital (wages) is necessitated by their previous conversion into money. In the accumulation of capital, the conversion into additional variable capital therefore takes place in the sphere of circulation, or during the time of circulation. Consequently it seems that the accumulation thus achieved is owed to the latter.

Within the sphere of circulation capital passes through the two antithetical phases C—M and M—C; it is immaterial in what order. Hence its time of circulation is likewise divided into two parts, viz.: the time it requires for its conversion from commodities into money, and that which it requires for its conversion from money into commodities. We have already learned from the analysis of the simple circulation of commodities (Buch I, Kap. III)[a] that C—M, the sale, is the most difficult part of its metamorphosis and that therefore under ordinary conditions it takes up the greater part of its time of circulation. As money, value exists in its always convertible form. As a commodity it must first be transformed into money before it can assume this form of direct convertibility and hence of constant readiness for action. However, in capital's process of circulation, its phase M—C has to do with its transformation into commodities which constitute defi-

---

[a] English edition: Vol. I, Ch. III (present edition, Vol. 35).

nite elements of productive capital in a given enterprise. The means of production may not be available in the market and must first be produced or they must be procured from distant markets or their ordinary supply has become irregular or prices have changed, etc., in short there are a multitude of circumstances which are not noticeable in the simple change of form $M — C$, but which nevertheless require now more, now less time also for this part of the circulation phase. $C — M$ and $M — C$ may be separate not only in time but also in space; the market for buying and the market for selling may be located apart. In the case of factories for instance buyer and seller are frequently different persons. In the production of commodities, circulation is as necessary as production itself, so that circulation agents are just as much needed as production agents. The process of reproduction includes both functions of capital, therefore it includes the necessity of having representatives of these functions, either in the person of the capitalist himself or of wage labourers, his agents. But this furnishes no ground for confusing the agents of circulation with those of production, any more than it furnishes ground for confusing the functions of commodity capital and money capital with those of productive capital. The agents of circulation must be paid by the agents of production. But if the capitalists, who sell to and buy from one another, create neither values nor products by these acts, this state of affairs is not changed if they are enabled or compelled by the volume of their business to shift this function on to others. In some businesses the buyers and sellers get paid in the form of percentages on the profits. All talk about their being paid by the consumer does not help matters. The consumers can pay only in so far as they themselves, as agents of production, produce an equivalent in commodities or appropriate it from production agents either on the basis of some legal title (as their co-partners, etc.) or by personal services.

There is a difference between $C — M$ and $M — C$ which has nothing to do with the difference in forms of commodities and money but arises from the capitalist character of production. Intrinsically both $C — M$ and $M — C$ are mere conversions of given value from one form into another. But $C' — M'$ is at the same time a realisation of the surplus value contained in C'. $M — C$ however is not. Hence selling is more important than buying. Under normal conditions $M — C$ is an act necessary for the self-expansion of the value expressed in M, but it is not a realisation of surplus value; it is the introduction to its production, not an afterword.

The form in which a commodity exists, its existence as a use value, sets definite limits to the circulation of commodity capital $C' - M'$. Use values are perishable by nature. Hence, if they are not productively or individually consumed within a certain time, depending on what they are intended for, in other words, if they are not sold within a certain period, they spoil and lose with their use value the property of being vehicles of exchange value. The capital value contained in them, hence also the surplus value accrued in it, gets lost. The use values do not remain the carriers of perennial self-expanding capital value unless they are constantly renewed and reproduced, are replaced by new use values of the same or of some other order. The sale of the use values in the form of finished commodities, hence their entry into productive or individual consumption effected through this sale, is however the ever recurring condition of their reproduction. They must change their old use form within a definite time in order to continue their existence in a new form. Exchange value maintains itself only by means of this constant renewal of its body. The use values of various commodities spoil sooner or later; the interval between their production and consumption may therefore be comparatively long or short; hence they can persist without spoiling in the circulation phase $C - M$ for a shorter or longer term in the form of commodity capital, can endure a shorter or a longer time of circulation as commodities. The limit of the circulation time of a commodity capital imposed by the spoiling of the body of the commodity is the absolute limit of this part of the time of circulation, or of the time of circulation of commodity capital as such. The more perishable a commodity and the sooner after its production it must therefore be consumed and hence sold, the more restricted is its capacity for removal from its place of production, the narrower therefore is the spatial sphere of its circulation, the more localised are the markets where it can be sold. For this reason the more perishable a commodity and the greater the absolute restriction of its time of circulation as commodity on account of its physical properties, the less is it suited to be an object of capitalist production. Such a commodity can come within its grasp only in thickly populated districts or to the extent that improved transportation facilities eliminate distance. But the concentration of the production of any article in the hands of a few and in a populous district may create a relatively large market even for such articles as are the products of large breweries, dairies, etc.

Chapter VI

THE COSTS OF CIRCULATION

I. GENUINE COSTS OF CIRCULATION

1. THE TIME OF PURCHASE AND SALE

The transformations of the forms of capital from commodities into money and from money into commodities are at the same time transactions of the capitalist, acts of purchase and sale. The time in which these transformations of forms take place constitutes subjectively, from the standpoint of the capitalist, the time of purchase and sale; it is the time during which he performs the functions of a seller and buyer in the market. Just as the time of circulation of capital is a necessary segment of its time of reproduction, so the time in which the capitalist buys and sells and scours the market is a necessary part of the time in which he functions as a capitalist, i. e., as personified capital. It is a part of his business hours.

(Since we have assumed that commodities are bought and sold at their values, these acts constitute merely the conversion of a certain value from one form into another, from the commodity form into the money form or from the money form into the commodity form — a change in the state of being. If commodities are sold at their values, then the magnitudes of value in the hands of the buyer and seller remain unchanged. Only the form of existence of value is changed. If the commodities are not sold at their values, then the sum of the converted values remains unchanged; the plus on one side is a minus on the other.

The metamorphoses C — M and M — C are transactions between buyers and sellers; they require time to conclude their bargains, the more so as a struggle goes on in which each seeks to get the best of the other, and it is businessmen who face one another here; and "WHEN GREEK MEETS GREEK THEN COMES THE TUG OF WAR". [a] To effect a change in the state of being costs time and labour power, not for the purpose of creating value, however, but in order to accomplish the conversion of value

---

[a] A paraphrase of "When Greeks join'd Greeks then was the tug of war!" (Nathaniel Lee, *The Rival Queens, or the Death of Alexander the Great*, Act IV, Scene 2).

from one form into another. The mutual attempt to appropriate an extra slice of this value on this occasion changes nothing. This labour, increased by the evil designs on either side, does not create any value, just as the work performed in a judicial proceeding does not increase the value of the subject-matter of the suit. Matters stand with this labour — which is a necessary element in the capitalist process of production as a whole, including circulation or included by it — as they stand, say, with the work of combustion of some substance used for the generation of heat. This work of combustion does not generate any heat, although it is a necessary element in the process of combustion. In order, e. g., to consume coal as fuel, I must combine it with oxygen, and for this purpose must transform it from the solid into the gaseous state (for in the carbonic acid gas, the result of the combustion, coal is in the gaseous state); consequently, I must bring about a physical change in the form of its existence or in its state of being. The separation of carbon molecules, which are united into a solid mass, and the splitting up of these molecules into their separate atoms must precede the new combination, and this requires a certain expenditure of energy which thus is not transformed into heat but taken from it. Therefore, if the owners of the commodities are not capitalists but independent direct producers, the time employed in buying and selling is a diminution of their labour time, and for this reason such transactions used to be deferred (in ancient and mediaeval times) to holidays.

Of course the dimensions assumed by the conversion of commodities in the hands of the capitalists cannot transform this labour — which does not create any value but is merely instrumental in changing the form of value — into labour productive of value. Nor can the miracle of this transubstantiation be accomplished by a transposition, i. e., by the industrial capitalists making this "work of combustion" the exclusive business of third persons, who are paid by them, instead of performing it themselves. These third persons will of course not tender their labour power to the capitalists out of sheer love for them. It is a matter of indifference to the rent collector of a real-estate owner or the messenger of a bank that their labour does not add one iota or tittle to the value of either the rent or the gold pieces carried to another bank by the bagful.)[10]

To the capitalist who has others working for him, buying and sell-

---

[10] The text in parentheses is taken from a note at the end of Manuscript VIII.

ing becomes a primary function. Since he appropriates the product of many on a large social scale, he must sell it on the same scale and then reconvert it from money into elements of production. Now as before neither the time of purchase nor of sale creates any value. The function of merchant's capital gives rise to an illusion. But without going into this at length here this much is plain from the start: If by a division of labour a function, unproductive in itself although a necessary element of reproduction, is transformed from an incidental occupation of many into the exclusive occupation of a few, into their special business, the nature of this function itself is not changed. *One* merchant (here considered a mere agent attending to the change of form of commodities, a mere buyer and seller) may by his operations shorten the time of purchase and sale for *many* producers. In such case he should be regarded as a machine which reduces useless expenditure of energy or helps to set production time free.[11]

In order to simplify the matter (since we shall not discuss the merchant as a capitalist and merchant's capital until later) we shall assume that this buying and selling agent is a man who sells his labour. He expends his labour power and labour time in the operations C — M and M — C. And he makes his living that way, just as another does by spinning or by making pills. He performs a necessary function, because the process of reproduction itself includes unproductive functions. He works as well as the next man, but intrinsically his labour creates neither value nor product. He belongs himself to the *faux frais* of production. His usefulness does not consist in transforming an unproductive function into a productive one, nor unproductive into productive labour. It would be a miracle if such a transformation could be accomplished by the mere transfer of a function. His useful-

---

[11] "The costs of commerce, although necessary, must be regarded as an onerous outlay" (Quesnay, *Analyse du Tableau économique*, in Daire, *Physiocrates*, Part I, Paris, 1846, p. 71). According to Quesnay, the "profit" which the competition among merchants produces, in that it compels them "to content themselves with a smaller reward or gain ... is, strictly speaking, nothing but a *prevention of loss* for the seller at first hand and for the buyer-consumer. Now, a prevention of loss on the costs of commerce is not a *real product* or an accession of wealth through commerce, if considered simply as an exchange, whether with or without the cost of transportation" (pp. 145, 146). "The costs of commerce are always paid by those who sell the products and who would enjoy the full prices paid for them by the buyers, if there were no intermediate expenses" (p. 163). The proprietors and producers are "*salariants*" (payers of wages), the merchants are "*salariés*" (recipients of wages) (p. 164, Quesnay, *Dialogues sur le Commerce et sur les Travaux des Artisans*, in Daire, *Physiocrates*, Part I, Paris, 1846).[21] [Marx quotes Quesnay in French.]

ness consists rather in the fact that a smaller part of society's labour power and labour time is tied up in this unproductive function. More. We shall assume that he is a mere wage labourer, maybe even one of the better paid. Whatever his pay, as a wage labourer he works part of his time for nothing. He may receive daily the value of the product of eight working hours, yet functions ten. But the two hours of surplus labour he performs do not produce value any more than his eight hours of necessary labour, although by means of the latter a part of the social product is transferred to him. In the first place, looking at it from the standpoint of society, labour power is used up now as before for ten hours in a mere function of circulation. It cannot be used for anything else, not for productive labour. In the second place, however, society does not pay for those two hours of surplus labour, although they are spent by the individual who performs this labour. Society does not appropriate any extra product or value thereby. But the costs of circulation, which he represents, are reduced by one-fifth, from ten hours to eight. Society does not pay any equivalent for one-fifth of this active time of circulation, of which he is the agent. But if this man is employed by a capitalist, then the non-payment of these two hours reduces the costs of circulation of *his* capital, which constitute a deduction from his income. For the capitalist this is a positive gain, because the negative limit for the self-expansion of his capital value is thereby reduced. So long as small independent producers of commodities spend a part of their own time in buying and selling, this represents nothing but time spent during the intervals between their productive function or diminution of their time of production.

At all events the time consumed for this purpose constitutes one of the costs of circulation which adds nothing to the converted values. It is the cost of converting them from the commodity form into the money form. The capitalist producer of commodities acting as an agent of circulation differs from the direct producer of commodities only in the fact that he buys and sells on a larger scale and therefore his function as such agent assumes greater dimensions. And if the volume of his business compels or enables him to buy (hire) circulation agents of his own to serve as wage labourers, the nature of the case is not changed thereby. A certain amount of labour power and labour time must be expended in the process of circulation (so far as it is merely a change of form). But this now appears as an additional outlay of capital. A part of the variable capital must be laid out in the purchase of this labour power functioning only in circulation. This advance of capital creates neither product nor value. It reduces *pro tanto* the dimensions in which the advanced capital functions productively. It is as though one part of the product were transformed into a machine which buys and sells the rest of the product. This machine brings about a reduction of the product. It does not participate in the production process, although it can diminish the labour power, etc., spent on circulation. It constitutes merely a part of the costs of circulation.

2. BOOKKEEPING

Apart from the actual buying and selling, labour time is expended in bookkeeping, which besides absorbs objectified labour such as pens, ink, paper, desks, office paraphernalia. This function, therefore, exacts the expenditure on the one hand of labour power and on the other of instruments of labour. It is the same condition of things as obtains in the case of the time of purchase and sale.

As unity within its circuits, as value in motion, whether in the sphere of production or in either phase of the sphere of circulation, capital exists ideally only in the form of money of account, primarily in the mind of the producer of commodities, the capitalist producer of commodities. This movement is fixed and controlled by bookkeeping, which also includes the determination of prices, or the calculation of the prices of commodities. The movement of production, especially of the production of surplus value — in which the commodities figure only as depositories of value, as the names of things whose ideal existence as values is crystallised in money of account — thus is symbolically reflected in imagination. So long as the individual producer of commodities keeps account only in his head (for instance, a peasant; the bookkeeping tenant farmer was not produced until the rise of capitalist agriculture), or books his expenditures, receipts, due dates of payments, etc., only incidentally, outside of his production time, it is palpably clear that this function and the instruments of labour consumed by it, such as paper, etc., represent additional consumption of labour time and instruments of labour which are necessary, but constitute a deduction from the time available for productive consumption as well as from the instruments of labour which function in the real process of production, enter into the creation of products and value.[12] The nature of the function itself is not changed — neither by the dimensions which it assumes on account of its concentration in the hands of the capitalist producer of commodities and the fact that instead of appearing as the function of many small commodity producers it appears as the function of *one* capitalist, as a function within a process of large-scale production; nor by its divorcement from those productive functions of which it formed an appendage, nor by its conversion into an independent function of special agents exclusively entrusted with it.

Division of labour and assumption of independence do not make a function one that creates products and value if it was not so intrinsically, hence before it became independent. If a capitalist invests his capital anew, he must invest a part of it in hiring a bookkeeper, etc., and in the wherewithal of bookkeeping. If his capital is already functioning, is engaged in the process of its own constant reproduction, he must continually reconvert a part of his product into a bookkeeper, clerks, and the like, by transforming that part into money. That part of his capital is withdrawn from the process of production and belongs in the costs of circulation, deductions from the total yield (including the labour power itself that is expended exclusively for this function).

But there is a certain difference between the costs incidental to bookkeeping, or the unproductive expenditure of labour time on the one hand and those of mere buying and selling time on the other. The latter arise only from the definite social form of the process of production, from the fact that it is the process of production of commodities. Bookkeeping, as the control and ideal synthesis of the process, be-

---

[12] In the Middle Ages we find bookkeeping for agriculture only in the monasteries. But we have seen (Buch I, S. 343)[a] that a bookkeeper was installed for agriculture as early as the primitive Indian communities. Bookkeeping is there made the independent and exclusive function of a communal officer. This division of labour saves time, effort, and expense, but production and bookkeeping in the sphere of production remain as much two different things as the cargo of a ship and the bill of lading. In the person of the bookkeeper, a part of the labour power of the community is withdrawn from production, and the costs of his function are not made good by his own labour but by a deduction from the communal product. What is true of the bookkeeper of an Indian community is true *mutatis mutandis* of the bookkeeper of the capitalist. //From Manuscript II.//

---

[a] This page refers to the first German edition of Volume One of *Capital* published in 1867. See present edition, Vol. 35 (*Capital*, Vol. I, Ch. XIV, 4).

comes the more necessary the more the process assumes a social scale and loses its purely individual character. It is therefore more necessary in capitalist production than in the scattered production of handicraft and peasant economy, more necessary in collective production than in capitalist production. But the costs of bookkeeping drop as production becomes concentrated and bookkeeping becomes social.

We are concerned here only with the general character of the costs of circulation, which arise out of the metamorphosis of forms alone. It is superfluous to discuss here all their forms in detail. But how forms which belong in the sphere of pure changes of the form of value and hence originate from the particular social form of the process of production, forms which in the case of the individual commodity producer are only transient, barely perceptible elements, run alongside his productive functions or become intertwined with them — how these can strike the eye as the huge costs of circulation can be seen from just the money taken in and paid out when these operations have become independent and concentrated on a large scale as the exclusive function of banks, etc., or of cashiers in individual businesses. But it must be firmly borne in mind that these costs of circulation are not changed in character by their change in appearance.

3. MONEY

Whether a product is fabricated as a commodity or not, it is always a material form of wealth, a use value intended for individual or productive consumption. Its value as a commodity is ideally expressed in its price, which does not change its actual use form in the least. But the fact that certain commodities like gold and silver function as money and as such reside exclusively in the process of circulation (even in the form of hoards, reserve funds, etc., they remain in the sphere of circulation, although latently) is a pure product of the particular social form of the process of production, the process of production of commodities. Since under capitalist production products assume the general form of commodities, and the overwhelming mass of products is created as commodities and must therefore assume the form of money, and since the vast bulk of the commodities, the part of social wealth functioning as commodities, grows continually, it follows that the quantity of gold and silver functioning as means of circulation, paying medium, reserve fund, etc., likewise increases. These commodities performing the function of money enter into neither individual nor productive consumption. They represent social labour fixed in a form in which it serves as a mere circulation machine. Besides the fact that a part of the social wealth has been condemned to assume this unproductive form, the wearing down of the money demands its constant replacement, or the conversion of more social labour, in the form of products, into more gold and silver. These replacement costs are considerable in capitalistically developed nations, because in general the portion of wealth tied up in the form of money is tremendous. Gold and silver as money commodities mean circulation costs to society which arise solely out of the social form of production. They are *faux frais* of commodity production in general, and they increase with the development of this production, especially of capitalist production. They represent a part of the social wealth that must be sacrificed to the process of circulation.[13]

II. COSTS OF STORAGE

Costs of circulation, which originate in a mere change of form of value, in circulation, ideally considered, do not enter into the value of commodities. The parts of capital expended as such costs are merely deductions from the productively expended capital so far as the capitalist is concerned. The costs of circulation which we shall consider now are of a different nature. They may arise from processes of production which are only continued in circulation, the productive character of which is hence merely concealed by the circulation form. On the other hand they may be, from the standpoint of society, mere costs, unproductive expenditure of living or objectified labour, but for that very reason they may become productive of value for the individual capitalist, may constitute an addition to the selling price of his commodities. This already follows from the fact that these costs are different in different spheres of production, and here and there even for different individual capitals in one and the same sphere of production. By being added to the prices of commodities they are distributed in proportion to the amount to be borne by each individual capitalist. But all labour which adds value can also add surplus value, and will

[13]*"The money circulating in a country is a certain portion of the capital of the country, absolutely withdrawn from productive purposes, in order to facilitate or increase the productiveness of the remainder. A certain amount of wealth is, therefore, as necessary in order to adopt gold as a circulating medium, as it is to make a machine in order to facilitate any other production"* (*Economist*, Vol. V, p. 520).

always add surplus value under capitalist production, as the value created by labour depends on the amount of the labour itself, whereas the surplus value created by it depends on the extent to which the capitalist pays for it. Consequently costs which enhance the price of a commodity without adding to its use value, which therefore are to be classed as the *faux frais* of production so far as society is concerned, may be a source of enrichment to the individual capitalist. On the other hand, as this addition to the price of the commodity merely distributes these costs of circulation equally, they do not thereby cease to be unproductive in character. For instance insurance companies divide the losses of individual capitalists among the capitalist class. But this does not prevent these equalised losses from remaining losses so far as the aggregate social capital is concerned.

1. FORMATION OF SUPPLY IN GENERAL

During its existence as commodity capital or its stay in the market, in other words, during the interval between the process of production, from which it emerges, and the process of consumption, into which it enters, the product constitutes a commodity supply. As a commodity in the market, and therefore in the shape of a supply, commodity capital figures in a dual capacity in each circuit: one time as the commodity product of that capital in process whose circuit is being examined; the other time however as the commodity product of another capital, which must be available in the market to be bought and converted into productive capital. It is, indeed, possible that this last-named commodity capital is not produced until ordered. In that event an interruption occurs until it has been produced. But the flow of the process of production and reproduction requires that a certain mass of commodities (means of production) should always be in the market, should therefore form a supply. Productive capital likewise comprises the purchase of labour power, and the money form is here only the value form of the means of subsistence, the greater part of which the labourer must find at hand in the market. We shall discuss this more in detail further on in this paragraph. But at this point the following is already clear. As far as concerns capital value in process which has been transformed into a commodity and must now be sold or reconverted into money, which therefore functions for the moment as commodity capital in the market, the condition in which it constitutes a supply is to be described as an inexpedient, involuntary stay there. The quicker the sale is effected the more smoothly runs the process of reproduction. Delay in the form conversion of $C' - M'$ impedes the real exchange of matter which must take place in the circuit of capital, as well as its further functioning as productive capital. On the other hand, so far as $M - C$ is concerned, the constant presence of commodities in the market, commodity supply, appears as a condition of the flow of the process of reproduction and of the investment of new or additional capital.

The abidance of the commodity capital as a commodity supply in the market requires buildings, stores, storage places, warehouses, in other words, an expenditure of constant capital; furthermore the payment of labour power for placing the commodities in storage. Besides, commodities spoil and are exposed to the injurious influences of the elements. Additional capital must be invested, partly in instruments of labour, in an objectified form, and partly in labour power to protect the commodities against the above.[14]

Thus the existence of capital in its form of commodity capital and hence of commodity supply gives rise to costs which must be classed as costs of circulation, since they do not come within the sphere of production. These costs of circulation differ from those mentioned under I by the fact that they enter to a certain extent into the value of the commodities, i. e., they increase the prices of commodities. At all events the capital and labour power which serve the need of preserving and storing the commodity supply are withdrawn from the direct process of production. On the other hand the capitals thus employed, including labour power as a constituent of capital, must be replaced out of the social product. Their expenditure has therefore the effect of diminishing the productive power of labour, so that a greater amount of capital and labour is required to obtain a particular useful effect. They are *unproductive costs*.

As the costs of circulation necessitated by the formation of a commodity supply are due merely to the time required for the conversion

---

[14] Corbet calculates, in 1841, that the cost of storing wheat for a season of nine months amounts to a loss of $^1/_2$% in quantity, 3% for interest on the price of wheat, 2% for warehouse rental, 1% for sifting and drayage, $^1/_2$% for delivery, together 7%, or 3 s. 6d. on a price of 50 s. per quarter (Th. Corbet, *An Inquiry into the Causes and Modes of the Wealth of Individuals, etc.*, London, 1841, [p. 140]).[22] According to the testimony of Liverpool merchants before the Railway Commission, the (net) costs of grain storage in 1865 amounted to about 2d. per quarter per month, or 9d. or 10d. a ton (*Royal Commission on Railways*, 1867. Evidence, p. 19, No. 331).

of existing values from the commodity form into the money form, hence merely to the particular social form of the production process (i. e., are due only to the fact that the product is brought forth as a commodity and must therefore undergo the transformation into money), these costs completely share the character of the circulation costs enumerated under I. On the other hand the value of the commodities is here preserved or increased only because the use value, the product itself, is placed in definite objective conditions which cost capital outlay, and is subjected to operations which bring additional labour to bear on the use values. However the computation of the values of commodities, the bookkeeping incidental to this process, the transactions of purchase and sale, do not affect the use value in which the commodity value exists. They have to do only with the form of the commodity value. Although in the case submitted here[a] the costs of forming a supply (which is here done involuntarily) arise only from a delay in the change of form and from its necessity, still these costs differ from those mentioned under I, in that their purpose is not a change in the form of the value, but the preservation of the value existing in the commodity as a product, a utility, and which cannot be preserved in any other way than by preserving the product, the use value, itself. The use value is neither raised nor increased here; on the contrary, it diminishes. But its diminution is restricted and it is preserved. Neither is the advanced value contained in the commodity increased here; but new labour, objectified and living, is added.

We have now to investigate furthermore to what extent these costs arise from the peculiar nature of commodity production in general and from commodity production in its general, absolute form, i. e., capitalist commodity production; and to what extent on the other hand they are common to all social production and merely assume a special shape, a special form of appearance, in capitalist production.

Adam Smith entertained the splendid notion that the formation of a supply was a phenomenon peculiar to capitalist production.[15] More recent economists, for instance Lalor, insist on the contrary that it declines with the development of capitalist production. Sismondi even regards it as one of the drawbacks of the latter.[23]

As a matter of fact, supplies exist in three forms: in the form of pro-

---

[15] Book II, Introduction. [A. Smith, *An Inquiry into the Nature and Causes of the Wealth of Nations.*]

---

[a] i. e., Corbet's calculations given in Footnote 14.

ductive capital, in the form of a fund for individual consumption, and in the form of a commodity supply or commodity capital. The supply in one form decreases relatively when it increases in another, although its quantity may increase absolutely in all three forms simultaneously.

It is plain from the outset that wherever production is carried on for the direct satisfaction of the needs of the producer and only to a minor extent for exchange or sale, hence where the social product does not assume the form of commodities at all or only to a rather small degree, the supply in the form of commodities, or commodity supply, forms only a small and insignificant part of wealth. But here the consumption fund is relatively large, especially that of the means of subsistence proper. One need but take a look at old-fashioned peasant economy. There the overwhelming part of the product is transformed directly into supplies of means of production or means of subsistence, without becoming supplies of commodities, for the very reason that it remains in the hands of its owner. It does not assume the form of a commodity supply and for this reason Adam Smith declares that there is no supply in societies based on this mode of production. He confuses the form of the supply with the supply itself and believes that society hitherto lived from hand to mouth or trusted to the hap of the morrow.[16] This is a naïve misunderstanding.

A supply in the form of productive capital exists in the shape of means of production, which are already in the process of production or at least in the hands of the producer, hence latently already in the process of production. It was seen previously that with the development of the productivity of labour and therefore also with the development of the capitalist mode of production — which develops the

[16] Instead of a supply arising only upon and from the conversion of the product into a commodity, and of the consumption supply into a commodity supply, as Adam Smith wrongly imagines, this change of form, on the contrary, causes most violent crises in the economy of the producers during the transition from production for one's own needs to commodity production. In India, for instance, "the disposition to hoard largely the grain for which little could be got in years of abundance" was observed until very recent times (*Return. Bengal and Orissa Famine, H. of C., 1867*, I, pp., 230-31, No. 74). The sudden increase in the demand for cotton, jute, etc., due to the American Civil War,[24] led in many parts of India to a severe restriction of rice culture, a rise in the price of rice, and a sale of the producers' old rice supplies. To this must be added the unexampled export of rice to Australia, Madagascar, etc., in 1864-66. This accounts for the acute character of the famine of 1866, which cost the lives of a million people in the district of Orissa alone (loc. cit., [pp.] 174, 175, 213, 214, and III: *Papers relating to the Famine in Behar*, pp. 32, 33, where the "DRAIN OF OLD STOCKS" is emphasised as one of the causes of the famine). //From Manuscript II.//

social productive power of labour more than all previous modes of production — there is a steady increase in the mass of means of production (buildings, machinery, etc.) which are incorporated once and for all in the process in the form of instruments of labour, and perform with steady repetition their function in it for a longer or shorter time. It was also observed that this increase is at the same time the premise and consequence of the development of the social productive power of labour. The growth, not only absolute but also relative, of wealth in this form (cf. Buch I, Kap. XXIII, 2)[a] is characteristic above all of the capitalist mode of production. The material forms of existence of constant capital, the means of production, do not however consist only of such instruments of labour but also of materials of labour in various stages of processing, and of auxiliary materials. With the enlargement of the scale of production and the increase in the productive power of labour through co-operation, division of labour, machinery, etc., grows the quantity of raw materials, auxiliary materials, etc., entering into the daily process of reproduction. These elements must be ready at hand at the place of production. The volume of this supply existing in the form of productive capital increases therefore absolutely. In order that the process may keep going — apart from the fact whether this supply can be renewed daily or only at fixed intervals — there must always be a greater accumulation of ready raw material, etc., at the place of production than is used up, say, daily or weekly. The continuity of the process requires that the presence of its conditions should not be jeopardised by possible interruptions when making purchases daily, nor depend on whether the product is sold daily or weekly, and hence is reconvertible into its elements of production only irregularly. But it is evident that productive capital may be latent or form a supply in quite different proportions. There is for instance a great difference whether a spinning-mill owner must have on hand a supply of cotton or coal for three months or for one. Patently this supply, while increasing absolutely, may decrease relatively.

This depends on various conditions, all of which practically amount to a demand for greater rapidity, regularity, and reliability in furnishing the necessary amount of raw material, so that no interruption will ever occur. The less these conditions are complied with, hence the less rapid, regular, and reliable the supplies, the greater

---

[a] English edition: Vol. I, Ch. XXV, 2 (present edition, Vol. 35).

must be the latent part of the productive capital, that is to say, the supply of raw material, etc., in the hands of the producer, waiting to be worked up. These conditions are inversely proportional to the degree of development of capitalist production, and hence of the productive power of social labour. The same applies therefore to the supply in this form.

However that which appears here as a decrease of the supply (for instance, in Lalor) is in part merely a decrease of the supply in the form of commodity capital, or of the commodity supply proper; it is consequently only a change of form of the same supply. If for instance a great quantity of coal is produced every day in a certain country, and therefore the scale and the energy of operation of the coal industry are great, the spinner does not need a large store of coal in order to ensure the continuity of his production. The steady and certain renewal of the coal supply makes this unnecessary. In the second place the rapidity with which the product of one process may be transferred as means of production to another process depends on the development of the transport and communication facilities. The cheapness of transportation is of great importance in this question. The continually renewed transport of coal from the mine to the spinning-mill for instance would be more expensive than the storing up of a larger supply of coal for a longer time when the price of transportation is relatively cheaper. These two circumstances examined so far arise from the process of production itself. In the third place the development of the credit system also exerts an influence. The less the spinner is dependent on the direct sale of his yarn for the renewal of his supply of cotton, coal, etc.— and this direct dependence will be the smaller, the more developed the credit system is — the smaller relatively these supplies can be and yet ensure a continuous production of yarn on a given scale, a production independent of the hazards of the sale of yarn. In the fourth place, however, many raw materials, semi-finished goods, etc., require rather long periods of time for their production. This applies especially to all raw materials furnished by agriculture. If no interruption of the process of production is to take place, a certain amount of raw materials must be on hand for the entire period in which no new products can take the place of the old. If this supply decreases in the hands of the industrial capitalist, it proves merely that it increases in the hands of the merchant in the form of commodity supply. The development of transportation for instance makes it possible rapidly to ship the cotton lying, say, in Liverpool's import warehouses to Manchester, so that the manufacturer can renew his supply in comparatively small portions, as and when needed. But in that case the cotton remains in so much larger quantities as commodity supply in the hands of the Liverpool merchants. It is therefore merely a change in the form of the supply, and this Lalor and others overlooked. And if you consider the social capital, the same quantity of products exists in either case in the form of supply. The quantity required for a single country during the period of, say, one year decreases as transportation improves. If a large number of sailing vessels and steamers ply between America and England, England's opportunities to renew its cotton supply are increased while the average quantity to be held in storage in England decreases. The same effect is produced by the development of the world market and the consequent multiplication of the sources of supply of the same merchandise. The article is supplied piecemeal from various countries and at various intervals.

2. THE COMMODITY SUPPLY PROPER

We have already seen that under capitalist production the product assumes the general form of a commodity, and the more so the more that production grows in size and depth. Consequently, even if production retains the same volume, the far greater part of the products exists in the shape of commodities, compared with either the former modes of production or the capitalist mode of production at a less developed stage. But every commodity — therefore also every commodity capital, which is only commodity, but commodity serving as the form of existence of capital value — constitutes an element of the commodity supply, unless it passes immediately from its sphere of production into productive or individual consumption, that is, while it lies in the market in the interval. If the volume of production remains the same, the commodity supply (i. e., this isolation and fixation of the commodity form of the product) grows therefore of itself concomitantly with capitalist production. We have seen above that this is merely a change of form of the supply, that is to say, the supply in the form of commodities increases on the one hand because on the other the supply in the form intended directly for production or consumption decreases. It is merely a changed social form of the supply. If at the same time it is not only the relative magnitude of the commodity supply compared with the aggregate social product that increases but also its absolute magnitude, that is so because the mass of the aggregate product grows with the growth of capitalist production.

With the development of capitalist production, the scale of production is determined less and less by the direct demand for the product and more and more by the amount of capital available in the hands of the individual capitalist, by the urge for self-expansion inherent in his capital and by the need of continuity and expansion of the process of production. Thus in each particular branch of production there is a necessary increase in the mass of products available in the market in the shape of commodities, i. e., in search of buyers. The amount of capital fixed for a shorter or longer period in the form of commodity capital grows. Hence the commodity supply also grows.

Finally the majority of the members of society are transformed into wage labourers, into people who live from hand to mouth, who receive their wages weekly and spend them daily, who therefore must have their means of subsistence made available to them in the shape of a supply. Although the separate elements of this supply may be in continuous flow, a part of them must always stagnate in order that the supply as a whole may remain in a state of flux.

All these moments have their origin in the form of production and in the incident change of form which the product must undergo in the process of circulation.

Whatever may be the social form of the products supply, its preservation requires outlays for buildings, vessels, etc., which are facilities for storing the product; also for means of production and labour, more or less of which must be expended, according to the nature of the product, in order to combat injurious influences. The more concentrated socially the supply is, the smaller relatively are the costs. These outlays always constitute a part of the social labour, in either objectified or living form — hence in the capitalist form outlays of capital — which do not enter into the formation of the product itself and thus are deductions from the product. They are necessary, these unproductive expenses of social wealth. They are the costs of preserving the social product regardless of whether its existence as an element of the commodity supply stems merely from the social form of production, hence from the commodity form and its necessary change of form, or whether we regard the commodity supply merely as a special form of the supply of products, which is common to all societies, although not in the form of a *commodity* supply, that form of products supply belonging in the process of circulation.

It may now be asked to what extent these costs enter into the values of commodities.

If the capitalist has converted the capital advanced by him in the form of means of production and labour power into a product, into a definite quantity of commodities ready for sale, and these commodities remain in stock unsold, then we have a case of not only the stagnation of the process of self-expansion of his capital value during this period. The costs of preserving this supply in buildings, of additional labour, etc., mean a positive loss. The buyer he would ultimately find would laugh in his face if he were to say to him: "I could not sell my goods for six months, and their preservation during that period did not only keep so and so much of my capital idle, but also cost me so and so much extra expense." "*Tant pis pour vous!*"[a] the buyer would say. "Right here alongside of you is another seller whose wares were completed only the day before yesterday. Your articles are shop-worn and probably more or less damaged by the ravages of time. Therefore you will have to sell cheaper than your competitor."

The conditions under which a commodity exists are not in the least affected by whether its producer is the real producer or a capitalist producer, hence actually only the representative of the real producer. He has to turn his product into money. The expenses incurred by him because of the fixation of the product in the form of commodities are a part of his individual speculations with which the buyer of the commodities has no concern. The latter does not pay him for the time of circulation of his commodities. Even when the capitalist keeps his goods intentionally off the market, in times of an actual or anticipated revolution in values, it depends on the advent of this revolution in values, on the correctness or incorrectness of his speculation, whether he will recover his additional costs or not. But the revolution in values does not ensue in consequence of his additional costs. Hence in so far as the formation of a supply entails a stagnation of circulation, the expense incurred thereby does not add to the value of the commodities. On the other hand there cannot be any supply without a stay in the sphere of circulation, without capital staying for a longer or shorter time in its commodity form; hence no supply without stagnation of circulation, just as no money can circulate without the formation of a money reserve. Hence no commodity circulation without commodity supply. If the capitalist does not come face to face with this neces-

---

[a] So much the worse for you!

sity in C′ — M′, he will encounter it in M — C; if not with regard to his own commodity capital, then with regard to that of other capitalists, who produce means of production for him and means of subsistence for his labourers.

Whether the formation of a supply is voluntary or involuntary, that is to say, whether the commodity producer keeps a supply intentionally or whether his products form a supply in consequence of the sales resistance offered by the conditions of the process of circulation itself cannot affect the matter essentially, it would seem. But for the solution of this problem it is useful to know what distinguishes voluntary from involuntary supply formation. Involuntary supply formation arises from, or is identical with, a stagnation of the circulation which is independent of the knowledge of the commodity producer and thwarts his will. And what characterises the voluntary formation of a supply? In both instances the seller seeks to get rid of his commodity as fast as ever. He always offers his product for sale as a commodity. If he were to withdraw it from sale, it would be only a potential (δυνάμει), not an actual (ἐνεργεία) element of the commodity supply. To him the commodity as such is as much a depository of exchange value as ever and as such can act only by and after stripping off its commodity form and assuming the money form.

The commodity supply must be of a certain volume in order to satisfy the demand during a given period. A continual extension of the circle of buyers is counted upon. For instance, in order to last for one day, a part of the commodities in the market must constantly remain in the commodity form while the remainder is fluent, turns into money. True, the part which stagnates while the rest is fluent decreases steadily, just as the size of the supply itself decreases until it is all sold. The stagnation of commodities thus counts as a requisite condition of their sale. The volume must furthermore be larger than the average sale or the average demand. Otherwise the excess over these averages could not be satisfied. On the other hand the supply must constantly be renewed, because it is constantly being drawn on. This renewal cannot come from anywhere in the last instance except from production, from a supply of commodities. It is immaterial whether this comes from abroad or not. The renewal depends on the periods required by the commodities for their reproduction. The commodity supply must last all that time. The fact that it does not remain in the hands of the original producer but passes through various reservoirs, from the wholesaler to the retailer, changes merely the appearance and not the nature of the thing. From the point of view of society, a part of the capital retains in both instances the form of a commodity supply until the commodities enter productive or individual consumption. The producer himself tries to keep a stock corresponding to his average demand in order not to depend directly on production and to ensure for himself a steady clientele. Purchase periods corresponding to the periods of production are formed and the commodities constitute supplies for longer or shorter times, until they can be replaced by new commodities of the same kind. Constancy and continuity of the process of circulation, and therefore of the process of reproduction, which includes the process of circulation, are safeguarded only by the formation of such supplies.

It must be remembered that $C' - M'$ may have been transacted for the producer of C, even if C is still in the market. If the producer were to keep his own commodities in stock until they are sold to the ultimate consumer, he would have to set two capitals in motion, one as the producer of the commodities and one as a merchant. As far as the commodity itself is concerned, whether we look upon it as an individual commodity or as a component part of social capital, it is immaterial whether the costs of forming the supply must be borne by its producer or by a series of merchants, from A to Z.

Since the commodity supply is nothing but the commodity form of the product which at a particular level of social production would exist either as a productive supply (latent production fund) or as a consumption fund (reserve of means of consumption) if it did not exist as a commodity supply, the expenses required for its preservation, that is, the costs of supply formation — i. e., objectified or living labour spent for this purpose — are merely expenses incurred for maintaining either the social fund for production or the social fund for consumption. The increase in the value of commodities caused by them distributes these costs simply *pro rata* over the different commodities, since the costs differ with different kinds of commodities. And the costs of supply formation are as much as ever deductions from the social wealth, although they constitute one of the conditions of its existence.

Only to the extent that the commodity supply is a premise of commodity circulation and is itself a form necessarily arising in commodity circulation, only in so far as this apparent stagnation is therefore a form of the movement itself, just as the formation of a money reserve is a premise of money circulation — only to that extent is such stagnation normal. But as soon as the commodities lying in the reservoirs of circulation do not make room for the swiftly succeeding wave of production, so that the reservoirs become over-stocked, the commodity supply expands in consequence of the stagnation in circulation just as the hoards increase when money circulation is clogged. It does not make any difference whether this jam occurs in the warehouses of the industrial capitalist or in the storerooms of the merchant. The commodity supply is in that case not a prerequisite of uninterrupted sale, but a consequence of the impossibility of selling the goods. The costs are the same, but since they now arise purely out of the form, that is to say, out of the necessity of transforming the commodities into money and out of the difficulty of going through this metamorphosis, they do not enter into the values of the commodities but constitute deductions, losses of value in the realisation of the value. Since the normal and abnormal forms of the supply do not differ in form and both clog circulation, these phenomena may be confused and deceive the agent of production himself so much the more since for the producer the process of circulation of his capital may continue while that of his commodities which have changed hands and now belong to merchants may be arrested. If production and consumption swell, other things being equal, then the commodity supply swells likewise. It is renewed and absorbed just as fast, but its size is greater. Hence the bulging size of the commodity supply, for which stagnant circulation is responsible, may be mistaken for a symptom of the expansion of the process of reproduction, especially when the development of the credit system makes it possible to wrap the real movement in mystery.

The costs of supply formation consist: 1) of a quantitative diminution of the mass of the products (for instance in the case of a flour supply); 2) of a deterioration of quality; 3) of the objectified and living labour required for the preservation of the supply.

III. COSTS OF TRANSPORTATION

It is not necessary to go here into all the details of the costs of circulation, such as packing, sorting, etc. The general law is that *all costs of circulation which arise only from changes in the forms of commodities do not add to their value.* They are merely expenses incurred in the realisation of the value or in its conversion from one form into another. The capital spent to meet those costs (including the labour done under its control) belongs among the *faux frais* of capitalist production. They must be replaced from the surplus product and constitute, as far as the entire capitalist class is concerned, a deduction from the surplus value or surplus product, just as the time a labourer needs for the purchase of his means of subsistence is lost time. But the costs of transportation play a too important part to pass them by without a few brief remarks.

Within the circuit of capital and the metamorphosis of commodities, which forms a part of that circuit, an interchange of matter takes place in social labour. This interchange of matter may necessitate a change of location of products, their real motion from one place to another. Still, circulation of commodities can take place without physical motion by them, and there can be transportation of products without circulation of commodities, and even without a direct exchange of products. A house sold by A to B does not wander from one place to another, although it circulates as a commodity. Movable commodity values, such as cotton or pig iron, may lie in the same storage dump at a time when they are passing through dozens of circulation processes, are bought and resold by speculators.[17] What really does move here is the title of ownership in goods, not the goods themselves. On the other hand, transportation played a prominent role in the land of the Incas,[20] although the social product neither circulated as a commodity nor was distributed by means of barter.

Consequently, although the transportation industry when based on capitalist production appears as a cause of circulation costs, this special form of appearance does not alter the matter in the least.

Quantities of products are not increased by transportation. Nor, with a few exceptions, is the possible alteration of their natural qualities, brought about by transportation, an intentional useful effect; it is rather an unavoidable evil. But the use value of things is realised only in their consumption, and their consumption may necessitate a change of location of these things, hence may require an additional process of production, in the transport industry. The productive capital invested in this industry imparts value to the transported products, partly by transferring value from the means of transportation, partly by adding value through the labour performed in transport.

[17] Storch calls this "circulation factice".

This last-named increment of value splits, as it does in all capitalist production, into a replacement of wages and into surplus value.

Within each process of production, a great role is played by the change of location of the subject of labour and the required instruments of labour and labour power—such as cotton trucked from the carding to the spinning room or coal hoisted from the shaft to the surface. The transition of the finished product as finished goods from one independent place of production to another located at a distance shows the same phenomenon, only on a larger scale. The transport of the products from one productive establishment to another is furthermore followed by the passage of the finished products from the sphere of production to that of consumption. The product is not ready for consumption until it has completed these movements.

As was shown above, the general law of commodity production holds: The productivity of labour is inversely proportional to the value created by it. This is true of the transport industry as well as of any other. The smaller the amount of dead and living labour required for the transportation of commodities over a certain distance, the greater the productive power of labour, and vice versa.[18]

The absolute magnitude of the value which transportation adds to the commodities stands in inverse proportion to the productive power of the transport industry and in direct proportion to the distance travelled, other conditions remaining the same.

The relative part of the value added to the prices of commodities by the costs of transportation, other conditions remaining the same, is directly proportional to their cubic content and weight. But there are many modifying factors. Transportation requires, for instance, more or less important precautionary measures, and therefore more or less

---

[18] Ricardo quotes Say, who considers it one of the blessings of commerce that by means of the costs of transportation it increases the price, or the value, of products. "Commerce," writes Say, "enables us to obtain a commodity in the place where it is to be found, and to convey it to another where it is to be consumed; it therefore gives us the power of increasing the value of the commodity, by the whole difference between its price in the first of these places, and its price in the second." [25] Ricardo remarks with reference to this: * "True, but how is this additional value given to it? By adding to the cost of production, first, the expenses of conveyance; secondly, the profit on the advances of capital made by the merchant. The commodity is only more valuable, for the same reason that every other commodity may become more valuable, because more labour is expended on its production and conveyance before it is purchased by the consumer. This must not be mentioned as one of the advantages of commerce" * (Ricardo, *Principles of Political Economy*, 3rd ed., London, 1821, pp. 309, 310).

expenditure of labour and instruments of labour, depending on how fragile, perishable, explosive, etc., the articles are. Here the railway kings show greater ingenuity in the invention of fantastic species than do botanists and zoologists. The classification of goods on English railways, for example, fills volumes and, in principle, rests on the general tendency to transform the diversified natural properties of goods into just as many ills of transportation and routine pretexts for fraudulent charges.

"Glass, which was formerly worth £11 per CRATE,[a] is now worth only £2 since the improvements which have taken place in manufactures, and since the abolition of the duty; but the rate for carriage is the same as it was formerly, and higher than it was previously, when carried by canal. Formerly, manufacturers ... had glass and glass wares for the plumbers' trade carried at about 10 s. per ton, within 50 miles of Birmingham. At the present time, the rate to cover risk of breakage is three times that amount... The companies always resist any claim that is made for breakages." [19]

The fact that furthermore the relative part of the value added to an article by the costs of transportation is inversely proportional to its value furnishes special grounds to the railway kings to tax articles in direct proportion to their values. The complaints of the industrialists and merchants on this score are found on every page of the testimony given in the report quoted.

The capitalist mode of production reduces the costs of transportation of the individual commodity by the development of the means of transportation and communication, as well as by the concentration — increasing scale — of transportation. It increases that part of the living and objectified social labour which is expended in the transport of commodities, firstly by converting the great majority of all products into commodities, secondly, by substituting distant for local markets.

The circulation, i. e., the actual locomotion of commodities in space, resolves itself into the transport of commodities. The transport industry forms on the one hand an independent branch of production and thus a separate sphere of investment of productive capital. On the other hand its distinguishing feature is that it appears as a continuation of a process of production *within* the process of circulation and *for* the process of circulation.

[19] *Royal Commission on Railways*, p. 31, No. 630.

---

[a] In the German original, the meaning of this English word is explained in parentheses.

Part II

THE TURNOVER OF CAPITAL

Chapter VII

THE TURNOVER TIME AND THE NUMBER
OF TURNOVERS

We have seen that the entire time of turnover of a given capital is equal to the sum of its time of circulation and its time of production. It is the period of time from the moment of the advance of capital value in a definite form to the return of the functioning capital value in the same form.

The compelling motive of capitalist production is always the self-expansion of the value advanced, no matter whether this value is advanced in its independent form, i. e., in the money form, or in commodities, in which case its value form possesses only ideal independence in the price of the advanced commodities. In both cases this capital value passes through various forms of existence during its circular movement. Its identity with itself is fixed in the books of the capitalists, or in the form of money of account.

Whether we take the form M ... M' or the form P ... P, the implication is (1) that the advanced value performs the function of capital value and has created surplus value; (2) that after completing its process it has returned to the form in which it began it. The self-expansion of the value advanced M and at the same time the return of capital to this form (the money form) is plainly visible in M ... M'. But the same takes place in the second form. For the starting-point of P is the existence of the elements of production, of commodities having a given value. The form includes the self-expansion of this value (C' and M') and the return to the original form, for in the second P the advanced value has again the form of the elements of production in which it was originally advanced.

We have seen previously: "If production be capitalistic in form, so, too, will be reproduction. Just as in the former the labour process figures but as a means towards the self-expansion of capital, so in the latter it figures but as a means of reproducing as capital — i. e., as self-expanding value,— the value advanced" (Buch I, Kap. XXI, S. 588).[a]

The three forms (I) M ... M′, (II) P ... P, and (III) C′ ... C′, present the following distinctions: in form II, P ... P, the renewal of the process, the process of reproduction, is expressed as a reality, while in form I only as a potentiality. But both differ from form III in that with them the advanced capital value — advanced either in the form of money or of material elements of production — is the starting-point and therefore also the returning point. In M ... M′ the return is expressed by M′ = M + m. If the process is renewed on the same scale, M is again the starting-point and m does not enter into it, but shows merely that M has self-expanded as capital and hence created a surplus value, m, but cast it off. In the form P ... P capital value P advanced in the form of elements of production is likewise the starting-point. This form includes its self-expansion. If simple reproduction takes place, the same capital value renews the same process in the same form P. If accumulation takes place, then P′ (= in magnitude of value to M′ = to C′) re-opens the process as an expanded capital value. But the process begins again with the advanced capital value in its initial form, although with a greater capital value than before. In form III, on the contrary, the capital value does not begin the process as an advanced, but as a value already expanded, as the aggregate wealth existing in the form of commodities, of which the advanced capital value is but a part. This last form ̃is important for Part III, in which the movements of the individual capitals are discussed in connection with the movement of the aggregate social capital. But it is not to be used in connection with the turnover of capital, which always begins with the advance of capital value, whether in the form of money or commodities, and which always necessitates the return of the rotating capital value in the form in which it was advanced. Of the circuits I and II, the former is of service in a study primarily of the influence of the turnover on the formation of surplus value and the latter in a study of its influence on the creation of the product.

Economists have little distinguished between the different forms of

---

[a] English edition: Vol. I, Ch. XXIII (present edition, Vol. 35).

circuits, nor have they examined them individually with relation to the turnover of capital. They generally consider the form M ... M′, because it dominates the individual capitalist and aids him in his calculations, even if money is the starting-point only in the shape of money of account. Others start with outlays in the form of elements of production to the point when returns are received, without alluding at all to the form of the returns, whether made in commodities or money. For instance:

* "The Economic Cycle ... [is] the whole course of production, from the time that outlays are made till returns are received. In agriculture, seedtime is its commencement, and harvesting its ending" * [a] (S.P. Newman, *Elements of Political Economy*, Andover and New York, [1835], p. 81). [26]

Others begin with C′ (the third form):

"The world of trade may be conceived to revolve in what we shall call an economic cycle, which accomplishes one revolution, by business coming round again, through its successive transactions, to the point from which it set out. Its commencement may be dated from the point at which the capitalist has obtained those returns, by which his capital is replaced to him: whence he proceeds anew to engage his workmen; to distribute among them, in wages, their maintenance, or rather, the power of lifting it; to obtain from them, in finished work, the articles in which he specially deals; to bring these articles to market and there terminate the orbit of one set of movements, by effecting a sale, and receiving, in its proceeds, a return for the whole outlays of the period" (Th. Chalmers, *On Political Economy*, 2nd ed., Glasgow, 1832, p. 85). [27]

As soon as the entire capital value invested by some individual capitalist in any branch of production whatever has described its circuit, it finds itself once more in its initial form and can now repeat the same process. It must repeat it, if the value is to perpetuate itself as capital value and to create surplus value. An individual circuit is but a constantly repeated section in the life of a capital; hence a period. At the end of the period M ... M′ capital has once more the form of money capital, which passes anew through that series of changes of form in which its process of reproduction, or self-expansion, is included. At the end of the period P ... P capital resumes the form of elements of production, which are the prerequisites for a renewal of its circuit. A circuit performed by a capital and meant to be a periodical process, not an individual act, is called its turnover. The duration of this turnover is determined by the sum of its time of production and its time of circulation. This time total constitutes the time of turnover of the capital. It thus measures the interval of time between one cir-

---

[a] In the original, this quotation from Newman is given both in German and in English.

cuit period of the entire capital value and the next, the periodicity in the process of life of capital or, if you like, the time of the renewal, the repetition, of the process of self-expansion, or production, of one and the same capital value.

Apart from the individual adventures which may accelerate or shorten the time of turnover of certain capitals, this time differs in the different spheres of investment.

Just as the working day is the natural unit for measuring the function of labour power, so the year is the natural unit for measuring the turnovers of functioning capital. The natural basis of this unit is the circumstance that the most important crops of the temperate zone, which is the mother country of capitalist production, are annual products.

If we designate the year as the unit of measure of the turnover time by T, the time of turnover of a given capital by t, and the number of its turnovers by n, then $n = \frac{T}{t}$. If, for instance, the time of turnover t is 3 months, then n is equal to $^{12}/_3$, or 4; capital is turned over four times per year. If t = 18 months, then $n = ^{12}/_{18} = ^2/_3$, or capital completes only two-thirds of its turnover in one year. If its time of turnover is several years, it is computed in multiples of one year.

From the point of view of the capitalist, the time of turnover of his capital is the time for which he must advance his capital in order to create surplus value with it and receive it back in its original shape.

Before examining more closely the influence of the turnover on the processes of production and self-expansion, we must investigate two new forms which accrue to capital from the process of circulation and affect the form of its turnover.

Chapter VIII

FIXED CAPITAL AND CIRCULATING CAPITAL

I. DISTINCTIONS OF FORM

We have seen (Buch I, Kap. VI) [a] that, in relation to the products toward the creation of which it contributes, a portion of the constant capital retains that definite use form in which it enters into the process of production. Hence it performs the same functions for a longer

---

[a] English edition: Vol. I, Ch. VIII (see present edition, Vol. 35).

or shorter period, in ever repeated labour processes. This applies for instance to industrial buildings, machinery, etc.— in short to all things which we comprise under the name of *instruments of labour*. This part of constant capital yields up value to the product in proportion as it loses its own exchange value together with its own use value. This delivery of value, or this transition of the value of such a means of production to the product which it helps to create is determined by a calculation of averages. It is measured by the average duration of its function, from the moment that the means of production enters into the process of production to the moment that it is completely spent, dead and gone, and must be replaced by a new sample of the same kind, or reproduced.

This, then, is the peculiarity of this part of constant capital, of the labour instruments proper:

A part of capital has been advanced in the form of constant capital, i. e., of means of production, which function as factors of the labour process so long as they retain the independent use form in which they enter this process. The finished product, and therefore also the creators of the product, so far as they have been transformed into product, is thrust out of the process of production and passes as a commodity from the sphere of production to the sphere of circulation. But the instruments of labour never leave the sphere of production, once they have entered it. Their function holds them there. A portion of the advanced capital value becomes *fixed* in this form determined by the function of the instruments of labour in the process. In the performance of this function, and thus by the wear and tear of the instruments of labour, a part of their value passes on to the product, while the other remains fixed in the instruments of labour and thus in the process of production. The value fixed in this way decreases steadily, until the instrument of labour is worn out, its value having been distributed during a shorter or longer period over a mass of products originating from a series of constantly repeated labour processes. But so long as it is still effective and need not yet be replaced by a new one of the same kind, a certain amount of constant capital value remains fixed in it, while the other part of the value originally fixed in it is transferred to the product and therefore circulates as a component part of the commodity supply. The longer an instrument of labour lasts, the slower it wears out, the longer will its constant capital value remain fixed in this use form. But whatever may be its durability, the proportion in which it yields value is always inverse to the entire time it functions. If of two machines of equal value one wears out in five years and the other in ten, then the first yields twice as much value in the same time as the second.

This portion of the capital value fixed in the instrument of labour circulates as well as any other. We have seen in general that all capital value is constantly in circulation, and that in this sense all capital is circulating capital. But the circulation of the portion of capital which we are now studying is peculiar. In the first place it does not circulate in its use form, but it is merely its value that circulates, and this takes place gradually, piecemeal, in proportion as it passes from it to the product, which circulates as a commodity. During the entire period of its functioning, a part of its value remains fixed in it, independently of the commodities which it helps to produce. It is this peculiarity which gives to this portion of constant capital the form of *fixed capital*. All other material parts of the capital advanced in the process of production form by way of contrast the *circulating*, or *fluid, capital*.

Some means of production do not enter materially into the product. Such are auxiliary materials, which are consumed by the instruments of labour proper in the performance of their functions, like coal consumed by a steam-engine; or which merely assist in the operation, like gas for lighting, etc. It is only their value which forms a part of the value of the products. The product circulates in its own circulation the value of these means of production. This feature they have in common with fixed capital. But they are entirely consumed in every labour process which they enter and must therefore be wholly replaced by new means of production of the same kind in every new labour process. They do not preserve their independent use form while performing their function. Hence while they function no portion of capital value remains fixed in their old use form, their bodily form, either. The circumstance that this portion of the auxiliary materials does not pass bodily into the product but enters into the value of the product only according to its own value, as a portion of that value, and what hangs together with this, namely, that the function of these substances is strictly confined to the sphere of production, has misled economists like Ramsay (who at the same time got fixed capital mixed up with constant capital) to classify them as fixed capital. [28]

That part of the means of production which bodily enters into the product, i. e., raw materials, etc., thus assumes in part forms which enable it later to enter into individual consumption as articles of use.

The instruments of labour properly so called, the material vehicles of the fixed capital, are consumed only productively and cannot enter into individual consumption, because they do not enter into the product, or the use value, which they help to create but retain their independent form with reference to it until they are completely worn out. The means of transportation are an exception to this rule. The useful effect which they produce during the performance of their productive function, hence during their stay in the sphere of production, the change of location, passes simultaneously into the individual consumption of, for instance, the passenger. He pays for their use in the same way in which he pays for the use of other articles of consumption. We have seen[a] that for instance in chemical manufacture raw and auxiliary materials blend. The same applies to instruments of labour and auxiliary and raw materials. Similarly in agriculture the substances added for the improvement of the soil pass partly into the plants raised and help to form the product. On the other hand their effect is distributed over a lengthy period, say four or five years. A portion of them therefore passes bodily into the product and thus immediately transfers its value to the product while the other portion remains fixed in its old use form and retains its value. It persists as a means of production and consequently keeps the form of fixed capital. As a beast of toil an ox is fixed capital. If he is eaten, he no longer functions as an instrument of labour, nor as fixed capital either.

What determines that a portion of the capital value invested in means of production is endowed with the character of fixed capital is exclusively the peculiar manner in which this value circulates. This specific manner of circulation arises from the specific manner in which the instrument of labour transmits its value to the product, or in which it behaves as a creator of values during the process of production. This manner again arises from the special way in which the instruments of labour function in the labour process.

We know that a use value which emerges as a product from one labour process enters into another as a means of production.[b] It is only the functioning of a product as an instrument of labour in the process of production that makes it fixed capital. But when it itself only just emerges from a process, it is in no way fixed capital. For instance a machine, as a product or commodity of the machine-manufacturer,

---

[a] See present edition, Vol. 35 (*Capital*, Vol. I, Ch. VII, 1). - [b] Ibid.

belongs to his commodity capital. It does not become fixed capital until it is employed productively in the hands of its purchaser, the capitalist.

All other circumstances being equal, the degree of fixity increases with the durability of the instrument of labour. It is this durability that determines the magnitude of the difference between the capital value fixed in instruments of labour and that part of its value which it yields to the product in repeated labour processes. The slower this value is yielded — and value is given up by the instrument of labour in every repetition of the labour process — the larger is the fixed capital and the greater the difference between the capital employed in the process of production and the capital consumed in it. As soon as this difference has disappeared the instrument of labour has outlived its usefulness and has lost with its use value also its value. It has ceased to be the depository of value. Since an instrument of labour, like every other material carrier of constant capital, gives up value to the product only to the extent that together with its use value it loses its value, it is evident that the more slowly its use value is lost, the longer it lasts in the process of production, the longer is the period in which constant capital value remains fixed in it.

If a means of production which is not an instrument of labour strictly speaking, such as auxiliary substances, raw material, partly finished articles, etc., behaves with regard to value yield and hence manner of circulation of its value in the same way as the instruments of labour, then it is likewise a material depository, a form of existence, of fixed capital. This is the case with the above-mentioned improvements of the soil, which add to it chemical substances whose influence is distributed over several periods of production or years. Here a portion of the value continues to exist alongside the product, in its independent form or in the form of fixed capital, while another portion of the value has been delivered to the product and therefore circulates with it. In this case it is not only a portion of the value of the fixed capital which enters into the product, but also the use value, the substance, in which this portion of value exists.

Apart from the fundamental mistake — the mixing up of the categories of fixed and circulating capital with the categories of constant and variable capital — the confusion of the economists hitherto in the definitions of concepts is based first of all on the following points:

One turns certain properties materially inherent in instruments of labour into direct properties of fixed capital; for instance physical immobility, say, of a house. However it is always easy to prove in such case that other instruments of labour, which as such are likewise fixed capital, possess the opposite property; for instance physical mobility, say, of a ship.

Or one confuses the economic definiteness of form which arises from the circulation of value with an objective property; as if things which in themselves are not capital at all but rather become so only under definite social conditions could *in themselves* and in their very nature be capital in some definite form, fixed or circulating. We have seen (Buch I, Kap. V)ᵃ that the means of production in every labour process, regardless of the social conditions in which it takes place, are divided into instruments of labour and subjects of labour. But both of them become capital only under the capitalist mode of production, when they become "productive capital", as shown in the preceding part. Thus the distinction between instruments of labour and subject of labour, which is grounded on the nature of the labour process, is reflected in a new form: the distinction between fixed capital and circulating capital. It is only then that a thing which performs the function of an instrument of labour becomes fixed capital. If owing to its material properties it can function also in other capacities than that of instrument of labour, it may be fixed capital or not, depending on the specific function it performs. Cattle as beasts of toil are fixed capital; as beef cattle they are raw material which finally enters into circulation as a product; hence they are circulating, not fixed capital.

The mere fixation of a means of production for a considerable length of time in repeated labour processes, which however are connected, continuous, and therefore form a production period — i. e., the entire time of production required to finish a certain product — obliges the capitalist, just as fixed capital does, to make his advances for a longer or shorter term, but this does not make his capital fixed capital. Seeds for instance are not fixed capital, but only raw material which is held for about a year in the process of production. All capital is held in the process of production so long as it functions as productive capital, and so are therefore all elements of productive capital, whatever their material forms, their functions and the modes of circulation of their values. Whether this period of fixation lasts a long or

---

ᵃ English edition: Vol. I, Ch. VII (present edition, Vol. 35).

a short time — a matter depending on the kind of process of production involved or the useful effect aimed at — this does not effect the distinction between fixed and circulating capital. [20]

A part of the instruments of labour, which includes the general conditions of labour, is either localised as soon as it enters the process of production as an instrument of labour, i. e., is prepared for its productive function, such as for instance machinery, or is produced from the outset in its immovable, localised form, such as improvements of the soil, factory buildings, blast furnaces, canals, railways, etc. The constant attachment of the instrument of labour to the process of production in which it is to function is here also due to its physical mode of existence. On the other hand an instrument of labour may physically change continually from place to place, may move about, and nevertheless be constantly in the process of production; for instance a locomotive, a ship, beasts of burden, etc. Neither does immobility in the one case bestow upon it the character of fixed capital, nor does mobility in the other case deprive it of this character. But the fact that some instruments of labour are localised, attached to the soil by their roots, assigns to this portion of fixed capital a peculiar role in the economy of nations. They cannot be sent abroad, cannot circulate as commodities in the world market. Title to this fixed capital may change, it may be bought and sold, and to this extent may circulate ideally. These titles of ownership may even circulate in foreign markets, for instance in the form of stocks. But a change of the persons owning this class of fixed capital does not alter the relation of the immovable, materially fixed part of the national wealth to its movable part. [21]

The peculiar circulation of fixed capital results in a peculiar turnover. That part of the value which it loses in its bodily form by wear and tear circulates as a part of the value of the product. The product converts itself by means of its circulation from a commodity into money; hence the same applies to the value part of the instrument of labour circulated by the product, and this value drips down in the form of money from the process of circulation in proportion as this in-

[20] On account of the difficulty of determining what is fixed and what circulating capital, Herr Lorenz Stein thinks that this distinction is meant only to facilitate the treatment of the subject.

[21] End of Manuscript IV, beginning of Manuscript II.

strument of labour ceases to be a depository of value in the process of production. Its value thus acquires a double existence. One part of it remains attached to its use form or bodily form belonging in the process of production. The other part detaches itself from that form in the shape of money. In the performance of its function that part of the value of an instrument of labour which exists in its bodily form constantly decreases, while that which is transformed into money constantly increases until the instrument of labour is at last exhausted and its entire value, detached from its corpse, is converted into money. Here the peculiarity in the turnover of this element of productive capital becomes apparent. The transformation of its value into money keeps pace with the pupation into money of the commodity which is the carrier of its value. But its reconversion from the money form into a use form proceeds separately from the reconversion of the commodities into other elements of their production and is determined rather by its own period of reproduction, that is, by the time during which the instrument of labour wears out and must be replaced by another of the same kind. If a machine worth £10,000 lasts for, say, a period of ten years, then the period of turnover of the value originally advanced for it amounts to ten years. It need not be renewed and continues to function in its bodily form until this period has expired. In the meantime its value circulates piecemeal as a part of the value of the commodities whose continuous production it serves, and it is thus gradually transformed into money until finally at the end of ten years it entirely assumes the form of money and is reconverted from money into a machine, in other words, has completed its turnover. Until this time of reproduction arrives, its value is gradually accumulated, in the form of a money reserve fund to start with.

The remaining elements of productive capital consist partly of those elements of constant capital which exist as auxiliary and raw materials, partly of variable capital invested in labour power.

The analysis of the labour process and of the process of producing surplus value (Buch I, Kap. V)[a] showed that these different components behave quite differently as creators of products and as creators of values. The value of that part of constant capital which consists of auxiliary and raw materials — the same as of that part which consists of instruments of labour — re-appears in the value of the product as

---

[a] English edition: Vol. I, Ch. VII (present edition, Vol. 35).

only transferred value, while labour power adds an equivalent of its value to the product by means of the labour process, in other words, actually reproduces its value. Furthermore, one part of the auxiliary substances — fuel, lighting gas, etc.— is consumed in the process of labour without entering bodily into the product, while the other part of them enters bodily into the product and forms its material substance. But all these differences are immaterial so far as the circulation and therefore the mode of turnover is concerned. Since auxiliary and raw materials are entirely consumed in the creation of the product, they transfer their value entirely to the product. Hence this value is circulated in its entirety by the product, transforms itself into money and from money back into the elements of production of the commodity. Its turnover is not interrupted, as is that of fixed capital, but passes uninterruptedly through the entire circuit of its forms, so that these elements of productive capital are continually renewed *in natura*.

As for the variable component of productive capital, which is invested in labour power, be it noted that labour power is purchased for a definite period of time. As soon as the capitalist has bought it and embodied it in the process of production, it forms a component part of his capital, its variable component. Labour power acts daily during a period of time in which it adds to the product not only its own value for the whole day but also a surplus value in excess of it. We shall not consider this surplus value for the present. After labour power has been bought and it has performed its function, say for a week, its purchase must be constantly renewed within the customary intervals of time. The equivalent of its value, which the labour power adds to the product during its functioning and which is transformed into money in consequence of the circulation of the product, must continually be reconverted from money into labour power or continually pass through the complete circuit of its forms, that is, must be turned over, if the circuit of continuous production is not to be interrupted.

Hence that part of the value of the productive capital which has been advanced for labour power is entirely transferred to the product (we constantly leave the question of surplus value out of consideration here), passes with it through the two metamorphoses belonging in the sphere of circulation and always remains incorporated in the process of production by virtue of this continuous renewal. Hence, however different otherwise may be the relation between labour power, so far as the creation of value is concerned, and the component parts of constant capital which *do not constitute fixed* capital, this kind of turnover of its value labour power shares with them, in contradistinction to fixed capital. These components of the productive capital — the parts of its value invested in labour power and in means of production which do not constitute fixed capital — by reason of their common turnover characteristics confront the fixed capital as *circulating* or *fluid* capital.

We have already seen [a] that the money which the capitalist pays to the labourer for the use of his labour power is in fact only the general equivalent form of the means of subsistence required by the labourer. To this extent, the variable capital consists in substance of means of subsistence. But in this case, where we are discussing turnover, it is a question of form. The capitalist does not buy the labourer's means of subsistence but his labour power. And that which forms the variable part of his capital is not the labourer's means of subsistence but his labour power in action. What the capitalist consumes productively in the labour process is the labour power itself and not the labourer's means of subsistence. It is the labourer himself who converts the money received for his labour power into means of subsistence, in order to reconvert them into labour power, to keep alive, just as the capitalist for instance converts a part of the surplus value of the commodities he sells for money into means of subsistence for himself without thereby warranting the statement that the purchaser of his commodities pays him in means of subsistence. Even if the labourer is paid a part of his wages in means of subsistence, *in natura*, this nowadays amounts to a second transaction. He sells his labour power at a certain price, with the understanding that he shall receive a part of this price in means of subsistence. This changes merely the form of the payment, but not the fact that what he actually sells is his labour power. It is a second transaction, which does not take place between the labourer and the capitalist, but between the labourer as a buyer of commodities and the capitalist as a seller of commodities, while in the first transaction the labourer is a seller of a commodity (his labour power) and the capitalist its buyer. It is exactly the same as if a capitalist, on selling his commodity, say, a machine, to an iron works, has it replaced by some other commodity, say, iron. It is therefore not the labourer's means of subsistence which acquire the definite character of circulating capital as opposed to fixed capital. Nor is it his labour power. It is rather that part of the value of productive capital which

---

[a] K. Marx, *Capital*, Vol. I, Ch. VI (present edition, Vol. 35).

is invested in labour power and which, by virtue of the form of its turn-over, receives this character in common with some, and in contrast with other, component parts of the constant capital.

The value of the circulating capital — in labour power and means of production — is advanced only for the time during which the product is in process of production, in accordance with the scale of production determined by the volume of the fixed capital. This value enters entirely into the product, is therefore fully returned by its sale from the sphere of circulation, and can be advanced anew. The labour power and means of production, in which the circulating component of capital exists, are withdrawn from circulation to the extent required for the creation and sale of the finished product, but they must be continually replaced and renewed by purchasing them back, by reconverting them from the money form into the elements of production. They are withdrawn from the market in smaller quantities at a time than the elements of fixed capital, but they must be withdrawn again from it so much the more frequently and the advance of capital invested in them must be renewed at shorter intervals. This constant renewal is effected by the continuous conversion of the product which circulates their entire value. And finally, they pass through the entire circuit of metamorphoses, not only so far as their value is concerned but also their material form. They are perpetually reconverted from commodities into the elements of production of the same commodities.

Together with its own value, labour power always adds to the product surplus value, the embodiment of unpaid labour. This is continuously circulated by the finished product and converted into money just as are other elements of its value. But here, where we are primarily concerned with the turnover of capital value, and not with that of the surplus value occurring at the same time, we dismiss the latter for the present.

From the foregoing one may conclude the following:

1. The definiteness of form of fixed and circulating capital arises merely from the different turnovers of the capital value, functioning in the process of production, or of the *productive capital*. This difference in turnover arises in its turn from the different manner in which the various components of productive capital transfer their value to the product; it is not due to the different parts played by these components in the generation of product value, nor to their characteristic behaviour in the process of self-expansion. Finally the difference in the delivery of value to the product — and therefore the different

manner in which this value is circulated by the product and is renewed in its original bodily form through the metamorphoses of the product — arises from the difference of the material shapes in which the productive capital exists, one portion of it being entirely consumed during the creation of an individual product and the other being used up only gradually. Hence it is only the productive capital which can be divided into fixed and circulating capital. But this antithesis does not apply to the other two modes of existence of industrial capital, that is to say, commodity capital and money capital, nor does it exist as an antithesis of these two modes to productive capital. It exists only *for productive capital and within its sphere*. No matter how much money capital and commodity capital may function as capital and no matter how fluently they may circulate, they cannot become circulating capital as distinct from fixed capital until they are transformed into circulating components of productive capital. But because these two forms of capital dwell in the sphere of circulation, political economy, as we shall see, has been misled since the time of Adam Smith into lumping them together with the circulating part of productive capital and assigning them to the category of circulating capital. They are indeed circulation capital in contrast to productive capital, but they are not circulating capital in contrast to fixed capital.

2. The turnover of the fixed component part of capital, and therefore also the time of turnover necessary for it, comprises several turnovers of the circulating constituents of capital. In the time during which the fixed capital turns over once, the circulating capital turns over several times. One of the component parts of the value of the productive capital acquires the definiteness of form of fixed capital only in case the means of production in which it exists is not wholly worn out in the time required for the fabrication of the product and its expulsion from the process of production as a commodity. One part of its value must remain tied up in the form of the still preserved old use form, while the other part is circulated by the finished product, and this circulation on the contrary simultaneously circulates the entire value of the fluid component parts of the capital.

3. The value part of the productive capital, the part invested in fixed capital, is advanced in one lump sum for the entire period of employment of that part of the means of production of which the fixed capital consists. Hence this value is thrown into the circulation by the capitalist all at one time. But it is withdrawn again from the circula-

tion only piecemeal and gradually by realising the parts of value which the fixed capital adds piecemeal to the commodities. On the other hand the means of production themselves, in which a component part of the productive capital becomes fixed, are withdrawn from the circulation all at one time to be embodied in the process of production for the entire period in which they function. But they do not require for this period any replacement by new samples of the same kind, do not require reproduction. They continue for a longer or shorter period to contribute to the creation of the commodities thrown into circulation without withdrawing from circulation the elements of their own renewal. Hence they do not require from the capitalist a renewal of his advance during this period. Finally the capital value invested in fixed capital does not pass bodily through the circuit of its forms, during the functioning period of the means of production in which this capital value exists, but only as concerns its value, and even this it does only in parts and gradually. In other words, a portion of its value is continually circulated and converted into money as a part of the value of the commodities, without being reconverted from money into its original bodily form. This reconversion of money into the bodily form of the means of production does not take place until the end of its functioning period, when the means of production has been completely consumed.

4. The elements of circulating capital are as permanently fixed in the process of production — if it is to be uninterrupted — as the elements of fixed capital. But the elements of circulating capital thus fixed are continually renewed *in natura* (the means of production by new products of the same kind, labour power by constantly renewed purchases) while in the case of the elements of fixed capital neither they themselves are renewed nor need their purchases be renewed so long as they continue to exist. There are always raw and auxiliary materials in the process of production, but always new products of the same kind, after the old elements have been consumed in the creation of the finished product. Labour power likewise always exists in the process of production, but only by means of ever new purchases, frequently involving changes of persons. But the same identical buildings, machines, etc., continue to function, during repeated turnovers of the circulating capital, in the same repeated processes of production.

II. COMPONENTS, REPLACEMENT, REPAIR,
AND ACCUMULATION OF FIXED CAPITAL

In any investment of capital the separate elements of the fixed capital have different lifetimes, and therefore different turnover times. In a railway, for instance, the rails, sleepers, earthworks, terminals, bridges, tunnels, locomotives, and carriages have different functional periods and times of reproduction, hence the capital advanced for them has different times of turnover. For a great number of years, buildings, platforms, water tanks, viaducts, tunnels, cuttings, dams, in short everything called WORKS OF ART in the English railway industry do not require any renewal. The things which wear out most are the tracks and the ROLLING STOCK. [a]

Originally in the construction of modern railways it was the prevailing opinion, nursed by the most prominent practical engineers, that a railway would last a century and that the wear and tear of the rails was so imperceptible that it could be ignored for all financial and other practical purposes; 100 to 150 years was supposed to be the life of good rails. But it was soon found that the life of a rail, which naturally depends on the speed of the locomotives, the weight and number of trains, the diameter of the rails, and on a multitude of other attendant circumstances, did not exceed an average of 20 years. In some railway terminals, great traffic centres, the rails even wear out every year. About 1867 began the introduction of steel rails, which cost about twice as much as iron rails but which last more than twice as long. The lifetime of wooden sleepers was from 12 to 15 years. It was also ascertained with regard to the rolling stock that freight cars wear out much faster than passenger cars. The life of a locomotive was estimated in 1867 to be about 10 to 12 years.

The wear and tear is first of all a result of use. As a rule "the wear of the rails is proportionate to the number of trains" (R. C., No. 17645). [22] With increased speed the wear and tear of a railway increased in a higher ratio than the square of the speed; that is to say, if you doubled the speed of the engine, you more than quadrupled the cost of wear and tear of the road (R. C., No 17046).

---

[22] The quotations marked R. C. are from: *Royal Commission on Railways. Minutes of Evidence taken before the Commissioners. Presented to both Houses of Parliament*, London, 1867.—The questions and answers are numbered and the numbers given here.

---

[a] In the original, this English term is given in parentheses after its German equivalent.

Wear and tear is furthermore caused by the action of natural forces. For instance sleepers suffer not only from actual wear but also from rot.

"The cost of maintaining the road does not depend so much upon the wear and tear of the traffic passing over it, as upon the quality of wood, iron, bricks and mortars exposed to the atmosphere. A month of severe winter would do more damage to the road of a railway than a year's traffic" (R. P. Williams, "On the Maintenance of Permanent Way." Paper read at the Institution of Civil Engineers, Autumn, 1867 [29]).

Finally, here as everywhere else in modern industry, the moral depreciation plays a role. After the lapse of ten years, one can generally buy the same number of cars and locomotives for £30,000 that would previously have cost £40,000. Depreciation in the rolling stock must be set at 25 per cent of the market price even when there is no depreciation whatever in its use value (Lardner, *Railway Economy*, [p. 120]).

"Tube bridges will not be replaced in their present form."

(Because now there are better forms for such bridges.)

"Ordinary repairs, taking away gradually, and replacing are not practicable" (W. B. Adams, *Roads and Rails*, London, 1862, [p. 136]). [30]

The instruments of labour are largely modified all the time by the progress of industry. Hence they are not replaced in their original, but in their modified form. On the one hand the mass of the fixed capital invested in a certain bodily form and endowed in that form with a certain average life constitutes one reason for the only gradual pace of the introduction of new machinery, etc., and therefore an obstacle to the rapid general introduction of improved instruments of labour. On the other hand competition compels the replacement of the old instruments of labour by new ones before the expiration of their natural life, especially when decisive changes occur. Such premature renewals of factory equipment on a rather large social scale are mainly enforced by catastrophes or crises.

By wear and tear (moral depreciation excepted) is meant that part of value which the fixed capital, on being used, gradually transmits to the product, in proportion to its average loss of use value.

This wear and tear takes place partly in such a way that the fixed capital has a certain average durability. It is advanced for this entire period in one sum. After the termination of this period it must be totally replaced. So far as living instruments of labour are concerned, for instance horses, their reproduction is timed by nature itself. Their average lifetime as instruments of labour is determined by laws of nature. As soon as this term has expired the worn-out items must be replaced by new ones. A horse cannot be raplaced piecemeal; it must be replaced by another horse.

Other elements of fixed capital permit of a periodical or partial renewal. In this instance partial or periodical replacement must be distinguished from gradual extension of the business.

The fixed capital consists in part of homogeneous constituents which do not however last the same length of time but are renewed piecemeal at various intervals. This is true for instance of the rails in railway stations, which must be replaced more often than those of the remainder of the trackage. It also applies to the sleepers, which on the Belgian railways had to be renewed in the forties at the rate of 8% annually, according to Lardner, so that all the sleepers were renewed in the course of $12^1/_2$ years. Hence we have here the following situation: a certain sum is advanced for a certain kind of fixed capital for say ten years. This expenditure is made at one time. But a definite part of this fixed capital, the value of which has entered into the value of the product and been converted with it into money, is replaced *in natura* every year, while the remainder continues to exist in its original bodily form. It is this advance in one sum and the only partial reproduction in bodily form which distinguish this capital, as fixed, from circulating capital.

Other pieces of the fixed capital consist of heterogeneous components, which wear out in unequal periods of time and must so be replaced. This applies particularly to machines. What we have just said concerning the different durabilities of different constituent parts of a fixed capital applies in this case to the durability of different component parts of any machine figuring as a piece of this fixed capital.

With regard to the gradual extension of the business in the course of the partial renewal, we make the following remarks. Although, as we have seen, the fixed capital continues to perform its functions in the process of production *in natura*, a part of its value, proportionate to the average wear and tear, has circulated with the product, has been converted into money, and forms an element in the money reserve fund intended for the replacement of the capital pending its reproduction *in natura*. This part of the value of the fixed capital transformed into money may serve to extend the business or to make improvements in the machinery which will increase the efficiency of the latter. Thus reproduction takes place in larger or smaller periods of time, and this is, from the standpoint of society, reproduction on an enlarged scale—extensive if the field of production is extended; intensive if the means of production is made more effective. This reproduction on an extended scale does not result from accumulation—transformation of surplus value into capital—but from the reconversion of the value which has branched off, detached itself in the form of money from the body of the fixed capital into new additional or at least more effective fixed capital of the same kind. Of course it depends partly on the specific nature of the business, to what extent and in what proportions it is capable of such gradual addition, hence also in what amount a reserve fund must be collected to be reinvested in this way, and what period of time this requires. To what extent furthermore improvements in the details of existing machinery can be made, depends of course on the nature of these improvements and the construction of the machine itself. How well this point is considered at the very outset in the construction of railways is shown by Adams:

"The whole structure should be set out on the principle which governs the bee-hive—capacity for indefinite extension. Any fixed and decided symmetrical structure is to be deprecated, as needing subsequent pulling down in case of enlargement" (p. 123).

This depends largely on the available space. In the case of some buildings additional storeys may be built; in the case of others lateral extension, hence more land, is required. Within capitalist production there is on the one side much waste of material, on the other much impracticable lateral extension of this sort (partly to the injury of the labour power) in the gradual expansion of the business, because nothing is undertaken according to a social plan, but everything depends on the infinitely different conditions, means, etc., with which the individual capitalist operates. This results in a great waste of the productive forces.

This piecemeal re-investment of the money reserve fund (i. e., of that part of the fixed capital which has been reconverted into money) is easiest in agriculture. A field of production of a given area is here capable of the greatest possible gradual absorption of capital. The same applies to where there is natural reproduction, as in cattle breeding.

Fixed capital entails special maintenance costs. A part of this maintenance is provided by the labour process itself; fixed capital spoils, if it is not employed in the labour process (see Buch I, Kap. VI, S. 196 and Kap. XIII, S. 423,[a] on wear and tear of machinery when not in use). The English law therefore explicitly treats it as WASTE, [b] if rented lands are not cultivated according to the custom of the land (W. A. Holdsworth, Barrister at Law, *The Law of Landlord and Tenant*, London, 1857, p. 96).

This maintenance resulting from use in the labour process is a free gift inherent in the nature of living labour. Moreover the preservative power of labour is of a two-fold character. On the one hand it preserves the value of the materials of labour by transferring it to the product, on the other hand it preserves the value of the instruments of labour without transferring this value to the product, by preserving their use value through their activity in the process of production.

The fixed capital however requires also a positive expenditure of labour for its maintenance in good repair. The machinery must be cleaned from time to time. It is a question here of additional labour without which the machinery becomes useless, of merely warding off the noxious influences of the elements, which are inseparable from the process of production; hence it is a question of keeping the machinery literally in working order. It goes without saying that the normal durability of fixed capital is calculated on the supposition that all the conditions under which it can perform its functions normally during that time are fulfilled, just as we assume, in placing a man's life at 30 years on the average, that he will wash himself. It is here not a question of replacing the labour contained in the machine, but of constant additional labour made necessary by its use. It is not a question of labour performed by the machine, but of labour spent on it, of labour in which it is not an agent of production but raw material. The capital expended for this labour must be classed as circulating capital, although it does not enter into the labour process proper to which the product owes its existence. This labour must be continually expended in production, hence its value must be continually replaced by that of the product. The capital invested in it belongs in that part of circulating capital which has to cover the unproductive costs and is to be distributed over the produced values according to an annual average calculation. We have seen[c] that in industry proper this labour of

[a] English edition: Vol. I, chapters VIII and XV.- [b] In the original, this English word is given in parentheses after its German equivalent.- [c] K. Marx, *Capital*, Vol. I, Ch. XV, 4 (present edition, Vol. 35).

cleaning is performed by the working men gratis, during the rest periods, and for that very reason often also during the process of production itself, and most accidents can be traced to this source. This labour does not figure in the price of the product. As far as that goes the consumer receives it gratis. On the other hand the capitalist thus does not pay the maintenance costs of his machine. The labourer pays *in persona*, and this is one of the mysteries of the self-preservation of capital, which in point of fact constitute a legal claim by the labourer on the machinery, on the strength of which he is a co-owner of the machine even from the standpoint of bourgeois law. [31] However, in various branches of production, in which the machinery must be removed from the process of production for the purpose of cleaning and where therefore the cleaning cannot be performed inbetween, as for instance in the case of locomotives, this maintenance work counts as current expenses and is therefore an element of circulating capital. For instance a goods engine should not run more than 3 days without being kept one day in the shed. If you attempt to wash out the boiler before it has cooled down that is very injurious (R. C., No. 17823).

The actual repairs or patchwork require expenditures of capital and labour which are not contained in the originally advanced capital and cannot therefore be replaced and covered, at least not always, by the gradual replacement of the value of the fixed capital. For instance if the value of the fixed capital = £10,000 and its total life = 10 years, then these £10,000, having been entirely converted into money after the lapse of ten years, will replace only the value of the capital originally invested, but they do not replace the capital, or labour, added in the meantime for repairs. This is an additional component part of the value, which is not advanced all at one time but whenever a need for it arises, and the various times for advancing it are in the very nature of things accidental. All fixed capital demands such subsequent, dosed out, additional outlay of capital for instruments of labour and labour power.

The damage which separate parts of the machinery, etc., may incur is naturally accidental and so are therefore the repairs involved. Nevertheless two kinds of repairs are to be distinguished in the general mass, which are of a more or less fixed character and fall within various periods of the life of fixed capital. These are the ailments of childhood and the far more numerous ailments of the post-middle durability period. A machine for instance may be commissioned in ever so perfect a condition, still actual use will reveal shortcomings which must be remedied by subsequent labour. On the other hand the more a machine passes beyond the mid-durability point, the more therefore the normal wear and tear has accumulated and the more the material of which it is made has been worn out and become decrepit, the more numerous and considerable will be the repairs required to keep it going for the remainder of its average durability. It is the same with an old man, who incurs more medical expenses to keep from dying prematurely than a young and strong man. So in spite of its accidental character repair work is unevenly distributed over the various periods of life of fixed capital.

From the foregoing and from the generally accidental character of repair work on machines it follows:

In one respect the actual expenditure of labour power and instruments of labour on repairs is accidental, like the circumstances which necessitate these repairs; the amount of the repairs needed is unevenly distributed over the different periods of fixed capital's life. In other respects it is taken for granted in estimating the average life of fixed capital that it is constantly kept in good working order, partly by cleaning (including the cleaning of the premises), partly by repairs as often as required. The transfer of value through wear and tear of fixed capital is calculated on its average life, but this average life itself is based on the assumption that the additional capital required for maintenance purposes is continually advanced.

But then it is also evident that the value added by this extra expenditure of capital and labour cannot enter into the price of the commodities concerned at the same time as it is incurred. For example, a cotton spinner cannot sell his yarn dearer this week than last, because one of his wheels broke or a belt tore this week. The general costs of spinning have not been changed in any way by this accident in some individual factory. Here, as in all determinations of value, the average decides. Experience shows the average occurrence of such accidents and the average volume of the maintenance and repair work necessary during the average life of the fixed capital invested in a given branch of business. This average expense is distributed over the average life and added to the price of the product in corresponding aliquot parts; hence it is replaced by means of its sale.

The additional capital which is thus replaced belongs to the circulating capital, although the manner of its expenditure is irregular. As it is of paramount importance to remedy every damage to machinery immediately, every comparatively large factory employs in addition to the regular factory force special personnel — engineers, carpenters, mechanics, lock-smiths, etc. Their wages are a part of the variable capital and the value of their labour is distributed over the product. On the other hand the required expenses for means of production are calculated on the basis of the above-mentioned average, according to which they form continually a part of the value of the product, although they are actually advanced in irregular periods and therefore enter into the product or the fixed capital in irregular periods. This capital, expended in repairs properly so called, is in many respects a capital *sui generis*, which can be classed neither as circulating nor as fixed capital, but belongs with greater justification to the former, since it figures among the running expenses.

The manner of bookkeeping does not of course change in any way the actual state of affairs booked. But it is important to note that customarily many lines of business figure the costs of repairs together with the actual wear and tear of the fixed capital in the following manner: Let the advanced fixed capital be £10,000 and its durability 15 years. The annual wear and tear is then £$666^2/_3$. But the depreciation is calculated on a durability of only ten years; in other words, £1,000 are added annually to the price of the produced commodities for wear and tear of the fixed capital, instead of £$666^2/_3$. Thus £$333^1/_3$ are reserved for repairs, etc. (The figures 10 and 15 are chosen only by way of illustration.) This amount is spent on an average for repairs, so that the fixed capital may last 15 years. Such a calculation naturally does not prevent the fixed capital and the additional capital spent on repairs from belonging to different categories. On the strength of this mode of calculation it was assumed for instance that the lowest cost estimate for the maintenance and replacement of steamships was 15% annually, the time of reproduction being therefore $6^2/_3$ years. In the sixties, the English government indemnified the Peninsular and Oriental Co. at the annual rate of 16%, corresponding to a reproduction time of $6^1/_4$ years. On railways the average life of a locomotive is 10 years, but the depreciation, counting in repairs, is taken as $12^1/_2$%, which brings down its durability to 8 years. In the case of passenger and goods cars, the estimate is 9%, or a durability of $11^1/_9$ years.

Legislation has everywhere drawn a distinction, in leases of houses and other objects which represent fixed capital to their owners and are leased as such, between normal depreciation which is the result of time, the action of the elements, and normal wear, and between those occasional repairs which are required from time to time for maintenance during the normal life of the house and during its normal use. As a rule, the former are borne by the owner, the latter by the tenant. Repairs are further divided into ordinary and substantial ones. The last-named are partly a renewal of the fixed capital in its bodily form, and they fall likewise on the shoulders of the owner, unless the lease explicitly states the contrary. Take for instance the English law:

"A tenant from year to year [...] is not bound to do more than keep the premises wind and watertight, when that can be done without 'substantial' repairs; and generally to do repairs coming fairly under the head 'ordinary'. Even with respect to those parts of the premises which are the subject of 'ordinary' repairs, regard must be had to their age and general state, and condition, when he took possession, for he is not bound to replace old and worn-out materials with new ones, nor to make good the inevitable depreciation resulting from time and ordinary wear and tear" (Holdsworth, *Law of Landlord and Tenant*, pp. 90-91).

Entirely different from the replacement of wear and tear and from the work of maintenance and repair is *insurance*, which relates to destruction caused by extraordinary phenomena of nature, fire, flood, etc. This must be made good out of the surplus value and is a deduction from it. Or, considered from the point of view of society as a whole, there must be continuous overproduction, that is, production on a larger scale than is necessary for the simple replacement and reproduction of the existing wealth, quite apart from the increase in population, so as to be in possession of the means of production required to compensate for the extraordinary destruction caused by accidents and natural forces.

In point of fact only the smallest part of the capital needed for replacement consists of the money reserve fund. The most substantial part consists in the extension of the scale of production itself, which partly is actual expansion and partly belongs to the normal volume of production in those branches of industry which produce the fixed capital. For instance a machine factory must arrange things so that the factories of its customers can annually be extended and that a number of them will always stand in need of total or partial reproduction.

On determining the wear and tear as well as the costs of repairs, according to the social average, great disparity necessarily appears, even in the case of capital investments of equal size, operating otherwise under equal conditions and in the same branch of production. In practice a machine, etc., lasts with one capitalist longer than the average period, while with another it does not last so long. With the one the costs of repairs are above, with the other below average, etc. But the addition to the price of the commodities resulting from wear and tear and from costs of repairs is the same and is determined by the average. The one therefore gets more out of this additional price than he really added, the other less. The circumstance, as well as all others which result in different gains for different capitalists in the same line of business with the same degree of exploitation of labour power, tends to enhance the difficulty of understanding the true nature of surplus value.

The boundary-line between repairs proper and replacement, between costs of maintenance and costs of renewal, is somewhat fluid. Hence the eternal dispute, for instance on the railways, as to whether certain expenses are for repairs or for replacement, whether they must be defrayed from current expenditures or from the original stock. A transfer of expenses for repairs to capital account instead of revenue account is the well-known method by which railway directors artificially inflate their dividends. However, here too experience has already furnished the most important bases for estimation. The subsequent labour required during the early life of a railway for example

"ought not to be denominated repairs, but should be considered as an essential part of the construction of the railway, and in the financial accounts should be debited to capital, [...] not being expenses due to wear and tear, or to the legitimate operation of the traffic, but to the original and inevitable incompleteness of the construction of the line" (Lardner, loc. cit., p. 40).

"The only sound way is to charge each year's revenue with the depreciation necessarily suffered to earn the revenue, whether the amount is actually spent or not" (Captain Fitzmaurice, "Committee of Inquiry on Caledonian Railway," published in *Money Market Review*, 1868).[32]

The separation of the replacement and maintenance of fixed capital becomes practically impossible and purposeless in agriculture, at least when not operated by steam.

"Wherever there is a complete, though not excessive, supply of implements" (of agricultural and other implements and farm appliances of every description) "it is the custom to estimate the annual wear and tear and maintenance of the implements, according to the different existing conditions, at a general average of 15 to 25 per cent of the original stock" (Kirchhof, *Handbuch der landwirthschaftlichen Betriebslehre*, Dessau, 1852, p. 137).[33]

In the case of the rolling stock of a railway, repairs and replacement cannot be separated at all.

"We maintain our stock by number. Whatever number of engines we have we maintain that. If one is destroyed by age, and it is better to build a new one, we build it at the expense of revenue, of course, taking credit for the materials of the old one as far as they go.... There is a great deal left; there are the wheels, the axles, the boilers, and in fact a great deal of the old engine is left" (D. Gooch, Chairman of Great Western Railway Co., R. C., Nos. 17327, 17329). "Repairing means renewing; I do not believe in the word replacement...; once a railway company has bought a vehicle or an engine, it ought to be repaired, and in that way admit of going on for ever" (No. 17784). "We calculate $8^1/_2$ d. per English train mile for the cost of the locomotives. The engines are maintained for ever out of this $8^1/_2$ d. We rebuild our engines. If you purchase an engine entirely it would be spending more money than is necessary ... yet there is always a pair of wheels or an axle or some portion of the engine which comes in, and hence it cheapens the cost of producing a practically new engine" (No. 17790). "I am at this moment turning out a new engine every week, or practically a new engine, for it has a new boiler, cylinder, or framing" (No. 17823. Archibald Sturrock, LOCOMOTIVE SUPERINTENDENT OF GREAT NORTHERN RAILWAY, IN R. C., 1867).

The same with coaches:

"In the course of time the stock of engines and vehicles is continually repaired. New wheels are put on at one time, and a new body at another. The different moving parts most subject to wear are gradually renewed; and the engines and vehicles may be conceived even to be subject to such a succession of repairs, that in many of them not a vestige of the original materials remains.... Even in this case, however, the old materials of coaches or engines are more or less worked up into other vehicles or engines, and never totally disappear from the road. The movable capital therefore may be considered to be in a state of continual reproduction; and that which, in the case of the permanent way, must take place altogether at a future epoch, when the entire road will have to be relaid, takes place in the rolling stock gradually from year to year. Its existence is perennial, and it is in a constant state of rejuvenescence" (Lardner, op. cit, pp. 115-16).

This process, which Lardner here describes relative to a railway, does not fit the case of an individual factory, but may well serve as an illustration of continuous, partial reproduction of fixed capital intermingled with repairs within an entire branch of industry or even within the aggregate production considered on a social scale.

Here is proof of the lengths to which adroit boards of directors may go in manipulating the terms repairs and replacement for the purpose of extracting dividends. According to the above-quoted paper read by R. P. Williams, various English railway companies wrote off the following sums from the revenue account, as averages over a number of years, for repairs and maintenance of the permanent way and buildings (per English mile of track annually).

London & North Western	£370
Midland	£225
London & South Western	£257
Great Northern	£360

Lancashire & Yorkshire £377
South Eastern £263
Brighton £266
Manchester & Sheffield . . . .£200 [34]

These differences arise only to a very minor degree from differences in the actual expenses; they are due almost exclusively to different methods of calculation, according to whether items of expense are debited to the capital or the revenue account. Williams says in so many words:

"A smaller charge is adopted because its adoption is necessary for a good dividend, and the larger charge is put forward because it can be supported by reason of revenue being superior." [29]

In certain cases the wear and tear, and therefore its replacement, is practically infinitesimal so that nothing but costs of repairs have to be charged. Lardner's statements below relative to WORKS OF ART in the railway apply in general to all such durable structures as canals, docks, iron and stone bridges, etc.

"That wear and tear which, being due to the slow operation of time acting upon the more solid structures, produces an effect altogether insensible when observed through short periods, but which, after a long interval of time, such, for example, as centuries, must necessitate the reconstruction of some or all even of the most solid structures. These changes may not unaptly be assimilated to the periodical and secular inequalities which take place in the movements of the great bodies of the universe. The operation of time upon the more massive works of art upon the railway, such as the bridges, tunnels, viaducts, etc., afford examples of what may be called the secular wear and tear. The more rapid and visible deterioration, which is made good by repairs or reconstruction effected at shorter intervals, is analogous to the periodic inequalities. In the annual repairs is included the casual damage which the exterior of the more solid and durable works may from time to time sustain; but, independently of these repairs, age produces its effects even on these structures, and an epoch must arrive, however remote it be, at which they would be reduced to a state which will necessitate their reconstruction. For financial and economical purposes such an epoch is perhaps too remote to render it necessary to bring it into practical calculation" (Lardner, loc. cit., pp. 38, 39).

This applies to all similar structures of secular duration, in which cases therefore the capital advanced need not be gradually replaced commensurate with their wear and tear, but only the annual average costs of maintenance and repair need be transferred to the prices of the product.

Although, as we have seen, a greater part of the money returning for the replacement of the wear and tear of the fixed capital is annually, or even in shorter intervals, reconverted into its bodily form, nevertheless every single capitalist requires a sinking fund for that part of his fixed capital which falls due for reproduction only after a lapse of years but must then be entirely replaced. A considerable component part of the fixed capital precludes piecemeal reproduction because of its peculiar properties. Besides, in cases where the reproduction takes place piecemeal in such a way that at short intervals new stock is added to the depreciated old stock, a previous accumulation of money of a greater or smaller amount, depending on the specific character of the branch of production is necessary before the replacement can be effected. Not just any sum of money will suffice for this purpose; a definite amount is needed.

If we study this question on the assumption of simple circulation of money, without regard to the credit system, of which we shall treat later,[35] then the mechanism of this movement is as follows: It was shown in the first book (Kap. III, 3a)[a] that the proportion in which the aggregate mass of money is distributed over a hoard and means of circulation varies steadily, if one part of the money available in society constantly lies fallow as a hoard, while another performs the functions of a medium of circulation or of an immediate reserve fund of the directly circulating money. Now in our case money that must be accumulated as a hoard in the hands of a relatively big capitalist in rather large amounts is thrown all at once into circulation on the purchase of the fixed capital. It then divides again in society into medium of circulation and hoard. By means of the sinking fund, in which the value of the fixed capital flows back to its starting-point in proportion to its wear and tear, a part of the circulating money again forms a hoard, for a longer or shorter period, in the hands of the same capitalist whose hoard had, upon the purchase of the fixed capital, been transformed into a medium of circulation and passed away from him. It is a continually changing distribution of the hoard which exists in society and alternately functions as a medium of circulation and then is separated again, as a hoard, from the mass of the circulating money. With the development of the credit system, which necessarily runs parallel with the development of modern industry and capitalist production, this money no longer serves as a hoard but as capital; however not in the hands of its owner but of other capitalists at whose disposal it has been placed.

---

[a] English edition: Ch. III, 3a (present edition, Vol. 35).

Chapter IX

THE AGGREGATE TURNOVER OF ADVANCED CAPITAL. CYCLES OF TURNOVER

We have seen that the fixed and circulating component parts of productive capital are turned over in various ways and at various periods, also that the different constituents of the fixed capital of a business have different periods of turnover, depending on their different durabilities and therefore on their different times of reproduction. (On the real or apparent difference in the turnover of different constituents of circulating capital in the same business, see the close of this chapter, under 6.)

1) The aggregate turnover of an advanced capital is the average turnover of its various constituent parts; the mode of its calculation is given later. Inasmuch as it is merely a question of different periods of time, nothing is easier than to compute their average. But

2) we have here not alone quantitative but also qualitative difference.

The circulating capital entering into the process of production transfers its entire value to the product and must therefore be continually replaced *in natura* by the sale of the product, if the process of production is to proceed without interruption. The fixed capital entering into the process of production transfers only a part of its value (the wear and tear) to the product and despite this wear and tear continues functioning in the process of production. Therefore it need not be replaced *in natura* until the lapse of intervals of various duration, at any rate not as frequently as the circulating capital. This necessity of replacement, the reproduction term, is not only quantitatively different for the various constituent parts of fixed capital, but, as we have seen, a part of the perennial fixed capital, that which lasts longer, may be replaced annually or at shorter intervals and added *in natura* to the old fixed capital. In the case of fixed capital of different properties the replacement can take place only all at once at the end of its period of durability.

It is therefore necessary to reduce the specific turnovers of the various parts of fixed capital to a homogeneous form of turnover, so that they will remain different only quantitatively, namely, according to duration of turnover.

This qualitative identity does not come about if we take as our starting-point P ... P, the form of the continuous process of production. For definite elements of P must be constantly replaced *in natura* while others need not. However the form M ... M′ undoubtedly yields this identity of turnover. Take for instance a machine worth £10,000, which lasts ten years of which $^1/_{10}$ = £1,000 is annually reconverted into money. These £1,000 have been converted in the course of one year from money capital into productive capital and commodity capital, and then reconverted from this into money capital. They have returned to their original form, the money form, just like the circulating capital, if we study the latter in this form, and it is immaterial here whether this money capital of £1,000 is once more converted at the end of the year into the bodily form of a machine or not. In calculating the aggregate turnover of the advanced productive capital we therefore fix all its elements in the money form, so that the return to that form concludes the turnover. We assume that value is always advanced in money, even in the continuous process of production, where this money form of value is only that of money of account. Thus we can compute the average.

3) It follows that even if by far the greater part of the advanced productive capital consists of fixed capital whose period of reproduction, hence also of turnover, comprises a cycle of many years, the capital value turned over during the year may, on account of the repeated turnovers of the circulating capital within the same year, be larger than the aggregate value of the advanced capital.

Suppose the fixed capital = £80,000 and its period of reproduction = 10 years, so that £8,000 of it annually return to their money form, or it completes $^1/_{10}$ of its turnover. Suppose further the circulating capital = £20,000, and its turnover is completed five times per year. The total capital would then be £100,000. The turned-over fixed capital = £8,000, the turned-over circulating capital = 5 x £20,000 = £100,000. Then the capital turned over during one year = £108,000, or £8,000 more than the advanced capital. $1 + {}^2/_{25}$ of the capital have been turned over.

4) Therefore the *turnover time of the value* of the advanced capital differs from its actual time of reproduction or from the actual time of turnover of its component parts. Take for instance a capital of £4,000 and let it turn over, say, five times a year. The turned-over capital is

then 5 x £4,000 = £20,000. But what returns at the end of each turn-over to be advanced anew is the originally advanced capital of £4,000. Its magnitude is not changed by the number of turnover periods, during which it performs anew its functions as capital. (Apart from surplus value.)

In the illustration under No. 3, then, the sums assumedly returned into the hands of the capitalist at the end of one year are (a) a sum of values amounting to £20,000 which he invests again in the circulat-ing constituents of the capital, and (b) a sum of £8,000 which has been set free by wear and tear from the value of the advanced fixed capital; simultaneously this same fixed capital remains in the process of production, but with the reduced value of £72,000 instead of £80,000. The process of production therefore would have to be conti-nued for nine years more, before the advanced fixed capital outlived its term and ceased to function as a creator of products and values, so that it would have to be replaced. The advanced capital value, then, has to pass through a cycle of turnovers, in the present case a cycle of ten annual ones, and this cycle is determined by the lifetime, hence the reproduction or turnover time, of the applied fixed capital.

As the magnitude of the value and the durability of the applied fixed capital develop with the development of the capitalist mode of production, the lifetime of industry and of industrial capital lengthens in each particular field of investment to a period of many years, say of ten years on an average. Whereas the development of fixed capital extends this life on the one hand it is shortened on the other by the continuous revolution in the means of production, which likewise in-cessantly gains momentum with the development of the capitalist mode of production. This involves a change in the means of produc-tion and the necessity of their constant replacement, on account of moral depreciation, long before they expire physically. One may as-sume that in the essential branches of large-scale industry this life cycle now averages ten years. However we are not concerned here with the exact figure. This much is evident: the cycle of interconnected turn-overs embracing a number of years, in which capital is held fast by its fixed constituent part, furnishes a material basis for the periodic crises. During this cycle business undergoes successive periods of de-pression, medium activity, precipitancy, crisis. True, periods in which capital is invested differ greatly and far from coincide in time.

But a crisis always forms the starting-point of large new investments. Therefore, from the point of view of society as a whole, more or less, a new material basis for the next turnover cycle.[22a)]

5) On the way to calculate the turnovers, an American economist states [37]:

"In some trades the whole capital embarked is turned or circulated several times within the year. In others a part is turned oftener than once a year, another part less often. It is the average period which his entire capital takes in passing through his hands, or making one revolution, from which a capitalist must calculate his profits. Suppose, for example, that a person engaged in a particular business has one half of his capital invested in buildings and machinery, so as to be turned only once in ten years; that one-fourth more, the cost of his tools, etc., is turned once in two years; and the remaining fourth, employed in paying wages and purchasing material, is turned twice in one year. Say that his entire capital is $50,000. Then his annual expenditure will be:

$$\frac{50,000}{2} = \$25,000: 10 = \$\ 2,500$$

$$\frac{50,000}{4} = \quad 12,500: \ 2 = \quad 6,250$$

$$\frac{50,000}{4} = \quad 12,500 \times 2 = \ 25,000$$

$$\overline{\hspace{6cm}}$$

$$\$33,750$$

... the mean term in which his capital is turned being sixteen months [38] ....

"Take another case, ... say that one-fourth of the entire capital circulates in ten years, one-fourth in one year, and one half twice in the year. Then the annual expenditure will be,

$$\$12,500: 10 = \$\ 1,250$$
$$12,500 \quad\ = \quad 12,500$$
$$25,000 \times 2 = \quad 50,000$$

$$\overline{\hspace{6cm}}$$

Turned over in 1 year $63,750 "

(Scrope, *Pol. Econ.*, edit. Alonzo Potter, New York, 1841, pp. 142, 143).

6) Real and apparent differences in the turnover of the various parts of capital.

The same Scrope says in the same passage:

"The capital laid out by a manufacturer, farmer, or tradesman in the payment of his labourer's wages, circulates most rapidly, being turned perhaps once a week (if his men are paid weekly), by the weekly receipts on his bills or sales. That invested in his materials and stock in hand circulates less quickly, being turned perhaps twice, per-

[22a)] "Urban production is bound to a cycle of days, rural production on the contrary to one of years" (Adam H. Müller, *Die Elemente der Staatskunst*, Berlin, 1809, III, p. 178).[36] This is the naïve conception of industry and agriculture held by the romantic school.

haps four times in the year, according to the time consumed between his purchases of the one and sales of the other, supposing him to buy and sell on equal credits. The capital invested in his implements and machinery circulates still more slowly, being turned, that is, consumed and renewed, on the average, perhaps but once in five or ten years; though there are many tools that are worn out in one set of operations. The capital which is embarked in buildings, as mills, shops, warehouses, barns, in roads, irrigation, etc., may appear scarcely to circulate at all. But, in truth, these things are, to the full, as much as those we have enumerated, consumed in contributing to production, and must be reproduced in order to enable the producer to continue his operations; with this only difference, that they are consumed and reproduced by slower degrees than the rest ... and the capital invested in them may be turned perhaps every twenty or fifty years" [pp. 141-42].

Scrope confuses here the difference in the flow of certain parts of the circulating capital, brought about for the individual capitalist by terms of payment and conditions of credit, with the difference in the turnovers due to the nature of capital. He says that wages must be paid weekly out of the weekly receipts from paid sales or bills. It must be noted here in the first place that certain differences occur relative to wages themselves, depending on the length of the term of payment, that is, the length of time for which the labourer must give credit to the capitalist, whether wages are payable every week, month, three months, six months, etc. In this case, the law expounded before, holds good, to the effect that "the quantity of the means of payment required for all periodical payments" (hence of the money capital to be advanced at one time) "is in inverse proportion to the length of their periods" (Buch I, Kap. III, 3b, Seite 124).[39]

In the second place, it is not only the new value added in the process of production by the week's labour which enters completely into the weekly product, but also the value of the raw and auxiliary materials consumed by the weekly product. This value circulates with the product containing it. It assumes the form of money through the sale of the product and must be reconverted into the same elements of production. This applies as much to the labour power as to the raw and auxiliary materials. But we have already seen (Chapter VI, II, 1) that continuity of production requires a supply of means of production different for different branches of business, and different within one and the same branch of business for different component parts of this element of the circulating capital, for instance, for coal and cotton. Hence, although these materials must be continually replaced *in natura*, they need not always be bought anew. The frequency of purchases depends on the size of the available stock, on the time it takes to exhaust it. In the case of labour power there is no such storing of a supply. The reconversion into money of the part of capital laid out in labour power goes hand in hand with that of the capital invested in raw and auxiliary materials. But the reconversion of the money, on the one hand into labour power, on the other into raw materials, proceeds separately on account of the special terms of purchase and payment of these two constituents, one of them being bought as a productive supply for long periods, the other, labour power, for shorter periods, for instance a week. On the other hand the capitalist must keep a stock of finished commodities besides a stock of materials for production. Let us leave sales difficulties, etc. aside. A certain quantity of goods must be produced, say, on order. While the last portion of this lot is being produced, the finished products are waiting in the warehouse until the order can be completely filled. Other differences in the turnover of circulating capital arise whenever some of its separate elements must stay in some preliminary stage of the process of production (drying of wood, etc.) longer than others.

The credit system, to which Scrope here refers, as well as commercial capital, modifies the turnover for the individual capitalist. On a social scale it modifies the turnover only in so far as it does not accelerate merely production but also consumption.

Chapter X

THEORIES OF FIXED AND CIRCULATING CAPITAL. THE PHYSIOCRATS AND ADAM SMITH

In Quesnay the distinction between fixed and circulating capital presents itself as *avances primitives* and *avances annuelles*. He correctly represents this distinction as one existing within productive capital, capital directly engaged in the process of production. As he regards the capital employed in agriculture, the capital of the farmer, as the only really productive capital, he draws these distinctions only for the capital of the farmer. This also accounts for the annual period of turnover of one part of the capital, and the more than annual (decennial) period of the other part. In the course of the development the Physiocrats incidentally applied these distinctions also to other kinds of capital and to industrial capital in general. The distinction between annual advances and others of two or more years' duration has retained such importance for society that many economists, even after Adam Smith, return to this definition.

The difference between these two kinds of advances does not arise until advanced money has been transformed into the elements of productive capital. It is a difference that exists solely within productive capital. It therefore never occurs to Quesnay to classify money either among the original or the annual advances. As advances for production, i. e., as productive capital, both of them stand opposed to money as well as the commodities existing in the market. Furthermore the difference between these two elements of productive capital is correctly reduced in Quesnay to the different manner in which they enter into the value of the finished product, hence to the different manner in which their values are circulated together with those of the products, and hence to the different manner of their replacement or their reproduction, the value of the one, being wholly replaced annually, that of the other partly and at longer intervals.[23]

The only progress made by Adam Smith is the generalisation of the categories. With him it no longer applies to one special form of capital, the farmer's capital, but to every form of productive capital. Hence it follows as a matter of course that the distinction derived from agriculture between an annual turnover and one of two or more years' duration is superseded by the general distinction into different periods of turnover, one turnover of the fixed capital always comprising more than one turnover of the circulating capital, regardless of the periods of turnover of the circulating capital, whether they be annual, more than annual, or less than annual. Thus in Adam Smith

---

[23] Cf. Quesnay, *Analyse du Tableau économique (Physiocrates*, éd. Daire, 1. partie, Paris, 1846). There we read, for instance: "The annual advances consist of the expenses incurred annually for the labour of cultivation; these advances must be distinguished from the original advances, which form the fund for the establishment of the farming enterprise" (p. 59). In the works of the later Physiocrats these advances are sometimes termed directly capital: *Capital ou avances.* Dupont de Nemours, *Maximes du docteur Quesnay, ou Résumé de ses principes d'économie sociale* (Daire, I, p. 391); furthermore Le Trosne writes: "As a result of the greater or smaller durability of the works of human labour, a nation possesses a substantial fund of wealth independent of its annual reproduction, this fund forming a capital—accumulated over a long period and originally paid with products—which is continually preserved and augmented" (Daire, II, pp. 928-29).[a] Turgot employs the term capital more regularly for *avances*, and identifies the *avances* of the manufacturers still more with those of the farmers (Turgot, *Réflexions sur la formation et la distribution des richesses*, 1766).[40]

---

[a] Marx quotes Quesnay and Le Trosne in French.

the *avances annuelles* transform themselves into circulating capital, and the *avances primitives* into fixed capital. But his progress is confined to this generalisation of the categories. His implementation is far inferior to that of Quesnay.

The crudely empirical manner in which Smith broaches the investigation engenders at the very outset a lack of clarity:

* "There are two different ways in which a capital may be employed so as to yield a revenue or profit to its employer" (*Wealth of Nations*, Book II, Chap. I, p. 189, Aberdeen edition, 1848).*

The ways in which value may be invested so as to perform the functions of capital, to yield surplus value to its owner, are as different and varied as the spheres of investment of capital. It is a question of the different branches of production in which capital may be invested. If put in this way, the question implies still more. It includes the question of the way in which value, even if it is not invested as productive capital, can function as capital for its owner, for instance as interest-bearing capital, merchants' capital, etc. At this point we are already miles away from the real subject of the analysis, viz., the question of how the division of *productive* capital into its different elements, apart from their different spheres of investment, affects their turnover.

Adam Smith immediately continues:

* "First, it may be employed in raising, manufacturing, or purchasing goods, and selling them again with a profit." *

Adam Smith does not tell us anything else here than that capital may be employed in agriculture, manufacture, and commerce. He speaks therefore only of the different spheres of investment of capital, including such in which, as in commerce, capital is not directly embodied in the process of production, hence does not function as productive capital. In so doing he abandons the foundation on which the Physiocrats base the distinctions within productive capital and their effect on the turnover. More. He uses merchants' capital as an illustration in a problem which concerns exclusively differences within the *productive* capital in the product- and value-creating process, which in turn cause differences in its turnover and reproduction.

He continues:

* "The capital employed in this manner yields no revenue or profit to its employer, while it either remains in his possession or continues in the same shape." *

"THE CAPITAL EMPLOYED IN THIS MANNER!" But Smith speaks of capital invested in agriculture, in industry, and he tells us later that a capital so employed divides into fixed and circulating capital! Hence investment of capital in this manner cannot make fixed or circulating capital of it.

Or does he mean to say that capital employed in order to produce goods and to sell these at a profit must be sold after its transformation into goods and by means of the sale must in the first place pass from the possession of the seller into that of the buyer, and in the second place change from its bodily form, goods, into its money form, so that it is of no use to its owner so long as it either remains in his possession or continues in the same shape? In that case, the whole thing amounts to this: The capital value that formerly functioned in the form of productive capital, in a form peculiar to the process of production, now functions as commodity capital and money capital, in forms peculiar to the process of circulation, where it is no longer either fixed or circulating capital. And this applies equally to those elements of value which are added by raw and auxiliary material, i. e., by circulating capital, and to those which are added by the wear and tear of instruments of labour, hence by fixed capital. We do not get any nearer to the difference between fixed and circulating capital in this way.

Further:

* "The goods of the merchant yield him no revenue or profit till he sells them for money, and the money yields him as little till it is again exchanged for goods. His capital is continually going from him in one shape, and returning to him in another, and it is only by means of such circulation, or successive exchanges, that it can yield him any profit. Such capitals therefore may very properly be called circulating capitals." *

What Adam Smith here defines as circulating capital is what I want to call *capital of circulation*, capital in a form pertinent to the process of circulation, to a change of form by means of exchange (a change of substance and change of hands), hence commodity capital and money capital, as distinguished from its form pertinent to the process of production, that of productive capital. These are not different kinds into which the industrial capitalist divides his capital, but different forms over and over again assumed and stripped off successively by the same advanced capital value during its *curriculum vitae*. Adam Smith lumps this together — and this is a big step back compared to the Physiocrats — with the distinctions in form which arise in the sphere of circulation of capital value, in its circular course through its successive forms, while the capital value exists in the form of *productive* capital; and they arise because of the different ways in which the different elements of productive capital take part in the formation of values and transfer their value to the product. We shall see below the consequences of this basic confusion of productive capital and capital in the sphere of circulation (commodity capital and money capital) on the one hand, with fixed and circulating capital on the other. The capital value advanced in fixed capital is as much circulated by the product as that which has been advanced in the circulating capital, and both are equally converted into money capital by the circulation of the commodity capital. The difference evolves only from the fact that the value of the fixed capital circulates piecemeal and therefore must likewise be replaced piecemeal, at shorter or longer intervals, must be reproduced in its bodily form.

That by circulating capital Adam Smith means here nothing but capital of circulation, i. e., capital value in the forms pertaining to the process of circulation (commodity capital and money capital) is shown by his singularly ill-chosen illustration. He selects for this purpose a kind of capital which does not belong at all in the process of production, but whose abode is exclusively the sphere of circulation, which consists solely of capital of circulation — merchants' capital.

How absurd it is to start out with an illustration in which capital does not figure altogether as productive capital is stated right afterwards by him himself:

* "The capital of a merchant [...] is altogether a circulating capital." *

Yet we are told later on that the difference between circulating and fixed capital evolves out of essential differences within the productive capital itself. On the one hand Adam Smith has the distinction of the Physiocrats in mind, on the other the different forms assumed by capital value in its circuit. And both these things are higgledy-piggledy jumbled together.

But how a profit is to come into existence by changes of form of money and commodities, by a mere transformation of value from one of these forms into another is more than anyone can tell. And an explanation becomes absolutely impossible because he starts out here with merchants' capital, which moves only in the sphere of circulation. We shall return to this later. Let us first hear what he has to say about fixed capital.

* "Secondly, it" (capital) "may be employed in the improvement of land, in the purchase of useful machines and instruments of trade, or in suchlike things as yield a revenue or profit without changing masters, or circulating any further. Such capitals, therefore, may very properly be called fixed capitals. Different occupations require very different proportions between the fixed and circulating capitals employed in them.... Some part of the capital of every master artificer or manufacturer must be fixed in the instruments of his trade. This part, however, is very small in some, and very great in others.... The far greater part of the capital of all such master artificers" (such as tailors, shoemakers, weavers) "however is circulated, either in the wages of their workmen, or in the price of their materials, and to be repaid with a profit by the price of the work." *

Apart from the naïve determination of the source of profit, weakness and confusion become at once apparent from the following: To a machine manufacturer for example the machine is his product, which circulates as commodity capital, or in Adam Smith's words, "IS PARTED WITH, CHANGES MASTERS, CIRCULATES FURTHER". According to his own definition therefore this machine would not be fixed but circulating capital. This confusion is again due to the fact that Smith mixes up the distinction between fixed and circulating capital evolved out of the manifold circulation of the various elements of productive capital, with differences in the form assumed by the same capital which functions as *productive* capital within the process of production and as circulation capital, that is to say, as commodity capital or as money capital, within the sphere of circulation. Consequently with Adam Smith things can function as fixed capital (as instruments of labour, elements of productive capital), or as "circulating" capital, commodity capital (as products thrust out of the sphere of production into that of circulation), all depending on the position they occupy in the life process of capital.

But Adam Smith suddenly changes the entire basis of his classification, and contradicts the text with which he had opened the entire investigation a few lines previously. This refers particularly to the statement:

* "There are two different ways in which a capital may be employed so as to yield a revenue or a profit to its employer," *

namely as circulating or as fixed capital. According to that, these are therefore different methods of employing different capitals independent of one another, such as capitals that can be employed either in industry or in agriculture. And then we read:

* "Different occupations require very different proportions between the fixed and circulating capitals employed in them." *

Fixed and circulating capital are now no longer different, independent investments of capital but different portions of the same productive capital, which form different parts of the total value of this capital in different spheres of investment. Hence we have here differences arising from an appropriate division of the *productive* capital itself and therefore valid only with respect to it. But this runs counter to the circumstance that merchants' capital, being merely circulating capital, is opposed to fixed capital, for Adam Smith says himself:

"The capital of a merchant [...] is altogether a circulating capital."

It is indeed a capital performing its functions solely within the sphere of circulation and as such stands opposed in general to productive capital, the capital embodied in the process of production. But for this very reason it cannot be contrasted as the fluid (circulating) component part of productive capital to its fixed component part.

In the illustrations Smith gives he designates the "INSTRUMENTS OF TRADE" as fixed capital, and the portion of capital laid out in wages and raw materials, including auxiliary materials, as circulating capital ("REPAID WITH A PROFIT BY THE PRICE OF THE WORK").

And so he starts out, in the first place, from the various constituents of the labour process, from labour power (labour) and raw materials on the one hand, and instruments of labour on the other. But these are constituents of capital, because a sum of value which is to function as capital is invested in them. To this extent they are material elements, modes of existence of *productive* capital, that is to say, of capital functioning in the process of production. But why is one of these parts called fixed? Because

* "some part of the capital [...] must be fixed in the instruments of trade".*

But the other part is also fixed — in wages and raw materials. Machines however and

* "instruments of trade ... suchlike things ... yield a revenue or profit without changing masters, or circulating any further. Such capitals, therefore, may very properly be called fixed capitals." *

Take for instance the mining industry. No raw material at all is used there, because the subject of labour, such as copper, is a product of nature, which must first be appropriated by labour. The copper to be first appropriated, the product of the process, which circulates later as a commodity, or commodity capital, does not form an element of productive capital. No part of its value is invested in it. On the other hand the other elements of the productive process, labour power and auxiliary materials such as coal, water, etc., do not enter materially into the product, either. The coal is entirely consumed and only its value enters into the product, just as a part of the value of the machine, etc., enters into it. Finally, the labourer remains as independent vis-à-vis the product, the copper, as the machine; except that the value which he produces by means of his labour is now a component part of the value of the copper. Hence in this illustration not a single constituent of productive capital changes "MASTERS",[a] nor is any of them circulated further, because none of them enter materially into the product. What becomes of the circulating capital in this case? According to Adam Smith's own definition the entire capital employed in a copper mine consists of fixed capital and nothing else.

Let us take on the other hand a different industry, one which utilises raw materials that form the substance of its product, and auxiliary materials that enter into the product bodily and not only as so much value, as is the case with fuel coal. The product, for instance the yarn, changes hands together with the raw material, the cotton, composing it, and passes from the process of production into that of consumption. But so long as the cotton functions as an element of productive capital, its owner does not sell it, but processes it, has it made into yarn. He does not part with it. Or, to use Smith's crudely erroneous and trivial terms, he does not make any profit BY PARTING WITH IT, BY ITS CHANGING MASTERS, OR BY CIRCULATING IT. He does not permit his materials to circulate any more than his machines. They are fixed in the process of production, the same as the spinning machines and the factory buildings. Indeed, a part of the productive capital must be just as continually fixed in the form of coal, cotton, etc., as in the form of instruments of labour. The difference is only that for instance the cot-

---

[a] Marx gives this English term in parentheses after its German equivalent.

ton, coal, etc., required for one week's yarn production, are always entirely consumed in the manufacture of the weekly product, so that new cotton, coal, etc., must be supplied in their place; in other words, these elements of productive capital, although remaining identical in kind, always consist of new specimens of the same kind, while the same individual spinning machine or the same individual factory building continues its participation in a whole series of weekly productions without being replaced by a new specimen of its kind. As elements of the productive capital all its constituent parts are continually fixed in the process of production, for it cannot proceed without them. And all the elements of productive capital, whether fixed or circulating, equally confront, as productive capital, the capital of circulation, i. e., commodity capital and money capital.

It is the same with labour power. A part of the productive capital must be continually fixed in it, and it is the same identical labour powers, just as it is the same machines, that are everywhere employed for a certain length of time by the same capitalist. The difference between labour power and machines in this case is not that the machines are bought once and for all (which is not so when they are paid for in instalments), while the labourer is not. The difference is rather that the labour expended by the labourer enters wholly into the value of the product, while the value of the machines enters only piecemeal.

Smith confuses different definitions when he says of circulating capital as opposed to fixed:

* "The capital employed in this manner yields no revenue or profit to its employer, while it either remains in his possession or continues in the same shape." *

He places the merely formal metamorphosis of the commodity, which the product, the commodity capital, undergoes in the sphere of circulation and which brings about the change of hands of the commodities, on the same level as the bodily metamorphosis, which the various elements of productive capital undergo during the process of production. He indiscriminately jumbles together the transformation of commodities into money and of money into commodities, or purchase and sale, with the transformation of elements of production into products. His illustration for circulating capital is merchants' capital, which is converted from commodities into money and from money into commodities — the change of form C—M—C pertaining to the circulation of commodities. But this change of form within the circulation signifies for the industrial capital in action that the commodities into which the money is reconverted are elements of production (instruments of labour and labour power), that, therefore, the change of form renders the function of industrial capital continuous, renders the process of production a continuous one, or a process of reproduction. This entire change of form takes place in *circulation*. It is this change of form that brings about the real passage of the commodities from hand to hand. But the metamorphoses gone through by productive capital within its process of production are on the contrary metamorphoses that pertain to the *labour process* and are necessary to transform the elements of production into the desired product. Adam Smith clings to the fact that a part of the means of production (the instruments of labour proper) serve in the labour process ("YIELD A PROFIT TO THEIR MASTER," as he erroneously expresses it) without changing their bodily form and wear out only by degrees; while the other part, the materials, change and by virtue of this very change attain their destination as means of production. This difference in the behaviour of the elements of productive capital in the labour process forms however only the point of departure of the difference between fixed and non-fixed capital, not this difference itself. That follows from the fact alone that this different behaviour exists in equal measure under all modes of production, capitalist and non-capitalist. To this different behaviour of material elements corresponds however the *transmission of value* to the product, and to this in turn corresponds the replacement of value by the sale of the product. That and that alone is what constitutes the difference in question. Hence capital is not called fixed because it is fixed in the instruments of labour but because a part of its value laid out in instruments of labour remains fixed in them, while the other part circulates as a component part of the value of the product.

"If it" (the stock) "is employed in procuring future profit, it must procure this profit either by staying with him" (the employer), "or by going from him. In the one case it is a fixed, in the other it is a circulating capital" (p. 189).

What strikes one here above all is the crudely empirical conception of profit derived from the outlook of the ordinary capitalist, which wholly contradicts the better esoteric understanding of Adam Smith. Not only the price of the materials and that of the labour power is replaced in the price of the product, but also that part of value which is transferred by wear and tear from the instruments of labour to the product. Under no circumstances does this replacement yield profit. Whether a value advanced for the production of a commodity is re- placed entirely or piecemeal, at one time or gradually, by the sale of that commodity, cannot change anything except the manner and time of replacement. But in no event can it transform that which is common to both, the replacement of value, into a creation of surplus value. At the bottom of it all lies the commonly held idea that, because surplus value is not realised until the product is sold, until it circulates, it originates only from sales, from the circulation. Indeed the different manner of origination of profit is in this case but a wrong way of expressing the fact that the different elements of productive capital serve differently, that as productive elements they act diffe- rently in the labour process. It the end, the difference is not derived from the process of labour or self-expansion, not from the function of productive capital itself, but it is supposed to apply only subjectively to the individual capitalist, to whom one part of capital serves a use- ful purpose in one way, while another part does so in another way.

Quesnay, on the other hand, had derived these differences from the process of reproduction and its necessities. In order that this process may be continuous, the value of the annual advances must annually be replaced in full out of the value of the annual product, while the value of the investment capital need be replaced only piecemeal, so that it requires complete replacement and therefore complete repro- duction only in a period of, say, ten years (by new material of the same kind). Consequently Adam Smith falls far below Quesnay.

So there is therefore absolutely nothing left to Adam Smith for a definition of fixed capital except that it is instruments of labour which do not change their shape in the process of production and continue to serve in production until they are worn out, as opposed to the products in the formation of which they assist. He forgets that all elements of productive capital continually confront in their bodily form (as instruments of labour, materials, and labour power) the pro- duct and the product circulating as a commodity, and that the differ- ence between the part consisting of materials and labour power and that consisting of instruments of labour is only this: with regard to la- bour power, that it is always purchased afresh (not bought for the time it lasts, as are the instruments of labour); with regard to the ma- terials, that it is not the same identical materials that function in the labour process throughout, but always new materials of the same kind. At the same time the false impression is created that the value of the fixed capital does not participate in the circulation, although of course Adam Smith previously explained the wear and tear of fixed capital as a part of the price of the product.

In opposing circulating capital to fixed, no emphasis is placed on the fact that this opposition exists solely because it is that constituent part of productive capital which must be *wholly* replaced out of the value of the product and must therefore fully share in its metamorphoses, while this is not so in the case of the fixed capital. Instead the circulating capital is jumbled together with those forms which capital assumes on passing from the sphere of production to that of circulation, as commodity capital and money capital. But both forms, commodity capital as well as money capital, are carriers of the value of both the fixed and the circulating component parts of productive capital. Both of them are capital of circulation, as distinguished from productive capital, but not circulating (fluid) capital as distinguished from fixed capital.

Finally, owing to the wholly erroneous explanation that profit is made by fixed capital staying in the process of production, and by circulating capital leaving it and being circulated, and also on account of the identity of form assumed in the *turnover* by the variable capital and the circulating constituent of the constant capital, their essential difference in the *process of self-expansion* and of the formation of surplus value is hidden, so that the entire secret of capitalist production is obscured still more. The common designation "circulating capital" abolishes this essential difference. Political economy subsequently went still farther by holding fast not to the antithesis between variable and constant capital but to the antithesis between fixed and circulating capital as the essential and sole delimitation.

After Adam Smith has designated fixed and circulating capital as two particular ways of investing capital, each of which yields a profit by itself, he says:

"No fixed capital can yield any revenue but by means of a circulating capital. The most useful machines and instruments of trade will produce nothing without the circulating capital which affords the materials they are employed upon, and the maintenance of the workmen who employ them" (p. 188).

Here it becomes apparent what the previously used expressions

"YIELD A REVENUE", "MAKE A PROFIT", etc., signify, viz., that both parts of
capital serve as creators of product.

Adam Smith then gives the following illustration:

*"That part of the capital of the farmer which is employed in the instruments of ag-
riculture is a fixed, that which is employed in the wages and maintenance of his labouring servants is a circulating capital." *

(Here the difference between fixed and circulating capital is correctly applied only to difference in circulation, to the turnovers of different constituent parts of productive capital.)

*"He makes a profit of the one by keeping it in his own possession, and of the other
by parting with it. The price or value of his labouring cattle is a fixed capital"*

(here he is again correct when he says it is the value, not the material element, to which the difference applies)

*"in the same manner as that of the instruments of husbandry; their maintenance"
(that of the labouring cattle) "is a circulating capital in the same manner as that of the
labouring servants. The farmer makes his profit by keeping the labouring cattle, and by
parting with their maintenance."*

(The farmer keeps the fodder of the cattle, he does not sell it. He
uses it to feed the cattle, while he uses up the cattle themselves as instruments of labour. The difference is only this: The fodder that goes
for the maintenance of the labouring cattle is consumed wholly and
must be continually replaced by new cattle fodder out of the products
of agriculture or by their sale; the cattle themselves are replaced only
as each head becomes incapacitated for work.)

*"Both the price and the maintenance of the cattle which are bought in and fat-
tened, not for labour but for sale, are a circulating capital. The farmer makes his profit
by parting with them." *

(Every producer of commodities, hence likewise the capitalist producer, sells his product, the result of his process of production, but this
is no reason why this product should form a part of either the fixed or
the circulating component of his *productive* capital. The product now
exists rather in that form in which it is thrust out of the process of production and must function as commodity capital. The fattened stock
function in the process of production as raw material, not as in-

struments of labour like the labouring cattle. Hence the fattened cattle enter into the product as substance, and their whole value enters into it, just as that of the auxiliary material //its fodder//. The fattened cattle are therefore a circulating part of the productive capital, but not because the sold product, the fattened cattle, have the same bodily form as the raw material, the cattle not yet fattened. This is accidental. At the same time Adam Smith might have seen by this illustration that it is not the material form of the element of production but its function within the process of production that determines the value contained in it as fixed or circulating.)

* "The whole value of the seed too is properly a fixed capital. Though it goes backwards and forwards between the ground and the granary, it never changes masters, and therefore it does not properly circulate. The farmer makes his profit not by its sale, but by its increase." *

At this point the utter thoughtlessness of the Smithian distinction reveals itself. According to him seed would be fixed capital, if there would be no "CHANGE OF MASTERS", that is to say, if the seed is directly replaced out of the annual product, is deducted from it. On the other hand it would be circulating capital, if the entire product were sold and with a part of its value seed of another owner were bought. In the one case there is a "CHANGE OF MASTERS", in the other there is not. Smith once more confuses here circulating and commodity capital. The product is the material vehicle of the commodity capital, but of course only that part of it which actually enters into the circulation and does not re-enter directly into the process of production from which it emerged as a product.

Whether the seed is directly deducted from the product as a part of it or the entire product is sold and a part of its value converted in the purchase of another man's seed — in either case it is mere replacement that takes place and no profit is made by this replacement. In the one case the seed enters into circulation as a commodity together with the remainder of the product; in the other it figures only in bookkeeping as a component part of the value of the advanced capital. But in both cases it remains a circulating constituent of the productive capital. The seed is entirely consumed to get the product ready, and it must be entirely replaced out of the product to make reproduction possible.

"Hence raw material and auxiliary substances lose the characteristic form with which they are clothed on entering the labour process. It is otherwise with the instruments of labour. Tools, machines, workshops, and vessels, are of use in the labour process, only so long as they retain their original shape, and are ready each morning to renew the process with their shape unchanged. And just as during their lifetime, that is to say, during the continued labour process in which they serve, they retain their shape independent of the product, so too, they do after their death. The corpses of machines, tools, workshops, etc., are always separate and distinct from the product they helped to turn out" (Buch I, Kap. VI, S. 192).[a]

These different ways in which means of production are consumed to form the product, some of them preserving their independent shape vis-à-vis the product, others changing or losing it entirely— this difference pertaining to the labour process as such and therefore just as well to labour processes aimed at satisfying merely one's own needs, e.g., the needs of the patriarchal family, without any exchange, without production of commodities — are falsified by Adam Smith. He does so 1) by introducing here the totally irrelevant definition of profit, claiming that some of the means of production yield a profit to their owner by preserving their form, while the others do so by losing it; 2) by jumbling together the alterations of a part of the elements of production in the labour process with the change of form (purchase and sale) that is characteristic of the exchange of products, of commodity circulation, and which at the same time includes a change in the ownership of the circulating commodities.

The turnover presupposes reproduction effected by circulation, hence by the sale of the product, by its conversion into money and its reconversion from money into its elements of production. But since a part of the capitalist producer's own product again directly serves him as means of production, he appears as a seller of it to himself, and that is how the matter figures in his books. In that case this part of the reproduction is not brought about by circulation but proceeds directly. However the part of the product thus serving again as means of production replaces circulating, not fixed capital, since 1) its value passes wholly into the product, and 2) it itself has been wholly replaced *in natura* by a new specimen out of the new product.

Adam Smith tells us now what circulating and fixed capital consist of. He enumerates the things, the material elements, which form

---

[a] *Capital*, Vol. I, Ch. VIII (present edition, Vol. 35).

fixed, and those which form circulating capital, as if this definiteness were inherent in these things materially, by nature, and did not rather spring from their definite function within the capitalist process of production. And yet in the same chapter (Book II, Chapter I) he makes the remark that although a certain thing, e. g., a dwelling, which is reserved for "immediate consumption,"

*"may yield a revenue to its proprietor, and thereby serve *in the function of a capital* to him, it cannot yield any to the public, nor serve in the function of a capital to it, and the revenue of the whole body of the people can never be in the smallest degree increased by it" (p. 186).*

Here, then, Adam Smith clearly states that the property of being capital is not inherent in things as such and in any case, but is a function with which they may or may not be invested, according to circumstances. But what is true of capital in general is also true of its subdivisions.

The same things form constituent parts of the circulating or fixed capital, depending on what function they perform in the labour process. A head of cattle for instance, as labouring cattle (instrument of labour), represents the material mode of existence of fixed capital, while as cattle for fattening (raw material) it is a constituent part of the farmer's circulating capital. On the other hand the same thing may now function as a constituent part of productive capital and now belong to the fund for direct consumption. A house for instance when performing the function of a workshop, is a fixed component part of productive capital; when serving as a dwelling it is in no wise a form of capital. The same instruments of labour may in many cases serve either as means of production or as means of consumption.

It was one of the errors following from Adam Smith's idea that the property of being fixed or circulating capital was conceived as inherent in the things themselves. The mere analysis of the labour process (Buch I, Kap. V) [a] shows that the definitions of instruments of labour, materials of labour, and product change according to the various roles played by one and the same thing in the process. The definitions of fixed and non-fixed capital are based in their turn on the definite roles played by these elements in the labour process, and therefore also in the value formation process.

In the second place, on enumerating the things fixed and circulating

---

[a] English edition: Vol. I, Ch. VII (present edition, Vol. 35).

capitals consist of, it becomes fully apparent that Smith lumps together the distinction — valid and making sense only with regard to
productive capital (capital in its productive form) — between the
fixed and circulating components of the same, with the distinction between productive capital and those forms which pertain to capital in
its process of circulation, viz., commodity capital and money capital.
He says in the same passage (pp. 187, 188):

* "The circulating capital consists ... of the provisions, materials, and finished work
of all kinds that are in the hands of their respective dealers, and of the money that is necessary for circulating and distributing them, etc." *

Indeed, if we look more closely we observe that here, contrary to
his previous statements, circulating capital is again equated to commodity capital and money capital, that is to say, to two forms of capital which do not belong in the process of production at all, which do
not form circulating (fluid) capital as opposed to fixed, but capital of
circulation as opposed to productive capital. It is only *alongside* these
that the constituents of productive capital advanced in materials
(raw materials or semi-finished products) and really incorporated in
the process of production then play a role again. He says:

* "... The third and last of the three portions into which the general stock of the society naturally divides itself, is the circulating capital, of which the characteristic is,
that it affords a revenue only by circulating or changing masters. It is composed likewise of four parts: first of the money..." *

(but money is never a form of productive capital, of capital functioning in the productive process; it is always only one of the forms assumed by capital within its process of circulation);

* "secondly, of the stock of provisions which are in the possession of the butcher, the
grazier, the farmer ... from the sale of which they expect to derive a profit.... Fourthly
and lastly, of the work which is made up and completed, but which is still in the hands
of the merchant and manufacturer". And, "thirdly, of the materials, whether altogether rude, or more or less manufactured, of clothes, furniture, and buildings, which
are not yet made up into any of those three shapes, but which remain in the hands of
the growers, the manufacturers, the mercers and drapers, the timber-merchants, the
carpenters and joiners, the brick-makers, etc." *

Nos. 2 and 4 contain nothing but products which have been thrust
out as such from the process of production and must be sold, in short,
which now function as commodities, hence as commodity capital,

and which therefore have a form and occupy a place in the process in which they are not elements of productive capital, no matter what may be their eventual destination, i. e., whether, in order to answer their purpose (use value), they should finally be allotted to individual or productive consumption. The products mentioned in 2 are food-stuffs, in 4 all other finished products, which in turn consist only of finished instruments of labour or finished articles of consumption (foodstuffs other than those mentioned under 2).

The fact that Smith at the same time speaks of the merchant shows his confusion. Once the producer sells his product to the merchant, it no longer constitutes any form of his capital. From the point of view of society, it is indeed still commodity capital, although in other hands than those of its producer; but for the very reason that it is a commodity capital it is neither fixed nor circulating capital.

In every kind of production not meant for the satisfaction of the producer's direct needs, the product must circulate as a commodity, i. e., it must be sold, not in order to make a profit on it, but that the producer may be able to live at all. Under capitalist production there is to be added the circumstance that when a commodity is sold the surplus value embodied in it is also realised. The product emerges as a commodity from the process of production and is therefore neither a fixed nor a circulating element of this process.

Incidentally, Smith here argues against himself. The finished products, whatever their material form or their use value, their useful effect, are all commodity capital here, hence capital in a form characteristic of the process of circulation. Being in this form, they are not constituent parts of any productive capital their owner may have. This does not in the least prevent them from *becoming*, right after their sale, in the hands of their purchaser, constituent parts of productive capital, either fixed or circulating. Here it is evident that things which for a certain time appear in the market as commodity capital, as opposed to productive capital, may or may not function as circulating or fixed constituents of productive capital after they have been removed from the market.

The product of the cotton spinner, yarn, is the commodity form of his capital, is commodity capital as far as he is concerned. It cannot function again as a constituent part of his productive capital, neither as material of labour nor as an instrument of labour. But in the hands of the weaver who buys it, it is incorporated in the productive capital of the latter as one of its circulating constituent parts. For the spinner, however, the yarn is the depository of the value of part of his fixed as well as circulating capital (apart from the surplus value). In the same way a machine, the product of a machine manufacturer, is the commodity form of his capital, is commodity capital to him. And so long as it stays in this form it is neither circulating nor fixed capital. But if sold to a manufacturer for use it becomes a fixed component part of a productive capital. Even if by virtue of its use form the product can partly re-enter as means of production into the process from which it originated, e. g., coal into coal production, precisely that part of the output of coal which is intended for sale represents neither circulating nor fixed capital but commodity capital.

On the other hand a product, due to its use form, may be wholly incapable of forming any element of productive capital, either as material of labour or as an instrument of labour. For instance any means of subsistence. Nevertheless it is commodity capital for its producer, is the carrier of the value of his fixed as well as circulating capital; and of the one or the other according to whether the capital employed in its production has to be replaced in whole or in part, has transferred its value to the product in whole or in part.

With Smith, in No. 3, the raw material (material not worked up, semi-finished products, auxiliary substances) does not figure on the one hand as a component part embodied in the productive capital, but actually only as a special kind of use values of which the social product can at all consist, as a special kind of commodities existing alongside the other material constituent parts, means of subsistence, etc., enumerated under Nos. 2 and 4. On the other hand these materials are indeed cited as incorporated in the productive capital and therefore as elements of it in the hands of the producer. The confusion is evidenced by the fact that they are partly conceived as functioning in the hands of the producer ("IN THE HANDS OF THE GROWERS, THE MANUFAC-TURERS, ETC."), and partly in the hands of merchants ("MERCERS, DRAPERS, TIMBER-MERCHANTS"), where they are merely commodity capital, not component parts of productive capital.

Indeed, Adam Smith wholly forgets here, in enumerating the elements of circulating capital, the distinction — applying only to the productive capital — between fixed and circulating capital. He rather places commodity capital and money capital, i. e., the two forms of capital typical of the process of circulation, in opposition to the productive capital, but that quite unconsciously.

Finally, it is a striking fact that Adam Smith forgets to mention labour power when counting off the constituent parts of circulating capital. There are two reasons for this.

We have just seen that, apart from money capital, circulating capital is only another name for commodity capital. But to the extent that labour power circulates in the market, it is not capital, no form of commodity capital. It is not capital at all; the labourer is not a capitalist, although he brings a commodity to market, namely his own skin. Not until labour power has been sold, been incorporated in the process of production, hence not until it has ceased to circulate as a commodity, does it become a constituent of productive capital—variable capital as the source of surplus value, a circulating component part of productive capital with reference to the turnover of the capital value invested in it. Since Smith here confuses the circulating capital with commodity capital, he cannot bring labour power under the head of circulating capital. Hence the variable capital here appears in the form of the commodities the labourer buys with his wages, viz., means of subsistence. In this form the capital value invested in wages is supposed to belong to circulating capital. That which is incorporated in the process of production is labour power, the labourer himself, not the means of subsistence wherewith the labourer maintains himself. True, we have seen (Buch I, Kap. XXI)[a] that from the point of view of society the reproduction of the labourer himself by means of his individual consumption is likewise part of the process of reproduction of social capital. But this does not apply to the individual, isolated process of production which we are studying here. The "ACQUIRED AND USEFUL ABILITIES" (p. 187) which Smith mentions under the head of fixed capital are on the contrary component parts of circulating capital, since they are ABILITIES of the wage labourer and he has sold his labour together with its ABILITIES.

It is a great mistake on the part of Adam Smith to divide the entire social wealth into 1) a fund for immediate consumption, 2) fixed capital, and 3) circulating capital. According to the above, wealth would have to be divided into 1) a consumption fund which does not form any part of functioning social capital although parts of it *can* continually function as capital; and 2) capital. Accordingly one part of the wealth functions as capital, the other as non-capital, or consumption fund. And here appears the absolute necessity that all capital be either fixed or circulating, somewhat like the natural necessity that

---

[a] English edition: Vol. I, Ch. XXIII (present edition, Vol. 35).

a mammal be male or female. But we have seen that the antithesis between fixed and circulating capital applies solely to the elements of
productive capital, that consequently there is besides these a considerable amount of capital — commodity capital and money capital —
that exists in a form in which it *can be* neither fixed nor circulating.

Inasmuch as under capitalist production the entire mass of social
products circulates in the market as commodity capital, with the exception of that part of the products which is directly used up again by
the individual capitalist producers in its bodily form as means of production without being sold or bought, it is evident that not only the
fixed and circulating elements of productive capital, but likewise all
the elements of the consumption fund are derived from the commodity capital. This is tantamount to saying that on the basis of capitalist production both means of production and articles of consumption
first appear as commodity capital, even though they are intended for
later use as means of production or articles of consumption, just as labour power itself is found in the market as a commodity, although not
as commodity capital.

This accounts for the following new confusion in Adam Smith. He
says:

* "Of these four parts" *

(of the circulating capital, i. e., of capital in its forms of commodity
capital and money capital belonging in the process of circulation, two
parts which are turned into four by the material distinctions Adam
Smith makes between the constituent parts of commodity capital)

* "three — provisions, materials, and finished work, are either annually or in a longer or shorter period, regularly withdrawn from it and placed either in the fixed capital, or in the stock reserved for immediate consumption. Every fixed capital is both originally derived from, and requires to be continually supported by, a circulating capital. All useful machines and instruments of trade are originally derived from a circulating capital which furnishes the materials of which they are made and the maintenance
of the workmen who make them. They require, too, a capital of the same kind to keep
them in constant repair" (p. 188).*

With the exception of that part of the product which is constantly
consumed again as means of production directly by its producers, the
following general proposition applies to capitalist production: All
products reach the market as commodities and therefore circulate for
the capitalist as the commodity form of his capital, as commodity cap-

ital, regardless of whether these products must or can function in their bodily form, in accordance with their use values, as elements of productive capital (of the process of production), as means of production and therefore as fixed or circulating elements of productive capital; or whether they can serve only as means of individual, not of productive, consumption. All products are thrown upon the market as commodities; all means of production or consumption, all elements of productive and individual consumption, must therefore be extracted from the market by purchasing them as commodities. This truism is of course correct. It applies for this reason to the fixed as well as the circulating elements of productive capital, to instruments of labour as well as material of labour in all forms. (This, moreover, ignores the fact that there are elements of productive capital which are furnished by nature, are not products.) A machine is bought in the market, as is cotton. But it does not follow from this by any means that every fixed capital stems originally from some circulating capital; that follows only from the Smithian confusion of capital of circulation with circulating or fluid, i. e., non-fixed capital. Besides, Smith actually refutes himself. According to him himself, machines, as commodities, form a part of No. 4 of the circulating capital. Hence to say that they come from the circulating capital means only that they functioned as commodity capital before they functioned as machines, but that materially they are derived from themselves; so is cotton, as the circulating element of some spinner's capital, derived from the cotton in the market. But if Adam Smith in his further exposition derives fixed capital from circulating capital for the reason that labour and raw material are required to build machines, it must be borne in mind that in the first place, instruments of labour, hence fixed capital, are also required to build machines, and in the second place fixed capital, such as machinery, etc., is likewise required to make raw materials, since productive capital always includes instruments of labour, but not always material of labour. He himself says immediately afterwards:

* "Land, mines, and fisheries, require all both a fixed and a circulating capital to cultivate them;" *

(thus he admits that not only circulating but also fixed capital is required for the production of raw material)

* "and" * (new error at this point) * "their produce replaces with a profit, not only those capitals, but *all the others in the society*" (p. 188).*

This is entirely wrong. Their produce furnishes the raw material, auxiliary material, etc., for all other branches of industry. But their value does not replace the value of all other social capitals; it replaces only their own capital value (+ the surplus value). Adam Smith is here again in the grip of his physiocratic reminiscences.

Considered socially it is true that that part of the commodity capital which consists of products that can serve only as instruments of labour must — unless they have been produced to no purpose, cannot be sold — sooner or later function as instruments of labour, i. e., with capitalist production as their basis, they must, whenever they cease to be commodities, form real, as before they formed prospective, elements of the fixed part of the social productive capital.

There is a distinction here, arising from the bodily form of the product.

A spinning machine for instance has no use value, unless it is used for spinning, unless therefore it functions as an element of production and consequently, from the point of view of the capitalist, as a fixed component part of a productive capital. But a spinning machine is movable. It may be exported from the country in which it was produced and sold abroad directly or indirectly for raw materials, etc., or for champagne. In that case it has functioned only as commodity capital in the country in which it was produced, but never as fixed capital, not even after its sale.

Products however which are localised by being anchored in the soil, and can therefore be used only locally, such as factory buildings, railways, bridges, tunnels, docks, etc., soil improvements, etc., cannot be exported bodily, neck and crop. They are not movable. They are either useless, or as soon as they have been sold must function as fixed capital in the country that produced them. To their capitalist producer, who builds factories or improves land for speculative sale, these things are forms of his commodity capital, or, according to Adam Smith, forms of circulating capital. But viewed socially these things — if they are not to be useless — must ultimately function as fixed capital in that very country, in some local process of production. From this it does not follow in the least that immovables are in themselves fixed capital. They may belong, as dwelling houses, etc., to the consumption fund, and in that case they are no part whatever of the social capital, although they constitute an element of the social wealth of which capital is only a part. The producer of these things, to speak in the language of Adam Smith, makes a profit by their sale. And so they are circulating capital! Their practical utiliser, their ultimate purchaser, can use them only by applying them in the process of production. And so they are fixed capital!

Titles to property, for instance railway shares, may change hands every day, and their owner may make a profit by their sale even in foreign countries, so that titles to property are exportable, although the railway itself is not. Nevertheless these things must either lie fallow in the very country in which they are localised, or function as a fixed component of some productive capital. In the same way manufacturer A may make a profit by selling his factory to manufacturer B, but this does not prevent the factory from functioning as fixed capital the same as before.

Therefore, while the locally fixed instruments of labour, which cannot be detached from the soil, will nevertheless, in all probability, have to function as fixed capital in that very country, though they may function as commodity capital for their producer and not constitute any elements of *his* fixed capital (which is made up as far as he is concerned of the instruments of labour he needs for the construction of buildings, railways, etc.), one should not by any means draw the contrary conclusion that fixed capital necessarily consists of immovables. A ship and a locomotive are effective only through their motion; yet they function, not for him who produced them, but for him who applies them as fixed capital. On the other hand things which are most decidedly fixed in the process of production, live and die in it and never leave it any more after once entering it, are circulating component parts of the productive capital. Such are for instance the coal consumed to drive the machine in the process of production, the gas used to light the factory, etc. They are circulating capital not because they bodily leave the process of production together with the product and circulate as commodities, but because their value enters wholly into that of the commodity which they help to produce and which therefore must be entirely replaced out of the proceeds of the sale of the commodity.

In the passage last quoted from Adam Smith, notice must also be taken of the following phrase:

* "A circulating capital which furnishes ... the maintenance of the workmen who make them" * (machines, etc.).

With the Physiocrats that part of capital which is advanced for wages figures correctly under the *avances annuelles* as distinguished from the *avances primitives*. On the other hand it is not the labour power itself that appears with them as a constituent part of the productive capital employed by the farmer, but the means of subsistence (THE MAINTENANCE OF THE WORKMEN, as Smith calls it) given to the farm labourers. This hangs together exactly with their specific doctrine. For according to them the value part added to the product by labour (quite like the value part added to the product by raw material, instruments of labour, etc., in short, by all the material components of constant capital) is equal only to the value of the means of subsistence paid to the labourers and necessarily consumed for the maintenance of their ability to function as labour power. Their very doctrine stands in the way of their discovering the distinction between constant and variable capital. If it is labour that produces surplus value (in addition to reproducing its own price), then it does so in industry as well as in agriculture. But since, according to their system, labour produces surplus value only in one branch of production, namely agriculture, it does not arise out of labour but out of the special activity (assistance) of nature in this branch. And only for this reason agricultural labour is to them productive labour, as distinct from the other kinds of labour.

Adam Smith classifies the means of subsistence of labourers as circulating capital in contradistinction to fixed capital:

1) Because he confuses circulating as distinguished from fixed capital with forms of capital pertaining to the sphere of circulation, with capital of circulation — a confusion uncritically accepted by his successors. He therefore mixes up commodity capital and the circulating component of productive capital, and in that case it is a matter of course that whenever the social product assumes the form of commodities, the means of subsistence of the labourers as well as those of the non-labourers, the materials as well as the instruments of labour themselves, must be supplied out of the commodity capital.

2) But the physiocratic conception too lurks in Smith's analysis, although it contradicts the esoteric — really scientific — part of his own exposition.

Generally speaking the advanced capital is converted into productive capital, i. e., it assumes the form of elements of production which are themselves the products of past labour. (Among them labour power.) Capital can function in the process of production only in this form. Now, if instead of labour power itself, into which the variable part of capital has been converted, we take the labourer's means of subsistence, it is evident that these means as such do not differ, so far as the formation of value is concerned, from the other elements of productive capital, from the raw materials and the food of the labouring cattle, on which ground Smith in one of the passages quoted above places them, after the manner of the Physiocrats, on the same level. The means of subsistence cannot themselves expand their own value or add any surplus value to it. Their value, like that of the other elements of the productive capital, can re-appear only in the value of the product. They cannot add any more to its value than they have themselves. Like raw materials, semi-finished goods, etc., they differ from fixed capital composed of instruments of labour only in that they are entirely consumed in the product (at least as far as concerns the capitalist who pays for them) in the formation of which they participate and that therefore their value must be replaced as a whole, while in the case of the fixed capital this takes place only gradually, piecemeal. The part of productive capital advanced in labour power (or in the labourer's means of subsistence) differs here only materially and not in respect of the process of labour and production of surplus value from the other material elements of productive capital. It differs only in so far as it falls into the category of circulating capital together with one part of the objective creators of the product (MATERIALS Adam Smith calls them generally), as opposed to the other part of these objective product creators, which belongs in the category of fixed capital.

The fact that the capital laid out in wages belongs in the circulating part of productive capital and, unlike the fixed component of productive capital, shares the quality of fluidity with a part of the objective product creators, the raw materials, etc., has nothing whatever to do with the role played in the process of self-expansion by this variable part, as distinct from the constant part of capital. This refers only to how this part of the advanced capital value is to be replaced, renewed, hence reproduced out of the value of the product by means of the circulation. The purchase and repurchase of labour power belong in the process of circulation. But it is only within the process of production that the value laid out in labour power is converted (not for the labourer but for the capitalist) from a definite, constant magnitude into a variable one, and only thus the advanced value is converted altogether into capital value, into capital, into self-expanding value. But by classing, like Smith, the value expended for the means of subsistence of the labourers, instead of the value laid out in labour power, as the circulating component of productive capital, the understanding of the distinction between variable and constant capital, and thus the understanding of the capitalist process of production in general, is rendered impossible. This part of capital's character as variable capital in contrast to the constant capital, spent for material creators of the product, is buried beneath the determination that the part of the capital invested in labour power belongs, as far as the turnover is concerned, in the circulating part of productive capital. And the burial is brought to completion by enumerating the labourer's means of subsistence instead of his labour power as an element of productive capital. It is immaterial whether the value of the labour power is advanced in money or directly in means of subsistence. However under capitalist production the latter can be but an exception.[24]

By thus establishing the definition of circulating capital as being the determinant of the capital value laid out for labour power — this physiocratic definition without the premise of the Physiocrats — Adam Smith fortunately killed among his followers the understanding that that part of capital which is spent on labour power is variable capital. The more profound and correct ideas developed by him elsewhere did not prevail, but this blunder of his did. Indeed, other writers after him went even further. They were not content to make it the decisive definition of the part of capital invested in labour power to be circulating as opposed to fixed capital; they made it the essential definition of circulating capital to be invested in means of subsistence for labourers. Naturally associated with this is the doctrine that the labour fund,[a] consisting of the necessary means of subsistence, is of a definite magnitude, which on the one hand physically limits the share of the labourers in the social product, but on the other has to be fully expended in the purchase of labour power.

---

[24] To what extent Adam Smith has blocked his own way to an understanding of the role of labour power in the process of self-expansion of value is proven by the following sentence, which in the manner of the Physiocrats places the labour of labourers on a level with that of labouring cattle. "NOT ONLY HIS" (THE FARMER'S) "LABOURING SERVANTS, BUT HIS LABOURING CATTLE ARE PRODUCTIVE LABOURERS" ([A. Smith, *Wealth of Nations*,] Book II, Ch. V, p. 243).

---

[a] K. Marx, *Capital*, Vol. I, Ch. XXIV, 5 (present edition, Vol. 35).

Chapter XI

THEORIES OF FIXED AND CIRCULATING CAPITAL. RICARDO

Ricardo introduces the distinction between fixed and circulating capital merely for the purpose of illustrating the exceptions to the rule of value, namely, cases where the rate of wages affects prices. The discussion of this point is reserved for Book III.[a]

But the original lack of clarity is apparent at the outset in the following immaterial juxtaposition:

"This difference in the degree of durability of fixed capital, *and* this variety in the proportions in which the two sorts of capital may be combined."[25)b]

And if we ask him which two sorts of capital he is referring to, we are told:

"The proportions, too, in which the capital that is to support labour, and the capital that is invested in tools, machinery, and buildings, may be variously combined."[26)]

In other words, fixed capital = instruments of labour and circulating capital = capital laid out in labour. "Capital that is to support labour" is a senseless expression culled from Adam Smith. On the one hand the circulating capital is here lumped together with the variable capital, i. e., with that part of productive capital which is laid out in labour. But on the other hand doubly erroneous definitions arise for the reason that the antithesis is not derived from the process of self-expansion of value — constant and variable capital — but from the process of circulation (Adam Smith's old confusion).

First: The differences in the degree of durability of fixed capital and the differences arising from capital being composed of constant and variable capital are conceived as being of equal significance. But the last-named difference determines the difference in the production of surplus value; the first-named on the other hand, so far as the process of self-expansion is concerned, refers only to the manner in which a particular value is transferred from a means of production to the product; so far as the process of circulation is concerned, this difference refers only to the period of the renewal of the expended capital,

---

[25)] *Principles*, p. 25.
[26)] l. c.

---

[a] *Capital*, Vol. III, Ch. XI (present edition, Vol. 37). - [b] Here and below Marx quotes Ricardo in German in the text and gives English original in the footnotes.

or, from another point of view, to the time for which it has been advanced. If instead of seeing through the internal machinery of the capitalist process of production one considers merely the accomplished
phenomena, then these distinctions actually coincide. In the distribution of the social surplus value among the various capitals invested in
different branches of industry, the differences in the different periods
of time for which capital is advanced (for instance the various degrees
of durability of fixed capital) and the different organic compositions
of capital (and therefore also the different circulations of constant and
variable capital) contribute equally toward an equalisation of the general rate of profit and the conversion of values into prices of production.

Secondly: From the point of view of the process of circulation, we
have on one side the instruments of labour — fixed capital, on the
other the material of labour and wages — circulating capital. But
from the point of view of the process of labour and self-expansion, we
have on one side means of production (instruments of labour and material of labour) — constant capital; on the other, labour power —
variable capital. It is wholly immaterial for the organic composition
of capital (Buch I, Kap. XXIII, 2, S. 647)[a] whether a specified quantity of value of constant capital consists of many instruments of labour
and little material of labour or of much material of labour and few instruments of labour, while everything depends on the ratio of the capital laid out in means of production to that laid out in labour power.
Vice versa: from the point of view of the process of circulation, of the
distinction between fixed and circulating capital, it is just as immaterial in what proportions a particular quantity of value of circulating
capital divides into material of labour and wages. From one of these
points of view the material of labour is classed in the same category
with the instruments of labour, as opposed to the capital value laid out
in labour power; from the other viewpoint the part of capital laid out
in labour power ranges with that laid out in material of labour, as opposed to that laid out in instruments of labour.

For this reason the part of the capital value laid out in material of
labour (raw and auxiliary materials) does not appear on either side in
Ricardo. It disappears entirely; for it will not do to class it with fixed
capital, because its mode of circulation coincides entirely with that of
the part of capital laid out in labour power. And on the other hand it
should not be placed alongside circulating capital, because in that

---

[a] English edition: Vol. I, Ch. XXV, 2 (see present edition, Vol. 35).

event the identification of the antithesis of fixed and circulating capital with that of constant and variable capital, which had been handed down by Adam Smith and is tacitly retained, would abolish itself. Ricardo has too much logical instinct not to feel this, and for this reason that part of capital vanishes entirely from his sight.

It is to be noted at this point that the capitalist, to use the jargon of political economy, advances the capital laid out in wages for various periods of time, according to whether he pays these wages weekly, monthly, or quarterly. But as a matter of fact the reverse takes place. It is the labourer who advances his labour to the capitalist for a week, a month, or three months, according to whether he is paid by the week, by the month, or every three months. If the capitalist *bought* labour power instead of paying for it, in other words, if he paid the labourer his wages in advance for a day, a week, a month, or a quarter, he would be justified in claiming that he advanced wages for those periods. But since he pays after the labour *has* lasted for days, weeks, or months, instead of buying it and paying for the time which it *is* to last, the whole thing amounts to a capitalist *quid pro quo*, and the advance which the labourer gives to the capitalist in labour is turned into an advance of money given to the labourer by the capitalist. It does not alter the case in the least that the capitalist gets back the product itself or its value (together with the surplus value embodied in it) from circulation, or realises it, only after a relatively long or short period of time, according to the different periods required for its manufacture or for its circulation. The seller of a commodity does not care a rap what its buyer is going to do with it. The capitalist does not get a machine cheaper because he must advance its entire value at one shot, while this value returns to him only gradually and piecemeal from circulation; nor does he pay more for cotton because its value enters entirely into the value of the product into which it is made and is therefore replaced fully and at one time by the sale of the product.

Let us return to Ricardo.

1. The characteristic feature of variable capital is that a definite, given (and as such constant) part of capital, a given sum of values (assumed to be equal in value to the labour power, although it does not matter here whether the wages are equal, more or less than the value of the labour power), is exchanged for a self-expanding, value-creating power, viz., labour power, which not only reproduces its value, paid by the capitalist, but simultaneously produces a surplus value, a value not existing previously and not paid for by any equiva-

lent. This characteristic property of the part of capital laid out for wages, which distinguishes it *toto coelo* as variable capital from constant capital, disappears whenever the part of capital expended on wages is considered solely from the point of view of the process of circulation and thus appears as circulating capital in contradistinction to the fixed capital laid out in instruments of labour. This is apparent if only from the fact that it is then brought under one head — that of circulating capital — together with the component part of the constant capital laid out in material of labour and opposed to the other component of the constant capital — that laid out in instruments of labour. Surplus value, hence the very circumstance which converts the laid-out sum of value into capital, is entirely ignored thereby. Similarly the fact is ignored that the part of the value added to the product by the capital laid out in wages is newly produced (and therefore really reproduced), while the part of the value which the raw material adds to the product is not newly produced, not really reproduced, but only preserved in the value of the product, conserved, and hence merely reappears as a component part of the value of the product. The distinction, as now seen from the point of view of the contrast between fixed and circulating capital, consists simply in this: The value of the instruments of labour used for the production of a commodity enters only partially into the value of the commodity and is therefore only partially replaced by its sale, hence is replaced altogether only piecemeal and gradually. On the other hand the value of the labour power and subjects of labour (raw materials, etc.) used for the production of a commodity entirely enters into it and is therefore entirely replaced by its sale. In this respect, as far as the process of circulation is concerned, one part of capital presents itself as fixed, the other as fluid, or circulating. In both cases it is a matter of transferring given, advanced values to the product and of their replacement by the sale of the product. The difference now depends only on whether the transfer of value, and consequently the replacement of the value, takes place piecemeal and gradually, or in bulk. The absolutely decisive distinction between the variable and constant capital is thereby blotted out, hence the whole secret of the production of surplus value and of capitalist production, the circumstances which transform certain values and the things in which they present themselves into capital, are obliterated. All constituent parts of capital are then distinguished merely by their mode of circulation (and, of course, circulation of commodities concerns itself solely with already existing, given values); and the capital laid out in wages shares a peculiar mode of circulation with the part of capital laid out in raw materials, semifinished products, auxiliary materials, as opposed to the part of capital laid out in instruments of labour.

It is therefore understandable why bourgeois political economy instinctively clung to Adam Smith's confusion of the categories "constant and variable capital" with the categories "fixed and circulating", and repeated it parrotlike, without criticism, from generation to generation for a century. The part of capital laid out for wages is no longer in the least distinguished by bourgeois political economy from the part of capital laid out for raw materials, and differs only formally from constant capital — on the point of whether it is circulated piecemeal or in one lump by the product. Thereby the basis for an understanding of the real movement of capitalist production, and hence of capitalist exploitation, is buried at one stroke. It is but a question of the reappearance of advanced values.

Ricardo's uncritical adoption of the Smithian confusion is not only more disturbing than it is in the later apologists, in whom the confusion of ideas is rather something not disturbing, but also than in Adam Smith himself, because Ricardo, in contrast to Smith, is more consistent and incisive in his analysis of value and surplus value, and indeed upholds the esoteric Adam Smith against the exoteric Adam Smith.

Among the Physiocrats there is no such confusion. The distinction between *avances annuelles* and *avances primitives* refers only to the different periods of reproduction of the different components of capital, especially of agricultural capital, while their views on the production of surplus value form a part of their theory that is independent of these distinctions, a part they hold up as the strong point of the theory. The formation of surplus value is not explained as originating from capital as such, but is attributed to one particular sphere of the production of capital, agriculture.

2. The essential point in the definition of variable capital — and therefore for the conversion of any sum of values into cap.al — is that the capitalist exchanges a definite, given (and in this sense constant) magnitude of value for value-creating power, a magnitude of value for the production, self-expansion, of value. Whether the capitalist pays the labourer in money or in means of subsistence does not affect this basic definition. It only alters the mode of existence of the value advanced by the capitalist which in one case exists in the form of

money for which the labourer buys himself his means of subsistence in the market, in the other case in the form of means of subsistence which he consumes directly. Developed capitalist production rests indeed on the assumption that the labourer is paid in money, just as in general it presupposes the process of production brought about by the process of circulation, hence presupposes the monetary system. But the creation of surplus value — and consequently the capitalisation of the advanced sum of values — has its source neither in the money form of wages nor in the form of wages paid in kind, nor in the capital laid out in the purchase of labour power. It arises out of the exchange of value for value-creating power, out of the conversion of a constant into a variable magnitude.

The greater or smaller fixity of the instruments of labour depends on their degree of durability, hence on a physical property. Other circumstances being equal, they will wear out sooner or later, will therefore function a longer or a shorter time as fixed capital, according to their durability. But it is by no means solely on account of this physical property of durability that they function as fixed capital. The raw material in metal factories is just as durable as the machines used in manufacturing, and more durable than many component parts of these machines, such as leather and wood. Nevertheless the metal serving as raw material forms a part of the circulating capital, while the instrument of labour, although probably built of the same metal, is a part of the fixed capital when in use. Consequently it is not because of the material, physical nature, nor the relatively great or small speed with which it wears out that a metal is put now in the category of fixed, now in that of circulating capital. This distinction is rather due to the role played by it in the process of production, being a subject of labour in one case and an instrument of labour in the other.

The function of an instrument of labour in the process of production requires that on the average it should serve for a longer or shorter period in ever renewed labour processes. Its very function therefore prescribes that the stuff of which it is composed should be more or less durable. But it is not the durability of the material of which it is fabricated that by itself makes it fixed capital. The same stuff, when raw material, becomes circulating capital, and among economists who confuse the distinction between commodity capital and productive capital with the distinction between circulating and fixed capital, the same stuff, the same machine, is circulating capital as product and fixed capital as instrument of labour.

Although it is not the durability of the material of which it is fabricated that makes an instrument of labour fixed capital, nevertheless its role as such an instrument requires that it should be composed of relatively durable material. The durability of its material is therefore a condition of its function as an instrument of labour, and consequently the material basis of the mode of circulation which renders it fixed capital. Other things being equal, the higher or lower degree of wear and tear of the stuff it is made of impresses upon it in a higher or lower degree the stamp of fixedness, is therefore very closely interwoven with its quality of being fixed capital.

If the part of capital laid out in labour power is considered exclusively from the point of view of circulating capital, hence in contrast with fixed capital, and if consequently the distinctions between constant and variable capital are lumped with those between fixed and circulating capital, then it is natural — supposing that material reality of the instrument of labour forms an essential basis of its character of fixed capital — to derive its character of circulating capital, in contrast with the fixed capital, from the material reality of the capital invested in labour power, and then again to determine the circulating capital with the aid of the material reality of the variable capital.

The real substance of the capital laid out in wages is labour itself, active, value-creating labour power, living labour, which the capitalist exchanges for dead, objectified labour and embodies in his capital, by which means, and by which alone, the value in his hands turns into self-expanding value. But this power of self-expansion is not sold by the capitalist. It is always only a constituent part of his productive capital, the same as his instruments of labour, it is never a part of his commodity capital, as for instance the finished product which he sells. In the process of production the instruments of labour, as components of the productive capital, are not opposed to labour power as fixed capital any more than materials of labour and auxiliary substances are identified with it as circulating capital. Labour power confronts both of them as a personal factor, while those are objective factors — speaking from the point of view of the labour process. Both of them stand opposed to labour power, as constant capital to variable capital — speaking from the point of view of the process of self-expansion of value. Or, if mention is to be made here of a material difference, so far as it affects the process of circulation, it is only this: It follows from the nature of value, which is nothing but objectified labour, and from the nature of active labour power, which is nothing but labour in pro-

cess of objectification, that labour power continually creates value
and surplus value during the time it functions; that what on the part
of labour power appears as motion, as a creation of value, appears on
the part of its product in a state of rest, as created value. If the labour
power has performed its function, capital no longer consists of labour
power on the one side and means of production on the other. The capital value that was invested in labour power is now value which
(+ surplus value) was added to the product. In order to repeat the
process, the product must be sold and new labour power constantly
bought with the proceeds and incorporated in the productive capital.
This then gives to the part of capital invested in labour power, and to
that invested in material of labour, etc., the character of circulating
capital as opposed to the capital remaining fixed in the instruments of
labour.

But if, on the contrary, the secondary definition of the circulating
capital, which it shares with a part of the constant capital (raw and auxiliary materials), is made the essential definition of the part of capital laid out in labour power, to wit, that the value laid out in it is
transferred in full to the product in whose creation it is consumed,
and not gradually and piecemeal as in the case of the fixed capital,
and that consequently it must be replaced in full by the sale of the
product — then the part of the capital laid out in wages must likewise
consist, materially, not of active labour power but of the material elements which the labourer buys with his wages, i. e., it must consist of
that part of the social commodity capital which passes into the consumption of the labourer, viz., of means of subsistence. In that case
the fixed capital consists of the more slowly perishable instruments of
labour which therefore have to be replaced more slowly, and the capital laid out in labour power consists of the means of subsistence,
which must be replaced more rapidly.

However, the borderline between greater or lesser perishableness is
very vague and indistinct.

* "The food and clothing consumed by the labourer, the buildings in which he
works, the implements with which his labour is assisted, are all of a perishable nature.
There is however a vast difference in the time for which these different capitals will endure: a steam-engine will last longer than a ship, a ship than the clothing of the labourer,
and the clothing of the labourer longer than the food which he consumes." * [27)a]

[27)] Ricardo, [*Principles*,] *etc.*, p. 26.

[a] Here and below Marx quotes Ricardo in German in the text and gives English
original in the footnotes.

Ricardo forgets to mention the house in which the labourer lives, his furniture, his tools of consumption, such as knives, forks, dishes, etc., all of which have the same quality of durability as the instruments of labour. The same things, the same kinds of things, appear in one place as articles of consumption and in another as instruments of labour.

The difference, as stated by Ricardo, is this:

   * "According as capital is rapidly perishable and requires to be frequently reproduced, or is of slow consumption, it is classed under the heads of circulating, or fixed capital." * [28)]

And he adds this note:

   *"A division not essential, and in which the line of demarcation cannot be accurately drawn." *[29)]

Thus we have once more happily arrived in the camp of the Physiocrats, where the distinction between *avances annuelles* and *avances primitives* was one referring to the time of consumption, and consequently also to the different times of reproduction of the capital employed. Only, what with them constitutes an important phenomenon of social production and is described in the *Tableau économique* in connection with the process of circulation, becomes here a subjective and, in Ricardo's own words, superfluous distinction.

Once the part of capital invested in labour differs from that invested in instruments of labour only by its period of reproduction and hence its term of circulation, and once one part consists of means of subsistence and the other of instruments of labour so that those differ from these only in being more rapidly perishable, there being various degrees of durability within the first group itself, all *differentia specifica* between capital invested in labour power and capital invested in means of production is naturally obliterated.

This wholly contradicts Ricardo's doctrine of value, likewise his theory of profit, which is in fact a theory of surplus value. In general he considers the distinction between fixed and circulating capital only to the extent that different proportions of both of them in equally large capitals invested in different branches of production influence the law of value, particularly the extent to which an increase or decrease of wages in consequence of these conditions affects prices. But even within this restricted investigation he commits the gravest errors on account of his confusing fixed and circulating with constant and

---

[28)] [Ibid.]
[29)] [Ibid.]

variable capital. Indeed, he starts his analysis on an entirely wrong basis. In the first place, in so far as the part of the capital value laid out in labour power has to be classified under the head of circulating capital, the definitions of circulating capital itself are wrongly developed, particularly the circumstances which place the part of capital laid out in labour under this head. In the second place there is a confusion of the definition according to which the part of capital invested in labour is variable capital with the definition according to which it is circulating capital, as opposed to fixed capital.

It is evident at the outset that the definition of capital invested in labour power as circulating or fluid capital is a secondary one, obliterating its *differentia specifica* in the process of production. For in this definition, on the one hand, the capitals invested in labour are of the same importance as those invested in raw material, etc. A classification which identifies a part of the constant capital with the variable capital does not deal with the *differentia specifica* of variable capital in opposition to constant capital. On the other hand the parts of capital laid out in labour are indeed opposed to those invested in instruments of labour, but not in the least with reference to the fact that these parts enter into the production of value in quite different ways, but with reference to the fact that both transfer their value to the product, but in different periods of time.

In all of these cases the point at issue is *how* a given value, laid out in the process of production of commodities, whether it be wages, the price of raw materials, or that of instruments of labour, is transferred to the product, hence is circulated by the product, and returned to its starting-point by the sale of the product, or is replaced. The only difference lies here in the "*how*", in the particular manner of the transfer, and therefore also of the circulation of this value.

Whether the price of labour power previously stipulated by contract in each individual case is paid in money or means of subsistence does not alter in any way its character of being a definite and given price. However it is evident in the case of wages paid in money that the money itself does not pass into the process of production in the way that the value as well as the material of the means of production do. But if on the other hand the means of subsistence which the labourer buys with his wages are directly classed in the same category, alongside raw materials, etc., as the material form of circulating capital and are opposed to the instruments of labour, then the matter assumes a different aspect. If the value of these things, of the means of production, is transferred to the product in the labour process, the value of those other things, the means of subsistence, reappears in the labour power that consumes them and is likewise transferred to the product by the functioning of this power. In both these cases it is equally a question of the mere reappearance, in the product, of the values advanced during production. (The Physiocrats took this seriously and therefore denied that industrial labour created surplus value.) Thus the previously quoted [a] passage from Wayland.

"It matters not in what form capital reappears... The various kinds of food, clothing, and shelter, necessary for the existence and comfort of the human being, are also changed. They are consumed, from time to time, and their value reappears, etc." (*Elements of Pol. Econ.*, pp. 31, 32). [41]

The capital values advanced for production in the form of both means of production and means of subsistence reappear here equally in the value of the product. Thus the transformation of the capitalist process of production into a complete mystery is happily accomplished and the origin of the surplus value existing in the product is entirely withdrawn from view.

Furthermore this brings to completion the fetishism peculiar to bourgeois political economy, the fetishism which metamorphoses the social, economic character impressed on things in the process of social production into a natural character stemming from the material nature of those things. For instance, "instruments of labour are fixed capital", is a scholastic definition, which leads to contradictions and confusion. Just as was demonstrated in the case of the labour process (Buch I, Kap. V), [b] that it depends wholly on the role which the material components play in a particular labour process, on their function — whether they function as instruments of labour, material of labour, or products — so instruments of labour are fixed capital only if the process of production is really a capitalist process of production and the means of production are therefore really capital and possess economic definiteness, the social character of capital. And in the second place, they are fixed capital only if they transfer their value to the product in a particular way. If not, they remain instruments of labour without being fixed capital. In the same way if auxiliary materials like manure give up value in the same peculiar manner as the greater part of the instruments of labour, they become fixed capital although they are not instruments of labour. It is not a question here

[a] See *Capital*, Vol. I, Ch. VIII, Note 4 (present edition, Vol. 35).-
[b] Ibid., Ch. VII.

of definitions, which things must be made to fit. We are dealing here with definite functions which must be expressed in definite categories.

If to be capital laid out in wages is considered one of the qualities of means of subsistence as such under all circumstances, then it will also be a quality of this "circulating" capital "TO SUPPORT LABOUR"[a] //Ricardo, p. 25//. If the means of subsistence were not "capital" they would not support labour power; whereas it is precisely their quality of capital that endows them with the faculty of supporting *capital* by the labour of others.

If means of subsistence as such are circulating capital— after the latter has been converted into wages— it follows further that the magnitude of wages depends on the ratio of the number of labourers to the given amount of circulating capital— a favourite economic proposition— while as a matter of fact the quantity of means of subsistence withdrawn from the market by the labourer, and the quantity of means of subsistence available for the consumption of the capitalist, depend on the ratio of the surplus value to the price of labour.

Ricardo, like Barton, [29a] everywhere confounds the relation of variable to constant capital with that of circulating to fixed capital. We shall see later to what extent this vitiates his investigation of the rate of profit. [b]

Ricardo furthermore identifies the differences which arise in the turnover from other causes than the distinction between fixed and circulating capital with this distinction:

"It is also to be observed that the circulating capital may circulate, or be returned to its employer, in very unequal times. The wheat bought by a farmer to sow is comparatively a fixed capital to the wheat purchased by a baker to make into loaves. The one leaves it in the ground, and can obtain no return for a year; the other can get it ground into flour, sell it as bread to his customers, and have his capital free, to renew the same, or commence any other employment in a week." [30]

It is characteristic here that wheat, although not serving as a means of subsistence but as raw material when used for sowing, is in the first place circulating capital, because in itself it is a means of sub-

---

[29a] *Observations on the Circumstances Which Influence the Condition of the Labouring Classes of Society*, London, 1817.[42] A pertinent passage is quoted in Book I, p. 655, Note 79. [See *Capital*, Vol. I, Ch. XXV, 3 (present edition, Vol. 35).]

[30] [D. Ricardo, *Principles, etc.*,] pp. 26, 27.

---

[a] In the original the English phrase is given after its German equivalent.- [b] See present edition, Vol. 37 (*Capital*, Vol. III, Ch. I-III).

sistence, and in the second place fixed capital, because its return takes over a year. However it is not only the more or less slow or rapid return which makes a fixed capital of a means of production, but also the definite manner in which it transfers its value to the product.

The confusion created by Adam Smith has brought about the following results:

1. The distinction between fixed and circulating capital is confused with that between productive capital and commodity capital. For instance the same machine is considered circulating capital when in the market as a commodity, and fixed capital when incorporated in the process of production. Moreover, it is absolutely impossible to ascertain why one kind of capital should be more fixed or circulating than another.

2. All circulating capital is identified with capital laid out or to be laid out in wages. This is so in John Stewart Mill, [a][43] and others.

3. The distinction between variable and constant capital, which was previously mistaken by Barton, Ricardo, and others for that between circulating and fixed capital, is finally wholly reduced to this last-named distinction, for instance in Ramsay, [28] where all means of production, raw materials, etc., as well as instruments of labour are fixed capital, and only capital laid out in wages is circulating capital. [b] But because the reduction takes place in this form, the real distinction between constant and variable capital is not understood.

4. The latter-day British, especially Scottish, economists, who look upon all things from the inexpressibly narrow-minded point of view of a bank clerk, such as MacLeod, [c] Patterson, [d] and others, transform the distinction between fixed and circulating capital into one between MONEY AT CALL and MONEY NOT AT CALL ([between] deposit money that can be withdrawn without prior notification and money, whose withdrawal requires such notification).

---

[a] J. St. Mill, *Essays on Some Unsettled Questions of Political Economy*, London, 1844, p. 164.- [b] G. Ramsay, *An Essay on the Distribution of Wealth*, Edinburgh, 1836, pp. 21-24.- [c] H. D. MacLeod, *The Elements of Political Economy*, London, 1858, pp. 76-80.- [d] R. H. Patterson, *The Science of Finance. A Practical Treatise*, Edinburgh and London, 1868, pp. 129-44.

Chapter XII

THE WORKING PERIOD

Let us take two branches of business with working days of equal length, say, of ten hours each, one of them a cotton spinning-mill, the other a locomotive works. In one of these branches a definite quantity of finished product, cotton yarn, is turned out daily or weekly; in the other, the labour process has to be repeated for perhaps three months in order to manufacture a finished product, a locomotive. In one case the product is discrete in nature, and each day or week the same labour starts over again. In the other case the labour process is continuous and extends over a rather great number of daily labour processes which, in their interconnection, in the continuity of their operation, bring forth a finished product only after a rather long period of time. Although the duration of the daily labour process is the same here, there is a very marked difference in the duration of the productive act, i. e., in the duration of the repeated labour processes required to get out a finished product, to market it as a commodity, hence to convert it from productive into commodity capital. The distinction between fixed and circulating capital has nothing to do with this. The distinction indicated would exist even if the very same proportions of fixed and circulating capital were employed in both branches of business.

These differences in the duration of the productive act can be observed not only between different spheres of production, but also within one and the same sphere of production, depending on the amount of product to be turned out. An ordinary dwelling house is built in less time than a large factory and therefore requires fewer continuous labour processes. While the building of a locomotive takes three months, that of an armoured man-of-war requires one year or more. It takes nearly a year to produce grain and several years to raise big cattle, while timber growing needs from 12 to 100 years. A few months will suffice for a country road, while a railway is a job of years. An ordinary carpet is made in about a week, but a *Gobelin* takes years, etc. Hence the time consumed in the performance of the productive act varies infinitely.

The difference in the duration of the productive act must evidently give rise to a difference in the velocity of the turnover, if invested capitals are equal, in other words, must make a difference in the time for which a certain capital is advanced. Assume that a spinning-mill and a locomotive works employ the same amount of capital, that the ratio of their constant to their variable capital is the same, likewise the proportion between the fixed and circulating parts of the capitals, and that lastly their working day is of equal length and its division into necessary and surplus labour the same. In order to eliminate, furthermore, all the circumstances arising out of the process of circulation and having no bearing on the present case, let us suppose that both the yarn and the locomotive are made to order and will be paid on delivery of the finished product. At the end of the week, on delivery of the finished yarn, the spinning-mill owner recovers his outlay for circulating capital (leaving the surplus value out of consideration), likewise the fixed capital's wear and tear incorporated in the value of the yarn. He can therefore repeat the same circuit anew with the same capital. It has completed its turnover. The locomotive manufacturer on the other hand must lay out ever new capital for wages and raw material every week for three months in succession, and it is only after three months, after the delivery of the locomotive, that the circulating capital, meanwhile gradually laid out in one and the same productive act for the manufacture of one and the same commodity, once more exists in a form in which it can renew its circuit. The wear and tear of his machinery during these three months is likewise replaced only now. The expenditure of the one is made for one week, that of the other is the weekly expenditure multiplied by 12. All other circumstances being assumed as equal, the one must have twelve times as much circulating capital at his disposal as the other.

It is however immaterial here that the capitals advanced weekly are equal. Whatever the amount of the advanced capital, it is advanced for only one week in the one case and for twelve weeks in the other, and the above periods must respectively elapse before it can be used for a new operation, before the same operation can be repeated with it, or a different one inaugurated.

The difference in the velocity of the turnover, or in the length of time for which the individual capital must be advanced before the same capital value can be employed in a new labour or self-expansion process, arises here from the following circumstances:

Granted the manufacture of a locomotive or of any other machine requires 100 working days. So far as the labourers employed in the manufacture of yarn or the building of locomotives are concerned, the 100 working days constitute in either case a discontinuous (discrete) magnitude, consisting, according to our assumption, of 100 consecutive separate ten-hour labour processes. But so far as the product — the machine — is concerned, these 100 working days form a continuous magnitude, a working day of 1,000 working hours, one single connected act of production. I call such a working day which is composed of a more or less numerous succession of connected working days a *working period*. When we speak of a working day we mean the length of working time during which the labourer must daily spend his labour power, must work day by day. But when we speak of a working period we mean the number of connected working days required in a certain branch of industry for the manufacture of a finished product. In this case the product of every working day is but a partial one, which is further worked upon from day to day and only at the end of the longer or shorter working period receives its finished form, is a finished use value.

Interruptions, disturbances of the process of social production, in consequence for instance of crises, have therefore very different effects on labour products of a discrete nature and on those that require for their production a prolonged connected period. In the one case all that happens is that today's production of a certain quantity of yarn, coal, etc., is not followed by tomorrow's new production of yarn, coal, etc. Not so in the case of ships, buildings, railways, etc. Here it is not only the day's work but an entire connected act of production that is interrupted. If the job is not continued, the means of production and labour already consumed in its production are wasted. Even if it is resumed, a deterioration has inevitably set in in the meantime.

For the entire length of the working period, the part of the value daily transferred to the product by the fixed capital accumulates in layers, as it were, until the product is finished. And here the difference between fixed and circulating capital is revealed at the same time in its practical significance. Fixed capital is advanced in the process of production for a comparatively long period; it need not be renewed until after the expiration of perhaps a period of several years. Whether a steam-engine transfers its value daily piecemeal to some yarn, the product of a discrete labour process, or for three months to a locomotive, the product of a continuous act of production, is immaterial as far as laying out the capital required for the purchase of the steam-engine is concerned. In the one case its value flows back in small doses, for instance weekly, in the other case in larger quantities, for instance quarterly. But in either case the renewal of the steam-engine may take place only after some 20 years. So long as every individual period within which the value of the steam-engine is returned piecemeal by the sale of the product is shorter than the lifetime of the engine itself, the latter continues to function in the process of production for several working periods.

It is different with the circulating components of the advanced capital. The labour power bought for a definite week is expended in the course of the same week and is objectified in the product. It must be paid for at the end of the week. And this investment of capital in labour power is repeated every week during the three months; yet the expenditure of this part of the capital during the one week does not enable the capitalist to settle for the purchase of the labour the following week. Every week additional capital must be expended to pay for labour power, and, leaving aside the question of credit, the capitalist must be able to lay out wages for three months, even if he pays them only in weekly doses. It is the same with the other portion of circulating capital, the raw and auxiliary materials. One layer of labour after another is piled up on the product. It is not alone the value of the expended labour power that is continually being transferred to the product during the labour process, but also surplus value. This product, however, is unfinished, it has not yet the form of a finished commodity, hence it cannot yet circulate. This applies likewise to the capital value transferred in layers from the raw and auxiliary materials to the product.

Depending on the length of the working period exacted by the specific nature of the product or by the useful effect to be achieved in its manufacture, a continuous additional investment of circulating capital (wages and raw and auxiliary materials) is required, no part of which is in a form capable of circulation and hence of promoting a renewal of the same operation. Every part is on the contrary held fast successively in the sphere of production as a component of the nascent product, tied up in the form of productive capital. Now, the time of turnover is equal to the sum of the time of production and the time of circulation of the capital. Hence a prolongation of the time of production reduces the velocity of the turnover quite as much as a prolongation of the time of circulation. In the present case however the following two points must be noted:

Firstly: The prolonged stay in the sphere of production. The capital advanced for instance for labour, raw material, etc., during the first week, as well as the portions of value transferred to the product by the fixed capital, are held fast in the sphere of production for the entire term of three months, and, being incorporated in an only nascent, still unfinished product, cannot pass into circulation as commodities.

Secondly: Since the working period required for the performance of the productive act lasts three months, and forms in fact only one connected labour process, a new' dose of circulating capital must be continually added week after week to the preceding amount. The total of the successively advanced additional capital grows therefore with the length of the working period.

We have assumed that capitals of equal size are invested in spinning and machine-building, that these capitals contain equal proportions of constant and variable, fixed and circulating capital, that the working days are of equal length, in brief, that all conditions are equal except the duration of the working period. In the first week, the outlay for both is the same, but the product of the spinner can be sold and the proceeds of the sale used to buy new labour power, new raw materials, etc.; in short, production can be resumed on the same scale. The machine-manufacturer on the other hand cannot reconvert the circulating capital expended in the first week into money and resume operations with it until three months later, when his product is finished. There is therefore first a difference in the return of the identical quantities of capital invested. But in the second place identical amounts of productive capital are employed during the three months in both spinning and machine-building. However the magnitude of the outlay of capital in the case of the yarn manufacturer is quite different from that of the machine-builder; for in the one case the same capital is rapidly renewed and the same operation can therefore be repeated, while in the other case the renewal of the capital is relatively slow, so that ever new quantities of capital must be added to the old up to the time of its renewal. Consequently there is a difference not only in the length of time of renewal of definite portions of capital, or in the length of time for which the capital is advanced, but also in the quantity of the capital to be advanced according to the duration of the labour process (although the capitals employed daily or weekly are equal). This circumstance is worthy of note for the reason that the term of the advance may be prolonged, as we shall see in the cases treated in the next chapter, without thereby necessitating a corresponding increase in the amount of the capital to be advanced. The capital must be advanced for a longer time, and a larger amount of capital is tied up in the form of productive capital.

At the less developed stages of capitalist production, undertakings requiring a long working period, and hence a large investment of capital for a long time, such as the building of roads, canals, etc., especially when they can be carried out only on a large scale, are either not carried out on a capitalist basis at all, but rather at communal or state expense (in earlier times generally by forced labour, so far as the labour power was concerned). Or objects whose production requires a lengthy working period are fabricated only for the smallest part by recourse to the private means of the capitalist himself. For instance, in the building of a house, the private person for whom it is built makes a number of partial advance payments to the building contractor. He therefore actually pays for the house piecemeal, in proportion as the productive process progresses. But in the advanced capitalist era, when on the one hand huge capitals are concentrated in the hands of single individuals, while on the other the associated capitalist (joint-stock companies) appears side by side with the individual capitalist and a credit system has simultaneously been developed, a capitalist building contractor builds only in exceptional cases on the order of private individuals. His business nowadays is to build whole rows of houses and entire sections of cities for the market, just as it is the business of individual capitalists to build railways as contractors.

To what extent capitalist production has revolutionised the building of houses in London is shown by the testimony of a builder before the Bank Acts Committee of 1857. When he was young, he said, houses were generally built to order and the payments made in instalments to the contractor as certain stages of the building were being completed. Very little was built on speculation. Contractors used to assent to such operations mainly to keep their men in constant employment and thus hold them together. In the last 40 years all that has changed. Very little is now built to order. Anyone wanting a new house picks one from among those built on speculation or still in process of construction. The builder no longer works for his customers but for the market. Like every other industrial capitalist he is compelled to have finished articles in the market. While formerly a builder had perhaps three or four houses building at a time on speculation, he must now buy a large plot of ground (which in continental language means rent it for 99 years, as a rule), build from 100 to 200 houses on it, and thus embark on an enterprise which exceeds his resources twenty to fifty times. The funds are procured through mortgaging and the money is placed at the disposal of the contractor as the buildings proceed. Then, if a crisis comes along and interrupts the payment of the advance instalments, the entire enterprise generally collapses. At best, the houses remain unfinished until better times arrive; at the worst they are sold at auction for half their cost. Without speculative building, and on a large scale at that, no contractor can get along today. The profit from just building is extremely small. His main profit comes from raising the ground rent, from careful selection and skilled utilisation of the building terrain. It is by this method of speculation anticipating the demand for houses that almost the whole of Belgravia and Tyburnia, and the countless thousands of villas round London have been built. (Abbreviated from the Report of the Select Committee on Bank Acts, Part I, 1857, Evidence, Questions 5413-18; 5435-36.)

The execution of enterprises requiring working periods of considerable length and operations on a large scale does not fall fully within the province of capitalist production until the concentration of capital becomes very pronounced, and the development of the credit system offers to the capitalist, on the other hand, the convenient expedient of advancing and thus risking other people's capital instead of his own. It goes without saying that whether the capital advanced in production belongs to him who uses it or does not has no effect on the velocity or time of turnover.

Conditions such as co-operation, division of labour, application of machinery, which augment the product of the individual working day, shorten at the same time the working period of connected acts of production. Thus machinery shortens the building time of houses, bridges, etc.; mowers, threshers, etc., reduce the working period required to transform ripe grain into the finished product. Greater speed due to improved shipbuilding cuts the turnover time of capital invested in shipping. But improvements that shorten the working period and thereby the time during which circulating capital must be advanced generally go hand in hand with an increased outlay of fixed capital. On the other hand the working period in certain branches of production may be diminished by the mere extension of co-operation.

The completion of a railway is expedited by setting afoot huge armies of labourers and thus tackling the job in many spots at once. The time of turnover is lessened in that case by an increase of the advanced capital. More means of production and more labour power must be united under the command of the capitalist.

Whereas the shortening of the working period is thus mostly connected with an increase of the capital advanced for this abbreviated time — the shorter the term of advance the greater the capital advanced — it must here be recalled that regardless of the existing amount of social capital, the essential point is the degree in which the means of production and subsistence, or the disposal of them, are scattered or concentrated in the hands of individual capitalists, in other words, the degree of concentration of capitals already attained. Inasmuch as credit promotes, accelerates and enhances the concentration of capital in one hand, it contributes to the shortening of the working period and thus of the turnover time.

In branches of production in which the working period, whether continuous or discontinuous, is prescribed by definite natural conditions, no shortening by the above-mentioned means can take place.

"In regard to quicker returns, this term cannot be made to apply to corn crops, as one return only can be made per annum. In respect to stock, we will simply ask, how is the return of two- and three-year-old sheep, and four- and five-year-old oxen to be quickened"(W. Walter Good, *Political, Agricultural, and Commercial Fallacies*, London, 1866, p. 325). [44]

The necessity of securing ready money as soon as possible (for instance to meet fixed obligations, such as taxes, ground rent, etc.) solves this problem, e. g., by selling or slaughtering cattle before they have reached the economically normal age, to the great detriment of agriculture. This also brings about in the end a rise in the price of meat.

"Men who have mainly reared cattle for supplying the pastures of the Midland counties in summer, and the yards of the eastern counties in winter ... have become so crippled through the uncertainty and lowness in the prices of corn that they are glad to take advantage of the high prices of butter and cheese; the former they take to market weekly to help to pay current expenses, and draw on the other from some factor, who takes the cheese when fit to move, and, of course, nearly at his own price. For this reason, remembering that farming is governed by the principles of political economy, the calves which used to come south from the dairying counties for rearing, are now largely sacrificed at times at a week and ten days old, in the shambles of Birmingham, Manchester, Liverpool, and other large neighbouring towns. If, however, malt had been free from duty, not only would farmers have made more profit and therefore been able to keep their stock till it got older and heavier, but it would have been substituted for milk for rearing by men who did not keep cows, and thus the present alarming scarcity of young cattle which has befallen the nation would have been largely averted. What these little men now say, in reply to recommendations to rear, is, 'We know very well it would pay to rear on milk, but it would first require us to put our hands in our purse, which we cannot do, and then we should have to wait a long time for a return, instead of getting it at once by dairying'" (ibid., pp. 11 and 12).

If the prolongation of the turnover has such consequences even for the small English farmers, it is easy to see what disarrangement it must produce among the small peasants of the continent.

The part of the value transferred in layers by the fixed capital to the product accumulates, and the return of this part is delayed, in proportion to the length of the working period and thus also of the period of time required for the completion of the commodity capable of circulation. But this delay does not cause a renewed outlay of fixed capital. The machine continues to function in the process of production, whether the replacement of its wear and tear in the form of money returns slowly or rapidly. It is different with the circulating capital. Not only must capital be tied up for a rather long time, in proportion to the length of the working period, but new capital must be continually advanced in the shape of wages, and raw and auxiliary materials. A delayed return has therefore a different effect on each. No matter whether the return is rapid or slow, the fixed capital continues to function. But the circulating capital becomes unable to perform its functions, if the return is delayed, if it is tied up in the form of unsold, or unfinished and as yet unsalable products, and if no additional capital is at hand for its renewal *in natura*.

"While the peasant farmer starves, his cattle thrive. Repeated showers had fallen in the country, and the forage was abundant. The Hindoo peasant will perish by hunger beside a fat bullock. The prescriptions of superstition, which appear cruel to the individual, are conservative for the community; and the preservation of the labouring cattle secures the power of cultivation, and the sources of future life and wealth. It may sound harsh and sad to say so, but in India it is more easy to replace a man than an ox" (Return, East India. Madras and Orissa Famine. No. 4, p. 44).

Compare with the preceding the utterance of Manava Dharma Sastra, [45] Chapter X, § 62.

"Desertion of life, without reward, for the sake of preserving a priest or a cow ... may cause the beatitude of those base-born tribes."

Naturally, it is impossible to deliver a five-year-old animal before the lapse of five years. But what *is* possible, within certain limits, is getting animals ready for their destination in less time by changing the way of treating them. This is precisely what Bakewell accomplished. Formerly English sheep, like the French as late as 1855, were not fit for the butcher until four or five years old. According to the Bakewell system, sheep may be fattened when only one year old and in every case have reached their full growth before the end of the second year. By careful selection, Bakewell, a Dishley Grange farmer, reduced the skeleton of sheep to the minimum required for their existence. His sheep are called the New Leicesters.

"The breeder can now send three to market in the same space of time that it formerly took him to prepare one; and if they are not taller, they are broader, rounder, and have a greater development in those parts which give most flesh. [...] Almost all their weight is pure meat" (Lavergne, *The Rural Economy of England, etc.*, 1855, p. 20).

The methods which shorten the working period are applicable in various branches of industry to a widely varying extent and do not eliminate the time differences of the various working periods. To stick to our illustration, the working period required for the building of a locomotive may be absolutely shortened by the employment of new machine-tools. But if at the same time the finished product turned out daily or weekly by a cotton-spinning mill is still more rapidly increased by improved processes, then the working period in machine-building, compared with that in spinning, has nevertheless grown relatively in length.

Chapter XIII

THE TIME OF PRODUCTION

Working time is always production time, that is to say, time during which capital is held fast in the sphere of production. But vice versa, not all time during which capital is engaged in the process of production is necessarily working time.

It is here not a question of interruptions of the labour process necessitated by natural limitations of the labour power itself, although we have seen to what extent the mere circumstance that fixed capital — factory buildings, machinery, etc.— lies idle during pauses in

the labour process,[a] became one of the motives for an unnatural prolongation of the labour process and for day and night work. We are
dealing here rather with interruptions independent of the length of
the labour process, brought about by the very nature of the product
and its fabrication, during which the subject of labour is for a longer
or shorter time subjected to natural processes, must undergo physical,
chemical and physiological changes, during which the labour process
is entirely or partially suspended.

For instance grape after being pressed must ferment awhile and
then rest for some time in order to reach a certain degree of perfection. In many branches of industry the product must pass through
a drying process, for instance in pottery, or be exposed to certain conditions in order to change its chemical properties, as for instance in
bleaching. Winter grain needs about nine months to mature. Between the time of sowing and harvesting the labour process is almost
entirely suspended. In timber-raising, after the sowing and the incidental preliminary work are completed, the seed requires about 100
years to be transformed into a finished product and during all that
time it stands in comparatively very little need of the action of labour.

In all these cases additional labour is drawn on only occasionally
during a large portion of the time of production. The condition described in the previous chapter, where additional capital and labour
must be supplied to the capital already tied up in the process of production, obtains here only with longer or shorter intervals.

In all these cases therefore the production time of the advanced capital consists of two periods: one period during which the capital is engaged in the labour process and a second period during which its
form of existence — that of an unfinished product —·is abandoned to
the sway of natural processes, without being at that time in the labour
process. Nor does it matter in the least that these two periods of time
may cross or wedge into one another here and there. The working
period and the production period do not coincide in these cases. The
production period is longer than the working period. But the product
is not finished, not ready, hence not fit to be converted from the form
of productive into that of commodity capital until the production
period is completed. Consequently the length of the turnover period
increases in proportion to the length of the production time that does
not consist of working time. In so far as the production time in excess

---

[a] K. Marx, *Capital*, Vol. I, Ch. X, 4, 5 (see present edition, Vol. 35).

of the working time is not fixed by natural laws given once and for all, such as govern the maturing of grain, the growth of an oak, etc., the period of turnover can often be more or less shortened by an artificial reduction of the production time. Such instances are the introduction of chemical bleaching instead of bleaching on the green and more efficient drying apparatus. Or, in tanning, where the penetration of the tannic acid into the skins, by the old method, took from six to eighteen months, while the new method, by means of an air-pump, does it in only one and a half to two months (J. G. Courcelle-Seneuil, *Traité théorique et pratique des entreprises industrielles, etc.*, Paris, 1857, 2-me éd. [p. 49] [46]). The most magnificent illustration of an artificial abbreviation of the time of production taken up exclusively with natural processes is furnished by the history of iron manufacture, more especially the conversion of pig iron into steel during the last 100 years, from the puddling process discovered about 1780 to the modern Bessemer process and the latest methods introduced since. The time of production has been brought down tremendously, but the investment of fixed capital has increased in proportion.

A peculiar illustration of the divergence of the production time from the working time is furnished by the American manufacture of shoe-lasts. In this case a considerable portion of the unproductive costs arises from having to hold the timber at least eighteen months before it is dry enough to work, so as to prevent subsequent warping. During this time the wood does not pass through any other labour process. The period of turnover of the invested capital is therefore not determined solely by the time required for the manufacture of the lasts but also by the time during which it lies unproductive in the shape of drying wood. It stays 18 months in the process of production before it can enter into the labour process proper. This example shows at the same time that the times of turnover of different parts of the aggregate circulating capital may differ in consequence of conditions which do not arise within the sphere of circulation but owe their origin to the production process.

The difference between production time and working time becomes especially apparent in agriculture. In our moderate climates the land bears grain once a year. Shortening or lengthening the period of production (for winter grain it averages nine months) itself depends on the alternation of good and bad seasons, and for this reason cannot be accurately determined and controlled beforehand as in industry proper. Only such by-products as milk, cheese, etc., can steadily be produced and sold in comparatively short periods. On the other hand, working time data are as follows:

"The number of working days in the various regions of Germany, with due regard to the climatic and other determining conditions, will for the three main working periods presumably be: For the spring period, from the middle of March or beginning of April to the middle of May, about 50 to 60 working days; for the summer period, from the beginning of June to the end of August, 65 to 80; and for the autumn period, from the beginning of September to the end of October, or the middle or end of November, 55 to 75 working days. For the winter, only the jobs customary for that time, such as the hauling of manure, wood, market goods, building materials, etc., are to be noted" (F. Kirchhof, *Handbuch der landwirthschaftlichen Betriebslehre*, Dessau, 1852, S. 160). [33]

The more unfavourable the climate, the more congested is the working period in agriculture, and hence the shorter is the time in which capital and labour are expended. Take Russia for instance. In some of the northern districts of that country field labour is possible only from 130 to 150 days throughout the year, and it may be imagined what a loss Russia would sustain if 50 out of the 65 millions of her European population remained without work during the six or eight months of the winter, when agricultural labour is at a standstill. Apart from the 200,000 peasants who work in the 10,500 factories of Russia, local domestic industries have everywhere developed in the villages. There are villages in which all the peasants have been for generations weavers, tanners, shoemakers, locksmiths, cutlers, etc. This is particularly the case in the gubernias of Moscow, Vladimir, Kaluga, Kostroma, and Petersburg. By the way, this domestic industry is being pressed more and more into the service of capitalist production. The weavers for instance are supplied with warp and woof directly by merchants or through middlemen. (Abbreviated from the Reports by H. M. Secretaries of Embassy and Legation, on the Manufactures, Commerce, etc., No. 8, 1865, pp. 86 and 87.) We see here that the divergence of the production period from the working period, the latter being but a part of the former, constitutes the natural basis for the combination of agriculture with subsidiary rural industries, and that these subsidiary industries in turn offer points of vantage to the capitalist, who intrudes first in the person of the merchant. When capitalist production later accomplishes the separation of manufacture and agriculture, the rural labourer becomes ever more dependent on merely casual accessory employment and his condition deteriorates thereby. For capital, as will be seen later, all differences in the turnover are evened out. Not so for the labourer.

In most branches of industry proper, of mining, transportation, etc., operations proceed evenly, the working time being the same year in year out and the outlay of capital passing daily into the circulation process being uniformly distributed, apart from such abnormal interruptions as fluctuations of prices, business dislocations, etc. Likewise the return of the circulating capital or its renewal is evenly distributed throughout the year, market conditions otherwise remaining the same. Yet there is in the course of the various periods of the year the greatest inequality in the outlay of circulating capital in such capital investments in which the working time constitutes only a part of the production time, while the return takes place only in bulk at a time fixed by natural conditions. If the scale of business is the same, i.e., if the amount of advanced circulating capital is the same, it must be advanced in larger quantities at a time and for longer periods than in enterprises with continuous working periods. There is also a considerably greater difference here between the life of the fixed capital and the time in which it really functions productively. Due to the difference between working time and production time, the time of employment of the applied fixed capital is of course likewise continually interrupted for a longer or shorter time, for instance in agriculture in the case of labouring cattle, implements and machines. In so far as this fixed capital consists of draught animals, it requires continually the same, or nearly the same, expenditure for feed, etc., as it does during the time they work. In the case of dead stock non-use also brings on a certain amount of depreciation. Hence the product is in general increasing in price, since the transfer of value to it is not calculated according to the time during which the fixed capital functions but according to the time during which it depreciates in value. In branches of production such as these, the idling of the fixed capital, whether combined with current expenses or not, forms as much a condition of its normal employment as for instance the loss of a certain quantity of cotton in spinning; and in the same way the labour power expended unproductively but unavoidably in any labour process under normal technical conditions counts just as well as that expended productively. Every improvement which reduces the unproductive expenditure of instruments of labour, raw material, and labour power also reduces the value of the product.

In agriculture we have a combination of both the longer working period and the great difference between working time and production time. Hodgskin rightly remarks:

"The difference of time" //although he does not differentiate here between working time and production time// "required to complete the products of agriculture, and of other species of labour," is "the main cause of the great dependence of the agriculturists. They cannot bring their commodities to market in less time than a year. For that whole period they are obliged to borrow of the shoemaker, the tailor, the smith, the wheelwright, and the various other labourers, whose products they cannot dispense with, but which are completed in a few days or weeks. Owing to this natural circumstance, and owing to the more rapid increase of the wealth produced by other labour than that of agriculture, the monopolisers of all the land, though they have also monopolised legislation, have not been able to save themselves and their servants, the farmers, from becoming the most dependent class of men in the community" (Thomas Hodgskin, *Popular Political Economy*, London, 1827, p. 147, note).[47]

All methods by which in agriculture on the one hand the expenditures for wages and instruments of labour are distributed more evenly over the entire year, while on the other the turnover is shortened by raising a greater variety of crops, thus making different harvests possible throughout the year, require an increase of the circulating capital advanced in production, invested in wages, fertilisers, seed, etc. This is the case in the transition from the three-field system with fallow land to the system of crop rotation without fallow. It applies furthermore to the *cultures dérobées* of Flanders.

"The root crops are planted in *culture dérobée*; the same field yields in succession first grain, flax, colza, for the wants of man, and after they are harvested root crops are sown for the maintenance of cattle. This system, which permits the keeping of horned cattle in the stables, yields a considerable amount of manure and thus becomes the pivot of crop rotation. More than a third of the cultivated area in sandy districts is taken up with *cultures dérobées*; it is just as if the cultivated area had been increased by one-third."

Apart from root crops, clover and other fodder plants are likewise used for this purpose.

"Agriculture, being thus carried to a point where it turns into horticulture, naturally requires a considerable investment of capital. This capital, estimated in England at 250 francs per hectare, must be almost 500 francs in Flanders, a figure which good farmers will undoubtedly consider far too low, judging by their own lands" (*Essai sur l'économie rurale de la Belgique*, par Émile de Laveleye, Bruxelles, 1863, pp. 59, 60, 63).[48]

Take finally timber-growing.

"The production of timber differs from most of the other branches of production essentially in that here the forces of nature act independently and do not require the power of man or capital when the increase is natural. Even in places where forests are propagated artificially the expenditure of human and capital energy is inconsiderable compared with the action of the natural forces. Besides, a forest will still thrive in soils and on sites where grain no longer gets along or where its cultivation no longer pays. Furthermore forestry engaged in as a regular economy requires a larger area than grain culture, because small plots do not permit of proper forestry methods, largely prevent the enjoyment of the secondary uses to which the land can be put, make forest protection more difficult, etc. But the productive process extends over such long periods that it exceeds the planning of an individual farm and in certain cases surpasses the entire span of a human life. The capital invested in the purchase of forest land"

//in the case of communal production this capital becomes unnecessary, the question then being simply what acreage the community can spare from its sowing and grazing area for forestry//

"will not yield substantial returns until after a long period, and even then is turned over only partially. With forests producing certain species of trees the complete turnover takes as much as 150 years. Besides, a properly managed timber-growing establishment itself demands a supply of standing timber which amounts to ten to forty times the annual yield. Unless a man has therefore still other sources of income and owns vast tracts of forest land, he cannot engage in regular forestry" (Kirchhof, p. 58).

The long production time (which comprises a relatively small period of working time) and the great length of the periods of turnover entailed make forestry an industry of little attraction to private and therefore capitalist enterprise, the latter being essentially private even if the associated capitalist takes the place of the individual capitalist. The development of culture and of industry in general has ever evinced itself in such energetic destruction of forests that everything done by it conversely for their preservation and restoration appears infinitesimal.

The following passage in the above quotation from Kirchhof is particularly worthy of note:

"Besides, a properly managed timber-growing establishment itself demands a supply of standing timber which amounts to ten to forty times the annual yield."

In other words, a turnover occurs once in ten to forty or more years.

The same applies to stock raising. A part of the herd (supply of cattle) remains in the process of production, while another part is sold annually as a product. In this case only a part of the capital is turned over every year, just as in the case of fixed capital: machinery, labouring cattle, etc. Although this capital is a capital fixed in the process of production for a long time, and thus prolongs the turnover of the total capital, it is not a fixed capital in the strict definition of the term.

What is here called a supply — a certain amount of standing timber or livestock — exists relatively in the process of production (simultaneously as instruments of labour and material of labour); in accordance with the natural conditions of its reproduction under proper management, a considerable part of this supply must always be available in this form.

A similar influence on the turnover is exerted by another kind of supply, which is productive capital only potentially, but which, owing to the nature of this economy, must be accumulated in more or less considerable quantities and hence advanced for purposes of production for a long term, although it enters into the actual process of production only gradually. In this class belongs for instance manure before it is hauled to the field, furthermore grain, hay, etc., and such supplies of means of subsistence as are employed in the production of cattle.

"A considerable part of the working capital is contained in the farm's supplies. But these may lose more or less of their value, if the precautionary measures necessary for their preservation in good condition are not properly observed. Lack of attention may even result in the total loss of a part of the produce supplies for the farm. For this reason, a careful inspection of the barns, feed and grain lofts, and cellars becomes indispensable, the store rooms must always be well closed, kept clean, ventilated, etc. The grain and other crops held in storage must be thoroughly turned over from time to time; potatoes and beets must be protected against frost, rain, and rot" (Kirchhof, p. 292). "In calculating one's own requirements, especially for the keeping of cattle, the distribution must be made according to the product obtained and its intended use. One must not only consider covering one's ordinary needs but also see to it that there is a proportionate reserve for extraordinary cases. If it is then found that the demand cannot be fully met by one's own production, it becomes necessary to reflect first whether the deficiency cannot be covered by other products (substitutes), or by the cheaper procurement of such in place of the deficient ones. For instance if there should happen to be a shortage of hay, this might be made good by roots and an admixture of straw. In general, the intrinsic value and market price of the various crops must always be kept in mind in such cases, and consumption regulated accordingly. If for instance oats are high, while peas and rye are relatively low, it will pay to substitute peas or rye for a part of the oats intended for horses and to sell the oats thus saved" (ibid., p. 300).

It was previously stated, when discussing the formation of a supply,[a] that a definite quantity, big or small, of potential productive capital is required, i. e., of means of production intended for use in production, which must be available in bigger or smaller quantities for the purpose of entering by and by into the productive process. The remark was incidentally made that, given a certain business or capi-

---

[a] See this volume, pp. 141-47.

talist enterprise of definite proportions, the magnitude of this productive supply depends on the greater or lesser difficulties of its renewal, the relative nearness of markets of supply, the development of transportation and communication facilities, etc. All these circumstances affect the minimum of capital which must be available in the form of a productive supply, hence affect the length of time for which the capital must be advanced and the amount of capital to be advanced at one time. This amount, which affects also the turnover, is determined by the longer or shorter time during which a circulating capital is tied up in the form of a productive supply as merely potential productive capital. On the other hand, inasmuch as this stagnation depends on the greater or smaller possibility of rapid replacement, on market conditions, etc., it arises itself out of the time of circulation, out of circumstances that belong in the sphere of circulation.

"Furthermore, all such implements and accessories as hand tools, sieves, baskets, ropes, wagon grease, nails, etc., must be the more available for immediate replacement, the less there is opportunity for purchasing them nearby without delay. Finally, the entire supply of implements must be carefully overhauled every winter, and new purchases or repairs found necessary must be provided for at once. Whether or not one is to keep a great or small supply of articles of equipment is to be settled mainly by local conditions. Wherever there are no artisans or stores in the vicinity, it is necessary to keep larger supplies than in places where these are to be had on the spot or nearby. But if the necessary supplies are procured in large quantities at a time, then, other circumstances being equal, one generally gets the benefit of cheaper purchases, provided an appropriate time has been chosen to make them. True, the rotating working capital is thereby shorn of a correspondingly larger sum, all at once, which cannot always be well spared in the business" (Kirchhof, p. 301).

The difference between production time and working time admits of many variations, as we have seen. For the circulating capital it may be production time before it enters into the labour process proper (production of lasts); or it may be production time after it has passed through the labour process proper (wine, seed grain); or the production time is occasionally interrupted by working time (agriculture, timber-growing). A large portion of the product fit for circulation remains incorporated in the active process of production, while a much smaller part enters into annual circulation (timber-growing and cattle raising); the longer or shorter period of time for which a circulating capital must be invested in the form of potential productive capital, hence also the larger or smaller amount of this capital to be advanced at one time, depends partly on the kind of productive process (agriculture), and partly on the proximity of markets, etc., in short, on circumstances pertinent to the sphere of circulation.

We shall see later (Book III), what senseless theories MacCulloch, James Mill, etc., arrived at as a result of the attempt to identify the production time diverging from working time with the latter, an attempt which in turn is due to a misapplication of the theory of value.

———

The turnover cycle which we considered above is determined by the durability of the fixed capital advanced for the process of production. Since this cycle extends over a number of years, it comprises a series of either annual turnovers of fixed capital or of turnovers repeated during the year.

In agriculture such a cycle of turnovers arises out of the system of crop rotation.

"The duration of the lease must in no case be less than the time of completion of the adopted system of crop rotation. Hence one always calculates 3, 6, 9, etc., in the three-field system. In that system with clean fallow, a field is cultivated only four times in six years, being sown to winter and summer grain in the years of cultivation, and, if the properties of the soil require or permit it, to wheat and rye, barley and oats successively. Every species of grain differs in its yield from the others on the same soil, every one of them has a different value and is sold at a different price. For this reason the yield of a field is different every year it is cultivated, and different in the first half of the rotation (the first three years) from that of the second. Even the average yield of one period of rotation is not equal to that of another, for fertility does not depend solely on the good quality of the soil, but also on the weather each year, just as prices depend on a multitude of changing conditions. If one now calculates the income from a field by taking into account the average fertility and the average prices for the entire six-year rotation period, one finds the total income of one year in either period of the rotation. But this is not so if the proceeds are calculated only for half of the time of rotation, that is to say, for three years; for then the total income figures would not coincide. It follows from the foregoing that a lease of land worked by the three-field system should run for at least six years. It is however always still more desirable for lessor and lessee that the duration of the lease should be a multiple of the duration of the lease" //sic!//; "hence that it should be 12, 18, and ever more years instead of 6 years in a system of three fields and 14, 28 years instead of 7 in a system of seven fields" (Kirchhof, pp. 117, 118).

//At this place the manuscript contains the note: "The English system of crop rotation. Give a note here."//

Chapter XIV·

THE TIME OF CIRCULATION

All circumstances considered so far which distinguish the periods of turnover of different capitals invested in different branches of industry and hence also the periods for which capital must be advanced, originate in the process of production itself, such as the difference between fixed and circulating capital, the difference in the working periods, etc. But the time of turnover of capital is equal to the sum of its production time plus its circulation, or rotation, time. It is therefore a matter of course that a difference in the time of circulation causes a difference in the time of turnover and hence in the length of the period of turnover. This becomes most evident either on comparing two different investments of capital in which all circumstances modifying the turnover are equal except the time of circulation, or on selecting a given capital with a given proportion of fixed and circulating capital, a given working period, etc., with only the times of circulation varying hypothetically.

One of the sections of the time of circulation — relatively the most decisive — consists of the time of selling, the period during which capital exists in the state of commodity capital. The time of circulation, and hence the period of turnover in general, are long or short depending on the relative length of this selling time. An additional outlay of capital may become necessary as a result of expenses of storage, etc. It is clear at the very start that the time required for the sale of finished goods may differ considerably for the individual capitalists in one and the same branch of production. Hence it may differ not only for the aggregate capitals invested in the various branches of industry, but also for the various independent capitals, which are in fact merely parts of the aggregate capital invested in the same sphere of production but which have made themselves independent. Other circumstances remaining equal, the period of selling will vary for the same individual capital with the general fluctuations of the market or with its fluctuations in that particular line of business. We shall not dwell on this point any longer. We merely state this simple fact: All circumstances which in general give rise to differences in the periods of turnover of the capitals invested in different branches of industry bring in their train differences also in the turnover of the various individual capitals operating in the same business, provided these circumstances operate individually (for instance, if one capitalist has an opportunity to sell more rapidly than his competitor, if one employs more methods shortening the working periods than the other, etc.).

One cause which acts permanently in differentiating the times of selling, and thus the periods of turnover in general, is the distance of the market in which a commodity is sold from its place of production. During the entire trip to the market, capital finds itself fettered in the state of commodity capital. If goods are made to order, up to the time of delivery; if they are not made to order, there must be added to the time of the trip to the market the time during which the goods are in the market waiting to be sold. The improvement of the means of communication and transportation cuts down absolutely the wandering period of the commodities but does not eliminate the relative difference in the time of circulation of different commodity capitals arising from their peregrinations, nor that of different portions of the same commodity capital which migrate to different markets. For instance the improved sailing vessels and steamships, which shorten travelling, do so equally for near and distant ports. The relative difference remains, although often diminished. But the relative differences may be displaced by the development of the means of transportation and communication in a way that does not correspond to the geographical distances. For instance a railway which leads from a place of production to an inland centre of population may relatively or absolutely lengthen the distance to a nearer inland point not connected by rail, as compared to the one which geographically is more remote. In the same way the same circumstances may alter the relative distance of places of production from the larger markets, which explains the deterioration of old and the rise of new centres of production because of changes in communication and transportation facilities. (To this must be added the circumstances that long hauls are relatively cheaper than short ones.) Simultaneously with the development of transport facilities not only is the velocity of movement in space accelerated and thereby the spatial distance shortened in terms of time. Not only is there a development of the mass of communication facilities, so that for instance many vessels sail simultaneously for the same port, or several trains travel simultaneously on different railways between the same two points, but freight vessels may clear on consecutive days of the same week from Liverpool for New York for example, or goods trains may start at different hours of the same day from Manchester to London. True, the absolute velocity — hence this part of the time of circulation — is not altered by this latter circumstance, a certain definite capacity of the means of transportation being given. But successive shipments of commodities can start their passage at shorter intervals of time and thus reach the market one after another without accumulating in large quantities as potential commodity capital before actual shipment. Hence the return of capital likewise is distributed over shorter successive periods of time, so that a part is continually transformed into money capital, while the other circulates as commodity capital. By distributing the return over several successive periods the total time of circulation and hence also the turnover are abridged. The first to increase is the frequency with which the means of transportation function, for instance the number of railway trains, as existing places of production produce more and become greater centres of production. The development tends in the direction of the already existing market, that is to say, towards the great centres of production, and population, towards ports of export, etc. On the other hand these particularly great traffic facilities and the resultant acceleration of the capital turnover (since it is conditional on the time of circulation) give rise to quicker concentration of both the centres of production and the markets. Along with this concentration of masses of men and capital thus accelerated at certain points, there is the concentration of these masses of capital in the hands of a few. Simultaneously one may note again a shifting and relocation of places of production and of markets as a result of the changes in their relative positions caused by the transformations in transport facilities. A place of production which once had a special advantage by being located on some highway or canal may now find itself relegated to a single sidetrack, which runs trains only at relatively long intervals, while another place, which formerly was remote from the main arteries of traffic, may now be situated at the junction of several railways. This second locality is on the upgrade, the former on the downgrade. Changes in the means of transportation thus engender local differences in the time of circulation of commodities, in the opportunity to buy, sell, etc., or an already existing local differentiation is distributed differently. The importance of this circumstance for the turnover of capital is evidenced by the wrangling of the commercial and industrial representatives of the various localities with the railway managements. (See for instance the above-quoted Bluebook of the Railway Committee.[a])

All branches of production which by the nature of their product are dependent mainly on local consumption, such as breweries, are therefore developed to the greatest extent in the principal centres of population. The more rapid turnover of capital compensates here in part for the circumstance that a number of conditions of production, building lots, etc., are more expensive.

Whereas on the one hand the improvement of the means of transportation and communication brought about by the progress of capitalist production reduces the time of circulation of particular quantities of commodities, the same progress and the opportunities created by the development of transport and communication facilities make it imperative, conversely, to work for ever more remote markets, in a word — for the world market. The mass of commodities in transit for distant places grows enormously, and with it therefore grows, both absolutely and relatively, that part of social capital which remains continually for long periods in the stage of commodity capital, within the time of circulation. There is a simultaneous growth of that portion of social wealth which, instead of serving as direct means of production, is invested in means of transportation and communication and in the fixed and circulating capital required for their operation.

The mere relative length of the transit of the commodities from their place of production to their market produces a difference not only in the first part of the circulation time, the selling time, but also in its second part, the reconversion of the money into the elements of the productive capital, the buying time. Suppose a 'commodity is shipped to India. This requires, say, four months. Let us assume that the selling time is equal to zero, i. e., the commodities are made to order and are paid for on delivery to the agent of the producer. The return of the money (no matter in what form) requires another four months. Thus it takes altogether eight months before a capital can again function as productive capital, renew the same operation. The differences in the turnover thus occasioned form one of the material bases of the various terms of credit, just as oversea commerce in general, for instance in Venice and Genoa, is one of the sources of the credit system, properly speaking.

---

[a] See this volume, pp. 154-55.

"The crisis of 1847 enabled the banking and mercantile community of that time to reduce the India and China usance" (time allowed for the currency of bills of exchange between there and Europe) "from ten months' date to six months' sight, and the lapse of twenty years with all the accelerations of speed and establishment of telegraphs [...] renders necessary [...] a further reduction" from six months' sight to four months' date as a first step to four months' sight. "The voyage of a sailing vessel *via* the Cape from Calcutta to London is, on the average, under 90 days. An usance of four months' sight would be equal to a currency of say 150 days. The present usance of six months' sight is equal to a currency of say 210 days" (*London Economist*, June 16, 1866).

On the other hand:

"The Brazilian usance remains at two and three months' sight, bills from Antwerp are drawn" (on London) "at three months' date, and even Manchester and Bradford draw upon London at three months and longer dates. By tacit consent, a fair opportunity is afforded to the merchant of realising the proceeds of his merchandise, not indeed before, but within a reasonable time of, the bills drawn against it fall due. In this view, the present usance for Indian bills cannot be considered excessive. Indian produce for the most part being sold in London with three months' prompt, and allowing for loss of time in effecting sales, cannot be realised much within five months, while another period of five months will have previously elapsed (on an average) between the time of purchase in India and of delivery in the English warehouse. We have here a period of ten months, whereas the bill drawn against the goods does not live beyond seven months" (ibid., June 30, 1866).

"On July 2, 1866, five big London banks dealing mainly with India and China, and the Paris *Comptoir d'Escompte*, gave notice that from the 1st January, 1867, their branches and agencies in the East will only buy and sell bills of exchange at a term not exceeding four months' sight" (ibid., July 7, 1866).

However this reduction miscarried and had to be abandoned. //Since then the Suez Canal has revolutionised all this.//

It is a matter of course that with the longer time of commodity circulation the risk of a change of prices in the market increases, since the period in which price changes can take place is lengthened.

Differences in the time of circulation, partly individual between the various separate capitals of the same branch of business, partly between different branches of business according to the different usances, when payment is not made in spot cash, arise from the different terms of payment in buying and selling. We shall not dwell any longer here on this point, which is of importance to the credit system.

Differences in the turnover time arise also from the size of contracts for the delivery of goods, and their size grows with the extent and scale of capitalist production. A contract of delivery, being a transaction between buyer and seller, is an operation pertaining to the market, the sphere of circulation. The differences in the time of turnover arising here stem therefore from the sphere of circulation, but react immediately on the sphere of production, and do so apart from all terms of payment and conditions of credit, hence also in the case of cash payment. For instance coal, cotton, yarn, etc., are discrete products. Every day supplies its quantum of finished product. But if the master-spinner or the mine-owner accepts contracts for the delivery of such large quantities of products as require, say, a period of four or six weeks of consecutive working days, then this is quite the same, so far as the time of advancement of capital is concerned, as if a continuous working period of four or six weeks had been introduced in this labour process. It is of course assumed here that the entire quantity ordered is to be delivered in one bulk, or at least is paid for only after total delivery. Individually considered, every day has thus furnished its definite quantum of finished product. But this finished quantum is only a part of the quantity contracted for. While in this case the portion finished so far is no longer in the process of production, still it lies in the warehouse as potential capital only.

Now let us take up the second stage of the time of circulation, the buying time, or that period in which capital is reconverted from the money form into the elements of productive capital. During this period it must persist for a shorter or longer time in its condition of money capital, hence a certain portion of the total capital advanced must all the time be in the condition of money capital, although this portion consists of constantly changing elements. For instance, of the total capital advanced in a certain business, $n \times £100$ must be available in the form of money capital, so that, while all the constituent parts of these $n \times £100$ are continually converted into productive capital, this sum is nevertheless just as continually replenished by the influx from the circulation, from the realised commodity capital. A definite part of the advanced capital value is therefore continually in the condition of money capital, i. e., a form not pertaining to its sphere of production but its sphere of circulation.

We have already seen that the prolongation of the time for which capital is fettered in the form of commodity capital on account of the distance of the market results in direct delay of the return of the money and consequently also of the transformation of the capital from money capital into productive capital.

We have furthermore seen (Chapter VI) with reference to the purchase of commodities, that the time of buying, the greater or smaller distance from the main sources of the raw material, makes it necessary to purchase raw material for a longer period and have it available in the form of a productive supply, of latent or potential productive capital; that in consequence it increases the amount of capital to be advanced at one time, and the time for which it must be advanced, if the scale of production remains otherwise the same.

A similar effect is produced in various branches of business by the more or less prolonged periods in which rather large quantities of raw material are thrown on the market. In London for example great auction sales of wool take place every three months, and the wool market is controlled by them. The cotton market on the other hand is on the whole restocked continuously, if not uniformly, from harvest to harvest. Such periods determine the principal dates when these raw materials are bought. Their effect is particularly great on speculative purchases necessitating advances for longer or shorter periods for these elements of production, just as the nature of the produced commodities acts on the speculative, intentional withholding of a product for a longer or shorter term in the form of potential commodity capital.

"The agriculturist must also be a speculator to a certain extent and therefore hold back the sale of his products if prevailing conditions so suggest..."

Here follow a few general rules.

"However in the sale of the products, it all depends mainly on the person, the product itself, and the locality. Anyone who, besides being skilful and lucky"(!), "is provided with sufficient working capital will not be blamed if for once he keeps his grain crop stored as long as a year when prices are unusually low. On the other hand a man who lacks working capital or is altogether devoid"(!) "of speculative spirit will try to get the current average prices and will be compelled to sell as soon and as often as opportunity presents itself. It will almost always mean a loss to keep wool stored longer than a year, while corn and oil seed may be stored for several years without detriment to their properties and high quality. Products generally subject to severe fluctuation at short intervals, for instance oil seed, hops, teasel and the like, may be stored to good advantage during years in which the selling price is far below the price of production. It is least permissible to postpone the sale of articles whose preservation involves daily expense, such as fatted cattle, or which are perishable, such as fruit, potatoes, etc. In various localities a certain product fetches its lowest average price in certain seasons, its highest in others. Thus, in some parts the average price of corn is lower around St. Martin's Day than between Christmas and Easter. Furthermore some products sell well in certain localities only at certain times, as is the case with wool in the wool markets of those localities where the wool trade at other times is dull, etc." (Kirchhof, p. 302).

In the study of the second half of the time of circulation, during which money is reconverted into the elements of productive capital, it is not only this transformation, taken by itself, that should be given consideration, not only the time within which the money returns, according to the distance of the market in which the product is sold. What must also be considered, and primarily so, is the amount of that part of the advanced capital which is always to be available in the form of money, in the condition of money capital.

Apart from all speculation, the volume of the purchases of those commodities which must always be available as a productive supply depends on the times of the renewal of this supply, hence on circumstances which in their turn are dependent on market conditions and which therefore are different for different raw materials. In these cases money must be advanced from time to time in rather large quantities and in lump sums. It returns more or less rapidly, but always in instalments, according to the turnover of the capital. One portion of it, namely the part reconverted into wages, is just as continually expended again at short intervals. But another portion, namely that which is to be reconverted into raw material, etc., must be accumulated for rather long periods, as a reserve fund for either buying or paying. Therefore it exists in the form of money capital, although the volume in which it exists as such changes.

We shall see in the next chapter that other circumstances arising either from the process of production or that of circulation make it necessary for a certain portion of the advanced capital to be available in the form of money. In general it must be noted that the economists are very prone to forget not only that a part of the capital required in a business passes successively through the three stages of money capital, productive capital, and commodity capital, but also that different portions of it continuously and simultaneously possess these forms, although the relative magnitudes of these portions vary all the time. It is especially the part always available as money capital that is forgotten by the economists, although precisely this circumstance is highly essential for an understanding of bourgeois economy and consequently makes its importance felt as such also in practice.

Chapter XV

EFFECT OF THE TIME
OF TURNOVER ON THE MAGNITUDE
OF ADVANCED CAPITAL

In this chapter and in the next, the sixteenth, we deal with the influence of the time of turnover on the self-expansion of capital.

Take the commodity capital which is the product of a working period of, say, nine weeks. Let us, for the time being, leave aside that portion of the value of the product which is added to it by the average wear and tear of the fixed capital, and also the surplus value added to the product during the process of production. The value of this product is then equal to that of the circulating capital advanced for its production, i. e., of the wages and the raw and auxiliary materials consumed in its production. Let this value be £900, so that the weekly outlay is £100. The period of production, which here coincides with the working period, is therefore 9 weeks. It is immaterial whether it is assumed that this is the working period of a continuous product, or whether it is a continuous working period for a discrete product, so long as the quantity of discrete product brought to market at one time costs 9 weeks' labour. Let the time of circulation be 3 weeks. Then the entire period of turnover is 12 weeks. At the end of 9 weeks the advanced productive capital is converted into commodity capital, but now it stays for three weeks in the period of circulation. The new period of production therefore cannot start before the beginning of the 13th week, and production would be at a standstill for three weeks, or for a quarter of the entire period of turnover. It again does not make any difference whether it is assumed that it takes so long on an average to sell the product, or that this length of time is bound up with the remoteness of the market or the terms of payment for the goods sold. Production would be standing still for 3 weeks every 3 months, making it $4 \times 3 = 12$ weeks in a year, which means 3 months, or one-quarter, of the annual period of turnover. Hence, if production is to be continuous and carried along on the same scale week after week, there is only this alternative:

Either the scale of production must be reduced, so that the £900 suffice to keep the work going both during the working period and the time of circulation of the first turnover. A second working period, hence also a second period of turnover, is then commenced with the

10th week, before the first period of turnover is completed, for the period of turnover is twelve weeks, and the working period nine weeks. A sum of £900 distributed over 12 weeks makes £75 per week. It is evident in the first place that such a reduced scale of business pre-supposes changed dimensions of the fixed capital and therefore, on the whole, a curtailment of the business. In the second place, it is questionable whether such a reduction can take place at all, for in each business there exists, commensurate with the development of its production, a normal minimum of invested capital essential to main-tain its capacity to compete. This normal minimum grows steadily with the advance of capitalist production, and hence it is not fixed. There are numerous intermediate grades between the normal mini-mum existing at any particular time and the ever increasing normal maximum, a medium which permits of many different scales of capi-tal investment. Within the limits of this medium reductions may take place, their lowest limit being the prevailing normal minimum.

When there is a hitch in production, when the markets are over-stocked, and when raw materials rise in price, etc., the normal outlay of circulating capital is restricted — once the pattern of the fixed capi-tal has been set — by cutting down working time to, say, one half. On the other hand, in times of prosperity, the pattern of the fixed capital given, there is an abnormal expansion of the circulating capital, partly through the extension of working time and partly through its intensification. In businesses which have, from the outset, to reckon with such fluctuations, the situation is relieved partly by recourse to the above measures and partly by employing simultaneously a great-er number of labourers, in combination with the application of re-serve fixed capital, such as reserve locomotives on railways, etc. How-ever, such abnormal fluctuations are not considered here, where we assume normal conditions.

In order to make production continuous, therefore, the expendi-ture of the same circulating capital is here distributed over a longer period, over 12 weeks instead of 9. In every section of time there con-sequently functions a reduced productive capital. The circulating portion of the productive capital is reduced from 100 to 75, or one-quarter. The total amount by which the productive capital function-ing for a working period of 9 weeks is reduced $= 9 \times 25 = £225$, or $^1/_4$ of £900. But the ratio of the time of circulation to that of turnover is likewise $^3/_{12} = ^1/_4$. It follows therefore: If production is not to be interrupted during the time of circulation of the productive capital transformed into commodity capital, if it is rather to be carried on si-multaneously and continuously week after week, and if no special cir-culating capital is available for this purpose, it can be done only by curtailing productive operations, by reducing the fluid component of the functioning productive capital. The portion of fluid capital thus set free for production during the time of circulation is to the total ad-vanced fluid capital as the time of circulation is to the period of turno-ver. This applies, as has already been stated, only to branches of pro-duction in which the labour process is carried on on the same scale week after week, where therefore no varying amounts of capital are to be invested in different working periods, as for instance in agriculture.

If on the other hand we assume that the nature of the business ex-cludes a reduction of the scale of production, and thus of the fluid ca-pital to be advanced each week, then continuity of production can be secured only by additional fluid capital, in the above-named case of £300. During the twelve-week turnover period, £1,200 are successi-vely invested, and £300 are one-quarter of this sum as 3 weeks are of 12. At the end of the working period of 9 weeks the capital value of £900 has been converted from the form of productive into that of commodity capital. Its working period is concluded, but it cannot be re-opened with the same capital. During the three weeks in which it stays in the sphere of circulation, functioning as commodity capital, it is in the same state, so far as the process of production is concerned, as if it did not exist at all. We rule out in the present case all credit rela-tions and take for granted that the capitalist operates only with his own money. But during the time the capital advanced for the first working period, having completed its process of production, stays 3 weeks in the process of circulation, there functions an additional ca-pital investment of £300, so that the continuity of production is not broken.

Now, the following must be noted in this connection:

Firstly: The working period of the capital of £900 first advanced is completed at the close of 9 weeks and it does not return until after 3 weeks are up, that is to say, at the beginning of the 13th week. But a new working period is immediately begun with the additional capi-tal of £300. By this means continuity of production is maintained.

Secondly: The functions of the original capital of £900 and of the capital of £300 newly added at the close of the first nine-week working period, inaugurating the second working period after the conclusion of the first without any interruption, are, or at least could be, clearly distinguished in the first period of turnover, while they cross each other in the course of the second period of turnover.

Let us make this matter plainer.

First period of turnover of 12 weeks. First working period of 9 weeks; the turnover of the capital advanced for this is completed at the beginning of the 13th week. During the last 3 weeks the additional capital of £300 functions, opening the second working period of 9 weeks.

Second period of turnover. At the beginning of the 13th week, £900 have returned and are able to begin a new turnover. But the second working period has already been opened in the 10th week by the additional £300. At the start of the 13th week, thanks to this, one-third of the working period is already over and £300 has been converted from productive capital into product. Since only 6 weeks more are required for the completion of the second working period, only two-thirds of the returned capital of £900, or only £600, can enter into the productive process of the second working period. £300 of the original £900 are set free to play the same role which the additional capital of £300 played in the first working period. At the close of the 6th week of the second period of turnover the second working period is up. The capital of £900 advanced in it returns after 3 weeks, or at the end of the 9th week of the second 12-week period of turnover. During the 3 weeks of its period of circulation, the freed capital of £300 comes into action. This begins the third working period of a capital of £900 in the 7th week of the second period of turnover, or the 19th week of the year.

Third period of turnover. At the close of the 9th week of the second period of turnover there is a new reflux of £900. But the third working period has already commenced in the 7th week of the previous period of turnover, and 6 weeks have already elapsed. The third working period, then, lasts only another 3 weeks. Hence only £300 of the returned £900 enter into the productive process. The fourth working period fills out the remaining 9 weeks of this period of turnover and thus the 37th week of the year begins simultaneously the fourth period of turnover and the fifth working period.

In order to simplify the calculation in this case let us assume a working period of 5 weeks and a period of circulation of 5 weeks, making a turnover period of 10 weeks. Figure the year as composed of 50 weeks and the capital outlay per week as £100. A working period then requires a circulating capital of £500 and the time of circulation an additional capital of £500. The working periods and times of turnover then are as follows:

Working period	Week	£ in goods	Returned
1st	1st-5th	500	End of 10th week
2nd	6th-10th	500	,, ,, 15th ,,
3rd	11th-15th	500	,, ,, 20th ,,
4th	16th-20th	500	,, ,, 25th ,,
5th	21st-25th	500	,, ,, 30th ,,

and so forth

If the time of circulation is zero, so that the period of turnover is equal to the working period, then the number of turnovers is equal to the number of working periods of the year. In the case of a 5-week working period this would make $^{50}/_5 = 10$ weeks, and the value of the capital turned over would be $500 \times 10 = 5,000$. In our table, in which we have assumed a circulation time of 5 weeks, the total value of the commodities produced per year would also be £5,000, but $^1/_{10}$ of this = £500 would always be in the form of commodity capital, and would not return until after 5 weeks. At the end of the year the product of the tenth working period (the 46th to the 50th working week) would have completed its time of turnover only by half, and its time of circulation would fall within the first 5 weeks of the next year.

Now let us take a third illustration: Working period 6 weeks, time of circulation 3 weeks, weekly advance during labour process £100.

1st working period: 1st-6th week. At the end of the 6th week a commodity capital of £600, returned at the end of the 9th week.

2nd working period: 7th-12th week. During the 7th-9th week £300 of additional capital is advanced. At the end of the 9th week, return of £600. Of this, £300 are advanced during the 10th-12th week. At the end of the 12th week therefore £300 are free and £600 are in the form of commodity capital, returnable at the end of the 15th week.

3rd working period: 13th-18th week. During the 13th-15th week, advance of above £300, then reflux of £600, of which £300 are advanced for the 16th-18th week. At the end of the 18th week, £300 are free in money form; £600 on hand as commodity capital which returns at the end of the 21st week. (See the more detailed presentation of this case under II, below.)

In other words during 9 working periods (= 54 weeks) 600 × 9 = £5,400 worth of commodities are produced. At the end of the ninth working period the capitalist has £300 in money and £600 in commodities which have not yet completed their time of circulation.

A comparison of these three illustrations shows, first, that a successive release of capital I of £500 and of additional capital II of likewise £500 takes place only in the second illustration, so that these two portions of capital move separately and apart from each other. But this is so only because we have made the very exceptional assumption that the working period and the time of circulation form two equal halves of the turnover period. In all other cases, whatever the difference between the two constituents of the period of turnover, the movements of the two capitals cross each other, as in illustrations I and III, beginning with the second period of turnover. The additional capital II, with a portion of capital I, then forms the capital functioning in the second turnover period, while the remainder of capital I is set free to perform the original function of capital II. The capital operating during the circulation time of the commodity capital is not identical, in this case, with the capital II originally advanced for this purpose, but it is of the same value and forms the same aliquot part of the total capital advanced.

Secondly: The capital which functioned during the working period lies idle during the time of circulation. In the second illustration the capital functions during the 5 weeks of the working period and lies idle during the 5 weeks of the circulation time. Therefore the entire time during which capital I lies idle here amounts to one half of the year. It is the additional capital II that appears during this time having, in the case before us, also in its turn lain idle half a year. But the additional capital required to ensure the continuity of production during the time of circulation is not determined by the aggregate amount, or sum total, of the times of circulation during the year, but only by the ratio of the time of circulation to the period of turnover. (We assume, of course, that all the turnovers take place under the same conditions.) For this reason £500 of additional capital, and not £2,500, are required in the second illustration. This is simply due to the fact that the additional capital enters just as well into the turnover as the capital originally advanced, and that it therefore makes up its magnitude just as the other by the number of its turnovers.

Thirdly: The circumstances here considered are not affected by whether the time of production is longer than the working time or not. True, the aggregate of the periods of turnover is prolonged thereby, but this extension does not necessitate any additional capital for the labour process. The additional capital serves merely the purpose of filling the gaps in the labour process that arise on account of the time of circulation. Hence it is there simply to protect production against interruptions, originating in the time of circulation. Interruptions arising from the specific conditions of production are to be eliminated in another way, which need not be discussed at this point. There are however establishments in which work is carried on only intermittently, to order, so that there may be intervals between the working periods. In such cases, the need for additional capital is *pro tanto* eliminated. On the other hand in most cases of seasonal work there is a certain limit for the time of reflux. The same work cannot be renewed next year with the same capital, if the circulation time of this capital has not, in the meantime, run out. On the contrary the time of circulation may also be shorter than the interval between two periods of production. In that event the capital lies fallow, unless it is meanwhile employed otherwise.

Fourthly: The capital advanced for a certain working period — for instance the £600 in the third illustration — is invested partly in raw and auxiliary materials, in a productive supply for the working period, in constant circulating capital, and partly in variable circulating capital, in the payment of labour itself. The portion laid out in constant circulating capital may not exist for the same length of time in the form of a productive supply; the raw material for instance may not be on hand for the entire working period, coal may be procured only every two weeks. However, as credit is still out of the question here, this portion of capital, in so far as it is not available in the form of a productive supply, must be kept on hand in the form of money so that it can be converted into a productive supply as and when needed. This does not alter the magnitude of the constant circulating capital value advanced for 6 weeks. On the other hand — regardless of the money supply for unforeseen expenses, the reserve fund proper for the elimination of disturbances — wages are paid in shorter intervals, mostly weekly. Therefore unless the capitalist compels the labourer to advance his labour for a longer time, the capital required for wages must be on hand in the form of money. During the reflux of the capital a portion must therefore be retained in money form for the payment of the labour, while the remaining portion may be converted into productive supply.

The additional capital is divided exactly like the original. But it is distinguished from capital I by the fact that (apart from credit relations) in order to be available for its own working period it must be advanced during the entire duration of the first working period of capital I, into which it does not enter. During this time it can already be converted, at least in part, into constant circulating capital, having been advanced for the entire period of turnover. To what extent it assumes this form or how long it persists in the form of additional money capital until this conversion becomes necessary, will depend partly on the special conditions of production of definite lines of business, partly on local conditions, partly on the price fluctuations of raw material, etc. If social capital is viewed in its entirety, a more or less considerable part of this additional capital will always be for a rather long time in the state of money capital. But as for that portion of capital II which is to be advanced for wages, it is always converted only gradually into labour power, as small working periods expire and are paid for. This portion of capital II, then, is available in the form of money capital during the entire working period, until by its conversion into labour power it takes part in the function of productive capital.

Consequently, the accession of the additional capital required for the transformation of the circulation time of capital I into time of production, increases not only the magnitude of the advanced capital and the length of time for which the aggregate capital must necessarily be advanced, but also, and specifically so, that portion of the advanced capital which exists as money supply, which hence exists in the state of money capital and has the form of potential money capital.

The same thing also takes place — as far as it concerns both the advance in the form of a productive supply and in that of a money supply — when the separation of capital into two parts made necessary by the time of circulation, namely, into capital for the first working period and replacement capital for the time of circulation, is not caused by the increase of the capital laid out but by a decrease of the scale of production. The amount of capital tied up in the money form grows here still more in relation to the scale of production.

What is achieved in general by this separation of capital into an originally productive and an additional capital is a continuous succession of the working periods, the constant function of an equal portion of the advanced capital as productive capital.

Let us look at the second illustration. The capital continuously employed in the process of production amounts to £500. As the working period = 5 weeks it operates ten times during 50 weeks (taken as a ·year). Hence its product, apart from surplus value, is 10 × £500 = £5,000. From the standpoint of a capital working directly and uninterruptedly in the process of production — a capital value of £500 — the time of circulation seems to be brought to nought. The period of turnover coincides with the working period, and the time of circulation is assumed to be equal to zero.

But if the capital of £500 were regularly interrupted in its productive activity by a 5-week circulation time, so that it would again become capable of production only after the close of the entire 10-week turnover period, we should have 5 turnovers of ten weeks each in the 50 weeks of the year. These would comprise five 5-week periods of production, or a sum of 25 productive weeks with a total product worth 5 × £500 = £2,500, and five 5-week periods of circulation, or a total circulation time of likewise 25 weeks. If we say in this case that the capital of £500 has been turned over five times in the year, it will be clear and obvious that during half of each period of turnover this capital of £500 did not function at all as a productive capital and that, all in all, it performed its function only during one half of the year, but did not function at all during the other half.

In our illustration the replacement capital of £500 appears on the scene during those five periods of circulation and the turnover is thus expanded from £2,500 to £5,000. But now the advanced capital is £1,000 instead of £500. 5,000 divided by 1,000 is 5. Hence, there are five turnovers instead of ten. And that is just the way people figure. But when it is said that the capital of £1,000 has been turned over five times during the year, the recollection of the time of circulation disappears from the hollow skulls of the capitalists and a confused idea is formed that this capital has served continuously in the production process during the five successive turnovers. But if we say that the capital of £1,000 has been turned over five times this includes both the time of circulation and the time of production. Indeed, if £1,000 had really been continuously active in the process of production, the product would, according to our assumptions, have to be £10,000 instead of £5,000. But in order to have £1,000 continuously in the process of production, £2,000 would have to be advanced. The economists, who as a general rule have nothing clear to say in reference to the mechanism of the turnover, always overlook this main point, to wit, that only a part of the industrial capital can actually be engaged in the process of production if production is to proceed uninterruptedly. While one part is in the period of production, another must always be in the period of circulation. Or in other words, one part can perform the function of productive capital only on condition that another part is withdrawn from production proper in the form of commodity or money capital. In overlooking this, the significance and role of money capital is entirely ignored.

We have now to ascertain what differences in the turnover arise if the two sections of the period of turnover, the working period and the circulation period, are equal, or if the working period is greater or smaller than the circulation period, and, furthermore, what effect this has on the tie-up of capital in the form of money capital.

We assume the capital advanced weekly to be in all cases £100, and the period of turnover 9 weeks, so that the capital to be advanced for each period of turnover is £900.

I. THE WORKING PERIOD EQUAL
TO THE CIRCULATION PERIOD

Although this case occurs in reality only as an accidental exception, it must serve as our point of departure in this investigation, because here relations shape themselves in the simplest and most intelligible way.

The two capitals (capital I advanced for the first working period, and additional capital II, which functions during the circulation period of capital I) relieve one another in their movements without crossing. With the exception of the first period, either of the two capitals is therefore advanced only for its own period of turnover. Let the period of turnover be 9 weeks, as indicated in the following illustrations, so that the working period and the circulation period are each $4\frac{1}{2}$ weeks. Then we have the following annual diagram.

Table I

CAPITAL I

Periods of Turnover		Working Periods	Advance	Periods of Circulation	
I. 1st-9th	week	1st-4th $^1/_2$ week	£ 450	4th $^1/_2$-9th	week
II. 10th-18th	,,	10th-13th $^1/_2$,,	£ 450	13th $^1/_2$-18th	,,
III. 19th-27th	,,	19th-22nd $^1/_2$,,	£ 450	22nd $^1/_2$-27th	,,
IV. 28th-36th	,,	28th-31st $^1/_2$,,	£ 450	31st $^1/_2$-36th	,,
V. 37th-45th	,,	37th-40th $^1/_2$,,	£ 450	40th $^1/_2$-45th	,,
VI. 46th-(54th)	,,	46th-49th $^1/_2$,,	£ 450	49th $^1/_2$-(54th)	,,[31]

CAPITAL II

Periods of Turnover	Working Periods	Advance	Periods of Circulation	
I. 4th $^1/_2$-13th $^1/_2$ week	4th $^1/_2$-9th week	£ 450	10th-13th $^1/_2$	week
II. 13th $^1/_2$-22nd $^1/_2$,,	13th $^1/_2$-18th ,,	£ 450	19th-22nd $^1/_2$	,,
III. 22nd $^1/_2$-31st $^1/_2$,,	22nd $^1/_2$-27th ,,	£ 450	28th-31st $^1/_2$	,,
IV. 31st $^1/_2$-40th $^1/_2$,,	31st $^1/_2$-36th ,,	£ 450	37th-40th $^1/_2$	,,
V. 40th $^1/_2$-49th $^1/_2$,,	40th $^1/_2$-45th ,,	£ 450	46th-49th $^1/_2$	,,
VI. 49th $^1/_2$-(58th $^1/_2$) ,,	49th $^1/_2$-(54th) ,,	£ 450	(55th-58th $^1/_2$)	,,

Within the 51 weeks which here stand for one year, capital I runs through six full working periods, producing 6 × 450 = £2,700 worth of commodities, and capital II producing in five full working periods 5 × 450 = £2,250 worth of commodities. In addition, capital II produced, within the last 1 $^1/_2$ weeks of the year (middle of the 50th to the end of the 51st week), an extra £150 worth. The aggregate product in 51 weeks is worth £5,100. So far as the direct production of surplus value is concerned, which takes place only during the working period, the aggregate capital of £900 would have been turned over 5 $^2/_3$ times (5 $^2/_3$ × 900 = £5,100). But if we consider the real turnover, capital I has been turned over 5 $^2/_3$ times, since at the close of the 51st week it still has 3 weeks to go of its sixth period of turnover; 5 $^2/_3$ × 450 = £2,550; and capital II turned over 5 $^1/_6$ times, since it has completed only 1 $^1/_2$ weeks of its sixth period of turnover, so that 7 $^1/_2$ weeks of it run into the next year; 5 $^1/_6$ × 450 = £2,325; real aggregate turnover: £4,875.

[31] The weeks falling within the second year of turnover are put in parentheses.

Let us consider capital I and capital II as two capitals wholly independent of one another. They are entirely independent in their movements; these movements complement one another merely because
their working and circulating periods directly relieve one another.
They may be regarded as two totally independent capitals belonging
to different capitalists.

Capital I has completed five full turnovers and two-thirds of its
sixth turnover period. At the end of the year it has the form of commodity capital, which is 3 weeks short of its normal realisation. During this time it cannot enter into the process of production. It functions as commodity capital, it circulates. It has completed only $^2/_3$ of
its last period of turnover. This is expressed as follows: It has been
turned over only $^2/_3$ of a time, only $^2/_3$ of its total value have performed
a complete turnover. We say that £450 complete their turnover in
9 weeks, hence £300 do in 6 weeks. But in this mode of expression the
organic relations between the two specifically different components of
the turnover time are ignored. The exact meaning of the expression
that the advanced capital of £450 has made $5\,^2/_3$ turnovers is merely
that it has accomplished five turnovers fully and only $^2/_3$ of the sixth.
On the other hand the expression that the turned-over capital = $5\,^2/_3$
times the advanced capital — hence, in the above case,
$5\,^2/_3 \times$ £450 = £2,550 — is correct, meaning that unless this capital
of £450 were complemented by another capital of £450, one portion
of it would have to be in the process of production while another in
the process of circulation. If the time of turnover is to be expressed in
terms of the quantity of capital turned over, it can always be expressed
only in terms of a quantity of existing value (in fact, of finished
product). The circumstance that the advanced capital is not in a condition in which it may re-open the process of production finds expression
in the fact that only a part of it is in a state capable of production or that,
in order to be in a state of uninterrupted production, the capital would
have to be divided into a portion which would be continually in the
period of production and into another which would be continually in the
period of circulation, depending upon the relation of these periods
to each other. It is the same law which determines the quantity of the
constantly functioning productive capital by the ratio of the time of
circulation to the time of turnover.

By the end of the 51st week, which we regard here as the end of
the year, £150 of capital II have been advanced to the production of
an unfinished lot of goods. Another part of it exists in the form of cir-

culating constant capital — raw materials, etc.— i. e., in a form in which it can function as productive capital in the production process. But a third part of it exists in the form of money, at least the amount of the wages for the remainder of the working period (3 weeks), which is not paid, however, until the end of each week. Now, although at the beginning of a new year, hence of a new turnover cycle, this portion of the capital is not in the form of productive capital but in that of money capital, in which it cannot take part in the process of production, at the opening of the new turnover circulating variable capital, i. e., living labour power, is nevertheless active in the process of production. This is due to the fact that labour power is not paid until the end of the week, although bought at the beginning of the working period, say, per week, and so consumed. Money serves here as a means of payment. For this reason it is still as money in the hands of the capitalist, on the one hand, while, on the other hand, labour power, the commodity into which money is being transformed, is already active in the process of production, so that the same capital value appears here doubly.

If we look merely at the working periods,

$$\text{capital I produces} \quad 6 \ \times 450 = £2,700$$
$$\text{capital II} \quad \text{"} \quad 5\,^1/_3 \times 450 = £2,400$$
$$\text{hence together} \quad 5\,^2/_3 \times 900 = £5,100.$$

Hence the total advanced capital of £900 has functioned $5\,^2/_3$ times throughout the year as productive capital. It is immaterial for the production of surplus value whether there are always £450 in the production process and always £450 in the circulation process, or whether £900 function $4\,^1/_2$ weeks in the process of production and the following $4\,^1/_2$ weeks in the process of circulation.

On the other hand, if we consider the periods of turnover, there has been turned over:

$$\text{capital I,} \quad 5\,^2/_3 \times 450 = £2,550$$
$$\text{capital II,} \quad 5\,^1/_6 \times 450 = £2,325$$
$$\text{hence the total capital} \quad 5\,^5/_{12} \times 900 = £4,875.$$

For the number of turnovers of the total capital is equal to the sum of the amounts turned over by I and II, divided by the sum of I and II.

It is to be noted that if capitals I and II were independent of each other they would nevertheless form merely different independent portions of the social capital advanced in the same sphere of production. Hence if the social capital within this sphere of production were composed *solely* of I and II, the same calculation would apply to the turnover of the social capital in this sphere as applies here to the two constituent parts I and II of the same private capital. Going further, every portion of the entire social capital invested in any particular sphere of production may be so calculated. But in the last analysis, the number of turnovers made by the entire social capital is equal to the sum of the capitals turned over in the various spheres of production divided by the sum of the capitals advanced in those spheres.

It must further be noted that just as capitals I and II in the same private business have here, strictly speaking, different turnover years (the cycle of turnover of capital II beginning $4\,^1/_2$ weeks later than that of capital I, so that the year of I ends $4\,^1/_2$ weeks earlier than that of II), so the various private capitals in the same sphere of production begin their operations at totally different periods and therefore conclude their turnover years at different times of the year. The same calculation of averages that we employed above for I and II suffices also here to bring down the turnover years of the various independent portions of the social capital to one uniform turnover year.

II. THE WORKING PERIOD GREATER
THAN THE PERIOD OF CIRCULATION

The working and turnover periods of capitals I and II cross one another instead of relieving one another. Simultaneously some capital is set free. This was not so in the previously considered case.

But this does not alter the fact that, as before, 1) the number of working periods of the total capital advanced is equal to the sum of the value of the annual product of both advanced portions of capital divided by the total capital advanced, and 2) the number of turnovers made by the total capital is equal to the sum of the two amounts turned over divided by the sum of the two advanced capitals. Here too we must consider both portions of capital as if they performed turnover movements entirely independent of each other.

Thus, we assume once more that £100 are to be advanced weekly to the labour process. Let the working period last 6 weeks, requiring therefore every time an advance of £600 (capital I). Let the period of circulation be 3 weeks, so that the period of turnover is 9 weeks, as before. Let capital II of £300 step in during the three-week circulation period of capital I. Considering both capitals as independent of each other, we find the schedule of the annual turnover to be as follows:

Table II
CAPITAL I, £ 600

Periods of Turnover	Working Periods	Advance	Periods of Circulation
I. 1st-9th week	1st-6th week	£ 600	7th-9th week
II. 10th-18th ,,	10th-15th ,,	£ 600	16th-18th ,,
III. 19th-27th ,,	19th-24th ,,	£ 600	25th-27th ,,
IV. 28th-36th ,,	28th-33rd ,,	£ 600	34th-36th ,,
V. 37th-45th ,,	37th-42nd ,,	£ 600	43rd-45th ,,
VI. 46th-(54th) ,,	46th-51st ,,	£ 600	(52nd-54th) ,,

ADDITIONAL CAPITAL II, £ 300

Periods of Turnover	Working Periods	Advance	Periods of Circulation
I. 7th-15th week	7th-9th week	£ 300	10th-15th week
II. 16th-24th ,,	16th-18th ,,	£ 300	19th-24th ,,
III. 25th-33rd ,,	25th-27th ,,	£ 300	28th-33rd ,,
IV. 34th-42nd ,,	34th-36th ,,	£ 300	37th-42nd ,,
V. 43rd-51st ,,	43rd-45th ,,	£ 300	46th-51st ,,

The process of production continues uninterruptedly the whole year round on the same scale. The two capitals I and II remain entirely separate. But in order to represent them as separate, we had to tear apart their real intersections and intertwinings, and thus also to change the number of turnovers. For according to the above table the amounts turned over would be:

by capital I, $5\,^2/_3 \times 600 = £3,400$ and
by capital II, $5 \times 300 = £1,500$

hence by the total capital $5\,^4/_9 \times 900 = £4,900.$

But this is not correct, for, as we shall see, the actual periods of production and circulation do not absolutely coincide with those of the above schedule, in which it was mainly a question of presenting capitals I and II as independent of each other.

In reality, for example, capital II has no working and circulating periods separate and distinct from those of capital I. The working period is 6 weeks, the circulation period 3 weeks. Since capital II amounts to only £300, it can suffice only for a part of the working period. This is indeed the case. At the end of the 6th week a product valued at £600 passes into circulation and returns in money form at the close of the 9th week. Then, at the opening of the 7th week, capital II begins its activity, and covers the requirements of the next working period, the 7th to 9th week. But according to our assumption the working period is only half up at the end of the 9th week. Hence capital I of £600 having just returned, at the beginning of the 10th week, once more enters into operation and with its £300 supplies the advances needed for the 10th to 12th week. This disposes of the second working period. A product value of £600 is in circulation and will return at the close of the 15th week. At the same time, £300, the amount of the original capital II, are set free and are able to function in the first half of the following working period, that is to say, in the 13th to 15th week. After the lapse of these weeks the £600 return; £300 of them suffice for the remainder of the working period, and £300 remain for the following working period.

The thing therefore works as follows:

First period of turnover: 1st-9th week.
   1st working period: 1st-6th week. Capital I, £600, performs its
      function.
   1st period of circulation: 7th-9th week. End of 9th week, £600 return.

Second period of turnover: 7th-15th week.
   2nd working period: 7th-12th week.
      First half: 7th-9th week. Capital II, £300, performs its function.
      End of 9th week, £600 return in money form (capital I).

Second half: 10th-12th week. £300 of capital I perform their function.

The other £300 of capital I remain freed.

2nd period of circulation: 13th-15th week.

End of 15th week, £600 (half taken from capital I, half from capital II) return in the form of money.

Third period of turnover: 13th-21st week.

3rd working period: 13th-18th week.

First half: 13th-15th week. The freed £300 perform their function. End of 15th week, £600 return in money form.

Second half: 16th-18th week, £300 of the returned £600 function, the other £300 again remain freed.

3rd period of circulation: 19th-21st week at the close of which £600 again return in money form. In these £600 capital I and capital II are now indistinguishably fused.

And so there are eight full turnover periods of a capital of £600 (I: 1st-9th week; II: 7th-15th; III: 13th-21st; IV: 19th-27th; V: 25th-33rd; VI: 31st-39th; VII: 37th-45th; VIII: 43rd-51st week) to the end of the 51st week. But as the 49th-51st weeks fall within the eighth period of circulation, the £300 of freed capital must step in and keep production going. Thus the turnover at the end of the year is as follows: £600 have completed their circuit eight times, making £4,800. In addition we have the product of the last 3 weeks (49th-51st), which, however, has completed only one-third of its circuit of 9 weeks, so that in the sum turned over it counts for only one-third of its amount, £100. If, then, the annual product of 51 weeks = £5,100, the capital turned over is only 4,800 + 100 = £4,900. The total capital advanced, £900, has therefore been turned over $5\,^4/_9$ times, a trifle more than in the first case.

In the present example we assumed a case in which the working time = $^2/_3$ and the circulation time = $^1/_3$ of the period of turnover, i. e., the working time was a simple multiple of the circulation time. The question now is whether capital is likewise set free, in the way shown above, when this assumption is not made.

Let us assume a working time = 5 weeks, a circulation time = 4 weeks, and a capital advance = £100 per week.

First period of turnover: 1st-9th week.

1st working period: 1st-5th week. Capital I = £500 performs its function.

1st circulation period: 6th-9th week. End of 9th week, £500 return in money form.

Second period of turnover: 6th-14th week.

2nd working period: 6th-10th week.

First section: 6th-9th week. Capital II = £400, performs its function. End of 9th week, capital I = £500 returns in money form.

Second section: 10th week. £100 of the returned £500 perform their function. The remaining £400 are set free for the following working period.

2nd circulation period: 11th-14th week. End of 14th week, £500 return in money form.

Up to the end of the 14th week (11th-14th), the £400 set free above perform their function; £100 of the £500 then returned fill the requirements of the third working period (11th-15th week), so that £400 are once more released for the fourth working period. The same thing is repeated in every working period; at its beginning £400 are ready at hand, sufficing for the first 4 weeks. End of the 4th week, £500 return in money form, only £100 of which are needed for the last week, while the other £400 remain free for the next working period.

Let us further assume a working period of 7 weeks, with a capital I of £700; a circulation period of 2 weeks, with a capital II of £200.

In that case the first period of turnover lasts from the 1st to the 9th week; its first working period from the 1st to the 7th week, with an advance of £700, its first circulation period from the 8th to the 9th week. End of the 9th week, £700 flow back in money form.

The second period of turnover, from the 8th to the 16th week, contains the second working period of the 8th to the 14th week. The requirements of the 8th and 9th weeks of this period are covered by capital II. End of the 9th week, the above £700 return. Up to the close of this working period (10th-14th week), £500 of this sum are used up; £200 remain free for the next working period. The second circulation period lasts from the 15th to the 16th week. End of the 16th week, £700 return once more. From now on, the same thing is repeated in every working period. The need for capital during the first two weeks is covered by the £200 set free at the close of the preceding working period; at the close of the second week £700 return; but only 5 weeks remain of the working period, so that it can consume only £500; therefore £200 always remain free for the next working period.

We find, then, that in the given case, where the working period has been assumed to be greater than the circulation period, a money capital will at all events have been set free at the close of each working period, which is of the same magnitude as capital II advanced for the circulation period. In our three illustrations capital II was £300 in the first, £400 in the second, and £200 in the third. Accordingly, the capital set free at the close of each working period was £300, £400 and £200 respectively.

III. THE WORKING PERIOD SMALLER
THAN THE CIRCULATION PERIOD

We begin by assuming once more a period of turnover of 9 weeks, of which 3 weeks are assigned to the working period with an available capital I of £300. Let the circulation period be 6 weeks. For these 6 weeks, an additional capital of £600 is required, which we may divide in turn into two capitals of £300, each of them meeting the requirements of one working period. We then have three capitals of £300 each, of which £300 are always engaged in production, while £600 circulate.

Table III
CAPITAL I

Periods of Turnover		Working Periods		Periods of Circulation	
I. 1st-9th	week	1st-3rd	week	4th-9th	week
II. 10th-18th	,,	10th-12th	,,	13th-18th	,,
III. 19th-27th	,,	19th-21st	,,	22nd-27th	,,
IV. 28th-36th	,,	28th-30th	,,	31st-36th	,,
V. 37th-45th	,,	37th-39th	,,	40th-45th	,,
VI. 46th-(54th)	,,	46th-48th	,,	49th-(54th)	,,

CAPITAL II

Periods of Turnover			Working Periods			Periods of Circulation		
I.	4th-12th	week	4th-6th	week		7th-12th	week	
II.	13th-21st	,,	13th-15th	,,		16th-21st	,,	
III.	22nd-30th	,,	22nd-24th	,,		25th-30th	,,	
IV.	31st-39th	,,	31st-33rd	,,		34th-39th	,,	
V.	40th-48th	,,	40th-42nd	,,		43rd-48th	,,	
VI.	49th-(57th)	,,	49th-51st	,,		(52nd-57th)	,,	

CAPITAL III

Periods of Turnover			Working Periods			Periods of Circulation		
I.	7th-15th	week	7th-9th	week		10th-15th	week	
II.	16th-24th	,,	16th-18th	,,		19th-24th	,,	
III.	25th-33rd	,,	25th-27th	,,		28th-33rd	,,	
IV.	34th-42nd	,,	34th-36th	,,		37th-42nd	,,	
V.	43rd-51st	,,	43rd-45th	,,		46th-51st	,,	

We have here the exact counterpart of Case I, with the only difference that now three capitals relieve one another instead of two. There is no intersection or intertwining of capitals. Each one of them can be traced separately to the end of the year. Just as in Case I, no capital is set free at the close of a working period. Capital I is completely laid out at the end of the 3rd week, returns entirely at the end of the 9th, and resumes its functions at the beginning of the 10th week. Similarly with capitals II and III. The regular and complete relief excludes any release of capital.

The total turnover is as follows:

$$
\begin{array}{lll}
\text{capital I} & £300 \times 5\,^2/_3 = £1,700 \\
\text{capital II} & £300 \times 5\,^1/_3 = £1,600 \\
\text{capital III} & £300 \times 5 = £1,500 \\
\hline
\text{Total capital} & £900 \times 5\,^1/_3 = £4,800.
\end{array}
$$

Let us now also take an illustration in which the circulation period is not an exact multiple of the working period. For instance, working period—4 weeks, circulation period—5 weeks. The corresponding amounts of capital would then be: capital I—£400; capital II—£400; capital III—£100. We present only the first three turnovers.

Table IV

CAPITAL I

Periods of Turnover		Working Periods		Periods of Circulation	
I. 1st-9th	week	1st-4th	week	5th-9th	week
II. 9th-17th	,,	9th, 10th-12th	,,	13th-17th	,,
III. 17th-25th	,,	17th, 18th-20th	,,	21st-25th	,,

CAPITAL II

Periods of Turnover		Working Periods		Periods of Circulation	
I. 5th-13th	week	5th-8th	week	9th-13th	week
II. 13th-21st	,,	13th, 14th-16th	,,	17th-21st	,,
III. 21st-29th	,,	21th, 22nd-24th	,,	25th-29th	,,

CAPITAL III

Periods of Turnover		Working Periods		Periods of Circulation	
I. 9th-17th	week	9th	week	10th-17th	week
II. 17th-25th	,,	17th	,,	18th-25th	,,
III. 25th-33rd	,,	25th	,,	26th-33rd	,,

There is in this case an intertwining of capitals in so far as the working period of capital III, which has no independent working period, because it suffices for only one week, coincides with the first working week of capital I. On the other hand an amount of £100, equal to capital III, is set free at the close of the working period of both capital I and II. For if capital III fills up the first week of the second and all succeeding working periods of capital I and £400, the entire capital I, return at the close of this first week, then only 3 weeks and a corresponding capital investment of £300 will remain for the rest of the working period of capital I. The £100 thus set free suffice for the first week of the immediately following working period of capital II; at the end of that week the entire capital II of £400 returns. But since the working period already started can absorb only another £300, £100 are once more disengaged at its close. And so forth. We have, then, a release of capital at the close of a working period whenever the circulation period is not a simple multiple of the working period. And this liberated capital is equal to that portion of the capital which has to fill up the excess of the circulation period over the working period or over a multiple of working periods.

In all cases investigated it was assumed that both the working period and the circulation period remain the same throughout the year in any of the businesses here examined. This assumption was necessary if we wished to ascertain the influence of the time of circulation on the turnover and advancement of capital. That in reality this assumption is not so unconditionally valid, and that it frequently is not valid at all does not alter the case in the least.

In this entire part we have discussed only the turnovers of the circulating capital, not those of the fixed, for the simple reason that the question at issue has nothing to do with fixed capital. The instruments of labour, etc., employed in the process of production form only fixed capital, inasmuch as their time of employment exceeds the period of turnover of the circulating capital; inasmuch as the period of time during which these instruments of labour continue to serve in perpetually repeated labour processes is greater than the period of turnover of the circulating capital, and hence equal to n periods of turnover of the circulating capital. Regardless of whether the total time represented by these n periods of turnover of the circulating capital is longer or shorter, that portion of the productive capital which was advanced for this time in fixed capital is not advanced anew during its course. It continues its functions in its old use form. The difference is merely this: In proportion to the varying length of a single *working period* of each period of turnover of the circulating capital, the fixed capital gives up a greater or smaller part of its original value to the product of that working period, and, proportionally to the duration of the circulation time of each period of turnover, this value part of the fixed capital given up to the product returns quicker or slower in money form. The nature of the subject we are discussing in this part — the turnover of the circulating portion of productive capital — derives from the very nature of this portion. The circulating capital employed in a working period cannot be applied in a new working period until it has completed its turnover, until it has been transformed into commodity capital, from that into money capital, and from that back into productive capital. Hence, in order that the first working period may be immediately followed by a second, capital must be advanced anew and converted into the circulating elements of productive capital, and its quantity must be sufficient to fill the void occasioned by the circulation period of the circulating capital advanced for the first working period. This is the source of the influence exerted by the length of the working period of the circulating capital over the scale of the labour process and over the division of the advanced capital or the addition of new portions of capital. This was precisely what we had to examine in this part.

IV. CONCLUSIONS

From the preceding investigation it follows that

A. The different portions into which capital must be divided in order that one part of it may be continually in the working period while others are in the period of circulation, relieve one another, like different independent individual capitals, in two cases: (1) when the working period is equal to the period of circulation, so that the period of turnover is divided into two equal sections; (2) when the period of circulation is longer than the working period, but at the same time is a simple multiple of the working period, so that one period of circulation = n working periods, in which case n must be a whole number. In these cases no portion of the successively advanced capital is set free.

B. On the other hand in all cases in which (1) the period of circulation is longer than the working period without being a simple multiple of it, and (2) in which the working period is longer than the circulation period, a portion of the total circulating capital is set free continually and periodically at the close of each working period, beginning with the second turnover. This freed capital is equal to that portion of the total capital which has been advanced for the circulation period, provided the working period is longer than the period of circulation; and equal to that portion of the capital which has to fill up the excess of the circulation period over the working period or over a multiple of working periods, provided the circulation period is longer than the working period.

C. It follows that for the aggregate social capital, so far as its circulating part is concerned, the release of capital must be the rule, while the mere alternation of portions of capital functioning successively in the production process must be the exception. For the equality of the working and circulation periods, or the equality of the period of circulation and a simple multiple of the working period, this regular proportionality of the two components of the period of turnover has absolutely nothing to do with the nature of the case and for this reason it can occur on the whole only as a matter of exception.

A very considerable portion of the social circulating capital, which is turned over several times a year, will therefore periodically exist in the form of released capital during the annual turnover cycle.

It is furthermore evident that, all other circumstances being equal, the magnitude of the released capital grows with the volume of the labour process or with the scale of production, hence with the development of capitalist production in general. In the case cited under *B*, (2), because the total advanced capital increases; in *B*, (1), because with the development of capitalist production the length of the period of circulation grows, hence also the period of turnover in those cases where the working period is less than the period of circulation, and there is no regular ratio between the two periods.

In the first case for instance we had to invest £100 per week. This required £600 for a working period of 6 weeks, £300 for a circulation period of 3 weeks, totalling £900. In that case £300 are released continually. On the other hand if £300 are invested weekly, we have £1,800 for the working period and £900 for the circulation period. Hence £900 instead of £300 are periodically set free.

D. A total capital of, say, £900 must be divided into two portions, as above, £600 for the working period and £300 for the period of circulation. That portion which is really invested in the labour process is thus reduced by one-third, from £900 to £600; consequently, the scale of production is diminished by one-third. On the other hand the £300 function only to make the working period continuous, in order that £100 may be invested every week of the year in the labour process.

Abstractly speaking, it is all the same whether £600 work during $6 \times 8 = 48$ weeks (product = £4,800) or whether the total capital of £900 is expended during 6 weeks in the labour process and then lies idle during the 3-week period of circulation. In the latter case, it would be working in the course of the 48 weeks, $5^1/_3 \times 6 = 32$ weeks (product = $5^1/_5 \times 900 = $ £4,800), and lie idle for 16 weeks. But, apart from the greater spoilage of the fixed capital during the idle 16 weeks and apart from the appreciation of labour, which must be paid during the entire year, even if employed only during a part of it, such a regular interruption of the process of production is altogether irreconcilable with the operations of modern big industry. This continuity is itself a productive power of labour.

Now, if we take a closer look at the released, or rather suspended, capital, we find that a considerable part of it must always be in the form of money capital. Let us adhere to our illustration: Working period — 6 weeks, period of circulation — 3 weeks, investment per week — £100. In the middle of the second working period, end of the 9th week, £600 return, and only £300 of them must be invested for the remainder of the working period. At the end of the second working period, £300 are therefore released. In what state are these £300? We shall assume that $^1/_3$ is invested for wages and $^2/_3$ for raw and auxiliary materials. Then £200 of the returned £600 exist in the form of money for wages and £400 in the form of a productive supply, in the form of elements of the constant circulating productive capital. But since only one half of this productive supply is required for the second half of the second working period, the other half exists for 3 weeks in the form of an excessive productive supply, i. e., of a supply exceeding the requirements of one working period. But the capitalist knows that he needs only one half, or £200, of this portion(= £400) of the returned capital for the current working period. It will therefore depend on market conditions whether he will immediately reconvert these £200, in whole or in part, into an excessive productive supply, or keep them entirely or partially in the form of money capital in anticipation of a more favourable market. On the other hand it goes without saying that the portion to be laid out for wages (= £200) is retained in the form of money. The capitalist cannot store labour power in warehouses after he has bought it, as he may do with the raw material. He must incorporate it in the process of production and pay for it at the end of the week. At any rate these £100 of the released capital of £300 will therefore have the form of money capital set free, i. e., not required for the working period. The capital released in the form of money capital must therefore be at least equal to the variable portion of capital invested in wages. At a maximum, it may comprise the entire released capital. In reality it fluctuates constantly between this minimum and maximum.

The money capital thus released by the mere mechanism of the turnover movement (together with the money capital freed by the successive reflux of fixed capital and the money capital required in every labour process for variable capital) must play an important role as soon as the credit system develops and must at the same time form one of the latter's foundations.

Let us assume that the time of circulation in our illustration is shortened from 3 to 2 weeks. This is not to be a normal change, but due, say, to prosperous times, shorter terms of payment, etc. The capital of £600, which is laid out during the working period, returns one week earlier than needed. It is therefore released for this week. Furthermore, in the middle of the working period, as before, £300 are released (a portion of those £600), but for 4 weeks instead of 3. There are, then, on the money market £600 for one week and £300 for 4 instead of 3 weeks. As this concerns not one capitalist alone but many and occurs in various periods in different businesses, more available money capital makes its appearance in the market. If this condition lasts for some time, production will be expanded wherever feasible. Capitalists operating on borrowed money will exercise less demand on the money market, which eases it as much as increased supply; or finally the sums which have become superfluous for the mechanism are thrown definitely on the money market.

In consequence of the contraction of the time of circulation from 3 weeks to 2, and consequently of the period of turnover from 9 weeks to 8, one-ninth of the total capital advanced becomes superfluous. The 6-week working period can now be kept going as continuously with £800 as formerly with £900. One portion of the value of the commodity capital, equal to £100, once it has been reconverted into money, persists therefore in the state of money capital without performing any more functions as a part of the capital advanced for the process of production. While the scale of production and other conditions, such as prices, etc., remain the same, the sum of value of the advanced capital is reduced from £900 to £800. The remainder of the originally advanced value amounting to £100 is eliminated in the form of money capital. As such it enters the money market and forms an additional portion of the capitals functioning here.

This shows the way in which a plethora of money capital may arise — and not only in the sense that the supply of money capital is greater than the demand; this is always only a relative plethora, which occurs for instance in the "melancholy period" opening a new cycle after the end of a crisis. But also in the sense that a definite portion of the capital value advanced becomes superfluous for the operation of the entire process of social reproduction (which includes the process of circulation) and is therefore eliminated in the form of money capital — a plethora brought about by the mere contraction of the period of turnover, while the scale of production and prices remain the same. The amount of money in circulation, whether great or small, does not influence it in the least.

Let us assume on the contrary that the period of circulation is prolonged from, say, 3 weeks to 5. In that case at the very next turnover the reflux of the advanced capital takes place 2 weeks too late. The last part of the process of production of this working period cannot be carried on further by the mechanism of the turnover of the advanced capital itself. Should this condition last any length of time, a contraction of the process of production, a reduction of its volume, might take place, just as an extension occurred in the previous case. But in order to continue the process on the same scale, the advanced capital would have to be increased by $^2/_9 = £200$ for the entire term of the prolongation of the circulation period. This additional capital can be obtained only from the money market. If the lengthening of the period of circulation applies to one or several big branches of business, it may exert pressure on the money market, unless this effect is paralysed by some counter-effect. In this case it is likewise evident and obvious that this pressure, like that plethora before, had nothing whatever to do with a movement either of prices of the commodities or the mass of the existing circulating medium.

//The preparation of this chapter for publication presented no small number of difficulties. Firmly grounded as Marx was in algebra, he did not get the knack of handling figures, particularly commercial arithmetic, although there exists a thick batch of copybooks containing numerous examples of all kinds of commercial computations which he had solved himself. But knowledge of the various methods of calculation and exercise in daily practical commercial arithmetic are by no means the same, and consequently Marx got so tangled up in his computations of turnovers that besides places left uncompleted a number of things were incorrect and contradictory. In the tables reproduced above I have preserved only the simplest and arithmetically correct data. My reason for doing so was mainly the following.

The uncertain results of these painstaking calculations led Marx to attach unwarranted importance to a circumstance, which, in my opinion, has actually little significance. I refer to what he calls the "release" of money capital. The actual state of affairs, based on the above assumptions, is this:

No matter what may be the ratio between the working period and circulation time, hence between capital I and capital II, the capital required for one working period, i. e., a sum equal to capital I, returns to the capitalist, in the form of money, after the end of the first turnover and thereafter at regular intervals equal to the duration of one working period.

If the working period = 5 weeks, the circulation time = 4 weeks, and capital I = £500, then a sum of money equal to £500 returns each time at the end of the 9th, 14th, 19th, 24th, 29th week, etc.

If. the working period = 6 weeks, the circulation time = 3 weeks, and capital I = £600, then £600 return at the end of the 9th, 15th, 21st, 27th, 33rd week, etc.

Finally, if the working period = 4 weeks, the circulation time = 5 weeks, and capital I = £400, then £400 are returned at the end of the 9th, 13th, 17th, 21st, 25th week, etc.

Whether any, and if so how much, of this returned money is superfluous for the current working period, and thus released, is immaterial. It is assumed that production continues uninterruptedly on the current scale, and in order that this may come about money must be available and must therefore return, whether "released" or not. If production is interrupted, release stops likewise.

In other words: There is indeed a release of money, a formation therefore of latent, merely potential, capital in the form of money. But it takes place under all circumstances and not only under the special conditions set forth in the text; and it comes about on a larger scale than that assumed in the text. So far as circulating capital I is concerned, the industrial capitalist is in the same situation at the end of each turnover as when he established his business: he has all of it in his hands in one bulk, while he can convert it back into productive capital only gradually.

The essential point in the text is the proof that on the one hand a considerable portion of the industrial capital must always be available in the form of money and that on the other hand a still more considerable portion must temporarily assume the form of money. The proof is, if anything, rendered stronger by these additional remarks of mine.— *F. E.* //

V. THE EFFECT OF A CHANGE OF PRICES

We have just assumed unaltered prices and an unaltered scale of production on the one hand, and a contraction or expansion of the time of circulation on the other. Now let us suppose on the contrary an unaltered period of turnover and an unaltered scale of production, and on the other hand price changes, i. e., rise or fall of prices of raw materials, auxiliary substances, and labour, or of the two first-named elements alone. Take it that the price of raw and auxiliary materials, as well as wages, fall by one half. In that case the capital to be advanced in our example would be £50 instead of £100 per week, and that for the 9-week turnover period would be £450 instead of £900. £450 of the advanced capital value are eliminated first of all in the form of money capital, but the process of production continues on the same scale, with the same period of turnover, and with the previous division of the latter. The annual output likewise remains the same but its value has been cut in half. This change, which is accompanied by a change in the supply and demand of money capital, is brought about neither by an acceleration of the circulation, nor by a change in the quantity of circulating money. On the contrary. A fall by half in the value, or price, of the elements of productive capital would first have the effect of diminishing by half the capital value to be advanced for the continuation of Business X on the same scale as before, and hence only one half of the money would have to be thrown on the market by Business X, since Business X advances this capital value first in the form of money, i. e., as money capital. The amount of money thrown into circulation would decrease because the prices of the elements of production fell. This would be the first effect.

In the second place however one half of the originally advanced capital value of £900 = £450, which (a) passed successively through the forms of money capital, productive capital, and commodity capital, and (b) existed simultaneously and constantly side by side partly in the form of money capital, partly in that of productive capital, and partly in that of commodity capital, would be eliminated from the circuit of Business X and thus come into the money market as additional money capital, affecting it as an additional constituent. These released £450 act as money capital, not because they have become superfluous money for the operation of Business X but because they are a constituent part of the original capital value, and hence are intended to function further as capital and not to be expended as mere means of circulation. The best method of letting them operate as capital is that of throwing them as money capital on the money market. On the other hand the scale of production (apart from fixed capital) might be doubled. In that case a productive process of double the previous volume would be carried on with the same advanced capital of £900.

If on the other hand the prices of the fluid elements of productive capital were to increase by one half, £150 instead of £100 or £1,350 instead of £900 would be required per week. It would take an additional capital of £450 to carry on the business on the same scale, and this would exert a *pro tanto* pressure on the money market, big or small depending on its condition. If all the capital available on this market were then already engaged, there would be increased competition for available capital. If a portion of it were unemployed, it would *pro tanto* be called into action.

But, in the third place, given a certain scale of production, the turnover velocity and the prices of the elements of the circulating productive capital remaining the same, the price of the products of Business X may rise or fall. If the price of the commodities supplied by Business X falls, the price of its commodity capital of £600, which it constantly threw into circulation, drops to, say, £500. Hence one-sixth of the value of the advanced capital does not return from the process of circulation. (The surplus value contained in the commodity capital is not considered here.) It is lost in that process. But since the value, or price, of the elements of production remains the same, this reflux of £500 suffices only to replace $5/_6$ of the capital of £600 constantly engaged in the process of production. It would therefore require an additional money capital of £100 to continue production on the same scale.

Vice versa, if the price of the product of Business X were to rise, then the price of the £600 commodity capital would be increased, say, to £700. One-seventh of this price = £100 does not originate in the process of production, is not advanced in this process, but derives from the process of circulation. But only £600 are needed to replace the elements of production. Hence, release of £100.

It does not fall within the scope of the investigation hitherto made to ascertain why, in the first case, the period of turnover is shortened or lengthened, and why in the second case the prices of raw materials and labour, and in the third, the prices of the products supplied, rise or fall.

But the following does belong in it:

First Case. Unchanged Scale of Production, Unchanged Prices of the Elements of Production and of Products, a Change in the Period of Circulation and Thus of Turnover.

According to the assumptions of our example, $^1/_9$ less of the total advanced capital is needed as a result of the contraction of the period of circulation, so that the total capital is reduced from £900 to £800 and £100 of money capital is eliminated.

Business X supplies, just as before, the same six weeks' product of the same value of £600, and as work continues year in year out without interruption, it supplies in 51 weeks the same quantity of products, valued at £5,100. There is, then, no change so far as the quantity and price of the product thrown into circulation by this business are concerned, nor in the time when it throws its product on the market. But £100 are eliminated because due to the contraction of the circulation period the requirements of the process are satisfied with only £800 instead of the former £900. The £100 of eliminated capital exist in the form of money capital. But they do not by any means represent that portion of the advanced capital which would have to function constantly in the form of money capital. Let us assume that $^4/_5 = £480$ of the advanced circulating capital I = £600 are constantly invested in productive materials and $^1/_5 = £120$ in wages. Then the weekly investment in materials of production would be £80 and in wages £20. Capital II = £300 should then also be divided into $^4/_5 = £240$ for materials of production and $^1/_5 = £60$ for wages. The capital invested in wages must always be advanced in the form of money. As soon as the commodity product, worth £600, has been reconverted into the money form, or sold, £480 of it can be transformed into materials of production (productive supply), but £120 retain their money form in order to serve for the payment of wages for 6 weeks. These £120 are the minimum of the returning capital of £600, which must always be renewed and replaced in the form of money capital and therefore must always be kept on hand as that portion of the advanced capital which functions in the form of money.

Now, if £100 of the £300 periodically released for three weeks, and likewise divisible into £240 for productive supply and £60 for wages, are eliminated, completely thrust out of the turnover mechanism, in the form of money capital by shortening the circulation time, where does the money for this money capital of £100 come from? Only one-fifth of this amount consists of money capital periodically set free within the turnovers. But $^4/_5 = $ £80 are already replaced by an additional productive supply of the same value. In what manner is this additional productive supply converted into money, and where does the money for this conversion come from?

If the abridged period of circulation has become a fact, then only £400 of the above £600, instead of £480, are reconverted into productive supply. The remainder, £80, is retained in its money form and constitutes, together with the above £20 for wages, the £100 of eliminated capital. Although these £100 come from the sphere of circulation through the sale of the £600 worth of commodity capital and are now withdrawn from it by not being re-invested in wages and elements of production, it must not be forgotten that, being in the money form, they are once more in that form in which they were originally thrown into circulation. In the beginning £900 were invested in productive supply and wages. Now only £800 are necessary to carry out the same productive process. The £100 thus released in money now form a new, employment-seeking money capital, a new constituent part of the money market. True, they have already previously been periodically in the form of released money capital and of additional productive capital, but these latent states were themselves the requisites for the execution of the process of production, because they were the requisites for its continuity. Now they are no longer needed for that purpose and for this reason form new money capital and a constituent part of the money market, although they by no means form either an additional element of the available social money supply (for they existed at the beginning of the business and were thrown by it into the circulation), or a newly accumulated hoard.

These £100 are now in actual fact withdrawn from circulation inasmuch as they are a part of the advanced money capital that is no longer employed in the same business. But this withdrawal is possible only because the conversion of the commodity capital into money, and of this money into productive capital, C′ — M — C, is accelerated by one week, so that the circulation of the money operating in this process is likewise hastened. They have been withdrawn from it because they are no longer needed for the turnover of capital X.

It has been assumed here that the advanced capital belongs to him who employs it. Had he borrowed it nothing would be changed. With the shortening of the time of circulation he would have to borrow only £800 instead of £900. The £100, if returned to the lender, would as before form £100 of new money capital, only in the hands of Y instead of X. Should capitalist X receive £480 worth of materials of production on credit, so that he has to advance only £120 in money for wages out of his own pocket, he would now have to procure £80 worth of productive materials less on credit and this sum would constitute superfluous commodity capital for the capitalist granting the credit, while capitalist X would have eliminated £20 in money.

The additional supply for production is now reduced by $^1/_3$. It consisted of £240 constituting $^4/_5$ of £300, the additional capital II, but now it is only £160, i. e., additional supply for 2 instead of 3 weeks. It is now renewed every 2 weeks instead of every 3, but only for 2 instead of 3 weeks. The purchases, for instance in the cotton market, are thus more frequent and smaller. The same amount of cotton is withdrawn from the market, for the quantity of the product remains the same. But the withdrawals are distributed differently in time, extending over a longer period. Supposing that it is a question of 3 months or 2. If the annual consumption of cotton amounts to 1,200 bales, the sales in the first case will be:

January	1	300 bales,	left in storage			900	bales
April	1	300	,,	,, ,,	,,	600	,,
July	1	300	,,	,, ,,	,,	300	,,
October	1	300	,,	,, ,,	,,	0	,,

But in the second case:

January	1	sold 200,	in storage		1,000	bales
March	1	,, 200,	,,	,,	800	,,
May	1	,, 200,	,,	,,	600	,,
July	1	,, 200,	,,	,,	400	,,
September	1	,, 200,	,,	,,	200	,,
November	1	,, 200,	,,	,,	0	,,

So the money invested in cotton only returns completely one month later, in November instead of October. If therefore $^1/_9$ of the advanced capital = £100 is eliminated in the form of money capital by the contraction of the circulation time and thus of the turnover, and if these £100 are composed of £20 worth of periodically superfluous money capital for the payment of weekly wages, and of £80 which existed as periodically superfluous productive supply for one week, then the diminished superfluous productive supply in the hands of the manufacturer corresponds, so far as these £80 are concerned, to an enlarged commodity supply in the hands of the cotton dealer. The longer this cotton lies in the latter's warehouse as a commodity, the less it lies in the storeroom of the manufacturer as a productive supply.

Hitherto we presupposed that the contraction of the time of circulation in Business X was due to the fact that X sold his commodities quicker, received his money for them sooner, or, in the event of credit, was given shorter terms of payment. The contraction was therefore attributed to a quicker sale of the commodities, to a quicker transformation of commodity capital into money capital, $C' - M$, the first phase of the process of circulation. But it might also derive from the second phase, $M - C$, and hence from a simultaneous change, be it in the working period or in the time of circulation of capitals Y, Z, etc., which supply capitalist X with the productive elements of his circulating capital.

For instance if cotton, coal, etc., with the old methods of transport, are 3 weeks in transit from their place of production or storage to the place of production of capitalist X, then X's productive supply must last at least for 3 weeks, until the arrival of new supplies. So long as cotton and coal are in transit, they cannot serve as means of production. They are then rather a subject of labour for the transport industry and the capital employed in it; they are also commodity capital in process of circulation for the producer of coal or the dealer in cotton. Suppose improvements in transport reduce the transit to 2 weeks. Then the productive supply can be changed from a three-weekly into a fortnightly supply. This releases the additional advanced capital of £80 set aside for this purpose and likewise the £20 for wages, because the turned-over capital of £600 returns one week sooner.

On the other hand if for instance the working period of the capital which supplies the raw materials is cut down (examples of which were given in the preceding chapters), so that the possibility arises of renewing the supply of raw materials in less time, then the productive supply may be reduced and the interval between periods of renewal shortened.

If, vice versa, the time of circulation, and thus the period of turnover, are prolonged, then it is necessary to advance additional capital.

This must come out of the pocket of the capitalist himself if he has any additional capital. But it will then be invested in some form or other as a part of the money market. To make it available, it must be stripped of its old form. For instance stocks must be sold, deposits withdrawn, so that in this case too the money market is indirectly affected. Or he must borrow it. As for that part of the additional capital which is needed for wages, it must under normal conditions always be advanced in the form of money capital, and for that purpose the capitalist X exerts his share of direct pressure on the money market. But this is indispensable for the part which must be invested in materials of production only if he must pay for them in cash. If he can get them on credit, this does not have any direct influence on the money market, because the additional capital is then advanced directly as a productive supply and not in the first instance as money capital. But if the lender throws the bill of exchange received from X directly on the money market, discounts it, etc., this would influence the money market indirectly, through someone else. If, however, he uses this note to cover a debt not yet due for instance, this additional advanced capital does not affect the money market either directly or indirectly.

Second Case. A Change in the Price of Materials of Production, All Other Circumstances Remaining the Same.

We have just assumed that the total capital of £900 was $^4/_5$ invested in materials of production ($= £720$) and $^1/_5$ in wages ($= £180$).

If the materials of production drop to half, they require for the 6-week working period only £240 instead of £480, and for the additional capital No. II only £120 instead of £240. Capital I is thus reduced from £600 to £240 + £120 = £360, and capital II from £300 to £120 + £60 = £180. The total capital of £900 is therefore reduced to £360 + £180 = £540. A sum of £360 is therefore released.

This eliminated and now unemployed capital, or money capital seeking employment in the money market, is nothing but a portion of the capital of £900 originally advanced as money capital, which, due to the fall in the prices of the elements of production, into which it is periodically reconverted, has become superfluous if the business is not to be expanded but carried on on the same scale. If this fall in prices were not due to accidental circumstances (a particularly rich harvest, over-supply, etc.) but to an increase of productive power in the branch of production which furnishes the raw materials, then this money capital would be an absolute addition to the money market, and to the capital available in the form of money capital in general, because it would no longer constitute an integral part of the capital already invested.

Third Case. A Change in the Market Price of the Product Itself.

In the case of a fall in prices a portion of the capital is lost, and must consequently be made good by a new advance of money capital. This loss of the seller may be a gain to the buyer. Directly, if the market price of the product has fallen merely because of an accidental fluctuation, and afterwards rises once more to its normal level. Indirectly, if the change of prices is caused by a change of value reacting on the old product and if this product passes again, as an element of production, into another sphere of production and there releases capital *pro tanto*. In either case the capital lost by X, and for whose replacement he exerts pressure on the money market, may be supplied to him by his business friends as new additional capital. All that takes place then is a transfer.

If, on the contrary, the price of the product rises, a portion of the capital which was not advanced is taken out of circulation. This is not an organic part of the capital advanced in the process of production and unless production is expanded therefore constitutes money capital eliminated. As we have assumed here that the prices of the elements of the product were given before it was brought to market as commodity capital, a real change of value might have caused the rise of prices since it acted retroactively, causing a subsequent rise in the price of, say, raw materials. In that event capitalist X would realise a gain on his product circulating as commodity capital and on his available productive supply. This gain would give him an additional capital, which would now be needed for the continuation of his business with the new and higher prices of the elements of production.

Or the rise of prices is but temporary. What capitalist X then needs by way of additional capital becomes released capital for the other side, in so far as X's product forms an element of production for other branches of business. What the one has lost the other has gained.

Chapter XVI

THE TURNOVER OF VARIABLE CAPITAL

I. THE ANNUAL RATE OF SURPLUS VALUE

Let us assume a circulating capital of £2,500, $^4/_5$ of which, or £2,000, are constant capital (materials of production) and $^1/_5 = $ £500 is variable capital invested in wages.

Let the period of turnover be 5 weeks; the working period 4 weeks, the period of circulation 1 week. Then capital I = £2,000, consisting of £1,600 of constant capital and £400 of variable capital; capital II = £500, £400 of which are constant and £100 variable. In every working week a capital of £500 is invested. In a year of 50 weeks an annual product of $50 \times 500 = $ £25,000 is manufactured. Capital I of £2,000, constantly employed in the working period, is therefore turned over $12^1/_2$ times. $12^1/_2 \times 2,000 = $ £25,000. Of these £25,000 $^4/_5 = $ £20,000 are constant capital laid out in means of production, and $^1/_5 = $ £5,000 is variable capital laid out in wages. The total capital of £2,500 is thus turned over $\frac{25,000}{2,500} = 10$ times.

The variable circulating capital expended in production can serve afresh in the process of circulation only to the extent that the product in which its value is reproduced has been sold, converted from a commodity capital into a money capital, in order to be once more laid out in payment of labour power. But the same is true of the constant circulating capital (materials of production) invested in production, the value of which reappears in the product as a portion of its value. What these two portions — the variable and the constant part of the circulating capital — have in common and what distinguishes them from the fixed capital is not that the value transferred from them to the product is circulated by the commodity capital, i. e., through the circulation of the product as a commodity. One portion of the value of the product, and thus of the product circulating as a commodity, of the commodity capital, always consists of the wear and tear of the fixed capital, that is to say, of that portion of the value of the fixed capital which is transferred to the product during the process of production. The difference is really this: The fixed capital continues to function in the process of production in its old use form for a longer or shorter cycle of turnover periods of the circulating capital (= constant circulating + variable circulating capital), while every turnover is conditioned on the replacement of the entire circulating capital passing from the sphere of production — in the form of commodity capital — into the sphere of circulation. The constant circulating and variable circulating capital have the first phase of circulation, C′ — M′, in common. In the second phase they separate. The money into which the commodity is reconverted is in part transformed into a productive supply (constant circulating capital). Depending on the different terms of purchase of its constituent parts, one portion of the money may sooner, another later, be converted from money into materials of production, but finally it is wholly consumed that way. Another portion of the money realised by the sale of the commodity is held in the form of a money supply, in order to be gradually expended in payment of the labour power incorporated in the process of production. This part constitutes the variable circulating capital. Nevertheless the entire replacement of either portion always originates from the turnover of the capital, from its conversion into a product, from a product into a commodity, from a commodity into money. This is the reason why, in the preceding chapter, the turnover of the circulating capital, constant and variable, was treated jointly and separately without paying any regard to the fixed capital.

In the question which we shall now take up, we must go a step farther and proceed with the variable portion of the circulating capital as though it alone constituted the circulating capital. In other words, we leave out of consideration the constant circulating capital which is turned over together with it.

A sum of £2,500 has been advanced and the value of the annual product is £25,000. But the variable portion of the circulating capital is £500; therefore the variable capital contained in £25,000 amounts to $\frac{25,000}{5} = £5,000$. If we divide these £5,000 by £500, we find that the number of turnovers is 10, just as it is in the case of the total capital of £2,500.

Here, where it is only a question of the production of surplus value, it is absolutely correct to make this average calculation, according to which the value of the annual product is divided by the value of the advanced capital and not by the value of that portion of this capital which is employed constantly in one working period (thus, in the present case not by 400 but by 500, not by capital I but by capital I + capital II). We shall see later that, from another point of view, the calculation is not quite exact, just as this average calculation generally is not quite exact. That is to say, it serves well enough for the practical purposes of the capitalist, but it does not express exactly or properly all the real circumstances of the turnover.

We have hitherto ignored one part of the value of the commodity capital, namely the surplus value contained in it, which was produced during the process of production and incorporated in the product. To this we have now to direct our attention.

Suppose the variable capital of £100 invested weekly produces a surplus value of 100% = £100, then the variable capital of £500 invested over a 5-week turnover period produces £500 of surplus value, i. e., one half of the working day consists of surplus labour.

But if £500 of variable capital produce a surplus value of £500, then £5,000 produce 10 × 500 = £5,000 in surplus value. But the advanced variable capital amounts to £500. The ratio of the total surplus value produced during one year to the sum of value of the advanced variable capital is what we call the annual rate of surplus value. In the case at hand it is $\frac{5,000}{500} = 1,000\%$. If we analyse this rate more closely, we find that it is equal to the rate of surplus value produced by the advanced variable capital during one period of turnover, multiplied by the number of turnovers of the variable capital (which coincides with the number of turnovers of the entire circulating capital).

The variable capital advanced in the case before us for one period of turnover is £500; the surplus value produced during this period is likewise £500. The rate of surplus value for one period of turnover is therefore $\frac{500s}{500v} = 100\%$. This 100%, multiplied by 10, the number of turnovers in one year, makes $\frac{5,000s}{500v} = 1,000\%$.

That refers to the annual rate of surplus value. As for the amount of surplus value obtained during a specified period of turnover, it is equal to the value of the variable capital advanced during this period, or £500 in the present case, multiplied by the rate of surplus value, in the present case therefore $500 \times \frac{100}{100} = 500 \times 1 = £500$. If the advanced capital were £1,500, then with the same rate of surplus value the amount of surplus value would be $1,500 \times \frac{100}{100} = £1,500$.

We shall apply the term capital A to the variable capital of £500, which is turned over ten times per year, producing an annual surplus value of £5,000 for which, therefore, the yearly rate of surplus value = 1,000%.

Now let us assume that another variable capital, B, of £5,000, is advanced for one whole year (i. e., here for 50 weeks), so that it is turned over only once a year. We assume furthermore that at the end of the year the product is paid for on the same day that it is finished, so that the money capital, into which it is converted, returns on the same day. The circulation period is then zero, the period of turnover = the working period, namely = 1 year. As in the preceding case there is to be found in the labour process each week a variable capital of £100, or of £5,000 in 50 weeks. Let the rate of surplus value be the same, or 100%, i. e., let one half of the working day of the same length consist of surplus labour. If we consider 5 weeks, the invested variable capital is £500, the rate of surplus value 100% and therefore the amount of surplus value produced in 5 weeks £500. The quantity of labour power here exploited, and the intensity of its exploitation, are assumed to be exactly the same as those of capital A.

Each week the invested variable capital of £100 produces a surplus value of £100, hence in 50 weeks the invested capital of $50 \times 100 = $ £5,000 produces a surplus value of £5,000. The amount of surplus value produced annually is the same as in the previous case, £5,000, but the yearly rate of surplus value is entirely different. It is equal to the surplus value produced in one year divided by the advanced variable capital: $\frac{5,000s}{5,000v} = 100\%$, while in the case of capital A it was 1,000%.

In the case of both capitals A and B, we have invested a variable capital of £100 a week. The degree of self-expansion, or the rate of surplus value, is likewise the same, 100%, and so is the magnitude of the variable capital, £100. The same quantity of labour power is exploited, the volume and degree of exploitation are equal in both cases, the working days are the same and equally divided into necessary labour and surplus labour. The amount of variable capital employed in the course of the year is £5,000 in either case; it sets the same amount of labour in motion, and extracts the same amount of surplus value, £5,000, from the labour power set in motion by these two equal capitals. Nevertheless there is a difference of 900% in the annual rate of surplus value of the two capitals A and B.

This phenomenon creates the impression, at all events, that the rate of surplus value depends not only on the quantity and intensity of exploitation of the labour power set in motion by the variable capital, but besides on inexplicable influences arising from the process of circulation. And it has indeed been so interpreted, and has — if not in this its pure form, then at least in its more complicated and disguised form, that of the annual rate of profit — completely routed the Ricardian school since the beginning of the twenties.[a]

The strangeness of this phenomenon disappears at once when we place capitals A and B in exactly the same conditions, not only seemingly but actually. These equal conditions exist only when the variable capital B in its entire volume is expended for the payment of labour power in the same period of time as capital A.

In that case the £5,000 of capital B are invested for 5 weeks, £1,000 per week makes an investment of £50,000 per year. The surplus value is then likewise £50,000, according to our premises. The turned-over capital of £50,000 divided by the advanced capital of £5,000 makes the number of turnovers 10. The rate of surplus value $= \frac{5,000s}{5,000v} = 100\%$, multiplied by the number of turnovers, 10, makes the annual rate of surplus value $= \frac{50,000s}{5,000v} = \frac{10}{1} = 1,000\%$. Now the annual rates of surplus value are alike for A and B, namely, 1,000%, but the amounts of the surplus value are £50,000 in the case of B, and £5,000 in the case of A. The amounts of the surplus value produced are now in the same proportion to one another as the advanced capital values B and A, to wit: 5,000:500 = 10:1. But capital B has set in motion ten times as much labour power as capital A within the same time.

Only the variable capital actually employed in the labour process produces surplus value and to it apply all laws relating to surplus value, including therefore the law according to which the quantity of surplus value, its rate being given, is determined by the relative magnitude of the variable capital.[b]

The labour process itself is measured by time. If the length of the working day is given (as here, where we assume all conditions relating to A and B to be equal, in order to elucidate the difference in the annual rate of surplus value), the working week consists of a definite number of working days. Or we may consider any working period, for instance this working period of 5 weeks, as one single working day of, say, 300 hours, if the working day = 10 hours and the week = 6 days. We must further multiply this number by the number of labourers who are employed conjointly every day simultaneously in the same labour process. If that number is taken as 10, there will be 60 × 10 = 600 hours in one week, and a working period of 5 weeks

---

[a] See present edition, Vol. 31, pp. 36-77 and Vol. 32, pp. 258-373. - [b] Ibid., Vol. 35 (*Capital*, Vol. I, Ch. XI).

would have 600 × 5 = 3,000 hours. The rate of surplus value and the length of the working day being the same, variable capitals of equal magnitude are therefore employed, if equal quantities of labour power (a labour power of the same price multiplied by the number of labourers) are set in motion in the same time.

Let us now return to our original examples. In both cases, A and B, equal variable capitals of £100 per week are invested every week throughout the year. The invested variable capitals actually functioning in the labour process are therefore equal, but the advanced variable capitals are very unequal. In the case of A, £500 are advanced for every 5 weeks, of which £100 are employed every week. In the case of B, £5,000 must be advanced for the first 5-week period, of which only £100 per week, or only £500 in 5 weeks, or $^1/_{10}$ of the advanced capital, is employed. In the second 5-week period £4,500 must be advanced, but only £500 of this are employed, etc. The variable capital advanced for a definite period of time is converted into employed, hence actually functioning and operative variable capital only to the extent that it really steps into the sections of that period of time taken up by the labour process, to the extent that it really functions in the labour process. In the intermediate time, in which a portion of it is advanced in order to be employed later, this portion is practically non-existent for the labour process and has therefore no influence on the formation of either value or surplus value. Take for instance capital A, of £500. It is advanced for 5 weeks, but every week only £100 enter successively into the labour process. In the first week $^1/_5$ of this capital is employed; $^4/_5$ are advanced without being employed, although they must be in stock, and therefore advanced, for the labour processes of the following 4 weeks.

The circumstances which differentiate the relation between the advanced and the employed variable capital affect the production of surplus value — the rate of surplus value being given — only to the extent, and only by reason of the fact that they differentiate the quantity of variable capital which can be really employed in a stated period of time, for instance in one week, 5 weeks, etc. The advanced variable capital functions as variable capital only to the extent and only during the time that it is actually employed, and not during the time in which it remains in stock, is advanced, without being employed. But all the circumstances which differentiate the relation between the advanced and the employed variable capital come down to the difference of the periods of turnover (determined by the difference of either the working period, or the circulation period, or both). The law of the production of surplus value states that equal quantities of functioning variable capital produce equal quantities of surplus value if the rate of surplus value is the same. If, then, equal quantities of variable capital are employed by the capitals A and B in equal periods of time with equal rates of surplus value, they must generate equal quantities of surplus value in equal periods of time, no matter how different the ratio of this variable capital employed during a definite period of time to the variable capital advanced during the same time, and no matter therefore how different the ratio of the quantities of surplus value produced, not to the employed but to the advanced variable capital in general. The difference of this ratio, far from contradicting the laws of the production of surplus value that have been demonstrated, rather corroborates them and is one of their inevitable consequences.

Let us consider the first 5-week productive period of capital B. At the end of the fifth week £500 have been employed and consumed. The value of the product is £1,000, hence $\frac{500s}{500v} = 100\%$. Just the same as with capital A. The fact that, in the case of capital A, the surplus value is realised together with the advanced capital, while in the case of B it is not, does not concern us here, where it is only a question of the production of surplus value and of its ratio to the variable capital advanced during its production. But if on the contrary we calculate the ratio of surplus value in B, not to that portion of the advanced capital of £5,000 which has been employed and hence consumed during its production, but to this total advanced capital itself, we find that it is $\frac{500s}{5,000v} = \frac{1}{10} = 10\%$. Hence it is 10% for capital B and 100% for capital A, i. e., tenfold. If it were said that this difference in the rate of surplus value for equal capitals, which have set in motion equal quantities of labour equally divided at that into paid and unpaid labour, is contrary to the laws of the production of surplus value, the answer would be simple and prompted by a mere glance at the actual relations: In the case of A, the actual rate of surplus value is expressed, i. e., the relation of a surplus value produced in 5 weeks by a variable capital of £500, to this variable capital of £500. In the case of B on the other hand the calculation is of a kind which has nothing to do either with the production of surplus value or with the determination of its corresponding rate of surplus value. For the £500 of sur-

plus value produced by a variable capital of £500 are not calculated
with reference to the £500 of variable capital advanced during their
production, but with reference to a capital of £5,000, $^9/_{10}$ of which,
or £4,500, have nothing whatever to do with the production of this
surplus value of £500, but are on the contrary intended to function
gradually in the course of the following 45 weeks, so that they do not
exist at all so far as the production of the first 5 weeks is concerned,
which alone is at issue in this instance. Hence in this case the difference in the rates of surplus value of A and B presents no problem at
all.

Let us now compare the annual rates of surplus value for capitals
B and A. For capital B it is $\frac{5,000s}{5,000v} = 100\%$; for capital A it
is $\frac{5,000s}{500v} = 1,000\%$. But the ratio of the rates of surplus value
is the same as before. There we had

$$\frac{\text{Rate of Surplus Value of Capital B}}{\text{Rate of Surplus Value of Capital A}} = \frac{10\%}{100\%}$$

Now we have

$$\frac{\text{Annual Rate of Surplus Value of Capital B}}{\text{Annual Rate of Surplus Value of Capital A}} = \frac{100\%}{1,000\%}$$

But $10\% : 100\% = 100\% : 1,000\%$, so that the proportion is the
same.

But now the problem has changed. The annual rate of capital B,
$\frac{5,000s}{5,000v} = 100\%$, offers not the slightest deviation—not even the
semblance of a deviation—from the laws of production known to us
and of the rate of surplus value corresponding to them. During the year 5,000v have been advanced and productively consumed, and they have produced 5,000s. The rate of surplus value
therefore equals the above fraction, $\frac{5,000s}{5,000v} = 100\%$. The annual
rate agrees with the actual rate of surplus value. In this case it
is therefore not capital B but capital A which presents an anomaly
that has to be explained.

We have here the rate of surplus value $\frac{5,000s}{500v} = 1,000\%$. But
while in the first case 500s, the product of 5 weeks, was calculated for

an advanced capital of £5,000, $^9/_{10}$ of which were not employed in its production, we have now 5,000s calculated for 500v, i. e., for only $^1/_{10}$ of the variable capital actually employed in the production of 5,000s; for the 5,000s are the product of a variable capital of £5,000 productively consumed during 50 weeks, not that of a capital of £500 consumed in one single period of 5 weeks. In the first case the surplus value produced in 5 weeks had been calculated for a capital advanced for 50 weeks, a capital ten times as large as the one consumed during the 5 weeks. Now the surplus value produced in 50 weeks is calculated for a capital advanced for 5 weeks, a capital ten times smaller than the one consumed in 50 weeks.

Capital A, of £500, is never advanced for more than 5 weeks. At the end of this time it returns and can renew the same process in the course of the year ten times, as it makes ten turnovers. Two conclusions follow from this.

Firstly: The capital advanced in the case of A is only five times larger than that portion of capital which is constantly employed in the productive process of one week. On the other hand capital B which is turned over only once in 50 weeks and must therefore be advanced for 50 weeks, is 50 times larger than that one of its portions which can constantly be employed for one week. The turnover therefore modifies the relation between the capital advanced during the year for the process of production and the capital constantly employable for a definite period of production, say, a week. Here we have, then, the first case, in which the surplus value of 5 weeks is not calculated for the capital employed during these 5 weeks, but for a capital ten times larger, employed for 50 weeks.

Secondly: The 5-week period of turnover of capital A comprises only $^1/_{10}$ of the year, so that one year contains ten such turnover periods, in which capital A of £500 is successively re-invested. The employed capital is here equal to the capital advanced for 5 weeks, multiplied by the number of periods of turnover per year. The capital employed during the year is 500 × 10 = £5,000. The capital advanced during the year = $\frac{5,000}{10}$ = £500. Indeed, although the £500 are always re-employed, the sum advanced every 5 weeks never exceeds these same £500. On the other hand in case of capital B only £500 are employed during 5 weeks and advanced for these 5 weeks. But as the period of turnover in this case = 50 weeks, the capital employed in one year is equal to the capital advanced for 50 weeks and not to that advanced for every 5 weeks. The annually produced quantity of surplus value, given the rate of surplus value, is however commensurate with the capital employed during the year, not with the capital advanced during the year. Hence it is not larger for this capital of £5,000, which is turned over once a year, than it is for the capital of £500, which is turned over ten times a year. And it is so big only because the capital turned over once a year is itself ten times larger than the capital turned over ten times a year.

The variable capital turned over during one year — hence the portion of the annual product, or of the annual expenditure equal to that portion — is the variable capital actually employed, productively consumed, during that year. It follows therefore that if the variable capital A turned over annually and the variable capital B turned over annually are equal and employed under equal conditions of self-expansion, so that the rate of surplus value is the same for both of them, then the quantity of surplus value produced annually must likewise be the same for both of them. Hence the rate of surplus value calculated for a year must also be the same, since the amounts of capital employed are the same, so far as the rate is expressed by $\frac{\text{quantity of surplus value produced annually}}{\text{variable capital turned over annually}}$. Or, expressed generally: Whatever the relative magnitude of the turned-over variable capitals, the rate of the surplus value produced by them in the course of the year is determined by the rate of surplus value at which the respective capitals have worked in average periods (say, the average of a week or day).

This is the only consequence of the laws of production of surplus value and of the determination of the rate of surplus value.

Let us now see further what is expressed by the ratio:

$$\frac{\text{capital turned over annually}}{\text{capital advanced}}$$

(taking into account, as we have said before, only the variable capital). The division shows the number of turnovers made by the capital advanced in one year.

In the case of capital A we have:

$$\frac{\text{£5,000 of capital turned over annually}}{\text{£500 of capital advanced}}$$

In the case of capital B we have:

$$\frac{\text{£5,000 of capital turned over annually}}{\text{£5,000 of capital advanced}}$$

In both ratios the numerator expresses the advanced capital multiplied by the *number* of turnovers; in the case of A, 500 × 10; in the case of B, 5,000 × 1. Or it may be multiplied by the inverted *time* of turnover calculated for one year. The time of turnover for A is $^1/_{10}$ of a year; the inverted time of turnover is $^{10}/_1$ years; hence 500 × $^{10}/_1$ = 5,000. In the case of B, 5,000 × $^1/_1$ = 5,000. The denominator expresses the turned-over capital multiplied by the inverted *number* of turnovers; in the case of A, 5,000 × $^1/_{10}$; in the case of B, 5,000 × $^1/_1$.

The respective quantities of labour (the sum of the paid and unpaid labour), which are set in motion by the two variable capitals turned over annually, are equal in this case, because the turned-over capitals themselves are equal and their rates of self-expansion are likewise equal.

The ratio of the variable capital turned over annually to the variable capital advanced indicates 1) the ratio of the capital to be advanced to the variable capital employed during a definite working period. If the number of turnovers is 10, as in the case of A, and the year assumed to have 50 weeks, then the period of turnover is 5 weeks. For these 5 weeks variable capital must be advanced and the capital advanced for 5 weeks must be 5 times as large as the variable capital employed during one week. That is to say, only $^1/_5$ of the advanced capital (in this case £ 500) can be employed in the course of one week. On the other hand, in the case of capital B, where the number of turnovers = $^1/_1$, the time of turnover is 1 year, or 50 weeks. The ratio of the advanced capital to the capital employed weekly is therefore 50 : 1. If matters were the same for B as they are for A, then B would have to invest £ 1,000 per week instead of £ 100. 2) It follows that B has employed ten times as much capital (£ 5,000) as A to set in motion the same quantity of variable capital and hence — the rate of surplus value being given — of labour (paid and unpaid), and thus to produce also the same quantity of surplus value during the year. The real rate of surplus value expresses nothing but the ratio of the variable capital employed during a definite period to the surplus value produced in the same time; or the quantity of unpaid labour set in motion by the variable capital employed during this time. It has absolutely nothing to do with that portion of the variable capital which is advanced during the time in which it is not employed. Hence it has likewise nothing to do with the ratio between that portion of variable capital which is advanced during a definite period of time and that portion which is employed during the same period of time — a ratio that is modified and differentiated for different capitals by the turnover period.

It follows rather from what has been set forth above that the annual rate of surplus value coincides only in one single case with the real rate of surplus value which expresses the degree of exploitation of labour; namely in the case when the advanced capital is turned over only once a year and the capital advanced is thus equal to the capital turned over in the course of the year, when therefore the ratio of the quantity of the surplus value produced during the year to the capital employed during the year in this production coincides and is identical with the ratio of the quantity of surplus value produced during the year to the capital advanced during the year.

A) The annual rate of surplus value is equal to the

$$\frac{\text{quantity of surplus value produced during the year}}{\text{variable capital advanced}}.$$

But the quantity of the surplus value produced during the year is equal to the real rate of surplus value multiplied by the variable capital employed in its production. The capital employed in the production of the annual quantity of surplus value is equal to the advanced capital multiplied by the number of its turnovers, which we shall call n. Formula A is therefore transformed into the following:

B) The annual rate of surplus value is equal to the

$$\frac{\text{real rate of surplus value} \times \text{variable capital advanced} \times n}{\text{variable capital advanced}}$$

For instance, in the case of capital $B = \frac{100 \times 5,000 \times 1}{5,000}$, or 100% Only when n is equal to 1, that is, when the variable capital advanced is turned over only once a year, and hence equal to the capital employed or turned over during a year, the annual rate of surplus value is equal to its real rate.

Let us call the annual rate of surplus value S′, the real rate of surplus value s′, the advanced variable capital v, the number of turnovers n. Then $S' = \frac{s'vn}{v} = s'n$. In other words, $S' = s'n$, and $= s'$ only when $n = 1$, and hence $S' = s' \times 1 = s'$.

It follows furthermore that the annual rate of surplus value is always equal to $s'n$, i. e., to the real rate of surplus value produced in one period of turnover by the variable capital consumed during that period, multiplied by the number of turnovers of this variable capital during one year, or (what amounts to the same) multiplied by its inverted *time* of turnover calculated for one year. (If the variable capital is turned over ten times per year, then its time of turnover is $^1/_{10}$ of a year, its inverted time of turnover therefore $^{10}/_1$ or 10.)

It follows furthermore that $S' = s'$ when $n = 1$. S' is greater than s' when n is greater than 1; i. e., when the advanced capital is turned over more than once a year or the turned-over capital is greater than the capital advanced.

Finally, S' is smaller than s' when n is smaller than 1, that is, when the capital turned over during the year is only a part of the advanced capital, so that the period of turnover is longer than one year.

Let us dwell a moment on this last case.

We retain all the premises of our former illustration, except that the period of turnover is lengthened to 55 weeks. The labour process requires a variable capital of £100 per week, hence £5,500 for the period of turnover, and produces every week 100s; s' is therefore 100%, as before. The number of turnovers, n, is here $^{50}/_{55}$ or $^{10}/_{11}$, because the time of turnover is $1 + ^1/_{10}$ of the year (of 50 weeks), or $^{11}/_{10}$

years. $S' = \dfrac{100\% \times 5,500 \times {}^{10}/_{11}}{5,500} = 100 \times {}^{10}/_{11} = \dfrac{1,000}{11} = 90\,{}^{10}/_{11}\,\%.$

It is therefore smaller than 100%. Indeed, if the annual rate of surplus value were 100%, then during the year 5,500v would produce 5,500s, whereas $^{11}/_{10}$ years are required for that. The 5,500v produce only 5,000s during one year, therefore the annual rate of

surplus value $= \dfrac{5,000s}{5,500v} = {}^{10}/_{11} = 90\,{}^{10}/_{11}\,\%.$

The annual rate of surplus value, or the comparison between the surplus value produced during one year and the variable capital *advanced* in general (as distinguished from the variable capital *turned over* during the year), is therefore not merely a subjective comparison; the actual movement of the capital itself gives rise to this contraposition. So far as the owner of capital A is concerned, his advanced variable capital of £500 has returned to him at the end of the year, and £5,000 of surplus value in addition. It is not the quantity of capital employed by him during the year, but the quantity returning to him periodically that expresses the magnitude of his advanced capital. It is immaterial for the present issue whether at the end of the year the capital exists partly as a productive supply, or partly as money or commodity capital, and in what proportions it may have been divided into these different parts. So far as the owner of capital B is concerned, £ 5,000, his advanced capital, has returned to him besides £ 5,000 in surplus value. For the owner of capital C (the last considered, worth £ 5,500) surplus value to the amount of £ 5,000 has been produced during the year (£ 5,000 invested and rate of surplus value 100%), but his advanced capital has not yet returned to him, nor has his produced surplus value.

$S' = s' n$ indicates that the rate of surplus value valid for the variable capital employed during one period of turnover, to wit,

$$\frac{\text{quantity of surplus value produced in one turnover period,}}{\text{variable capital employed in one turnover period}}$$

must be multiplied by the number of turnover periods, or of the periods of reproduction of the advanced variable capital, by the number of periods in which it renews its circuit.

We have already seen (Buch I, Kap. IV[a]) (The Transformation of Money into Capital), and furthermore (Buch I, Kap. XXI[b]) (Simple Reproduction), that the capital value is in general advanced, not expended, as this value, having passed through the various phases of its circuit, returns to its point of departure, and at that enriched by surplus value. This characterises it as advanced. The time that elapses from the moment of its departure to the moment of its return is the time for which it was advanced. The entire circular movement described by capital value, measured by the time from its advance to its return, constitutes its turnover, and the duration of this turnover is a period of turnover. When this period has expired and the circuit is completed, the same capital value can renew the same circuit, can therefore expand anew, can create surplus value. If the variable capital is turned over ten times in one year, as in the case of capital A, then the same advance of capital begets in the course of one year ten times the quantity of surplus value that corresponds to one period of turnover.

One must get a clear conception of the nature of this advance from the standpoint of capitalist society.

Capital A, which is annually turned over ten times, is advanced ten times during one year. It is advanced anew for every new period of turnover. But at the same time, during the year A never advances more than this same capital value of £ 500 and in actual fact never disposes of more than these £ 500 for the productive process exam-

---

[a] English edition: Vol. I, chapters IV-VI (present edition, Vol. 35). - [b] Ibid., Ch. XXIII.

ined by us. As soon as these £ 500 have completed one circuit A makes them start anew the same circuit; by its very nature capital preserves its character of capital only because it always functions as capital in successive production processes. It is, moreover, never advanced for more than 5 weeks. Should the turnover last longer, it proves inadequate. Should the turnover be curtailed, a part becomes superfluous. Not ten capitals of £ 500 are advanced, but *one* capital of £ 500 is advanced ten times at successive intervals. The annual rate of surplus value is therefore not calculated for ten advances of a capital of £ 500 or for £ 5,000, but for one advance of a capital of £ 500. It is the same as if 1 taler circulates ten times and yet never represents more than one single taler in circulation, although it performs the function of 10 talers. But in the pocket which holds it after each change of hands it retains the same identical value of 1 taler as before.

In the same way capital A indicates at each successive return, and likewise on its return at the end of the year, that its owner has operated always with the same capital value of £ 500. Hence only £ 500 return to him each time. His advanced capital is therefore never more than £ 500. Hence the advanced capital of £ 500 forms the denominator of the fraction which expresses the annual rate of surplus value. We had for it the above formula $S' = \frac{s'vn}{v} = s'n$. Since the real rate of surplus value $s' = \frac{s}{v}$, the quantity of surplus value divided by the variable capital which produced it, we may substitute $\frac{s}{v}$ for the value of s' in $s'n$, and get the other formula $S' = \frac{sn}{v}$.

But by its ten-fold turnover and thus the ten-fold renewal of its advance, the capital of £ 500 performs the function of a ten times larger capital, of a capital of £ 5,000, just as 500 talers which circulate ten times per year perform the same function as 5,000 talers which circulate only once.

II. THE TURNOVER OF THE INDIVIDUAL VARIABLE CAPITAL

"Whatever the form of the process of production in a society, it must be a continuous process, must continue to go periodically through the same phases... When viewed, therefore, as a connected whole, and as flowing on with incessant renewal, every social process of production is, at the same time, a process of reproduction... As a periodic increment of the capital advanced, or periodic fruit of capital in process, surplus value acquires the form of a *revenue* flowing out of capital" (Buch I, Kap. XXI, pp. 588, 589).[a]

In the case of capital A we have 10 five-week turnover periods. In the first period of turnover £ 500 of variable capital are advanced; i. e., £ 100 are weekly converted into labour power, so that £ 500 are spent on labour power at the end of the first turnover period. These £ 500, originally a part of the total capital advanced, have ceased to be capital. They are paid out in wages. The labourers in their turn pay them out in the purchase of means of subsistence, consuming means of subsistence worth £ 500. A quantity of commodities of that value is therefore annihilated (what the labourer may save up in money, etc., is not capital either). As far as concerns the labourer, this quantity of commodities has been consumed unproductively, except inasmuch as it preserves the efficacy of his labour power, an instrument indispensable to the capitalist.

In the second place, however, these £ 500 have been transformed, for the capitalist, into labour power of the same value (or price). Labour power is consumed by him productively in the labour process. At the end of 5 weeks a product valued at £ 1,000 has been created. Half of this, £ 500, is the reproduced value of the variable capital expended in payment of labour power. The other half, £ 500, is newly produced surplus value. But the 5-weekly labour power, through exchange for which a portion of the capital was converted into variable capital, is likewise expended, consumed, although productively. The labour which was active yesterday is not the same that is active today. Its value plus that of the surplus value created by it exists now as the value of a thing distinct from labour power, to wit, of a product. But by converting the product into money, that portion of its value which is equal to the value of the variable capital advanced can once more be exchanged for labour power and thus again function as variable capital. The fact that the same workmen, i. e., the same bearers of labour power, are given employment not only by the reproduced capital value but also by that which has been reconverted into the form of money is immaterial. It is possible for the capitalist to hire different workmen for the second period of turnover.

In actual fact therefore a capital of £ 5,000, and not of £ 500, is expended successively in wages during the ten periods of turnover of 5 weeks each, and these wages will again be spent by the labourers to

---

[a] English edition: Vol. I, Ch. XXIII (present edition, Vol. 35).

buy means of subsistence. The capital of £ 5,000 so advanced is consumed. It ceases to exist. On the other hand labour power worth £ 5,000, not £ 500, is incorporated successively in the productive process and reproduces not only its own value of £ 5,000, but produces over and above that a surplus value of £ 5,000. The variable capital of £ 500 advanced during the second period of turnover is not the identical capital of £ 500 that had been advanced during the first period of turnover. That has been consumed, spent in wages. But it is *replaced* by new variable capital of £ 500, which was produced in the first period of turnover in the form of commodities, and reconverted into money. This new money capital of £ 500 is therefore the money form of the quantity of commodities newly produced in the first period of turnover. The fact that an identical sum of money, £ 500, is again in the hands of the capitalist, i. e., apart from the surplus value, precisely as much money capital as he had originally advanced, conceals the circumstance that he is operating with a newly produced capital. (As for the other constituents of value of the commodity capital, which replace the constant parts of capital, their value is not newly produced, but only the form is changed in which this value exists.)

Let us take the third period of turnover. Here it is evident that the capital of £ 500, advanced for a third time, is not an old but a newly produced capital, for it is the money form of the quantity of commodities produced in the second, not the first, period of turnover, i. e., of that portion of this quantity of commodities whose value is equal to that of the advanced variable capital. The quantity of commodities produced in the first period of turnover is sold. A part of its value equal to the variable portion of the value of the advanced capital was transformed into the new labour power of the second period of turnover; it produced a new quantity of commodities, which were sold in their turn and a portion of whose value constitutes the capital of £ 500 advanced in the third turnover period.

And so forth during the ten periods of turnover. In the course of these, newly produced quantities of commodities (whose value, inasmuch as it replaces variable capital, is also newly produced, and does not merely re-appear as in the case of the constant circulating part of the capital) are thrown upon the market every 5 weeks, in order to incorporate ever new labour power in the process of production.

Therefore what is accomplished by the ten-fold turnover of the advanced variable capital of £ 500 is not that this capital of £ 500 can be productively consumed ten times, or that a variable capital lasting for 5 weeks can be employed for 50 weeks. Rather, 10 × £500 of variable capital is employed in the 50 weeks, and the capital of £500 always lasts only for 5 weeks and must be replaced at the end of the 5 weeks by a newly produced capital of £500. This applies equally to capitals A and B. But at this point the difference begins.

At the end of the first period of 5 weeks a variable capital of £500 has been advanced and expended by B as well as A. Both A and B have converted its value into labour power and replaced it by that portion of the value of the product newly created by this labour power which is equal to the value of the advanced variable capital of £500. For both B and A the labour power has not only replaced the value of the expended variable capital of £500 by a new value of the same amount, but also added a surplus value which, according to our assumption, is of the same magnitude.

But in the case of B the value product, which replaces the advanced variable capital and adds to it a surplus value, is not in the form in which it can function anew as productive, or variable, capital. It is in such a form in the case of A. And up to the end of the year B does not possess the variable capital expended in the first 5 and every subsequent 5 weeks, although it has been replaced by newly produced value plus surplus value, in the form in which it can again function as productive, or variable, capital. True, its *value* is replaced by new value, hence renewed, but the *form* of its value (in this case the absolute form of value, its money form) is not renewed.

For the second period of 5 weeks (and thus for every succeeding 5 weeks of the year) another £500 must again be available, the same as for the first period. Hence, regardless of credit relations, £5,000 must be available at the beginning of the year as a latent advanced money capital, although they are really expended, turned into labour power, only gradually, in the course of the year.

But because in the case of A the circuit, the turnover of the advanced capital, is consummated, the replacement value after the lapse of the first 5 weeks is already in the form in which it can set new labour power in motion for a term of 5 weeks — in its original form, the money form.

In the cases of both A and B new labour power is consumed in the second 5-week period and a new capital of £500 is spent in payment of this labour power. The means of subsistence of the labourers, paid with the first £500, are gone; at all events their value had vanished from the hands of the capitalist. With the second £500 new labour power is bought, new means of subsistence withdrawn from the market. In short, it is a new capital of £ 500 that is being expended, not the old. But in the case of A this new capital of £ 500 is the money form of the newly produced substitute for the value of the formerly expended £ 500, while in the case of B, this substitute is in a form in which it cannot function as variable capital. It is there, but not in the form of variable capital. For the continuation of the process of production for the next 5 weeks an additional capital of £ 500 must therefore be available and advanced in the here indispensable form of money. Thus, during 50 weeks, both A and B expend an equal amount of variable capital, pay for and consume an equal quantity of labour power. But B must pay for it with an advanced capital equal to its total value of £ 5,000, while A pays for it successively with the ever renewed money form of the value substitute, produced every 5 weeks, for the capital of £ 500 advanced for every 5 weeks. In no case is more money capital advanced here than is required for 5 weeks, i. e., never more than that advanced for the first 5 weeks, viz., £ 500. These £ 500 last for the entire year. It is therefore clear that, the degree of exploitation of labour and the real rate of surplus value being the same, the annual rates [of surplus value] of A and B must be inversely proportional to the magnitudes of the variable money capitals which have to be advanced in order to set in motion the same amount of labour power during the year.

$$A: \frac{5,000s}{500v} = 1,000\%; \qquad B: \frac{5,000s}{5,000v} = 100\%.$$

But $500v : 5,000v = 1 : 10 = 100\% : 1,000\%$.

The difference is due to the difference in the periods of turnover, i. e., the periods in which the value substitute of the variable capital employed for a definite time can function anew as capital, hence as a new capital. In the case of B as well as A, there is the same replacement of value for the variable capital employed during the same periods. There is also the same increment of surplus value during the same periods. But in the case of B, while every 5 weeks there is a replacement of the value of £500 and a surplus value of £500, this value substitute does not constitute a new capital, because it does not exist in the form of money. In the case of A the old capital value is not only replaced by a new one, but is rehabilitated in its money form, hence replaced as a new capital capable of performing its function.

The conversion, sooner or later, of the value substitute into money, and thus into the form in which variable capital is advanced, is obviously an immaterial circumstance, so far as the production of surplus value itself is concerned. This production depends on the magnitude of the variable capital employed and the degree of exploitation of labour. But that circumstance modifies the magnitude of the money capital which must be advanced in order to set a definite quantum of labour power in motion during the year, and therefore it determines the annual rate of surplus value.

III. THE TURNOVER OF THE VARIABLE CAPITAL
FROM THE SOCIAL POINT OF VIEW

Let us look at this matter for a moment from the point of view of society. The labourer costs, say, £1 per week, the working day is 10 hours. In case of A as well as B 100 labourers are employed during a year (£100 for 100 labourers per week, or £500 for 5 weeks, or £5,000 for 50 weeks), and each one of them works 60 hours per week of 6 days. So 100 labourers work 6,000 hours per week and 300,000 hours in 50 weeks. This labour power is taken hold of by A and B and therefore cannot be expended by society for anything else. To this extent the matter is the same socially with both A and B. Furthermore: In the cases of both A and B the 100 labourers employed by either side receive a yearly wage of £5,000 (or, together for the 200 labourers, £10,000) and withdraw from society means of subsistence to that amount. So far the matter is therefore socially the same in the case of both A and B. Since the labourers in either case are paid by the week, they weekly withdraw their means of subsistence from society and, in either case, throw a weekly equivalent in money into circulation. But here the difference begins.

First. The money which the A labourer throws into circulation is not only, as it is for the B labourer, the money form of the value of his labour power (in fact a means of payment for labour already performed); it is, counting from the second turnover period after the opening of the business, the money form *of his own value* (= the price of the labour power plus the surplus value) created during the first period of turnover, by which his labour is paid during the second period of turnover. This is not the case with the B labourer. As far as the latter is concerned, the money is here, true enough, a medium of payment for work already done by him, but this work done is not paid for with the value which it itself produced and which was turned into money (not with the money form of the value the labour itself has produced). This cannot be done until the beginning of the second year, when the B labourer is paid with the value produced by him in the preceding year and turned into money.

The shorter the period of turnover of capital — the shorter therefore the intervals at which it is reproduced throughout the year — the quicker is the variable portion of the capital, originally advanced by the capitalist in the form of money, transformed into the money form of the value (including, besides, surplus value) created by the labourer to replace this variable capital; the shorter is the time for which the capitalist must advance money out of his own funds, and the smaller is the capital advanced by him in general in proportion to the given scale of production; and the greater comparatively is the quantity of surplus value which he extracts during the year with a given rate of surplus value, because he can buy the labourer so much more frequently with the money form of the value created by that labourer and can so much more frequently set his labour into motion again.

If the scale of production is given, the absolute magnitude of the advanced variable money capital (and of the circulating capital in general) decreases proportionately to the decrease of the turnover period, while the annual rate of surplus value increases. If the magnitude of the advanced capital is given, the scale of production grows; hence, if the rate of surplus value is given, the absolute quantity of surplus value created in one period of turnover likewise grows, simultaneously with the rise in the annual rate of surplus value effected by the shortening of the periods of reproduction. It generally follows from the foregoing investigation that the different lengths of the turnover periods make it necessary for money capital to be advanced in very different amounts in order to set in motion the same quantity of productive circulating capital and the same quantity of labour with the same degree of exploitation of labour.

Second — and this is interlinked with the first difference — the B and A labourers pay for the means of subsistence which they buy with the variable capital that has been transformed in their hands into a medium of circulation. For instance they not only withdraw wheat from the market, but also replace it with an equivalent in money. But since the money wherewith the B labourer pays for his means of subsistence, which he withdraws from the market, is not the money form of a value produced and thrown by him on the market during the year, as it is in the case of the A labourer, he supplies the seller of the means of subsistence with money, but not with commodities — be they means of production or means of subsistence — which this seller could buy with the proceeds of the sale, as he can in the case of A. The market is therefore stripped of labour power, means of subsistence for this labour power, fixed capital in the form of instruments of labour used in the case of B, and of materials of production, and to replace them an equivalent in money is thrown on the market; but during the year no product is thrown on the market with which to replace the material elements of productive capital withdrawn from it. If we conceive society as being not capitalist but communist, there will be no money capital at all in the first place, nor the disguises cloaking the transactions arising on account of it. The question then comes down to the need of society to calculate beforehand how much labour, means of production, and means of subsistence it can invest, without detriment, in such lines of business as for instance the building of railways, which do not furnish any means of production or subsistence, nor produce any useful effect for a long time, a year or more, while they extract labour, means of production and means of subsistence from the total annual production. In capitalist society however where social reason always asserts itself only *post festum* great disturbances may and must constantly occur. On the one hand pressure is brought to bear on the money market, while on the other, an easy money market calls such enterprises into being *en masse*, thus creating the very circumstances which later give rise to pressure on the money market. Pressure is brought to bear on the money market, since large advances of money capital are constantly needed here for long periods of time. And this regardless of the fact that industrialists and merchants throw the money capital necessary to carry on their business into speculative railway schemes, etc., and make it good by borrowing in the money market.

On the other hand pressure on society's available productive capital. Since elements of productive capital are for ever being withdrawn from the market and only an equivalent in money is thrown on the market in their place, the effective demand rises without itself furnishing any element of supply. Hence a rise in the prices of productive materials as well as means of subsistence. To this must be added that stock-jobbing is a regular practice and capital is transferred on a large scale. A band of speculators, contractors, engineers, lawyers, etc., enrich themselves. They create a strong demand for articles of consumption on the market, wages rising at the same time. So far as foodstuffs are involved, agriculture too is stimulated. But as these foodstuffs cannot be suddenly increased in the course of the year, their import grows, just as that of exotic foods in general (coffee, sugar, wine, etc.) and of articles of luxury. Hence excessive imports and speculation in this line of the import business. Meanwhile, in those branches of industry in which production can be rapidly expanded (manufacture proper, mining, etc.), climbing prices give rise to sudden expansion soon followed by collapse. The same effect is produced in the labour market, attracting great numbers of the latent relative surplus population, and even of the employed labourers, to the new lines of business. In general such large-scale undertakings as railways withdraw a definite quantity of labour power from the labour market, which can come only from such lines of business as agriculture, etc., where only strong lads are needed. This still continues even after the new enterprises have become established lines of business and the migratory working class needed for them has already been formed, as for instance in the case of a temporary rise above the average in the scale of railway construction. A portion of the reserve army of labourers, which kept wages down, is absorbed. A general rise in wages ensues, even in the hitherto well employed sections of the labour market. This lasts until the inevitable crash again releases the reserve army of labour and wages are once more depressed to their minimum, and lower.[32]

Inasmuch as the length, great or small, of the period of turnover depends on the working period proper, that is, the period necessary to get the product ready for the market, it is based on the existing material conditions of production specific for the various investments of capital. In agriculture they assume more of the character of natural

[32] In the manuscript, the following note is here inserted for future amplification: "Contradiction in the capitalist mode of production: the labourers as buyers of commodities are important for the market. But as sellers of their own commodity — labour power — capitalist society tends to keep them down to the minimum price.— Further contradiction: the periods in which capitalist production exerts all its forces regularly turn out to be periods of overproduction, because production potentials can never be utilised to such an extent that more value may not only be produced but also realised; but the sale of commodities, the realisation of commodity capital and thus of surplus value, is limited, not by the consumer requirements of society in general, but by the consumer requirements of a society in which the vast majority are always poor and must always remain poor. However, this pertains to the next part."

conditions of production, in manufacture and the greater part of the mining industry they vary with the social development of the process of production itself.

Inasmuch as the length of the working period depends on the size of the supply (the quantitative volume in which the product is generally thrown upon the market as commodities), it is conventional in character. But the convention itself has its material basis in the scale of production, and is therefore accidental only when examined singly.

Finally, inasmuch as the length of the turnover period hinges on that of the period of circulation, it is partly dependent on the incessant change of market conditions, the greater or lesser ease of selling, and the resultant necessity of throwing part of the product on nearer or remoter markets. Apart from the volume of the demand in general, the movement of prices is here of cardinal importance since sales are intentionally restricted when prices are falling, while production proceeds; vice versa, production and sales keep pace when prices are rising or sales can be made in advance. But we must consider the actual distance of the place of production from the market as the real material basis.

For instance English cotton goods or yarn are sold to India. Suppose the export merchant himself pays the English cotton manufacturer (the export merchant does so willingly only if the money market is strong. But when the manufacturer himself replaces his money capital by some credit transaction, things are not so good). The exporter sells his cotton goods later in the Indian market, from where his advanced capital is remitted to him. Up to this remittance the case runs the very same course as when the length of the working period necessitated the advance of new money capital to maintain the production process on a given scale. The money capital with which the manufacturer pays his labourers and renews the other elements of his circulating capital is not the money form of the yarn produced by him. This cannot be the case until the value of this yarn has returned to England in the form of money or products. It is additional money capital as before. The only difference is that, instead of the manufacturer, it is advanced by the merchant, who in turn may well have obtained it by means of credit operations. Similarly, before this money is thrown on the market, or simultaneously with this, no additional product has been put on the English market that could be bought with this money and would enter the sphere of productive or individual consumption. If this situation continues for a rather long period of time and on a rather large scale, it must have the same effect as the previously mentioned prolongation of the working period.

Now it may be that in India the yarn is again sold on credit. With this credit products are bought in India and sent as return shipment to England or drafts remitted for this amount. If this condition is protracted, the Indian money market comes under pressure and the reaction on England may here produce a crisis. This crisis, in its turn, even if combined with the export of precious metals to India, calls forth a new crisis in that country on account of the bankruptcy of English firms and their Indian branches, which had received credit from Indian banks. Thus a crisis occurs simultaneously in the market in which the balance of trade is *favourable*, as well as in the one in which it is *unfavourable*. This phenomenon may be still more complicated. Assume for instance that England has sent silver bullion to India but India's English creditors are now urgently collecting their debts in that country, and India will soon after have to ship its silver bullion back to England.

It is possible that the export trade to India and the import trade from India may approximately balance each other, although the volume of the import trade (except under special circumstances, such as an increase in cotton prices, etc.) is determined and stimulated by the export trade. The balance of trade between England and India may seem equilibrated or may disclose slight oscillations in either direction. But as soon as the crisis breaks out in England it turns out that unsold cotton goods are stored in India (hence have not been transformed from commodity capital into money capital — an overproduction to this extent), and that on the other hand there are stored up in England unsold supplies of Indian goods, and, moreover, a great portion of the sold and consumed supplies is not yet paid. Hence what appears as a crisis on the money market is in reality an expression of abnormal conditions in the very process of production and reproduction.

Third. So far as the employed circulating capital itself (constant and variable) is concerned, the length of the period of turnover, since it derives from the working period, makes this difference: In the case of several turnovers during one year, an element of the variable or constant circulating capital may be supplied through its own product, for instance in the production of coal, the ready-made clothes business, etc. In other cases this cannot occur, at least not within the year.

Chapter XVII

THE CIRCULATION OF SURPLUS VALUE

We have just seen that a difference in the period of turnover causes a difference in the annual rate of surplus value, even if the mass of the annually produced surplus value is the same.

But there are furthermore necessarily differences in the capitalisation of surplus value, in *accumulation*, and also in the quantity of surplus value produced during the year, while the rate of surplus value remains the same.

To begin with, we note that capital A (in the illustration of the preceding chapter) has a current periodical revenue, so that with the exception of the period of turnover inaugurating the business, it pays for its own consumption within the year out of its production of surplus value, and need not cover it by advances out of its own funds. But the latter has to be done in the case of B. While it produces as much surplus value in the same intervals of time as A, the surplus value is not realised and therefore cannot be consumed either productively or individually. So far as individual consumption is concerned, the surplus value is anticipated. Funds for that purpose must be advanced.

One portion of the productive capital, which it is difficult to classify, namely the additional capital required for the repair and maintenance of the fixed capital, is now likewise seen in a new light.[a]

In the case of A this portion of capital is not advanced — in full or for the greater part — at the beginning of production. It need not be available or even in existence. It comes out of the business itself by a direct transformation of surplus value into capital, i. e., by its direct employment as capital. A part of the surplus value which is not only periodically generated but also realised during the year can defray the expenditures that must be incurred for repairs, etc. A portion of the capital needed to carry on the business on its original scale is thus produced in the course of business by the business itself by means of capitalising part of the surplus value. This is impossible for the capitalist B. The portion of the capital in question must in his case form a part of the capital originally advanced. In both cases this portion will figure in the books of the capitalists as an advanced capital, which it really is, since according to our assumption it forms a part of the productive capital required for maintaining the business on a certain

---

[a] See this volume, pp. 178-79.

scale. But it makes all the difference in the world out of which funds it is advanced. In the case of B it is really a part of the capital to be originally advanced or held available. In the case of A on the other hand it is a part of the surplus value used as capital. This last case shows us that not only the accumulated capital but also a portion of the originally advanced capital may simply be capitalised surplus value.

As soon as the development of credit interferes, the relation between originally advanced capital and capitalised surplus value becomes still more complicated. For instance from not having sufficient capital of his own at the very outset for this purpose, A borrows from banker C a portion of the productive capital with which he starts in business or continues it during the year. Banker C lends him a sum of money which consists only of surplus value deposited with the banker by capitalists D, E, F, etc. As far as A is concerned there is as yet no question of accumulated capital. But with regard to D, E, F, etc., A is, in fact, nothing but an agent capitalising surplus value appropriated by them.

We have seen (Buch I, Kap. XXII[a]) that accumulation, the conversion of surplus value into capital, is essentially a process of reproduction on a progressively increasing scale, whether this expansion is expressed extensively in the form of an addition of new factories to the old, or intensively by the enlargement of the existing scale of operation.

The expansion of the scale of production may proceed in small portions, a part of the surplus value being used for improvements which either simply increase the productive power of the labour employed or permit at the same time of its more intensive exploitation. Or, where the working day is not legally limited, an additional expenditure of circulating capital (in materials of production and wages) suffices to enhance the production scale without an expansion of the fixed capital, whose daily time of employment is thus merely lengthened, while its period of turnover is correspondingly shortened. Or the capitalised surplus value may, under favourable market conditions, permit of speculation in raw materials, operations for which the capital originally advanced would not have been sufficient, etc.

However it is clear that in cases where the greater number of periods of turnover brings with it a more frequent realisation of surplus value during the year, there will be periods in which there can be nei-

---

[a] English edition: Vol. I, Ch. XXIV (present edition, Vol. 35).

ther a prolongation of the working day nor an introduction of improvements in details; on the other hand a proportional expansion of the whole business, partly by expanding its entire plant, the buildings for example, partly by enlarging the cultivated areas in agriculture, is possible only within certain more or less narrow limits and, besides, requires such a volume of additional capital as can be supplied only by several years' accumulation of surplus value.

Along with the real accumulation or conversion of surplus value into productive capital (and a corresponding reproduction on an extended scale), there is, then, an accumulation of money, a raking together of a portion of the surplus value in the form of latent money capital, which is not intended to function as additional active capital until later, when it swells to a certain volume.

That is how the matter looks from the standpoint of the individual capitalist. But simultaneously with the development of capitalist production the credit system also develops. The money capital which the capitalist cannot as yet employ in his own business is employed by others, who pay him interest for its use. It serves him as money capital in its specific meaning, as a kind of capital distinguished from productive capital. But it serves as capital in another's hands. It is plain that with the more frequent realisation of surplus value and the rising scale on which it is produced, there is an increase in the proportion of new money capital or money as capital thrown upon the money market and then absorbed — at least the greater part of it — by extended production.

The simplest form in which the additional latent money capital may be represented is that of a hoard. It may be that this hoard is additional gold or silver secured directly or indirectly in exchange with countries producing precious metals. And only in this manner does the hoarded money in a country grow absolutely. On the other hand it may be — and is so in the majority of cases — that this hoard is nothing but money which has been withdrawn from circulation at home and has assumed the form of a hoard in the hands of individual capitalists. It is furthermore possible that this latent money capital consists only of tokens of value — we still ignore credit money at this point — or of mere claims of capitalists (titles) against third persons conferred by legal documents. In all such cases, whatever may be the form of existence of this additional money capital, it represents, so far as it is capital *in spe*, nothing but additional and reserved legal titles of capitalists to future annual additional social production.

"The mass of real accumulated wealth, in point of magnitude ... is so utterly insignificant when compared with the powers of production of the same society in whatever state of civilisation, or even compared with the actual consumption for even a few years of that society, that the great attention of legislators and political economists should be directed to 'productive powers' and their future free development, and not, as hitherto, to the mere accumulated wealth that strikes the eye. Of what is called accumulated wealth, by far the greater part is only nominal, consisting not of any real things, ships, houses, cottons, improvements on land, but of mere demands on the future annual productive powers of society, engendered and perpetuated by the expedients or institutions of insecurity... The use of such articles" (accumulations of physical things or actual wealth) "as a mere means of appropriating to their possessors the wealth to be created by the future productive powers of society, being that alone of which the natural laws of distribution would, without force, gradually deprive them, or, if aided by co-operative labour, would in a very few years deprive them" (William Thompson, *An Inquiry into the Principles of the Distribution of Wealth*, London, 1850, p. 453. This book originally appeared in 1824).

"It is little thought, by most persons not at all suspected, how very small a proportion, either in extent or influence, the actual accumulations of society bear to human productive powers, even to the ordinary consumption of a few years of a single generation. The reason is obvious; but the effect very pernicious. The wealth that is annually consumed, disappearing with its consumption, is seen but for a moment, and makes no impression but during the act of enjoyment or use. But that part of wealth which is of slow consumption, furniture, machinery, buildings, from childhood to old age stand out before the eye, the durable monuments of human exertion. By means of the possession of this fixed, permanent, or slowly consumed, part of national wealth, of the land and materials to work upon, the tools to work with, the houses to shelter whilst working, the holders of these articles command for their own benefit the yearly productive powers of all the really efficient productive labourers of society, though these articles may bear ever so small a proportion to the recurring products of that labour. The population of Britain and Ireland being twenty millions, the average consumption of each individual, man, woman, and child, is probably about twenty pounds, making four hundred millions of wealth, the product of labour annually consumed. The whole amount of the accumulated capital of these countries, it has been estimated, does not exceed twelve hundred millions, or three times the year's labour of the community; or, if equally divided, sixty pounds capital for every individual. 'Tis with the proportions, rather than with the absolute accurate amount of these estimated sums, we are concerned. The interest of this capital stock would support the whole population in the same comfort in which they now exist, for about two months of one year, and the whole accumulated capital itself would maintain them in idleness (could purchasers be found) for three years! at the end of which time, without houses, clothes, or food, they must starve, or become the slaves of those who supported them in the three years' idleness. As three years to the life of one healthy generation, say forty years, so is the magnitude and importance of the actual wealth, the accumulated capital of even the wealthiest community, to their productive powers, to the productive powers of only one generation; not of what, under judicious arrangements of equal security, they might produce, particularly with the aid of co-operative labour, but of what, under the defective and depressing expedients of insecurity, they do absolutely produce!.. The seeming mighty mass of existing capital to maintain and perpetuate which (or rather the command of the products of yearly labour which it serves as the means of engrossing)... in its present state of forced division, are all the horrible machinery, the vices, crimes, and miseries of insecurity, sought to be perpetuated. As nothing can be accumulated without first supplying necessaries, and as the great current of human inclination is to enjoyment; hence the comparatively trifling amount of the actual wealth of society at any particular moment. 'Tis an eternal round of production and consumption. From the amount of this immense mass of annual consumption and production, the handful of actual accumulation would hardly be missed; and yet it is to this handful, and not to the mass of productive powers that attention has chiefly been directed. This handful, however, having been seized upon by a few, and been made the instrument of converting to their use the constantly recurring annual products of the labour of the great majority of their fellow creatures; hence, in the opinion of these few, the paramount importance of such an instrument... About one-third part of the annual products of the labour of these countries is now abstracted from the producers, under the name of public burdens, and unproductively consumed by those who give no equivalent, that is to say, none satisfactory to the producers... With the accumulated masses, particularly when held forth in the hands of a few individuals, the vulgar eye has been always struck. The annually produced and consumed masses, like the eternal and incalculable waves of a mighty river, roll on and are lost in the forgotten ocean of consumption. On this eternal consumption, however, are dependent, not only for almost all gratifications, but even for existence, the whole human race. The quantity and distribution of these yearly products ought to be the paramount objects of consideration. The actual accumulation is altogether of secondary importance, and derives almost the whole of that importance from its influence on the distribution of the yearly productions... Actual accumulations and distributions have been always considered" (in Thompson's works) "in reference, and subordinate, to the power of producing. In almost all other systems, the power of producing has been considered in reference, and subordinate, to actual accumulations, and to the perpetuating of the existing modes of distribution. In comparison to the preservation of this actual distribution, the ever recurring misery or happiness of the whole human race has been considered as unworthy of regard. To perpetuate the results of force, fraud, and chance, has been called security; and to the support of this spurious security, have all the productive powers of the human race been unrelentingly sacrificed" (ibid., pp. 440-43).

––––––––––

For reproduction only two normal cases are possible, apart from disturbances, which interfere with reproduction even on a fixed scale.

There is either reproduction on a simple scale.

Or there is capitalisation of surplus value, accumulation.

I. SIMPLE REPRODUCTION

In the case of simple reproduction the surplus value produced and realised annually, or periodically, if there are several turnovers during the year, is consumed individually, i. e., unproductively, by its owner, the capitalist.

The circumstance that the value of the product consists in part of surplus value and in part of that portion of value which is formed by the variable capital reproduced in the product plus the constant capital consumed by it, does not alter anything whatever either in the quantity or in the value of the total product, which constantly steps into circulation as commodity capital and is just as constantly withdrawn from it, in order to be productively or individually consumed, i. e., to serve as means of production or consumption. If constant capital is left aside, only the distribution of the annual product between the labourers and the capitalists is affected thereby.

Even if simple reproduction is assumed, a portion of the surplus value must therefore always exist in the form of money and not of products, because otherwise it could not be converted for purposes of consumption from money into products. This conversion of the surplus value from its original commodity form into money must be further analysed at this place. In order to simplify the matter, we shall presuppose the most elementary form of the problem, namely the exclusive circulation of metal coin, of money which is a real equivalent.

According to the laws of the simple circulation of commodities (developed in Buch I, Kap. III[a]), the mass of the metal coin existing in a country must not only be sufficient to circulate the commodities, but must also suffice to meet the currency fluctuations, which arise partly from fluctuations in the velocity of the circulation, partly from a change in the prices of commodities, partly from the various and varying proportions in which the money functions as a medium of payment or as a medium of circulation proper. The proportion in which the existing quantity of money is split into a hoard and money in circulation varies continually, but the total quantity of money is always equal to the sum of the money hoarded and the money circulating. This quantity of money (quantity of precious metal) is a gradually accumulated hoard of society. Since a portion of this hoard is consumed by wear and tear, it must be replaced annually, the same as any other product. This takes place in reality by a direct or indirect exchange of a part of the annual product of a particular country for the product of countries producing gold and silver. However, this

---

[a] See present edition, Vol. 35.

international character of the transaction conceals its simple course. In order to reduce the problem to its simplest and most lucid expression, it must be assumed that the production of gold and silver takes place in that particular country itself, that therefore the production of gold and silver constitutes a part of the total social production within every country.

Apart from the gold and silver produced for articles of luxury, the minimum of their annual production must be equal to the wear of metal coin annually occasioned by the circulation of money. Furthermore, if the sum of the values of the annually produced and circulating quantity of commodities increases, the annual production of gold and silver must likewise increase, inasmuch as the increased sum of the values of the circulating commodities and the quantity of money required for their circulation (and the corresponding formation of a hoard) are not made good by a greater velocity of money currency and a more comprehensive function of money as a medium of payment, i. e., by a greater mutual balancing of purchases and sales without the intervention of actual money.

A portion of the social labour power and a portion of the social means of production must therefore be expended annually in the production of gold and silver.

The capitalists who are engaged in the production of gold and silver and who, according to our assumption of simple reproduction, carry on their production only within the bounds of the annual average wear and tear and the annual average consumption of gold and silver entailed thereby, throw their surplus value — which they consume annually, according to our assumption, without capitalising any of it — directly into circulation in the money form, which is its natural form; unlike the other branches of production, where it is the converted form of the product.

Furthermore, as far as wages are concerned — the money form in which the variable capital is advanced — they are also not replaced by the sale of the product, by its conversion into money, but by a product itself whose natural form is from the outset that of money.

Finally, the same applies also to that portion of the product of precious metals which is equal to the value of the periodically consumed constant capital, both the constant circulating and the constant fixed capital consumed during the year.

Let us consider the circuit, or turnover, of the capital invested in the production of precious metals first in the form of M — C...

P ... M'. Since C in M — C consists not only of labour power and means of production but also of fixed capital, only a part of whose value is consumed in P, it is evident that M', the product, is a sum of money equal to the variable capital laid out in wages plus the circulating constant capital laid out in means of production plus a portion of the value equivalent to the worn-out fixed capital plus the surplus value. If the sum were smaller, the general value of gold remaining the same, then the mine would be unproductive or, if this got to be generally the case, the value of gold compared with the value of commodities that remains unchanged would subsequently rise; i. e., the prices of commodities would fall, so that henceforth the amount of money laid out in M — C would be smaller.

If we consider at first only the circulating portion of capital advanced in M, the starting-point of M — C ... P ... M', we find that a certain sum of money is advanced, thrown into circulation for the payment of labour power and the purchase of materials of production. But this sum is not withdrawn from circulation by the circuit of *this* capital, in order to be thrown into it anew. The product is money even in its natural form; there is no need therefore of transforming it into money by means of exchange, by a process of circulation. It passes from the process of production into the sphere of circulation, not in the form of commodity capital which has to be reconverted into money capital, but as a money capital which is to be reconverted into productive capital, i. e., which is to buy fresh labour power and materials of production. The money form of the circulating capital consumed in labour power and means of production is replaced, not by the sale of the product, but by the natural form of the product itself; hence, not by once more withdrawing its value from circulation in money form, but by additional, newly produced money.

Let us suppose that this circulating capital is £500, the period of turnover 5 weeks, the working period 4 weeks, the period of circulation only 1 week. From the outset, money for 5 weeks must be partly advanced for a productive supply and partly be ready to be paid out gradually in wages. At the beginning of the 6th week, £400 will have returned and £100 will have been released. This is constantly repeated. Here, as in previous cases, £100 will always be found in released form during a certain time of the turnover. But they consist of additional, newly produced, money, the same as the other £400. We have in this case 10 turnovers per year and the annual product is £5,000 in gold. (The period of circulation is not constituted, in this case, by the

time required for the conversion of commodities into money, but by
that required for the conversion of money into the elements of production.)

In the case of every other capital of £500 turned over under the
same conditions, the ever renewed money form is the converted form
of the commodity capital produced, a capital which is thrown into
circulation every 4 weeks and which by its sale — that is to say, by
a periodical withdrawal of the quantity of money it represented when
it originally entered into the process — assumes this money form
anew over and over again. Here, on the contrary, in every turnover
period a new additional sum of £500 in money is thrown from the
process of production itself into circulation in order to withdraw
from it continually materials of production and labour power. This
money thrown into circulation is not withdrawn from it again by the
circuit which this capital describes, but is rather increased by quantities of gold constantly produced anew.

Let us look at the variable portion of this circulating capital and assume that it is, as before, £100. Then these £100 would be sufficient
in the ordinary production of commodities, with 10 turnovers, to pay
continually for the labour power. Here, in the production of gold, the
same amount is sufficient. But the £100 of the reflux, with which the
labour power is paid every 5 weeks, are not a converted form of its
product but a portion of this ever renewed product itself. The producer of gold pays his labourers directly with a portion of the gold
they themselves produced. The £1,000 thus expended annually in labour power and thrown by the labourers into circulation do not return therefore via this circulation to their starting-point.

Furthermore, so far as the fixed capital is concerned, it requires the
investment of a comparatively large money capital on the original establishment of the business, and this capital is thus thrown into circulation. Like all fixed capital it returns only piecemeal in the course of
years. But it returns as a direct portion of the product, of the gold, not
by the sale of the product and its consequent conversion into money.
In other words, it gradually assumes its money form not by a withdrawal of money from the circulation but by an accumulation of
a corresponding portion of the product. The money capital so restored is not a quantity of money gradually withdrawn from the circulation to compensate for the sum originally thrown into it for the fixed
capital. It is an additional sum of money.

Finally, as concerns the surplus value, it is likewise equal to a cer-

tain portion of the new gold product, which is thrown into circulation in every new period of turnover in order to be unproductively
expended, according to our assumption, on means of subsistence and
articles of luxury.

But according to our assumption, the entire annual production of
gold — which continually withdraws labour power and materials of
production, but no money, from the market, while continuously adding fresh quantities of money to it — merely replaces the money worn
out during the year, hence only keeps intact the quantity of social
money which exists constantly, although in varying portions, in the
two forms of hoarded money and money in circulation.

According to the law of the circulation of commodities, the quantity of money must be equal to the amount of money required for circulation plus a certain amount held in the form of a hoard, which increases or decreases as the circulation contracts or expands, and serves
especially for the formation of the requisite reserve funds of means
of payment. What must be paid in money in so far as there is no balancing of accounts — is the value of the commodities. The fact that
a portion of this value consists of surplus value, that is to say, did not
cost the seller of the commodities anything, does not alter the matter
in any way. Let us suppose that the producers are all independent
owners of their means of production, so that circulation takes place
between the immediate producers themselves. Apart from the constant portion of their capital, their annual value product might then be
divided into two parts, analogous with capitalist conditions: Part a,
replacing only the necessary means of subsistence, and part b, consumed partly in articles of luxury, partly for an expansion of production. Part a then represents the variable capital, part b the surplus
value. But this division would remain without influence on the magnitude of the sum of money required for the circulation of their total
product. Other circumstances remaining equal, the value of the circulating mass of commodities would be the same, and thus also the
amount of money required for that value. They would also have to
have the same money reserves if the turnover periods are equally divided, i. e., the same portion of their capital would always have to be
held in the form of money, because their production, according to our
assumption, would be commodity production, the same as before.
Hence the fact that a portion of the value of the commodities consists
of surplus value would change absolutely nothing in the quantity of
the money required for the running of the business.

An opponent of Tooke, who clings to the formula $M — C — M'$, asks him how the capitalist manages always to withdraw more money from circulation than he throws into it. Mind you! The question at issue here is not the *formation* of surplus value. This, the only secret, is a matter of course from the capitalist standpoint. The sum of values employed would not be capital if it did not enrich itself by means of surplus value. But as it is capital by assumption, surplus value is taken for granted.

The question, then, is not where the surplus value comes from but whence the money comes into which it is turned.

But in bourgeois economics, the existence of surplus value is self-understood. It is therefore not only assumed but also connected with the further assumption that a part of the mass of commodities thrown into circulation is a surplus product, hence representing a value which the capitalist did not throw into circulation as part of his capital; that, consequently, with his product the capitalist throws into circulation a surplus over and above his capital, and that he withdraws this surplus from it.

The commodity capital, which the capitalist throws into circulation, has a greater value (it is not explained and remains obscure where this comes from, but from the standpoint of this capitalist *c'est un fait*[a]) than the productive capital which he withdrew from circulation in the form of labour power plus means of production. On the basis of this assumption it is evident why not only capitalist A, but also B, C, D, etc., are always able to withdraw more value from circulation by the exchange of their commodities than the value of the capital originally and repeatedly advanced by them. A, B, C, D, etc., continuously throw a greater commodity value into circulation in the form of commodity capital — this operation is as many-sided as the various independently functioning capitals — than they withdraw from it in the form of productive capital. Hence they have constantly to divide among themselves a sum of values (i. e., everyone, on his part, has to withdraw from circulation a productive capital) equal to the sum of values of the productive capitals they respectively advanced; and just as constantly they have to divide among themselves a sum of values which they all, from all sides, throw into circulation in the form of commodities representing the respective excesses of the commodity values above the values of their elements of production.

---

[a] it is a fact

But the commodity capital must be turned into money before its re-conversion into productive capital and before the surplus value contained in it is spent. Where does the money for this purpose come from? This question seems difficult at the first glance, and neither Tooke nor any one else has answered it so far.

Let the circulating capital of £500 advanced in the form of money capital, whatever its period of turnover, now stand for the total circulating capital of society, that is, of the capitalist class. Let the surplus value be £100. How can the entire capitalist class manage to draw continually £600 out of circulation, when it continually throws only £500 into it?

After the money capital of £500 has been converted into productive capital, the latter transforms itself within the process of production into commodities worth £600 and there are in circulation not only commodities valued at £500, equal to the money capital originally advanced, but also a newly produced surplus value of £100.

This additional surplus value of £100 is thrown into circulation in the form of commodities. No doubt about that. But such an operation does not by any means furnish the additional money for the circulation of this additional commodity value.

It will not do to obviate this difficulty by plausible subterfuges.

For instance: So far as the constant circulating capital is concerned, it is obvious that not all invest it simultaneously. While capitalist A sells his commodities, so that his advanced capital assumes the form of money, there is on the other hand the available money capital of the buyer B which assumes the form of his means of production — precisely what A is producing. By the same act through which A restores the money form to his produced commodity capital, B returns his capital to its productive form, transforms it from money form into means of production and labour power; the same amount of money functions in the two-sided process as in every simple purchase C — M. On the other hand when A reconverts his money into means of production, he buys from C, and this man pays B with it, etc., and thus the transaction would be explained. But:

None of the laws established with reference to the quantity of the circulating money in the circulation of commodities (Buch I, Kap. III[a]), are changed in any way by the capitalist character of the process of production.

---

[a] See present edition, Vol. 35.

Hence, when one says that the circulating capital of society to be advanced in the form of money amounts to £500, one has already taken into account that this is on the one hand the sum simultaneously advanced, and that on the other hand it sets in motion more productive capital than £500 because it serves alternately as the money fund of various productive capitals. This manner of explanation, then, assumes the money, whose existence it is called upon to explain, as already existing.—

It might be further said: Capitalist A produces articles which capitalist B consumes individually, unproductively. B's money therefore turns A's commodity capital into money and thus the same sum of money serves to realise B's surplus value and A's circulating constant capital. But in that case the question that still awaits solution is assumed still more directly to have been solved, namely: where does B get the money that makes up his revenue? How did he himself realise this portion of the surplus value of his product?

It might also be said that the part of the circulating variable capital which A steadily advances to his labourers returns to him steadily from the circulation, and only a varying part of it always stays with him for the payment of wages. But a certain time elapses between the expenditure and the reflux, and meanwhile the money paid out for wages might, among other uses, serve for the realisation of surplus value.

But we know in the first place that the longer this time the greater must be the supply of money which capitalist A has to keep constantly *in petto*. In the second place the labourer spends the money, buys commodities for it and thus converts into money *pro tanto* the surplus value contained in them. Consequently the same money that is advanced in the form of variable capital serves *pro tanto* also the purpose of turning surplus value into money. Without penetrating any further into the question at this point, let this suffice: the consumption of the entire capitalist class and its retainers keeps step with that of the working class; hence simultaneously with the money thrown into circulation by the labourers the capitalists too must throw money into it, in order to spend their surplus value as revenue; hence money must be withdrawn from circulation for it. This explanation would serve merely to reduce, but not eliminate, the quantity of money required.

Finally, it might be said: A large amount of money is constantly thrown into circulation when fixed capital is first invested, and it is recovered from the circulation only gradually, piecemeal, after a lapse of years, by him who threw it into circulation. Cannot this sum suffice to convert the surplus value into money?

The answer to this must be that perhaps the sum of £500 (which includes hoard formation for needed reserve funds) implies its employment as fixed capital, if not by him who threw it into circulation, then by somebody else. Besides, it is already assumed in regard to the amount expended for the procurement of products serving as fixed capital that the surplus value contained in them is also paid, and the question is precisely where this money comes from.

The general reply has already been given: If a mass of commodities worth x times £1,000 has to circulate, it changes absolutely nothing in the quantity of the money required for this circulation whether the value of this mass of commodities contains any surplus value or not, whether this mass of commodities has been produced capitalistically or not. *The problem itself therefore does not exist.* All other conditions being given, such as velocity of the currency of money, etc., a definite sum of money is required in order to circulate commodities worth x times £1,000 quite independently of how much or how little of this value falls to the share of the direct producers of these commodities. So far as any problem exists here, it coincides with the general problem: Where does the money required for the circulation of the commodities of a country come from?

However, from the point of view of capitalist production, the *semblance* of a special problem does indeed exist. In the present case it is the capitalist who appears as the point of departure, who throws money into circulation. The money which the labourer expends for the payment of his means of subsistence existed previously as the money form of the variable capital and was therefore thrown originally into circulation by the capitalist as a means of buying or paying for labour power. The capitalist furthermore throws into circulation the money which constitutes originally the money form of his constant, fixed and circulating, capital; he expends it as a means of purchase or payment for instruments of labour and materials of production. But beyond this the capitalist no longer appears as the starting-point of the quantity of money in circulation. Now, there are only two points of departure: the capitalist and the labourer. All third categories of persons must either receive money for their services from these two classes or, to the extent that they receive it without any services in return, they are joint owners of the surplus value in the form of rent, interest, etc. That the surplus value does not all stay in the pocket of the industrial capitalist but must be shared by him with other persons, has nothing to do with the present question. The question is how he turns his surplus value into money, not how the proceeds are later divided. For our purposes the capitalist may as well still be regarded as the sole owner of the surplus value. As for the labourer, it has already been said that he is but the secondary, while the capitalist is the primary, starting-point of the money thrown by the labourer into circulation. The money first advanced as variable capital is going through its second circulation when the labourer spends it to pay for means of subsistence.

The capitalist class remains consequently the sole point of departure of the circulation of money. If it needs £400 for the payment of means of production and £100 for the payment of labour power, it throws £500 into circulation. But the surplus value incorporated in the product, with a rate of surplus value of 100%, is equal in value to £100. How can the capitalist class continually draw £600 out of circulation, when it continually throws only £500 into it? Nothing comes from nothing. The capitalist class as a whole cannot draw out of circulation what was not previously thrown into it.

We disregard here the fact that the sum of £400 may suffice, when turned over ten times, to circulate means of production valued at £4,000 and labour power valued at £1,000, and that the other £100 may likewise suffice for the circulation of £1,000 worth of surplus value. The ratio of the sum of money to the value of the commodities circulated by it is immaterial here. The problem remains the same. Unless the same pieces of money circulate several times, a capital of £5,000 must be thrown into circulation, and £1,000 is required to convert the surplus value into money. The question is where this money comes from, whether it is £1,000 or £100. In any event it is in excess of the money capital thrown into circulation.

Indeed, paradoxical as it may appear at first sight, it is the capitalist class itself that throws the money into circulation which serves for the realisation of the surplus value incorporated in the commodities. But, *nota bene*, it does not throw it into circulation as advanced money, hence not as capital. It spends it as a means of purchase for its individual consumption. The money is not therefore advanced by the capitalist class, although it is the point of departure of its circulation.

Let us take some individual capitalist who is starting in business, a farmer for instance. During the first year, he advances a money capital of, say, £5,000, paying £4,000 for means of production, and

£1,000 for labour power. Let the rate of surplus value be 100%, the amount of surplus value appropriated by him £1,000. The above £5,000 comprise all the money he advances as money capital. But the man must also live, and he does not take in any money until the end of the year. Take it that his consumption amounts to £1,000. These he must have in his possession. He may say that he has to advance himself these £1,000 during the first year. But this advance, which here has only a subjective meaning, denotes nothing else but that he must pay for his individual consumption during the first year out of his own pocket instead of defraying it out of the gratuitous production of his labourers. He does not advance this money as capital. He spends it, pays it out for an equivalent in means of subsistence which he consumes. This value has been spent by him in money, thrown into circulation and withdrawn from it in the form of commodity values. These commodity values he has consumed. He has thus ceased to bear any relation to their value. The money with which he paid for this value exists now as an element of the circulating money. But he has withdrawn the value of this money from circulation in the form of products, and this value is now destroyed together with the products in which it existed. It's all gone. But at the end of the year he throws commodities worth £6,000 into circulation and sells them. By this means he recovers: 1) his advanced money capital of £5,000; 2) the surplus value of £1,000 turned into money. He has advanced as capital, has thrown into circulation, £5,000, and he withdraws from it £6,000—£5,000 of which cover his capital, and £1,000 his surplus value. The last £1,000 are turned into money with the money which he himself has thrown into circulation, which he did not advance, but spent as a consumer, not as a capitalist. They now return to him as the money form of the surplus value produced by him. And henceforth this operation is repeated every year. But beginning with the second year, the £1,000 which he spends are constantly the converted form, the money form, of the surplus value produced by him. He spends them annually and they return to him annually.

If his capital were turned over more frequently a year, it would not alter this state of affairs, but would affect the length of time, and hence the amount which he would have to throw into circulation for his individual consumption over and above his advanced money capital.

This money is not thrown into circulation by the capitalist as capital. But it is a decided trait of the capitalist to be able to live on means in his possession until surplus value begins to return.

In the present case we assumed that the sum of money which the capitalist throws into circulation to pay for his individual consumption until the first return of his capital is exactly equal to the surplus value which he produced and hence must turn into money. This is obviously an arbitrary assumption so far as the individual capitalist is concerned. But it must be correct when applied to the entire capitalist class if simple reproduction is assumed. It only expresses the same thing as the assumption, namely that the entire surplus value, and it alone — hence no fraction of the original capital stock — is consumed unproductively.

It had been previously assumed that the total production of precious metals (taken to be equal to £500) sufficed only for the replacement of the wear and tear of the money.

The capitalists producing gold possess their entire product in gold — that portion which replaces constant capital as well as that which replaces variable capital, and also that consisting of surplus value. A portion of the social surplus value therefore consists of gold, and not of a product which is turned into gold only in the process of circulation. It consists from the outset of gold and is thrown into circulation in order to draw products out of it. The same applies here to wages, to variable capital, and to the replacement of the advanced constant capital. Hence, whereas one part of the capitalist class throws into circulation commodities greater in value (greater by the amount of the surplus value) than the money capital advanced by them, another part of the capitalists throws into circulation money of greater value (greater by the amount of the surplus value) than that of the commodities which they constantly withdraw from circulation for the production of gold. Whereas one part of the capitalists constantly pumps more money out of circulation than it pours into it, the part that produces gold constantly pumps more money into it than it takes out in means of production.

Although a part of this product of £500 in gold is surplus value of the gold producers, the entire sum is, nonetheless, intended only to replace the money necessary for the circulation of the commodities. It is immaterial for this purpose how much of this sum turns into money the surplus value incorporated in the commodities, and how much of it their other value constituents.

Transferring the production of gold from one country to another produces no change whatever in the matter. One part of the social labour power and the social means of production of country A is converted into a product, for instance linen, valued at £500, which is exported to country B in order to buy gold there. The productive capital thus employed in the country A throws no more commodities — as distinct from money — upon the market of country A than it would if it were employed directly in the production of gold. This product of A represents £500 in gold and enters into the circulation of this country only as money. That portion of the social surplus value which is contained in this product exists for country A directly in the form of money, and never in any other form. Although for the gold-producing capitalists only a part of the product represents surplus value, and another part the replacement capital, still the question of how much of this gold, outside the circulating constant capital, replaces variable capital and how much of it represents surplus value depends exclusively on the respective ratios of wages and surplus value to the value of the circulating commodities. The part which forms surplus value is distributed among the diverse members of the capitalist class. Although that part is continually spent by them for individual consumption and recovered by the sale of new products — it is precisely this purchase and sale that circulates among them the money required for the conversion of the surplus value into money — there is nevertheless a portion of the social surplus value in the form of money, even if in varying proportions, in the pockets of the capitalists, just as a portion of the wages stays at least during part of the week in the pockets of the labourers in the form of money. And this part is not limited by that part of the money product which originally forms the surplus value of the gold-producing capitalists, but, as we have said, is limited by the proportion in which the above product of £500 is generally distributed between capitalists and labourers, and in which the commodity supply to be circulated consists of surplus value and the other constituents of value.

However, that portion of surplus value which does not exist in other commodities but alongside of them in the form of money, consists of a portion of the annually produced gold only to the extent that a portion of the annual production of gold circulates for the realisation of the surplus value. The other portion of money, which is continually in the hands of the capitalist class in varying portions, as the money form of their surplus value, is not an element of the annually produced gold, but of the mass of money previously accumulated in the country.

According to our assumption the annual production of gold, £500, just covers the annual wear of money. If we keep in mind only these £500, and ignore that portion of the annually produced mass of commodities which is circulated by means of previously accumulated money, the surplus value produced in commodity form will find in the circulation process money for its conversion into money for the simple reason that on the other side surplus value is annually produced in the form of gold. The same applies to the other parts of the gold product of £500 which replace the advanced money capital.

Now, two things are to be noted here.

In the first place, it follows that the surplus value spent by the capitalists as money, as well as the variable and other productive capital advanced by them in money, is actually the product of labourers, namely of the labourers engaged in the production of gold. They produce anew not only that portion of the gold product which is "advanced" to them as wages but also that portion of the gold product in which the surplus value of the capitalist gold producers is directly represented. Finally, as for that portion of the gold product which replaces only the constant capital value advanced for its production, it re-appears in the form of money (or product in general) only through the annual work of the labourers. When the business started, it was originally expended by the capitalist in the form of money, which was not newly produced but formed a part of the circulating mass of social money. But to the extent that it is replaced by a new product, by additional gold, it is the annual product of the labourer. The advance on the part of the capitalist appears here, too, merely as a form which owes its existence to the fact that the labourer is neither the owner of his own means of production nor able to command, during production, the means of subsistence produced by other labourers.

In the second place, however, as far as concerns that mass of money which exists independently of this annual replacement of £500, partly in the form of a hoard and partly in the form of circulating money, things must be, i. e., must have been originally, with it just as they are annually with regard to these £500. We shall return to this point at the close of this sub-section. [a] But before then we wish to make a few additional remarks.

---

[a] See this volume, p. 342.

We have seen during our study of the turnover that, other circumstances remaining equal, changes in the length of the periods of turnover require changes in the amounts of money capital, in order to carry on production on the same scale. The elasticity of the money circulation must therefore be sufficient to adapt itself to this alternation of expansion and contraction.

If we furthermore assume other circumstances as remaining equal — including the length, intensity, and productivity of the working day — but *a different division of the value of the product* between wages and surplus value, so that either the former rises and the latter falls, or vice versa, the mass of the circulating money is not affected thereby. This change can take place without any expansion or contraction of the mass of money in circulation. Let us consider particularly the case in which there is a general rise in wages, so that, under the assumptions made, there will be a general fall in the rate of surplus value, but besides this, also according to our assumption, there will be no change in the value of the circulating mass of commodities. In this case there naturally is an increase in the money capital which must be advanced as variable capital, hence in the amount of money which performs this function. But the surplus value, and therefore also the amount of money required for its realisation, decreases by exactly the same amount by which the amount of money required for the function of variable capital increases. The amount of money required for the realisation of the commodity value is not affected thereby, any more than this commodity value itself. The cost price of the commodity rises for the individual capitalist but its social price of production remains unchanged. What is changed is the proportion in which, apart from the constant part of the value, the price of the production of commodities is divided into wages and profit.

But, it is argued, a greater outlay of variable money capital (the value of the money is, of course, considered constant) implies a larger amount of money in the hands of the labourers. This causes a greater demand for commodities on the part of the labourers. This, in turn, leads to a rise in the price of commodities.— Or it is said: If wages rise, the capitalists raise the prices of their commodities.— In either case, the general rise in wages causes a rise in commodity prices.

Hence a greater amount of money is needed for the circulation of the commodities, no matter how the rise in prices is explained.

Reply to the first formulation: in consequence of a rise in wages, the demand of the labourers for the necessities of life will rise particularly. Their demand for articles of luxury will increase to a lesser degree, or a demand will develop for things which formerly did not come within the scope of their consumption. The sudden and large-scale increase in the demand for the necessary means of subsistence will doubtless raise their prices immediately. The consequence: a greater part of the social capital will be employed in the production of necessities of life and a smaller in the production of luxuries, since these fall in price on account of the decrease in surplus value and the consequent decrease in the demand of the capitalists for these articles. On the other hand as the labourers themselves buy articles of luxury, the rise in their wages — within these limits — does not promote an increase in the prices of the necessities of life but simply displaces buyers of luxuries. More luxuries than before are consumed by labourers, and relatively fewer by capitalists. *Voilà tout.*[a] After some oscillations the value of the mass of circulating commodities is the same as before. — As for the momentary fluctuations, they will not have any other effect than to throw unemployed money capital into domestic circulation, capital which hitherto sought employment in speculative deals on the stock-exchange or in foreign countries.

Reply to the second formulation: If it were in the power of the capitalist producers to raise the prices of their commodities at will, they could and would do so without a rise in wages. Wages would never rise if commodity prices fell. The capitalist class would never resist the TRADE-UNIONS, if it could always and under all circumstances do what it is now doing by way of exception, under definite, special, so to say, local, circumstances, to wit, avail itself of every rise in wages in order to raise prices of commodities much higher yet and thus pocket greater profits.

The assertion that the capitalists can raise the prices of luxuries, because the demand for them decreases (in consequence of the reduced demand of the capitalists whose means for purchasing such articles have decreased) would be a very unique application of the law of supply and demand. Since it is not a mere displacement of luxury buyers, a displacement of capitalists by labourers — and so far as this dis-

---

[a] That's all.

placement does occur, the demand of the labourers does not stimulate a rise in the prices of the necessities of life, for the labourers cannot spend that portion of their increased wages for necessities which they spend for luxuries — the prices of luxuries fall in consequence of reduced demand. Capital is therefore withdrawn from the production of luxury articles, until their supply is reduced to dimensions corresponding to their altered role in the process of social production. With their production thus reduced, they rise in price — their value otherwise unchanged — to their normal level. So long as this contraction, or this process of levelling, lasts and the prices of necessities rise, as much capital is supplied to the production of the latter as is withdrawn from the other branch of production, until the demand is satisfied. Then the equilibrium is restored and the end of the whole process is that the social capital, and therefore also the money capital, is divided in a different proportion between the production of the necessities of life and that of luxury articles.

The entire objection is a bugbear set up by the capitalists and their economic sycophants.

The facts which serve as the pretext for this bugbear are of three kinds:

1) It is a general law of money circulation that, other things being equal, the quantity of money in circulation increases with a rise in the sum of the prices of circulating commodities, irrespective of whether this augmentation of the totality of prices applies to the same quantity of commodities or to a greater quantity. The effect is then confused with the cause. Wages rise (although the rise is rare, and proportional only in exceptional cases) with the rising prices of the necessities of life. Wage advances are the consequence, not the cause, of advances in the prices of commodities.

2) In the case of a partial, or local, rise of wages — that is, a rise only in some branches of production — a local rise in the prices of the products of these branches may follow. But even this depends on many circumstances. For instance that wages were not abnormally depressed and that therefore the rate of profit was not abnormally high; that the market for these goods is not narrowed by the rise in prices (hence a contraction of their supply previous to raising their prices is not necessary), etc.

3) In the case of a general rise in wages the price of the produced commodities rises in branches of industry where the variable capital

preponderates, but falls on the other hand in branches where the constant, or fixed, capital preponderates.

We found in our study of the simple circulation of commodities (Buch I, Kap. III, 2[a]) that, though the money form of any definite quantity of commodities is only transient within the process of circulation, still the money transiently in the hands of one man during the metamorphosis of a certain commodity necessarily passes into the hands of another, so that in the first instance commodities are not only exchanged all-sidedly, or replace one another, but this replacement is promoted and accompanied by an all-sided precipitation of money. "When one commodity replaces another, the money commodity always sticks to the hands of some third person. Circulation sweats money from every pore" (Buch I, S. 92[a]). The same identical fact is expressed, on the basis of the capitalist production of commodities, by a portion of capital constantly existing in the form of money capital, and a portion of surplus value constantly being found in the hands of its owners, likewise in the form of money.

Apart from this, the *circuit of money* — that is, the *return* of money to its point of departure — being a phase of the turnover of capital, is a phenomenon entirely different from, and even the opposite of, the *currency of money*,[33] which expresses its steady *departure* from the starting-point by changing hands again and again (Buch I, S. 94.[b])

---

[33] Although the Physiocrats still confuse these two phenomena, they were the first to emphasise the reflux of money to its starting-point as the essential form of circulation of capital, as that form of circulation which promotes reproduction. "Cast a glance at the *Tableau Économique* and you will see that the productive class provides the money with which the other classes buy products from it, and that they return this money to it when they come back next year to make the same purchases... You see, then, no other circle here but that of expenditure followed by reproduction, and of reproduction followed by expenditure, a circle described by the circulation of money, which measures expenditure and reproduction" (Quesnay, *Dialogues sur le Commerce et sur les Travaux des Artisans*, Daire édition, *Physiocrates*, I, pp. 208, 209). "It is this continual advance and return of capitals which should be called the circulation of money, this useful and fertile circulation which gives life to all the labours of society, which maintains the activity and life of the body politic, and which is quite rightly compared to the circulation of blood in the animal body" (Turgot, *Réflexions, etc., Oeuvres*, Daire édition, I, p. 45). [Marx quotes in French.]

---

[a] English edition: Vol. I, Ch. III., 2a (present edition, Vol. 35). - [b] Ibid., 2b.

Nevertheless, an accelerated turnover implies *eo ipso* an accelerated currency.

First concerning the variable capital: If a certain money capital of, say, £ 500 is turned over in the form of variable capital ten times a year, it is evident that this aliquot part of the quantity of money in circulation circulates ten times its value, or £ 5,000. It circulates ten times a year between the capitalist and the labourer. The labourer is paid, and pays, ten times a year with the same aliquot part of the circulating quantity of money. If the same variable capital were turned over only once a year, the scale of production remaining the same, there would be only one turnover of £ 5,000.

Furthermore: Let the constant portion of the circulating capital be equal to £ 1,000. If the capital is turned over ten times, the capitalist sells his commodity, and therefore also the constant circulating portion of its value, ten times a year. The same aliquot part of the circulating quantity of money (equal to £ 1,000) passes ten times per annum from the hands of its owners into those of the capitalist. This money changes hands ten times. Secondly, the capitalist buys means of production ten times a year. This again makes ten circulations of the money from one hand into another. With a sum of money amounting to £ 1,000, the industrial capitalist sells £ 10,000 worth of commodities, and again buys £ 10,000 worth of commodities. By means of 20 circulations of £ 1,000 in money a commodity supply of £ 20,000 is circulated.

Finally, with an acceleration of the turnover, the portion of money which realises the surplus value also circulates faster.

But, conversely, an acceleration in money circulation does not necessarily imply a more rapid turnover of capital, and therefore of money, i.e., it does not necessarily imply a contraction and more rapid renewal of the reproduction process.

A more rapid circulation of money takes place whenever a larger number of transactions are performed with the same amount of money. This may also take place under the same periods of capital reproduction as a result of changes in the technical facilities for the circulation of money. Furthermore, there may be an increase in the number of transactions in which money circulates without representing actual exchanges of commodities (marginal transactions on the stock-exchange, etc.). On the other hand some circulations of money may be entirely eliminated. For instance where the agriculturist is himself a landowner, there is no circulation of money between the farmer and the landlord; where the industrial capitalist is himself the owner of the capital, there is no circulation of money between him and creditors.

————————

As for the primitive formation of a money hoard in a country, and its appropriation by a few, it is unnecessary to discuss it in detail at this point.

The capitalist mode of production — its basis being wage labour, the payment of the labourer in money, and in general the transformation of payments in kind into money payments — can assume greater dimensions and achieve greater perfection only where there is available in the country a quantity of money sufficient for circulation and the formation of a hoard (reserve fund, etc.) promoted by it. This is the historical premise, although it is not to be taken to mean that first a sufficient hoard is formed and then capitalist production begins. It develops simultaneously with the development of the conditions necessary for it, and one of these conditions is a sufficient supply of precious metals. Hence the increased supply of precious metals since the sixteenth century is an essential element in the history of the development of capitalist production. But so far as the necessary further supply of money material on the basis of capitalist production is concerned, we see surplus value incorporated in products thrown into circulation without the money required for their conversion into money, on the one hand, and on the other surplus value in the form of gold without previous transformation of products into money.

The additional commodities to be converted into money find the necessary amount of money at hand, because on the other side additional gold (and silver) intended for conversion into commodities is thrown into circulation, not by means of exchange, but by production itself.

II. ACCUMULATION AND REPRODUCTION ON AN EXTENDED SCALE

Since accumulation takes place in the form of reproduction on an extended scale, it is evident that it does not offer any new problem with regard to money circulation.

In the first place, as far as the additional money capital required for the functioning of the increasing productive capital is concerned, that is supplied by the portion of the realised surplus value thrown into circulation by the capitalists as money capital, not as the money form of the revenue. The money is already in the hands of the capitalists. Only its employment is different.

Now, however, in consequence of the additional productive capital, its product, an additional mass of commodities is thrown into circulation. Together with this additional quantity of commodities, a part of the additional money needed for its realisation is thrown into circulation, inasmuch as the value of this mass of commodities is equal to that of the productive capital consumed in their production. This additional amount of money has been advanced precisely as additional money capital, and therefore returns to the capitalist through the turnover of his capital. Here the same question as above re-appears. Where does the additional money come from with which to realise the additional surplus value now contained in the form of commodities?

The general reply is again the same. The sum total of the prices of the circulating commodities has been increased, not because the prices of a given quantity of commodities have risen, but because the mass of the commodities now circulating is greater than that of the previously circulating commodities, without it being offset by a fall in prices. The additional money required for the circulation of this greater quantity of commodities of greater value must be secured either by greater economy in the use of the circulating quantity of money — whether by balancing the payments, etc., by measures which accelerate the circulation of the same coins — or by the transformation of money from the form of a hoard into that of a circulating medium. The latter does not only imply that idle money capital begins to function as a means of purchase or payment, or that money capital, already functioning as a reserve fund while performing this function for its owner, actively circulates for society (as is the case with bank deposits which are continually lent), thus performing a double function. It also implies that the stagnating reserve funds of coins are economised.

"So that money as coin may flow continuously, coin must continuously congeal into money. The continual movement of coin implies its perpetual stagnation in larger or smaller amounts in reserve funds of coin which arise everywhere within the framework of circulation and which are at the same time a condition of circulation. The formation, distribution, dissolution and re-formation of these funds constantly changes; existing funds disappear continuously and their disapperance is a continuous fact. This unceasing transformation of coin into money and of money into coin was expressed by Adam Smith when he said that, in addition to the particular commodity he sells, every commodity owner must always keep in stock a certain amount of the general commodity with which he buys. We have seen that $M — C$, the second member of the circuit $C — M — C$, splits up into a series of purchases, which are not effected all at once but successively over a period of time, so that one part of M circulates as coin, while the other part remains at rest as money. In this case, money is in fact only suspended coin and the various component parts of the coinage in circulation appear, constantly changing, now in one form, now in another. The first transformation of the medium of circulation into money constitutes therefore merely a technical aspect of the circulation of money" (Karl Marx, *Zur Kritik der Politischen Oekonomie*, 1859, S. 105, 106.[a] — "Coin" as distinguished from money is here employed to indicate money in its function of a mere medium of circulation in contrast with its other functions.)

To the extent that all these measures do not suffice, additional gold must be produced, or, what amounts to the same, a part of the additional product exchanged, directly or indirectly, for gold — the product of countries in which precious metals are mined.

The entire amount of labour power and social means of production expended in the annual production of gold and silver intended as instruments of circulation constitutes a bulky item of the *faux frais*[b] of the capitalist mode of production, of the production of commodities in general. It is an equivalent abstraction from social utilisation of as many additional means of production and consumption as possible, i. e., of real wealth. To the extent that the costs of this expensive machinery of circulation are decreased, the given scale of production or the given degree of its extension remaining constant, the productive power of social labour is *eo ipso* increased. Hence, so far as the expediences developing with the credit system have this effect, they increase capitalist wealth directly, either by performing a large portion of the social production and labour process without any intervention of real money, or by raising the functional capacity of the quantity of money really functioning.

This disposes also of the absurd question whether capitalist production in its present volume would be possible without the credit system

---
[a] See present edition, Vol. 29. p. 360. - [b] overhead costs

(even if regarded only from this point of view), that is, with the circulation of metallic coin alone. Evidently this is not the case. It would rather have encountered barriers in the volume of production of precious metals. On the other hand one must not entertain any fantastic illusions on the productive power of the credit system, so far as it supplies or sets in motion money capital. A further analysis of this question is out of place here.

———

We have now to investigate the case in which there takes place no real accumulation, i. e., no direct expansion of the scale of production, but where a part of the realised surplus value is accumulated for a longer or shorter time as a money reserve fund, in order to be transformed later into productive capital.

Inasmuch as the money so accumulating is additional money, the matter needs no explanation. It can only be a portion of the excessive gold brought from gold-producing countries. In this connection it must be noted that the home product, in exchange for which this gold is imported, is no longer available in the country in question. It has been exported to foreign countries in exchange for gold.

But if we assume that the same amount of money is still in the country as before, then the accumulated and accumulating money has accrued from the circulation. Only its function is changed. It has been converted from money in currency into latent money capital gradually taking shape.

The money which is accumulated in this case is the money form of sold commodities, and moreover of that part of their value which constitutes surplus value for their owner. (The credit system is here assumed to be non-existent.) The capitalist who accumulates this money has sold *pro tanto* without buying.

If we look upon this process merely as an individual phenomenon, there is nothing to explain. A part of the capitalists keeps a portion of the money realised by the sale of its product without withdrawing products from the market in return. Another part of them on the other hand transforms its money wholly into products, with the exception of the constantly recurring money capital required for running the business. One portion of the products thrown upon the market as vehicles of surplus value consists of means of production, or of the real elements of variable capital, the necessary means of subsistence. It can therefore serve immediately for the expansion of production. For it has not been premised in the least that one part of the capitalists accumulates money capital, while the other consumes its surplus value entirely, but only that one part does its accumulating in the shape of money, forms latent money capital, while the other part accumulates genuinely, that is to say, enlarges the scale of production, genuinely expands its productive capital. The available quantity of money remains sufficient for the requirements of circulation, even if, alternately, one part of the capitalists accumulates money, while the other enlarges the scale of production, and vice versa. Moreover, the accumulation of money on one side may proceed even without cash money by the mere accumulation of outstanding claims.

But the difficulty arises when we assume not an individual, but a general accumulation of money capital on the part of the capitalist class. Apart from this class, according to our assumption — the general and exclusive domination of capitalist production — there is no other class at all except the working class. All that the working class buys is equal to the sum total of its wages, equal to the sum total of the variable capital advanced by the entire capitalist class. This money flows back to the capitalist class by the sale of its product to the working class. Its variable capital thus resumes its money form. Let the sum total of the variable capital be x times £ 100, i. e., the sum total of the variable capital employed, not advanced, during the year. The question now under consideration is not affected by how much or how little money, depending on the velocity of the turnover, is needed to advance this variable capital value during the year. The capitalist class buys with these x times £ 100 of capital a certain amount of labour power, or pays wages to a certain number of labourers — first transaction. The labourers buy with this same sum a certain quantity of commodities from the capitalists, whereby the sum of x times £ 100 flows back into the hands of the capitalists — second transaction. And this is constantly repeated. This amount of x times £ 100, therefore, can never enable the working class to buy the part of the product which represents the constant capital, not to mention the part which represents the surplus value of the capitalist class. With these x times £ 100 the labourers can never buy more than a part of the value of the social product equal to that part of the value which represents the value of the advanced variable capital.

Apart from the case in which this universal accumulation of money expresses nothing but the distribution of the precious metal additionally introduced, in whatever proportion, among the various individual capitalists, how is the entire capitalist class then supposed to accumulate money?

They would all have to sell a portion of their product without buying anything in return. There is nothing mysterious about the fact that they all have a certain fund of money which they throw into circulation as a medium of circulation for their consumption, and a certain portion of which returns to each one of them from the circulation. But in that case this money fund exists precisely as a fund for circulation, as a result of the conversion of the surplus value into money, and does not by any means exist as latent money capital.

If we view the matter as it takes place in reality, we find that the latent money capital, which is accumulated for future use, consists:

1) Of deposits in banks; and it is a comparatively trifling sum which is really at the disposal of the bank. Money capital is accumulated here only nominally. What is actually accumulated is outstanding claims which can be converted into money (if ever) only because a certain balance arises between the money withdrawn and the money deposited. It is only a relatively small sum that the bank holds in its hands in money.

2) Of government securities. These are not capital at all, but merely outstanding claims on the annual product of the nation.

3) Of stocks. Those which are not fakes are titles of ownership of some corporative real capital and drafts on the surplus value accruing annually from it.

There is no accumulation of money in any of these cases. What appears on the one side as an accumulation of money capital appears on the other as a continual actual expenditure of money. It is immaterial whether the money is spent by him who owns it, or by others, his debtors.

On the basis of capitalist production the formation of a hoard as such is never an end in itself but the result either of a stagnation of the circulation — larger amounts of money than is generally the case assuming the form of a hoard — or of accumulations necessitated by the turnover; or, finally, the hoard is merely the creation of money capital existing temporarily in latent form and intended to function as productive capital.

If therefore on the one hand a portion of the surplus value realised in money is withdrawn from circulation and accumulated as a hoard, another part of the surplus value is at the same time continually converted into productive capital. With the exception of the distribution of additional precious metals among the members of the capitalist class, accumulation in the form of money never takes place simultaneously at all points.

What is true of the portion of the annual product which represents surplus value in the form of commodities, is also true of the other portion of it. A certain sum of money is required for its circulation. This sum of money belongs to the capitalist class quite as much as the annually produced quantity of commodities which represents surplus value. It is originally thrown into circulation by the capitalist class itself. It is constantly redistributed among its members by means of the circulation itself. Just as in the case of the circulation of coin in general, a portion of this sum stagnates at ever varying points, while another portion continually circulates. Whether a part of this accumulation is intentional, for the purpose of forming money capital, or not, does not alter things.

No notice has been taken here of those adventures of circulation in which one capitalist grasps a portion of the surplus value, or even of the capital, of another, thereby bringing about one-sided accumulation and centralisation of money capital as well as of productive capital. For instance a part of the snatched surplus value accumulated by A as money capital may be a part of the surplus value of B which does not return to him.

Part III

THE REPRODUCTION AND CIRCULATION
OF THE AGGREGATE SOCIAL CAPITAL

Chapter XVIII [34]

INTRODUCTION

I. THE SUBJECT INVESTIGATED

The direct process of the production of capital is its labour and self-expansion process, the process whose result is the commodity product and whose compelling motive is the production of surplus value.

The process of reproduction of capital comprises this direct process of production as well as the two phases of the circulation process proper, i. e., the entire circuit which, as a periodic process — a process which constantly repeats itself in definite periods — constitutes the turnover of capital.

Whether we study the circuit in the form of M ... M' or that of P ... P, the direct process of production P itself always forms but one link in this circuit. In the one form it appears as a promoter of the process of circulation; in the other the process of circulation appears as its promoter. Its continuous renewal, the continuous re-appearance of capital as productive capital, is in either case determined by its transformations in the process of circulation. On the other hand the continuously renewed process of production is the condition of the transformations which the capital undergoes ever anew in the sphere of circulation, of its alternate appearance as money capital and commodity capital.

Every individual capital forms, however, but an individualised fraction, a fraction endowed with individual life, as it were, of the aggregate social capital, just as every individual capitalist is but an individual element of the capitalist class. The movement of the social capital consists of the totality of the movements of its individualised fractional parts, the turnovers of the individual capitals. Just as the metamorphosis of the individual commodity is a link in the series of metamorphoses of the commodity world — the circulation of commodities — so the metamorphosis of the individual capital, its turnover, is a link in the circuit described by social capital.

This total process comprises both the productive consumption (the direct process of production) together with the conversions of form (materially considered, exchanges) which bring it about, and the individual consumption together with the conversions of form or exchanges by which it is brought about. It includes on the one hand the conversion of variable capital into labour power, and therefore the incorporation of labour power in the process of capitalist production. Here the labourer acts as the seller of his commodity, labour power, and the capitalist as its buyer. But on the other hand the sale of the commodities embraces also their purchase by the working class, hence their individual consumption. Here the working class appears as buyer and the capitalists as sellers of commodities to the labourers.

The circulation of the commodity capital includes the circulation of surplus value, hence also the purchases and sales by which the capitalists effect their individual consumption, the consumption of surplus value.

The circuit of the individual capitals in their aggregate as social capital, hence considered in its totality, comprises not only the circulation of capital but also the general circulation of commodities. The latter can originally consist of only two components: 1) the circuit of capital proper and 2) the circuit of the commodities which enter into individual consumption, consequently of the commodities for which the labourer expends his wages and the capitalist his surplus value (or a part of it). At any rate, the circuit of capital comprises also the circulation of the surplus value, since the latter is a part of the commodity capital, and likewise the conversion of the variable capital into labour power, the payment of wages. But the expenditure of this surplus value and wages for commodities does not form a link in the circulation of capital, although at least the expenditure of wages is essential for this circulation.

In Book I the process of capitalist production was analysed as an individual act as well as a process of reproduction: the production of surplus value and the production of capital itself. The changes of form and substance experienced by capital in the sphere of circulation were assumed without dwelling upon them. It was presupposed therefore that on the one hand the capitalist sells the product at its value and on the other that he finds within the sphere of circulation the objective means of production for restarting or continuing the process. The only act within the sphere of circulation on which we dwelt there was the purchase and sale of labour power as the fundamental condition of capitalist production.

In the first part of this Book II, the various forms were considered which capital assumes in its circuit, and the various forms of this circuit itself. The circulation time must now be added to the working time discussed in Book I.

In the second part, the circuit was studied as being periodic, i. e., as a turnover. It was shown on the one hand in what manner the various constituents of capital (fixed and circulating) accomplish the circuit of forms in different periods of time and in different ways; on the other hand the circumstances were examined by which the different lengths of the working period and circulation period are conditioned. The influence was shown which the period of the circuit and the different proportions of its component parts exert upon the dimensions of the production process itself and upon the annual rate of surplus value. Indeed, while it was the successive forms continually assumed and discarded by capital in its circuit that were studied in Part I, it was shown in Part II how a capital of a given magnitude is simultaneously, though in varying proportions, divided, within this flow and succession of forms, into different forms: productive capital, money capital, and commodity capital, so that they not only alternate with one another, but different portions of the total capital value are constantly side by side and function in these different states. Especially money capital came forward with distinctive features not shown in Book I. Certain laws were found according to which diverse large components of a given capital must be continually advanced and renewed — depending on the conditions of the turnover — in the form of money capital in order to keep a productive capital of a given size constantly functioning.

But in both the first and the second parts it was always only a question of some individual capital, of the movement of some individualised part of social capital.

However the circuits of the individual capitals intertwine, presuppose and necessitate one another, and form, precisely in this interlacing, the movement of the total social capital. Just as in the simple circulation of commodities the total metamorphosis of a commodity appeared as a link in the series of metamorphoses of the world of commodities, so now the metamorphosis of the individual capital appears as a link in the series of metamorphoses of the social capital. But while simple commodity circulation by no means necessarily comprises the circulation of the capital—since it may take place on the basis of non-capitalist production—the circuit of the total social capital, as was noted, comprises also the commodity circulation lying outside the circuit of the individual capital, i. e., the circulation of commodities which do not represent capital.

We have now to study the process of circulation (which in its entirety is a form of the process of reproduction) of the individual capitals as components of the total social capital, that is to say, the process of circulation of this total social capital.

II. THE ROLE OF MONEY CAPITAL

//Although the following belongs in a later section of this part, we shall analyse it immediately, namely, the money capital considered as a constituent part of the aggregate social capital.//

In the study of the turnover of the individual capital money capital revealed two aspects.

In the first place, it constitutes the form in which every individual capital appears upon the scene and opens its process as capital. It therefore appears as the *primus motor*, lending impetus to the entire process.

In the second place, that portion of the advanced capital value which must be continually advanced and renewed in the form of money differs in its ratio to the productive capital which it sets in motion, i. e., in its ratio to the continuous scale of production, depending on the particular length of the period of turnover and the particular ratio between its two component parts—the working period and the period of circulation. But whatever this ratio may be, the portion of the capital value in process which can continually function as productive capital is limited in any event by that portion of the advanced capital value which must always exist beside the productive capital in the form of money. It is here merely a question of the normal turnover, an abstract average. Additional money capital required to compensate for interruptions of the circulation is excepted.

On the first point. Commodity production presupposes commodity circulation, and commodity circulation presupposes the expression of commodities in money, the circulation of money; the splitting of a commodity into commodity and money is a law of the expression of the product as a commodity.[a] Similarly the capitalist production of commodities — whether considered socially or individually — presupposes capital in the form of money, or money capital, both as the *primus motor* of every incipient business, and as its continual motor. The circulating capital especially implies that the money capital acts with constant repetition at short intervals as a motor. The entire advanced capital value, that is to say, all the elements of capital, consisting of commodities, labour power, instruments of labour, and materials of production, must be bought over and over again with money. What is true here of the individual capital is also true of the social capital, which functions only in the form of many individual capitals. But as we showed in Book I, it does not at all follow from this that capital's field of operation, the scale of production, depends — even on a capitalist basis — for its *absolute* limits on the amount of functioning money capital.

Incorporated in capital are elements of production whose expansion within certain limits is independent of the magnitude of the advanced money capital. Though payment of labour power be the same, it can be exploited more or less extensively or intensively. If the money capital is increased with this greater exploitation (that is, if wages are raised), it is not increased proportionately, hence not at all *pro tanto*.

The productively exploited natural materials — the soil, the seas, ores, forests, etc.— which do not constitute elements of capital value, are more intensively or extensively exploited with a greater exertion of the same amount of labour power, without an increased advance of money capital. The real elements of productive capital are thus multiplied without requiring an additional money capital. But so far as such an addition becomes necessary for additional auxiliary materials, the money capital in which the capital value is advanced is not increased proportionately to the augmented effectiveness of the productive capital, hence is *pro tanto* not at all increased.

The same instruments of labour, and thus the same fixed capital, can be used more effectively by an extension of the time they are daily[b] used and by a greater intensity of their employment, without an additional outlay of money for fixed capital. There is, in that case, only a more rapid turnover of the fixed capital, but then the elements of its reproduction are supplied more rapidly.

---

[a] See K. Marx, *Capital*, Vol. I, Ch. II-III (present edition, Vol. 35). - [b] More precisely: annually.

Apart from the natural materials, it is possible to incorporate in the production process natural forces, which do not cost anything, to act as agents with more or less heightened effect. The degree of their effectiveness depends on methods and scientific developments which cost the capitalist nothing.

The same is true of the social combination of labour power in the process of production and of the accumulated skill of the individual labourers. Carey calculates that the landowner never receives enough, because he is not paid for all the capital or labour put into the soil since time immemorial in order to give it its present productivity. (Of course, no mention is made of the productivity of which the soil is robbed.) Accordingly each individual labourer would have to be paid in conformity with the work which it cost the entire human race to evolve a modern mechanic out of a savage. On the contrary one should think that if all the unpaid labour put into the soil and converted into money by the landowner and capitalist is totalled up, all the capital ever invested in this soil has been paid back over and over again with usurious interest, so that society has long ago redeemed landed property over and over again.

True enough, the increase in the productive power of labour, so far as it does not imply an additional investment of capital value, augments in the first instance only the quantity of the product, not its value, except in so far as it makes it possible to reproduce more constant capital with the same labour and thus to preserve its value. But it forms at the same time new material for capital, hence the basis of increased accumulation of capital.

So far as the organisation of social labour itself, and thus the increase in the social productive power of labour, requires large-scale production and therefore the advance of large quantities of money capital by individual capitalists, we have shown in Book I [a] that this is accomplished in part by the centralisation of capitals in a few hands, without necessitating an absolute increase in the magnitude of the functioning capital values, and consequently also in the magnitude of the money capital in which they are advanced. The magnitude of the individual capitals can increase by centralisation in the hands of a few without a growth of their social sum total. It is only a changed distribution of the individual capitals.

---

[a] English edition: Vol. I, Ch. XXV, 2 and Ch. XXXII (present edition, Vol. 35).

Finally, we have shown in the preceding part that a shortening of the period of turnover permits of setting in motion either the same productive capital with less money capital or more productive capital with the same money capital.

But evidently all this has nothing to do with the question of money capital itself. It shows only that the advanced capital — a given sum of values consisting in its free form, in its value form, of a certain sum of money — includes, after its conversion into productive capital, productive powers whose limits are not set by the limits of its value, but which on the contrary may operate within certain bounds with differing degrees of extensiveness or intensiveness. If the prices of the elements of production — the means of production and labour power — are given, the magnitude of the money capital required for the purchase of a definite quantity of these elements of production existing as commodities is determined. Or the magnitude of value of the capital to be advanced is determined. But the extent to which this capital acts as a creator of values and products is elastic and variable.

On the second point. It is self-evident that the part of the social labour and means of production which must be annually expended for the production or purchase of money in order to replace worn-off coin is *pro tanto* a diminution of the volume of social production. But as for the money value which functions partly as a medium of circulation, partly as a hoard, it is simply there, acquired, present alongside the labour power, the produced means of production, and the natural sources of wealth. It cannot be regarded as a limit set to these things. By its transformation into elements of production, by its exchange with other nations, the scale of production might be extended. This presupposes, however, that money continues as before to play its role of universal money.[a]

To set the productive capital in motion requires more or less money capital, depending on the length of the period of turnover. We have also seen that the division of the period of turnover into working time and circulation time requires an increase of the capital latent or suspended in the form of money.

Inasmuch as the period of turnover is determined by the length of the working period, it is determined, other conditions remaining equal, by the material nature of the process of production, hence not by the specific social character of this process of production. How-

---

[a] Cf. K. Marx, *Capital*, Vol. I, Ch. III, 3c (present edition, Vol. 35).

ever, on the basis of capitalist production, more extensive operations of comparatively long duration necessitate large advances of money capital for a rather long time. Production in such spheres depends therefore on the magnitude of the money capital which the individual capitalist has at his disposal. This barrier is broken down by the credit system and the associations connected with it, e. g., the stock companies. Disturbances in the money market therefore put such establishments out of business, while these same establishments, in their turn, produce disturbances in the money market.

When social production is the basis, the scale must be ascertained on which those operations—which withdraw labour power and means of production for a long time without supplying any product as a useful effect in the interim—can be carried on without injuring branches of production which not only withdraw labour power and means of production continually, or several times a year, but also supply means of subsistence and of production. Under social as well as capitalist production, the labourers in branches of business with shorter working periods will as before withdraw products only for a short time without giving any products in return; while branches of business with long working periods continually withdraw products for a longer time before they return anything. This circumstance, then, arises from the material conditions of the particular labour process, not from its social form. In the case of social production, money capital is eliminated. Society distributes labour power and means of production to the different branches of production. The producers may, for all it matters, receive paper vouchers entitling them to withdraw from the social supplies of consumer goods a quantity corresponding to their labour time. These vouchers are not money. They do not circulate.

We see that inasmuch as the need for money capital originates in the length of the working period, it is conditioned by two things: *First*, that money in general is the form in which every individual capital (apart from credit) must make its appearance in order to transform itself into productive capital; this follows from the nature of capitalist production and of commodity production in general.—*Second*, the magnitude of the required money advance is due to the circumstance that labour power and means of production are continually withdrawn from society for a comparatively long time without any return to it, during that period, of products convertible into money. The first condition, that the capital to be advanced must be advanced in the form of money, is not eliminated by the form of this money itself, whether it is metal money, credit money, token money, etc. The second condition is in no way affected by what money medium or in what form of production labour, means of subsistence, and means of production are withdrawn without the return of some equivalent to the circulation.

Chapter XIX[35)]

FORMER PRESENTATIONS OF THE SUBJECT

I. THE PHYSIOCRATS

Quesnay's *Tableau économique* [49] shows in a few broad outlines how the annual result of the national production, representing a definite value, is distributed by means of the circulation in such a way that, other things being equal, simple reproduction, i. e., reproduction on the same scale, can take place. The starting-point of the period of production is properly the preceding year's harvest. The innumerable individual acts of circulation are at once brought together in their characteristic social mass movement — the circulation between great functionally determined economic classes of society. We are here interested in the following: A portion of the total product — being, like every other portion of it, a use object, it is a new result of last year's labour — is at the same time only the depository of old capital value re-appearing in the same natural form. It does not circulate but remains in the hands of its producers, the class of farmers, in order to resume there its service as capital. In this portion of the year's product, the constant capital, Quesnay includes impertinent elements, but he strikes upon the main thing, thanks to the limitations of his horizon, within which agriculture is the only sphere of investment of human labour producing surplus value, hence the only really productive one from the capitalist point of view. The economic process of reproduction, whatever may be its specific social character, always becomes intertwined in this sphere (agriculture) with a natural process of reproduction. The obvious conditions of the latter throw light on those of the former, and keep off a confusion of thought which is called forth by the mirage of circulation.

[35)] Beginning of Manuscript VIII.

The label of a system differs from that of other articles, among other things, by the fact that it cheats not only the buyer but often also the seller. Quesnay himself and his immediate disciples believed in their feudal shop-sign. So do our academic pedants even this day and hour. But as a matter of fact the system of the Physiocrats is the first systematic conception of capitalist production. The representative of industrial capital — the class of farmers — directs the entire economic movement. Agriculture is carried on capitalistically, that is to say, it is the enterprise of a capitalist farmer on a large scale; the direct cultivator of the soil is the wage labourer. Production creates not only articles of use but also their value; its compelling motive is the procurement of surplus value, whose birthplace is the sphere of production, not of circulation. Among the three classes which figure as the vehicles of the social process of reproduction brought about by the circulation, the immediate exploiter of "productive" labour, the producer of surplus value, the capitalist farmer, is distinguished from those who merely appropriate the surplus value.

The capitalist character of the physiocratic system excited opposition even during its florescence: on the one side it was challenged by Linguet [50] and Mably, on the other by the champions of the small freeholders.

———

Adam Smith's retrogression [36] in the analysis of the process of reproduction is so much the more remarkable because he not only elaborates upon Quesnay's correct analyses, generalising his "*avances primitives*" and "*avances annuelles*" for instance and calling them respectively "fixed" and "circulating" capital, [37] but even relapses in spots entirely into physiocratic errors. For instance in order to demonstrate that the farmer produces more value than any other sort of capitalist, he says:

[36] *Kapital*, Band I, 2. Ausgabe, S. 612, Note 32.[a]

[37] Some Physiocrats had paved the way for him even here, especially Turgot. The latter uses the term capital for *avances* more frequently than Quesnay and the other Physiocrats and identifies still more the *avances*, or *capitaux*, of the manufacturers with those of the farmers. For instance: "Like these" (the *entrepreneurs-manufacturers*), "they" (*les fermiers*, i. e., the capitalist farmers) "must receive in addition to returning capitals, etc." (Turgot, *Oeuvres*, Daire édition, Paris, 1844, Vol. I, p. 40).

———

[a] English edition: Vol. I, Ch. XXIV, 2 (present edition, Vol. 35).

"No equal capital puts into motion a greater quantity of **productive** labour than that of the farmer. Not only his labouring servants, but his labouring cattle are productive labourers." //Fine compliment for the labouring servants!// "In agriculture too nature *labours* along with man; and though *her labour costs no expense*, its produce has *its value, as well as that of the most expensive workmen*. The most important operations of agriculture seem intended not so much to increase, though they do that too, as to direct the fertility of nature towards the production of the plants most profitable to man. A field overgrown with briars and brambles may frequently produce as great a quantity of vegetables as the best cultivated vineyard or corn field. Planting and tillage frequently regulate more than they animate the active fertility of nature; and after all their labour, a great part of the work always remains to be done by her. The labourers and labouring cattle" (!), "therefore, employed in agriculture, not only occasion, like the workmen in manufactures, the reproduction of a value equal to their own consumption, or to the capital which employs them, together with its owners' profits; but of a much greater value. Over and above the capital of the farmer and all its profits, they regularly occasion the reproduction of the rent of the landlord. This rent may be considered as the produce of those powers of nature the use of which the landlord lends to the farmer. It is greater or smaller according to the supposed extent of those powers, or, in other words, according to the supposed natural or improved fertility of the land. It is the work of nature which remains after deducting or compensating everything which can be regarded as the work of man. It is seldom less than a fourth, and frequently more than a third of the whole produce. No equal quantity of productive labour employed in manufactures can ever occasion so great a reproduction. In them nature does nothing; man does all; and the reproduction must always be in proportion to the strength of the agents that occasion it. The capital employed in agriculture, therefore, not only puts into motion a greater quantity of productive labour than any equal capital employed in manufactures, but in proportion, too, to the quantity of productive labour which it employs, it adds a much greater value to the annual produce of the land and labour of the country, to the real wealth and revenue of its inhabitants" (Book II, Ch. 5, p. 242).

Adam Smith says in Book II, Ch. 1:

"The whole value of the seed, too, is properly a fixed capital.

Here, then, capital = capital value; it exists in a "fixed" form.

"Though it [the seed] goes backwards and forwards between the ground and the granary, it never changes masters, and therefore does not properly circulate. The farmer makes his profit, not by its sale, but by its increase" (p. 186).

The absurdity of the thing lies here in the fact that Smith does not, like Quesnay before him, see the re-appearance of the value of constant capital in a renewed form, and hence fails to see an important element of the process of reproduction, but merely offers one more illustration, and a wrong one at that, of his distinction between circulating and fixed capital.— In Smith's translation of "*avances primitives*" and "*avances annuelles*" as "fixed capital" and "circulating capital", the progress consists in the word "capital", the concept of which is generalised, and becomes independent of the special consideration for the "agricultural" sphere of application of the Physiocrats; the retrogression consists in the fact that "fixed" and "circulating" are regarded as the over-riding distinction, and are so maintained.

II. ADAM SMITH

1. SMITH'S GENERAL POINTS OF VIEW

Adam Smith says in Book I, Ch. 6, p. 42:

"In every society the price of every commodity finally resolves itself into some one or other, or all of those three parts" (wages, profit, rent); "and in every improved society, all the three enter more or less, as component parts, into the price of the far greater part of commodities." [38]

Or, as he continues, p. 43:

"Wages, profit, and rent, are the *three original sources* of all revenue as well as of *all exchangeable value*."

Below we shall discuss in greater detail this doctrine of Adam Smith concerning "the component parts of the price of commodities", or of "all exchangeable value".

He says furthermore:

"Since this is the case, it has been observed, with regard to every particular commodity, taken separately; it must be so with regard to all the commodities which compose the *whole annual produce* of the land and labour of every country, taken complexly. The *whole price or exchangeable value* of that annual produce, must *resolve itself* into the same three parts, and *be parcelled out* among the different inhabitants of the country, either as the *wages* of their labour, the *profits* of their stock, or the *rent* of their land" (Book II, Ch. 2, p. 190).

---

[38] In order that the reader may not misconstrue the meaning of the phrase "the price of the far greater part of commodities", the following shows how Adam Smith himself explains this term. For instance, no rent enters into the price of sea fish, only wages and profit; only wages enter into the price of Scotch pebbles. He says: "In some parts of Scotland a few poor people make a trade of gathering, along the sea-shore, those little variegated stones commonly known by the name of Scotch Pebbles. The price which is paid to them by the stone-cutter is altogether the wages of their labour; neither rent nor profit makes any part of it."

After Adam Smith has thus resolved the price of all commodities individually, as well as "the whole price or exchangeable value ... of the annual produce of the land and labour of every country", into wages, profit and rent, the three sources of revenue for wage labourers, capitalists and landowners, he must needs smuggle in a fourth element by a circuitous route, namely the element of capital. This is accomplished by drawing a distinction between gross and net revenue:

"The *gross* revenue of all the inhabitants of a great country comprehends the *whole annual produce* of their land and labour; the *neat* revenue, what remains free to them *after deducting the expense of maintaining*; first, their *fixed*; and secondly, their *circulating capital*; or what, without encroaching upon their capital, they can place in their stock reserved for immediate consumption, or spend upon their subsistence, conveniences, and amusements. Their real wealth too is in proportion, not to their gross, but to their neat revenue" (ibid., p. 190).

On this we comment as follows:

1) Adam Smith expressly deals here only with simple reproduction, not reproduction on an extended scale, or accumulation. He speaks only of expenses for MAINTAINING [a] the capital in operation. The "neat" income is equal to that portion of the annual product, whether of society or of the individual capitalist, which can pass into the "fund for consumption", but the size of this fund must not ENCROACH UPON CAPITAL [b] in operation. One portion of the value of both the individual and the social product, then, is resolved neither into wages nor into profit nor into rent, but into capital.

2) Adam Smith flees from his own theory by means of a play upon words, the distinction between gross and net revenue. The individual capitalist as well as the entire capitalist class, or the so-called nation, receive in place of the capital consumed in production a commodity product whose value — it can be represented by the proportional parts of this product — replaces on the one hand the expended capital value and thus forms an income, or still more literally, revenue (*revenu*, past participle of *revenir* — to come back), but, *nota bene*, a revenue upon capital, or income upon capital; on the other hand components of the value product which are "parcelled out among the different inhabitants of the country, either as the wages of their labour,

---

[a] In the original, this English word is given in parentheses after its German equivalent. - [b] In the original, these English words are given in parentheses after their German equivalent.

the profits of their stock, or the rent of their land", a thing commonly called income. Hence the value of the entire product constitutes
somebody's income — either of the individual capitalist or of the
whole country, but it is on the one hand an income upon capital, and
on the other a "revenue" different from the latter. Consequently, the
thing which is eliminated in the analysis of the value of the commodity into its component parts is brought back through a side door —
the ambiguity of the word "revenue". But only such value constituents of the product can be "taken in" as already exist in it. If the
capital is to come in as revenue, capital must first have been expended.
Adam Smith says furthermore:

> "The lowest ordinary rate of profit must always be something more than what is
> sufficient to compensate the occasional losses to which every employment of stock is ex-
> posed. It is this surplus only which is neat or clear profit."

//What capitalist understands by profit, necessary expenditure of
capital?//

> "What is called gross profit comprehends frequently, not only this surplus,
> but what is retained for compensating such extraordinary losses" (Book I, Ch. 9,
> p. 72).

But this means nothing else than that a part of the surplus value,
considered as a part of the gross profit, must form an insurance fund
for the production. This insurance fund is created by a portion of the
surplus labour, which to that extent produces capital directly, that is
to say, the fund intended for reproduction. As regards the expense for
"maintaining" the fixed capital, etc. (see the above quotations), the
replacement of the consumed fixed capital by a new one is not a new
outlay of capital, but only a renewal of the old capital value in a new
form. And as far as the repair of the fixed capital is concerned, which
Adam Smith counts likewise among the costs of maintenance, this expense goes in with the price of the capital advanced. The fact that the
capitalist, instead of having to invest this all at one time, invests it
gradually, as required, during the functioning of the capital, and can
invest it out of profits already pocketed, does not change the source of
this profit. The value constituent from which it derives proves only
that the labourer delivers surplus labour for the insurance fund as
well as for the repair fund.[51]
Adam Smith then tells us that one should exclude from the net revenue, i. e., from the revenue in its specific meaning, the entire fixed cap-

ital, and also the entire portion of the circulating capital which is required for the maintenance and repair of the fixed capital, and for its renewal, in fact all capital not in a bodily form intended for the consumption fund.

"The whole expense of maintaining the fixed capital, must evidently be excluded from the neat revenue of the society. Neither the materials necessary for supporting their useful machines and instruments of trade ... nor the produce of the labour necessary for fashioning those materials into the proper form, can ever make any part of it. The *price* of that labour may indeed make a part of it; as the workmen so employed may place the whole value of their wages in their stock reserved for immediate consumption. But in other sorts of labour, both the *price*" //i. e., the wages paid for this labour// "and the *produce*" //in which this labour is incorporated// "go to this stock, the price to that of the workmen, the produce to that of other people, whose subsistence, conveniences, and amusements, are augmented by the labour of those workmen" (Book II, Ch. 2, pp. 190, 191).

Adam Smith comes here upon a very important distinction between the labourers employed in the production of *means of production* and those employed in the immediate production of *articles of consumption*. The value of the commodities produced by the first-named contains a constituent part which is equal to the sum of the wages, i. e., equal to the value of the part of capital invested in the purchase of labour power. This part of value exists bodily as a certain quota of the means of production produced by the labourers. The money received by them as wages is their revenue, but their labour has not produced any goods which are consumable, either for themselves or for others. Hence these products are not an element of that part of the annual product which is intended to form a social consumption fund, in which alone a "neat revenue" can be realised. Adam Smith forgets to add here that the same thing that applies to wages is also true of that constituent of the value of the means of production which, being surplus value, forms the revenue (first and foremost) of the industrial capitalist under the categories of profit and rent. These value components likewise exist in means of production, articles which cannot be consumed. They cannot raise articles of consumption produced by the second kind of labourers in a quantity corresponding to their price until they have been converted into money; only then can they transfer those articles to the individual consumption fund of their owners. But so much the more should Adam Smith have seen that that part of the value of the annually begotten means of production which is equal to the value of the means of production functioning within this sphere of production—the means of production with which means of production are made—hence a portion of value equal to the value of the constant capital employed here, is absolutely excluded from being a value constituent forming revenue, not only on account of the natural form in which it exists, but also on account of its functioning as capital.

With regard to the second kind of labourers—who directly produce articles of consumption—Adam Smith's definitions are not quite exact. For he says that in these kinds of labour, both the price of labour and the product GO TO [a] the stock reserved for immediate consumption,

"the *price*" (i. e., the money received in wages) "to that of the *workmen*, the *produce* to THAT OF *OTHER PEOPLE*[a] whose subsistence, conveniences and amusements, are augmented by the labour of those workmen".

But the labourer cannot live on the "*price*" of his labour, the money in which his wages are paid; he realises this money by buying articles of consumption with it. These may in part consist of classes of commodities produced by himself. On the other hand his own product may be such as goes only into the consumption of the exploiters of labour.

After Adam Smith has thus entirely excluded the fixed capital from the "neat revenue" of a country, he continues:

"But though the whole expense of maintaining the fixed capital is thus necessarily excluded from the neat revenue of the society, it is not the same case with that of maintaining the circulating capital. Of the four parts of which this latter capital is composed, money, provisions, materials, and finished work, the three last, it has already been observed, are regularly withdrawn from it, and placed either in the fixed capital of the society, or in their stock reserved for immediate consumption. Whatever portion of those consumable goods is not employed in maintaining the former" //the fixed capital// "goes all to the latter" // the fund for immediate consumption//, "and makes a part of the neat revenue of the society. The maintenance of those three parts of the circulating capital, therefore, withdraws no portion of the annual produce from the neat revenue of the society, besides what is necessary for maintaining the fixed capital" (Book II, Ch. 2, pp. [191,] 192).

It is sheer tautology to say that that portion of the circulating capital which does not serve for the production of means of production

---

[a] In the original, these English words are given in parentheses after their German equivalent.

goes into that of articles of consumption, in other words, into that part of the annual product which is intended to form society's consumption fund. However, the immediately following passage is important:

"The circulating capital of a society is in this respect different from that of an individual. That of an individual is totally excluded from making any part of his neat revenue, which must consist altogether in his profits. But though the circulating capital of every individual makes a part of that of the society to which he belongs, it is not upon that account totally excluded from making a part likewise of their neat revenue. Though the whole goods in a merchant's shop must by no means be placed in his own stock reserved for immediate consumption, they may in that of other people, who, from a revenue derived from other funds, may regularly replace their value to him, together with its profits, without occasioning any diminution either of his capital or of theirs" (ibid).

And so we learn here that:

1) Just as the fixed capital, and the circulating capital required for its reproduction (he forgets the function) and maintenance, are totally excluded from the net revenue of every individual capitalist, which can consist only of his profit, so is the circulating capital employed in the production of articles of consumption. Hence that portion of his commodity product which replaces his capital cannot resolve itself into constituents of value which form any revenue for him.

2) The circulating capital of every individual capitalist constitutes a part of society's circulating capital, the same as every individual fixed capital.

3) The circulating capital of society, while representing only the sum of the individual circulating capitals, has a character different from that of the circulating capital of every individual capitalist. The latter circulating capital can never form a part *of his own revenue*; however a portion of the first-named circulating capital (namely that consisting of consumable goods) may at the same time form a portion of the *revenue of society* or, as he has expressed it above, it must not necessarily reduce the net revenue of society by a portion of the annual product. Indeed, that which Adam Smith here calls circulating capital consists of the annually produced commodity capital, which is thrown into circulation annually by the capitalists producing articles of consumption. This entire annual commodity product of theirs consists of consumable goods and therefore forms the fund in which the net revenues of society (including wages) are realised or expended. Instead of choosing for his illustration the goods in a merchant's shop,

Adam Smith should have selected the masses of goods stored away in the warehouses of the industrial capitalists.

Now if Adam Smith had welded together the snatches of thought which forced themselves upon him at first in the study of the reproduction of that which he calls fixed, and now of that which he calls circulating capital, he would have arrived at the following result:

I. The annual product of society consists of two departments; one of them comprises the means of production, the other the articles of consumption. Each must be treated separately.

II. The aggregate value of that part of the annual product which consists of *means of production* is divided as follows: One portion of the value represents only the value of the means of production consumed in the fabrication of these means of production; it is but capital value re-appearing in a renewed form; another portion is equal to the value of the capital laid out in labour power, or equal to the sum of the wages paid by the capitalists in this sphere of production. Finally, a third portion of the value is the source of profits, including ground rent, of the industrial capitalists in this category.

The first constituent part, according to Adam Smith the reproduced portion of the fixed capital of all the individual capitals employed in this first department, is "totally excluded from making any part of the neat revenue", either of the individual capitalist or of society. It always functions as capital, never as revenue. To that extent the "fixed capital" of every individual capitalist is in no way different from the fixed capital of society. But the other portions of the value of the annual product of society consisting of means of production — portions of value which therefore exist in aliquot parts of this aggregate quantity of means of production — form indeed simultaneously *revenues for all agents engaged in this production*, wages for the labourers, profits and rents for the capitalists. But they form *capital*, not revenue, *for society*, although the annual product of society consists only of the sums of the products of the individual capitalists who belong to that society. By nature they are generally fit to function only as means of production, and even those which, if need be, might be able to function as articles of consumption are intended for service as raw or auxiliary materials of new production. But they serve as such — hence as capital — not in the hands of their producers, but in those of their users, namely:

III. The capitalists of the second department, the direct producers of *articles of consumption*. They replace for these capitalists the capital consumed in the production of articles of consumption (so far as this capital is not converted into labour power, and hence is not the sum of the wages of the labourers of this second department), while this consumed capital, which now exists in the form of articles of consumption in the hands of the capitalists producing them, in its turn —socially speaking— *forms the consumption fund in which the capitalists and labourers of the first department realise their revenue.*

If Adam Smith had continued his analysis to this point but little would have been lacking for the solution of the whole problem. He almost hit the nail on the head, for he had already observed that certain value parts of *one* kind (means of production) of the commodity capitals constituting the total annual product of society indeed form revenue for the individual labourers and capitalists engaged in their production, but do not form a constituent part of the revenue of society; while a value part of the *other* kind (articles of consumption), although representing capital value for its individual owners, the capitalists engaged in this sphere of investment, is only a part of the social revenue.

But this much is evident from the foregoing:

First: Although the social capital is only equal to the sum of the individual capitals, and for this reason the annual commodity product (or commodity capital) of society is equal to the sum of commodity products of these individual capitals; and although therefore the analysis of the value of the commodities into its component parts, valid for every individual commodity capital, must also be valid for the commodity capital of all society — and actually proves valid in the end — the form of appearance which these component parts assume in the aggregate social process of reproduction is *different*.

Second: Even on the basis of simple reproduction there takes place not merely a production of wages (variable capital) and surplus value, but direct production of new constant capital value, although the working day consists of only two parts, one in which the labourer replaces the variable capital, in fact producing an equivalent for the purchase of his labour power, and another in which he produces surplus value (profit, rent, etc.).

The daily labour which is expended in the reproduction of means of production — and whose value is composed of wages and surplus value — realises itself in new means of production which replace the constant part of capital laid out in the production of articles of consumption.

The main difficulties, the greater part of which has been solved in the preceding text, are not encountered in studying accumulation but simple reproduction. For this reason, Adam Smith (Book II) and Quesnay (*Tableau économique*) before him make simple reproduction their starting-point, whenever it is a question of the movement of the annual product of society and its reproduction through circulation.

2. ADAM SMITH RESOLVES EXCHANGE VALUE INTO V + S

Adam Smith's dogma that the price or "EXCHANGEABLE VALUE"[a] of any single commodity — and therefore of all commodities in the aggregate constituting the annual product of society (he rightly assumes capitalist production everywhere) — is made up of three "COMPONENT PARTS"[a] or "RESOLVES ITSELF INTO"[a] wages, profit, and rent, can be reduced to this: that the commodity value = v + s, i. e., is equal to the value of the advanced variable capital plus the surplus value. And we may undertake this reduction of profit and rent to a common unit called s with the express permission of Adam Smith, as shown by the following quotations, in which we at first leave aside all minor points, i. e., any apparent or real deviation from the dogma that commodity value consists exclusively of those elements which we call v + s.

In manufacture:

"The value which the workmen add to the materials ... resolves itself ... into two parts, of which the one pays their wages, the other the profits of their employer upon the whole stock of materials and wages which he advanced" (Book I, Ch. 6, p. 41).

"Though the manufacturer //the manufacturing worker// has his wages advanced to him by his master, he, in reality, costs him no expense, the value of those wages being generally restored" (RESERVED), "together with a profit, in the improved value of the subject upon which his labour is bestowed" (Book II, Ch. 3, p. 221).

That portion of the capital (STOCK) which is laid out

"in maintaining productive hands ... after having served in the function of a capital to him //the employer// "...constitutes a revenue to them" //the labourers// (Book II, Ch. 3, p. 223).

Adam Smith says explicitly in the chapter just quoted:

---

[a] In the original, these English words are given in parentheses after their German equivalent.

"The whole annual produce of the land and labour of every country ... NATURALLY [a] divides itself into two parts. One of them, and frequently the largest, is, in the first place, destined for replacing a capital, or for renewing the provisions, materials, and finished work, which had been withdrawn from a capital; the other for constituting a revenue either to the owner of this capital, as the *profit of his stock*; or to some other person, as the rent of his *land*" (p. 222).

Only one part of the capital, so Adam Smith has just informed us, forms at the same time a revenue for somebody, namely that which is invested in the purchase of productive hands. This part — the variable capital — first "serves in the function of a capital" in the hands of its employer and for him and then it "constitutes a revenue" for the productive labourer himself. The capitalist transforms a portion of his capital value into labour power and precisely thereby into variable capital; it is only due to this transformation that not alone this portion of capital but his entire capital functions as industrial capital. The labourer — the seller of labour power — receives its value in the form of wages. In his hands labour power is but a saleable commodity, a commodity by the sale of which he lives, which therefore is the sole source of his revenue; labour power functions as a variable capital only in the hands of its buyer, the capitalist, and the capitalist advances its purchase price only apparently, since its value has been previously supplied to him by the labourer.

After Adam Smith has thus shown us that the value of a product in manufacture = v + s (s standing for the profit of the capitalist), he tells us that in agriculture the labourers besides

"the reproduction of a value equal to their own consumption, or to the " //variable// "capital which employs them, together with its owners' profits..." — furthermore, "over and above the capital of the farmer and all its *profits* regularly occasion the reproduction of the *rent* of the landlord" (Book II, Ch. 5, p. 243).

The fact that the rent passes into the hands of the landlord is wholly immaterial for the question under consideration. Before it can pass into his hands, it must be in those of the farmer, i. e., of the industrial capitalist. It must form a component part of the value of the product before it becomes a revenue for anyone. Rent as well as profit are therefore, according to Adam Smith himself, but component parts of surplus value and these the productive labourer reproduces continually together with his own wages, i. e., with the value of the variable capital. Hence rent and profit are parts of the surplus value s,

---

[a] In the original, this English word is given in parentheses after its German equivalent.

and thus, with Adam Smith, the price of all commodities resolves itself into v + s.

The dogma that the price of all commodities (hence also of the annual commodity product) resolves itself into wages plus profit plus ground rent, assumes even in the intermittent esoteric constituents of Smith's work the form that the value of every commodity, hence also that of society's annual commodity product, = v + s, = the capital value laid out in labour power and continually reproduced by the labourers, plus the surplus value added by the labourers through their work.

This final result of Adam Smith reveals to us at the same time — see further down — the source of his one-sided analysis of the component parts into which the value of a commodity resolves itself. The circumstance that they are at the same time different sources of revenue for different classes engaged in production has nothing to do with the determination of the magnitude of each of these component parts and of the sum of their values.

All kinds of *quid pro quo*'s are jumbled together when Adam Smith says:

"Wages, profit, and rent, are the three original sources of all revenue as well as of all exchangeable value. All other revenue is ultimately derived from some one or other of these" (Book I, Ch. 6, p. 43).

1) All members of society not directly engaged in reproduction, with or without labour, can obtain their share of the annual commodity product — in other words, their articles of consumption — primarily only out of the hands of those classes to which the product first accrues — productive labourers, industrial capitalists, and landlords. To that extent their revenues are materially derived from wages (of the productive labourers), profit, and rent, and appear therefore as derivative vis-à-vis those primary revenues. But on the other hand the recipients of these revenues, derived in this sense, draw them by virtue of their social functions — as a king, priest, professor, prostitute, soldier, etc., and they may, therefore, regard these functions as the original sources of their revenue.

2) — and here Adam Smith's ridiculous blunder reaches its climax. After starting by correctly defining the component parts of the value of the commodities and the sum of the value product incorporated in them, and then demonstrating how these component parts form so

many different sources of revenue,[39] after thus deriving the revenues from the value, he proceeds in the opposite direction — and this remains the predominant conception with him — and turns the revenues from "COMPONENT PARTS"[a] into "*original sources* of all exchangeable value", thereby throwing the doors wide open to vulgar economy. (See our Roscher.[b])[52]

3. THE CONSTANT PART OF CAPITAL

Let us now see how Adam Smith tries to spirit the constant part of the capital value away from the commodity value.

"In the price of corn, for example, one part pays the rent of the landlord."

The origin of this constituent of value has no more to do with the circumstance that it is paid to the landlord and forms a revenue for him in the shape of rent than the origin of the other constituents of value has to do with the fact that as profit and wages they form sources of revenue.

"Another [part] pays the wages or maintenance of the labourers" //"and labouring cattle!" he adds// "employed in producing it, and the third pays the profit of the farmer. These three parts seem" //they seem indeed// "either immediately or ultimately to make up the whole price of corn."[40]

This entire price, i. e., the determination of its magnitude, is absolutely independent of its distribution among three kinds of people.

"A fourth part, it may perhaps be thought, is necessary for replacing the stock of the farmer, or for compensating the wear and tear of his labouring cattle, and other in-

---

[39] I reproduce this sentence verbatim from the manuscript, although it seems to contradict, in its present context, both what precedes and immediately follows. This apparent contradiction is resolved further down in No. 4: Capital and Revenue in Adam Smith.— *F. E.*

[40] We ignore the fact that Adam Smith was here particularly unfortunate in the choice of his example. The value of the corn resolves itself into wages, profit, and rent only because the food consumed by the labouring cattle is depicted as wages of the labouring cattle, and the labouring cattle as wage labourers, so that the wage labourer on his part is also depicted as labouring cattle. //Added from Manuscript II.//

---

[a] In the original, these English words are given in parentheses after their German equivalent. - [b] W. Roscher, *System der Volkswirtschaft*. Band I: *Die Grundlagen der Nationalökonomie*. Dritte, vermehrte und verbesserte Auflage, Stuttgart und Augsburg, 1858.

struments of husbandry. But it must be considered that the price of any instrument of husbandry, such as a labouring horse, is itself made up of the same three parts: the rent of the land upon which he is reared, the labour of tending and rearing him, and the profits of the farmer who advances both the rent of this land, and the wages of this labour. Though the price of the corn, therefore, may pay the price as well as the maintenance of the horse, the whole price still resolves itself either immediately or ultimately into the same three parts of rent, labour" //he means wages//, "and profit" (Book I, Ch. 6, p. 42).

This is verbatim all that Adam Smith has to say in support of his astonishing doctrine. His proof consists simply in the repetition of the same assertion. He admits, for instance, that the price of corn does not only consist of v + s, but also of the price of the means of production consumed in the production of corn, hence of a capital value not invested in labour power by the farmer. But, he says, the prices of all these means of production resolve themselves into v + s, the same as the price of corn. He forgets, however, to add: and, moreover, into the prices of the means of production consumed in their own creation. He refers us from one branch of production to another, and from that to a third. The contention that the entire price of commodities resolves itself "immediately" or "ULTIMATELY" [a] into v + s would not be a hollow subterfuge only if he were able to demonstrate that the commodities whose price resolves itself immediately into c (price of consumed means of production) + v + s, are ultimately compensated by commodities which completely replace those "consumed means of production", and which are themselves produced by the mere outlay of variable capital, i. e., by a mere investment of capital in labour power. The price of these last commodity products would then be immediately v + s. Consequently the price of the former, c + v + s, where c stands for the constant part of capital, would also be ultimately resolvable into v + s. Adam Smith himself did not believe that he had furnished such a proof by his example of the collectors of Scotch PEBBLES[b], who, according to him, 1) do not generate surplus value of any description, but produce only their own wages, and 2) do not employ any means of production (they do, however, employ them, such as baskets, sacks, and other containers for carrying the pebbles).

We have already seen above that Adam Smith himself later on overthrows his own theory, without however being conscious of his contradictions. But their source is to be found precisely in his scien-

---

[a] In the original, this English word is given in parentheses after its German equivalent. - [b] See this volume, p. 360, footnote [38]).

tific premises. The capital converted into labour produces a greater value than its own. How? Says Adam Smith: by the labourers imparting during the process of production to the things on which they work a value which forms not only an equivalent for their own purchase price, but also a surplus value (profit and rent) apportioned not to them but to their employers. But that is all they accomplish, and all they can accomplish. And what is true of the industrial labour of one day is true of the labour set in motion by the entire capitalist class during one year. Hence the aggregate mass of the annual value produced by society can resolve itself only into v + s, into an equivalent by which the labourers replace the capital value expended for the purchase of their own labour power, and into an additional value which they must deliver over and above this to their employers. But these two elements of commodity value form at the same time sources of revenue for the various classes engaged in reproduction: the first is the source of wages, the revenue of the labourers; the second that of surplus value, a portion of which is retained by the industrial capitalist in the form of profit, while another is given up by him as rent, the revenue of the landlord. Where, then, should yet another part of value come from, when the annual value product contains no other elements than v + s? We are proceeding here from simple reproduction. Since the entire quantity of annual labour resolves itself into labour needed for the reproduction of the capital value laid out in labour power, and into labour needed for the creation of surplus value, where should the labour for the production of a capital value not laid out in labour power come from?

The case is as follows:

1) Adam Smith determines the value of a commodity by the amount of labour which the wage labourer ADDS [a] to the subject of labour. He says literally: "to the materials", since he is dealing with manufacture, which itself is working up products of labour. But this does not alter the matter. The value which the labourer adds to a thing (and this "ADDS" is the expression of Adam Smith) is entirely independent of whether or not this object to which value is added had itself any value *before* this addition. The labourer therefore produces a value in the form of a commodity. This, according to Adam Smith, is partly an equivalent for his wages, and this part, then, is determined by the magnitude of value of his wages; depending on that mag-

[a] In the original, this English word is given in parentheses after its German equivalent.

nitude he has to add labour in order to produce or reproduce a value equal to that of his wages. On the other hand the labourer adds more labour over and above the limit so drawn, and this creates surplus value for the capitalist employing him. Whether this surplus value remains entirely in the hands of the capitalist or parts of it are yielded by him to third persons, does not in the least alter either the qualitative (that it is at all surplus value) or the quantitative (magnitude) determination of the surplus value added by the wage labourer. It is value the same as any other portion of the value of the product, but it differs in that the labourer has not received any equivalent for it, nor will receive any later on, in that, on the contrary, this value is appropriated by the capitalist without any equivalent. The total value of a commodity is determined by the quantity of labour expended by the labourer in its production; one portion of this total value is determined by the fact that it is equal to the value of the wages, i. e., an equivalent for them. The second part, the surplus value, is, therefore, necessarily likewise determined as equal to the total value of the product minus that part of its value which is equivalent to the wages; hence equal to the excess of the value produced in the making of the commodity over that part of the value contained in it which is an equivalent for his wages.

2) That which is true of a commodity produced in some individual industrial establishment by any individual labourer is true of the annual product of all branches of business as a whole. That which is true of the day's work of some individual productive labourer is true of the year's work set in motion by the entire class of productive labourers. It "fixes" (Adam Smith's expression) in the annual product a total value determined by the quantity of the annual labour expended, and this total value resolves itself into one portion determined by that part of the annual labour wherewith the working class creates an equivalent of its annual wages, in fact, these wages themselves; and into another portion determined by the additional annual labour by which the labourer creates surplus value for the capitalist class. The annual value product contained in the annual product consists therefore of but two elements: namely, the equivalent of the annual wages received by the working class, and the surplus value annually provided for the capitalist class. Now, the annual wages are the revenue of the working class, and the annual quantity of surplus value the revenue of the capitalist class; hence both of them represent the relative shares in the annual fund for consumption (this view is correct when

describing simple reproduction) and are realised in it. There is, then, no room left anywhere for the constant capital value, for the reproduction of the capital functioning in the form of means of production. And Adam Smith states explicitly in the introduction to his work that all portions of the value of commodities which serve as revenue coincide with the annual product of labour intended for the social fund for consumption:

"To explain in what has consisted the revenue of the great body of the people, or what has been the nature of those funds, which... have SUPPLIED [a] their annual consumption, is the object of these first Four Books" (p. 12).

And in the very first sentence of the introduction we read:

"The annual labour of every nation is the fund, which originally supplies it with all the necessaries and conveniences of life which it annually consumes, [and] which consists always either in the immediate produce of that labour, or in what is purchased with that produce from other nations" (p. 11).

Now Adam Smith's first mistake consists in equating the *value* of the annual *product* to the *newly produced annual value*. The latter is *only* the product of labour of the past year; the former includes, besides, all elements of value consumed in the making of the annual product, but which *were produced in the preceding and partly even earlier years*: means of production whose value merely *re-appears* — which, as far as their value is concerned, have been neither produced nor reproduced by the labour expended in the past year. By this confusion Adam Smith spirits away the constant portion of the value of the annual product. This confusion rests on another error in his fundamental conception: he does not distinguish the two-fold nature of labour itself: of labour which creates value by expending labour power, and of labour as concrete, useful work which creates articles of use (use values). The total quantity of the commodities fabricated annually, in other words, the *total annual product* is the product of the *useful* labour active during the past year; it is only due to the fact that socially employed labour was spent in a ramified system of useful kinds of labour that all these commodities exist; it is due to this fact alone that the value of the means of production consumed in the production of commodities and re-appearing in a new natural form is preserved in their total value. The total *annual product*, then, is the result of the *useful* labour expended during the year; but only a part of the *value* of the

[a] In the original, this English word is given in parentheses after its German equivalent.

annual *product* has been created during the year; this part is the annual *value product*, in which the quantity of labour set in motion during the year is represented.

Hence, if Adam Smith says in the passage just cited:

"The annual labour of every nation is the fund which originally supplies it with all the necessaries and conveniences of life which it annually consumes, etc.",

he takes the one-sided standpoint of solely useful labour, which has indeed given all these means of subsistence their consumable form. But he forgets that this was impossible without the assistance of instruments and subjects of labour supplied by former years, and that, therefore, the "annual labour", while it created value, did not create all the value of the products fabricated by it; that the value newly produced is smaller than the value of the product.

While we cannot reproach Adam Smith for going in this analysis no farther than all his successors (although a step in the right direction could already be discerned among the Physiocrats), he subsequently gets lost in a chaos and this mainly because his "esoteric" conception of the value of commodities in general is constantly contravened by exoteric conceptions, which on the whole prevail with him, and yet his scientific instinct permits the esoteric standpoint to re-appear from time to time.

4. CAPITAL AND REVENUE IN ADAM SMITH

That portion of the value of every commodity (and therefore also of the annual product) which is but an equivalent of the wages is equal to the capital advanced by the capitalist for labour power, i. e., is equal to the variable portion of the total capital advanced. The capitalist recovers this portion of the capital value through a portion of the newly produced value of the commodities supplied by the wage labourers. Whether the variable capital is advanced in the sense that the capitalist pays the labourer in money for his share in a product which is not yet ready for sale or which, though ready, has not yet been sold by the capitalist, or whether he pays him with money already obtained by the sale of commodities previously supplied by the labourer, or whether he has drawn this money in advance by means of credit — in all these cases the capitalist expends variable capital, which passes into the hands of the labourers in the form of money, and on the other hand he possesses the equivalent of this capital value in that portion of the value of his commodities in which the labourer has produced anew his share of its total value, in other words, in which he has produced the value of his own wages. Instead of giving him this portion of the value in the bodily form of his own product, the capitalist pays it to him in money. For the capitalist the variable portion of his advanced capital value now exists in the form of commodities, while the labourer has received the equivalent for his sold labour power in the form of money.

Now while that portion of the capital advanced by the capitalist, which has been converted by the purchase of labour power into variable capital, functions in the process of production itself as operative labour power and by the expenditure of this power is produced anew as a new value, in the form of commodities, i. e., is reproduced — hence a reproduction, or new production, of advanced capital value — the labourer spends the value, or price, of his sold labour power on means of subsistence, on means for the reproduction of his labour power. An amount of money equal to the variable capital forms his income, hence his revenue, which lasts only so long as he can sell his labour power to the capitalist.

The commodity of the wage labourer — his own labour power — serves as a commodity only to the extent that it is incorporated in the capital of the capitalist, acts as capital; on the other hand the capital expended by the capitalist as money capital in the purchase of labour power functions as a revenue in the hands of the seller of labour power, the wage labourer.

Various processes of circulation and production intermingle here, which Adam Smith does not distinguish.

First: Acts pertaining to the process of *circulation*. The labourer sells his commodity — labour power — to the capitalist; the money with which the capitalist buys it is from his point of view money invested for the production of surplus value, hence money capital; it is not spent but advanced. (This is the real meaning of "advance" — the *avance* of the Physiocrats — no matter where the capitalist gets the money. Every value which the capitalist pays out for the purposes of the production process is advanced from his point of view, regardless of whether this takes place before or *post festum*; it is advanced to the process of production itself.) The same takes place here as in every other sale of commodities: The seller gives away a use value (in this case his labour power) and receives its value (realises its price) in money; the buyer gives away his money and receives in return the commodity itself—in this case labour power.

Second: In the process of *production* the purchased labour power now forms a part of the functioning capital, and the labourer himself serves here merely as a special natural form of this capital, distinguished from its elements existing in the natural form of means of production. During the process, by expending his labour power, the labourer adds value to the means of production which he converts into products equal to the value of his labour power (exclusive of surplus value); he therefore reproduces for the capitalist in the form of commodities that portion of his capital which has been, or has to be, advanced by him for wages, produces for him an equivalent of the latter; hence he produces for the capitalist that capital which the latter can "advance" once more for the purchase of labour power.

Third: In the sale of a commodity one portion of its selling price replaces the variable capital advanced by the capitalist, whereby on the one hand he is enabled anew to buy labour power, and the labourer on the other hand to sell it anew.

In all purchases and sales of commodities—so far as only these transactions are under discussion—it is quite immaterial what becomes of the proceeds the seller receives for his commodities, and what becomes of the bought articles of use in the hands of the buyer. Hence, so far as the mere process of circulation is concerned, it is quite immaterial that the labour power bought by the capitalist reproduces capital value for him, and that on the other hand the money received by the labourer as the purchase price of his labour power constitutes his revenue. The magnitude of value of the labourer's article of commerce, his labour power, is not affected either by its forming "revenue" for him or by the fact that the use of this article of commerce by the buyer reproduces capital value for this buyer.

Since the value of the labour power—i. e., the adequate selling price of this commodity—is determined by the quantity of labour required for its reproduction, and this quantity of labour itself is here determined by that needed for the production of the necessary means of subsistence of the labourer, hence for the maintenance of his existence, the wages become the revenue on which the labourer has to live.

It is entirely wrong, when Adam Smith says (p. 223):

"*That portion of the stock* which is laid out in maintaining productive hands ... after having served in the function of a capital to him" //the capitalist// "...constitutes a revenue to them" //the labourers//.

The *money* with which the capitalist pays for the labour power purchased by him "serves in the function of a capital to him", since he thereby incorporates labour power in the material constituents of his capital and thus enables his capital to function altogether as productive capital. We must make this distinction: The labour power is a *commodity*, not capital, in the hands of the labourer, and it constitutes for him a revenue so long as he can continuously repeat its sale; it functions as capital *after* its sale, in the hands of the capitalist, during the process of production itself. That which here serves twice is labour power: as a commodity which is sold at its value, in the hands of the labourer; as a power-producing value and use value, in the hands of the capitalist who has bought it. But the labourer does not receive the money from the capitalist until after he has given him the use of his labour power, after it has already been realised in the value of the product of labour. The capitalist possesses this value before he pays for it. Hence it is not the money which functions twice: first, as the money form of the variable capital, and then as wages. On the contrary it is labour power which has functioned twice: first, as a *commodity* in the sale of labour power (in stipulating the amount of wages to be paid, money acts merely as an ideal measure of value and need not even be in the hands of the capitalist); secondly, in the process of production, in which it functions as *capital*, i. e., as an element, in the hands of the capitalist, creating use value and value. Labour power already supplied, in the form of commodities, the equivalent which is to be paid to the labourer, before it is paid by the capitalist to the labourer in money form. Hence the labourer himself creates the fund out of which the capitalist pays him. But this is not all.

The money which the labourer receives is spent by him in order to maintain his labour power, or — viewing the capitalist class and the working class in their totality — in order to preserve for the capitalist the instrument by means of which alone he can remain a capitalist.

Thus the continuous purchase and sale of labour power perpetuates on the one hand labour power as an element of capital, by virtue of which the latter appears as the creator of commodities, articles of use having value, by virtue of which, furthermore, that portion of capital which buys labour power is continually restored by labour power's own product, and consequently the labourer himself constantly creates the fund of capital out of which he is paid. On the other hand the constant sale of labour power becomes the source, ever renewing itself, of the maintenance of the labourer, and hence his labour power appears as that faculty through which he secures the revenue by which he lives. Revenue in this case signifies nothing else than an appropriation of values effected by ever repeated sales of a commodity (labour power), these values serving only for the continual reproduction of the commodity to be sold. And to this extent Smith is right when he says that the portion of the value of the product created by the labourer himself, for which the capitalist pays him an equivalent in the form of wages, becomes the source of revenue for the labourer. But this does not alter the nature or magnitude of this portion of the value of the commodity any more than the value of the means of production is changed by the fact that they function as capital values, or the nature and length of a straight line are changed by the fact that it serves as the base of some triangle or as the diameter of some ellipse. The value of labour power remains quite as independently definite as that of those means of production. This portion of the value of a commodity neither *consists of* revenue as an independent factor constituting this value part nor does it *resolve itself* into revenue. While this new value constantly reproduced by the labourer constitutes a source of revenue for him, his revenue conversely is not a constituent of the new value produced by him. The magnitude of the share paid to him of the new value created by him determines the value magnitude of his revenue, not vice versa. The fact that this part of the newly created value forms a revenue for him, indicates merely what becomes of it, shows the character of its application, and has no more to do with its formation than with that of any other value. If my receipts are ten talers a week that changes nothing in the *nature* of the value of the ten talers, nor in the *magnitude* of their value. As in the case of every other commodity so in that of labour power its value is determined by the amount of labour necessary for its reproduction; that the amount of this labour is determined by the value of the labourer's necessary means of subsistence, hence is equal to the labour required for the reproduction of the very conditions of his life — that is peculiar for this commodity (labour power), but no more peculiar than the fact that the value of labouring cattle is determined by the value of the means of subsistence necessary for its maintenance, i. e., by the amount of human labour necessary to produce these means of subsistence.

But it is this category of "revenue" which is to blame for all the harmful confusion in Adam Smith. The various kinds of revenue form with him the "COMPONENT PARTS"[a] of the annually produced, newly created commodity value, while, vice versa, the two parts into which this commodity value resolves itself *for the capitalist* — the equivalent of his variable capital advanced in the form of money when purchasing labour, and the other portion of the value, the surplus value, which likewise belongs to him but did not cost him anything — form sources of revenue. The equivalent of the variable capital is advanced again for labour power and to that extent forms a revenue for the labourer in the shape of wages; since the other portion, the surplus value, does not serve to replace any advance of capital for the capitalist, it may be spent by him in articles of consumption (both necessities and luxuries) or consumed as revenue instead of forming capital value of any description. Commodity value itself is the preliminary condition of this revenue, and its component parts differ, from the point of view of the capitalist, only to the extent that they constitute either an equivalent *for* or an excess *over* the variable capital value advanced by him. Both of them consist of nothing but labour power expended during the production of commodities, rendered fluent in labour. They consist of outlay, not income or revenue — of outlay of labour.

In accordance with the *quid pro quo*, by which the revenue becomes the source of commodity value instead of the commodity value being the source of revenue, the value of commodities now has the appearance of being "composed" of the various kinds of revenue; these revenues are determined independently of one another, and the total value of commodities is determined by the addition of the values of these revenues. But now the question is how to determine the value of each of these revenues which are supposed to form commodity value. In the case of wages it can be done, for wages represent the value of their commodity, labour power, and this value is determinable (the same as that of all other commodities) by the labour required for the reproduction of this commodity. But surplus value, or, as Adam Smith has it, its two forms, profit and rent, how are they determined? Here Adam Smith has but empty phrases to offer. At one time he represents wages and surplus value (or wages and profit) as component parts of the value, or price, of commodities; at another, and almost

---

[a] After these English words Marx gives their German equivalent.

in the same breath, as parts into which the price of commodities "RE-SOLVES ITSELF"[a]; but this means on the contrary that the commodity value is the thing given first and that different parts of this given value fall in the form of different revenues to the share of different persons engaged in the production process. This is by no means identical with the notion that value is composed of these three "component parts". If I determine the lengths of three different straight lines independently, and then form out of these three lines as "component parts" a fourth straight line equal to their sum, it is by no means the same procedure as when I have some given straight line before me and for some purpose divide it, "resolve" it, so to say, into three different parts. In the first case, the length of the line changes throughout with the lengths of the three lines whose sum it is; in the second case, the lengths of the three parts of the line are from the outset limited by the fact that they are parts of a line of the given length.

As a matter of fact, if we adhere to that part of Smith's exposition which is correct, namely, that *the value newly created by the annual labour* and contained in the annual social commodity product (the same as in every individual commodity, or every daily, weekly, etc., product) is equal to the value of the variable capital advanced (i. e., to the value part intended to purchase new labour power) plus the surplus value which the capitalist can realise in means of his individual consumption — simple reproduction being assumed and other circumstances remaining the same; if we furthermore keep in mind that Adam Smith lumps together labour, so far as it creates value and is an expenditure of labour power, and labour, so far as it creates use value, i. e., is expended in a useful, appropriate manner — then the entire conception amounts to this: The value of every commodity is the product of labour; hence this is also true of the value of the product of the annual labour or of the value of society's annual commodity product. But since all labour resolves itself 1) into necessary labour time, in which the labourer reproduces merely an equivalent for the capital advanced in the purchase of his labour power, and 2) into surplus labour, by which he supplies the capitalist with a value for which the latter does not give any equivalent, hence surplus value, it follows that all commodity value can resolve itself only into these two component parts, so that ultimately it forms a revenue for the work-

---

[a] In the original, these English words are given in parentheses after their German equivalent.

ing class in the form of wages, and for the capitalist class in the form of surplus value. As for the constant capital value, i. e., the value of the means of production consumed in the creation of the annual product, it cannot be explained how this value gets into that of the new product (except for the phrase that the capitalist charges the buyer with it in the sale of his goods), but ULTIMATELY,[a] since the means of production are themselves products of labour, this portion of value can, in turn, consist only of an equivalent of the variable capital and of surplus value, of a product of necessary labour and of surplus labour. The fact that the values of these means of production function in the hands of their employers as capital values does not prevent them from having "originally", in the hands of others if we go to the bottom of the matter — even though at some previous time — resolved themselves into the same two portions of value, hence into two different sources of revenue.

One point herein is correct: that the matter presents itself differently in the movement of social capital, i. e., of the totality of individual capitals, from the way it presents itself for each individual capital considered separately, hence from the standpoint of each individual capitalist. For the latter the value of commodities resolves itself into 1) a constant element (a fourth one, as Adam Smith says), and 2) the sum of wages and surplus value, or wages, profit, and ground rent. But from the point of view of society the fourth element of Adam Smith, the constant capital value, disappears.

5. RECAPITULATION

The absurd formula that the three revenues, wages, profit, and rent, form the three "component parts" of the value of commodities originates with Adam Smith from the more plausible idea that the value of commodities "RESOLVES ITSELF"[b] into these three component parts. This is likewise incorrect, even granted that the value of commodities is divisible only into an equivalent of the consumed labour power and the surplus value created by it. But the mistake rests here too on a deeper, a true foundation. Capitalist production is based on the fact that the productive labourer sells his own labour power, as

---

[a] In the original, this English word is given after its German equivalent. - [b] In the original, these English words are given before their German equivalent.

his commodity, to the capitalist, in whose hands it then functions merely as an element of his productive capital. This transaction, which pertains to circulation — the sale and purchase of labour power — not only inaugurates the process of production, but also determines implicitly its specific character. The production of a use value, and even that of a commodity (for this can be carried on also by independent productive labourers), is here only a means of producing absolute and relative surplus value for a capitalist. For this reason we have seen in the analysis of the process of production that the production of absolute and relative surplus value determines 1) the duration of the daily labour process and 2) the entire social and technical configuration of the capitalist process of production. Within this process there is realised the distinction between the mere conservation of value (of the constant capital value), the actual reproduction of advanced value (equivalent of labour power), and the production of surplus value, i. e., of value for which the capitalist has neither advanced an equivalent previously nor will advance one *post festum*.

The appropriation of surplus value — a value in excess of the equivalent of the value advanced by the capitalist — although inaugurated by the purchase and sale of labour power, is an act performed within the process of production itself, and forms an essential element of it.

The introductory act, which constitutes an act of circulation — the purchase and sale of labour power — itself rests on a distribution of the *elements* of production which preceded and presupposed the distribution of the social *products*, namely on the separation of labour power as a commodity of the labourer from the means of production as the property of non-labourers.

However this appropriation of surplus value, or this separation of the production of value into a reproduction of advanced value and a production of new value (surplus value) which does not replace any equivalent, does not alter in any way the substance of value itself or the nature of the production of value. The substance of value is and remains nothing but expended labour power — labour independent of the specific, useful character of this labour — and the production of value is nothing but the process of this expenditure. A serf for instance expends his labour power for six days, labours for six days, and the fact of this expenditure as such is not altered by the circumstance that he may be working three days for himself, on his own field, and three days for his lord, on the field of the latter. Both his voluntary labour for himself and his forced labour for his lord are equally labour; so far as this labour is considered with reference to the values, or to the useful articles created by it, there is no difference in his six days of labour. The difference refers merely to the different conditions by which the expenditure of his labour power during both halves of his labour time of six days is called forth. The same applies to the necessary and surplus labour of the wage labourer.

The process of production expires in the commodity. The fact that labour power was expended in its fabrication now appears as a material property of the commodity, as the property of possessing value. The magnitude of this value is measured by the amount of labour expended; the value of a commodity resolves itself into nothing else besides and is not composed of anything else. If I have drawn a straight line of definite length, I have, to start with, "produced" a straight line (true, only symbolically, as I know beforehand) by resort to the art of drawing, which is practised in accordance with certain rules (laws) independent of myself. If I divide this line into three sections (which may correspond to a certain problem), every one of these sections remains a straight line, and the entire line, whose sections they are, does not resolve itself by this division into anything different from a straight line, for instance into some kind of curve. Neither can I divide a line of a given length in such a way that the sum of its parts is greater than the undivided line itself; hence the length of the undivided line is not determined by any arbitrarily fixed lengths of its parts. Vice versa, the relative lengths of these parts are limited from the outset by the size of the line whose parts they are.

In this a commodity produced by a capitalist does not differ in any way from that produced by an independent labourer or by communities of working people or by slaves. But in the present case the entire product of labour, as well as its entire value, belongs to the capitalist. Like every other producer he has to convert his commodity by sale into money before he can manipulate it further; he must convert it into the form of the universal equivalent.

Let us examine the commodity product before it is converted into money. It belongs wholly to the capitalist. On the other hand as a useful product of labour, a use value, it is entirely the product of a past labour process. Not so its value. One portion of this value is but the value of the means of production expended in the production of the commodity and re-appearing in a new form. This value has not been produced during the process of production of this commodity, for the means of production possessed this value before the process of production, independently of it; they entered into this process as the vehicles of this value; it is only its form of appearance that has been renewed and altered. This portion of the value of the commodity constitutes for the capitalist an equivalent of the portion of his constant capital value advanced and consumed in the production of the commodity. It existed previously in the form of means of production; it exists now as a component part of the value of the newly produced commodity. As soon as this commodity has been turned into money, the value now existing in the form of money must be reconverted into means of production, into its original form determined by the process of production and its function in it. Nothing is altered in the character of the value of a commodity by the function of this value as capital.

A second portion of the value of a commodity is the value of the labour power which the wage labourer sells to the capitalist. It is determined, the same as the value of the means of production, independently of the process of production into which labour power is to enter, and it is fixed in an act of circulation, the purchase and sale of labour power, before the latter enters the process of production. By means of his function — the expenditure of his labour power — the wage labourer produces a commodity value equal to the value which the capitalist has to pay him for the use of his labour power. He gives this value to the capitalist in the form of a commodity and is paid for it by him in money. That this portion of the commodity value is for the capitalist but an equivalent for the variable capital which he has to advance in wages does not alter in any way the fact that it is a commodity value newly created during the process of production and consisting of nothing but what surplus value consists of, namely, past expenditure of labour power. Nor is this truth affected by the fact that the value of the labour power paid by the capitalist to the labourer in the form of wages assumes the form of a revenue for the labourer, and that not only labour power is continually reproduced thereby but also the class of wage labourers as such, and thus the basis of the entire capitalist production.

However, the sum of these two portions of value does not comprise the whole of commodity value. There remains an excess over both of them — the surplus value. This, like the portion of value which replaces the variable capital advanced in wages, is a value newly created by the labourer during the process of production — congealed labour. But it does not cost the owner of the entire product, the capitalist,

anything. This circumstance actually permits the capitalist to consume the surplus value entirely as revenue, unless he has to surrender
parts of it to other participants — such as ground rent to the landlord,
in which case such portions constitute a revenue of such third persons.
This same circumstance was the compelling motive that induced our
capitalist to engage at all in the manufacture of commodities. But neither his original benevolent intention of snatching surplus value, nor
its subsequent expenditure as revenue by him or others affects the surplus value as such. They do not impair the fact that it is congealed
unpaid labour, nor the magnitude of this surplus value, which is determined by entirely different conditions.

However, if Adam Smith wanted to occupy himself, as he did, with
the role of the various parts of this value in the total process of reproduction, even while he was investigating the value of commodities, it
would be evident that while some particular parts function as revenue, others function just as continually as capital — and consequently, according to his logic, should have been designated as constituent parts of the commodity value, or parts into which this value
resolves itself.

Adam Smith identifies the production of commodities in general
with capitalist commodity production; the means of production are to
him from the outset "capital", labour is from the outset wage labour,
and therefore

"the number of useful and productive labourers ... is everywhere in proportion TO
THE QUANTITY OF CAPITAL STOCK WHICH IS EMPLOYED IN SETTING THEM TO WORK [a]"
(Introduction, p. 12).

In short, the various factors of the labour process — both objective
and personal — appear from the first with the masks characteristic of
the period of capitalist production. The analysis of the value of commodities therefore coincides directly with the consideration of the extent to which this value is on the one hand a mere equivalent of capital laid out, and on the other, to what extent it forms "free" value,
value not replacing any advanced capital value, or surplus value.
Compared from this point of view, parts of commodity value thus
transform themselves imperceptibly into its independent "component
parts", and finally into the "sources of all value". A further conclu-

---

[a] In the original, these English words are given in parentheses after their German equivalent.

sion is that commodity value is composed of, or "resolves itself" into, revenues of various kinds, so that the revenues do not consist of commodity values but the commodity value consists of "revenues". As little, however, as the nature of a commodity value as such, or of money as such, is changed through their functioning as capital value, just so little is the nature of a commodity value changed on account of its functioning later as a revenue for some particular person. The commodity with which Adam Smith has to deal is from the outset commodity capital (which comprises surplus value in addition to the capital value consumed in the production of the commodity); it is therefore a commodity produced capitalistically, the result of the capitalist process of production. It would have been necessary, then, to analyse first this process, and also the process of self-expansion and of the formation of value, which it includes. Since this process is in its turn premised by the circulation of commodities, its description requires also a preliminary and independent analysis of the commodity. However, even where Adam Smith at times hits "esoterically" upon the correct thing he always takes into consideration the formation of value only as incidental to the analysis of commodities, i. e., to the analysis of commodity capital.

III. LATER ECONOMISTS [41]

Ricardo reproduces the theory of Adam Smith almost verbatim:

> "It must be understood that all the productions of a country are consumed; but it makes the greatest difference imaginable whether they are consumed by those who reproduce, or by those who do not reproduce another value. When we say that revenue is saved, and added to capital, what we mean is, that the portion of revenue, so said to be added to the capital, is consumed by productive instead of unproductive labourers" (*Principles*, p. 163).

In fact Ricardo fully accepted the theory of Adam Smith concerning the resolution of the price of commodities into wages and surplus value (or variable capital and surplus value). The points of dispute with him are 1) the component parts of the surplus value: he eliminates ground rent as an essential element of it; 2) Ricardo *splits* the price of the commodity into these component parts. The magnitude of value is, then, the *prius*. The sum of component parts is assumed as

---

[41] From here to the end of the chapter, a supplement from Manuscript II.

a given magnitude, it is the starting-point, while Adam Smith frequently acts to the contrary, against his own better judgement, by *post festum* deducing the magnitude of value of the commodity through the sum of the component parts.

Ramsay makes the following remark against Ricardo:

"He seems always to consider the whole produce as divided between wages and profits, forgetting the part necessary for replacing fixed capital" (*An Essay on the Distribution of Wealth*, Edinburgh, 1836, p. 174).

By fixed capital Ramsay means the same thing that I mean by constant capital:

"Fixed capital exists in a form in which, though assisting to raise the future commodity, it does not maintain labourers" (p 59).

Adam Smith opposed the necessary conclusion of his resolution of the value of commodities, and therefore also of the value of the social annual product into wages and surplus value and therefore into mere revenue — the conclusion that in this event the entire annual product might be consumed. It is never the original thinkers that draw the absurd conclusions. They leave that to the Says and MacCullochs.

Say, indeed, settles the matter easy enough. That which is an advance of capital for one, is or was a revenue and net product for another. The difference between the gross and the net product is purely subjective, and

"thus the total value of all products has been distributed in society as revenue" (Say, *Traité d'Economie Politique*, 1817, II, p. 64). "The total value of every product is composed of the profits of the landowners, the capitalists, and those who ply industrial trades" //wages figure here as *profits des industrieux!*//, "who have contributed towards its production. This makes the revenue of society equal to the *gross value produced*, not equal to the net product of the soil, as was believed by the sect of the economists" //the Physiocrats// (p. 63).

Among others, Proudhon has appropriated this discovery of Say.

Storch, who likewise accepts Adam Smith's doctrine in principle, finds however that Say's practical application of it does not hold water.

"If it is admitted that the revenue of a nation is equal to its gross product, i. e., that no capital" //it should say: no constant capital// "is to be deducted, then it must also be admitted that this nation may consume unproductively the entire value of its annual product without the least detriment to its future revenue.... The products which represent the" //constant// "capital of a nation are not consumable" (Storch, *Considérations sur la nature du revenu national*, Paris, 1824, pp. 147, 150). [53]

However, Storch forgot to tell us how the existence of this constant portion of capital harmonises with the Smithian analysis of prices accepted by him, according to which the value of commodities contains only wages and surplus value, but no part of any constant capital. He realises only through Say that this analysis of prices leads to absurd results, and his own last word on the subject is

"that it is impossible to resolve the necessary price into its simplest elements" (*Cours d'Économie Politique*, Pétersbourg, 1815, II, p. 141).

Sismondi, who occupies himself particularly with the relation of capital to revenue, and in actual fact makes the peculiar formulation of this relation the *differentia specifica* of his *Nouveaux Principes*, did not say *one* scientific word, did not contribute one iota to the clarification of the problem.

Barton, Ramsay, and Cherbuliez [54] attempt to go beyond Smith's formulation. They founder because they pose the problem one-sidedly from the outset by failing to make clear the distinction between constant and variable capital value and between fixed and circulating capital.

John Stuart Mill likewise reproduces, with his usual pomposity, the doctrine handed down by Adam Smith to his followers.

As a result, the Smithian confusion of thought persists to this hour, and his dogma is one of the orthodox articles of faith of political economy.

Chapter XX

SIMPLE REPRODUCTION

I. THE FORMULATION OF THE QUESTION

If we study [42] the annual function of social capital—hence of the total capital of which the individual capitals form only fractional parts, whose movement is their individual movement and simultaneously an integrating link in the movement of the total capital—and

[42] From Manuscript II.

its results, i. e., if we study the commodity product furnished by society during the year, then it must become apparent how the process
of reproduction of the social capital takes place, what characteristics
distinguish this process of reproduction from the process of reproduction of an individual capital, and what characteristics are common to
both. The annual product includes those portions of the social product which replace capital, namely social reproduction, as well as
those which go to the consumption fund, those which are consumed
by labourers and capitalists, hence both productive and individual
consumption. It comprises also the reproduction (i. e., maintenance)
of the capitalist class and the working class, and thus the reproduction of the capitalist character of the entire process of production.

It is evidently the circulation formula $C' - \begin{cases} M-C...P...C' \\ m-c \end{cases}$

which we have to analyse, and consumption necessarily plays a role
in it; for the point of departure, $C' = C + c$, the commodity capital,
embraces both the constant and variable capital value, and the surplus value. Its movement therefore includes both individual and productive consumption. In the circuits $M - C ... P ... C' - M'$ and
$P ... C' - M' - C ... P$, the movement of the *capital* is the starting and fin-
ishing point. And of course this includes consumption, for the commodity, the product, must be sold. When this has assumedly been
done it is immaterial for the movement of the individual capital what
becomes of this commodity subsequently. On the other hand in the
movement of $C' ... C'$ the conditions of social reproduction are discerni-
ble precisely from the fact that it must be shown what becomes of
every portion of value of this total product, C'. In this case the total
process of reproduction includes the process of consumption brought
about by the circulation quite as much as the process of reproduction of the capital itself.

For our present purpose this process of reproduction must be studied from the point of view of the replacement of the value as well as
the substance of the individual component parts of C'. We cannot rest
content any longer, as we did in the analysis of the value of the product of the individual capital, with the *assumption* that the individual
capitalist can first convert the component parts of his capital into
money by the sale of his commodities, and then reconvert them into
productive capital by renewed purchase of the elements of production in the commodity market. Inasmuch as those elements of pro-

duction are by nature material, they represent as much a constituent of the social capital as the individual finished product, which is exchanged for them and replaced by them. Contrariwise the movement of that portion of the social commodity product which is consumed by the labourer in expending his wages, and by the capitalist in expending his surplus value, not only forms an integral part of the movement of the total product but intermingles with the movements of the individual capitals, and therefore this process cannot be explained by merely assuming it.

The question that confronts us directly is this: How is the *capital* consumed in production replaced in value out of the annual product and how does the movement of this replacement intertwine with the consumption of the surplus value by the capitalists and of the wages by the labourers? It is then first a matter of reproduction on a simple scale. It is furthermore assumed that products are exchanged at their values and also that there is no revolution in the values of the component parts of productive capital. The fact that prices diverge from values cannot, however, exert any influence on the movement of the social capital. On the whole, there is the same exchange of the same quantities of products, although the individual capitalists are involved in value relations no longer proportional to their respective advances and to the quantities of surplus value produced singly by every one of them. As for revolutions in value, they do not alter anything in the relations between the value components of the total annual product, provided they are universally and evenly distributed. To the extent however that they are partially and unevenly distributed, they represent disturbances which, in the *first* place, can be understood as such only as far as they are regarded as *divergences* from unchanged value relations; but, in the *second* place, once there is proof of the law according to which one portion of the value of the annual product replaces constant, and another portion variable capital, a revolution either in the value of the constant or that of the variable capital would not alter anything in this law. It would change merely the relative magnitudes of the portions of value which function in the one or the other capacity, because other values would have taken the places of the original ones.

So long as we looked upon the production of value and the value of the product of capital individually, the bodily form of the commodities produced was wholly immaterial for the analysis, whether it was machines, for instance, corn, or looking glasses. It was always but a matter of illustration, and any branch of production could have served that purpose equally well. What we dealt with was the immediate process of production itself, which presents itself at every point as the process of some individual capital. So far as the reproduction of capital was concerned, it was sufficient to assume that that portion of the product in commodities which represents capital value finds an opportunity in the sphere of circulation to reconvert itself into its elements of production and thus into its form of productive capital; just as it sufficed to assume that both the labourer and the capitalist find in the market those commodities on which they spend wages and surplus value. This merely formal manner of presentation is no longer adequate in the study of the total social capital and of the value of its products. The reconversion of one portion of the value of the product into capital and the passing of another portion into the individual consumption of the capitalist as well as the working class form a movement within the value of the product itself in which the result of the aggregate capital finds expression; and this movement is not only a replacement of value, but also a replacement in material and is therefore as much bound up with the relative proportions of the value components of the total social product as with their use value, their material shape.

Simple [43] reproduction, reproduction on the same scale, appears as an abstraction, inasmuch as on the one hand the absence of all accumulation or reproduction on an extended scale is a strange assumption in capitalist conditions, and on the other hand conditions of production do not remain exactly the same in different years (and this is assumed). The assumption is that a social capital of a given magnitude produces the same quantity of commodity value this year as last, and supplies the same quantum of wants, although the forms of the commodities may change in the process of reproduction. However, as far as accumulation does take place, simple reproduction is always a part of it, and can therefore be studied by itself, and is an actual factor of accumulation. The value of the annual product may decrease, although the quantity of use values may remain the same; or the value may remain the same although the quantity of the use values may decrease; or the quantity of value and of the reproduced use values may decrease simultaneously. All this amounts to reproduction

[43] From Manuscript VIII.

taking place either under more favourable conditions than before or under more difficult ones, which may result in imperfect — defective — reproduction. All this can refer only to the quantitative aspect of the various elements of reproduction, not to the role which they play as reproducing capital or as a reproduced revenue in the entire process.

II. THE TWO DEPARTMENTS OF SOCIAL PRODUCTION [44]

The total product, and therefore the total production, of society may be divided into two major departments:

I. *Means of production,* commodities having a form in which they must, or at least may, pass into productive consumption.

II. *Articles of consumption,* commodities having a form in which they pass into the individual consumption of the capitalist and the working class.

All the various branches of production pertaining to each of these two departments form one single great branch of production, that of the means of production in the one case, and that of articles of consumption in the other. The aggregate capital employed in each of these two branches of production constitutes a separate large department of the social capital.

In each department the capital consists of two component parts:

1) *Variable capital.* This capital, so far as its *value* is concerned, is equal to the value of the social labour power employed in this branch of production; in other words, it is equal to the sum of the wages paid for this labour power. So far as its substance is concerned, it consists of the labour power in action, i. e., of the living labour set in motion by this capital value.

2) *Constant capital.* This is the value of all the means of production employed for productive purposes in this branch. These, again, are divided into *fixed* capital, such as machines, instruments of labour, buildings, labouring cattle, etc., and *circulating* constant capital, such as materials of production: raw and auxiliary materials, semi-finished products, etc.

The value of the total annual product created with the aid of this capital in each of the two departments consists of one portion which represents the constant capital c consumed in the process of produc-

---

[44] Mainly from Manuscript II, the scheme from Manuscript VIII.

tion and only transferred to the product in accordance with its value, and of another portion added by the entire labour of the year. This latter portion is divided in turn into the replacement of the advanced variable capital v and the excess over and above it, which forms the surplus value s. And just as the value of every individual commodity, that of the entire annual product of each department consists of c + v + s.

Portion c of the value, representing the constant capital *consumed* in production, does not coincide with the value of the constant capital *employed* in production. True, the materials of production are entirely consumed and their values completely transferred to the product. But only a portion of the employed *fixed* capital is wholly consumed and its value thus transferred to the product. Another part of the fixed capital, such as machines, buildings, etc., continues to exist and function the same as before, though depreciated to the extent of the annual wear and tear. This persistent portion of the fixed capital does not exist for us, when we consider the value of the product. It is a portion of the capital value, which exists independently and alongside of this newly produced commodity value. This was shown previously in the analysis of the value of the product of individual capital (Buch I, Kap. VI, S. 192).[a] However, for the present we must leave aside the method of analysis employed there. We saw in the study of the value of the product of individual capital that the value of which the fixed capital was shorn through wear and tear is transferred to the commodity product created during the time of wear, irrespective of whether or not any portion of this fixed capital is replaced *in natura* during this time out of the value thus transferred. At this point in the study of the total social product and of its value, however, we are compelled, at least for the present, to leave out of account that portion of value which is transferred from the fixed capital to the annual product by wear and tear, unless this fixed capital is replaced *in natura* during the year. In one of the following sections of this chapter we shall discuss this point in particular.

———

We shall base our study of simple reproduction on the following scheme, in which c = constant capital, v = variable capital, and

———

[a] English edition: Vol. I, Ch. VIII (see present edition, Vol. 35).

s = surplus value, assuming the rate of surplus value $\frac{s}{v}$ to be 100%. The figures may indicate millions of marks, francs, or pounds sterling.

   I. Production of means of production:

   Capital . . . . . . $4,000_c + 1,000_v = 5,000$

   Commodity product $4,000_c + 1,000_v + 1,000_s = 6,000$,

existing in means of production.

   II. Production of articles of consumption:

   Capital . . . . . . $2,000_c + 500_v = 2,500$

   Commodity product $2,000_c + 500_v + 500_s = 3,000$,

existing in articles of consumption.

   Recapitulation: Total annual commodity product:

   I. $4,000_c + 1,000_v + 1,000_s = 6,000$ means of production.

   II. $2,000_c + 500_v + 500_s = 3,000$ articles of consumption.

Total value = 9,000, exclusive of the fixed capital persisting in its natural form, according to our assumption.

If we were now to examine the transformations necessary on the basis of simple reproduction, where the entire surplus value is unproductively consumed, and leave aside for the present the money circulation that brings them about, we should obtain at the outset three great points of support.

   1) The 500_v, representing wages of the labourers, and 500_s, representing surplus value of the capitalists, in department II, must be spent for articles of consumption. But their value exists in articles of consumption worth 1,000, held by the capitalists of department II, which replace the advanced 500_v and represent the 500_s. Consequently the wages and surplus value of department II are exchanged within this department for products of this same department. Thereby articles of consumption to the amount of $(500_v + 500_s)$ II = 1,000 drop out of the total product.

   2) The $1,000_v + 1,000_s$ of department I must likewise be spent for articles of consumption; in other words, for the product of department II. Hence they must be exchanged for the remainder of this product equal to the constant capital part, $2,000_c$. Department II receives in return an equal quantity of means of production, the product of I, in which the value of $1,000_v + 1,000_s$ of I is incorporated. Thereby $2,000$ II_c and $(1,000_v + 1,000_s)$ I drop out of the calculation.

   3) There still remain $4,000$ I_c. These consist of means of production which can be used only in department I to replace its consumed constant capital, and are therefore disposed of by mutual exchange between the individual capitalists of I, just as the $(500_v + 500_s)$ II by an

exchange between the labourers and capitalists, or between the individual capitalists of II.

Let this serve for the moment to facilitate the understanding of what follows.

III. EXCHANGE BETWEEN THE TWO DEPARTMENTS
$$I_{(V + S)} \text{ versus } II_C\text{[45]}$$

We begin with the great exchange between the two classes. $(1,000_v + 1,000_s)$ I — these values consisting, in the hands of their producers, of means of production in their bodily form, are exchanged for 2,000 II_c, for values consisting of articles of consumption in their bodily form. The capitalist class of II thereby reconverts its constant capital of 2,000 from the form of articles of consumption into that of means of production of articles of consumption, into a form in which it can once more function as a factor of the labour process and for purposes of self-expansion of value as constant capital value. On the other hand the equivalent of the labour power of I $(1,000_v)$ and the surplus value of the capitalists of I $(1,000_s)$ are realised thereby in articles of consumption; both of them are converted from their bodily form of means of production into a bodily form in which they can be consumed as revenue.

Now, this mutual exchange is accomplished by means of a circulation of money, which promotes it just as much as it renders its understanding difficult, but which is of decisive importance because the variable portion of capital must ever resume the form of money, as money capital converting itself from the form of money into labour power. The variable capital must be advanced in the form of money in all branches of production carried on at the entire periphery of society simultaneously alongside each other, regardless of whether they belong to category I or II. The capitalist buys the labour power before it enters into the process of production, but pays for it only at stipulated times, after it has been expended in the production of use values. He owns, together with the remainder of the value of the product, also that portion of it which is only an equivalent for the money expended in the payment of labour power, that portion of the value of the product which represents variable capital. In this portion of value the labourer has already supplied the capitalist with the equiv-

[45] Here Manuscript VIII is resumed.

alent of his wages. But it is the reconversion of commodities into money, their sale, which restores to the capitalist his variable capital in the form of money capital, which he may advance once more for the purchase of labour power.

In department I, then, the aggregate capitalist has paid £1,000 (I say £ solely to indicate that it is value in the *form of money*) equal to 1,000$_v$, to the labourers for the value of product I already existing as the v-portion, i. e., of the means of production created by them. With these £1,000 the labourers buy articles of consumption of the same value from capitalists II, thereby converting one half of the constant capital II into money; capitalists II, in their turn, buy with these £1,000 means of production, valued at 1,000, from capitalists I; thereby, as far as the latter are concerned, the variable capital value equal to 1,000$_v$, which, being part of their product, existed in the bodily form of means of production, is thus reconverted into money and can now function anew in the hands of capitalists I as money capital, which is transformed into labour power, hence into the most essential element of productive capital. In this way their variable capital flows back to them in the form of money, as a result of the realisation of some of their commodity capital.

As for the money required to exchange the s-portion of commodity capital I for the second half of constant capital II, it may be advanced in various ways. In reality this circulation embraces innumerable separate purchases and sales by the individual capitalists of both categories, the money coming in any event from these capitalists, since we have already accounted for the money put into circulation by the labourers. A capitalist of category II can buy, with the money capital he has besides his productive capital, means of production from capitalists of category I, and, vice versa, a capitalist of category I can buy, with money funds assigned for personal and not for capital expenditure, articles of consumption from capitalists of category II. A certain supply of money, to be used either for the advancement of capital or for the expenditure of revenue, must under all circumstances be assumed to exist beside the productive capital in the hands of the capitalists, as we have shown above in parts I and II. Let us assume — the proportion is wholly immaterial for our purpose — that one half of the money is advanced by capitalists II in the purchase of means of production for the replacement of their constant capital, while the other half is spent by capitalists I for articles of consumption. In that case department II advances £500 for the purchase of means of production from department I, thereby replacing (inclusive of the above £1,000 coming from the labourers of department I) $^3/_4$ of its constant capital *in natura*; with the £500 so obtained department I buys articles of consumption from II, thereby completing for one half of the s-portion of its commodity capital the circulation c — m — c, and thus realising its product in the consumption fund. By means of this second process the £500 return to the hands of II as money capital existing beside its productive capital. On the other hand I expends money to the amount of £500 for the purchase of II's articles of consumption in anticipation of the sale of that half of the s-portion of its commodity capital which is still lying in store as product. With the same £500 II buys from I means of production, thereby replacing *in natura* its entire constant capital (1,000 + 500 + 500 = 2,000), while I realises its entire surplus value in articles of consumption. On the whole, the entire exchange of commodities in the amount of £4,000 would be effected with a money circulation of £2,000, which amount is attained only because the entire annual product is described as exchanged in bulk, in a few large lots. The important point here is that II has not only reconverted its constant capital, reproduced in the form of articles of consumption, into the form of means of production, but has besides recovered the £500 which it had advanced to the circulation for the purchase of means of production; and that, similarly, I again possesses not only its variable capital, which it had reproduced in the form of means of production, in money form, as money capital once more directly convertible into labour power, but also the £500 expended in the purchase of articles of consumption in anticipation of the sale of the s-portion of its capital. But these £500 flow back to it not because of the expenditure incurred, but because of the subsequent sale of a part of its commodity product incorporating one half of its surplus value.

In both cases it is not only that the constant capital of II is reconverted from the form of a product into the bodily form of means of production, in which alone it can function as capital; and likewise it is not only that the variable portion of the capital of I is converted into its money form, and the surplus-value portion of the means of production of I into its consumable form, the form in which it can be used as revenue. It is also that the £500 of money capital, advanced by II in the purchase of means of production prior to selling the corresponding compensating portion of the value of its constant capital — existing in the form of means of consumption — flow back to II; and furthermore back to I flow the £500 which were expended *anticipando* by it for the purchase of articles of consumption. If the money advanced by II at the expense of the constant portion of its commodity product, and by I at the expense of the surplus-value portion of its commodity product, flows back to them, this is solely because the one class of capitalists throws £500 into circulation over and above the constant capital existing in the form of commodities in II, and the other class a like amount over and above the surplus value existing in the form of commodities in I. In the last analysis the two departments have mutually paid one another in full by the exchange of equivalents in the shape of their respective commodities. The money thrown into circulation by them in excess of the values of their commodities, as a means of effecting the exchange of these commodities, returns to each one of them out of the circulation in proportion to the quota which each of the two had thrown into circulation. Neither has grown a farthing richer thereby. II possessed a constant capital of 2,000 in the form of articles of consumption and 500 in money; now it possesses 2,000 in means of production + 500 in money, the same as before; in the same way I possesses, as before, a surplus value of 1,000 (consisting of commodities, means of production, now converted into a consumption fund) + 500 in money.

The general conclusion is this: Of the money which the industrial capitalists throw into circulation to accomplish their own commodity circulation, whether at the expense of the constant part of the commodity value or at the expense of the surplus value existing in the commodities to the extent that it is laid out as revenue, as much returns into the hands of the respective capitalists as was advanced by them for the money circulation.

As for the reconversion of the variable capital of class I into the form of money, this capital, after the capitalists of I invested it in wages, exists for them first in the form of commodities in which the labourers delivered it to them. They paid this capital in the form of money to these labourers as the price of their labour power. To this extent the capitalists have paid for that constituent part of the value of their commodity product which is equal to the variable capital expended in the form of money. They are, for this reason, the owners of this portion of the commodity product as well. But that part of the working class which is employed by them does not buy the means of production created by it; these labourers buy articles of consumption produced by II. Hence the variable capital advanced by the capitalists of I in the payment of labour power in money form does not return to them directly. It passes by means of purchases made by the labourers into the hands of the capitalist producers of the commodities necessary for and within the reach of working folks; in other words, it passes into the hands of capitalists II. And not until these expend the money in the purchase of means of production does it return by this circuitous route into the hands of capitalists I.

It follows that, on the basis of simple reproduction, the sum of the values of v + s of the commodity capital of I (and therefore a corresponding proportional part of the total commodity product of I) must be equal to the constant capital II_c, which is likewise taken as a proportional part of the total commodity product of department II; $I_{(v + s)} = II_c$.

IV. EXCHANGE WITHIN DEPARTMENT II.
NECESSITIES OF LIFE AND ARTICLES OF LUXURY

Of the value of the commodity product of department II there still remain to be studied the constituents v + s. This analysis has nothing to do with the most important question which occupies our attention here, namely to what extent the division of the value of every individual capitalist commodity product into c + v + s — even if brought about by different forms of appearance — applies also to the value of the total annual product. This question finds its answers on the one hand in the exchange of $I_{(v + s)}$ for II_c, and on the other hand in the investigation, to be made later,[a] of the reproduction of I_c in the annual product of I. Since $II_{(v + s)}$ exists in the bodily form of articles of consumption, since the variable capital advanced to the labourers in payment of their labour power must generally speaking be spent by them for articles of consumption, and since the s-portion of the value of commodities, on the assumption of simple reproduction, is practically spent as revenue for articles of consumption, it is *prima facie* evident that the labourers II buy back, with the wages received from the capitalists II, a portion of their own product, corresponding to the amount of the money value received as wages. Thereby the capitalist class II reconverts the money capital advanced by it in the payment of labour power into the form of money. It is quite the same as if it had paid the labourers in mere value tokens. As soon as the labourers

---

[a] See this volume, pp. 420-23.

would realise these value tokens by the purchase of a part of the commodities produced by them but belonging to the capitalists, these tokens would return into the hands of the capitalists. Only, these tokens do not merely represent value but possess it, in golden or silver embodiment. We shall analyse in greater detail later on this sort of reflux of variable capital advanced in the form of money by means of a process in which the working class appears as the purchaser and the capitalist class as the seller. Here however a different point is at issue, which must be discussed in connection with this return of the variable capital to its point of departure.

Category II of the annual production of commodities consists of a great variety of branches of production, which may, however, be divided into two great sub-divisions by their products:

a) Articles of consumption, which enter into the consumption of the working class, and, to the extent that they are necessities of life — even if frequently different in quality and value from those of the labourers — also form a portion of the consumption of the capitalist class. For our purposes we may call this entire sub-division consumer *necessities*, regardless of whether such a product as tobacco is really a consumer necessity from the physiological point of view. It suffices that it is habitually such.

b) Articles of *luxury*, which enter into the consumption of only the capitalist class and can therefore be exchanged only for spent surplus value, which never falls to the share of the labourer.

As far as the first category is concerned it is obvious that the variable capital advanced in the production of the commodities belonging in it must flow back in money form directly to that portion of the capitalist class II (i. e., the capitalists IIa) who have produced these necessities of life. They sell them to their own labourers to the amount of the variable capital paid to them in wages. This reflux is *direct* so far as this entire sub-division a of the capitalist class II is concerned, no matter how numerous the transactions may be between the capitalists of the various pertinent branches of industry, by means of which the returning variable capital is distributed *pro rata*. These are processes of circulation, whose means of circulation are supplied directly by the money expended by the labourers. It is different, however, with sub-division IIb. The entire portion of the value produced in this sub-division, $IIb_{(v+s)}$, exists in the bodily form of articles of luxury, i. e., articles which the labouring class can buy no more than it can buy commodity value I_v existing in the form of means of production, notwithstanding the fact that both the articles of luxury and the means of production are the products of these labourers. Hence the reflux by which the variable capital advanced in this sub-division returns to the capitalist producers in its money form cannot be direct but must be mediated, as in the case of I_v.

Let us assume for instance that $v = 500$ and $s = 500$, as we did in the case of the entire class II; but that the variable capital and the corresponding surplus value are distributed as follows:

Sub-division a, necessities of life: $v = 400$, $s = 400$; hence a quantity of commodities in consumer necessities of the value of $400_v + 400_s = 800$, or IIa $(400_v + 400_s)$.

Sub-division b, articles of luxury: of the value of $100_v + 100_s = 200$, or IIb $(100_v + 100_s)$.

The labourers of IIb have received 100 in money as payment for their labour power, or say £100. With this money they buy articles of consumption from capitalists IIa to the same amount. This class of capitalists buys with the same money £100 worth of the IIb commodities, and in this way the variable capital of capitalists IIb flows back to them in the form of money.

In IIa there are available once more 400_v in money, in the hands of the capitalists, obtained by exchange with their own labourers. Besides, a fourth of the part of the product representing surplus value has been transferred to the labourers of IIb, and in exchange IIb (100_v) have been received in the form of articles of luxury.

Now, assuming that the capitalists of IIa and IIb divide the expenditure of their revenue in the same proportion between necessities of life and luxuries — $3/5$ for necessities of life, for instance, and $2/5$ for luxuries — the capitalists of sub-class IIa will spend $3/5$ of their revenue from surplus value, amounting to 400_s, or 240, for their own products, necessities of life, and $2/5 = 160$ for articles of luxury. The capitalists of sub-class IIb will divide their surplus value of 100_s in the same way: $3/5 = 60$ for necessities, and $2/5 = 40$ for articles of luxury, the latter being produced and exchanged in their own sub-class.

The 160 in articles of luxury received by $(IIa)_s$ pass into the hands of the IIa capitalists in the following manner: As we have seen, 100 of the (IIa) 400_s were exchanged in the form of necessities of life for an equal amount of $(IIb)_v$, which exists as articles of luxury, and another 60, consisting of necessities of life, for (IIb) 60_s, consisting of luxuries. The total calculation then stands as follows:

IIa: $400_v + 400_s$;   IIb: $100_v + 100_s$.

1) 400_v (a) are consumed by the labourers of IIa, a part of whose product (necessities of life) they form. The labourers buy them from the capitalist producers of their own sub-division. These capitalists thereby recover £400 in money, which is the value of their variable capital of 400 paid by them to these same labourers as wages; they can now once more buy labour power with it.

2) A part of the 400_s (a), equal to the 100_v (b), $^1/_4$ of the surplus value (a), is realised in luxuries in the following way: The labourers (b) received from the capitalists of their sub-division (b) £100 in wages. With this amount they buy $^1/_4$ of the surplus value (a), i. e., commodities consisting of necessities of life. With this money the capitalists of (a) buy articles of luxury to the same amount, which equals 100_v (b), or one half of the entire output of luxuries. In this way the b capitalists get back their variable capital in the form of money and are enabled to resume reproduction by again purchasing labour power, since the entire constant capital of the whole category II has already been replaced by the exchange of $I_{(v+s)}$ for II_c. The labour power of the luxury workers is therefore saleable anew only because the part of their own product created as an equivalent for their wages is drawn by capitalists IIa into their consumption fund, is turned into money. (The same applies to the sale of the labour power of I, since the II_c for which $I_{(v+s)}$ is exchanged consists of both articles of luxury and necessities of life, and that which is renewed by means of $I_{(v+s)}$ constitutes the means of production of both luxuries and necessities.)

3) We now come to the exchange between a and b, which is merely exchange between the capitalists of the two sub-divisions. So far we have disposed of the variable capital (400_v) and part of the surplus value (100_s) in a, and the variable capital (100_v) in b. We have furthermore assumed that the average proportion of the expenditure of the capitalist revenue was in both classes $^2/_5$ for luxuries and $^3/_5$ for necessities. Apart from the 100 already expended for luxuries, the entire sub-division a still has to be allotted 60 for luxuries, and b has proportionately to be allotted 40.

$(IIa)_s$ is then divided into 240 for necessities and 160 for luxuries, or $240 + 160 = 400_s$ (IIa).

$(IIb)_s$ is divided into 60 for necessities and 40 for luxuries:

$60 + 40 = 100_s$ (IIb). The last 40 are consumed by this class out of its own product ($^2/_5$ of its surplus value); the 60 in necessities are obtained by this class through the exchange of 60 of its surplus value for 60_s (a).

We have, then, for the entire capitalist class II the following (v + s in sub-division a consisting of necessities, in b of luxuries):

IIa $(400_v + 400_s)$ + IIb $(100_v + 100_s)$ = 1,000; by this movement there is thus realised: 500_v (a + b) //realised in 400_v (a) and 100_s (a)// + 500_s (a + b) //realised in 300_s (a) + 100_v (b) + 100_s (b)// = 1,000.

For a and b, each considered by itself, we obtain the following realisation:

$$\text{a)} \quad \frac{v}{400_v \text{ (a)}} + \frac{s}{240_s \text{(a)} + 100_s \text{(b)} + 60_s \text{(b)}} = 800$$

$$\text{b)} \quad \frac{v}{100_s \text{(a)}} + \frac{s}{60_s \text{(a)} + 40_s \text{(b)}} \ldots = \frac{200}{1,000}.$$

If, for the sake of simplicity, we assume the same proportion between the variable and constant capital (which, by the way, is not at all necessary), we obtain for 400_v (a) a constant capital of 1,600, and for 100_v (b) a constant capital of 400. We then have the following two sub-divisions, a and b, in II:

$$\text{IIa)} \quad 1,600_c + 400_v + 400_s = 2,400$$
$$\text{IIb)} \quad 400_c + 100_v + 100_s = 600,$$

adding up to

$$2,000_c + 500_v + 500_s = 3,000.$$

Accordingly 1,600 of the 2,000 II_c in articles of consumption, which are exchanged for 2,000 $I_{(v+s)}$, are exchanged for means of production of necessities of life and 400 for means of production of luxuries.

The 2,000 $I_{(v+s)}$ would therefore break up into $(800_v + 800_s)$ I for a, equal to 1,600 means of production of necessities of life, and $(200_v + 200_s)$ I for b, equal to 400 means of production of luxuries.

A considerable part of the instruments of labour as such, as well as of the raw and auxiliary materials, etc., is the same for both departments. But so far as the exchange of the various portions of value of the total product $I_{(v+s)}$ is concerned, such a division would be wholly immaterial. Both the above 800_v of I and the 200_v of I are realised because the wages are spent for articles of consumption 1,000 II_c; hence the money capital advanced for this purpose is distributed evenly on its return among the capitalist producers of I, their advanced variable capital is replaced *pro rata* in money. On the other hand, so far as the realisation of the 1,000 I_s is concerned, the capitalists will here likewise draw uniformly (in proportion to the magnitude of their s) 600 IIa and 400 IIb in means of consumption out of the entire second half of $II_c = 1,000$; consequently those who replace the constant capital of IIa will draw:

480 $(^3/_5)$ out of 600_c (IIa) and 320 $(^2/_5)$ out of 400_c (IIb) = 800; those who replace the constant capital of IIb will draw:

120 $(^3/_5)$ out of 600_c (IIa) and 80 $(^2/_5)$ out of 400_c (IIb) = 200. Grand total = 1,000.

What is arbitrary here is the ratio of the variable to the constant capital of both I and II and so is the identity of this ratio for I and II and their sub-divisions. As for this identity, it has been assumed here merely for the sake of simplification, and it would not alter in any way the conditions of the problem and its solution if we were to assume different proportions. However, the necessary result of all this, on the assumption of simple reproduction, is the following:

1) That the new value created by the labour of one year (divisible into v + s) in the natural form of means of production is equal to the value of the constant capital c contained in the value of the product created by the other part of the annual labour and reproduced in the form of articles of consumption. If it were smaller than II_c, it would be impossible for II to replace its constant capital entirely; if it were greater, a surplus would remain unused. In either case, the assumption of simple reproduction would be violated.

2) That in the case of annual product which is reproduced in the form of articles of consumption, the variable capital v advanced in the form of money can be realised by its recipients, inasmuch as they are labourers producing luxuries, only in that portion of the necessities of life which embodies for their capitalist producers *prima facie* their surplus value; hence that v, laid out in the production of luxuries, is equal in value to a corresponding portion of s produced in the form of necessities of life, and hence must be smaller than the whole of this s, namely $(IIa)_s$, and that the variable capital advanced by the capitalist producers of luxuries returns to them in the form of money

only by means of the realisation of that v in this portion of s. This phenomenon is quite analogous to the realisation of $I_{(v+s)}$ in II_c, except that in the second case $(IIb)_v$ realises itself in a *part* of $(IIa)_s$ of the same value. These proportions remain qualitatively determinant in every distribution of the total annual product, since it actually enters into the process of the annual reproduction brought about by circulation. $I_{(v+s)}$ can be realised only in II_c, just as II_c can only be renewed in its function as a component part of productive capital by means of this realisation; in the same way, $(IIb)_v$ can be realised only in a portion of $(IIa)_s$ and $(IIb)_v$ can only thus be reconverted into the form of money capital. It goes without saying that this applies only to the extent that it all is really a result of the process of reproduction itself, i. e., to the extent that the capitalists of IIb, for instance, do not obtain money capital for v on credit from others. Quantitatively however the exchanges of the various portions of the annual product can take place in the proportions indicated above only so long as the scale and value relations in production remain stationary and so long as these strict relations are not altered by foreign commerce.

Now, if we were to say after the manner of Adam Smith that $I_{(v+s)}$ resolve themselves into II_c, and II_c resolves itself into $I_{(v+s)}$, or, as he used to say more frequently and still more absurdly, $I_{(v+s)}$ constitute component parts of the price (or "VALUE IN EXCHANGE", as he has it) of II_c and II_c constitutes the entire component part of the value of $I_{(v+s)}$, then one could and should likewise say that $(IIb)_v$ resolves itself into $(IIa)_s$, or $(IIa)_s$ into $(IIb)_v$, or $(IIb)_v$ forms a component part of the surplus value of IIa, and, vice versa, the surplus value thus resolves itself into wages, or into variable capital, and the variable capital forms a "component part" of the surplus value. This absurdity is indeed found in Adam Smith, since with him wages are determined by the value of the necessities of life, and these commodity values in their turn by the value of the wages (variable capital) and surplus value contained in them. He is so absorbed in the fractional parts into which the value product of one working day is divided on the basis of capitalism—namely into v + s—that he quite forgets that it is immaterial in simple commodity exchange whether the equivalents existing in various natural forms consist of paid or unpaid labour, since their production costs in either case the same amount of labour; and that it is also immaterial whether the commodity of A is a means of production and that of B an article of consumption and whether one commodity has to serve as a component part of capital after its sale while another passes into the consumption fund and, *secundum*[a] Adam, is consumed as revenue. The use to which the individual buyer puts his commodity does not come within the scope of commodity exchange, the sphere of circulation, and does not affect the value of the commodity. This is in no wise altered by the fact that in the analysis of the circulation of the total annual social product, the definite use for which it is intended, the factor of consumption of the various component parts of that product, must be taken into consideration.

In the exchange established above of $(IIb)_v$ for a portion of $(IIa)_s$ of the same value, and in the further exchanges between $(IIa)_s$ and $(IIb)_s$ it is by no means assumed that either the individual capitalists of IIa and IIb or their respective totalities divide their surplus value in the same proportion between necessary articles of consumption and articles of luxury. The one may spend more on this consumption, the other more on that. On the basis of simple reproduction it is merely assumed that a sum of values equal to the entire surplus value is realised in the consumption fund. The limits are thus given. Within each department the one may spend more in a, the other in b. But this may compensate itself mutually, so that the capitalist groups of a and b, taken as a whole, each participate in the same proportion in both. The value relations — the proportional shares of the two kinds of producers a and b in the total value of product II — consequently also a definite quantitative relation between the branches of production supplying those products — are however necessarily given in each concrete case; only the proportion chosen as an illustration is a hypothetical one. It would not alter the qualitative aspects if another illustration were selected; only the quantitative determinations would be altered. But if on account of any circumstances there arises an actual change in the relative magnitude of a and b, the conditions of simple reproduction would also change accordingly.

––––––––

Since $(IIb)_v$ is realised in an equivalent part of $(IIa)_s$, it follows that in proportion as the luxury part of the annual product grows, as therefore an increasing share of the labour power is absorbed in the production of luxuries, the reconversion of the variable capital ad-

––––––––
[a] according to

vanced in $(IIb)_v$ into money capital functioning anew as the money form of the variable capital, and thereby the existence and reproduction of the part of the working class employed in IIb — the supply to them of consumer necessities — depends upon the prodigality of the capitalist class, upon the exchange of a considerable portion of their surplus value for articles of luxury.

Every crisis at once lessens the consumption of luxuries. It retards, delays the reconversion of $(IIb)_v$ into money capital, permitting it only partially and thus throwing a certain number of the labourers employed in the production of luxuries out of work, while on the other hand it thus clogs the sale of consumer necessities and reduces it. And this without mentioning the unproductive labourers who are dismissed at the same time, labourers who receive for their services a portion of the capitalists' luxury expense fund (these labourers are themselves *pro tanto* luxuries) and who take part to a very considerable extent in the consumption of the necessities of life, etc. The reverse takes place in periods of prosperity, particularly during the times of bogus prosperity, in which the relative value of money, expressed in commodities, decreases also for other reasons (without any actual revolution in values), so that the prices of commodities rise independently of their own values. It is not alone the consumption of necessities of life which increases. The working class (now actively reinforced by its entire reserve army) also enjoys momentarily articles of luxury ordinarily beyond its reach, and those articles which at other times constitute for the greater part consumer "necessities" only for the capitalist class. This on its part calls forth a rise in prices.

It is sheer tautology to say that crises are caused by the scarcity of effective consumption, or of effective consumers. The capitalist system does not know any other modes of consumption than effective ones, except that of *sub forma pauperis* or of the "thief". That commodities are unsaleable means only that no effective purchasers have been found for them, i. e., consumers (since commodities are bought in the final analysis for productive or individual consumption). But if one were to attempt to give this tautology the semblance of a profounder justification by saying that the working class receives too small a portion of its own product and the evil would be remedied as soon as it receives a larger share of it and its wages increase in consequence, one could only remark that crises are always prepared by precisely a period in which wages rise generally and the working class actually gets a larger share of that part of the annual product which is intended for consumption. From the point of view of these advocates of sound and "simple" (!) common sense, such a period should rather remove the crisis. It appears, then, that capitalist production comprises conditions independent of good or bad will, conditions which permit the working class to enjoy that relative prosperity only momentarily, and at that always only as the harbinger of a coming crisis.[47]

We saw a while ago that the proportion between the production of consumer necessities and that of luxuries requires the division of $II_{(v+s)}$ between IIa and IIb, and thus of II_c between $(IIa)_c$ and $(IIb)_c$. Hence this division affects the character and the quantitative relations of production to their very roots, and is an essential determining factor of its general structure.

Simple reproduction is essentially directed toward consumption as an end, although the grabbing of surplus value appears as the compelling motive of the individual capitalists; but surplus value, whatever its relative magnitude may be, is after all supposed to serve here only for the individual consumption of the capitalist.

As simple reproduction is a part, and the most important one at that, of all annual reproduction on an extended scale, this motive remains as an accompaniment of and contrast to the self-enrichment motive as such. In reality the matter is more complicated, because PARTNERS[a] in the loot — the surplus value of the capitalist — figure as consumers independent of him.

V. THE MEDIATION OF EXCHANGE
BY THE CIRCULATION OF MONEY

So far as we have analysed circulation up to the present, it proceeded between the various classes of producers as indicated in the following scheme:

1) Between class I and class II:

$$\text{I. } 4{,}000_c + \underline{1{,}000_v + 1{,}000_s}$$

$$\text{II. } \ldots \ldots \ldots \ 2{,}000_c \ldots \ldots + 500_v + 500_s.$$

This disposes of the circulation of $II_c = 2{,}000$, which is exchanged for I $(1{,}000_v + 1000_s)$.

[47] *Ad notam* for possible followers of the Rodbertian theory of crises.— *F. E.*

[a] In the original, this English word is given in parentheses after its German equivalent.

Leaving aside for the present the 4,000 I_c there still remains the circulation of v + s within class II. Now $II_{(v+s)}$ is divided between the sub-classes IIa and IIb in the following manner:

2) II. $500_v + 500_s = a\ (400_v + 400_s) + b\ (100_v + 100_s)$.

The 400_v (a) circulate within its own sub-class; the labourers paid with it buy from their employers, the capitalists IIa, necessary means of subsistence produced by themselves.

Since the capitalists of both sub-classes spend $^3/_5$ of their surplus value in products of IIa (necessities) and $^2/_5$ in products of IIb (luxuries), the $^3/_5$ of the surplus value of a, or 240, are consumed within the sub-class IIa itself; likewise, $^2/_5$ of the surplus value of b (produced and existing in the form of articles of luxury), within the sub-class IIb.

There remains to be exchanged between IIa and IIb:
on the side of IIa: 160_s,
on the side of IIb: $100_v + 60_s$. These cancel each other. With their 100, received in the form of money wages, the labourers of IIb buy necessities of life in that amount from IIa. The IIb capitalists likewise buy necessities from IIa to the amount of $^3/_5$ of their surplus value, or 60. The IIa capitalists thus obtain the money required for investing, as above assumed, $^2/_5$ of their surplus value, or 160_s, in luxuries produced by IIb (100_v held by the IIb capitalists as a product replacing the wages paid by them, and 60_s). The scheme for this is therefore:

3) IIa. $//400_v// + //240_s// + \underline{\qquad 160_s \qquad}$
   b. . . . . $100_v + 60_s\ + //40_s//$,

the bracketed items circulating and being consumed only within their own sub-class.

The direct reflux of the money capital advanced in variable capital, which takes place only in the case of the capitalist department IIa producing necessities of life, is but an expression, modified by special conditions, of the previously mentioned general law that money advanced to the circulation by producers of commodities returns to them in the normal course of commodity circulation. From this it incidentally follows that if any money capitalist at all stands behind the producer of commodities and advances to the industrial capitalist money capital (in the strictest meaning of the word, i. e., capital value in the form of money), the real point of reflux for this money is the pocket of this money capitalist. Thus the mass of the circulating money belongs to that department of money capital which is organised and concentrated in the form of banks, etc., although the money circulates more or less through all hands. The way in which this department advances its capital necessitates the continual final reflux to it in the form of money, although this is once again brought about by the reconversion of the industrial capital into money capital.

The circulation of commodities always requires two things: Commodities which are thrown into circulation and money which is likewise thrown into it. "The process of circulation ... does not, like direct barter of products, become extinguished upon the use values changing places and hands. The money does not vanish on dropping out of the circuit of the metamorphosis of a given commodity. It is constantly being precipitated into new places in the arena of circulation vacated by other commodities," etc. (Buch I, Kap. III, S. 92).[a]

For instance in the circulation between II_c and $I_{(v+s)}$ we assumed that II had advanced £500 in money for it. In the innumerable processes of circulation, into which the circulation between large social groups of producers resolves itself, representatives of the various groups will at various times be the first to appear as buyers, and hence throw money into circulation. Quite apart from particular circumstances, this is necessitated by the difference, if nothing else, in the periods of production, and thus of the turnovers, of the various commodity capitals. So with these £500 II buys from I means of production of the same value and I buys from II articles of consumption valued at £500. Hence the money flows back to II, but this department does not in any way grow richer by this reflux. It had first thrown £500 in money into circulation and drew commodities of the same value out of it; then it sells £500 worth of commodities and draws the same amount of money out of circulation; thus the £500 flow back to it. As a matter of fact, II has thrown into circulation £500 in money and £500 in commodities, which is equal to £1,000. It draws out of the circulation £500 in commodities and £500 in money. The circulation requires for the handling of £500 in I commodities and £500 in II commodities only £500 in money; hence whoever advanced the money in the purchase of commodities from other producers recovers it when selling his own. Consequently if I had at first bought commodities from II for £500, and later sold to II commodities of the value of £500, these £500 would have returned to I instead of to II.

---

[a] See present edition, Vol. 35.

In class I the money invested in wages, i. e., the variable capital advanced in the form of money, does not return directly in this form but indirectly, by a detour. On the contrary, in II the £500 of wages return directly from the labourers to the capitalists, and this return is always direct in the case where purchase and sale take place repeatedly between the same persons in such a way that they are acting alternately as buyers and sellers of commodities. The capitalist of II pays for the labour power in money; he thereby incorporates labour power in his capital and assumes the role of an industrial capitalist in relation to his labourers as wage earners, but does so only by means of this act of circulation, which is for him merely a conversion of money capital into productive capital. Thereupon the labourer, who in the first instance was a seller, a dealer in his own labour power, appears in the second instance as a buyer, a possessor of money, in relation to the capitalist, who now acts as a seller of commodities. In this way the capitalist recovers the money invested by him in wages. As the sale of these commodities does not imply cheating, etc., but is an exchange of equivalents in commodities and money, it is not a process by which the capitalist enriches himself. He does not pay the labourer twice, first in money and then in commodities. His money returns to him as soon as the labourer exchanges it for his commodities.

However, the money capital converted into variable capital, i. e., the money advanced for wages, plays a prominent role in the circulation of money itself, since the labourers must live from hand to mouth and cannot give the industrial capitalists credit for any length of time. For this reason variable capital must be advanced in the form of money simultaneously at innumerable territorially different points in society at certain short intervals, such as a week, etc.— in periods of time that repeat themselves rather quickly (and the shorter these periods, the smaller relatively is the total amount of money thrown at one time into circulation through this channel) — whatever the various periods of turnover of the capitals in the different branches of industry. In every country with a capitalist production the money capital so advanced constitutes a relatively decisive share of the total circulation, the more so as the same money, before its reflux to its point of departure, passes through the most diverse channels and functions as a medium of circulation for countless other businesses.

Now let us consider the circulation between $I_{(v+s)}$ and II_c from a different angle.

Capitalists I advance £1,000 in the payment of wages. With this money the labourers buy £1,000 worth of means of subsistence from capitalists II. These in turn buy for the same money means of production from capitalists I. Capitalists I thus get back their variable capital in the form of money, while capitalists II have reconverted one half of their constant capital from the form of commodity capital into that of productive capital. Capitalists II advance another £500 in money to get means of production from I. The capitalists I spend this money on articles of consumption from II. These £500 thus return to capitalists II. They advance this amount again in order to reconvert the last quarter of their constant capital, converted into commodities, into its productive natural form. This money flows back to I and once more withdraws articles of consumption of the same amount from II. Thus the £500 return to II. The capitalists II are now as before in possession of £500 in money and £2,000 in constant capital, the latter having been newly converted from the form of commodity capital into that of productive capital. By means of £1,500 a quantity of commodities worth £5,000 has been circulated, namely: 1) I pays £1,000 to his labourers for their labour power of the same value; 2) with these same £1,000 the labourers buy means of subsistence from II; 3) with the same money II buys means of production from I, thereby restoring to I variable capital to the amount of £1,000 in the form of money; 4) II buys £500 worth of means of production from I; 5) with the same £500 I buys articles of consumption from II; 6) with the same £500 II buys means of production from I; 7) with the same £500 I buys means of subsistence from II. Thus £500 have returned to II, which had thrown them into circulation besides its £2,000 in commodities and for which it did not withdraw from circulation any equivalent in commodities.[48]

The exchange therefore takes the following course:

1) I pays £1,000 in money for labour power, hence for commodities = £1,000.

---

[48] This presentation differs somewhat from that given above (p. 374[a]). There I likewise throws an independent amount of £ 500 into circulation. Here II alone supplies the additional money for the circulation. But this does not alter the final result.— F. E.

---

[a] See this volume, p. 331.

2) The labourers buy with their wages amounting in money to
£1,000 articles of consumption from II; hence commodities = £1,000.

3) With the £1,000 received from the labourers II buys means of
production of the same value from I; hence commodities = £1,000.

In this way the £1,000 have returned to I as the money form of its
variable capital.

4) II buys £500 worth of means of production from I, hence commodities = £500.

5) With the same £500 I buys articles of consumption from II;
hence commodities = £500.

6) With the same £500 II buys means of production from I; hence
commodities = £500.

7) With the same £500 I buys articles of consumption from II;
hence commodities = £500.

Total amount of commodity values exchanged = £5,000.

The £500 advanced by II for the purchase have returned to it.
The result is as follows:

1) I possesses variable capital in the form of money to the amount
of £1,000, which it originally advanced to the circulation. It furthermore expended £1,000 for its individual consumption, in the shape of
its own products; i. e., it has spent the money which it had received
for the sale of means of production to the amount of £1,000.

On the other hand the natural form into which the variable capital
existing in the form of money must be transformed, i. e., labour power, has been maintained, reproduced and again made available by
consumption as the sole article of trade of its owners, which they must
sell in order to live. The relation of wage labourers and capitalists has
likewise been reproduced.

2) The constant capital of II is replaced *in natura*, and the £500
advanced by the same II to the circulation have returned to it.

As for the labourers I, the circulation is the simple one of
C—M—C:C′ (labour power) —M² (£1,000, money form of variable
capital I) —C³ (necessities of life to the amount of £1,000); these
£1,000 convert into money to the same amount of value the constant
capital II existing in the form of commodities, of means of subsistence.

As for the capitalists II, the process is C—M, the transformation of
a portion of their commodity product into the money form, from
which it is reconverted into the constituents of productive capital, namely into a portion of the means of production required by them.

In the money advance M (£500) made by capitalists II for the purchase of the other parts of the means of production, the money form of that portion of II_c which exists as yet in the form of commodities (articles of consumption) is anticipated; in the act $M — C$, in which II buys with M, and C is sold by I, the money (II) is converted into a portion of the productive capital, while C (I) passes through the act $C — M$, changes into money, which however does not represent any component part of capital value for I, but surplus value converted into money and expended solely for articles of consumption.

In the circuit $M — C \ldots P \ldots C' — M'$, the first act, $M — C$, is that of one capitalist, the last, $C' — M'$ (or part of it), is that of another; whether the C, by which M is converted into productive capital, represents a component of constant capital, of variable capital, or surplus value for the seller of C (who exchanges this C for money), is wholly immaterial for the commodity circulation itself.

Class I, so far as concerns the component v + s of its commodity product, draws more money out of the circulation than it has thrown in. In the first place, the £1,000 of variable capital return to it; in the second place, it sells means of production worth £500 (see above, exchange No. 4); one half of its surplus value is thus turned into money; then (exchange No. 6) it sells once more £500 worth of means of production, the second half of its surplus value, and thus the entire surplus value is withdrawn from circulation in the shape of money. Hence in succession: 1) variable capital reconverted into money = £1,000; 2) one half of the surplus value turned into money = £500; 3) the other half of the surplus value = £500; altogether $1,000_v + 1,000_s$ turned into money = £2,000. Although I threw only £1,000 into circulation (aside from those exchanges which promote the reproduction of I_c and which we shall have to analyse later), it has withdrawn double that amount from it. Of course s passes into other hands, (II), as soon as it has been converted into money, by being spent for articles of consumption. The capitalists of I withdrew only as much *in money* as they threw into it in value in the form of *commodities*; the fact that this value is surplus value, i. e., that it does not cost the capitalists anything, does not alter the value of these commodities in any way; so far as the exchange of values in commodity circulation is concerned, that fact is of no consequence at all. The existence of surplus value in money is of course transient, the same as all other forms which the advanced capital assumes in its metamorphoses. It lasts no longer than the interval between the conversion of commodities I into money and the subsequent conversion of the money I into commodities II.

If the turnovers had been assumed to be shorter — or, from the point of view of the simple circulation of commodities, the circulation of money more rapid — even less money would be ample to circulate the exchanged commodity values; the amount is always determined — if the number of successive exchanges is given — by the sum of the prices, or the sum of values, of the circulating commodities. It is immaterial in what proportion this sum of values consists of surplus value on the one hand, and of capital value on the other.

If the wages of I, in our illustration, were paid four times per year, we should have $4 \times 250 = 1,000$. Hence £250 in money would suffice for the circulation $I_v - \frac{1}{2} II_c$ and for that between the variable capital I_v and the labour power I. Likewise, if the circulation between I_s and II_c were to take place in four turnovers, it would require only £250, or in the aggregate a sum of money, or a money capital, of £500 for the circulation of commodities amounting to £5,000. In that case the surplus value would be converted into money four times successively, $\frac{1}{4}$ each time, instead of twice successively, one half each time.

If I instead of II should act as buyer in exchange No. 4 and expend £500 for articles of consumption of the same value, II would buy means of production with the same £500 in exchange No. 5; 6) I buys articles of consumption with the same £500; 7) II buys means of production with the same £500 so that the £500 finally return to I, the same as before to II. The surplus value is here converted into money by means of the money spent by the capitalist producers themselves for their individual consumption. This money represents the anticipated revenue, the anticipated receipts from the surplus value contained in the commodities still to be sold. The surplus value is not converted into money by the reflux of the £500; for aside from £1,000 in the form of commodities I_v, I threw £500 in money into circulation at the close of exchange No. 4, and this was additional money, so far as we know, and not the proceeds from the sale of commodities. If this money flows back to I, I merely gets back its additional money, and does not thereby convert its surplus value into money. The conversion of the surplus value I into money takes place only by the sale of the commodities I_s, in which it is incorporated, and lasts each time only until the money obtained by the sale of the commodities is expended anew in the purchase of articles of consumption.

With additional money (£500) I buys articles of consumption from II; this money was spent by I, which holds its equivalent in II commodities; the money returns for the first time by the purchase from I by II of commodities to the amount of £500; in other words, it returns as the equivalent of the commodities sold by I, but these commodities do not cost I anything, they constitute surplus value for I, and *thus the money thrown into circulation by this very department turns its own surplus value into money.* On buying for the second time (No. 6) I has likewise obtained its equivalent in II commodities. Take it, now, that II does not buy (No. 7) means of production from I. In that case I would have actually paid £1,000 for articles of consumption, thereby consuming its entire surplus value as revenue, namely 500 in its own I commodities (means of production) and 500 in money; on the other hand, it would still have £500 in its own commodities (means of production) in stock, and would have got rid of £500 in money.

On the contrary II would have reconverted three-fourths of its constant capital from the form of commodity capital into that of productive capital; but one-fourth (£500) would be held by it in the form of money capital, actually in the form of idle money, or of money which has suspended its function and is held in abeyance. Should this state of affairs last for any length of time, II would have to cut down its scale of reproduction by one-fourth.

However the 500 in means of production, which I has on its hands, are not surplus value existing in the form of commodities; they occupy the place of the £500 advanced in money, which I possessed aside from its £1,000 of surplus value in commodity form. In the form of money, they are always convertible; as commodities they are momentarily unsaleable. So much is evident: that simple reproduction — in which every element of productive capital must be replaced in both II and I — remains possible in this case only if the 500 golden birds, which I first sent flying, return to it.

If a capitalist (we have only industrial capitalists still to deal with here, who are the representatives of all others) spends money for articles of consumption, he is through with it, it goes the way of all flesh. It can flow back to him only if he fishes it out of circulation in exchange for commodities, i. e., for his commodity capital. As the value of his entire annual commodity product (his commodity capital), so that of every one of its elements, i. e., the value of every individual commodity, is divisible, as far as he is concerned, into constant capital value, variable capital value, and surplus value. The conversion into money of every individual commodity (as elements constituting the commodity product) is consequently at the same time such a conversion of a certain portion of the surplus value contained in the entire commodity product. In this case, then, it is literally true that the capitalist himself threw the money into circulation—when he spent it on articles of consumption—by which his surplus value is converted into money, or realised. Of course it is not a question of the identical coins but of a certain amount of hard cash equal to the one (or to a portion of the one) which he had previously thrown into circulation to satisfy his personal wants.

In practice this occurs in two ways: If the business has just been opened, in the current year, it will take quite a while, at least a few months, before the capitalist is able to use any portion of the receipts of his business for his personal consumption. But for all that he does not suspend his consumption for a single moment. He advances to himself (immaterial whether out of his own pocket or by means of credit from the pocket of somebody else) money in anticipation of surplus value still to be snatched by him; but in doing so he also advances a circulating medium for the realisation of surplus value to be realised later. If, on the contrary, the business has been running regularly for a longer period, payments and receipts are distributed over different terms throughout the year. But one thing continues uninterruptedly, namely, the consumption of the capitalist, which anticipates, and whose volume is computed on a definite proportion of, the customary or estimated revenue. With every portion of commodities sold, a portion of the surplus value to be produced annually is also realised. But if during the entire year only as much of the produced commodities is sold as is required to replace the constant and variable capital values contained in them, or if prices were to fall to such an extent that only the advanced capital value contained in the entire annual commodity product should be realised on its sale, then the anticipatory character of the expenditure of money in expectation of future surplus value would be clearly revealed. If our capitalist fails, his creditors and the court investigate whether his anticipated private expenditures were in proper proportion to the volume of his business and to the receipt of surplus value usually or normally corresponding to it.

So far as the entire capitalist class is concerned, the proposition that it must itself throw into circulation the money required for the realisation of its surplus value (correspondingly also for the circulation of its capital, constant and variable) not only fails to appear paradoxical, but stands forth as a necessary condition of the entire mechanism. For there are here only two classes: the working class disposing only of its labour power, and the capitalist class, which has a monopoly of the social means of production and money. It would rather be a paradox if the working class were to advance in the first instance from its own resources the money required for the realisation of the surplus value contained in the commodities. But the individual capitalist makes this advance only by acting as a buyer, *expending* money in the purchase of articles of consumption or *advancing* money in the purchase of elements of his productive capital, whether of labour power or means of production. He never parts with his money unless he gets an equivalent for it. He advances money to the circulation only in the same way as he advances commodities to it. He acts in both instances as the initial point of their circulation.

The actual process is obscured by two circumstances:

1) The appearance in the process of circulation of industrial capital of *merchant's capital* (the first form of which is always money, since the merchant as such does not create any "product" or "commodity") and of *money capital* as an object of manipulation by a special kind of capitalists.

2) The division of surplus value—which must always be first in the hands of the industrial capitalist—into various categories, the vehicles of which there appear, aside from the industrial capitalist, as the landlord (for ground rent), the usurer (for interest), etc., as well as the government and its employees, rentiers, etc. These gentry appear as buyers vis-à-vis the industrial capitalist and to that extent as converters of his commodities into money; they too throw "money" *pro parte* into the circulation and he gets it from them. But it is always forgotten from what source they derived it originally, and continue deriving it ever anew.

VI. THE CONSTANT CAPITAL
OF DEPARTMENT I[48a]

It remains for us to analyse the constant capital of department $I = 4,000_c$. This value is equal to the value—appearing anew in the

[48a] From here, Manuscript II.

commodity product I — of the means of production consumed in the creation of this quantity of commodities. This re-appearing value, which was not produced in the process of production of I, but entered into it during the preceding year as constant value, as the given value of its means of production, exists now in the entire part of commodity mass I not absorbed by category II. And the value of this quantity of commodities thus left in the hands of the I capitalists = $^2/_3$ of the value of their entire annual commodity product. In the case of the individual capitalist producing some particular means of production we could say: He sells his commodity product; he converts it into money. By converting it into money he has also reconverted into money the constant portion of the value of his product. With this portion of value converted into money he then buys his means of production once more from other sellers of commodities or transforms the constant portion of the value of his product into a natural form in which it can resume its function of productive constant capital. But now this assumption becomes impossible. The capitalist class of I comprises the totality of the capitalists producing means of production. Besides, the commodity product of 4,000, which is left in their hands, is a portion of the social product which cannot be exchanged for any other, because no such other portion of the annual product remains. With the exception of these 4,000, all the remainder has been disposed of. One portion has been absorbed by the social consumption fund, and another portion has to replace the constant capital of department II, which has already exchanged everything it could dispose of in an exchange with department I.

The difficulty is solved very easily if we remember that the entire commodity product I in its natural form consists of means of production, i. e., of the material elements of the constant capital itself. We meet here the same phenomenon which we witnessed before under II, only in a different aspect. In the case of II the entire commodity product consisted of articles of consumption. Hence one portion of it, measured by the wages plus surplus value contained in this product, could be consumed by its own producers. Here, in the case of I, the entire product consists of means of production, of buildings, machinery, vessels, raw and auxiliary materials, etc. One portion of them, namely that replacing the constant capital employed in this sphere, can therefore immediately function anew in its natural form as a component of the productive capital. So far as it goes into circulation, it circulates within class I. In II a part of the commodity product is individually consumed *in natura* by its own producers while in I a portion of the product is productively consumed *in natura* by its capitalist producers.

In the part of the commodity product $I = 4,000_c$ the constant capital value consumed in this category re-appears, and does so in a natural form in which it can immediately resume its function of productive constant capital. In II that portion of the commodity product of 3,000 whose value is equal to the wages plus the surplus value $(= 1,000)$ passes directly into the individual consumption of the capitalists and labourers of II, while on the other hand the constant capital value of this commodity product $(= 2,000)$ cannot re-enter the productive consumption of the II capitalists but must be replaced by exchange with I.

In I, on the contrary, that portion of its commodity product of 6,000 whose value is equal to the wages plus the surplus value $(= 2,000)$ does not pass into the individual consumption of its producers, and cannot do so on account of its natural form. It must first be exchanged with II. Contrariwise the constant portion of the value of this product $= 4,000$ exists in a natural form in which — taking the capitalist class I as a whole — it can immediately resume its function of constant capital of that class. In other words, the entire product of department I consists of use values which, on account of their natural form, can under a capitalist mode of production serve only as elements of constant capital. Hence one-third (2,000) of this product of 6,000 replaces the constant capital of department II, and the other two-thirds the constant capital of department I.

The constant capital I consists of a great number of different groups of capital invested in the various branches of production of means of production, so much in iron works, so much in coal-mines, etc. Every one of these groups of capital, or every one of these social group capitals, is in its turn composed of a larger or smaller number of independently functioning individual capitals. In the first place, the capital of society, for instance 7,500 (which may mean millions, etc.), is composed of various groups of capital; the social capital of 7,500 is divided into separate parts, every one of which is invested in a special branch of production; each portion of the social capital value invested in some particular branch of production consists, so far as its natural form is concerned, partly of means of production required in that particular sphere of production, partly of the labour power needed in that business and trained accordingly, variously modified by division of labour, according to the specific kind of labour to be performed in each individual sphere of production. The portion of social capital invested in each particular branch of production in its turn consists of the sum of the individual capitals invested in it and functioning independently. This patently applies to both departments, I as well as II.

As for the constant capital value re-appearing in I in the form of its commodity product, it re-enters in part as means of production into the particular sphere of production (or even into the individual business) from which it emerges as product; for instance corn into the production of corn, coal into the production of coal, iron in the form of machines into the production of iron, etc.

However since the partial products constituting the constant capital value I do not return directly to their particular or individual sphere of production, they merely change their place. They pass in their natural form to some other sphere of production of department I, while the product of other spheres of production of department I replaces them *in natura*. It is merely a change of place of these products. All of them re-enter as factors replacing constant capital in I, only instead of the same group of I they enter another. Since an exchange takes place here between the individual capitalist of I, it is an exchange of one natural form of constant capital for another natural form of constant capital, of one kind of means of production for other kinds of means of production. It is an exchange of the different individual parts of constant capital I among themselves. Products which do not serve directly as means of production in their own sphere are transferred from their place of production to another and thus mutually replace one another. In other words (similarly to what happens in the case of the surplus value II), every capitalist I draws from this quantity of commodities, proportionally to his share in the constant capital of 4,000, the means of production required by him. If production were social instead of capitalist, these products of department I would evidently just as regularly be redistributed as means of production to the various branches of this department, for purposes of reproduction, one portion remaining directly in that sphere of production from which it emerged as a product, another passing over to other places of production, thereby giving rise to a constant to-and-fro movement between the various places of production in this department.

VII. VARIABLE CAPITAL AND SURPLUS VALUE
IN BOTH DEPARTMENTS

The total value of the annually produced articles of consumption is thus equal to the variable capital value II reproduced during the year plus the newly produced surplus value II (i. e., equal to the value produced by II during the year) plus the variable capital value I reproduced during the year and the newly produced surplus value I (i. e., plus the value created by I during the year).

On the assumption of simple reproduction the total value of the annually produced articles of consumption is therefore equal to the annual value product, i. e., equal to the total value produced during the year by social labour, and this must be so, because in simple reproduction this entire value is consumed.

The total social working day is divided into two parts: 1) necessary labour, which creates in the course of the year a value of $1,500_v$; 2) surplus labour, which creates an additional value, or surplus value, of $1,500_s$. The sum of these values, 3,000, is equal to the value of the annually produced articles of consumption — 3,000. The total value of the articles of consumption produced during the year is therefore equal to the total value produced by the total social working day during the year, equal to the value of the social variable capital plus the social surplus value, equal to the total new product of the year.

But we know that even if these two magnitudes of value are equal, this in no way means that the total value of commodities II, the articles of consumption, has been produced in this department of social production. They are equal because the constant capital value reappearing in II is equal to the value newly produced by I (value of variable capital plus surplus value); therefore $I_{(v+s)}$ can buy the part of the product of II which represents the constant capital value for its producers (in department II). This shows, then, why the value of the product of capitalists II, from the point of view of society, may be resolved into $v + s$ although for these capitalists it is divided into $c + v + s$. This is so only because II_c is here equal to $I_{(v+s)}$, and because these two components of the social product interchange their natural forms by exchange, so that after this transformation II_c exists once more in means of production and $I_{(v+s)}$ in articles of consumption.

And it is this circumstance which induced Adam Smith to maintain that the value of the annual product resolves itself into $v + s$. This is true 1) only for that part of the annual product which consists of articles of consumption, and 2) it is not true in the sense that this total value is produced in II and that the value of its product is equal to the value of the variable capital advanced in II plus the surplus value produced in II. It is true only in the sense that $II_{(c+v+s)} = II_{(v+s)} + I_{(v+s)}$, or because $II_c = I_{(v+s)}$.

It follows furthermore:

The social working day (i. e., the labour expended by the entire working class during the whole year), like every individual working day, breaks up into only two parts, namely into necessary labour and surplus labour, and the value produced by this working day consequently likewise resolves itself into only two parts, namely into the value of the variable capital, or that portion of the value with which the labourer buys the means of his own reproduction, and the surplus value which the capitalist may spend for his own individual consumption. Nevertheless, from the point of view of society, one part of the social working day is spent exclusively on the *production of new constant capital*, namely of products exclusively intended to function as means of production in the labour process and hence as constant capital in the accompanying process of self-expansion of value. According to our assumption the total social working day presents itself as a money value of 3,000, of which only $^1/_3 = 1,000$ is produced in department II which manufactures articles of consumption, that is, the commodities in which the entire value of the variable capital and the entire surplus value of society are ultimately realised. Thus, according to this assumption, $^2/_3$ of the social working day are employed in the production of new constant capital. Although from the standpoint of the individual capitalists and labourers of department I these $^2/_3$ of the social working day serve merely for the production of variable capital value plus surplus value, the same as the last third of the social working day in department II, still from the point of view of society and likewise of the use value of the product, these $^2/_3$ of the social working day produce only replacement of constant capital in the process of productive consumption or already so consumed. Also when viewed individually, these $^2/_3$ of the working day, while producing a total value equal only to the value of the variable capital plus surplus value for the producer, nevertheless do not produce any use values of a kind on which wages or surplus value could be expended; for their products are means of production.

It must be noted in the first place that no portion of the social working day, whether in I or in II, serves for the production of the value of the constant capital employed and functioning in these two great spheres of production. They produce only additional value, $2,000 \, I_{(v+s)} + 1,000 \, II_{(v+s)}$, in addition to the value of the constant capital $= 4,000 \, I_c + 2,000 \, II_c$. The new value produced in the form of means of production is not yet constant capital. It merely is intended to function as such in the future.

The entire product of II — the articles of consumption — viewed concretely as a use value, in its natural form, is a product of the one-third of the social working day spent by II. It is the product of labour in its concrete form — such as the labour of weaving, baking, etc., performed in this department — the product of this labour, inasmuch as it functions as the subjective element of the labour process. As to the constant portion of the value of this product II, it re-appears only in a new use value, in a new natural form, the form of articles of consumption, while it existed previously in the form of means of production. Its value has been transferred by the labour process from its old natural form to its new natural form. But the *value* of these $^2/_3$ of the product value $= 2,000$ has not been produced in this year's self-expansion process of II.

Just as from the point of view of the labour process, the product of II is the result of newly functioning living labour and of the assumed means of production assigned to it, in which that labour materialises itself as in its objective conditions, so, from the point of view of the process of self-expansion, the value of the product of II $= 3,000$ is composed of a new value $(500_v + 500_s = 1,000)$ produced by the newly added $^1/_3$ of the social working day and of a constant value in which are objectified $^2/_3$ of a past social working day that had elapsed before the present process of production of II here under consideration. This portion of the value of the II product finds expression in a portion of the product itself. It exists in a quantity of articles of consumption worth $2,000 = {}^2/_3$ of a social working day. This is the new use form in which this value portion re-appears. The exchange of part of the articles of consumption equal to $2,000 \, II_c$ for means of production of $I = I \, (1,000_v + 1,000_s)$ thus really represents an exchange of two-thirds of an aggregate working day — which do not constitute any portion of this year's labour, and elapsed before this year — for $^2/_3$ of the working day newly added this year. Two-thirds of this year's so-cial working day could not be employed in the production of constant capital and at the same time constitute variable capital value plus surplus value for their own producers unless they were to be ex-changed for a portion of the value of the annually consumed articles of consumption, in which are incorporated $^2/_3$ of a working day spent and realised before this year. It is an exchange of $^2/_3$ of this year's working day for $^2/_3$ of a working day spent before this year, an ex-change of this year's labour time for last year's. This therefore ex-plains the riddle of how the value product of an entire social working day can resolve itself into variable capital value plus surplus value, al-though $^2/_3$ of this working day were not expended in the production of articles in which variable capital or surplus value can be realised, but rather in the production of means of production for the replace-ment of the capital consumed during the year. The explanation is simply that $^2/_3$ of the value of the product of II, in which the capital-ists and labourers of I realise the variable capital value plus surplus value produced by them (and which constitute $^2/_9$ of the value of the entire annual product), are, so far as their value is concerned, the product of $^2/_3$ of a social working day of a year prior to the current one.

The sum of the social product I and II — means of production and articles of consumption — is indeed, viewed from the standpoint of their use value, in their concrete, natural form, the product of this year's labour, but only to the extent that this labour itself is regarded as useful and concrete and not as an expenditure of labour power, as value-creating labour. And even the first is true only in the sense that the means of production have transformed themselves into new prod-ucts, into this year's products, solely by dint of the living labour add-ed on to them, operating on them. On the contrary, this year's la-bour could not have transformed itself into products without means of production independent of it, without instruments of labour and materials of production.

VIII. THE CONSTANT CAPITAL IN BOTH DEPARTMENTS

The analysis of the total value of the product of 9,000, and of the categories into which it is divided, does not present any greater diffi-culty than that of the value produced by an individual capital. On the contrary, they are identical.

The entire annual social product here contains three social working days, each of one year. The value expressed by each one of these working days is 3,000, so that the value expressed by the total product = $3 \times 3{,}000 = 9{,}000$.

Furthermore, the following portions of this working time have elapsed *prior* to the one-year process of production, the product of which we are now analysing: In department I $^4/_3$ of a working day (with a product worth 4,000), and in department II $^2/_3$ of a working day (with a product worth 2,000), making a total of 2 social working days with a product = 6,000. For this reason $4{,}000\ I_c + 2{,}000\ II_c = 6{,}000_c$ figure as the value of the means of production, or the constant capital value re-appearing in the total value of the social product.

Furthermore, $^1/_3$ of the social working day of one year newly added in department I is necessary labour, or labour replacing the value of the variable capital of $1{,}000\ I_v$ and paying the price of the labour employed by I. In the same way $^1/_6$ of a social working day in II is necessary with a value of 500. Hence $1{,}000\ I_v + 500\ II_v = 1{,}500_v$, expressing the value of one half of the social working day, is the value expression of the first half of the aggregate working day added this year and consisting of necessary labour.

Finally, in department I $^1/_3$ of the aggregate working day, with a product = 1,000, is surplus labour, and in department II $^1/_6$ of the working day, with a product = 500, is surplus labour. Together they constitute the other half of the added aggregate working day. Hence the total surplus value produced = $1{,}000\ I_s + 500\ II_s = 1{,}500_s$.

Thus:

The constant capital portion of the value of the social product (c):
Two working days expended prior to the process of production; value expression = 6,000.

Necessary labour (v) expended during the year:
One half of a working day expended on the annual production; value expression = 1,500.

Surplus labour (s) expended during the year:
One half of a working day expended on the annual production; value expression = 1,500.

Value produced by annual labour (v + s) = 3,000.

Total value of product (c + v + s) = 9,000.

The difficulty, then, does not consist in the analysis of the value of the social product itself. It arises in the comparison of the component parts of the *value* of the social product with its *material* constituents.

The constant, merely re-appearing portion of value is equal to the value of that part of this product which consists of means of *production* and is incorporated in that part.

The new value product of the year, equal to $v + s$, is equal to the value of that part of this product which consists of *articles of consumption* and is incorporated in it.

But with exceptions of no consequence here, means of production and articles of consumption are wholly different kinds of commodities, products of entirely different natural or use forms, and, therefore, products of wholly different classes of concrete labour. The labour which employs machinery in the production of means of subsistence is vastly different from the labour which makes machinery. The entire aggregate annual working day, whose value expression = 3,000, seems spent in the production of articles of consumption = 3,000, in which no constant portion of value re-appears, since these $3,000 = 1,500_v + 1,500_s$ resolve themselves only into variable capital value + surplus value. On the other hand the constant capital value of 6,000 re-appears in a class of products quite different from articles of consumption, namely in means of production, while as a matter of fact no part of the social working day seems spent in the production of these new products. It seems rather that the entire working day consists only of classes of labour which do not result in means of production but in articles of consumption. This mystery has already been cleared up. The value product of the year's labour is equal to the value of the products of department II, to the total value of the newly produced articles of consumption. But the value of these products is greater by $^2/_3$ than that portion of the annual labour which has been expended in the sphere of production of articles of consumption (department II). Only $^1/_3$ of the annual labour has been expended in their production. Two-thirds of this annual labour have been expended in the production of means of production, that is to say, in department I. The value product created during this time in I, equal to the variable capital value plus surplus value produced in I, is equal to the constant capital value of II re-appearing in articles of consumption of II. Hence they may be mutually exchanged and replaced *in natura*. The total value of the articles of consumption of II is therefore equal to the sum of the new value product of I + II, or $II_{(c+v+s)} =$

$I_{(v+s)} + II_{(v+s)}$, hence equal to the sum of the new values produced by the year's labour in the form of v plus s.

On the other hand the total value of the means of production (I) is equal to the sum of the constant capital value re-appearing in the form of means of production (I) and in that of articles of consumption (II); in other words, equal to the sum of the constant capital value re-appearing in the total product of society. This total value is equal in terms of value to $^4/_3$ of a working day preceding the process of production of I and $^2/_3$ of a working day preceding the process of production of II, in all equal to two aggregate working days.

The difficulty with the annual social product arises therefore from the fact that the constant portion of value is represented by a wholly different class of products — means of production — than the new value v + s added to this constant portion of value and represented by articles of consumption. Thus the appearance is created, so far as value is concerned, that $^2/_3$ of the consumed mass of products are found again in a new form as new product, without any labour having been expended by society in their production. This is not so in the case of an individual capital. Every individual capitalist employs some particular concrete kind of labour, which transforms the means of production peculiar to it into a product. Let, for instance, the capitalist be a machine-builder, the constant capital expended during the year = $6,000_c$, the variable = $1,500_v$, the surplus value = $1,500_s$; the product = 9,000, the product, say, 18 machines of 500 each. The entire product here exists in the same form, that of machines. (If he produces various kinds, each kind is calculated separately.) The entire commodity product is the result of the labour expended during the year in machine-building; it is a combination of the same concrete kind of labour with the same means of production. The various portions of the value of the product therefore present themselves in the same natural form: 12 machines embody $6,000_c$, 3 machines $1,500_v$, 3 machines $1,500_s$. In the present case it is evident that the value of the 12 machines = $6,000_c$, not because there is incorporated in these 12 machines only labour performed previously to the manufacture of these machines and not labour expended on building them. The value of the means of production for 18 machines did not of itself become transformed into 12 machines but the value of these 12 machines (consisting itself of $4,000_c + 1,000_v + 1,000_s$) is equal to the total value of the constant capital contained in the 18 machines. The machine-manufacturer must therefore sell 12 of the 18 machines in order to replace his expended constant capital, which he requires for the reproduction of 18 new machines. On the contrary, the thing would be inexplicable if, in spite of the fact that the labour expended was employed solely in the manufacture of machines, the result were to be: On the one hand 6 machines = $1,500_v + 1,500_s$, on the other iron, copper, screws, belts, etc., of a value amounting to $6,000_c$, i. e., the means of production of the machines in their natural form, which, as we know, the individual machine-building capitalist does not produce himself but must replace by way of the process of circulation. And yet it seems at first glance that the reproduction of the annual product of society takes place in this absurd way.

The product of an individual capital, i. e., of every fraction of the social capital endowed with a life of its own and functioning independently, has a natural form of one kind or another. The only condition is that this product must really have a use form, a use value, which gives it the imprint of a member of the world of commodities capable of circulation. It is completely immaterial and accidental whether or not it can re-enter as a means of production into the same process of production from which it emerged as a product; in other words, whether the portion of its value representing the constant part of the capital has a natural form in which it can actually function again as constant capital. If not, this portion of the value of the product is reconverted into the form of its material elements of production by means of sale and purchase and thus the constant capital is reproduced in the natural form capable of functioning.

It is different with the product of the aggregate social capital. All the material elements of reproduction must in their natural form constitute parts of this product. The consumed constant part of capital can be replaced by the aggregate production only to the extent that the entire constant part of the capital re-appearing in the product re-appears in the natural form of new means of production which can really function as constant capital. Hence, simple reproduction being assumed, the value of that portion of the product which consists of means of production must be equal to the constant portion of the value of social capital.

Furthermore: Considered individually, the capitalist produces in the value of his product by means of the newly added labour only his variable capital plus surplus value, while the constant part of the value is transferred to the product owing to the concrete character of the newly added labour.

Considered socially, that portion of the social working day which produces means of production, hence adding new value to them as well as transferring to them the value of the means of production consumed in their manufacture, creates nothing but new *constant capital* intended to replace that consumed in the shape of old means of production in both departments I and II. It creates only product intended for productive consumption. The entire value of this product, then, is only value which can function anew as constant capital, which can only buy back constant capital in its natural form, and which, for this reason, resolves itself, considered socially, neither into variable capital nor surplus value.

On the other hand that part of the social working day which produces articles of consumption does not create any portion of the social replacement capital. It creates only products intended, in their natural form, to realise the value of the variable capital and surplus value of I and II.

Speaking from the point of view of society, and therefore considering the aggregate product of society, which comprises both the reproduction of social capital and individual consumption, we must not lapse into the manner copied by Proudhon from bourgeois economy and look upon this matter as though a society with a capitalist mode of production, if viewed *en bloc*, as a totality, would lose this its specific historical and economic character. No, on the contrary. We have, in that case, to deal with the aggregate capitalist. The aggregate capital appears as the capital stock of all individual capitalists combined. This joint-stock company has in common with many other stock companies that everyone knows what he puts in, but *not* what he will get out of it.

IX. A RETROSPECT TO ADAM SMITH, STORCH, AND RAMSAY

The aggregate value of the social product amounts to $9,000 = 6,000_c + 1,500_v + 1,300_s$; in other words: 6,000 reproduce the value of the means of production and 3,000 that of the articles of consumption. The value of the social revenue $(v + s)$ amounts therefore to only $^1/_3$ of the value of the aggregate product, and the totality of consumers, labourers as well as capitalists, can draw commodities, products out of the total social product and incorporate them in their consumption fund only to the amount of this $^1/_3$. On the other hand 6,000, or $^2/_3$ of the value of the product, are the value of the constant capital which must be replaced *in natura*. Means of production to this amount must therefore again be incorporated in the production fund. Storch recognised this as essential without being able to prove it:

> "It is clear that the value of the annual product is divided partly into capital and part-ly into profits, and that each one of these portions of the value of the annual product is regularly employed in buying the products which the nation needs both for the mainte-nance of its capital and for replacing its consumption fund.... The products which constitute the *capital* of a nation *are not to be consumed*"[a] (Storch, *Considèrations sur la na-ture du revenu national*, Paris, 1824, pp. 134-35, 150).

Adam Smith, however, has promulgated this astounding dogma, which is believed to this day, not only in the previously mentioned form, according to which the entire value of the social product resolves itself into revenue, into wages plus surplus value, or, as he ex-presses it, into wages plus profit (interest) plus ground rent, but also in the still more popular form, according to which the *consumers* must "ULTIMATELY"[b] pay to the producers the *entire value of the product*. This is to this day one of the best-established commonplaces, or rather eternal truths, of the so-called science of political economy. This is il-lustrated in the following plausible manner: Take any article, for in-stance a linen shirt. First, the spinner of linen yarn has to pay the flax-grower the entire value of the flax, i. e., the value of flax-seed, fer-tilisers, labouring cattle feed, etc., plus that part of the value which the fixed capital, such as buildings, agricultural implements, etc., of the flax-grower gives up to the product; the wages paid in the produc-tion of the flax; the surplus value (profit, ground rent) embodied in the flax; finally the carriage costs of the flax from its place of produc-tion to the spinnery. Next, the weaver has to reimburse the spinner of the linen yarn not only for the price of the flax, but also for that por-tion of the value of machinery, buildings, etc., in short of the fixed cap-ital, which is transferred to the flax; furthermore, all the auxiliary materials consumed in the spinning process, the wages of the spin-ners, the surplus value, etc., and so the thing goes on with the

---

[a] Marx quotes Storch in French. - [b] In the original, this English word is given in parentheses after its German equivalent.

bleacher, the transportation costs of the finished linen, and finally the shirt manufacturer, who has to pay the entire price of all preceding producers, who supplied him only with his raw material. In his hands a further addition of value takes place, partly through the value of constant capital consumed in the manufacture of shirts in the shape of instruments of labour, auxiliary materials, etc., and partly through the labour expended, which adds the value of the shirt makers' wages plus the surplus value of the shirt manufacturer. Now let this entire product in shirts cost ultimately £100 and let this be the aliquot part of the value of the total annual product expended by society on shirts. The consumers of the shirts pay these £100, i. e., the value of all the means of production contained in the shirts, and of the wages plus surplus value of the flax-grower, spinner, weaver, bleacher, shirt manufacturer, and all carriers. This is absolutely correct. Indeed, every child can see that. But then it says: That's how matters stand with regard to the value of all other commodities. It should say: That's how matters stand with regard to the value of *all articles of consumption*, with regard to the value of that portion of the social product which passes into the consumption fund, i. e., with regard to that portion of the value of the social product which can be expended as revenue. True enough, the sum of the values of all these commodities is equal to the value of all the means of production (constant portions of capital) used up in them plus the value created by the labour last added (wages plus surplus value). Hence the totality of the consumers can pay for this entire sum of values because, although the value of each individual commodity is made up of c + v + s, nevertheless the sum of the values of all commodities passing into the consumption fund, taken at its maximum, can be equal only to that portion of the value of the social product which resolves itself into v + s, in other words, equal to that value which the labour expended during the year has added to the existing means of production — to the value of the constant capital. As for the value of the constant capital, we have seen that it is replaced out of the mass of social products in a two-fold way. First, through an exchange by capitalists II, who produce articles of consumption, with capitalists I, who produce the means of production for them. And here is the source of the saying that what is capital for the one is revenue for the other.[55] But this is not the actual state of affairs. The 2,000 II$_c$ existing in the shape of articles of consumption worth 2,000 constitute a constant capital value for the capitalist class of II. They therefore cannot consume this value themselves, although the product in accordance with its natural form is intended for consumption. On the other hand, the 2,000 $I_{(v+s)}$ are wages plus surplus value produced by capitalist and working class I. They exist in the natural form of means of production, of things in which their own value cannot be consumed. We have here, then, a sum of values to the amount of 4,000, one half of which, before and after the exchange, replaces only constant capital, while the other half forms only revenue.

In the second place, the constant capital of department I is replaced *in natura*, partly by exchange among capitalists I, partly by replacement *in natura* in each individual business.

The phrase that the value of the entire annual product must ultimately be paid by the consumer [56] would be correct only if consumer were taken to comprise two vastly different kinds: individual consumers and productive consumers. However that one portion of the product must be consumed *productively* means nothing but that it must *function as capital* and not be *consumed as revenue*.

If we divide the value of the aggregate product = 9,000 into $6,000_c + 1,500_v + 1,500_s$ and look upon the $3,000_{(v+s)}$ only in its quality of revenue, then, on the contrary, the variable capital seems to disappear and capital, socially speaking, to consist only of constant capital. For that which appeared originally as $1,500_v$ has resolved itself into a portion of the social revenue, into wages, the revenue of the working class, and its character of capital has thus vanished. This conclusion is actually drawn by Ramsay. According to him, capital, socially considered, consists only of fixed capital, but by fixed capital he means the constant capital, that quantity of values which consists of means of production, whether these means of production are instruments or materials of labour, such as raw materials, semi-finished products, auxiliary materials, etc. He calls the variable capital circulating capital:

* "Circulating capital consists exclusively of subsistence and other necessaries advanced to the workmen, previous to the completion of the produce of their labour... Fixed capital alone, not circulating, is properly speaking a source of national wealth... Circulating capital is not an immediate agent in production, nor even essential to it at all, but merely a convenience rendered necessary by the deplorable poverty of the mass of the people... Fixed capital alone constitutes an element of cost of production in a national point of view" * (Ramsay, l. c., pp. 23-26, *passim*).

Ramsay defines fixed capital, by which he means constant capital, more closely in the following words:

* "The length of time during which any portion of the product of that labour" * (namely LABOUR BESTOWED ON ANY COMMODITY) *"has existed as fixed capital; that is, in a form in which, though assisting to raise the future commodity, *it does not maintain labourers*" * (ibid., p. 59).

Here we see once more the calamity Adam Smith brings on by submerging the distinction between constant and variable capital in that between fixed capital and circulating capital. Ramsay's constant capital consists of instruments of labour, his circulating capital of means of subsistence. Both of them are commodities of a given value. The one can no more create surplus value than the other.

X. CAPITAL AND REVENUE: VARIABLE CAPITAL AND WAGES [49]

The entire annual reproduction, the entire product of the year is the product of the useful labour of that year. But the value of this total product is greater than that portion of the value in which the annual labour, the labour power expended during the current year, is incorporated. The *value product* of this year, the value newly created during this period in the form of commodities, is smaller than the *value of the product*, the aggregate value of the mass of commodities fabricated during the entire year. The difference obtained by deducting from the total value of the annual product that value which was added to it by the labour of the current year, is not really reproduced value but only value re-appearing in a new form of existence. It is value transferred to the annual product from value existing prior to it, which may be of an earlier or later date, according to the durability of the components of the constant capital which have participated in that year's social labour process, a value which may originate from the value of means of production which came into the world the previous year or in a number of years even previous to that. It is by all means a value transferred from means of production of former years to the product of the current year.

Take our scheme. We have, after the exchange of the elements hitherto considered between I and II, and within II:

[49] The following is from Manuscript VIII.

I. $4,000_c + 1,000_v + 1,000_s$ (the latter 2,000 realised in articles of consumption of II_c) = 6,000.

II. $2,000_c$ (reproduced by exchange with $I_{(v+s)}$) + $500_v + 500_s$ = 3,000.

Sum of values = 9,000.

Value newly produced during the year is contained only in v and s. The sum of the value product of this year is therefore equal to the sum of v + s, or $2,000\ I_{(v+s)} + 1,000\ II_{(v+s)} = 3,000$. All remaining value parts of the product of this year are merely value transferred from the value of earlier means of production consumed in the annual production. The current annual labour has not produced any value other than that of 3,000. That represents its entire annual value product.

Now, as we have seen, the $2,000\ I_{(v+s)}$ replace for class II its 2,000 II_c in the natural form of means of production. Two-thirds of the annual labour, then, expended in category I, have newly produced constant capital II, both its entire value and its natural form. From the standpoint of society, two-thirds of the labour expended during the year have created new constant capital value realised in the natural form appropriate for department II. Thus the greater portion of the annual labour of society has been spent in the production of new constant capital (capital value existing in the form of means of production) in order to replace the value of the constant capital expended in the production of articles of consumption. What distinguishes capitalist society in this case from the savage is not, as Senior[50] thinks, the privilege and peculiarity of the savage to expend his labour at times in a way that does not procure him any products resolvable (exchangeable) into revenue, i. e., into articles of consumption. No, the distinction consists in the following:

a) Capitalist society employs more of its available annual labour in the production of means of production (ergo, of constant capital) which are not resolvable into revenue in the form of wages or surplus value, but can function only as capital.

---

[50] "When the savage makes bows, he exercises an industry, but he does not practise abstinence" (Senior, *Principes fondamentaux de l'Economie Politique*,[57] trad. Arrivabene, Paris, 1836, pp. 342-43). "The more society progresses, the more abstinence is demanded" (ibid., p. 343). (Cf. *Das Kapital*, Buch I, Kap. XXII, 3, S. 619.[a])

---

[a] English edition: Vol. I, Ch. XXIV, 3 (present edition, Vol. 35).

b) When a savage makes bows, arrows, stone hammers, axes, baskets, etc., he knows very well that he did not spend the time so employed in the production of articles of consumption, but that he has thus stocked up the means of production he needs, and nothing else. Furthermore, a savage commits a grave economic sin by his utter indifference to waste of time, and, as Tyler[51] tells us, takes sometimes a whole month to make one arrow.

The current conception whereby some political economists seek to extricate themselves from the theoretical difficulty, i. e., the understanding of the real interconnections — that what is capital to one is revenue to another, and vice versa — is only partially correct and becomes utterly wrong (harbours therefore a complete misunderstanding of the entire process of exchange taking place in annual reproduction, hence also a misunderstanding of the actual basis of the partially correct) as soon as the character of universality is attributed to it.

We now summarise the actual relations on which the partial correctness of this conception rests, and in doing so the wrong conception of these relations will come to the surface at once.

1) The variable capital functions as capital in the hands of the capitalist and as revenue in the hands of the wage worker.

The variable capital exists at first in the hands of the capitalist as *money capital*; it performs the function of *money capital*, by his buying labour power with it. So long as it persists in his hands in the form of money, it is nothing but a given value existing in the form of money; hence a constant and not a variable magnitude. It is a variable capital only potentially, owing to its convertibility into labour power. It becomes real variable capital only after divesting itself of its money form, after being converted into labour power functioning as a component part of productive capital in the capitalist process.

Money, which first functioned as the money form of the variable capital for the capitalist, now functions in the hands of the labourer as the money form of his wages, which he exchanges for means of subsistence, hence as the money form of *revenue* derived from the constantly repeated sale of his labour power.

We have here but the simple fact that the *money* of the buyer, in this

[51] E. B. Tyler, *Forschungen über die Urgeschichte der Menschheit*, übersetzt von H. Müller, Leipzig, ohne Datum, S. 240. [58]

case the capitalist, passes from his hands into those of the seller, in this case the seller of labour power, the labourer. It is not a case of the variable *capital* functioning in a dual capacity, as capital for the capitalist and as revenue for the labourer. It is the same *money* which exists first in the hands of the capitalist as the money form of his variable capital, hence as potential variable capital, and which serves in the hands of the labourer as an equivalent for sold labour power as soon as the capitalist converts it into labour power. But the fact that the same money serves another useful purpose in the hands of the seller than in those of the buyer is a phenomenon peculiar to the purchase and sale of all commodities.

Apologetic economists present the matter in a wrong light, as is best seen if we keep our eyes fixed exclusively, without taking for the time being any notice of what follows, on the act of circulation $M — L$ ($= M — C$), the conversion of money into labour power on the part of the capitalist buyer, which is $L — M$ (equal to $C — M$), the conversion of the commodity labour power into money on the part of the seller, the labourer. They say: Here the same money realises two capitals; the buyer — the capitalist — converts his money capital into living labour power, which he incorporates in his productive capital; on the other hand the seller, the labourer, converts his commodity, labour power, into money, which he spends as revenue, and this enables him to keep on reselling his labour power and thereby to maintain it. His labour power, then, represents his capital in commodity form, which yields him a continuous revenue. Labour power is indeed his property (ever self-renewing, reproductive), not his capital. It is the only commodity which he can and must sell continually in order to live, and which acts as capital (variable) only in the hands of the buyer, the capitalist. The fact that a man is continually compelled to sell his labour power, i. e., himself, to another man proves, according to those economists, that he is a capitalist, because he constantly has "commodity" (himself) for sale. In that sense a slave is also a capitalist, although he is sold by another once and for all as a commodity; for it is in the nature of this commodity, a labouring slave, that its buyer does not only make it work anew every day, but also provides it with the means of subsistence that enable it to work ever anew. (Compare on this point Sismondi and Say in the letters to Malthus.[59]

2) And so, in the exchange of $1,000\ I_v + 1,000\ I_s$ for $2,000\ II_c$, what is constant capital for some ($2,000\ II_c$) becomes variable capital

and surplus value, hence generally revenue, for the others; and what is variable capital and surplus value $(2,000\ I_{(v+s)})$, hence generally revenue, for some becomes constant capital for the others.

Let us first look at the exchange of I_v for II_c, beginning with the point of view of the labourer.

The collective labourer of I has sold his labour power to the collective capitalist of I for 1,000; he receives this value in money, paid in the form of wages. With this money he buys from II articles of consumption for the same amount of value. Capitalist II confronts him only as a seller of commodities, and nothing else, even if the labourer buys from his own capitalist, as he does for instance in the exchange of 500 II_v, as we have seen above (p. 400[a]) [60]. The form of circulation through which his commodity, labour power, passes, is that of the simple circulation of commodities for the mere satisfaction of needs, for the purpose of consumption: C (labour power) — M — C (articles of consumption, commodities II). The result of this act of circulation is that the labourer maintains himself as labour power for capitalist I, and in order to continue maintaining himself as such he must continually renew the process L(C) — M — C. His wages are realised in articles of consumption, they are spent as revenue, and, taking the working class as a whole, are spent again and again as revenue.

Now let us look at the same exchange of I_v for II_c from the point of view of the capitalist. The entire commodity product of II consists of articles of consumption, hence of things intended to enter into annual consumption, hence to serve in the realisation of revenue for someone, in the present case for the collective labourer I. But for the collective capitalist II one portion of his commodity product, 2,000, is now the form of the constant capital value of his productive capital converted into commodities. This productive capital must be reconverted from this commodity form into its natural form, in which it may act again as the constant portion of a productive capital. What capitalist II has accomplished so far is that he has reconverted by means of sales to labourers I one half (= 1,000) of his constant capital value, which had been reproduced in the shape of commodities (articles of consumption), into the form of money. Hence it is not the variable capital I_v, which has been converted into this first half of the constant capital value II_c, but simply the money which functioned for I as money capital in the exchange for labour power and thus came into the possession of the seller of labour power, to whom it does not represent capital but revenue in the form of money, i. e., it is spent as a means of purchase of articles of consumption. Meanwhile, the money = 1,000, which has come into the hands of the II capitalists from labourers of I, cannot function as the constant element of productive capital II. It is only as yet the money form of his commodity capital to be commuted into fixed or circulating constituents of constant capital. So II buys with the money received from the labourers of I, the buyers of its commodities, means of production from I to the amount of 1,000. In this way the constant capital value II is renewed to the extent of one half of its total amount in its natural form, in which it can function once more as an element of productive capital II. The circulation in this instance took the course C — M — C: articles of consumption worth 1,000 — money = 1,000 — means of production worth 1,000.

But C — M — C represents here the movement of capital. C, when sold to the labourers, is converted into M, and this M is converted into means of production. It is the reconversion of commodities into the material elements of which this commodity is made. On the other hand just as capitalist II acts vis-à-vis I only as a buyer of commodities, so capitalist I acts only as a seller of commodities vis-à-vis II. I originally bought labour power worth 1,000 with 1,000 in money intended to function as variable capital. It has therefore received an equivalent for the $1,000_v$ which it expended in money form. This money now belongs to the labourer who spends it in purchases from II; I cannot get back this money, which thus found its way into the II treasury, unless it fishes it out of it again by the sale of commodities of the same value.

Department I first had a definite sum of money = 1,000 destined to function as variable capital; it functions as such by its conversion into labour power of the same value. But the labourer supplied it as a result of the process of production with a quantity of commodities (means of production) worth 6,000, of which $^1/_6$, or 1,000, are equivalent to the variable portion of capital advanced in money. The variable capital value functions no more as variable capital now in its commodity form than it did before in its form of money. It can do so only after its conversion into living labour power, and only so long as this labour power functions in the process of production. As money the variable capital value was only potential variable capital. But it had a form in which it was directly convertible into labour power. As a commodity the same variable capital value is still potential money value; it is restored to its original money form only by the sale of the commodities, and therefore by II buying for 1,000 commodities from I. The movement of the circulation is here as follows: $1,000_v$ (money) — labour power worth $1,000 — 1,000$ in commodities (equivalent of the variable capital) $— 1,000_v$ (money); hence $M — C...$ $C — M$ ($= M — L ... C — M$). The process of production intervening between $C ... C$ does not itself belong in the sphere of circulation. It does not figure in the mutual exchange of the various elements of the annual reproduction, although this exchange includes the reproduction of all the elements of productive capital, the constant elements as well as the variable element (labour power). All the participants in this exchange appear either as buyers or sellers or both. The labourers appear only as buyers of commodities, the capitalists alternately as buyers and sellers, and within certain limits either only as buyers of commodities or only as sellers of commodities.

Result: I possesses once more the variable value constituent of its capital in the form of money, from which alone it is directly convertible into labour power, i. e., it once more possesses the variable capital value in the sole form in which it can really be advanced as a variable element of its productive capital. On the other hand the labourer must again act as a seller of commodities, of his labour power, before he can act again as a buyer of commodities.

So far as the variable capital of category II (500 II_v) is concerned, the process of circulation between the capitalists and labourers of the same class of production takes place directly, since we look upon it as taking place between the collective capitalist II and the collective labourer II.

The collective capitalist II advances 500_v for the purchase of labour power of the same value. In this case the collective capitalist is a buyer, the collective labourer a seller. Thereupon the labourer appears with the proceeds of the sale of his labour power to act as a buyer of a part of the commodities produced by himself. Here the capitalist is therefore a seller. The labourer has replaced to the capitalist the money paid in the purchase of his labour power by means of a portion of commodity capital II produced, namely 500_v in commodities. The capitalist now holds in the form of commodities the same v which he had in the form of money before its conversion into labour power, while the labourer on the other hand has realised the value of his labour power in money and now, in his turn, realises this money by spending it as his revenue to defray his consumption in the purchase of part of the articles of consumption produced by himself. It is an exchange of the revenue of the labourer in money for a portion of commodities he has himself reproduced, namely 500_v of the capitalist. In this way this money returns to capitalist II as the money form of his variable capital. An equivalent value of revenue in the form of money here replaces variable capital value in the form of commodities.

The capitalist does not increase his wealth by taking away again the money paid by him to the labourer in the purchase of labour power when he sells him an equivalent quantity of commodities. He would indeed be paying the labourer twice if he were to pay him first 500 in the purchase of his labour power, and then in addition give him gratis a quantity of commodities worth 500, which the labourers produced for him. Vice versa, if the labourer were to produce for him nothing but an equivalent in commodities worth 500 for the price of his labour power of 500, the capitalist would be no better off after the transaction than before. But the labourer has reproduced a product of 3,000. He has preserved the constant portion of the value of the product, i. e., the value of the means of production used up in it = 2,000 by converting them into a new product. He has furthermore added to this given value a value of $1,000_{(v+s)}$. (The idea that the capitalist grows richer in the sense that he wins a surplus value by the reflux of the 500 in money is developed by Destutt de Tracy, as shown in detail in section XIII of this chapter.[61])

Through the purchase of 500 worth of articles of consumption by labourer II, capitalist II recovers the value of 500 II_v — which he just possessed in commodities — in money, the form in which he advanced it originally. The immediate result of this transaction, as of any other sale of commodities, is the conversion of a given value from the form of commodities into that of money. Nor is there anything special in the reflux thus effected of the money to its point of departure. If capitalist II had bought, with 500 in money, commodities from capitalist I, and then in turn sold to capitalist I commodities to the amount of 500, then 500 would have likewise returned to him in money. This sum of 500 in money would merely have served for the circulation of a quantity of commodities (1,000), and according to the general law previously expounded, the money would have returned to the one who put it into circulation for the purpose of exchanging this quantity of commodities.

But the 500 in money which flowed back to capitalist II are at one and the same time renewed potential variable capital in money form. Why is this so? Money, and therefore money capital, is potential variable capital only because and to the extent that it is convertible into labour power. The return of £500 in money to capitalist II is accompanied by the return of labour power II to the market. The return of both of these at opposite poles — hence also the re-appearance of 500 in money not only as money but also as variable capital in the form of money — is conditional on one and the same process. The money = 500 returns to capitalist II because he sold to labourer II articles of consumption amounting to 500, i. e., because the labourer spends his wages to maintain himself and his family and thus his labour power. In order to be able to live on and act again as a buyer of commodities he must again sell his labour power. The return of 500 in money to capitalist II is therefore at the same time a return, or an abiding, of the labour power in the capacity of a commodity purchasable with 500 in money, and thereby a return of 500 in money as potential variable capital.

As for category IIb, which produces articles of luxury, the case with v — (IIb)$_v$ — is the same as with I$_v$. The money, which renews for capitalists IIb their variable capital in the form of money, flows back to them in a roundabout way through capitalists IIa. But it nevertheless makes a difference whether the labourers buy their means of subsistence directly from the capitalist producers to whom they sell their labour power or whether they buy them from capitalists of another category, through whose agency the money returns to the former only by a circuitous route. Since the working class lives from hand to mouth, it buys as long as it has the means to buy. It is different with the capitalist, as for instance in the exchange of 1,000 II$_c$ for 1,000 I$_v$. The capitalist does not live from hand to mouth. His compelling motive is the utmost self-expansion of his capital. Now, if circumstances of any description seem to promise greater advantages to capitalist II in case he holds on to his money, or to part of it at least, for a while, instead of immediately renewing his constant capital, then the return of 1,000 II$_c$ (in money) to I is delayed; and so is the restoration of 1,000$_v$ to the form of money, and capitalist I can continue his business on the same scale only if he disposes of reserve money; and, generally speaking, reserve capital in the form of money is necessary to be able to work without interruption, regardless of the rapid or slow reflux of the variable capital value in money.

If the exchange of the various elements of the current annual reproduction is to be investigated, so are the results of the labour of the preceding year, of the labour of the year that has already come to a close. The process of production which resulted in this yearly product lies behind us; it is a thing of the past, incorporated in its product, and so much the more is this the case with the process of circulation, which precedes the process of production or runs parallel with it, the conversion of potential into real variable capital, i. e., the sale and purchase of labour power. The labour market is no longer a part of the commodity market, such as we have here before us. The labourer has here not only already sold his labour power, but besides the surplus value also supplied an equivalent of the price of his labour power in the shape of commodities. He has furthermore pocketed his wages and figures during the exchange only as a buyer of commodities (articles of consumption). On the other hand the annual product must contain all the elements of reproduction, restore all the elements of productive capital, above all its most important element, the variable capital. And we have seen indeed that the result of the exchange in regard to the variable capital is this: By spending his wages and consuming the purchased commodities, the labourer as a buyer of commodities maintains and reproduces his labour power, this being the only commodity which he has to sell. Just as the money advanced by the capitalist in the purchase of his labour power returns to him, so labour power returns to the labour market in its capacity of a commodity exchangeable for money. The result in the special case of $1,000\ I_v$ is that the capitalists of I hold $1,000_v$ in money and the labourers of I offer them 1,000 in labour power, so that the entire process of reproduction of I can be renewed. This is one result of the process of exchange.

On the other hand the expenditure of the wages of the labourers of I relieved II of articles of consumption to the amount of $1,000_c$, thus transforming them from the commodity form into the money form. Department II reconverted them into the bodily form of its constant capital by purchasing from I commodities $= 1,000_v$ and thus restoring to I in money form the value of its variable capital.

The variable capital of I passes through three metamorphoses, which do not appear at all in the exchange of the annual product or do so only suggestively.

1) The first form is $1,000\ I_v$ in money, which is converted into labour power of the same value. This conversion does not itself appear

in the exchange of commodities between I and II, but its result is seen in the fact that working class I confronts commodity seller II with 1,000 in money, just as working class II with 500 in money confronts commodity seller of 500 II_v in commodity form.

2) The second form, the only one in which variable capital actually varies, functions as variable capital, where value-creating force appears in the place of given value exchanged for it; it belongs exclusively to the process of production which is behind us.

3) The third form, in which the variable capital has justified itself as such in the result of the process of production, is the annual value product, which in the case of $I = 1,000_v + 1,000_s = 2,000 \, I_{(v+s)}$. In the place of its original value of 1,000 in money we have a value of double this amount, or 2,000, in commodities. The variable capital value of 1,000 in commodities is therefore only one half of the value produced by the variable capital as an element of the productive capital. The 1,000 I_v in commodities are an exact equivalent of the $1,000_v$ in money originally advanced by I and intended to be the variable part of the aggregate capital. But in the form of commodities they are money only potentially (they do not become so actually until they are sold), and still less directly are they variable money capital. They eventually become variable money capital by the sale of the commodity 1,000 I_v to II_c and by the early re-appearance of labour power as a purchasable commodity, as a material for which $1,000_v$ in money may be exchanged.

During all these transformations capitalist I continually holds the variable capital in his hands; 1) to start with as money capital; 2) then as an element of his productive capital; 3) still later as a portion of the value of his commodity capital, hence in the form of commodity value; 4) finally once more in money which is again confronted by the labour power for which it can be exchanged. During the labour process the capitalist is in possession of the variable capital as active value-creating labour power, but not as a value of a given magnitude. But since he never pays the labourer until his power has acted for a certain length of time, he already has in hand the value created by that power to replace itself plus the surplus value before he pays him.

As the variable capital always stays in the hands of the capitalist in some form or other, it cannot be claimed in any way that it converts itself into revenue for anyone. On the contrary, 1,000 I_v in commodities converts itself into money by its sale to II half of whose constant capital it re-places *in natura*.

What resolves itself into revenue is not variable capital I, or $1,000_v$ in money. This money has ceased to function as the money form of variable capital I as soon as it is converted into labour power, just as the money of any other buyer of commodities has ceased to represent anything belonging to him as soon as he has exchanged it for commodities of still other sellers. The conversions which the money received in wages goes through in the hands of the working class are not conversions of variable capital, but of the value of their labour power converted into money; just as the conversion of the value $(2,000\ I_{(v+s)})$ created by the labourer is only the conversion of a commodity belonging to the capitalist, which does not concern the labourer. However, the capitalist — and still more his theoretical interpreter, the political economist — can rid himself only with the greatest difficulty of the idea that the money paid to the labourer is still his, the capitalist's. If the capitalist is a producer of gold, then the variable portion of value — i. e., the equivalent in commodities which replaces for him the purchasing price of the labour — appears itself directly in the form of money and can therefore function anew as variable money capital without the circuitous route of a reflux. But so far as labourer II is concerned — aside from the labourer who produces articles of luxury — 500_v exists in commodities intended for the consumption of the labourer which he, considered as the collective labourer, buys directly again from the same collective capitalist to whom he sold his labour power. The variable portion of capital value II, so far as its natural form is concerned, consists of articles of consumption intended mostly for consumption by the working class. But it is not the variable capital which is spent in this form by the labourer; it is the wages, the money of the labourer, which precisely by its realisation in the articles of consumption restores to the capitalist the variable capital $500\ II_v$ in its money form. The variable capital II_v is reproduced in articles of consumption, the same as the constant capital $2,000\ II_c$. The one resolves itself no more into revenue than the other does. In either case it is the wages which resolve themselves into revenue.

However it is a momentous fact in the exchange of the annual product that by the expenditure of the wages as revenue there is restored to the form of money capital in the one case $1,000\ II_c$, likewise, by this circuitous route, $1,000\ I_v$ and ditto $500\ II_v$, hence constant and variable capital. (In the case of the variable capital partly by means of a direct and partly by means of an indirect reflux.)

XI. REPLACEMENT OF THE FIXED CAPITAL

In the analysis of the exchanges of the annual reproduction the following presents great difficulty. If we take the simplest form in which the matter may be presented, we get:

$$\text{(I)} \quad 4,000_c + 1,000_v + 1,000_s +$$
$$\text{(II)} \quad 2,000_c + 500_v + 500_s = 9,000.$$

This resolves itself finally into:

$$4,000 \ \text{I}_c + 2,000 \ \text{II}_c + 1,000 \ \text{I}_v + 500 \ \text{II}_v + 1,000 \ \text{I}_s +$$
$$+ 500 \ \text{II}_s = 6,000_c + 1,500_v + 1,500_s = 9,000.$$

One portion of the value of the constant capital, which consists of instruments of labour in the strict meaning of the term (as a distinct section of the means of production), is transferred from the instruments of labour to the product of labour (the commodity); these instruments of labour continue to function as elements of the productive capital, doing so in their old natural form. It is their wear and tear, the diminution in value gradually experienced by them during their continual functioning for a definite period, which re-appears as an element of the value of the commodities produced by means of them, which is transferred from the instrument of labour to the product of labour. With regard to the annual reproduction therefore only such component parts of fixed capital will from the first be given consideration as last longer than a year. If they are completely worn out within the year they must be completely replaced and renewed by the annual reproduction, and the point at issue does not concern them at all. It may happen in the case of machines and other more durable forms of fixed capital—and it frequently does happen—that certain parts of them must be replaced lock, stock and barrel within one year, although the building or machine in its entirety lasts much longer. These parts belong in one category with the elements of fixed capital which are to be replaced within one year.

This element of the value of commodities must not be confused with the costs of repair.[a] If a commodity is sold, this value element is turned into money, the same as all others. But after it has been turned

---

[a] See this volume, pp. 172-84.

into money, its difference from the other elements of value becomes apparent. The raw and auxiliary materials consumed in the production of commodities must be replaced *in natura* in order that the reproduction of commodities may begin (or that the process of production of commodities in general may be continuous). The labour power spent on them must also be replaced by fresh labour power. Consequently the money realised on the commodities must be continually reconverted into these elements of the productive capital, from the money form into the commodity form. It does not alter the matter if raw and auxiliary materials for instance are bought at certain intervals in larger quantities—so that they constitute productive supplies—and need not be bought anew during certain periods; and therefore—as long as they last—the money coming in through the sale of commodities, inasmuch as it is meant for this purpose, may accumulate and this portion of constant capital thus appears temporarily as money capital whose active function has been suspended. It is not a revenue capital; it is productive capital suspended in the form of money. The renewal of the means of production must go on all the time, although the form of this renewal—with reference to the circulation—may vary. The new purchase, the circulation operation by which they are renewed or replaced, may take place at more or at less prolonged intervals: then a large amount may be invested at one stroke, compensated by a corresponding productive supply. Or the intervals between purchases may be small: then follows a rapid succession of money expenditures in small doses, of small productive supplies. This does not alter the matter itself. The same applies to labour power. Where production is carried on continuously throughout the year on the same scale—continuous replacement of consumed labour power by new. Where work is seasonal, or different portions of labour are applied at different periods, as in agriculture—corresponding purchases of labour power, now in small, now in large amounts. But the money proceeds realised from the sale of commodities, so far as they turn into money that part of the commodity value which is equal to the wear and tear of fixed capital, are not reconverted into that component part of the productive capital whose diminution in value they cover. They settle down beside the productive capital and persist in the form of money. This precipitation of money is repeated, until the period of reproduction consisting of great or small numbers of years has elapsed, during which the fixed element of constant capital continues to function in the process of production in its old natural form. As soon as the fixed element, such as buildings, machinery, etc., has been worn out, and can no longer function in the process of production, its value exists alongside it fully replaced by money, by the sum of money precipitations, the values which had been gradually transferred from the fixed capital to the commodities in whose production it participated and which had assumed the form of money as a result of the sale of these commodities. This money then serves to replace the fixed capital (or its elements, since its various elements have different durabilities) *in natura* and thus really to renew this component part of the productive capital. This money is therefore the money form of a part of the constant capital value, of its fixed part. The formation of this hoard is thus itself an element of the capitalist process of reproduction; it is the reproduction and storing up — in the form of money — of the value of fixed capital, or its several elements, until the fixed capital has ceased to live and in consequence has given off its full value to the commodities produced and must now be replaced *in natura*. But this money loses only its form of a hoard and hence resumes its activity in the process of reproduction of capital brought about by the circulation as soon as it is reconverted into new elements of fixed capital to replace those that died off.

Just as simple commodity circulation is in no way identical with a mere exchange of products, the conversion of the annual commodity product can in no way resolve itself into a mere unmediated mutual exchange of its various components. Money plays a specific role in it, which finds expression particularly in the manner in which the value of the fixed capital is reproduced. (How different the matter would present itself if production were collective and no longer possessed the form of commodity production is left to a later analysis.)

Should we now return to our fundamental scheme, we shall get the following for class II: $2,000_c + 500_v + 500_s$. All the articles of consumption produced in the course of the year are in that case equal in value to 3,000; and every one of the different commodity elements in the total sum of the commodities is composed, so far as its value is concerned, of $^2/_{3c} + ^1/_{6v} + ^1/_{6s}$, or, in percentages, $66^2/_{3c} + 16^2/_{3v} + 16^2/_{3s}$. The various kinds of commodities of class II may contain different proportions of constant capital. Likewise the fixed portion of the constant capital may be different. The duration of the parts of the fixed capital and hence the annual wear and tear, or that portion of value which they transfer *pro rata* to the commodities in the production of which they participate, may also differ. But that is immaterial here. As to the process of social reproduction, it is only a question of exchange between classes II and I. These two classes here confront each other only in their social, mass relations. Therefore the proportional magnitude of part c of the value of commodity product II (the only one of consequence in the question now being discussed) gives the average proportion if all the branches of production classed under II are embraced.

Every kind of commodity (and they are largely the same kinds) whose aggregate value is classed under $2,000_c + 500_v + 500_s$ is therefore equal in value to $66^2/_3\%_{0c} + 16^2/_3\%_{0v} + 16^2/_3\%_{0s}$. This applies to every 100 of the commodities, whether classed under c, v or s.

The commodities in which the $2,000_c$ are incorporated may be further divided, in value, into:

1) $1,333^1/_{3c} + 333^1/_{3v} + 333^1/_{3s} = 2,000_c$;

similarly 500_v may be divided into:

2) $333^1/_{3c} + 83^1/_{3v} + 83^1/_{3s} = 500_v$;

and finally 500_s may be divided into:

3) $333^1/_{3c} + 83^1./_{3v} + 83^1/_{3s} = 500_s$.

Now, if we add the c's in 1, 2 and 3 we get $1,333^1/_{3c} + 333^1/_{3c} + 333^1/_{3c} = 2,000$. Similarly, $333^1/_{3v} + 83^1/_{3v} + 83^1/_{3v} = 500$. And the same in the case of s. The addition gives the same total value of 3,000, as above.

The entire constant capital value contained in the commodity mass II representing a value of 3,000 is therefore comprised in $2,000_c$, and neither 500_v nor 500_s hold an atom of it. The same is true of v and s respectively.

In other words, the entire share of commodity mass II that represents constant capital value and therefore is reconvertible either into its natural or its money form, exists in $2,000_c$. Everything referring to the exchange of the constant value of commodities II is therefore confined to the movement of 2,000 II_c. And this exchange can be made only with I $(1,000_v + 1,000_s)$.

Similarly, as regards class I, everything that bears on the exchange of the constant capital value of that class is to be confined to a consideration of 4,000 I_c.

Now, if to start with we take

$$\text{I. } 4,000_c + \underbrace{1,000_v + 1,000_s}$$

$$\text{II. . . . . } 2,000_c + 500_v + 500_s,$$

the exchange of the commodities 2,000 II_c for commodities of the same value I $(1,000_v + 1,000_s)$ would presuppose that the entire 2,000 II_c are reconverted *in natura* into the natural elements of the constant capital of II, produced by I. But the commodity value of 2,000, in which the latter exists, contains an element making good the diminution in value of the fixed capital, which is not to be replaced immediately *in natura* but converted into money, which gradually accumulates into a sum total until the time for the renewal of the fixed capital in its natural form arrives. Every year registers the demise of fixed capital which must be replaced in this or that individual business, or in this or that branch of industry. In the case of one and the same individual capital, this or that portion of its fixed capital must be replaced (since its different parts have different durabilities). On examining annual reproduction, even on a simple scale, i. e., disregarding all accumulation, we do not begin *ab ovo*. The year which we study is one in the course of many; it is not the first year after the birth of capitalist production. The various capitals invested in the manifold lines of production of class II therefore differ in age, and just as people functioning in these lines of production die annually, so a host of fixed capitals expire annually and must be renewed *in natura* out of the accumulated money fund. Therefore the exchange of 2,000 II_c for 2,000 $\text{I}_{(v + s)}$ includes a conversion of 2,000 II_c from its commodity form (articles of consumption) into natural elements which consist not only of raw and auxiliary materials but also of natural elements of fixed capital, such as machinery, tools, buildings, etc. The wear and tear, which must be replaced *in money* in the value of 2,000 II_c, therefore by no means corresponds to the amount of the functioning fixed capital, since a portion of this must be replaced *in natura* every year. But this assumes that the money necessary for this replacement was accumulated in former years by the capitalists of class II. However that very condition holds good in the same measure for the current year as for the preceding ones.

In the exchange between I $(1,000_v + 1,000_s)$ and 2,000 II_c it must be first noted that the sum of values $I_{(v+s)}$ does not contain any constant element of value, hence also no element of value to replace wear and tear, i. e., value that has been transmitted from the fixed component of the constant capital to the commodities in whose natural form $v + s$ exist. On the other hand this element exists in II_c, and it is precisely a part of this value element that owes its existence to fixed capital which is not to be converted immediately from the money form into its natural form, but has first to persist in the form of money. The exchange between I $(1,000_v + 1,000_s)$ and 2,000 II_c, therefore, at once presents the difficulty that the means of production of I, in whose natural form the $2,000_{(v+s)}$ exist, are to be exchanged to the full value of 2,000 for an equivalent in articles of consumption II, while on the other hand the 2,000 II_c of articles of consumption cannot be exchanged at their full value for means of production I $(1,000_v + 1,000_s)$ because an aliquot part of their value — equal to the wear and tear, or the value depreciation of the fixed capital that is to be replaced — must first be precipitated in the form of money that will not function any more as a medium of circulation during the current period of annual reproduction, which alone we are examining. But the money paying for this element of wear and tear incorporated in the commodity value 2,000 II_c can come only from class I, since II cannot pay for itself but effects payment precisely by selling its goods, and since presumably $I_{(v+s)}$ buys the whole of the commodities 2,000 II_c. Hence class I must by means of this purchase convert that wear and tear into money for II. But according . to the law previously evolved, money advanced to the circulation returns to the capitalist producer who later on throws an equal amount of commodities into circulation. It is evident that in buying II_c, I cannot give II commodities worth 2,000 and an additional amount of money on top of that once and for all (without any return of the same by way of the operation of exchange). Otherwise I would buy the commodity mass II_c above its value. If II actually exchanges its $2,000_c$ for I $(1,000_v + 1,000_s)$, it has no further claims on I, and the money circulating in this exchange returns to either I or II, depending on which of them threw it into circulation, i. e., which of them acted first as buyer. At the same time, in this case, II would have reconverted the entire value of its commodity capital into the natural form of means of production, while our assumption is that after its sale it would not reconvert an aliquot portion of it during the current period of annual reproduction from money into the natural form of fixed components of its constant capital. A money balance in favour of II could arise only if it sold 2,000 worth to I and bought less than 2,000 from I, say only 1,800. In that case I would have to make good the debit balance by 200 in money, which would not flow back to it, because it would not have withdrawn from circulation the money it had advanced to it by throwing into it commodities equal to 200. In such an event we would have a money fund for II, placed to the credit of the wear and tear of its fixed capital. But then we would have an overproduction of means of production to the amount of 200 on the other side, the side of I, and the basis of our scheme would be destroyed, namely reproduction on the same scale, where complete proportionality between the various systems of production is assumed. We would only have done away with one difficulty in order to create another one, much worse.

As this problem offers peculiar difficulties and has hitherto not been treated at all by the political economists, we shall examine *seriatim* all possible (at least seemingly possible) solutions, or rather formulations of the problem.

In the first place, we have just assumed that II sells commodities of the value of 2,000 to I, but buys from it only 1,800 worth. The commodity value $2,000 \text{ II}_c$ contains 200 for replacement of wear and tear, which must be stored up in the form of money. The value of $2,000 \text{ II}_c$ would thus be divided into 1,800, to be exchanged for means of production I, and 200, to replace wear and tear, which are to be kept in the form of money (after the sale of the $2,000_c$ to I). Expressed in terms of value, $2,000 \text{ II}_c = 1,800_c + 200_c(d)$, this d standing for *déchet | |*depreciation | |.

We would then have to study

Exchange

$$\text{I. } \underbrace{1,000_v + 1,000_s}$$

$$\text{II. } 1,800_c + 200_c \text{ (d).}$$

I buys with £1,000, which has gone to the labourers in wages for their labour power, $1,000 \text{ II}_c$ of articles of consumption. II buys with the same £1,000 means of production $1,000 \text{ I}_v$. Capitalists I thus recover their variable capital in the form of money and can employ it next year in the purchase of labour power to the same amount, i. e., they can replace the variable portion of their productive capital *in natura*.

Furthermore, II buys with advanced £400 means of production I_s, and I_s buys with the same £400 articles of consumption II_c. The £400 advanced to the circulation by the capitalists of II have thus returned to them, but only as an equivalent for sold commodities. I now buys articles of consumption for advanced £400; II buys from I £400 worth of means of production, whereupon these £400 flow back to I. So far, then, the account is as follows:

I throws into circulation $1,000_v + 800_s$ in commodities; it furthermore throws into circulation, in money, £1,000 in wages and £400 for exchange with II. After the exchange has been made, I has $1,000_v$ in money, 800_s exchanged for 800 II_c (articles of consumption) and £400 in money.

II throws into circulation $1,800_c$ in commodities (articles of consumption) and £400 in money. On the completion of the exchange it has 1,800 in commodities I (means of production) and £400 in money.

There still remain, on the side of I, 200_s (in means of production) and, on the side of II, $200_c(d)$ (in articles of consumption).

According to our assumption I buys with £200 the articles of consumption c (d) of the value of 200. But II holds on to these £200 since $200_c(d)$ represent wear and tear, and are not to be immediately reconverted into means of production. Therefore 200 I_s cannot be sold; $^1/_5$ of the surplus value I to be replaced cannot be realised, or converted, from its natural form of means of production into that of articles of consumption.

This not only contradicts our assumption of reproduction on a simple scale; it is by itself not a hypothesis which would explain the transformation of $200_c(d)$ into money. It means rather that it cannot be explained. Since it cannot be demonstrated in what manner $200_c(d)$ can be converted into money, it is assumed that I is obliging enough to do the conversion just because it is not able to convert its own remainder of 200_s into money. To conceive this as a normal operation of the exchange mechanism is tantamount to the notion that £200 fall every year from the clouds in order regularly to convert $200_c(d)$ into money.

But the absurdity of such a hypothesis does not strike one at once if I_s, instead of appearing, as it does in this case, in its primitive mode of existence — namely as a component part of the value of means of production, hence as a component part of the value of commodities which their capitalist producers must convert into money by sale — appears in the hands of the partners of the capitalists, for instance as ground rent in the hands of landowners or as interest in the hands of money lenders. But if that portion of the surplus value of commodities which the industrial capitalist has to yield as ground rent or interest to other co-owners of the surplus value cannot be realised for a long time by the sale of the commodities, then there is also an end to the payment of rent and interest, and the landowners or recipients of interest cannot therefore serve as *dei ex machina* [a] to convert at pleasure definite portions of the annual reproduction into money by spending rent and interest. The same is true of the expenditures of all so-called unproductive labourers — government officials, physicians, lawyers, etc., and others who as members of the "general public" "serve" the political economists by explaining what they left unexplained.

Nor does it improve matters if instead of direct exchange between I and II — between the two major departments of capitalist producers — the merchant is drawn in as mediator and helps to overcome all difficulties with his "money". In the present case for instance 200 I_s must be definitively disposed of to the industrial capitalists of II. It may pass through the hands of a number of merchants, but the last of them will find himself, according to the hypothesis, in the same predicament, vis-à-vis II, in which the capitalist producers of I were at the outset, i. e., they cannot sell the 200 I_s to II. And this stalled purchase sum cannot renew the same process with I.

We see here that, aside from our real purpose, it is absolutely necessary to view the process of reproduction in its basic form — in which obscuring minor circumstances have been eliminated — in order to get rid of the false subterfuges which furnish the semblance of "scientific" analysis when the process of social reproduction is immediately made the subject of the analysis in its complicated concrete form.

The law that, when reproduction proceeds normally (whether it be on a simple or on an extended scale), the money advanced by the capitalist producer to the circulation must return to its point of departure (whether the money is his own or borrowed) excludes once and for all the hypothesis that 200 II_c(d) is converted into money by means of money advanced by I.

---

[a] The plural of *deus ex machina* ("a deity from a machine"). In the ancient Greek and Roman theatre, the intervention of a god, brought in suddenly by stage machinery, to resolve an apparently insoluble conflict.

Having disposed of the hypothesis considered above, only such possibilities remain as, besides replacing the wear and tear portion in money, include also the replacement *in natura* of the wholly defunct fixed capital.

We assumed hitherto

a) that £1,000 paid in wages by I are spent by the labourers for II_c to the same amount, i. e., that they buy articles of consumption with them.

It is merely a statement of fact that these £1,000 are advanced by I in money. Wages must be paid in money by the respective capitalist producers. This money is then spent by the labourers for articles of consumption and serves the sellers of the articles of consumption as a medium of circulation in the conversion of their constant capital from commodity capital into productive capital. True, it passes through many channels (shopkeepers, house owners, tax collectors, unproductive labourers, such as physicians, etc., who are needed by the labourer himself) and hence it flows only in part directly from the hands of labourers I into those of capitalist class II. Its flow may be retarded more or less and the capitalist may therefore require a new money reserve. All this does not come under consideration in this basic form.

b) We assumed that at one time I advances another £400 in money for purchases from II and that this money returns to it, while at some other time II advances £400 for purchases from I and likewise recovers this money. This assumption must be made, for it would be arbitrary to presuppose the contrary, that capitalist class I or II should one-sidedly advance to the circulation the money necessary for the exchange of their commodities. Since we have shown under subtitle 1 that one should reject as absurd the hypothesis that I would throw additional money into the circulation in order to turn 200 $II_c(d)$ into money, it would appear that there was left only the seemingly still more absurd hypothesis that II itself was throwing the money into circulation, by which that constituent portion of the value of its commodities is converted into money which has to compensate the wear and tear of its fixed capital. For instance that portion of value which is lost by the spinning-machine of Mr. X in the process of production re-appears as a portion of the value of the yarn. The loss which his spinning-machine suffers in value, i. e., in wear and tear, on the one hand, should accumulate in his hands as money on the other. Now supposing that X buys for example £200 worth of cotton from Y and thus advances to the circulation £200 in money. Y then buys from him £200 worth of yarn, and these £200 now serve X as a fund to compensate the wear and tear of his machine. The thing would simply come down to this — that X, aside from his production, its product, and the sale of this product, keeps £200 *in petto* to make good to himself the depreciation of his spinning-machine, i. e., that in addition to losing £200 through the depreciation of his machine, he must also put up another £200 in money every year out of his own pocket in order to be able eventually to buy a new spinning-machine.

But the absurdity is only apparent. Class II consists of capitalists whose fixed capital is in the most diverse stages of its reproduction. In the case of some of them it has arrived at the stage where it must be entirely replaced *in natura*. In the case of the others it is more or less remote from that stage. All the members of the latter group have this in common, that their fixed capital is not actually reproduced, i. e., is not renewed *in natura*, is not replaced by a new specimen of the same kind, but that its value is successively accumulated in money. The first group is in quite the same (or almost the same, it does not matter here) position as when it started in business, when it came on the market with its money capital in order to convert it into constant (fixed and circulating) capital on the one hand and into labour power, into variable capital, on the other. They have once more to advance this money capital to the circulation, i. e., the value of constant fixed capital as well as that of the circulating and variable capital.

Hence, if we assume that half of the £400 thrown into circulation by capitalist class II for exchange with I comes from those capitalists of II who have to renew not only by means of their commodities their means of production pertaining to the circulating capital, but also, by means of their money, their fixed capital *in natura*, while the other half of capitalists II replaces *in natura* with its money only the circulating portion of its constant capital, but does not renew *in natura* its fixed capital, then there is no contradiction in the statement that these returning £400 (returning as soon as I buys articles of consumption for it) are variously distributed among these two sections of II. They return to class II, but they do not come back into the same hands and are distributed variously within this class, passing from one of its sections to another.

One section of II has, besides the part of the means of production covered in the long run by its commodities, converted £200 in money into new elements of fixed capital *in natura*. As was the case at the start of the business, the money thus spent returns to this section from the circulation only gradually over a number of years as the wear and tear portion of the value of the commodities to be produced by this fixed capital.

The other section of II however did not get any commodities from I for £200. But I pays it with the money which the first section of II spent for elements of its fixed capital. The first section of II has its fixed capital value once more in renewed natural form, while the second section is still engaged in accumulating it in money form for the subsequent replacement of its fixed capital *in natura*.

The basis on which we now have to proceed after the previous exchanges is the remainder of the commodities still to be exchanged by both sides: 400_s on the part of I, and 400_c on the part of II.[52] We assume that II advances 400 in money for the exchange of these commodities amounting to 800. One half of the 400 (= 200) must be laid out under all circumstances by that section of II_c which has accumulated 200 in money as the wear and tear value and which has to reconvert this money into the natural form of its fixed capital.

Just as constant capital value, variable capital value, and surplus value — into which the value of commodity capital II as well as I is divisible — may be represented by special proportional shares of commodities II and I respectively, so may, within the value of the constant capital itself, that portion of the value which is not yet to be converted into the natural form of the fixed capital, but is rather to be gradually accumulated for the time being in the form of money. A certain quantity of commodities II (in the present case therefore one half of the remainder = 200) is here only a vehicle of this wear and tear value, which has to be precipitated in money by means of exchange. (The first section of capitalists II, which renews fixed capital *in natura*, may already have realised in this way — with the wear and tear part of the mass of commodities of which here only the re-

---

[52] These figures again do not coincide with those previously assumed. But this is immaterial since it is merely a question of proportions.— *F. E.*

mainder still figures — a part of its wear and tear value, but it still has to realise 200 in money.)

As for the second half (= 200) of the £400 thrown into circulation by II in this final operation, it buys circulating components of constant capital from I. A portion of these £200 may be thrown into circulation by both sections of II, or only by the one which does not renew its fixed component of value *in natura*.

With these £400 there is thus extracted from I: 1) commodities amounting to £200, consisting only of elements of fixed capital; 2) commodities amounting to £200, replacing only natural elements of the circulating portion of the constant capital of II. So I has sold its entire annual commodity product, so far as it is to be sold to II; but the value of one-fifth of it, £400, is now held by I in the form of money. This money however is surplus value converted into money which must be spent as revenue for articles of consumption. Thus I buys with these £400 II's entire commodity value = 400. Hence this money flows back to II by setting its commodities in motion.

We shall now suppose three cases, in which we shall call the section of capitalists II which replaces its fixed capital *in natura* "section 1", and that section which stores up depreciation value of fixed capital in money form, "section 2". The three cases are the following: a) that a share of the 400 still existing with II as a remnant in the shape of commodities must replace certain shares of the circulating parts of the constant capital for sections 1 and 2 (say, $\frac{1}{2}$ for each); b) that section 1 has already sold all its commodities, while section 2 still has to sell 400; c) that section 2 has sold all but the 200 which are the bearers of the depreciation value.

Then we have the following distributions:

a) Of the commodity value = 400_c, still in the hands of II, section 1 holds 100 and section 2 — 300; 200 out of the 300 represent depreciation. In that case section 1 originally laid out 300 of the £400 in money now returned by I to get commodities from II, namely 200 in money, for which it secured elements of fixed capital *in natura* from I, and 100 in money for the promotion of its exchange of commodities with I. Section 2 on the other hand advanced only $\frac{1}{4}$ of the 400, i. e., 100, likewise for the promotion of its commodity exchange with I.

Section 1, then, advanced 300, and section 2 — 100 of the 400 in money.

Of these 400 there return however:

To section 1 — 100, i. e., only $\frac{1}{3}$ of the money advanced by it. But it has in place of the other $^2/_3$ a renewed fixed capital to the value of 200. Section 1 has given money to I for this element of fixed capital to the value of 200, but no subsequent commodities. So far as the 200 in money are concerned, section 1 confronts department I only as buyer, but not later on as seller. This money cannot therefore return to section 1; otherwise it would have received the elements of fixed capital from I as a gift.

With reference to the last third of the money advanced by it, section 1 first acted as a buyer of circulating constituent parts of its constant capital. With the same money I buys from it the remainder of its commodities worth 100. This money, then, flows back to it (section 1 of department II) because it acts as a vendor of commodities directly after having acted as a buyer. If this money did not return, then II (section 1) would have given to I, for commodities amounting to 100, first 100 in money, and then into the bargain, 100 in commodities, i. e., II would have given away its commodities to I as a present.

On the other hand section 2, which laid out 100 in money, receives back 300 in money: 100 because first as a buyer it threw 100 in money into circulation, and receives them back as a seller; 200, because it functions only as a seller of commodities to that amount, but not as a buyer. Hence the money cannot flow back to I. The fixed capital depreciation is thus balanced by the money thrown into circulation by II (section 1) in the purchase of elements of fixed capital. But it reaches the hands of section 2 not as money of section 1, but as money belonging to class I.

b) On this assumption the remainder of II_c is so distributed that section 1 has 200 in money and section 2 has 400 in commodities.

Section 1 has sold all of its commodities, but 200 in money are a transformed shape of the fixed component part of its constant capital which it has to renew *in natura*. Hence it acts here only as a buyer and receives instead of its money commodity I to the same value in natural elements of its fixed capital. Section 2 has to throw only £200 into circulation, as a maximum (if I does not advance any money for commodity exchange between I and II), since for half of its commodity value it is only a seller to I, not a buyer from I.

There return to section 2 from the circulation £400: 200, because it has advanced them as a buyer and receives them back as a seller of 200 in commodities; 200, because it sells commodities to the value of 200 to I without obtaining an equivalent in commodities from I.

c) Section 1 has 200 in money and 200_c in commodities. Section 2 has 200_c (d) in commodities.

On this supposition section 2 does not have any advance to make in money, because vis-à-vis I it no longer acts at all as buyer but only as seller, hence has to wait until someone buys from it.

Section 1 advances £400 in money: 200 for mutual commodity exchange with I, 200 as mere buyer from I. With the last £200 in money it purchases the elements of fixed capital.

With £200 in money I buys from section 1 commodities for 200, so that the latter thus recovers the £200 in money it had advanced for this commodity exchange. And I buys with the other £200, which it has likewise received from section 1, commodities to the value of 200 from section 2, whereby the latter's wear and tear of fixed capital is precipitated in the form of money.

The matter is not altered in the least if it is assumed that, in case c), class I instead of II (section 1) advances the 200 in money to promote the exchange of the existing commodities. If I buys in that event first 200 in commodities from II, section 2, on the assumption that this section has only this commodity remnant left to sell — then the £200 do not return to I, since II, section 2, does not act again as buyer. But II, section 1, has in that case £200 in money to spend in buying and 200 in commodities for exchange purposes, thus making a total of 400 for trading with I. £200 in money then return to I from II, section 1. If I again lays them out in the purchase of 200 in commodities from II, section 1, they return to I as soon as II, section 1, takes the second half of the 400 in commodities off I's hands. Section 1 (II) has spent £200 in money as a mere buyer of elements of fixed capital; they therefore do not return to it, but serve to turn the 200_c, the commodity remnant of II, section 2, into money, while the £200, the money laid out by I for the exchange of commodities, return to I via II, section 1, not via II, section 2. In the place of its commodities of 400 there has returned to it a commodity equivalent amounting to 400; the £200 in money advanced by it for the exchange of 800 in commodities have likewise returned to it. Everything is therefore all right.

———

The difficulty encountered in the exchange:

I. $1{,}000_v + 1{,}000_s$

has been reduced to the difficulty in exchanging

II. $2{,}000_c$

remainders:

I. .... 400_s.

II. (1) 200 in money + 200_c in commodities + (2) 200_c in commodities. Or, to make the matter still clearer:

I. $200_s + 200_s$.

II. (1) 200 in money + 200_c in commodities + (2) 200_c in commodities.

Since in II, section 1, 200_c in commodities are exchanged for 200 I_s (in commodities) and since all the money circulating in this exchange of 400 in commodities between I and II returns to him who advanced it, I or II, this money, being an element of the exchange between I and II, is actually not an element of the problem which is troubling us here. Or, to present it differently: Supposing in the exchange between 200 I_s (commodities) and 200 II_c (commodities of II, section 1) the money functions as a means of payment, not as a means of purchase and therefore also not as a "medium of circulation" in the strictest sense of the words. It is then clear, since the commodities 200 I_s and 200 II_c (section 1) are equal in magnitude of value, that means of production worth 200 are exchanged for articles of consumption worth 200, that money functions here only ideally, and that neither side really has to throw any money into circulation for the payment of any balance. Hence the problem presents itself in its pure form only when we strike off on both sides, I and II, the commodities 200 I_s and their equivalent, the commodities 200 II_c (section 1).

After the elimination of these two amounts of commodities of equal value (I and II), which balance each other, there is left for exchange a remainder in which the problem evinces its pure form, namely:

I. 200_s in commodities.

II. (1) 200_c in money plus (2) 200_c in commodities.

It is evident here that II, section 1, buys with 200 in money the component parts of its fixed capital, 200 I_s. The fixed capital of II, section 1, is thereby renewed *in natura*, and the surplus value of I, worth 200, is converted from the commodity form (means of production, or, more precisely, elements of fixed capital) into the money form. With this money I buys articles of consumption from II, section 2, and the result for II is that for section 1 a fixed component part of its constant capital has been renewed *in natura*, and that for section 2 another component part (which compensates for the depreciation of its fixed capital) has been precipitated in money form. And this continues every year until this last component part, too, has to be renewed *in natura*.

The condition precedent is here evidently that this fixed component part of constant capital II, which is reconverted into money to the full extent of its value and therefore must be renewed *in natura* each year (section 1), should be equal to the annual depreciation of the other fixed component part of constant capital II, which continues to function in its old natural form and whose wear and tear, depreciation in value, which it transfers to the commodities in whose production it is engaged, is first to be compensated in money. Such a balance would seem to be a law of reproduction on the same scale, which means in other words that in class I, which puts out the means of production, the proportional division of labour must remain unchanged, since it produces on the one hand circulating and on the other fixed component parts of the constant capital of department II.

Before we analyse this more closely we must see what turn the matter takes if the remainder of II_c (1) is not equal to the remainder of II_c (2), and may be larger or smaller. Let us study the two cases one after the other.

First Case

I. 200_s.

II. (1) 220_c (in money) + (2) 200_c (in commodities).

In this case II_c (1) buys with £200 in money the commodities 200 I_s, and I buys with the same money the commodities 200 II_c (2), i. e., that portion of the fixed capital which is to be precipitated in money. This portion is thus converted into money. But 20 II_c (1) in money cannot be reconverted into fixed capital *in natura*.

It seems this misfortune can be remedied by setting the remainder of I_s at 220 instead of at 200, so that only 1,780 instead of 1,800 of the 2,000 I would be disposed of by former exchange. We should then have:

I. 220_s.

II. (1) 220_c (in money) + (2) 200_c (in commodities).

II_c, section 1, buys with £220 in money the 220 I_s and I buys then with £200 the 200 II_c (2) in commodities. But now £20 in money remain on the side of I, a portion of surplus value which it can hold on to only in the form of money, without being able to spend it for articles of consumption. The difficulty is thus merely transferred from II_c, section 1, to I_s.

Let us now assume on the other hand that II_c, section 1, is smaller than II_c, section 2; then we have:

Second Case

I. 200_s (in commodities).

II. (1) 180_c (in money) + (2) 200_c (in commodities).

With £180 in money II (section 1) buys commodities, 180 I_s. With this money I buys commodities of the same value from II (section 2), hence 180 II_c (2). There remain 20 I_s unsaleable on one side, and also 20 II_c (2) on the other — commodities worth 40, not convertible into money.

It would not help us to make the remainder of I equal to 180. True, no surplus would then be left in I, but now as before an excess of 20 would remain in II_c (section 2), unsaleable, inconvertible into money.

In the first case, where II (1) is greater than II (2), there remains on the side of II_c (1) an excess in money not reconvertible into fixed capital; or, if the remainder I_s is assumed to be equal to II_c (1), there remains on the side of I_s the same excess in money, not convertible into articles of consumption.

In the second case, where II_c (1) is smaller than II_c (2), there remains a money deficit on the side of 200 I_s and II_c (2), and an equal excess of commodities on both sides, or, if the remainder of I_s is assumed to be equal to II_c (1), there remains a money deficit and an excess of commodities on the side of II_c (2).

If we assume the remainders of I_s always to be equal to II_c (1) — since production is determined by orders and reproduction is not altered in any way if one year there is a greater output of fixed component parts and the next a greater output of circulating component parts of constant capitals II and I — then in the first case I_s can be reconverted into articles of consumption only if I buys with it a portion of the surplus value of II and II accumulates it in money instead of consuming it; in the second case matters can be remedied only if I spends the money itself, an assumption, we have already rejected.

If II_c (1) is greater than II_c (2), foreign commodities must be imported to realise the money excess in I_s. If, conversely, II_c (1) is smaller than II_c (2), commodities II (articles of consumption) will have to be exported to realise the depreciation part of II_c in means of production. Consequently in either case foreign trade is necessary.

Even granted that for a study of reproduction on an unchanging scale it is to be supposed that the productivity of all lines of industry, hence also the proportional value relations of their commodities, remain constant, the two last-named cases, in which II_c (1) is either greater or smaller than II_c (2), will nevertheless always be of interest for production on an enlarged scale where these cases may infallibly be encountered.

3. RESULTS

The following is to be noted with reference to replacement of fixed capital:

If—all other things, and not only the scale of production, but above all the productivity of labour, remaining the same—a greater part of the fixed element of II_c expires than did the year before, and hence a greater part must be renewed *in natura*, then that part of the fixed capital which is as yet only on the way to its demise and is to be replaced meanwhile in money until its day of expiry, must shrink in the same proportion, inasmuch as it was assumed that the sum (and the sum of the value) of the fixed part of capital functioning in II remains the same. This however brings with it the following circumstances. *First*: If the greater part of commodity capital I consists of elements of the fixed capital of II_c, then a correspondingly smaller portion consists of circulating component parts of II_c, because the total production of I for II_c remains unchanged. If one of these parts increases the other decreases, and vice versa. On the other hand the total production of class II also retains the same volume. But how is this possible if its raw materials, semi-finished products, and auxiliary materials (i. e., the circulating elements of constant capital II) decrease? *Second*: The greater part of fixed capital II_c, restored in its money form, flows to I to be reconverted from its money form into its natural form. So there is a greater flow of money to I, aside from the money circulating between I and II merely for the exchange of their commodities; more money which is not instrumental in effecting mutual commodity exchange, but acts only one-sidedly in the function of a means of purchase. But then the mass of commodities of II_c, which is the bearer of the wear and tear equivalent — and thus the mass of commodities II that must only be exchanged for money I and not for commodities I — would also shrink proportionately. More money would have flown from II to I as mere means of purchase, and there would be fewer commodities II in relation to which I would have to function as a mere buyer. A greater portion of I_s — for I_v is already converted into commodities II — would not therefore be convertible into commodities II, but would persist in the form of money.

The opposite case, in which the reproduction of demises of fixed capital II in a certain year is less and on the contrary the depreciation part greater, needs no further discussion.

There would be a crisis — a crisis of overproduction — in spite of reproduction on an unchanging scale.

In short, if under simple reproduction and other unchanged conditions — particularly under unchanged productive power, total volume and intensity of labour — no constant proportion is assumed between expiring fixed capital (to be renewed) and fixed capital still continuing to function in its old natural form (merely adding to the products value in compensation of its depreciation), then, in the one case the mass of circulating component parts to be reproduced would remain the same while the mass of fixed component parts to be reproduced would be increased. Therefore the total production I would have to grow or, even aside from money relations, there would be a deficit in reproduction.

In the other case, if the size of fixed capital II to be reproduced *in natura* should proportionately decrease and hence the component part of fixed capital II, which must now be replaced only in money, should increase in the same ratio, then the quantity of the circulating component parts of constant capital II reproduced by I would remain unchanged, while that of the fixed component parts to be reproduced would decrease. Hence either decrease in aggregate production of I, or excess (as previously deficit) and excess that is not to be converted into money.

True, the same labour can, in the first case, turn out a greater product through increasing productivity, extension or intensity, and the deficit could thus be covered in that case. But such a change would not take place without a shifting of capital and labour from one line of production of I to another, and every such shift would call forth momentary disturbances. Furthermore (in so far as extension and intensification of labour would mount), I would have for exchange more of its own value for less of II's value. Hence there would be a depreciation of the product of I.

The reverse would take place in the second case, where I must curtail its production, which implies a crisis for its labourers and capitalists, or produce an excess, which again spells crisis. Such excess is not an evil in itself, but an advantage; however it is an evil under capitalist production.

Foreign trade could help out in either case: in the first case in order to convert commodities I held in the form of money into articles of consumption, and in the second case to dispose of the commodity excess. But since foreign trade does not merely replace certain elements (also with regard to value), it only transfers the contradictions to a wider sphere and gives them greater latitude.

Once the capitalist form of reproduction is abolished, it is only a matter of the volume of the expiring portion — expiring and therefore to be reproduced *in natura* — of fixed capital (the capital which in our illustration functions in the production of articles of consumption) varying in various successive years. If it is very large in a certain year (in excess of the average mortality, as is the case with human beings), then it is certainly so much smaller in the next year. The quantity of raw materials, semi-finished products, and auxiliary materials required for the annual production of the articles of consumption — provided other things remain equal — does not decrease in consequence. Hence the aggregate production of means of production would have to increase in the one case and decrease in the other. This can be remedied only by a continuous relative overproduction. There must be on the one hand a certain quantity of fixed capital produced in excess of that which is directly required; on the other hand, and particularly, there must be a supply of raw materials, etc., in excess of the direct annual requirements (this applies especially to means of subsistence). This sort of overproduction is tantamount to control by society over the material means of its own reproduction. But within capitalist society it is an element of anarchy.

This illustration of fixed capital, on the basis of an unchanged scale of reproduction, is striking. A disproportion in the production of fixed and circulating capital is one of the favourite arguments of the economists in explaining crises. That such a disproportion can and must arise even when the fixed capital is merely *preserved*, that it can and must do so on the assumption of ideal normal production on the basis

of simple reproduction of the already functioning social capital is
something new to them.

XII. THE REPRODUCTION
OF THE MONEY MATERIAL

One factor has so far been entirely disregarded, namely the annual
reproduction of gold and silver. As mere material for articles of luxury, gilding, etc., there is as little occasion for special mention of
them as there is of mentioning any other products. But they play an
important role as money material and hence as potential money. For
the sake of simplicity we here regard only gold as material for money.

According to older data the entire annual production of gold
amounted to 800,000-900,000 lbs, equal roundly to 1,100 or 1,250
million marks. But according to Soetbeer[53] it amounted to only
170,675 kilograms, valued at roundly 476 million marks, based on the
average for 1871 to 1875. Of this amount Australia supplied roundly
167, the United States 166, and Russia 93 million marks. The remainder is distributed over various countries in amounts of less than
10 million marks each. During the same period, the annual production of silver amounted to somewhat less than 2 million kilograms, valued at $354^1/_2$ million marks. Of this amount, Mexico supplied
roundly 108, the United States 102, South America 67, Germany 26
million, etc.

Among the countries with predominantly capitalist production
only the United States is a producer of gold and silver. The capitalist
countries of Europe obtain almost all their gold, and by far the greater part of their silver, from Australia, the United States, Mexico,
South America, and Russia.

But we take it that the gold mines are in a country with capitalist
production whose annual reproduction we are here analysing, and
for the following reasons:

Capitalist production does not exist at all without foreign commerce. But when one assumes normal annual reproduction on a given
scale one also assumes that foreign commerce only replaces home products by articles of other use or natural form, without affecting value
relations, hence without affecting either the value relations in which
the two categories, "means of production" and "articles of consump-

[53] Ad. Soetbeer, *Edelmetall-Produktion*, Gotha, 1879 [S. 112].

tion", mutually exchange, or the relations between constant capital, variable capital, and surplus value, into which the value of the product of each of these categories may be divided. The involvement of foreign commerce in analysing the annually reproduced value of products can therefore only confuse without contributing any new element of the problem, or of its solution. For this reason it must be entirely discarded. And consequently gold too is to be treated here as a direct element of annual reproduction and not as a commodity element imported from abroad by means of exchange.

The production of gold, like that of metals generally, belongs in class I, the category which embraces the production of means of production. Supposing the annual production of gold is equal to 30 (for convenience's sake; actually the figure is much too high compared to the other figures of our scheme). Let this value be divisible into $20_c + 5_v + 5_s$; 20_c are to be exchanged for other elements of I_c and this is to be studied later[a]; but the $5_v + 5_s$ (I) are to be exchanged for elements of II_c, i. e., articles of consumption.

As for the 5_v, every gold-producing establishment begins by buying labour power. This is done not with gold produced by this particular enterprise, but with a portion of the money supply in the country. The labourers buy with these 5_v articles of consumption from II, and the latter buys with this money means of production from I. Let II buy gold from I to the amount of 2 as commodity material, etc. (component part of its constant capital), then 2_v flow back to gold producers I in money which has already belonged to the circulation. If II does not buy any more material from I, then I buys from II by throwing its gold into circulation as money, since gold can buy any commodity. The difference is only that I does not act here as a seller, but only as a buyer. Gold miners I can always get rid of their commodity; it is always in a directly exchangeable form.

Let us assume that some producer of yarn has paid 5_v to his labourers, who create for him in return — aside from the surplus value — a yarn product = 5. For 5 the labourers buy from II_c, and the latter buys yarn from I for 5 in money, and thus 5_v flow back in money to the spinner of yarn. Now in the case assumed I g (as we shall designate the producers of gold) advances to his labourers 5_v in money which previously belonged to the circulation. The labourers spend it for necessities of life, but only 2 of the 5 return from II to I g. How-

---

[a] See Engels' footnote 55) on p. 472 of this volume.

ever I g can begin the process of reproduction anew, just as well as the producer of yarn. For his labourers have supplied him with 5 in gold, 2 of which he sold and 3 of which he still has, so that he has but to coin[54] them, or turn them into banknotes to have his entire variable capital again directly in his hands in money form, without the further intervention of II.

Even this first process of annual reproduction has wrought a change in the quantity of money actually or virtually belonging to the circulation. We assumed that II_c bought 2_v (I g) as material, and that I g has again laid out 3 — as the money form of his variable capital — within II. Hence 3 of the mass of money supplied by the new gold production remained within II and did not return to I. According to our assumption, II has satisfied its requirements in gold material. The 3 remain in its hands as a gold hoard. Since they cannot constitute any element of its constant capital, and since II had previously enough money capital for the purchase of labour power; since furthermore these additional 3 g, with the exception of the depreciation element, have no function to perform within II_c, for a portion of which they were exchanged (they could only serve to cover the depreciation element *pro tanto*, if II_c (1) should be smaller than II_c (2), which would be accidental); on the other hand, however, namely with the exception of the depreciation element, the entire commodity product II_c, must be exchanged for means of production $I_{(v+s)}$ — this money must be transferred in its entirety from II_c to II_s, no matter whether it exists in necessities of life or articles of luxury, and vice versa, corresponding commodity value must be transferred from II_s to II_c. Result: A portion of the surplus value is stored up as a money hoard.

In the second year of reproduction, provided the same proportion of annually produced gold continues to be used as material, 2 will again flow back to I g, and 3 will be replaced *in natura*, i. e., will be released again in II as a hoard, etc.

With reference to the variable capital in general: The capitalist I g, like every other capitalist, must continually advance this capital in money for the purchase of labour power. But so far as this v is concerned, it is not he but his labourers who have to buy from II. It can

---

[54] "A considerable quantity of GOLD BULLION[a] ... is taken direct to the mint at San Francisco by the owners." Reports of H. M. Secretaries of Embassy and Legation, 1879, Part III, p. 337.

---

[a] In the original, this English term is given in parentheses after its German equivalent.

therefore never happen that he should act as a buyer, throwing gold into II without the initiative of II. But to the extent that II buys material from him, and must convert constant capital II_c into gold material, a portion of $(I\ g)_v$ flows back to him from II in the same way that it does to other capitalists of I. And so far as this is not the case, he replaces his v in gold directly from his product. But to the extent that the v advanced in money does not flow back to him from II, a portion of the already available means of circulation (received from I and not returned to I) is converted in II into a hoard and for that reason a portion of its surplus value is not expended for articles of consumption. Since new gold-mines are continually opened or old ones reopened, a certain portion of the money to be laid out by I g in v is always part of the money existing prior to the new gold production; it is thrown by I g through his labourers into II, and unless it returns from II to I g it forms there an element of hoard formation.

But as for $(I\ g)_s$, I g can always act here as buyer. He throws his s in the shape of gold into circulation and withdraws from it in return articles of consumption II_c. In II the gold is used in part as material, and thus functions as a real element of the constant constituent portion c of the productive capital. When this is not the case it becomes once more an element of hoard formation as a part of II_s persisting in the form of money. We see, then, aside from I_c which we reserve for a later analysis,[55] that even simple reproduction, excluding accumulation proper, namely reproduction on an extended scale, necessarily includes the storing up, or hoarding, of money. And as this is annually repeated, it explains the assumption from which we started in the analysis of capitalist production, namely, that at the beginning of the reproduction a supply of money corresponding to the exchange of commodities is in the hands of capitalist classes I and II. Such an accumulation takes place even after deducting the amount of gold being lost through the depreciation of money in circulation.

It goes without saying that the more advanced capitalist production, the more money is accumulated in all hands, and therefore the smaller the quantity annually added to this hoard by the production of new gold, although the absolute quantity thus added may be considerable. We revert once more in general terms to the objection[a] raised

[55] The study of the exchange of newly produced gold within the constant capital of department I is not contained in the manuscript.— *F. E.*

---

[a] See this volume, p. 328-29.

against Tooke: How is it possible that every capitalist draws a surplus value in money out of the annual product, i.e., draws more money out of the circulation than he throws into it, since in the long run the capitalist class itself must be regarded as the source of all the money thrown into circulation?

We note on this point by summarising the ideas developed previously (in Chapter XVII):

1) The only assumption essential here, namely, that in general there is money enough for the exchange of the various elements of the mass of the annual reproduction, is not affected in any way by the fact that a portion of the commodity value consists of surplus value. Supposing that the entire production belonged to the labourers themselves and that their surplus labour were therefore only surplus labour for themselves, not for the capitalists, then the quantity of circulating commodity values would be the same and, other things being equal, would require the same amount of money for their circulation. The question in either case is therefore only: Where does the money come from to make possible the exchange of this total of commodity values? It is not at all: Where does the money come from to turn the surplus value into money?

It is true, to revert to it once more, that every individual commodity consists of $c + v + s$, and the circulation of the entire quantity of commodities therefore requires on the one hand a definite sum of money for the circulation of the capital $c + v$ and on the other hand another sum for the circulation of the revenue of the capitalists, the surplus value s. For the individual capitalist, as well as for the entire capitalist class, the money in which they advance capital is different from the money in which they spend their revenue. Where does the latter money come from? Simply from the mass of money in the hands of the capitalist class, hence by and large from the total mass of money in society, a portion of which circulates the revenue of the capitalists. We have already seen above that every capitalist establishing a new business recoups the money which he spent for his maintenance in articles of consumption as money serving to convert his surplus value into money, once his business is fairly under way. But generally speaking the whole difficulty has two sources:

In the first place, if we analyse only the circulation and the turnover of capital, thus regarding the capitalist merely as a personification of capital, not as a capitalist consumer and man about town, we see indeed that he is continually throwing surplus value into circulation as a component part of his commodity capital, but we never see money as a form of revenue in his hands. We never see him throwing money into circulation for the consumption of surplus value.

In the second place, if the capitalist class throws a certain amount of money into circulation in the shape of revenue, it looks as if it were paying an equivalent for this portion of the total annual product, and this portion thereby ceases to represent surplus value. But the surplus product in which the surplus value is represented does not cost the capitalist class anything. As a class, the capitalists possess and enjoy it gratuitously, and the circulation of money cannot alter this fact. The alteration brought about by this circulation consists merely in the fact that every capitalist, instead of consuming his surplus product *in natura*, a thing which is generally impossible, draws commodities of all sorts up to the amount of the surplus value he has appropriated out of the general stock of the annual surplus product of society and appropriates them. But the mechanism of the circulation has shown that while the capitalist class throws money into circulation for the purpose of spending its revenue, it also withdraws this money from the circulation, and can continue the same process over and over again; so that, considered as a class, capitalists remain as before in possession of the amount of money necessary for the conversion of surplus value into money. Hence, if the capitalist not only withdraws his surplus value from the commodity market in the form of commodities for his consumption fund, but at the same time gets back the money with which he has paid for these commodities, he has evidently withdrawn the commodities from circulation without paying an equivalent for them. They do not cost him anything, although he pays money for them. If I buy commodities for one pound sterling and the seller of the commodities gives me the pound back for surplus product which I got for nothing, it is obvious that I received the commodities gratis. The constant repetition of this operation does not alter the fact that I constantly withdraw commodities and constantly remain in possession of the pound, although I part with it temporarily to purchase commodities. The capitalist constantly gets this money back as a money equivalent of surplus value that has not cost him anything.

We have seen that with Adam Smith the entire value of the social product resolves itself into revenue, into v + s, so that the constant capital value is set down as zero. It follows necessarily that the money required for the circulation of the yearly revenue must also suffice for the circulation of the entire annual product, that therefore in our illustration the money required for the circulation of the articles of consumption worth 3,000 also suffices for the circulation of the entire annual product worth 9,000. This is indeed the opinion of Adam Smith, and it is repeated by Th. Tooke. This erroneous conception of the ratio of the quantity of money required for the realisation of revenue to the quantity of money required to circulate the entire social product is the necessary result of the uncomprehended, thoughtlessly conceived manner in which the various elements of material and value of the total annual product are reproduced and annually replaced. It has therefore already been refuted.

Let us listen to Smith and Tooke themselves.

Smith says in Book II, Ch. 2:

"The circulation of every country may be considered as divided into two different branches: the circulation of the dealers with one another, and the circulation between the dealers and the consumers. Though the same pieces of money, whether paper or metal, may be employed sometimes in the one circulation and sometimes in the other; yet as both are constantly going on at the same time, each requires a certain stock of money of one kind or another, to carry it on. The value of the goods circulated between the different dealers never can exceed the value of those circulated between the dealers and the consumers; whatever is bought by the dealers, being ultimately destined to be sold to the consumers. The circulation between the dealers, as it is carried on by wholesale, requires generally a pretty large sum for every particular transaction. That between the dealers and the consumers, on the contrary, as it is generally carried on by retail, frequently requires but very small ones, a shilling, or even a halfpenny, being often sufficient. But small sums circulate much faster than large ones... Though the annual purchases of all the consumers, therefore, are at least" //this "at least" is rich// "equal in value to those of all the dealers, they can generally be transacted with a much smaller quantity of money;" etc.

Th. Tooke remarks to this passage from Adam Smith (in *An Inquiry into the Currency Principle*, London, 1844, pp. 34 to 36 *passim* [62]):

"There can be no doubt that the distinction here made is substantially correct ... the interchange between dealers and consumers including the payment of wages, which constitute the PRINCIPAL MEANS[a] of the consumers... All the transactions between dealers and dealers, by which are to be understood all sales from the producer or importer, through all the stages of intermediate processes of manufacture or otherwise to the retail dealer or the exporting merchant, are resolvable into movements or transfers of capital. Now transfers of capital do not necessarily suppose, nor do actually as a matter of fact entail, in the great majority of transactions, a passing of money, that is, banknotes or coin — I mean bodily, and not by fiction — at the time of transfer... The total amount of the transactions between dealers and dealers must, in the last resort, be determined and limited by the amount of those between dealers and consumers."

---

[a] In the original, the words "principal means" are given in parentheses after their German equivalent.

If this last sentence stood by itself, one might think Tooke simply stated the fact that there was a ratio between the exchanges among dealers and those among dealers and consumers, in other words, between the value of the total annual revenue and the value of the capital with which it is produced. But this is not the case. He explicitly endorses the view of Adam Smith. A special criticism of his theory of circulation is therefore superfluous.

2) Every industrial capital, on beginning its career, throws at one fling money into circulation for its entire fixed constituent part, which it recovers but gradually, in the course of years, by the sale of its annual product. Thus it throws at first more money into circulation than it draws from it. This is repeated at every renewal of the entire capital *in natura*. It is repeated every year for a certain number of enterprises whose fixed capital is to be renewed *in natura*. It is repeated piecemeal at every repair, every only partial renewal of the fixed capital. While, then, on the one hand more money is withdrawn from circulation than is thrown into it, the opposite takes place on the other hand.

In all lines of industry whose production period — as distinguished from its working period — extends over a longer term, money is continually thrown into circulation during this period by the capitalist producers, partly in payment for labour power employed, partly in the purchase of means of production to be consumed. Means of production are thus directly withdrawn from the commodity market, and articles of consumption, partly indirectly, by the labourers spending their wages, and partly directly, by the capitalists, who do not by any means suspend their consumption, although they do not simultaneously throw any equivalent in commodities on the market. During this period the money thrown by them into circulation serves to convert commodity value, including the surplus value embodied in it, into money. This factor becomes very important at an advanced stage of capitalist production in the case of long-drawn out enterprises, such as are undertaken by stock companies, etc., for instance the construction of railways, canals, docks, large municipal buildings, iron shipbuilding, large-scale drainage of land, etc.

3) While the other capitalists, aside from the investment in fixed capital, draw more money out of the circulation than they threw into it on purchasing the labour power and the circulating elements, the gold- and silver-producing capitalists throw only money into the circulation, aside from the precious metal which serves as raw material,

while they withdraw only commodities from it. The constant capital, with the exception of the depreciated portion, the greater portion of the variable capital and the entire surplus value, save the hoard which may be accumulating in their own hands, are all thrown into circulation as money.

4) On the one hand all kinds of things circulate as commodities which were not produced during the given year, such as land lots, houses, etc.; furthermore goods whose period of production exceeds one year, such as cattle, timber, wine, etc. For this and other phenomena it is important to establish that aside from the quantity of money required for the immediate circulation there is always a certain quantity in a latent non-functioning state which may start functioning if the impulse is given. Furthermore, the value of such products circulates often piecemeal and gradually, like the value of houses in the rents over a number of years.

On the other hand not all movements of the process of reproduction are effected through the circulation of money. The entire process of production, once its elements have been procured, is excluded from circulation. All products which the producer himself consumes directly, whether individually or productively, are also excluded. Under this head comes also the feeding of agricultural labourers in kind.

Therefore the quantity of money which circulates the annual product, exists in society, having been gradually accumulated. It does not belong to the value produced during the given year, except perhaps the gold used to make good the loss of depreciated coins.

This exposition presupposes the exclusive circulation of precious metals as money, and in this circulation the simplest form of cash purchases and sales; although money can function also as a means of payment, and has actually done so in the course of history, even on the basis of circulating plain metal coin, and though a credit system and certain aspects of its mechanism have developed upon that basis.

This assumption is not made from mere considerations of method, although these are important enough, as demonstrated by the fact that Tooke and his school, as well as their opponents, were continually compelled in their controversies concerning the circulation of banknotes to revert to the hypothesis of a purely metallic circulation. They were forced to do so *post festum*[a] and did so very superficially,

---

[a] See this volume, p. 314.

which was unavoidable, because the point of departure in their analysis thus played merely the role of an incidental point.

But the simplest study of money circulation presented in its *primitive* form — and this is here an immanent element of the process of annual reproduction — demonstrates:

a) Developed capitalist production, and hence the domination of the wage system, being assumed, money capital obviously plays a prominent role, since it is the form in which the variable capital is advanced. In step with the development of the wage system, all products are transformed into commodities and must therefore — with a few important exceptions — pass in their entirety through the transformation into money as one phase of their movement. The quantity of circulating money must suffice for this conversion of commodities into money, and the greater part of this mass is furnished in the form of wages, of the money which is advanced by the industrial capitalists as the money form of the variable capital in payment for labour power, and which mainly functions in the hands of the labourers only as a medium of circulation (means of purchase). It is quite the opposite of natural economy[a] such as is predominant under every form of bondage (including serfdom), and still more so in more or less primitive communities, whether or not they are attended by conditions of bondage or slavery.

In the slave system, the money capital invested in the purchase of labour power plays the role of the money form of the fixed capital, which is but gradually replaced as the active period of the slave's life expires. Among the Athenians, therefore, the gain realised by a slave owner directly through the industrial employment of his slave, or indirectly by hiring him out to other industrial employers (e. g., for mining), was regarded merely as interest (plus amortisation) on the advanced money capital, just as the industrial capitalist under capitalist production places a portion of the surplus value plus the depreciation of his fixed capital to the account of interest and replacement of his fixed capital. This is also the rule with capitalists offering fixed capital (houses, machinery, etc.) for rent. Mere household slaves, whether they perform necessary services or are kept as luxuries for show, are not considered here. They correspond to the modern servant class. But the slave system too — so long as it is the dominant form of pro-

---

[a] "Natural economy" in the sense of the relative absence of commodity exchange; see this volume, pp. 120-22.

ductive labour in agriculture, manufacture, navigation, etc., as it was in the developed states of Greece and in Rome — preserves an element of natural economy. The slave market maintains its supply of the commodity labour power by war, piracy, etc., and this rapine is not promoted by a process of circulation, but by the actual appropriation of the labour power of others by direct physical compulsion. Even in the United States, after the conversion of the buffer territory between the wage labour states of the North and the slavery states of the South into a slave-breeding region for the South, where the slave thrown on the market thus became himself an element of the annual reproduction, this did not suffice for a long time, so that the African slave trade was continued as long as possible to satisfy the market.

b) The fluxes and refluxes of money taking place spontaneously on the basis of capitalist production in the exchange of the annual product; the one-time advances of fixed capitals to the full extent of their value and the successive extraction of this value from the circulation in the course of years, in other words, their gradual reconstitution in money form by the annual formation of hoards, a hoarding which is essentially different from the parallel accumulation of hoards based on the annual production of new gold; the different lengths of time for which, depending on the duration of the production period of the commodities, money must be advanced, and consequently always hoarded anew before it can be recovered from the circulation by the sale of the commodities; the different lengths of time for which money must be advanced, if only resulting from the different distances of the places of production from their markets; furthermore the differences in the magnitude and period of the reflux according to the condition or relative size of the productive supplies in the various lines of business and in the individual businesses of the same line, and hence the lengths of periods for which the elements of constant capital are bought, and all this during the year of reproduction — all these different aspects of spontaneous movement had only to be noted, and made conspicuous, through experience, in order to give rise to a methodical use of the mechanical appliances of the credit system and to a real fishing out of available loanable capitals.

To this must be added the difference between those lines of business whose production proceeds under otherwise normal conditions continuously on the same scale, and those which apply varying quantities of labour power in different periods of the year, such as agriculture.

XIII. DESTUTT DE TRACY'S THEORY OF REPRODUCTION[56]

Let us illustrate the confused and at the same time boastful thoughtlessness of political economists analysing social reproduction, with the example of the great logician Destutt de Tracy (cf. Buch I, p. 147, Note 30[a]), whom even Ricardo took seriously and called a VERY DISTINGUISHED WRITER (*Principles*, p. 333).

This "distinguished writer" gives the following explanations concerning the entire process of social reproduction and circulation:

"I will be asked how these industrial entrepreneurs can make such large profits, and whence they can draw them. I reply that it is through their selling everything that they produce at a higher price than it has cost them to produce; and that they sell it,

"1) to one another for the whole part of their consumption destined for the satisfaction of their needs, which they pay with a portion of their profits;

"2) to the wage labourers, both those whom they pay and those paid by the idle capitalists; in this way they draw back from these labourers their total wages, apart from their small savings;

"3) to the idle capitalists, who pay them with the part of their revenue which they have not already given to the labourers directly employed by them; so that all the rent which they annually pay them comes back to them in one or other of these ways" (Destutt de Tracy, *Traité de la volonté et de ses effets*, Paris, 1826, p. 239).

In other words, the capitalists enrich themselves firstly by mutually getting the best of one another in the exchange of the portion of their surplus value which they set apart for their individual consumption or consume as revenue. For instance, if this portion of their surplus value or of their profits is equal to £400, this sum of £400 is supposed to grow to, say, £500 by each stockholder of the £400 selling his share to another 25% in excess. But since all do the same, the result will be the same as if they had sold to one another at the real values. They merely need £500 in money for the circulation of commodities worth £400, and this would seem to be rather a method of impoverishing than of enriching themselves since it compels them to keep a large portion of their total wealth unproductively in the useless

---

[56] From Manuscript II.

---

[a] English edition: Vol. I, Ch. V (present edition, Vol. 35).

form of circulation media. The whole thing boils down to this, that despite the all-round nominal rise in the price of their commodities the capitalist class has only £400 worth of commodities to divide among themselves for their individual consumption, but that they do one another the favour of circulating £400 worth of commodities by means of a quantity of money which is required to circulate £500 worth of commodities.

And this quite aside from the fact that a "portion of their profits", and therefore in general a supply of commodities in which profit is represented, is here assumed. But Destutt undertook precisely to tell us where those profits come from. The quantity of money required to circulate the profit is a very subordinate question. The quantity of commodities in which the profit is represented seems to have its origin in the circumstance that the capitalists not only sell these commodities to one another, although even this much is quite fine and profound, but sell them to one another at prices which are too high. So we now know one source of the enrichment of the capitalists. It is on a par with the secret of the "Entspektor Bräsig" that the great poverty is due to the great *pauvreté*.

2) The same capitalists furthermore sell

"to the wage labourers, both those whom they pay and those paid by the idle capitalists; in this way they draw back from these labourers their total wages, apart from their small savings".

According to Monsieur Destutt, then, the reflux of the money capital, the form in which the capitalists have advanced wages to the labourers, is the second source of the enrichment of these capitalists.

If therefore the capitalists paid for instance £100 to their labourers as wages and if these same labourers then buy from the same capitalists commodities of this same value, of £100, so that the sum of £100 which the capitalists had advanced as buyers of labour power returns to the capitalists when they sell to the labourers £100 worth of commodities, the capitalists *get richer* thereby. It would appear to anyone endowed with ordinary common sense that they find themselves once more in possession of their £100, which they owned before this procedure. At the beginning of the procedure they have £100 in money. For these £100 they buy labour power. The labour bought produces for these £100 in money commodities of a value which, so far as we now know, amounts to £100. By selling the £100 worth of commodities to their labourers the capitalists recover £100 in money. The capitalists then have once more £100 in money, and the labourers have £100 worth of commodities which they have themselves produced. It is hard to understand how that can make the capitalists any richer. If the £100 in money did not flow back to them they would first have to pay to the labourers £100 in money for their labour and secondly to give them the product of this labour, £100 worth of articles of consumption, for nothing. The reflux of this money might therefore at best explain why the capitalists do not get poorer by this transaction, but by no means why they get richer by it.

To be sure it is another question how the capitalists come into possession of the £100 in money and why the labourers, instead of producing commodities for their own account, are compelled to exchange their labour power for these £100. But this, for a thinker of Destutt's calibre, is self-explanatory.

Destutt himself is not quite satisfied with the solution. After all, he did not tell us that one gets richer by spending a sum of money, £100, and then taking in again a sum of money amounting to £100; hence, by the reflux of £100 in money, which merely shows why the £100 in money do not get lost. He tells us that the capitalists get richer

"through their selling everything that they produce at a higher price than it has cost them to produce".

Consequently the capitalists must get richer also in their transactions with the labourers by selling to them too dear. Very well!

"They pay wages ... and all this flows back to them through the expenditures of all these people who pay them more" //for the products// "than they cost them" //the capitalists// "in wages" (ibid., p. 240).

In other words, the capitalists pay £100 in wages to the labourers, and then they sell to these labourers their own product at £120, so that they not only recover their £100 but also gain £20? That is impossible. The labourers can pay only with the money which they have received in the form of wages. If they get £100 in wages from the capitalists they can buy only £100 worth, not £120 worth. So this will not work. But there is still another way. The labourers buy from the capitalists commodities for £100, but actually receive commodities worth only £80. Then they are certainly cheated out of £20. And the capitalist has certainly gained £20, because he actually paid for the labour power 20% less than its value, or cut nominal wages 20% by a circuitous route.

The capitalist class would accomplish the same end if it paid the labourers at the start only £80 in wages and afterwards gave them for these £80 in money actually £80 worth of commodities. This seems to be the normal way, considering the class of capitalists as a whole, for according to Monsieur Destutt himself the labouring class must receive a "sufficient wage" (p. 219), since their wages must at least be adequate to maintain their existence and capacity to work, "to procure the barest subsistence" (p. 180). If the labourers do not receive such sufficient wages, that means, according to the same Destutt, "the death of industry" (p. 208), which does not seem therefore to be a way in which the capitalists can get richer. But whatever may be the scale of wages paid by the capitalists to the working class, they have a definite value, e. g., £80. If the capitalist class pays the labourers £80, then it has to supply them with commodities worth £80 for these £80, and the reflux of the £80 does not enrich it. If it pays them £100 in money and sells them £80 worth of commodities for £100, it pays them in money 25% more than their normal wage and supplies them in return with 25% less in commodities.

In other words, the fund from which the capitalist class in general derives its profits is supposedly made up of deductions from the normal wages by paying less than its value for labour power, i. e., less than the value of the means of subsistence required for their normal reproduction as wage labourers. If therefore normal wages were paid, which is supposed to be the case according to Destutt, there could be no profit fund for either the industrial or the idle capitalists.

Hence Monsieur Destutt would be compelled to reduce the entire secret of how the capitalist class gets richer to the following: by a deduction from wages. In that case the other surplus value funds, which he mentions under 1) and 3), would not exist.

Hence in all countries, in which the money wages of the labourers should be reduced to the value of the articles of consumption necessary for their subsistence as a class, there would be no consumption fund and no accumulation fund for the capitalists, and hence also no existence fund for the capitalist class, and hence also no capitalist class. And, according to Destutt, this should be the case in all wealthy and developed countries with an old civilisation, for in them, "in our ancient societies, the fund for the maintenance of wage labourers is ... an almost constant magnitude" (ibid., p. 202).

Even with a deduction from the wages, the capitalist does not enrich himself by first paying the labourer £100 in money and then supplying him with £80 worth of commodities for these £100, thus actually circulating £80 worth of commodities by means of £100, an excess of 25%. The capitalist gets richer by appropriating, besides the surplus value — that portion of the product in which surplus value is represented — 25% of that portion of the product which the labourer should receive in the form of wages. The capitalist class would not gain anything by the silly method Destutt conceived. It pays £100 in wages and gives back to the labourer for these £100 £80 worth of his own product. But in the next transaction it must again advance £100 for the same procedure. It would thus be indulging in the useless sport of advancing £100 in money and giving in exchange £80 in commodities, instead of advancing £80 in money and supplying in exchange for it £80 in commodities. That is to say, it would be continually advancing to no purpose a money capital which is 25% in excess of that required for the circulation of its variable capital, which is a very peculiar method of getting rich.

3) Finally the capitalist class sells

"to the idle capitalists, who pay them with the part of their revenue which they have not already given to the labourers directly employed by them, so that all the rent which they annually pay them" (the idle ones) "comes back to them in one or other of these ways".

We have seen above that the industrial capitalists

"pay with a portion of their profits the whole part of their consumption destined for the satisfaction of their needs"

Take it, then, that their profits are equal to £200. And let them use up, say, £100 of this in their individual consumption. But the other half = £100 does not belong to them; it belongs to the idle capitalists, i. e., to those who receive the ground rent, and to capitalists who lend money on interest. So they have to pay £100 in money to these people. Let us assume that the latter need £80 of this money for their individual consumption, and £20 for the hire of servants, etc. With those £80 they buy articles of consumption from the industrial capitalists. Thus while these capitalists part with products to the value of

£80, they receive back £80 in money, or $^4/_5$ of the £100 paid by them to the idle capitalists under the name of rent, interest, etc. Furthermore the servant class, the direct wage labourers of the idle capitalists, have received £20 from their masters. These servants likewise buy articles of consumption from the industrial capitalists to the amount of £20. In this way, while parting with products worth £20, these capitalists have £20 in money come back to them, the last fifth of the £100 which they paid to the idle capitalists for rent, interest, etc.

At the close of the transaction the industrial capitalists have recovered in money the £100 which they remitted to the idle capitalists in payment of rent, interest, etc. But one half of their surplus product = £100 passed meanwhile from their hands into the consumption fund of the idle capitalists.

It is evidently quite superfluous for the question now under discussion to bring in somehow or other the division of the £100 between the idle capitalists and their direct wage labourers. The matter is simple: their rent, interest, in short, their share in the surplus value = £200, is paid to them by the industrial capitalists in money to the amount of £100. With these £100 they buy directly or indirectly articles of consumption from the industrial capitalists. Thus they pay back to them the £100 in money and take from them articles of consumption worth £100.

This completes the reflux of the £100 paid by the industrial capitalists in money to the idle capitalists. Is this reflux of money a means of enriching the industrial capitalists, as Destutt imagines? Before the transaction they had a sum of values amounting to £200, 100 being money and 100 articles of consumption. After the transaction they have only one half of the original sum of values. They have once more the £100 in money, but they have lost the £100 in articles of consumption which have passed into the hands of the idle capitalists. Hence they are poorer by £100 instead of richer by £100. If instead of taking the circuitous route of first paying out £100 in money and then receiving this £100 in money back in payment of articles of consumption worth £100, they had paid rent, interest, etc., directly in the natural form of their products, there would be no £100 in money flowing back to them from the circulation, because they would not have thrown that amount of money into the circulation. *Via* payment in kind the matter would simply have taken this course: they would keep one half of the surplus product worth £200 for themselves and give the other half to the idle capitalists without any equivalent in return. Even Destutt would not have been tempted to declare this a means of getting richer.

Of course the land and capital borrowed by the industrial capitalists from the idle capitalists and for which they have to pay a portion of their surplus value in the form of ground rent, interest, etc., are profitable for them, for this constitutes one of the conditions of production of commodities in general and of that portion of the product which constitutes surplus product or in which surplus value is represented. This profit accrues from the use of the borrowed land and capital, not from the price paid for them. This price rather constitutes a deduction from it. Otherwise one would have to contend that the industrial capitalists would not get richer but poorer, if they were able to keep the other half of their surplus value for themselves instead of having to give it away. This is the confusion which results from mixing up such phenomena of circulation as a reflux of money with the distribution of the product, which is merely promoted by these phenomena of circulation.

And yet the same Destutt is shrewd enough to remark:

"Whence come the revenues of these idle men? Do the revenues not come out of the rent paid to them out of their profits by those who set the capitals of the former to work, i.e., by those who use the funds of the former to pay a labour which produces more than it costs, in a word, the men of industry? It is always necessary to hark back to them to find the source of all wealth. It is these who really feed the wage labourers employed by the former" (p. 246).

So now the payment of this rent, etc., is a deduction from the profit of the men of industry. Before it was a means wherewith they could enrich themselves.

But at least one consolation is left to our Destutt. These good industrialists handle the idle capitalists the same way they have been handling one another and the labourers. They sell them all commodities too dear, for instance, by 20%. Now there are two possibilities. The idlers either have other money resources aside from the £100 which they receive annually from the industrial capitalists, or they have not. In the first case the industrial capitalists sell them commodities worth £100 at a price of, say, £120. Consequently on selling their commodities they recover not only the £100 paid to the idlers but £20 besides, which constitute really new value for them. How does the account look now? They have given away £100 in commodities for nothing, because the £100 in money that they were paid in part for their commodities were their own money. Thus their own commodities have been paid with their own money. Hence they have lost £100. But they have also received an excess of £20 in the price of their commodities over and above their value, which makes £20 to the good. Balance this against the loss of £100, and you still have a loss of £80. Never a plus, always a minus. The cheating practised against the idlers has reduced the loss of the industrial capitalists, but for all that it has not transformed a diminution of their wealth into a means of enrichment. But this method cannot go on indefinitely, for the idlers cannot possibly pay year after year £120 in money if they take in only £100 in money year after year.

There remains the other method: The industrial capitalists sell commodities worth £80 in exchange for the £100 in money they paid to the idlers. In this case, the same as before, they still give away £80 for nothing, in the form of rent, interest, etc. By this fraudulent means the industrial capitalists have reduced their tribute to the idlers, but it still exists nevertheless and the idlers are in a position — according to the same theory proclaiming that prices depend on the good will of the sellers — to demand in the future £120 instead of £100, as formerly, for rent, interest, etc., on their land and capital.

This brilliant analysis is quite worthy of that deep thinker who copies on the one hand from Adam Smith that

"labour is the source of all wealth" (p. 242),

that the industrial capitalists

"employ their capital to pay labour which reproduces it with a profit" (p. 246),

and who concludes on the other hand that these industrial capitalists

"maintain all the others and alone augment the public fortune and create all our means of enjoyment" (p. 242),

that it is not the capitalists who are fed by the labourers, but the labourers who are fed by the capitalists, for the brilliant reason that the money with which the labourers are paid does not remain in their hands, but continually returns to the capitalists in payment of the commodities produced by the labourers.

"All they do is receive with one hand and return with the other. Their consumption must therefore be regarded as having been made by those who hire them" (p. 235).

After this exhaustive analysis of social reproduction and consumption, as being brought about by the circulation of money, Destutt continues:

"This is what perfects this *perpetuum mobile* of wealth, a movement which, though badly understood" (*mal connu*, I should say so!), "has justly been named circulation; for it is indeed a circuit and always returns to its point of departure. This is the point where production is consummated" (pp. 239, 240).

Destutt, THAT VERY DISTINGUISHED WRITER, *membre de l'Institut de France et de la Société Philosophique de Philadelphie,*[63] and in fact to a certain extent a luminary among the vulgar economists, finally requests his readers to admire the wonderful lucidity with which he has presented the course of social process, the flood of light which he has poured over the matter, and is even condescending enough to communicate to his readers, where all this light comes from. This must be read in the original:

"On remarquera, j'espère, combien cette manière de considérer la consommation de nos richesses est concordante avec tout ce que nous avons dit à propos de leur production et de leur distribution, et en même temps *quelle clarté elle répand sur toute la marche de la société.* D'où viennent cet accord et cette *lucidité?* De ce que nous avons rencontré la vérité. Cela rappelle l'effet de ces miroirs où les objets se peignent nettement et dans leurs justes proportions, quand on est placé dans leur vrai point-de-vue, et où tout paraît confus et désuni, quand on en est trop près ou trop loin" [a] (pp. 242, 243).

Voilà le crétinisme bourgeois dans toute sa béatitude! [b]

Chapter XXI[57)]

ACCUMULATION AND REPRODUCTION ON AN EXTENDED SCALE

It has been shown in Book I how accumulation works in the case of the individual capitalist. By the conversion of the commodity capital

---

[57)] From here to the end Manuscript VIII.

---

[a] "It will be noted, I hope, how much this manner of viewing the consumption of our wealth is in accord with all we have been saying concerning its production and distribution, and at the same time *how much light it throws on the entire course of society.* Whence this accord and this *lucidity?* From the fact that we have met truth face to face. This recalls the effect of those mirrors in which things are reflected accurately and in their true proportions when correctly focussed, but in which everything appears confused and disjointed when one is too close or too far away from them." - [b] There you have the bourgeois idiocy in all its beatitude!

into money the surplus product, in which the surplus value is represented, is also turned into money. The capitalist reconverts the so metamorphosed surplus value into additional natural elements of his productive capital. In the next cycle of production the increased capital furnishes an increased product. But what happens in the case of the individual capital must also show in the annual reproduction as a whole, just as we have seen it happen on analysing simple reproduction, namely, that the successive precipitation — in the case of individual capital — of its used-up fixed component parts in money which is being hoarded, also finds expression in the annual reproduction of society.

If a certain individual capital is equal to $400_c + 100_v$, and the annual surplus value is equal to 100, then the commodity product amounts to $400_c + 100_v + 100_s$. These 600 are converted into money. Of this money, again, 400_c are converted into the natural form of constant capital, 100_v into labour power, and — provided the entire surplus value is being accumulated — 100_s are converted besides into additional constant capital by transformation into natural elements of the productive capital. It is assumed in this case: 1) that this amount is sufficient under the given technical conditions either to expand the functioning constant capital or to establish a new industrial business. But it may also happen that surplus value must be converted into money and this money hoarded for a much longer time before this process, i. e., before real accumulation, expansion of production, can take place; 2) that production on an extended scale has actually been in process previously. For in order that the money (the surplus value hoarded in money form) may be converted into elements of productive capital, one must be able to buy these elements on the market as commodities. It makes no difference if they are not bought as finished products but made to order. They are not paid for until they are in existence and at any rate not until actual reproduction on an extended scale, an expansion of hitherto normal production, has taken place so far as they are concerned. They had to exist potentially, i. e., in their elements, as it requires only the impulse of an order, that is, the purchase of commodities before they actually exist and their anticipated sale, for their production really to take place. The money on the one side then calls forth extended reproduction on the other, because the possibility of it exists *without* money. For money in itself is not an element of real reproduction.

For instance, if capitalist A sells during one year or during a number of years certain quantities of commodities successively produced by him, he thereby converts into money also that portion of the commodities which is the vehicle of surplus value—the surplus product—or in other words the very surplus value produced by him in commodity form, accumulates it gradually, and thus forms for himself new potential money capital—potential because of its capacity and mission to be converted into elements of productive capital. But in actual fact he only engages in simple hoarding, which is not an element of actual reproduction. His activity at first consists only in successively withdrawing circulating money out of the circulation. Of course it is not impossible that the circulating money thus kept under lock and key by him was itself, before it entered into circulation, a portion of some other hoard. This hoard of A, which is potentially new money capital, is not additional social wealth, any more than it would be if it were spent in articles of consumption. But money withdrawn from circulation, which therefore previously existed in circulation, may have been stored up at some prior time as a component part of a hoard, may have been the money form of wages, may have converted means of production or other commodities into money or may have circulated portions of constant capital or the revenue of some capitalist. It is no more new wealth than money, considered from the standpoint of the simple circulation of commodities, is the vehicle not only of its actual value but also of its ten-fold value, because it was turned over ten times a day, realised ten different commodity values. The commodities exist without it, and it itself remains what it is (or becomes even less by depreciation) whether in one turnover or in ten. Only in the production of gold—inasmuch as the gold product contains a surplus product, a depository of surplus value—is new wealth (potential money) created, and it increases the money material of new potential money capitals only so far as the entire new money product enters into circulation.

Although this surplus value hoarded in the form of money is not additional new social wealth, it represents new potential money capital, on account of the function for which it is hoarded. (We shall see later that new money capital may arise also in a way other than the gradual conversion of surplus value into money.)

Money is withdrawn from circulation and stored up as a hoard by selling commodities without subsequent buying. If this operation is therefore conceived as a general process, it seems inexplicable where the buyers are to come from, since in that process everybody would want to sell in order to hoard, and none would want to buy. And it must be conceived as a general one, since every individual capital may be in the process of accumulation.

If we were to conceive the process of circulation between the various parts of the annual reproduction as taking place in a straight line — which would be wrong as it always consists with a few exceptions of mutually opposite movements — then we should have to start from the producer of gold (or silver) who buys without selling, and to assume that all others sell to him. In that case the entire yearly social surplus product (the bearer of the entire surplus value) would pass into his hands, and all the other capitalists would distribute among themselves *pro rata* his surplus product, which naturally exists in the form of money, the natural embodiment in gold of his surplus value. For that portion of the product of the gold producer which has to make good his active capital is already tied up and disposed of. The surplus value of the gold producer, created in the form of gold, would then be the sole fund from which all other capitalists would draw the material for the conversion of their annual surplus product into money. The magnitude of its value would then have to be equal to the entire annual surplus value of society, which must first assume the guise of a hoard. Absurd as these assumptions would be, they would do nothing more than explain the possibility of a universal simultaneous formation of a hoard, and would not get reproduction itself one step further, except on the part of the gold producer.

Before we resolve this seeming difficulty we must distinguish between the accumulation in department I (production of means of production) and in department II (production of articles of consumption). We shall start with I.

I. ACCUMULATION IN DEPARTMENT I

1. THE FORMATION OF A HOARD

It is evident that both the investments of capital in the numerous branches of industry constituting class I and the different individual investments of capital within each of these branches of industry, according to their age, i. e., the space of time during which they already have functioned, quite aside from their volumes, technical conditions, market conditions, etc., are in different stages of the process of successive transformation from surplus value into potential money capital, whether this money capital is to serve for the expansion of the active capital or for the establishment of new industrial enterprises—the two forms of expansion of production. One part of the capitalists therefore is continually converting its potential money capital, grown to an appropriate size, into productive capital, i. e., with the money hoarded by the conversion of surplus value into money it buys means of production, additional elements of constant capital. Another part of the capitalists is meanwhile still engaged in hoarding its potential money capital. Capitalists belonging to these two categories confront each other: some as buyers, the others as sellers, and each one of the two exclusively in one of these roles.

For instance, let A sell 600 (= $400_c + 100_v + 100_s$) to B (who may represent more than one buyer). A sells 600 in commodities for 600 in money, of which 100 are surplus value which he withdraws from circulation and hoards in the form of money. But these 100 in money are but the money form of the surplus product, which was the bearer of a value of 100. The formation of a hoard is no production at all, hence not an increment of production, either. The action of the capitalist consists here merely in withdrawing from circulation the 100 in money he grabbed by the sale of his surplus product, holding on to it and impounding it. This operation is carried on not alone by A, but at numerous points along the periphery of circulation by other capitalists, A', A'', A''', all of them working with equal zeal at this sort of hoard formation. These numerous points at which money is withdrawn from circulation and accumulated in numerous individual hoards or potential money capitals appear as so many obstacles to circulation, because they immobilise the money and deprive it of its capacity to circulate for a certain length of time. But it must be borne in mind that hoarding takes place in the simple circulation of commodities long before this is based on capitalist commodity production. The quantity of money existing in society is always greater than the part of it in actual circulation, although this swells or subsides according to circumstances. We find here again the same hoards, and the same formation of hoards, but now as an element immanent in the capitalist process of production.

One can understand the pleasure experienced when all these potential capitals within the credit system, by their concentration in the hands of banks, etc., become disposable, "LOANABLE CAPITAL", money capital, which indeed is no longer passive and music of the future,[64] but active capital growing rank.

However, A accomplishes the formation of a hoard only to the extent that he acts only as a seller, so far as his surplus product is concerned, and not afterward as a buyer. His successive production of surplus products, the vehicles of his surplus value to be converted into money, is therefore the premise of his forming a hoard. In the present case, where we are examining only the circulation within category I, the natural form of the surplus product, as that of the total product of which it is a part, is the natural form of an element of constant capital I, that is to say, it belongs in the category of means of production creating means of production. We shall see presently what becomes of it, what function it performs, in the hands of buyers B, B′, B″, etc.

It must be noted at this point first and foremost that although withdrawing money to the amount of his surplus value from circulation and hoarding it, A on the other hand throws commodities into it without withdrawing other commodities in return. The capitalists B, B′, B″, etc., are thereby enabled to throw money into circulation and withdraw only commodities from it. In the present case these commodities, according to their natural form and their destination, enter into the constant capital of B, B′, etc., as fixed or circulating element. We shall hear more about this anon when we deal with the buyers of the surplus product, with B, B′, etc.

———

Let us note by the way: Once more we find here, as we did in the case of simple reproduction, that the exchange of the various component parts of the annual product, i. e., their circulation (which must comprise at the same time the reproduction of the capital, and indeed its restoration in its various determinations, such as constant, variable, fixed, circulating, money and commodity capital) does not by any means presuppose mere purchase of commodities supplemented by a subsequent sale, or a sale supplemented by a subsequent purchase, so that there would actually be a bare exchange of commodity for commodity, as political economy assumes, especially the free-trade school since the Physiocrats and Adam Smith. We know that the fixed capital, once the expenditure for it is made, is not renewed during the entire period of its function, but continues to act in its old form, while its value is gradually precipitated in the form of money. Now we have seen that the periodical renewal of fixed capital II_c (the entire capital value II_c being converted into elements worth $I_{(v+s)}$) presupposes on the one hand the *mere purchase* of the fixed part of II_c, reconverted from the form of money into its natural form, to which corresponds the mere sale of I_s; and presupposes on the other hand the *mere sale* on the part of II_c, the sale of its fixed (depreciation) part of the value precipitated in money, to which corresponds the mere purchase of I_s. In order that the exchange may take place normally in this case, it must be assumed that the mere purchase on the part of II_c is equal in magnitude of value to the mere sale on the part of II_c, and that in the same way the mere sale of I_s to II_c, section 1, is equal to its mere purchase from II_c, section 2 (p. 440).[a] Otherwise simple reproduction is disturbed. A mere purchase here must be offset by a mere sale there. It must likewise be assumed in this case that the mere sale of that portion of I_s which forms the hoards of A, A′, A″ is balanced by the mere purchase of that portion of I_s which converts the hoards of B, B′ and B″ into elements of additional productive capital.

So far as the balance is restored by the fact that the buyer acts later on as a seller to the same amount of value, and vice versa, the money returns to the side that advanced it on purchasing, and which sold before it bought again. But the actual balance, so far as the exchange of commodities itself, the exchange of the various portions of the annual product is concerned, demands that the values of the commodities exchanged for one another be equal.

But inasmuch as only one-sided exchanges are made, a number of mere purchases on the one hand, a number of mere sales on the other — and we have seen that the normal exchange of the annual product on the basis of capitalism necessitates such one-sided metamorphoses — the balance can be maintained only on the assumption that in amount the value of the one-sided purchases and that of the one-sided sales tally. The fact that the production of commodities is the general form of capitalist production implies the role which money is playing in it not only as a medium of circulation, but also as money capital, and engenders certain conditions of normal exchange peculiar to this mode of production and therefore of the normal course of reproduction, whether it be on a simple or on an extended scale — conditions which change into so many conditions of abnormal course, into so many possibilities of crises, since a balance is itself an accident owing to the spontaneous nature of this production.

---

[a] See this volume, pp. 462-64.

We have also seen that in the exchange of I_v for a corresponding amount of value of II_c, there takes place in the end, precisely for II_c, a replacement of commodities II by an equivalent commodity value I, that therefore on the part of aggregate capitalist II the sale of his own commodities is subsequently supplemented by the purchase of commodities from I of the same amount of value. This replacement takes place. But what does not take place is an exchange between capitalists I and II of their respective goods. II_c sells its commodities to working class I. The latter confronts it one-sidedly, as a buyer of commodities, and it confronts that class one-sidedly as a seller of commodities. With the money proceeds so obtained II_c confronts aggregate capitalist I one-sidedly as a buyer of commodities, and aggregate capitalist I confronts it one-sidedly as a seller of commodities up to the amount of I_v. It is only by means of this sale of commodities that I finally reproduces its variable capital in the form of money capital. If capital I faces that of II one-sidedly as a seller of commodities to the amount of I_v, it faces working class I as a buyer of commodities purchasing their labour power. And if working class I faces capitalist II one-sidedly as a buyer of commodities (namely, as a buyer of means of subsistence), it faces capitalist I one-sidedly as a seller of commodities, namely, as a seller of its labour power.

The constant supply of labour power on the part of working class I, the reconversion of a portion of commodity capital I into the money form of variable capital, the replacement of a portion of commodity capital II by natural elements of constant capital II_c — all these necessary premises demand one another, but they are brought about by a very complicated process, including three processes of circulation which occur independently of one another but intermingle. This process is so complicated that it offers ever so many occasions for running abnormally.

2. THE ADDITIONAL CONSTANT CAPITAL

The surplus product, the bearer of surplus value, does not cost its appropriators, capitalists I, anything. They are by no manner of means obliged to advance any money or commodities in order to obtain it. Even among the Physiocrats an advance (*avance*) was the general form of value embodied in elements of productive capital. Hence what capitalists I advance is nothing but their constant and variable capital. The labourer not only preserves by his labour their constant capital; he not only replaces the value of their variable capital by a corresponding newly created portion of value in the form of commodities; by his surplus labour he supplies them with a surplus value existing in the form of surplus product. By the successive sale of this surplus product they form a hoard, additional potential money capital. In the case under consideration, this surplus product consists from the outset of means of production of means of production. It is only when it reaches the hands of B, B′, B″, etc. (I) that this surplus product functions as additional constant capital. But it is this *virtualiter* even before it is sold, even in the hands of the accumulators of hoards, A, A′, A″ (I). If we consider merely the amount of value of the reproduction on the part of I, we are still moving within the bounds of simple reproduction, for no additional capital has been set in motion to create this *virtualiter* additional constant capital (the surplus product), nor has any greater amount of surplus labour been expended than that on the basis of simple reproduction. The difference is here only in the form of the surplus labour performed, in the concrete nature of its particular useful character. It has been expended in means of production for I_c instead of II_c, in means of production of means of production instead of means of production of articles of consumption. In the case of simple reproduction it was assumed that the entire surplus value I is spent as revenue, hence in commodities II. Hence the surplus value consisted only of such means of production as have to replace constant capital II_c in its natural form. In order that the transition from simple to extended reproduction may take place, production in department I must be in a position to fabricate fewer elements of constant capital for II and so many the more for I. This transition, which does not always take place without difficulties, is facilitated by the fact that some of the products of I may serve as means of production in either department.

It follows, then, that, considering the matter merely from the angle of volume of values, the material substratum of extended reproduction is produced within simple reproduction. It is simply surplus labour of working class I expended directly in the production of means of production, in the creation of virtual additional capital I. The formation of virtual additional money capital on the part of A, A′ and A″ (I) — by the successive sale of their surplus product which was formed without any capitalist expenditure of money — is therefore simply the money form of additionally produced means of production I.

Consequently production of virtual additional capital expresses in our case (we shall see that it may also be formed in a quite different way) nothing but a phenomenon of the process of production itself, production, in a particular form, of elements of productive capital.

The production of additional virtual money capital on a large scale, at numerous points of the periphery of circulation, is therefore but a result and expression of multifarious production of virtually additional productive capital, whose rise does not itself require additional expenditure of money on the part of the industrial capitalist.

The successive transformation of this virtually additional productive capital into virtual money capital (hoard) on the part of A, A′, A″, etc. (I), occasioned by the successive sale of their surplus product — hence by repeated one-sided sale of commodities without a supplementing purchase — is accomplished by a repeated withdrawal of money from circulation and a corresponding formation of a hoard. Except in the case where the buyer is a gold producer, this hoarding does not in any way imply additional wealth in precious metals, but only a change in the function of money previously circulating. A while ago it functioned as a medium of circulation, now it functions as a hoard, as virtually new money capital in the process of formation. Thus the formation of additional money capital and the quantity of the precious metals existing in a country are not in any causal relation to each other.

Hence it follows furthermore: The greater the productive capital already functioning in a country (including the labour power, the producer of the surplus product, incorporated in it), the more developed the productive power of labour and thereby also the technical means for the rapid expansion of the production of means of production — the greater therefore the quantity of the surplus product both as to its value and as to the quantity of use values in which it is represented — so much the greater is

1) the virtually additional productive capital in the form of a surplus product in the hands of A, A′, A″, etc., and

2) the quantity of this surplus product transformed into money, and hence that of the virtually additional money capital in the hands of A, A′, A″. The fact that Fullarton for instance does not want to hear of overproduction in the ordinary sense but only of the overproduction of capital, meaning money capital, again shows how extremely little of the mechanism of their own system even the best bourgeois economists understand.

Whereas the surplus product, directly produced and appropriated by the capitalists A, A′, A″ (I), is the real basis of the accumulation of capital, i. e., of extended reproduction, although it does not actually function in this capacity until it reaches the hands of B, B′, B″, etc. (I), it is on the contrary absolutely unproductive in its chrysalis stage of money — as a hoard and virtual money capital in process of gradual formation — runs parallel with the process of production in this form, but lies outside of it. It is a DEAD WEIGHT[a] of capitalist production. The eagerness to utilise this surplus value accumulating as virtual money capital for the purpose of deriving profits or revenue from it finds its object accomplished in the credit system and "papers". Money capital thereby gains in another form an enormous influence on the course and the stupendous development of the capitalist system of production.

The surplus product converted into virtual money capital will grow so much more in volume, the greater was the total amount of already functioning capital whose functioning brought it into being. With the absolute increase of the volume of the annually reproduced virtual money capital its segmentation also becomes easier, so that it is more rapidly invested in any particular business, either in the hands of the same capitalist or in those of others (for instance members of the family, in the case of a partition of inherited property, etc.). By segmentation of money capital is meant here that it is wholly detached from the parent stock in order to be invested as a new money capital in a new and independent business.

While the sellers of the surplus product, A, A′, A″, etc. (I), have obtained it as a direct outcome of the process of production, which does not envisage any additional acts of circulation except the advance of constant and variable capital required also in simple reproduction; and while they thereby construct the real basis for reproduction on an extended scale, and in actual fact manufacture virtually additional capital, the attitude of B, B′, B″, etc. (I), is different. 1) Not until it reaches the hands of B, B′, B″, etc. (I), will the surplus product of A, A′, A″, etc., actually function as additional constant capital (we leave out of consideration for the present the other element of productive capital, the additional labour power, in other words, the additional variable capital). 2) In order that that surplus product may reach their hands an act of circulation is wanted — they must buy it.

---

[a] In the original, these English words are given in parentheses after their German equivalent.

In regard to point 1, it should be noted here that a major portion of the surplus product (virtually additional constant capital), although produced by A, A′, A″ (I) in a given year, may not function as industrial capital in the hands of B, B′, B″ (I) until the following year or still later. With reference to point 2, the question arises: Whence comes the money needed for the process of circulation?

Since the products created by B, B′, B″, etc. (I), re-enter *in natura* into their own process, it goes without saying that *pro tanto* a portion of their own surplus product is transferred directly (without any intervention of circulation) to their productive capital and becomes an additional element of constant capital. And *pro tanto* they do not effect the conversion of the surplus product of A, A′, etc. (I), into money. Aside from this, where does the money come from? We know that B, B′, B″, etc. (I), have formed their hoard in the same way as A, A′, etc., by the sale of their respective surplus products. Now they have arrived at the point where their hoarded, only virtual, money capital is to function effectively as additional money capital. But this is merely going round in circles. The question still remains: Where does the money come from which the B's (I) before withdrew from circulation and accumulated?

We know from the analysis of simple reproduction that capitalists I and II must have a certain amount of money at hand in order to be able to exchange their surplus product. In that case the money which served only as revenue to be spent for articles of consumption returned to the capitalists in the same measure in which they had advanced it for the exchange of their respective commodities. Here the same money re-appears, but performing a different function. The A's and B's (I) supply one another alternately with the money for converting surplus product into additional virtual money capital, and throw the newly formed money capital alternately back into circulation as a means of purchase.

The only assumption made in this case is that the amount of money in the country in question (the velocity of circulation, etc., being constant) should suffice for both the active circulation and the reserve hoard. As we have seen this is the same assumption as had to be made in the case of the simple circulation of commodities. Only the function of the hoards is different in the present case. Furthermore, the available amount of money must be larger, (1) because under capitalist production all the products (with the exception of newly produced precious metals and the few products consumed by the producer himself) are created as commodities and must therefore pass through the pupation stage of money; (2) because on a capitalist basis the quantity of the commodity capital and the magnitude of its value is not only absolutely greater but also grows with incomparably greater rapidity; (3) because an ever expanding variable capital must always be converted into money capital; (4) because the formation of new money capitals keeps pace with the extension of production, so that the material for corresponding hoard formation must be available.

If this is generally true of the first phase of capitalist production, in which even the credit system is mostly accompanied by metallic circulation, so it applies to the most developed phase of the credit system as well, to the extent that metallic circulation remains its basis. On the one hand an additional production of precious metals, being alternately abundant or scarce, may here exert a disturbing influence on the prices of commodities not only at long, but also at very short intervals. On the other hand the entire credit mechanism is continually occupied in reducing the actual metallic circulation to a relatively more and more decreasing minimum by means of sundry operations, methods, and technical devices. The artificiality of the entire machinery and the possibility of disturbing its normal course increase to the same extent.

The different B's, B''s, B'''s, etc. (I), whose virtual new money capital enters upon its function as active capital, may have to buy their products (portions of their surplus product) from one another, or to sell them to one another. *Pro tanto* the money advanced by them for the circulation of their surplus product flows back under normal conditions to the different B's in the same proportion in which they had advanced it for the circulation of their respective commodities. If the money circulates as a means of payment, then only balances are to be squared so far as the mutual purchases and sales do not cover one another. But it is important first and foremost to assume here, as everywhere, metallic circulation in its simplest, most primitive form, because then the flux and reflux, the squaring of balances, in short all elements appearing under the credit system as consciously regulated processes, present themselves as existing independently of the credit system, and the matter appears in primitive form instead of the later, reflected form.

3. THE ADDITIONAL VARIABLE CAPITAL

Hitherto we have been dealing only with additional constant capital. Now we must direct our attention to a consideration of the additional variable capital.

We have explained at great length in Book I that labour power is always available under the capitalist system of production, and that more labour can be rendered fluid, if necessary, without increasing the number of labourers or the quantity of labour power employed. We therefore need not go into this any further, but shall rather assume that the portion of the newly created money capital capable of being converted into variable capital will always find at hand the labour power into which it is to transform itself. It has also been explained in Book I that a given capital may expand its volume of production within certain limits without any accumulation. But here we are dealing with the accumulation of capital in its specific meaning, so that the expansion of production implies the conversion of surplus value into additional capital, and thus also an expansion of the capital forming the basis of production.

The gold producer can accumulate a portion of his golden surplus value as virtual money capital. As soon as it becomes sufficient in amount, he can transform it directly into new variable capital, without first having to sell his surplus product. He can likewise convert it into elements of the constant capital. But in the latter case he must find at hand the material elements of his constant capital. It is immaterial whether, as was assumed in our presentation hitherto, each producer works to stock up and then brings his finished product to the market or fills orders. The actual expansion of production, i. e., the surplus product, is assumed in either case, in the one case as actually available, in the other as virtually available, capable of delivery.

II. ACCUMULATION IN DEPARTMENT II

We have hitherto assumed that A, A', A'' (I) sell their surplus product to B, B', B'', etc., who belong to the same department I. But supposing A (I) converts his surplus product into money by selling it to one B in department II. This can be done only by A (I) selling means of production to B (II) without subsequently buying articles of consumption, i. e., only by a one-sided sale on A's part. Now whereas II_c cannot be converted from the commodity-capital form into the natural form of productive constant capital unless not only I_v but also at least a portion of I_s is exchanged for a portion of II_c, which II_c exists in the form of articles of consumption; but now A converts his I_s into money by not making this exchange but rather withdrawing from circulation the money obtained from II on the sale of his I_s instead of exchanging it in the purchase of articles of consumption II_c — then what we have on the part of A (I) is indeed a formation of additional virtual money capital, but on the other hand a portion of the constant capital of B (II) of equal magnitude of value is tied up in the form of commodity capital, unable to transform itself into the natural form of productive, constant capital. In other words, a portion of the commodities of B (II), and indeed *prima facie* a portion without the sale of which he cannot reconvert his constant capital entirely into its productive form, has become unsaleable. As fas as this portion is concerned there is therefore an overproduction, which, likewise as far as the same portion is concerned, clogs reproduction, even on the same scale.

In this case the additional virtual money capital on the side of A (I) is indeed a moneyed form of surplus product (surplus value), but the surplus product (surplus value) considered as such is here a phenomenon of simple reproduction, not yet of reproduction on an extended scale. $I_{(v+s)}$, for which this is true at all events of one portion of s, must ultimately be exchanged for II_c, in order that the reproduction of II_c may take place on the same scale. By the sale of his surplus product to B (II), A (I) has supplied to the latter a corresponding portion of the value of constant capital in its natural form. But at the same time he has rendered an equivalent portion of the commodities of B (II) unsaleable by withdrawing the money from circulation — by failing to complement his sale through subsequent purchase. Hence, if we survey the entire social reproduction, which comprises the capitalists of both I and II, the conversion of the surplus product of A (I) into virtual money capital expresses the impossibility of reconverting commodity capital of B (II) representing an equal amount of value into productive (constant) capital; hence not virtual production on an extended scale but an obstruction of simple reproduction, and so a deficit in simple reproduction. As the formation and sale of the surplus product of A (I) are normal phenomena of simple reproduction, we have here even on the basis of simple reproduction the following interdependent phenomena: Formation of virtual additional money capital in class I (hence underconsumption from the viewpoint of II); piling up of commodity supplies in class II which cannot be reconverted into productive capital (hence relative overproduction in II); excess of money capital in I and reproduction deficit in II.

Without pausing any longer at this point, we simply remark that we had assumed in the analysis of simple reproduction that the entire surplus value of I and II is spent as revenue. As a matter of fact however one portion of the surplus value is spent as revenue, and the other is converted into capital. Actual accumulation can take place only on this assumption. That accumulation should take place at the expense of consumption is, couched in such general terms, an illusion contradicting the nature of capitalist production. For it takes for granted that the aim and compelling motive of capitalist production is consumption, and not the snatching of surplus value and its capitalisation, i. e., accumulation.

———

Let us now take a closer look at the accumulation in department II.

The first difficulty with reference to II_c, i. e., its reconversion from a component part of commodity capital II into the natural form of constant capital II, concerns simple reproduction. Let us take the former scheme:

$(1,000_v + 1,000_s)$ I are exchanged for
$2,000 \ II_c$.

Now, if for instance one half of the surplus product of I, hence $\frac{1,000}{2}$ s or $500 \ I_s$ is reincorporated in department I as constant capital, then this portion of the surplus product, being detained in I, cannot replace any part of II_c. Instead of being converted into articles of consumption (and here in this section of the circulation between I and II the exchange is actually mutual, that is, there is a double change of position of the commodities, unlike the replacement of $1,000 \ II_c$ by $1,000 \ I_v$ effected by the labourers of I), it is made to serve as an additional means of production in I itself. It cannot perform this function simultaneously in I and II. The capitalist cannot spend the value of his surplus product for articles of consumption and at the same time consume the surplus product itself productively, i. e., incorporate it in his productive capital. Instead of $2,000 \ I_{(v+s)}$, only

1,500, namely $(1,000_v + 500_s)$ I, are therefore exchangeable for 2,000 II_c; 500 II_c cannot be reconverted from the commodity form into productive (constant) capital II. Hence there would be an overproduction in II, exactly equal in volume to the expansion of production in I. This overproduction in II might react to such an extent on I that even the reflux of the 1,000 spent by the labourers of I for articles of consumption of II might take place but partially, so that these 1,000 would not return to the hands of capitalists I in the form of variable money capital. These capitalists would thus find themselves hampered even in reproduction on an unchanging scale, and this by the bare attempt to expand it. And in this connection it must be taken into consideration that in I only simple reproduction had actually taken place and that its elements, as represented in our scheme, are only differently grouped with a view to expansion in the future, say, next year.

One might attempt to circumvent this difficulty in the following way: Far from being overproduction, the 500 II_c which are kept in stock by the capitalists and cannot be immediately converted into productive capital represent, on the contrary, a necessary element of reproduction, which we have so far neglected. We have seen that a money supply must be accumulated at many points, hence money must be withdrawn from circulation, partly for the purpose of making it possible to form new money capital in I, and partly to hold fast temporarily the value of the gradually depreciating fixed capital in the form of money. But since we placed all money and commodities from the very start exclusively into the hands of capitalists I and II when we drew up our scheme and since neither merchants, nor money changers, nor bankers, not merely consuming and not directly producing classes exist here, it follows that the constant formation of commodity stores in the hands of their respective producers is here indispensable to keep the machinery of reproduction going. The 500 II_c held in stock by capitalists II therefore represent the commodity supply of articles of consumption which ensures the continuity of the process of consumption implied in reproduction, here meaning the passage of one year to the next. The consumption fund, which is as yet in the hands of its sellers who are at the same time its producers, cannot fall one year to the point of zero in order to begin the next with zero, any more than such a thing can take place in the transition from today to tomorrow. Since such supplies of commodities must constantly be built up anew, though varying in volume, our capitalist producers II must have a reserve money capital, which enables them to continue their process of production although one portion of their productive capital is temporarily tied up in the shape of commodities. Our assumption is that they combine the whole business of trading with that of producing. Hence they must also have at their disposal the additional money capital, which is in the hands of the merchants when the individual functions in the process of reproduction are separated and distributed among the various kinds of capitalists.

To this one may object: 1) that the forming of such supplies and the necessity of doing so applies to all capitalists, those of I as well as of II. Considered as mere sellers of commodities, they differ only in that they sell different kinds of commodities. A supply of commodities II implies a previous supply of commodities I. If we neglect this supply on one side, we must also do so on the other. But if we take them into account on both sides, the problem is not altered in any way.

2) Just as a certain year closes on the part of II with a supply of commodities for the following year, so it was opened with a supply of commodities on the same part, taken over from the preceding year. In an analysis of annual reproduction, reduced to its most abstract form, we must therefore strike it out in both cases. If we leave to the given year its entire production, including the commodity supply to be yielded up for next year, and simultaneously take from it the supply of commodities transferred to it from the preceding year, we have before us the actual aggregate product of an average year as the subject of our analysis.

3) The simple circumstance that in the analysis of simple reproduction we did not stumble across the difficulty which is now to be surmounted proves that we are confronted by a specific phenomenon due solely to the different grouping (with reference to reproduction) of elements I, a changed grouping without which reproduction on an extended scale cannot take place at all.

III. SCHEMATIC PRESENTATION OF ACCUMULATION

We shall now study reproduction according to the following scheme:

Scheme a)
$$\text{I. } 4{,}000_c + 1{,}000_v + 1{,}000_s = 6{,}000$$
$$\text{II. } 1{,}500_c + 376_v + 376_s = 2{,}252$$
$$\left. \right\} \text{ Total} = 8{,}252.$$

We note in the first place that the sum total of the annual social product, $= 8{,}252$, is smaller than that of the first scheme, where it was 9,000. We might just as well assume a much larger sum, for instance one ten times larger. We have chosen a smaller sum than in our scheme I in order to make it conspicuously clear that reproduction on an enlarged scale (which is here regarded merely as production carried on with a larger investment of capital) has nothing to do with the absolute volume of the product, that for a given quantity of commodities it implies merely a different arrangement or a different definition of the functions of the various elements of a given product, so that it is but a simple reproduction so far as the value of the product is concerned. It is not the quantity but the qualitative determination of the given elements of simple reproduction which is changed, and this change is the material premise of a subsequent reproduction on an extended scale.[58]

We might vary the scheme by changing the ratio between the variable and constant capital. For instance as follows:

Scheme b)
$$\text{I. } 4{,}000_c + 875_v + 875_s = 5{,}750$$
$$\text{II. } 1{,}750_c + 376_v + 376_s = 2{,}502$$
$$\left. \right\} \text{ Total} = 8{,}252.$$

This scheme seems arranged for reproduction on a simple scale, the surplus value being entirely consumed as revenue and not accumulated. In either case, both a) and b), we have an annual product of the same magnitude of value, only under b) functionally its elements are

[58] This puts an end, once and for all, to the feud over the accumulation of capital between James Mill and S. Bailey, which we have discussed from another point of view in Book I (Kap. XXII, 5, S. 634, Note 65),[a] namely the feud concerning the possibility of extending the operation of industrial capital without changing its magnitude. We shall revert to this later.

[a] English edition, Vol. I, Ch. XXIV, 5 (present edition, Vol. 35).

grouped in such a way that reproduction is resumed on the same scale, while under a) the functional grouping forms the material basis of reproduction on an extended scale. Under b) $(875_v + 875_s)$ I = 1,750 $I_{(v+s)}$ are exchanged without any surplus for 1,750 II_c, while under a) the exchange of $(1,000_v + 1,000_s)$ I = 2,000 $I_{(v+s)}$ for 1,500 II_c leaves a surplus of 500 I_s for accumulation in class I.

Now let us analyse scheme a) more closely. Let us suppose that both I and II accumulate one half of their surplus value, that is to say, convert it into an element of additional capital, instead of spending it as revenue. As one half of 1,000 I_s = 500 are to be accumulated in one form or another, invested as additional money capital, i. e., converted into additional productive capital, only $(1,000_v + 500_s)$ I are spent as revenue. Hence only 1,500 figure here as the normal size of II_c. We need not further examine the exchange between 1,500 $I_{(v+s)}$ and 1,500 II_c, because this has already been done under the head of process of simple reproduction. Nor do 4,000 I_c require any attention, since their re-arrangement for the newly commencing reproduction (which this time occurs on an extended scale) was likewise discussed as a process of simple reproduction.

The only thing that remains to be examined by us is 500 I_s and $(376_v + 376_s)$ II, inasmuch as it is a matter on the one hand of the internal relations of both I and II and on the other of the movement between them. Since we have assumed that in II likewise one half of the surplus value is to be accumulated, 188 are to be converted here into capital, of which $^1/_4$ [a] = 47, or, to round it off, 48, are to be variable capital, so that 140 remain to be converted into constant capital.

Here we come across a new problem, whose very existence must appear strange to the current view that commodities of one kind are exchanged for commodities of another kind, or commodities for money and the same money again for commodities of another kind. The 140 II_s can be converted into productive capital only by replacing them with a portion of commodities of I_s of the same value. It is a matter of course that that portion of I_s which must be exchanged for II_s must consist of means of production, which may enter either into the production of both I and II, or exclusively into that of II. This replacement can be made feasible only by means of a one-sided purchase on the part of II, as the entire surplus product of 500 I_s, which we still

---

[a] This is an obvious slip of the pen; it should be one-fifth; this, however, does not affect the final conclusions.

have to examine, is to serve the purposes of accumulation within I, hence cannot be exchanged for commodities II; in other words, it cannot be simultaneously accumulated and consumed by I. Therefore II must buy 140 I_s for cash without recovering this money by a subsequent sale of its commodities to I. And this is a process which is continually repeating itself in every new annual production, so far as it is reproduction on an extended scale. Where in II is the source of the money for this?

It would rather seem that II is a very unprofitable field for the formation of new money capital which accompanies actual accumulation and necessitates it under capitalist production, and which at first actually presents itself as simple hoarding.

We have first 376 II_v. The money capital of 376, advanced in labour power, continually returns through the purchase of commodities II as variable capital in money form to capitalist II. This constant repetition of departure from and return to the starting-point, the pocket of the capitalist, does not add in any way to the money roving over this circuit. This, then, is not a source of the accumulation of money. Nor can this money be withdrawn from circulation in order to form hoarded, virtually new money capital.

But stop! Isn't there a chance here to make a little profit?

We must not forget that class II has this advantage over class I, that its labourers have to buy back from it the commodities produced by themselves. Class II is a buyer of labour power and at the same time a seller of the commodities to the owners of the labour power employed by it. Class II can therefore:

1) — and this it shares with the capitalists of class I — simply depress wages below their normal average level. By this means a portion of the money functioning as the money form of variable capital is released, and if this process is continually repeated, it might become a normal source of hoarding, and thus of virtually additional money capital in class II. Of course we are not referring to a casual swindle profit here, since we are treating of a normal formation of capital. But it must not be forgotten that the normal wages actually paid (which *ceteris paribus* determine the magnitude of the variable capital) are not paid by the capitalists out of the goodness of their hearts, but must be paid under given relations. This eliminates the above method of explanation. If we assume that 376_v is the variable capital to be laid out by class II, we have no right suddenly to sneak in the hy-

pothesis that it may pay only 350_v instead of 376_v, merely to elucidate a problem that has newly arisen.

2) On the other hand class II, taken as a whole, has the above-mentioned advantage over I that it is at the same time a buyer of labour power and a seller of its commodities to its own labourers. Every industrial country (for instance Britain and the U. S. A.) furnishes the most tangible proofs of the way in which this advantage may be exploited — by paying nominally the normal wages but grabbing, alias stealing, back part of them without an equivalent in commodities; by accomplishing the same thing either through the TRUCK SYSTEM or through a falsification of the medium of circulation (perhaps in a way too elusive for the law). (Take this opportunity to expatiate on this idea with some appropriate examples.) This is the same operation as under 1), only disguised and carried out by a detour. Therefore it must likewise be rejected, the same as the other. We are dealing here with actually paid, not nominally paid wages.

We see that in an objective analysis of the mechanism of capitalism certain stains still sticking to it with extraordinary tenacity cannot be used as a subterfuge to get over some theoretical difficulties. But strange to say, the great majority of my bourgeois critics upbraid me as though I have wronged the capitalists by assuming, for instance in Book I of *Capital*, that the capitalist pays labour power at its real value, a thing which he mostly does not do! (Here, exercising some of the magnanimity attributed to me, it would be appropriate to quote Schäffle.)

So with the 376 II_v we cannot get any nearer the goal we have mentioned.

But the 376 II_s seem to be in a still more precarious position. Here only capitalists of the same class, mutually buying and selling the articles of consumption they produced, confront one another. The money required for these transactions functions only as a medium of circulation and in the normal course of things must flow back to the interested parties in the same proportion in which they advanced it to the circulation, in order to cover the same route over and over again.

There seem to be only two ways by which this money can be withdrawn from circulation to form virtually additional money capital. Either one part of capitalists II cheats the other and thus robs them of their money. We know that no preliminary expansion of the circulating medium is necessary for the formation of new money capital. All that is necessary is that the money should be withdrawn from circulation by certain parties and hoarded. It would not alter the case if this money were stolen, so that the formation of additional money capital by one part of capitalists II would entail a positive loss of money by another part. The cheated capitalists II would have to live a little less gaily, that would be all.

Or a part of II_s represented by necessities of life is directly converted into new variable capital within department II. How that is done we shall examine at the close of this chapter (under No. IV).

1. FIRST ILLUSTRATION

A) Scheme of Simple Reproduction

$$\left. \begin{array}{l} \text{I. } 4{,}000_c + 1{,}000_v + 1{,}000_s = 6{,}000 \\ \text{II. } 2{,}000_c + 500_v + 500_s = 3{,}000 \end{array} \right\} \text{Total} = 9{,}000.$$

B) Initial Scheme for Reproduction on an Extended Scale

$$\left. \begin{array}{l} \text{I. } 4{,}000_c + 1{,}000_v + 1{,}000_s = 6{,}000 \\ \text{II. } 1{,}500_c + 750_v + 750_s = 3{,}000 \end{array} \right\} \text{Total} = 9{,}000.$$

Assuming that in scheme B one half of surplus value I, i. e., 500, is accumulated, we first receive $(1{,}000_v + 500_s)$ I, or $1{,}500\ I_{(v+s)}$ to be replaced by $1{,}500\ II_c$. There then remains in $I{:}4{,}000_c + 500_s$, the latter having to be accumulated. The replacement of $(1{,}000_v + 500_s)$ I by $1{,}500\ II_c$ is a process of simple reproduction, which has been examined previously.

Let us now assume that 400 of the 500 I_s are to be converted into constant capital, and 100 into variable capital. The exchange within I of the 400_s which are thus to be capitalised, has already been discussed. They can therefore be annexed to I_c without more ado and in that case we get for I:

$$4{,}400_c + 1{,}000_v + 100_s \text{ (the latter to be converted into } 100_v\text{)}.$$

II in turn buys from I for the purpose of accumulation the 100 I_s (existing in means of production) which now form additional constant capital II, while the 100 in money which it pays for them are converted into the money form of the additional variable capital of I. We then have for I a capital of $4{,}400_c + 1{,}100_v$ (the latter in money) $= 5{,}500$.

II has now $1{,}600_c$ for its constant capital. In order to put them to work, it must advance a further 50_v in money for the purchase of new labour power, so that its variable capital grows from 750 to 800. This expansion of the constant and variable capital of II by a total of 150 is supplied out of its surplus value. Hence only 600_s of the 750 II_s remain as a consumption fund for capitalists II, whose annual product is now divided as follows:

II. $1,600_c + 800_v + 600_s$ (consumption fund) = 3,000.

The 150_s produced in articles of consumption, which have been converted here into $(100_c + 50_v)$ II, go entirely in their natural form for the consumption of the labourers, 100 being consumed by the labourers of I (100 I_v), and 50 by the labourers of II (50 II_v), as explained above. As a matter of fact in II, where its total product is prepared in a form suitable for accumulation, a part greater by 100 of the surplus value in the form of *necessary* articles of consumption must be reproduced. If reproduction really starts on an extended scale, then the 100 of variable money capital I flow back through the hands of its working class to II, while II transfers 100_s in commodity supply to I and at the same time 50 in commodity supply to its own working class.

The arrangement changed for the purpose of accumulation is now as follows:

II. $4,400_c + 1,100_v + 500$ consumption fund = 6,000
II. $1,600_c + 800_v + 600$ consumption fund = 3,000

Total,   9,000 as above.

Of these amounts, the following are capital:

$$\left. \begin{array}{l} \text{I. } 4,400_c + 1,100_v \text{ (money)} = 5,500 \\ \text{II. } 1,600_c + 800_v \text{ (money)} = 2,400 \end{array} \right\} = 7,900,$$

while production started out with

$$\left. \begin{array}{l} \text{I. } 4,000_c + 1,000_v = 5,000 \\ \text{II. } 1,500_c + 750_v = 2,250 \end{array} \right\} = 7,250.$$

Now, if actual accumulation takes place on this basis, that is to say, if production really goes on with this augmented capital, we obtain at the end of the following year:

$$\left. \begin{array}{l} \text{I. } 4,400_c + 1,100_v + 1,100_s = 6,600 \\ \text{II. } 1,600_c + 800_s + 800_s = 3,200 \end{array} \right\} = 9,800.$$

Then let accumulation in I continue in the same proportion, so that 550_s are spent as revenue and 550_s accumulated. In that case $1,100 \; I_v$ are first replaced by $1,100 \; II_c$, and $550 \; I_s$ must be realised in an equal amount of commodities of II, making a total of $1,650 \; I_{(v+s)}$. But the constant capital II, which is to be replaced, is equal to only 1,600; hence the remaining 50 must be supplemented out of $800 \; II_s$. Leaving aside the money aspect for the present, we have as a result of this transaction:

I. $4,400_c + 550_s$ (to be capitalised); furthermore, realised in commodities II_c, the consumption fund of the capitalists and labourers $1,650_{(v+s)}$.

II. $1,650_c$ (50 added from II_s as indicated above) $+ 800_v + 750_s$ (consumption fund of the capitalists).

But if the old ratio of v:c is maintained in II, then additional 25_v must be laid out for 50_c, and these are to be taken from the 750_s. Then we have

$$\text{II.} \quad 1,650_c + 825_v + 725_s.$$

In I, 550_s must be capitalised. If the former ratio is maintained, 440 of this amount form constant capital and 110 variable capital. These 110 might be taken out of the $725 \; II_s$, i. e., articles of consumption to the value of 110 are consumed by labourers I instead of capitalists II, so that the latter are compelled to capitalise these 110_s which they cannot consume. This leaves $615 \; II_s$ of the $725 \; II_s$. But if II thus converts these 110 into additional constant capital, it requires an additional variable capital of 55. This again must be supplied by its surplus value. Subtracting this amount from $615 \; II_s$ leaves 560 for the consumption of capitalists II, and we now obtain the following capital value after accomplishing all actual and potential transfers:

I. $(4,400_c + 440_c) + (1,100_v + 110_v) = 4,840_c + 1,210_v = 6,050$
II. $(1,600_c + 50_c + 110_c) + (800_v + 25_v + 55_v) =$

$$= 1,760_c + 880_v = \frac{2,640}{8,690}$$

If things are to proceed normally, accumulation in II must take place more rapidly than in I, because otherwise the portion $I_{(v+s)}$ which must be converted into commodities II_c will grow more rapidly than II_c, for which alone it can be exchanged.

If reproduction is continued on this basis and conditions otherwise remain unchanged, we obtain at the end of the succeeding year:

$$\left. \begin{array}{l} \text{I. } 4,840_c + 1,210_v + 1,210_s = 7,260 \\ \text{II. } 1,760_c + 880_v + 880_s = 3,520 \end{array} \right\} = 10,780.$$

If the rate of division of the surplus value remains unchanged, there is first to be expended as revenue by I: $1,210_v$ and one half of $s = 605$, a total of $1,815$. This consumption fund is again larger than II_c by 55. These 55 must be deducted from 880_s, leaving 825. Furthermore, the conversion of 55 II_s into II_c implies another deduction from II_s for a corresponding variable capital $= 27^1/_2$, leaving for consumption $797^1/_2$ II_s.

I has now to capitalise 605_s. Of these 484 are constant and 121 variable. The last named are to be deducted from II_s, which is still equal to $797^1/_2$, leaving $676^1/_2$ II_s. II, then, converts another 121 into constant capital and requires another variable capital of $60^1/_2$ for it, which likewise comes out of $676^1/_2$, leaving 616 for consumption.

Then we have the following capital:

I. Constant $\quad 4,840 + 484 = 5,324.$
   Variable $\quad 1,210 + 121 = 1,331.$
II. Constant $\quad 1,760 + 55 + 121 = 1,936.$
   Variable $\quad 880 + 27^1/_2 + 60^1/_2 = 968.$

$$\text{Totals:} \left. \begin{array}{l} \text{I. } 5,324_c + 1,331_v = 6,655 \\ \text{II. } 1,936_c + 968_v = 2,904 \end{array} \right\} = 9,559.$$

And at the end of the year the product is

$$\left. \begin{array}{l} \text{I. } 5,324_c + 1,331_v + 1,331_s = 7,986 \\ \text{II. } 1,936_c + 968_v + 968_s = 3,872 \end{array} \right\} = 11,858.$$

Repeating the same calculation and rounding off the fractions, we get at the end of the succeeding year the following product:

$$\left. \begin{array}{l} \text{I. } 5,856_c + 1,464_v + 1,464_s = 8,784 \\ \text{II. } 2,129_c + 1,065_v + 1,065_s = 4,259 \end{array} \right\} = 13,043.$$

And at the end of the next succeeding year:

$$\left. \begin{array}{l} \text{I. } 6,442_c + 1,610_v + 1,610_s = 9,662 \\ \text{II. } 2,342_c + 1,172_v + 1,172_s = 4,686 \end{array} \right\} = 14,348.$$

In the course of five years of reproduction on an extended scale the aggregate capital of I and II has risen from $5,500_c + 1,750_v = 7,250$

to $8,784_c + 2,782_v = 11,566$; in other words, in the ratio of 100:160. The total surplus value was originally 1,750; it is now 2,782. The consumed surplus value was originally 500 for I and 600 for II, a total of 1,100. The previous year it was 732 for I and 745 for II, a total of 1,477. It has therefore grown in the ratio of 100:134.[65]

2. SECOND ILLUSTRATION

Now take the annual product of 9,000, which is altogether a commodity capital in the hands of the class of industrial capitalists in a form in which the general average ratio of the variable to the constant capital is that of 1:5. This presupposes a considerable development of capitalist production and accordingly of the productivity of social labour, a considerable previous increase in the scale of production, and finally a development of all the circumstances which produce a relative surplus population among the working class. The annual product will then be divided as follows, after rounding off the various fractions:

$$\left.\begin{array}{l} \text{I. } 5,000_c + 1,000_v + 1,000_s = 7,000 \\ \text{II. } 1,430_c + 285_v + 285_s = 2,000 \end{array}\right\} = 9,000.$$

Now take it that capitalist class I consumes one half of its surplus value $= 500$, and accumulates the other half. In that case $(1,000_v + 500_s)$ I $= 1,500$ would have to be converted into $1,500$ II_c. Since II_c here amounts to only 1,430, it is necessary to add 70 from the surplus value. Subtracting this sum from 285 II_s leaves 215 II_s. Then we have:

$$\text{I. } 5,000_c + 500_s \text{ (to be capitalised)} + 1,500_{(v + s)}$$

in the consumption fund of the capitalists and labourers.

$$\text{II. } 1,430_c + 70_s \text{ (to be capitalised)} + 285_v + 215_s.$$

As 70 II_s are directly annexed here to II_c, a variable capital of $^{70}/_5 = 14$ is required to set this additional constant capital in motion. These 14 must also come out of the 215 II_s, so that 201 II_s remain, and we have:

$$\text{II. } (1,430_c + 70_c) + (285_v + 14_v) + 201_s.$$

The exchange of $1,500$ $I_{(v + 1/2s)}$ for $1,500$ II_c is a process of simple reproduction, and nothing further need be said about it. However a few peculiarities remain to be noted here, which arise from the fact that in accumulating reproduction $I_{(v + 1/2s)}$ is not replaced solely by II_c, but by II_c plus a portion of II_s.

It goes without saying that as soon as we assume accumulation, $I_{(v + s)}$ is greater than II_c, not equal to II_c, as in simple reproduction. For in the first place, I incorporates a portion of its surplus product in its own productive capital and converts $5/6$ of it into constant capital, therefore cannot replace these $5/6$ simultaneously by articles of consumption II. In the second place, I has to supply out of its surplus product the material for the constant capital required for accumulation within II, just as II has to supply I with the material for the variable capital, which is to set in motion the portion of I's surplus product employed by I itself as additional constant capital. We know that the actual, and therefore also the additional, variable capital consists of labour power. It is not capitalist I who buys from II a supply of necessities of life or accumulates them for the additional labour power to be employed by him, as the slaveholder had to do. It is the labourers themselves who trade with II. But this does not prevent the articles of consumption of his additional labour power from being viewed by the capitalist as only so many means of production and maintenance of his eventual additional labour power, hence as the natural form of his variable capital. His own immediate operation, in the present case that of I, consists in merely storing up the new money capital required for the purchase of additional labour power. As soon as he has incorporated this in his capital, the money becomes a means of purchase of commodities II for this labour power, which must find these articles of consumption at hand.

By the by. Mr. Capitalist, as well as his press, is often dissatisfied with the way in which the labour power spends its money and with the commodities II in which it realises this money. On such occasions he philosophises, babbles of culture, and dabbles in philanthropical talk, for instance after the manner of Mr. Drummond, the Secretary of the British Embassy in Washington. According to him, *The Nation* //a journal// carried last October 1879 an interesting article, which contained among other things the following passages:

"The working people have not kept up in culture with the growth of invention, and they have had things showered on them which they do not know how to use, and thus make no market for." //Every capitalist naturally wants the labourer to buy his commodities.// "There is no reason why the working man should not desire as many com-

forts as the minister, lawyer, and doctor, who is earning the same amount as himself."
//This class of lawyers, ministers, and doctors have indeed to be satisfied with the mere
desire of many comforts!// "He does not do so, however. The problem remains, how to
raise him as a consumer by rational and healthful processes, not an easy one, as his
ambition does not go beyond a diminution of his hours of labour, the demagogues
rather inciting him to this than to raising his condition by the improvement of his mental and moral powers" (Reports of H. M.'s Secretaries of Embassy and Legation on
the Manufactures, Commerce, etc., of the Countries in which they reside. London,
1879, p. 404).

Long hours of labour seem to be the secret of the rational and
healthful processes, which are to raise the condition of the labourer
by an improvement of his mental and moral powers and to make
a rational consumer of him. In order to become a rational consumer
of the commodities of the capitalist, he should above all begin to let
his own capitalist consume his labour power irrationally and un-
healthfully — but the demagogue prevents him! What the capitalist
means by a rational consumption is evident wherever he is condescending enough to engage directly in the trade with his own labourers, in the TRUCK SYSTEM, which includes also the supplying of homes to
the labourers, so that the capitalist is at the same time a landlord for
them — a branch of business among many others.

The same Drummond, whose beautiful soul is enamoured of the
capitalist attempts to uplift the working class, tells in the same report
among other things of the cotton goods manufacture of the Lowell
and Lawrence Mills. The boarding and lodging houses for the factory
girls belong to the corporation or company owning the mills. The stew-
ardesses of these houses are in the employ of the same company
which prescribes them rules of conduct. No girl is permitted to stay
out after 10 p. m. Then comes a gem: a special police patrol the
grounds for the purpose of guarding against an infringement of those
rules. After 10 p. m. no girl can leave or enter. No girl may live anywhere but on the premises of the company, and every house on it
brings the company about 10 dollars per week in rent. And now we
see the rational consumer in his full glory:

"As the ever present piano is however to be found in many of the best appointed
working girls' boarding houses, music, song, and dance come in for a considerable
share of the operatives' attention at least among those who, after 10 hours' steady work
at the looms, need more relief from monotony than actual rest" (p. 412).

But the main secret of making a rational consumer out of the labourer is yet to be told. Mr. Drummond visits the cutlery works of Turner's Falls (Connecticut River), and Mr. Oakman, the treasurer of the concern, after telling him that especially American table cutlery beat the English in quality, continues:

"The time is coming that we will beat England as to prices also, we are ahead in quality now, that is acknowledged, but we must have lower prices, and shall have it the moment we get our steel at lower prices and have our labour down" (p. 427).

A reduction of wages and long hours of labour — that is the essence of the "rational and healthful processes" which are to raise the labourer to the dignity of a rational consumer, so that "he make a market for things showered upon him" by culture and growth of invention.

––––––––

Consequently, just as I has to supply the additional constant capital for II out of its surplus product, so II likewise supplies the additional variable capital for I. II accumulates for I and for itself, so far as the variable capital is concerned, by reproducing a greater portion of its total product, and hence especially of its surplus product, in the shape of necessary articles of consumption.

In production on the basis of increasing capital, $I_{(v+s)}$ must be equal to II_c plus that portion of the surplus product which is re-incorporated as capital, plus the additional portion of constant capital required for the expansion of the production in II; and the minimum of this expansion is that without which real accumulation, i. e., a real expansion of production in I itself, is unfeasible.

Reverting now to the case which we examined last, we find in it the peculiarity that II_c is smaller than $I_{(v+1/2s)}$, than that portion of product I which is spent as revenue for articles of consumption, so that on exchanging the 1,500 $I_{(v+s)}$ a portion of surplus product II = 70 is at once realised. As for II_c = 1,430, it must, all other conditions remaining the same, be replaced by an equal magnitude of value out of $I_{(v+s)}$, in order that simple reproduction may take place in II, and to that extent we need not pay any more attention to it here. It is different with the additional 70 II_s. What for I is merely a replacement of revenue by articles of consumption, merely commodity exchange meant for consumption, is for II not a mere reconversion of its constant capital from the form of commodity capital into its natural form, as it is in simple reproduction, but a direct process of accumulation, a transformation of a part of its surplus product from the form of articles of consumption into that of constant capital. If with £70 in money (money reserve for the conversion of surplus value) I buys the 70 II_s, and if II does not buy in exchange 70 I_s, but accumulates the £70 as money capital, then the latter is indeed always an expression of additional product (precisely of the surplus product of II, of which it is an aliquot part), although this is not a product which re-enters production; but in that case this accumulation of money on the part of II would at the same time express that 70 I_s in means of production are unsaleable. There would be a relative overproduction in I, corresponding to the simultaneous non-expansion of reproduction on the part of II.

But apart from this: Until the 70 in money, which came from I, return to it, wholly or in part, through the purchase of 70 I_s by II, this 70 in money figures wholly or in part as additional virtual money capital in the hands of II. This is true of every exchange between I and II, until the mutual replacement of their respective commodities has effected the return of the money to its starting-point. But in the normal course of things the money figures here only transiently in this role. In the credit system, however, where all temporarily released additional money is supposed to function at once actively as an additional money capital, such only temporarily released money capital may be enthralled, for instance, serve in new enterprises of I, while it should have to realise additional product held there in other enterprises. It must also be noted that the annexation of 70 I_s to constant capital II requires at the same time an expansion of variable capital II by 14. This implies — about the way it did in I, in the direct incorporation of surplus product I_s in capital I_c — that the reproduction in II is already in process with a tendency toward further capitalisation; in other words, it implies expansion of that portion of the surplus product which consists of necessary means of subsistence.

————

The product of 9,000 in the second illustration must, as we have seen, be distributed in the following manner for the purpose of reproduction, if 500 I_s are to be capitalised. In doing so we merely consider the commodities and neglect the money circulation.

I. $5,000_c + 500_s$ (to be capitalised) $+ 1,500_{(v + s)}$ consumption fund $= 7,000$ in commodities.

II. $1,500_c + 299_v + 201_s = 2,000$ in commodities. Grand total, 9,000 in commodities.

Capitalisation takes place in the following manner:

In I the 500_s which are being capitalised divide into $^5/_6 = 417_c + ^1/_6 = 83_v$. The 83_v draw an equal amount out of II_s, which buys elements of constant capital and adds them to II_c. An increase of II_c by 83 implies an increase of II_v by $^1/_5$ of $83 = 17$. We have, then, after this exchange:

I. $(5,000_c + 417_s)_c + (1,000_v + 83_s)_v = 5,417_c + 1,083_v = 6,500$
II. $(1,500_c + 83_s)_c + (299_v + 17_s)_v = 1,583_c + 316_v = 1,899$

$$\text{Total...} \quad 8,399.$$

The capital in I has grown from 6,000 to 6,500, or by $^1/_{12}$. That of II has grown from 1,715 to 1,899, or by not quite $^1/_9$.

The reproduction on this basis in the second year brings the capital at the end of that year to:

I. $(5,417_c + 452_s)_c + (1,083_v + 90_s)_v = 5,869_c + 1,173_v = 7,042$
II. $(1,583_c + 42_s + 90_s)_c + (316_v + 8_s + 18_s)_v = 1,715_c + 342_v = 2,057,$

and at the end of the third year, we have a product of

$$\text{I. } 5,869_c + 1,173_v + 1,173_s$$
$$\text{II. } 1,715_c + 342_v + 342_s.$$

If I accumulates one half of its surplus value, as before, we find that $I_{(v + 1/2s)}$ yields $1,173_v + 587_{(1/2s)} = 1,760$, i. e., more than the entire $1,715 \ II_c$, an excess of 45. This must again be balanced by transferring an equal amount of means of production to II_c, which thus grows by 45, necessitating an addition of $^1/_5 = 9$ to II_v. Furthermore, the capitalised $587 \ I_s$ divide into $^5/_6$ and $^1/_6$, i. e., 489_c and 98_v. The 98 imply in II a new addition of 98 to the constant capital, and this again an increase of variable capital II by $^1/_5 = 20$. Then we have:

II. $(5,869_c + 489_s)_c + (1,173_v + 98_s)_v = 6,358_c + 1,271_v = 7,629$
II. $(1,715_c + 45_s + 98_s)_c + (342_v + 9_s + 20_s)_v = 1,858_c + 371_v = 2,229$
$$\text{Total capital} = 9,858.$$

In three years of growing reproduction the total capital of I has increased from 6,000 to 7,629 and that of II from 1,715 to 2,229, the aggregate social capital from 7,715 to 9,858.

3. REPLACEMENT OF II$_c$ IN ACCUMULATION

In the exchange of $I_{(v+s)}$ for II_c we thus meet with various cases.

In simple reproduction both of them must be equal and replace one another, since otherwise simple reproduction cannot proceed without disturbance, as we have seen above.

In accumulation it is above all the rate of accumulation that must be considered. In the preceding cases we assumed that the rate of accumulation in $I = \frac{1}{2}s$ I, and also that it remained constant from year to year. We changed only the proportion in which this accumulated capital was divided into variable and constant capital. We then had three cases:

1) $I_{(v + 1/2s)} = II_c$, which is therefore smaller than $I_{(v+s)}$. This must always be so, otherwise I does not accumulate.

2) $I_{(v + 1/2s)}$ is greater than II_c. In this case the replacement is effected by adding a corresponding portion of II_s to II_c, so that this sum $= I_{(v + 1/2s)}$. Here the replacement for II is not a simple reproduction of its constant capital, but accumulation, an augmentation of its constant capital by that portion of its surplus product which it exchanges for means of production of I. This augmentation implies at the same time a corresponding addition to variable capital II out of its own surplus product.

3) $I_{(v + 1/2s)}$ is smaller than II_c. In this case II does not fully reproduce its constant capital by means of exchange and must make good the deficit by purchase from I. But this does not entail any further accumulation of variable capital II, since its constant capital is fully reproduced only by this operation. On the other hand that part of capitalists I, who accumulate only additional money capital, have already accomplished a portion of this accumulation by this transaction.

The premise of simple reproduction, that $I_{(v+s)} = II_c$, is not only incompatible with capitalist production, although this does not exclude the possibility that in an industrial cycle of 10-11 years some year may show a smaller total production than the preceding year, so that not even simple reproduction takes place compared to the preceding year. Besides that, considering the natural annual increase in population, simple reproduction could take place only to the extent that a correspondingly larger number of unproductive servants would partake of the 1,500 representing the aggregate surplus value. But accumulation of capital, real capitalist production, would be impossible under such circumstances. The fact of capitalist accumulation therefore excludes the possibility of II_c being equal to $I_{(v+s)}$. Nevertheless it might occur even with capitalist accumulation that, in consequence of the course taken by the processes of accumulation during a preceding series of periods of production, II_c might become not only equal but even bigger than $I_{(v+s)}$. This would mean an overproduction in II and could not be adjusted in any other way than by a great crash, in consequence of which some capital of II would get transferred to I.

Nor does it alter the relation of $I_{(v+s)}$ to II_c if a portion of constant capital II reproduces itself, as happens for instance in the use of home-grown seeds in agriculture. This portion of II_c is no more to be taken into consideration in the exchange between I and II than is I_c. Nor does it change matters if a part of the products of II is capable of entering into I as means of production. It is covered by a part of the means of production supplied by I, and this part must be deducted on both sides at the outset, if we wish to examine in pure and unobscured form the exchange between the two large classes of social production, the producers of means of production and the producers of articles of consumption.

Hence under capitalist production $I_{(v+s)}$ cannot be equal to II_c, in other words, the two cannot balance in mutual exchange. On the other hand, if $I\frac{s}{x}$ is taken as that portion of I_s which is spent by capitalists I as revenue, $I_{(v+\frac{s}{x})}$ may be equal to, larger, or smaller than II_c. But $I_{(v+\frac{s}{x})}$ must always be smaller than $II_{(c+s)}$ by as much as that portion of II_s which must be consumed under all circumstances by capitalist class II.

It must be noted that in this exposition of accumulation the value of the constant capital is not presented accurately so far as that capital is a part of the value of the commodity capital it helped to produce. The fixed portion of the newly accumulated constant capital enters into the commodity capital only gradually and periodically, according to the different natures of these fixed elements. Therefore whenever raw materials, semi-finished goods, etc., enter in huge quantities into the production of commodities, the commodity capital consists for the most part of replacements of the circulating constant components and of the variable capital. (On account of the turnover of the circulating component parts this way of presenting the matter may nevertheless be adopted. It is then assumed that the circulating portion together with the portion of value of the fixed capital transferred to it is turned over so often during the year that the aggregate sum of the commodities supplied is equal in value to all the capital entering into the annual production.) But wherever only auxiliary materials are used for mechanical industry, and no raw material, there the labour element = v must re-appear in the commodity capital as its larger constituent. While in the calculation of the rate of profit the surplus value is figured on the total capital, regardless of whether the fixed components periodically transfer much or little value to the product, the fixed portion of constant capital is to be included in the calculation of the value of any periodically created commodity capital only to the extent that on an average it yields value to the product on account of wear and tear.

IV. SUPPLEMENTARY REMARKS

The original source of the money for II is v + s of the gold production I exchanged for a part of II_c. The v + s of the producer of gold does not enter into II only to the extent that he accumulates surplus value or converts it into means of production I, i. e., to the extent that he expands his production. On the other hand, since the accumulation of money on the part of the gold producer himself leads ultimately to reproduction on an extended scale, a portion of the surplus value of gold production not spent as revenue passes as additional variable capital of the gold producer into II, promotes here the formation of new hoards or supplies new means with which to buy from I without selling to it direct. From the money derived from this $I_{(v + s)}$ of the production of gold that portion of the gold must be deducted which certain branches of production II need as raw material, etc., in short as an element for the replacement of their constant capital. An element for the preliminary formation of hoards — for the purpose of future extended reproduction — exists in the exchange between I and II: for I only if part of I_s is sold one-sidedly, without a balancing purchase, to II and serves here as additional constant capital II; for II, when the same is the case on the part of I for additional variable capital; furthermore, if a part of the surplus value spent by I as revenue is not covered by II_c, hence a part of II_s is bought with it and thus converted into money. If $I_{(v + \frac{s}{x})}$ is greater than II_c, then II_c need not for its simple reproduction replace in commodities from I what I consumed out of II_s. The question arises to what extent hoarding can take place within the sphere of exchange of capitalists II among themselves, an exchange which can consist only of a mutual exchange of II_s. We know that direct accumulation takes place within II by the direct conversion of a portion of II_s into variable capital (just as in I a portion of I_s is directly converted into constant capital). In the various age categories of accumulation within the various lines of business of II, and for the individual capitalists in each line of business, the matter is explained *mutatis mutandis* in the same way as in I. Some are still in the stage of hoarding, and sell without buying; the others are on the point of actual expansion of reproduction, and buy without selling. The additional variable money capital is, true enough, first invested in additional labour power, but this buys means of subsistence from the hoarding owners of the additional articles of consumption entering into the consumption of the labourers. From these owners, *pro rata* to their hoard formation, the money does not return to its point of departure. They hoard it.

NOTES
AND
INDEXES

NOTES

[1] In the second half of the 1850s Marx began to study the problems to be dealt with in Volume II of *Capital*, and continued this work in the 1860s, as is shown, amongst other things, by the Economic Manuscripts of 1861-63 and 1864-65 where the results of these investigations were still, in his words, in the form of preparatory outlines.

Later stages in Marx's work on this volume are described at length by Engels in his Preface to the First Edition, which he prepared for the press and published after Marx's death.

Manuscript I, written in the early half of 1865, was, in effect, the first composite version of the volume. According to Engels, "Some parts of the argument would be treated in detail, others of equal importance only indicated" in this manuscript (see this volume, p. 5).

From the end of 1868 to the middle of 1870 Marx prepared the second version of the volume — Manuscript II — which comprises all three parts (three sections, according to Engels) and "is the only somewhat complete elaboration of Book II" (see this volume, p.7).

After 1870 there followed a long interruption in the work on the volume, mainly as a result of the author's illness. Marx was able to resume his work only in 1877. Prior to 1881 he wrote several more manuscripts of varying size; most of them were versions of the beginning of the volume, and only the last represented a revised version of the third chapter of Manuscript II.

During the last two years of his life Marx did not work on Volume II.

After studying the content of Marx's manuscripts and considering the volume of material involved, Engels decided to divide Volume II into two portions and publish two separate volumes — Vol. II and Vol. III.

Engels edited the text with great discretion: according to his own words, he contented himself "with reproducing these manuscripts as literally as possible, changing the style only in places where Marx would have changed it himself, and interpolating explanatory sentences or connecting statements only where this was absolutely necessary, and where, besides, the meaning was clear beyond any doubt" (see this volume, pp. 5-6). Structural division was made according to the model used in the Second Edition of *Capital*, Vol. I (1872). The titles of parts and chapters were also provided by Engels.

The first German edition of Vol. II appeared in 1885, the second edition—in 1893.

Soon after the publication of the volume the newspaper *Le Socialiste* printed a review of it in its first number for August 29, 1885.

"The second volume of Marx's *Capital* has just been published in German thanks to the work done by Frederick Engels, his old friend and staunch associate. It was compiled on the basis of manuscripts left by Marx.

"In the first volume Marx examined the question of the production of capital; on the basis of a broad and comprehensive analysis he demonstrated that capital was just unpaid labour, in other words, labour stolen from the working class. Although many economists in Germany, France, Italy, Russia and America tried to criticise his book, not one of them could refute Marx's scientific proposition. To this day *Capital* remains the most formidable indictment written against capitalist society; and the fact that capital is a product of theft is now proved beyond doubt.

"In the second volume, which is expected so impatiently, Marx analyses the circulation of capital, that is, the manner in which the bourgeois divide among themselves the products they have stolen from the working class. After making a comprehensive study of all economic theories of ground rent he refuted all of them and formulated a new theory of rent.

"Marx's works are not text-books consisting of repetitions, neither are they volumes filled with the banal talk of representatives of various schools, such as the works of Mr. Leroy-Beaulieu and Co.; they are scientific books that must be studied thoroughly as mathematical treatises and works on physics or chemistry; for the moment, therefore, we are merely announcing the fact of publication, and after reading and re-reading it with a clear head we shall return to discuss it with our readers."

The first English edition of *Capital*, Vol. II was published in Chicago in 1907 by the Charles H. Kerr & Company in the translation of Ernest Untermann.— 1

[2] Engels did not have time to publish Marx's *Theories of Surplus Value* as the fourth volume of *Capital*. It was first published in 1905-10 by Karl Kautsky. In 1954-61 and 1962-64, the Institute of Marxism-Leninism of the CC CPSU in Moscow published in Russian a new edition of *Theories*... which differed from that of Kautsky. In 1956-62 this Russian edition was used by the Institute of Marxism-Leninism of the CC SUPG as the basis for the publication of *Theories*... in German.

In the present edition *Theories of Surplus Value* is published, according to MEGA [2], Abt. II, Bd. 3, Berlin, 1976-82, as part of the Economic Manuscript of 1861-63 (see present edition, vols 30-34).— 6

[3] From the numerous notebooks compiled by Marx in the period indicated by Engels, the Institute of Marxism-Leninism of the CC CPSU published nearly all the passages from Russian sources (see *Marx-Engels Archives*, vols XI-XII, XVI, Moscow, 1948, 1952, 1955, 1982) as well as *Mathematical Manuscripts* (Moscow, 1968). Marx's notebooks are published in full in Section IV of Marx-Engels Gesamtausgabe.— 7

[4] *State socialism*— a bourgeois-reformist and opportunist conception whose adherents reduced the essence of socialism to bourgeois state interference in economics and to a certain degree of regulation of social relations. Among its theoreticians were Louis

Blanc (France), Ferdinand Lassalle, Karl Rodbertus-Jagetzow (Germany) and others.

Armchair socialism (Kathedersozialismus) — a trend in German bourgeois political economy that emerged in Germany at the close of 1860s as a reaction to the growth of the working-class movement and the dissemination within it of the ideas of scientific socialism propounded by Marx and Engels. Under the banner of socialism its exponents (L. Brentano, A. Wagner, W. Zombart and others) preached bourgeois reformism; they asserted that any state, including the German Empire, had a super-class character and that with its help it was possible to achieve a considerable improvement in the condition of the working class through social reforms effected by governments. The armchair socialists called upon the workers to refrain from economic and political revolutionary struggle.— 9

5 Engels is referring to the letter written by K. Rodbertus to J. Zeller on March 14, 1875. Rodbertus died in 1875 but his letter to Zeller was not published until 1879.

A copy of *Briefe und Sozialpolitische Aufsätze* mentioned below (ed. by R. Meyer, Berlin, 1881), with Engels' remarks, was kept in Marx's personal library.— 10

6 *Mercantilism* — a school of bourgeois political economy, that emerged in the last third of the fifteenth century; it expressed the interests of the merchant bourgeoisie in the period of the primitive accumulation of capital, identified the wealth of the country with the accumulation of money, and attached primary importance in this to the state. Marx called the early period of mercantilism the monetary system.— 13, 66

7 In the 1861-63 manuscript Marx quotes Adam Smith in French according to *Recherches sur la nature et les causes de la richesse des nations* trad. par G. Garnier, Paris, 1802, t. 1, pp. 96-97, 99-100. Marx copied out passages from this book in his Paris notebook compiled in 1844. See MEGA ², Bd. IV/2, Berlin, 1981, S. 332-86. Marx had this French edition in his personal library.— 13

8 In the 1861-63 manuscript Marx gives this quotation from Adam Smith in English according to McCulloch's edition of 1828, Vol. I, pp. 109-10. Marx copied out passages from this book in notebooks VII and VIII, which he compiled in London in 1851 (MEGA ², Bd. IV/8, Berlin, 1986, S. 272, 279, 284-86), and in Notebook VII (London, 1859-63).— 13

9 Marx copied out passages from this pamphlet in Notebook XII (London, 1851).— 15

10 "This most incredible cobbler" — was the way John Wilson, the author of the pamphlet *Some Illustrations of Mr. McCulloch's Principles of Political Economy* (Edinburgh, 1826, p. 31), described McCulloch. See present edition, Vol. 32, pp. 374-400. Marx copied out passages from this pamphlet in Notebook VII (London, 1859-63).— 16

11 This refers to the social utopian theory expounded by Robert Owen in *The Book of the New Moral World* (Parts I-VII, London, 1836-44) and in other of his works. Owen was the only one among great utopian socialists who sought to realise socialist ideals with the participation of workers themselves, and he founded a number of communist colonies in the USA and Great Britain. Appraising the importance of Owen's activity for the English working-class movement in the first decades of the 19th century, Engels wrote: "Every social movement, every real advance in Eng-

land on behalf of the workers links itself unto the name of Robert Owen" (see present edition, Vol. 25, p. 251).— 17

[12] A copy of this book, which belonged to Engels (1850 edition) and contained Marx's remarks, has survived. From the 1824 edition Marx copied out passages in one of his Manchester notebooks for 1845.— 18

[13] Passages from Ravenstone's *Thoughts on the Funding System, and Its Effects* copied out by Marx in London in 1851 are to be found in Notebook IX (MEGA[2], Bd. IV/8, Berlin, 1986, S. 542-48).— 18

[14] Marx had this book by Roscoe and Schorlemmer in his personal library.— 19

[15] A reference to the *Peasant Reform* of 1861, which abolished serfdom in Russia and brought "freedom" to about 22.5 million peasants. Even after the official abolition of serfdom, however, part of the peasantry remained dependent on its former landlords. For the use of land these so-called temporarily obligated peasants had to perform corvée services and pay quit-rent. Under the law of December 28, 1881, peasants could redeem their allotments as of January 1, 1883, and corvée and quit-rent as they had previously existed were officially abolished. In actual fact, however, they continued to the beginning of the 20th century.— 39

[16] Marx had both volumes of this book by A. Chuprov in his personal library. His extracts from the first volume are extant.— 61

[17] The *monetary system*, an early form of mercantilism, consisting of a variety of economic measures applied by European states in the 17th and 18th centuries. Its advocates equated wealth with money and favoured policies designed to ensure an inflow of money into the country by maintaining an active trade balance and imposing protective tariffs. See also Note 6.— 68

[18] Marx quotes S. Bailey's book according to Notebook VII, which he compiled in London between 1859 and 1863.— 111

[19] Marx quotes S. de Sismondi from the notebook which he compiled between 1844 and 1847. MEGA[2], Bd. IV/3.— 116

[20] The *Inca state* existed between the early 15th and the mid-16th centuries on the territory that is now occupied by Peru, Equador, Bolivia and the northern part of Chile. It was a slave-owning state with considerable remnants of the primitive-communal system. The dominant tribe of the Incas was subdivided into 100 gentile communities which gradually assumed the character of rural (neighbouring) communities with a self-sustained natural economy. Social product was not produced as a commodity, but the movement of its various kinds between communities, though not in the form of trade, already played an important role.— 121, 153

[21] Marx copied out passages from Quesnay's work *Analyse du Tableau économique* in one of his notebooks compiled in London between 1859 and 1863 and in Notebook C (Beiheft C); the latter also contains excerpts from *Dialogues sur le commerce et sur les travaux des artisans*.— 135

[22] Passages from Th. Corbet's book, *An Inquiry into the Causes and Modes of the Wealth of Individuals; or the Principles of Trade and Speculation Explained*, were copied out by Marx in Notebook XVI, compiled in London in 1851.— 142

[23] See Lalor, *Money and Morals: a Book for the Times*, London, 1852, pp. 43, 44; Sis-

mondi, *Études sur l'économie politique*, t. 1, Bruxelles, 1837, p. 49, etc. Marx copied out passages from Lalor's book in Notebook VII (London, 1859-63); passages from Sismondi's book are quoted in one of his notebooks compiled in Brussels in 1845.— 143

²⁴ *The Civil War in America* broke out in April 1861. The Southern slaveholders rose against the Union and formed the Confederacy of the Southern States. The war was caused mainly by the conflict between the two social systems: the capitalist system of wage labour established in the North and the slave system dominant in the South. The Civil War, which had the nature of a bourgeois-democratic revolution, passed two stages in its development: the period of a constitutional war to maintain the Union, and the period of a revolutionary war to abolish slavery. The decisive role in the defeat of the Southern slaveholders and the victory of the North in April 1865 was played by the workers and farmers. Marx analysed the causes and the nature of the Civil War in America in articles published in the Vienna newspaper *Die Presse* (see present edition, Vol. 19).

The interruption of cotton imports from America as a result of the blockade of the Southern States by the Northern fleet caused a crisis in the cotton industry of several European countries. In England, for two or three years beginning in 1862, over 75 per cent of spinners and weavers in Lancashire, Cheshire and other counties were fully or partly unemployed. Despite privation and distress, the European proletariat gave all possible support to the American fighters against slavery.— 144

²⁵ D. Ricardo quotes the third edition of Say's *Traité d'économie politique, ou simple exposition de la manière dont se forment, se distribuent et se consomment, les richesses*, Paris, 1817, p. 433. Marx copied out passages from this book in one of his Paris notebooks for 1844 (MEGA², Bd. IV/2, Berlin, 1981, S. 301-27). Passages from the third edition of Ricardo's book are quoted by Marx in London notebooks IV (1850) (MEGA², Bd. IV/7, Berlin, 1983, S. 316-28) and VII (1851).

Marx had both books in his personal library.— 154

²⁶ Marx copied out passages from S. P. Newman's *Elements of Political Economy* in notebooks XV (1851) and XVII (1851-52), which he compiled in London.— 158

²⁷ Passages from Chalmers' book, *On Political Economy in Connexion with the Moral State and Moral Prospects of Society*, 2nd ed., Glasgow, 1832, are quoted by Marx in his London Notebook for 1851.— 158

²⁸ A reference to George Ramsay's work *An Essay on the Distribution of Wealth*, Edinburgh, London, 1836. Marx copied out passages from it in notebooks IX and X, compiled in London in 1851. MEGA², Bd. IV/8, Berlin, 1986, S. 643-47, 651-67. For details see present edition, Vol. 33, pp. 255-84.— 161, 229

²⁹ This quotation from R. P. Williams' work is given on p. 76 of the London Notebook for 1867-68, and is taken from *The Money Market Review*, December 21, 1867.— 173, 183

³⁰ Marx had this book by W. B. Adams in his personal library.— 173

³¹ *Bourgeois law*— a reference to the general meaning, content and purpose of bourgeois legislation protecting, above all, its main institute— private capitalist property in the instruments and means of production.— 177

³² Marx's excerpts from *The Money Market Review* for January 25, 1868, are exant.— 181

[33] Marx had this book by Friedrich Kirchhof in his personal library.— 181, 242

[34] In his excerpts from *The Money Market Review* Marx also mentions: North-eastern 206; in the column "Great Northern" he gives 310 instead of 360.— 183

[35] Marx investigates the system of capitalist credit in Parts IV and V of *Capital*, Vol. III (see present edition, Vol. 37).— 184

[36] Passages from H. Müller's book are quoted by Marx in one of his notebooks compiled in London in 1858.— 188

[37] This passage is taken from A. Potter's book *Political Economy: Its Objects, Uses, and Principles: Considered with Reference to the Condition of the American People*, New York, 1841. As is seen from the introduction, the greater part of this book is a reprint (with changes introduced by A. Potter) of the first ten chapters of J. P. Scrope's book *Principles of Political Economy...*, published in England in 1833.

Passages from Scrope's book as given by Potter are copied out by Marx in his London Notebook VII for 1859-63. Passages taken directly from Scrope's book are quoted in Marx's Notebook IX (1851). See MEGA ², Abt. IV, Bd. 8, Berlin, 1986, S. 592-96.— 188

[38] In the manuscript Marx points to the fallacy of such a method of calculating the period of the turnover of capital. The mean term of turnover (16 months) given in the quotation was calculated on the basis of a profit of 7.5 per cent on an aggregate capital of $50,000. Excluding profit, the turnover of capital is equal to 18 months.— 188

[39] Marx has, presumably, made a slip of the pen, since the quantity of the means of payment required for all periodical payments is not in inverse but in direct proportion to the length of their periods. Just such a proportion is established by William Petty, whom Marx quotes in Note 107 to Chapter 3 of Capital, Vol. I. The meaning of the concept "the period of payment" is also defined in this concrete example. In all German editions of *Capital*, Vol. II, published in recent years, including *Complete Works of K. Marx and F. Engels* in the languages of the original (Marx-Engels, Gesamtausgabe (MEGA), Zweite Abteilung, Band 5, Dietz Verlag, Berlin, 1983, S. 97), this passage has been corrected and reads as follows. "From the law of the rapidity of circulation of the means of payment, it follows that the quantity of the means of payment required for all periodical payments, whatever their source, is in *direct* proportion to the length of their periods."

See also present edition, Vol. 35.— 189

[40] Passages from Turgot's work *Réflexions sur la formation et la distribution des richesses* are to be found in Notebook VII, which Marx compiled in London between 1859 and 1863; excerpts from Dupont de Nemours' works are given in Notebook C (Beiheft C); excerpts from Le Trosne—in notebooks D and E (Beiheften); concerning passages copied out from Quesnay's works see Note 21.— 191

[41] Marx copied out passages from Wayland's book in Notebook VII (London, 1859-63).— 227

[42] Excerpts from Barton's book are to be found in Notebook IX, which Marx compiled in London in 1851. See MEGA ², Bd. IV/8, Berlin, 1986, S. 518-21.— 228

⁴³ Marx copied out passages from the book by J. St. Mill, *Essays on Some Unsettled Questions of Political Economy*, London, 1844, in his Manchester Notebook for 1845. See MEGA², Bd. IV/4, Berlin, 1988, S. 329-54.— 229

⁴⁴ Marx had a copy of this book in his personal library.— 237

⁴⁵ *Manava Dharma Sastra* (Manu laws) — an ancient Indian religious, legal and ritual code, similar to the Bible and the Koran, which determined the duties of every Hindu in keeping with the tenets of Brahmanism. The compilation of these laws, dating back to approximately the 3 cent. B. C., is attributed to Manu, the mythical "progenitor of men".

Marx is quoting from: *Manava Dharma Sastra, or the Institutes of Manu According to the Gloss of Kulluka Comprising the Indian System of Duties, Religious and Civil.* Third edition, Madras, 1863, p. 281.— 238

⁴⁶ Passages which Marx copied out from J. G. Courcelle-Seneuil's book are to be found in Notebook VII (London, 1859-63).— 241

⁴⁷ Marx copied out passages from Thomas Hodgskin's book in Notebook IX (London, 1851), MEGA², Bd. IV/8, Berlin, 1986, S. 549-62.— 244

⁴⁸ Marx is referring to the Brussels edition of this book. In his personal library there was a copy of it with remarks made on the indicated pages.— 244

⁴⁹ *Tableau économique* — a scheme of the reproduction and circulation of the total social product worked out by Quesnay. A more detailed analysis of the *Tableau économique* is given in Marx's Economic Manuscript of 1861-63 (present edition, Vol. 31, pp. 204-40) and in Chapter X, Part II of *Anti-Dühring*, which Engels wrote on the basis of Marx's manuscript (present edition, Vol. 25, pp. 211-43).— 357

⁵⁰ Concerning Linguet see present edition, Vol. 31, pp. 241-45.— 358

⁵¹ In the first edition of Volume II of *Capital* there followed one more paragraph: "As to the explanation of constant capital given by Smith, it is reduced to an assertion that constant capital is part of advanced industrial capital which is fixed in the process of production or, as Smith says on p. 187, 'gives revenue or profit without circulation or change of owner' or, as it is said on p. 185, 'remains in his [owner's] possession or petrifies in an unchanged form'."— 362

⁵² Marx copied out passages from the book by W. Roscher, *System der Volkswirtschaft.* Band I: *Die Grundlagen der Nationalökonomie*, Stuttgart und Augsburg, 1858, in Notebook VII, which he compiled in London between 1859 and 1863.— 371

⁵³ Passages which Marx copied out from Storch's works are to be found in his Brussels notebooks (see MEGA², Bd. IV/3).— 390

⁵⁴ Concerning Cherbuliez see present edition, Vol. 33, pp. 285-320.— 390

⁵⁵ Marx is referring to Smith's assertion that part of capital for an entrepreneur forms workers' revenue. For a detailed criticism of this proposition see this volume, pp. 378-79.— 434

⁵⁶ Marx is referring to the following phrase from A. Smith's *An Inquiry into the Nature and Causes of the Wealth of Nations*: "the whole annual produce of the land and labour of every country is, no doubt, ultimately destined for supplying the consumption of its inhabitants" (Vol. II, Book II, Ch. III).— 435

[57] Marx copied out passages from this book by Senior in one of his Brussels notebooks compiled in 1845. See MEGA [2], Bd. IV/3.— 437

[58] In his personal library Marx had the book by E. Tyler (Tylor) *Forschungen über die Urgeschichte der Menschheit und die Entwickelung der Civilisation*. Aus dem Engl. von H. Müller, Leipzig, 1847, in which he made his remarks. Compare with E. B. Tylor, *Researches into the Early History of Mankind and the Development of Civilisation*, London, 1865, pp. 198-99.— 438

[59] Marx is alluding to J. B. Say's *Lettres à Malthus sur différents sujets d'économie politique, notamment sur les causes de la stagnation générale du commerce*. Paris, London, 1820. (Marx had this book in his personal library.) — 439

[60] In the original: "p. 400" should read "p. 380"; a reference to the page of the first edition of *Capital*,Vol. II.— 440

[61] Marx is alluding to *Éléments d'idéologie* 4-e et 5-e parties par Destutt de Tracy; the text of this book which he had in his personal library, carries Marx's crossings-out and underlinings. Passages from it are to be found in the Paris notebook which Marx compiled in 1844 (see MEGA [2], Bd. IV/2, Berlin, 1981, S. 489-92).— 443

[62] Marx copied out passages from Th. Tooke's book, *An Inquiry into the Currency Principle* (London, 1844), in Notebook VII, which he compiled in London in 1851. See MEGA [2], Bd. IV/8, Berlin, 1986, pp. 199-211.— 475

[63] The *Institute of France* (l'Institute de France) — the country's most authoritative centre dealing with the arts and sciences; it comprises a number of leading academies and has existed since 1795. Destutt de Tracy was a member of the Académie des sciences morales et politiques.

The *Philosophic Society of Philadelphia* (la Société Philosophique de Philadelphie) — one of the oldest scientific societies in the USA, dating back to 1740.— 488

[64] The expression "music of the future" came into use after the publication in 1850 of Richard Wagner's book *An Artistic Work of the Future*; opponents of Wagner's views in the sphere of music adduced an ironical sense to this expression.— 493

[65] In the first and second editions of *Capital*, Vol. II, this paragraph reads as follows: "In the course of four years of reproduction on an extended scale, the aggregate capital of I and II has risen from $5,400c + 7,250$ to $8,784c + 2,782 = 11,566$, in other words, in the ratio of 100:160. The total surplus value was originally 1,750, it is now 2,782. The consumed surplus value was originally 500 for I and 535 for II, a total of 1,035; in the last year it was 732 for I and 958 for II, a total of 1,690. It has therefore grown in the ratio 100:163."

In the present edition this paragraph has been corrected.— 514

NAME INDEX

INDEX OF LITERARY
AND MYTHOLOGICAL
NAMES

Bräsig — a character in the German humorous writer Fritz Reuter's novel *Ut mine Stromtig.* — 481

INDEX OF QUOTED
AND MENTIONED
LITERATURE

WORKS BY KARL MARX AND FREDERICK ENGELS[a]

Marx, Karl

Capital. A Critical Analysis of Capitalist Production. Vol. I (present edition, Vol. 35) —
6, 15, 18, 31, 35, 46, 54, 58, 117, 130, 159, 164, 166, 184, 205, 323, 329, 350-51, 353,
354, 501, 509

— Das Kapital. Kritik der politischen Oekonomie. Erster Band. Buch I. Der
Produktionsprocess des Kapitals. Hamburg, 1867.— 7, 138

— Das Kapital. Kritik der politischen Oekonomie. Erster Band. Buch I. Der Produktionsprocess des Kapitals. Zweite verbesserte Auflage. Hamburg, 1872.— 9,
15, 35, 73, 85, 127, 145, 157, 176, 189, 204, 209, 218, 227-28, 306, 307-08, 319,
340, 358, 395, 412, 437, 506

Capital. A Critique of Political Economy. Vol. III (present edition, Vol. 37).— 6, 7-9,
15, 21, 22, 23, 217, 228, 248

A Contribution to the Critique of Political Economy. Part One (present edition, Vol. 29)
— Zur Kritik der Politischen Oekonomie. Erstes Heft. Berlin, 1859.— 6, 344

A Contribution to the Critique of Political Economy (present edition, vols 31-34).— 6, 9,
12-14, 16-17

The Crisis and the Counter-Revolution (present edition, Vol. 7)
— Die Krisis und die Kontrerevolution. *Neue Rheinische Zeitung*, Nr. 100, 12. September 1848.— 11

The Crisis in Berlin (present edition, Vol. 8)
— Die Berliner Krisis. In: *Neue Rheinische Zeitung*, Nr. 138, 9. November 1848.— 11

---

[a] Editions in the language of the original are given only in cases when they were
published during the author's lifetime.— *Ed.*

Legal Proceedings against the "Neue Rheinische Zeitung" (present edition, Vol. 7)
— Gerichtliche Untersuchung gegen die *Neue Rheinische Zeitung*, Nr. 37, 7. July 1848.— 11

The Poverty of Philosophy. Answer to the "Philosophy of Poverty" by M. Proudhon (present edition, Vol. 6)
— Das Elend der Philosophie. Antwort auf Proudhons "Philosophie des Elends". Deutsch von E. Bernstein und K. Kautsky. Mit Vorwort und Noten von Friedrich Engels. Stuttgart, 1885.— 10
— Misère de la philosophie. Réponse à la philosophie de la misère de M. Proudhon. Paris, Bruxelles, 1847.— 11, 17-18, 21

Theories of Surplus Value (present edition, vols 30-37).— 6, 16-17

Wage Labour and Capital (present edition, Vol. 9)
— Lohnarbeit und Kapital. In: *Neue Rheinische Zeitung*, Nr. 264-67, 269; 5.-8. und 11. April 1849.— 11

Engels, Frederick

The Agreement Debate (present edition, Vol. 7)
— Vereinbarungsdebatte. In: *Neue Rheinische Zeitung*, Nr. 39, 9. Juli 1848.— 11

The Agreement Debates (present edition, Vol. 7)
— Vereinbarungsdebatten. In: *Neue Rheinische Zeitung*, Nr. 34, 4. Juli 1848.— 11

The Agreement Debates on the District Estates (present edition, Vol. 7)
— Vereinbarungsdebatten über die Kreisstände. In: *Neue Rheinische Zeitung*, Nr. 56, 26. Juli 1848.— 11

The Danish-Prussian Armistice (present edition, Vol. 7)
— Der dänisch-preussische Waffenstillstand. In: *Neue Rheinische Zeitung*, Nr. 99, 10. September 1848.— 11

The Fall of the Government of Action (present edition, Vol. 7)
— Sturz des Ministeriums der That. In: *Neue Rheinische Zeitung*, Nr. 98, 9. September 1848, Special supplement.— 11

WORKS BY DIFFERENT AUTHORS

Adams, W. B. *Roads and Rails and Their Sequences, Physical and Moral.* London, 1862.— 173, 175

[Bailey, S.] *A Critical Dissertation on the Nature, Measures, and Causes of Value; Chiefly in Reference to the Writings of Mr. Ricardo and His Followers.* By the Author of Essays on the Formation and Publication of Opinions, &c, London, 1825.— 111

Barton, J. *Observations on the Circumstances Which Influence the Condition of the Labouring Classes of Society.* London, 1817.— 228

Chalmers, Th. *On Political Economy in Connexion with the Moral State and Moral Pros-*

pects of Society. Second edition, Glasgow, Edinburgh, Dublin and London, 1832.— 158

[Chuprov, A.] Чупровъ, А. Желѣзнодорожное хозяйство. [Том 1.] Его экономичес-
кія особенности и его отношенія къ интересамъ страны. Москва, 1875.— 61

Corbet, Th. *An Inquiry into the Causes and Modes of the Wealth of Individuals; or the Principles of Trade and Speculation Explained.* In two parts. London, 1841.— 142

Courcelle-Seneuil, J.-G. *Traité théorique et pratique des entreprises industrielles, commerci-
ales & agricoles ou Manuel des affaires.* Deuxième édition. Paris, 1857.— 241

Destutt de Tracy [A. L. C.] *Éleméns d'idéologie.* IVe et V^e parties. *Traité de la volonté
et de ses effets.* Paris, 1826.— 443, 480-88

Dupont de Nemours, P. S. *Maximes du docteur Quesnay, ou Résumé de ses principes d'économie
sociale.* In: *Physiocrates. Quesnay, Dupont de Nemours, Mercier de la Rivière, L'Abbé Baudeau, Le Trosne,* avec une introduction sur la doctrine des physiocrates, des commentaires et des notices historiques, par M. Eugène Daire. Première partie, Paris,
1846.— 191

Fitzmaurice. *Committee of Inquiry on Caledonian Railway.* In: *The Money Market Review,*
Vol. XVI, 25 January 1868.— 181

Good, W. W. *Political, Agricultural and Commercial Fallacies; or, the Prospect of the
Nation after Twenty Years' "Free-Trade".* London, [1866].— 237-38

Hodgskin, Th. *Popular Political Economy. Four Lectures Delivered at the London Mechanics' Institution.* London, 1827.— 244

Holdsworth, W. A. *The Law of Landlord and Tenant, with a Copious Collection of Useful
Forms.* London, 1857.— 176, 180

Kirchhof, F. *Handbuch der landwirthschaftlichen Betriebslehre. Ein Leitfaden für praktische
Landwirthe zur zweckmäßigen Einrichtung und Verwaltung der Landgüter.* Dessau, 1852.—
181, 242, 244-46, 247-48, 255

Lalor, J. *Money and Morals: a Book for the Times.* London, 1852.— 143, 145-47

Lardner, D. *Railway Economy: A Treatise on the New Art of Transport, Its Management,
Prospects, and Relations, Commercial, Financial, and Social.* London, 1850.— 173-74,
181-83

Laveleye, É. de. *Essai sur l'économie rurale de la Belgique.* Bruxelles, [1863].— 244

Lavergne, L. de. *The Rural Economy of England, Scotland, and Ireland.* Translated
from the French. With Notes by a Scottish farmer. Edinburgh and London, 1855.—
239

Le Trosne, G. F. *De l'intérèt social, par rapport à la valeur, à la circulation, à l'indus-
trie et au commerce intérieur et extérieur.* In: *Physiocrates. Quesnay, Dupont de Nemours, Mercier de la Rivière, L'Abbé Baudeau, Le Trosne,* avec une introduction sur la doctrine des
physiocrates, des commentaires et des notices historiques, par M. Eugène Daire.
Deuxième partie. Paris, 1846.— 191

Lee, N. *The Rival Queens; or, The Death of Alexander the Great.*— 133

Macleod, H. D. *The Elements of Political Economy.* London, 1858.— 229

Meyer, R. *Der Emancipationskampf des vierten Standes.* I. Band, Erste Abtheilung. Berlin, 1874.— 10

Mill, J. St. *Essays on Some Unsettled Questions of Political Economy.* London, 1844.— 229, 248

Müller, A. H. *Die Elemente der Staatskunst.* Dritter Theil. Berlin, 1809.— 188

Newman, S. P. *Elements of Political Economy.* Andover, New York, 1835.— 158

Patterson, R. H. *The Science of Finance.* A practical treatise. Edinburgh and London, 1868.— 229

Potter, A. *Political Economy: Its Objects, Uses, and Principles: Considered with Reference to the Condition of the American People.* New York [1841].— 188

Quesnay, F. *Analyse du Tableau économique.* In: *Physiocrates. Quesnay, Dupont de Nemours, Mercier de la Rivière, L'abbe Baudeau, Le Trosne,* avec une introduction sur la doctrine des Physiocrates, des commentaires et des notices historiques, par M. Eugène Daire. Première partie. Paris, 1846.— 105, 135, 191, 225, 340, 357, 368

— Dialogues sur le commerce et sur les travaux des artisans. In: *Physiocrates. Quesnay, Dupont de Nemours, Mercier de la Rivière, L'abbe Baudeau, Le Trosne,* avec une introduction sur la doctrine des Physiocrates, des commentaires et des notices historiques, par M. Eugène Daire. Première partie. Paris, 1846.— 135, 340

Ramsay, G. *An Essay on the Distribution of Wealth.* Edinburgh, London, 1836.— 229, 389, 435-36

Ravenstone, P. *Thoughts on the Funding System, and Its Effects.* London, 1824.— 18

Ricardo, D. *On the Principles of Political Economy, and Taxation.* Third edition. London, 1821.— 154, 217, 224-25, 228-29, 388, 480

Rodbertus-Jagetzow, [J. K.] *Briefe und Sozialpolitische Aufsätze.* Hrsg. von Rudolph Meyer. Bd. I. Berlin [1881].— 10, 11, 21
— *Einige Briefe von Dr. Rodbertus an J. Z.* In: *Zeitschrift für die gesamte Staatswissenschaft.* Hrsg. von Fricker-Leipzig, Schäffle-Stuttgart, A. Wagner-Berlin, Bd. 35. Tübingen, 1879.— 10-11

— *Das Kapital.* Vierter socialer Brief an von Kirchmann. Herausgegeben und eingeleitet von Theophil Kozak. Berlin, 1884.— 10
— *Sociale Briefe an von Kirchmann.* Dritter Brief: Widerlegung der Ricardo'schen Lehre von der Grundrente und Begründung einer neuen Rententheorie. Berlin, 1851.— 12

— *Zur Erkenntniss unsrer staatswirthschaftlichen Zustände.* Erstes Heft: Fünf Theoreme. Neubrandenburg und Friedland, 1842.— 10, 15, 23

Roscher, W. *System der Volkswirthschaft.* Band I: *Die Grundlagen der Nationalökonomie.* Ein Hand- und Lesebuch für Geschäftsmänner und Studierende. Dritte, vermehrte und verbesserte Auflage. Stuttgart und Augsburg, 1858.— 371

Roscoe, H. E. und Schorlemmer, C. *Ausführliches Lehrbuch der Chemie.* Erster Band. Nichtmetalle. Braunschweig, 1877.— 19

Say, J. B. *Lettres à M. Malthus, sur différens sujets d'économie politique, notamment sur les causes de la stagnation générale du commerce.* Paris, 1820.— 439

— *Traité d'économie politique, ou simple exposition de la manière dont se forment, se distribuent et se consomment les richesses;* Troisième édition, à laquelle se trouve joint un épitomé des principes fondamentaux de l'économie politique. Tome second. Paris, 1817.— 154, 389

Scrope, G. *Principles of Political Economy, Deduced from the Natural Laws of Social Welfare, and Applied to the Present State of Britain,* London, 1833.— 188, 189

Senior, N. W. *Principes fondamentaux de l'économie politique, tirés de leçons édites et inédites de Mr. N.-W. Senior, Professeur émérite d'économie politique à l'université d'Oxford, par le c-te Jean Arrivabene.* Paris, 1836.— 437

Sismondi, J. C. L. Simonde de. *Études sur l'économie politique.* Tome premier. Bruxelles, 1837.— 143

— *Nouveaux principes d'économie politique, ou de la richesse dans ses rapports avec la population;* par J.-C.-L. Simonde de Sismondi, Correspondant de l'Institut de France, de l'Académie impériale de Saint-Pétersbourg, de l'Académie royale des sciences de Prusse, membre honoraire de l'Université de Wilna, de l'Académie et de la Société des arts de Genève, des Académies italienne, des Georgofili, de Cagliari, de Pistoia, etc. Tome premier. Paris, 1819.— 22, 116-17, 390

Smith, A. *An Inquiry into the Nature and Causes of the Wealth of Nations.* With a life of the author, and introductory discourse, notes and supplementary dissertations. By J. R. McCulloch. Vol. 1-4, Edinburgh, 1828.— 13-14

— *An Inquiry into the Nature and Causes of the Wealth of Nations.* By Adam Smith, L. L. D. F. R. S. With a Memoir of the Author's Life. London, 1848.— 9, 143-44, 192, 193-98, 199, 201-02, 204-05, 206, 208-11, 212, 358-66, 369-72, 375-76, 378-79, 475

— *Recherches sur la nature et les causes de la richesse des nations.* Traduction nouvelle, avec des notes et observations; par Germain Garnier. T. I-V. Paris, 1802.— 13, 14

Soetbeer, A. *Edelmetall-Produktion und Werthverhältniss zwischen Gold und Silber seit der Entdeckung Amerika's bis zur Gegenwart* (Ergänzungsheft No. 57 zu "Petermann's Mittheilungen"). Gotha, 1879.— 469

The Source and Remedy of the National Difficulties, deduced from Principles of Political Economy, in A Letter to Lord John Russell, London, 1821.— 15-18

Storch, H. *Considérations sur la nature du revenu national.* Paris, 1824.— 389-90, 433

— *Cours d'économie politique, ou exposition des principes qui déterminent la prospérité des nations.* Tome second. St.-Pétersbourg, 1815.— 390

Thompson, W. *An Inquiry into the Principles of the Distribution of Wealth Most Conducive to Human Happiness; applied to the newly proposed system of voluntary equality of wealth.* London, 1824.— 17-18, 321

— *An Inquiry into the Principles of the Distribution of Wealth Most Conducive to Human Happiness.* A new edition. London, 1850.— 17-18, 321-22

Tooke, Th. *An Inquiry into the Currency Principle; the Connection of the Currency with Prices, and the Expediency of a Separation of Issue from Banking*. Second edition. London, 1844.— 475-76

Turgot, [A. R. J.] *Réflexions sur la formation et la distribution des richesses*. In: *Oeuvres de Turgot*. Nouvelle édition [...] Par M. Eugène Daire. Tome premier, Paris, 1844.— 191, 340, 358

Tyler [Tylor], E. B. *Forschungen über die Urgeschichte der Menschheit und die Entwickelung der Civilisation*. Aus dem Englischen von H. Müller. Leipzig.— 438

Wayland, Fr. *The Elements of Political Economy*. Boston, 1843.— 227

Williams, R. P. *On the Maintenance of Permanent Way*. In: *The Money Market Review,* December 2, 1867.— 173, 182-83
— *On the Maintenance and Renewal of Permanent Way*. In: *Minutes of Proceedings of the Institution of Civil Engineers; with abstracts of the discussions*. Vol. XXV. Session 1865-66. London, 1866.— 173, 182-83

[Wilson, J.] *Nature of Capital and Functions of Money*. In: *The Economist*, Vol. V, No. 193, May 8, 1847.— 140

DOCUMENTS

East India (Bengal and Orissa Famine). Papers and correspondence relative to the Famine in Bengal and Orissa, including the Report of the Famine Commission and the Minutes of the Lieutenant Governor of Bengal and the Governor General of India. (Presented to Parliament by Her Majesty's command.) Ordered, by the House of Commons, to be Printed, 31 May 1867.— 144

East India (Bengal and Orissa Famine). Papers relating to the Famine in Behar, including Mr. F. R. Cockerell's report. (Presented to Parliament by Her Majesty's command.) Part III. Ordered, by the House of Commons, to be printed, 31 May 1867.— 144

East India (Madras and Orissa Famine). Return to an address of the Honourable The House of Commons, dated 4 July 1867. Ordered, by the House of Commons, to be printed, 30 July 1867.— 238

Manava Dharma Sastra, or the institutes of Manu according to the gloss of Kulluka, comprising the Indian system of duties, religious and civil. Verbally translated from the original, with a preface by Sir William Jones, and collated with the sanskrit text, by Graves Chamney Haughton, Esq., M. A. F. R. S. &c. &c., Professor of Hindu Literature in the East India College. Third edition. Edited by the Revd. P. Percival. Madras, 1863.— 238

Report from the Select Committee on the Bank Acts; together with the proceedings of the committee minutes of evidence, appendix and index. Part I. Report and evidence. Ordered, by the House of Commons, to be Printed, 30 July 1857.— 235-36

Reports by Her Majesty's Secretaries of Embassy and Legation, on the manufactures, commerce &c., of the countries in which they reside. No. 8. Presented to both Houses of Parliament by Command of Her Majesty. 1865. London [1865].— 242

Reports by Her Majesty's Secretaries of Embassy and Legation, on the Manufactures, Commerce &c., of the countries in which they reside. Part III. Presented to both Houses of Parliament by command of Her Majesty. May 1879. London, 1879.— 471, 515-17

Royal Commission on Railways. Minutes of Evidence Taken Before the Commissioners, March 1865 to May 1866. Presented to both Houses of Parliament by command of Her Majesty. London, 1867.— 142, 155, 172, 177, 181-82, 252

ANONYMOUS ARTICLES AND REPORTS PUBLISHED IN PERIODIC EDITIONS

The Economist
- — No. 1190, June 16, 1866: *Practical Reforms Rendered Possible by the Crises. Shortening the Usance of Indian Bills.*— 253
- — No. 1192, June 30, 1866: *Usance of Indian Bills. To the Editor of the "Economist":* Signed: An East India Merchant.— 253
- — No. 1193, July 7, 1866: *The Shortened Usance of Indian Bills.*— 253

INDEX OF PERIODICALS

The Economist — a weekly journal on problems of economics and politics, mouthpiece of the industrialists, published in London from 1843.— 140, 253

The Money Market Review. A Weekly Commercial and Financial Journal — English weekly, published under this title from 1860 to 1921.— 173, 181, 183

Neue Rheinische Zeitung. Organ der Demokratie — a daily newspaper of the revolutionary-proletarian wing of the democrats during the 1848-49 revolution in Germany; it was published in Cologne under Marx's editorship from June 1, 1848 to May 19, 1849 (with an interval between 27 September and 12 October 1848); Engels was among its editors.— 11

Zeitschrift für die gesammte Staatswissenschaft — liberal political and economic review, published from 1844 to 1943 (with intervals) in Tübingen.— 10-11

Heterick Memorial Library
Ohio Northern University

	DUE	RETURNED		DUE	RETURNED
1.			13.		
2.			14.		
3.			15.		
4.			16.		
5.			17.		
6.			18.		
7.			19.		
8.			20.		
9.			21.		
10.			22.		
11.			23.		
12.			24.